A *Backwoods Home* Anthology:

The Seventeenth Year

Published by
Backwoods Home Magazine
P.O. Box 712
Gold Beach, OR 97444

ISBN: 978-0-9846222-2-1

Editor: Dave Duffy

Senior Editor: John Silveira

Art Director: Don Childers

Contributors: *Linda Gabris, Habeeb Salloum, Massad Ayoob, Kelly McCarthy, Jeffrey R. Yago, Jerry King, Corcceigh Green, Alice Brantley Yeager, James O. Yeager, George Erdosh, emet, David Lee, Sharon Palmer, Emily Buehler, John Silveira, Jackie Clay, Claire Wolfe, Dave Duffy, Charles Sanders, John Lo Cicero, Raymond Nones, Tom Kovach, Sylvia Gist, Roy Martin, Patrice Lewis, Ilene Duffy, Gail Butler, Daniel Motz, Richard Blunt, Roy Martin, Dorothy Ainsworth, Devon Winter, Allen Easterly*

Cover Art: Don Childers

Layout Design and Proofreading: Lisa Nourse, Rhoda Denning, Annie Tuttle, Ilene Duffy

For Olga Victoria Robertson,
who knew when to toil and
when to stop and smell the roses.

Contents —

Issue Number 97

Issue Number 98

Issue Number 99

Issue Number 100

Issue Number 101

Issue Number 102

Jan/Feb 2006
Issue #97
$4.95 US
$6.50 CAN

Backwoods Home magazine

practical ideas for self-reliant living

BIRD FLU — panic or hype?

Homemade breads
Nutritious potatoes
Emergency flashlights
Self publish your book

www.backwoodshome.com

My view

Talking to your kids about death

How do you talk to a child about the death of someone they love? How do you explain the impossible? It's a task many of us parents have had to do, and between issues it was my turn.

Eighty-seven-year-old Grandma, my wife's mom, died after an illness of several months. My wife, Ilene, and her sister, Cindy, as well as three of Grandma's closest friends, were with her to the very end. They even gave her permission to die as she gasped for her last breath. "It's okay, Mom; it's okay to go."

I waited several hours to tell my three sons, Jake, 14, Robby, 12, and Sam, 10, until we came home from work and school so they could be in the comfort and privacy of their own home. They loved Grandma, and had grown accustomed to the two-day car rides we made three or four times a year to stay with her at her Oxnard, California, home. Sammy was especially close to her. During our last visit, about 10 days before she died, Sam sat on the floor and played with toys beside Grandma's bed as she waged one last fight against the ailments that besieged her frail 75-pound body. It didn't matter if there was not a lot of conversation; he just wanted to be close to Grandma.

Grandma had had osteoporosis for many years, could barely read with the aid of a magnifying glass, heard about half of what you said through her hearing aids, and breathed during the last year with the aid of an oxygen hose that was strewn about the house as she slowly trekked throughout her spacious home. A fall and a broken leg a few months ago sounded her final lap in life.

But Grandma, ever the valiant leader who had raised her four daughters alone after her husband, Jules, died of heart failure while they were still young, brought her sense of humor into her final days. A week before her death, when her daughters, sensing the imminent, converged on her home from places like Oregon and Canada, she wryly quipped, "I hope I don't disappoint you." The exhausted daughters retired to the kitchen and laughed with relief. It was their mom's way of saying she knew what was going on and she could handle it.

"But I thought she was getting better," Sam protested through his tears when I broke the news to the boys. Kids never really understand until it slaps them in the face, no matter how much you prepare them.

Their own mom had been gone for two weeks to be with Grandma. They needed a Mom hug in the worst way, but I would have to do. We stayed up late that night and had tea and cocoa in the kitchen. Between bouts of tears that sent them into the bathroom so no one could see them cry, I told them how I still talked to my Dad 41 years after he had died, and that they could talk to Grandma anytime they wanted. "She'll hear you," I said, "just like my Dad still hears me now whenever I do something I think is pretty neat and whisper, "How'd you like that Dad?"

Grandma Myers with Duffy grandkids

I told them that at that very moment, I imagine Grandma is walking through some room where people are patting her on the back and shaking her hand and saying things like, "Congratulations Grandma! Nice run, lady, what a life you had! You gave it everything you had baby, beautiful, just a beautiful life." I said Grandma lived life to the fullest, raised four fine daughters, enjoyed a flock of great grandkids like them, and made the world a far better place than when she entered it. "She's done everything you could possibly do with the gift of life," I said, and I meant it. "She must be proud as heck, and we should be too."

In the morning, the boys, resilient as children are, ate a Dad-type breakfast of fried potatoes mixed with eight eggs, onions, garlic, and fresh tomatoes they had to go out in the rain to get from the garden, and they felt fine. No more tears. Over breakfast, the boys and I, in consultation by phone with Mom, decided to plant two trees in our yard for Grandma and my brother, Jim, who also died recently.

"A weeping willow," Jake said. "And a pear tree," Robby said, "to replace the one the bear broke down." "We'll tie a hammock between them," Mom suggested.

Later in the day, during our ongoing effort to improve writing skills by having them write themes on things that interest them, I suggested they write their essays about Grandma. They took to the task enthusiastically, and it became more therapy than writing lesson. "She would make us pumkin pies. She loved to see us eat," Robby wrote. "She was working on my blankit," Sam said, referring to a blanket Grandma knitted for him as she was dying. And Jake closed his theme with, "I loved Grandma very much and no one will ever replace her."

Grandma Kathy Myers died on Yom Kippur, the holiest day of the year for Jews. Legend has it that you go straight to heaven if you die on Yom Kippur.

I can believe that! Nice run Grandma! ***— Dave***

VINEGAR

A splash is all you need for healthful eating, natural healing, and sparkling home.

By Linda Gabris

Call me a sourpuss, if you will, but I love vinegar and can't imagine a day going by without calling upon one type or another for cooking, curing, or cleansing purposes.

Vinegar gets its name from Latin (*vinum* for wine and *acer* for sour) and is one of the oldest condiments in the world. It is believed to have been discovered quite by accident—wine exposed to air and voila, "sour wine" or vinegar came to be known. Too tart to drink, too precious to throw away, creative experimentation proved that soured wine had fascinating properties—one of them being the power to pickle!

Ancient Egyptians and Chinese used vinegar thousands of years before Christ, and its use is mentioned in both the Old and New Testaments. Traces of vinegar were discovered in an Egyptian vessel dating back 10,000 years. Babylonians used it for cleansing and preserving food, and in Rome legionaries drank vinegar before battle believing it gave them strength and courage. After the fighting was over, vinegar was applied as a disinfectant to cleanse wounds inflicted by swords.

When I was a kid, inexpensive distilled white vinegar was one of the handiest staples in my grandmother's pantry. Even though she depended upon it for nursing boils, cold sores, skin rashes, bug bites, nosebleeds, and dozens of other everyday nuisances as well as for housecleaning purposes, Grandma vouched that distilled white vinegar was far too strong for the stomach to handle.

Distilled white vinegar is not a healthy choice for table use because harsh chemicals and solvents are used during distillation to make the vinegar clear. Sometimes called "dead" vinegar, due to intense heat involved in the process, the life-giving "mother" is destroyed along with beneficial enzymes, minerals, and other nutrients like malic and tartaric acids, noted for flushing impurities from the body.

Even though it is not recommended for consumption, distilled white vinegar is environmentally friendly and easy on the budget, making it an excellent alternative to chemical cleaning solutions for ridding germs and unpleasant odors around the house.

For healthy eating and medicinal tonics, I learned from Grandma to reach for a jug of pure apple cider vinegar to do the trick. If you don't make your own apple cider vinegar as my grandmother did, make sure you purchase organic vinegar—one that has been fermented out of organically grown apples, un-pasteurized to preserve nutritional goodness. Read the label to ensure there are no chemicals, additives, or preservatives in the bottle.

An array of vinegars from around the world

Cider vinegar is recorded in Grandma's old doctoring journals as being useful tonic for many ailments including cold, flu, sore throat, and stuffy head. It is also good for flushing impurities from the kidneys, bladder, and liver.

Studies have indicated that apple cider vinegar helps relieve arthritic pain, either taken orally or applied on a hot compress. Patting a twisted ankle or sprain with a cloth that's been soaked in cider vinegar reduces swelling.

Apple cider vinegar is useful treatment for insomnia, constipation, nervousness, muscle cramps, and other afflictions—some of which are much less common today than in Grandmother's doctoring days. Her scribbles testify that it can be administered to expel intestinal worms and, when used as a hair rinse, rids head lice by dissolving nests.

I still depend on distilled white and apple cider vinegars for cleaning solutions and old remedies passed down to me from Grandmother, but over the years I have become a connoisseur of more exotic types of vinegar for dressing up meals. In my book, any cook can go from being good to gourmet simply by keeping an aromatic bottle or two of specialty vinegars close at hand.

Unlike my rural grandmother, I have access to larger supermarkets that offer vinegars from around the world. One of my favorite picks is balsamic vinegar from Italy.

Traditional balsamic is made from white Trebbiano grapes and aged, up to a hundred years, in a succession of casks made out of different woods, each instilling a particular flavor and aroma to the vinegar, thus its magical taste and pricier tag.

Malt vinegar with its English roots, is fermented out of barley and grain mash and flavored from casks of beech and birch. When purchasing, look for an organic label.

The quality of Champagne and wine vinegars is determined by the type of wines from which they're made. The best wine vinegars are made the slow, old-fashioned way in oak barrels with plenty of time to mature naturally. Reds and sherry vinegars are aged longer than whites. When purchasing, look for those derived from organic wines.

Tall bottle: Tarragon and garlic; small bottle: Mixed herbs

Some of the most interesting vinegars are those with Oriental roots made from glutinous rice like award-winning, double-fermented and twice distilled, organic Mirin—a thick, golden sweet vinegar that's said to be one of the purest in the world and can actually be sipped like sake.

When shopping for vinegar, use the same guidelines as for fine wine. Good organic vinegar should have a sharp, clean taste and pleasant bouquet and upon inhaling, its origin should be revealed. It should never be cloudy, smell like alcohol, or leave an unpleasant aftertaste. Like wine, it must be kept tightly corked in a cool place. Most vinegars today are 5% acetic acid, except Balsamic, which ideally is 6%.

Although vinegar is rooted in history as a preservative and disinfectant, only in more recent times has apple cider vinegar gained recognition as being a remarkable health booster. Studies have indicated that cider is a powerful detoxifying and purifying agent that provides the body with a wide range of minerals including potassium, phosphorus, sodium, magnesium, calcium, chlorine, sulfur, and iron, as well as a number of essential vitamins and beta-carotene.

Cider vinegar prevents high blood pressure by thinning blood and helps maintain healthy blood sugar levels as well as regulating metabolism, which is beneficial in achieving and maintaining weight loss. Because acetic acid in vinegar helps the body break down and digest rich, fatty foods, many cider vinegar-based diets have sprung into being.

Whether or not such diets work, they are not recommended. Overindulgence with any type of acid can cause harm, especially for those suffering from ulcers or other stomach disorders. Too much acid can wear down the stomach lining as well as cause tooth decay.

But the good news is, sensibly adding cider and other specialty vinegars to one's diet promotes healthier eating habits, which in turn lowers body fat. Substituting perky vinegar like cider or malt in place of butter, cream, cheese, or other heavy sauces on vegetables is one tasty way to cut fat from the diet.

Sprinkling herbal vinegars on salads is another refreshing way to shape up by cutting down on traditional oily dressings, and using fruity infusions instead of sweet sauces and whipped cream on desserts cuts calories drastically.

If you want to get on the sweet side of sour, all you have to do is enter the exciting world of vinegar. Following are some of the great things you can do with vinegar—from gourmet cooking tips to soothing sunburn and absorbing pet wet.

On the table

Old World wilts. Grandma always packed a wilt in her picnic basket because she claimed that cider vinegar destroyed bacteria in the digestive system. So if by chance anything got tainted in the sun, the wilt would ward off illness. I like wilts because they are refreshingly good. Wilts are versatile and easy to make. Just shred lettuce, cabbage, dandelion leaves, spinach, cucumber, or a mix of greens and put in an earthen or glass bowl. Boil 1 part cider vinegar to 2 parts water and sweeten with honey. Pour over greens and let steep until cold. Drain before serving.

Light, bright salads. You can cut down or eliminate oil by simply tossing greens with a shake of organic store-bought or homemade herbal vinegar. Making your own is as easy as pairing a herb with a vinegar and finding a neat little bottle with a tight fitting cork. See recipes.

Guilt-free desserts. In Italy, it is common practice to dip fresh strawberries into a little bowl of balsamic vinegar before eating. This is truly a must-try treat. Unlike traditional chocolate or caramel dunks, balsamic vinegar actually draws out and enhances flavor rather than masking it. Try sticking other fruits like banana slices, apple wedges, peach, or pear slices on toothpicks and dipping in balsamic for exciting variety.

Thirst quencher. Stir a tablespoon of apple cider or fruit vinegar (see recipes) into iced water for a tantalizing thirst quencher said to regulate body temperature and clear up bad complexion.

Diva dip. Cider, balsamic, or herbal vinegars poured into the dip bowl make a delightfully light substitute for sour cream, mayonnaise, and other fatty dips. You can dunk veggies until your heart's content.

Balsamic dip for bread. Here's a super quick and delicious Old World dish from Italy. Combine ½ cup balsamic vinegar, 3 tablespoons extra virgin olive oil, 5 cloves of roasted mashed garlic, and 1 teaspoon of freshly grated black pepper into a jar. Shake well and let draw in the fridge until the flavors meld. Serve with chunks of crusty bread for dipping. This makes a very elegant appetizer, easy picnic, or impromptu supper.

Getting the most out of soup stocks. Adding a squirt of white wine or apple cider vinegar—about 2 tablespoons per pound of bones—to the stock pot helps leach valuable calcium from the bones. There will be no sour taste, and you'll be on the plus side of calcium.

Potassium-rich tea. If your stamina needs improving, you may need more potassium in your diet. One teaspoon full of cider vinegar per cup of herbal tea can fill the bill. A dash in place of lemon perks up tea.

Salt substitute. Fill a small-holed salt shaker with cider, malt, or herbal vinegar and use in place of salt on raw onions, tomatoes, poached eggs, steamed vegetables, pasta, or anything else that normally draws you to the shaker. When not in use, keep tightly capped in the refrigerator.

Produce wash. Mix three parts distilled white vinegar to 1 part water in a spray bottle. Use to blast away germs from produce. After spraying, rinse well under cold running water. Store leftover spray, tightly capped, in fridge.

Making your own herb vinegar. Gather a few sprigs of fresh garden herbs—more for stronger vinegar. Basil, dill, rosemary, sage, tarragon, thyme, mint, chives, or whatever is handy in your herb patch. Wash, pat dry, and put in a sterilized bottle. Cover with apple cider, malt, or any wine vinegar or blend of vinegars you desire. Let draw for two weeks, then strain and bottle. Peeled garlic cloves, shallots, peppercorns, chilies, juniper berries, or other spices and seasonings can be added.

Fruit vinegar. Use raspberry, cranberries, blueberries, or choice of fruit in place of herbs. Create unique flavors by adding orange peel, lemon zest, pomegranate seeds, nutmeg pod, cinnamon stick, or other sweet things to the bottle. For the very best in fruit-infused vinegar, use white wine or Champagne vinegar.

In the medicine cupboard

Cold prevention medicine. Peel a knuckle of ginger root and put into a pint jar. Add peeled cloves of 1 head of garlic and two small chili peppers. Cover with cider vinegar that's been brought to a near boil. Cap tightly and store in fridge. Grandmother's suggested dosage: Take 1 teaspoon in half cup of water when you feel a cold coming on. Saves indefinitely under refrigeration. Makes good stir-fry sauce or enlivening sprinkle for rice dishes.

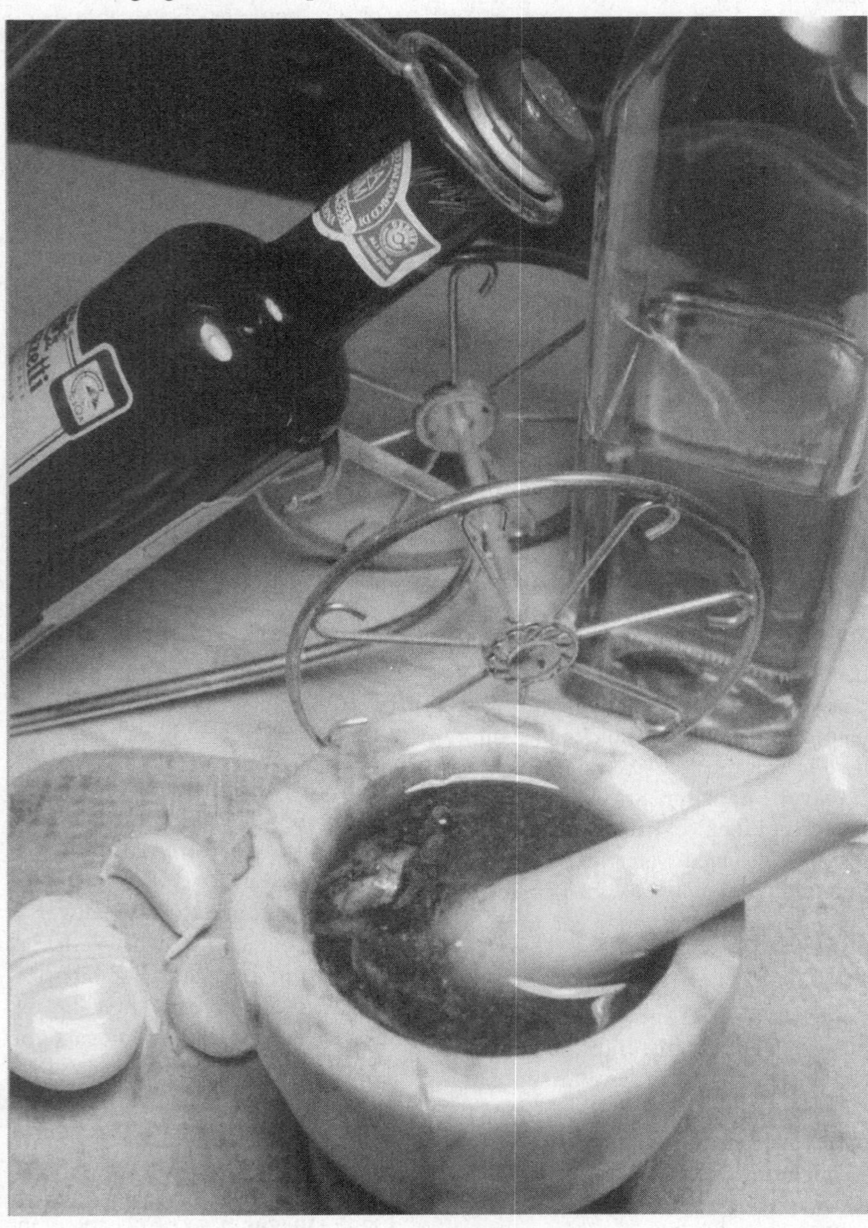

Making delicious balsamic dip

Cold and flu tonic. Mix 2 teaspoons of cider vinegar into 1 cup of boiling water and sweeten with honey to taste. When cool, sip slowly. Good for relieving cough and breaking up phlegm. For congestion, serve this mixture hot and inhale the steam.

Heartburn. One teaspoon of cider vinegar mixed into a glass of water taken with a spicy meal makes a reliable neutralizer—warding off heartburn.

Nosebleed. Soak sterile cloth in white distilled vinegar diluted with equal parts water and apply to stop bleeding. According to Grandma's old notes, the acid in the vinegar seals the broken vessel.

Headache. Bring ¼ cup white distilled or ½ cup apple cider vinegar and 1 cup of water to a boil. Add a generous handful of fresh or several spoons full of dried mint leaves and steep until infused. Cover head with a towel, hold over steaming liquid and inhale fumes. Good treatment for tension or sinus headache.

Itchy skin. Run a cool tub full of water and add 2 cups of white distilled vinegar. This is good for soothing heat rash, hives, mosquito bites, and swimmers itch. Cider vinegar works even better—if you have enough of the good stuff to spare.

Sunburn. Pat affected skin with a mixture of cider vinegar and water to cool and relieve pain. This helps prevent blistering and peeling.

Foot odor. Put about a pint of distilled white or cider vinegar into a basin of warm water and soak feet. This deodorizes and softens calluses at the same time. Rinsing socks in this solution after washing acts like a built-in odor eater.

Itchy scalp. Add a couple tablespoons distilled white, rice, or cider vinegar to a quart of warm water and use as final rinse after shampooing. Dissolves soap residue that causes dry, flaking scalp. Rosemary adds fragrance and shine to hair.

Around the house

Sparkling glass. Add distilled white vinegar to water when washing windows and glass decorations. Cuts grease and grime and deters buildup. A quarter cup added to rinse water leaves dishes squeaky clean.

Clean and disinfect chopping blocks. To remove meat, onions, garlic, fish, and other odors, rub with baking soda then sprinkle with white distilled vinegar. Let stand until fizzling stops, then rinse with scalding water and air dry.

Coffee pots. Half distilled white vinegar, half water. Run it through pot to remove lime and calcium deposits. Use in tea kettle, too.

Rid smoke, musky, and pet wet odors. To remove smoke or musky odors from clothes or blankets, add 2 cups white distilled vinegar to the final rinse water. Also rids mothball odor. To remove pet wet from carpets—sponge with equal parts white distilled vinegar and water.

Wash machine. To remove soap residue and scum from wash machine, let fill with hot water, add a quart of white distilled vinegar and let stand until soap and scum are dissolved. Then run the cycle through.

Ants. Grandma always said that an ant would never tread in the path of vinegar. Detour them with full strength white distilled vinegar.

Drains. Empty ½ cup baking soda into drain. Add 1 cup of white distilled vinegar. Let the carbon dioxide fizzle until its worn out. Rinse with boiling water. Gets rid of greasy odor and buildup.

Microwave oven. Put 1 cup of vinegar in microwave and nuke until boiling. Let set a few minutes. Remove and wipe steam—and odors—from oven. Soak kitchen scrub brushes in leftover hot vinegar to disinfect and remove odor. Δ

Healthy homemade breads with worldly flair

By Linda Gabris

My grandma always quipped that "bread in the breadbox was as rich as any person ever needed to be..." Of course, I'm sure that Grandmother's praises and deeply-rooted sentiments for the world's greatest staple evolved during the struggling eras of war, depression, rationing, and other hardships that she grew up in and raised her large family around. Meager times when a loaf of bread really was worth its weight in gold!

As a child, I didn't pay much mind to her old saying but today, whenever I'm kneading dough with the same passions passed down from Grandma, memory of her words bring a smile to my face and warm my heart, for really, what could be more precious than the joy of creating a loaf of bread to satisfy hunger pangs of loved ones.

Understanding the art of bread making, and taking note of the standard choices of ingredients normally called for in traditional recipes, is the first step in creating perfect loaves of bread every time. The principle ingredient is flour, which gives bread its basic bulk. There are so many types of flour to choose from that no two loaves ever have to be the same. You can use all-purpose, whole wheat, barley, buckwheat, rye, or other types of flour, or a blend of flours to achieve unique flavors, colors, textures, aromas, and nutritional values.

Yeast—a living microscopic plant—is the most mystifying substance on the pantry shelf and is the magical organism that "breathes life into breads and other risen baked goods." For most of my recipes, I prefer packaged instant, quick-rise yeast as it is the easiest to use and maintains shelf life longer than other types such as compressed yeast (known as cake or bulk yeast that is not pre-measured). If using other types of yeast, follow package directions.

Liquids act as binders. Common binders are: types of milk like whole, evaporated, or buttermilk; water; fruit juices, which are often used in sweeter types of breads; or vegetable water such as that drained off boiled potatoes and carrots which adds flavor, color, and nutrients. Grandma saved all her vegetable cooking water to use in breads and soups. I do, too, to cash in on extra vitamins, minerals, and other good things that might otherwise go down the drain. Liquids can be interchanged in most recipes to suit taste and availability. In recipes calling for milk, I usually use whole milk, but you can use two percent or other choice.

Sweeteners are often added to enhance taste. Common recipes call for honey, white or brown sugar, molasses, or corn syrup. Like liquids, these can be interchanged as desired.

Fat enriches the dough, produces tenderness, and adds mouthwatering flavor to the loaf. Butter, shortening, lard, margarine, or vegetable or olive oils can often stand in for one another. In the olden days, Grandmother used homemade lard rendered from pork or bear fat, which she vouched, was as good as any.

Salt is added to the liquid in which yeast is dissolved as it helps to activate the yeast, bringing it to life. If you're on a salt-free diet, you can omit salt, but your loaf may not rise quite as high.

Eggs, nuts, seeds, fruits, raisins, cheese, olives, onions, herbs, spices, and an endless array of other good things make the world of bread baking a very large one. I'm sure that every day in kitchens around the world, hundreds of exciting new recipes for homemade breads are created by whim and fancy, and sometimes by trial and error.

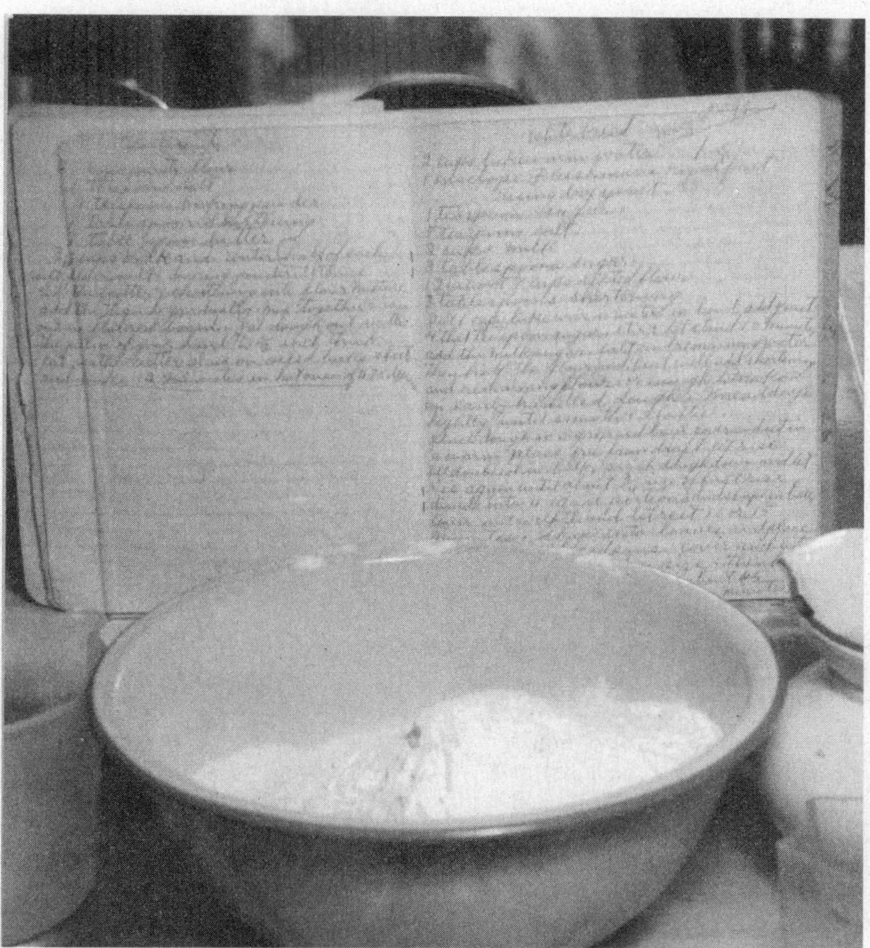

Basic ingredients for "Old flour sack white bread"

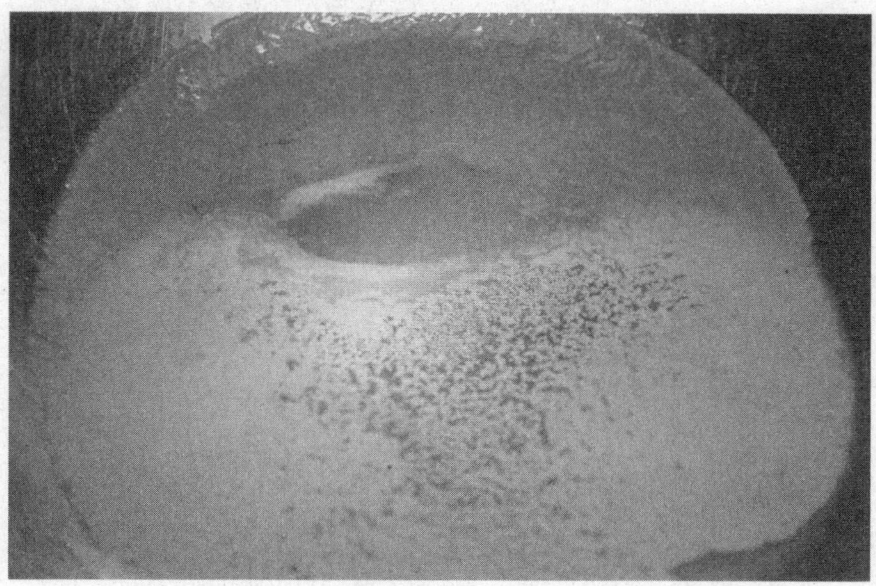

Yeast: The living organism that breathes life into bread. Here, it is activated in warm liquid.

The best breads in the world are loaves that are baked by loving hands. To enjoy the hobby of bread baking to the fullest, let your creative juices flow freely. When that happens, your bread will earn the highest praise, and you'll be very rich indeed.

But first... a few tips

- ➢Softening yeast in warm liquid ensures the highest rise.
- ➢Although some folks store flour in a cellar, cold room, or freezer, it should be brought to room temperature for best results. When flour is too cold it can stunt the growth of yeast.
- ➢Always knead the dough until smooth and elastic. Under-kneading can produce heavy, lumpy or uneven bread. Grandma always said that kneading was a special time for letting your heart be happy and giving thanks. Old World and modern day herbalists claim that kneading warm, pliable dough is a wonderful therapeutic workout for arthritic, weak, or lame hands.
- ➢It is important to let the dough rise in a warm place away from draft. When baking bread during colder weather, you can fill the kitchen sink with hot water, then set the bowl over the sink, cover with a tea towel to trap warmth in from the steam, and let rise. Do not use boiling water as it will be too hot and can actually kill the yeast. Some bakers set dough in a pre-warmed oven when the house is too cold or drafty. Just be sure that you do not let the oven get too hot or yeast can die.
- ➢Don't forget to punch the dough down and let it re-rise as called for in recipes. Some novice bakers tend to skip this important step and flat, heavy bread is often the tell-tale sign.

Flour is beaten in slowly, until liquid gathers up all the flour.

When all the flour has been gathered up, dough is turned out on floured board.

- ➢Use proper sized loaf pans. If the pan is too small, bread will spill over, losing shape and making a mess in the oven. If pans are too large, the loaves will be flat. If you end up with a bit of extra dough, form a ball and bake a small round loaf or pat the dough into a flat circle and fry in a skillet until golden. In Grandma's kitchen, these were known as scones and every so often, like Grandma, I will make an extra batch of bread dough especially for this purpose. Serve these tasty fried breads with jam for a hearty winter breakfast treat.
- ➢Remember Grandma's old test for doneness: rap with the finger, and it should sound hollow. The top of the loaf should be smooth, shiny and golden brown. Sides and bottom should be a little lighter in color.

Troubleshooting

- ➢When dough is too sticky to knead, add more flour by sprinkling it over the board and working it in with your hands. Don't worry about how much more flour is needed, just sprinkle until it feels right. If you can't "gather up" all the flour, sprinkle in a bit more warm liquid.
- ➢Follow the double in bulk rule. If you skip this important step, your bread will be too dense.
- ➢The most common cause of failed bread is expired yeast. Check the expiration date before using. Yeast really does die, losing its ability to cause expansion in the dough. Discard outdated yeast or packages that have suffered exposure to dampness.
- ➢If bread is pale at the end of baking time, leave it in the oven 10 to 15 minutes longer. If this doesn't produce the desired color, brush with beaten egg yolk. The most common cause is an oven that loses heat or one that has a broken thermostat. Since oven temperatures can vary, use given times as a general guideline and let your eyes, nose and fingers tell you when the bread is done to perfection.
- ➢If the bread sticks to the pan upon removal, grease more heavily next time around. If bread is too greasy, lighten up.

Try the recipes below for some of the world's greatest breads.

Old flour sack white bread

Here is a very old, very basic recipe for white bread that takes its name from where it originated. It was passed down to me from my grandmother, who said she copied the recipe off the back of an old flour sack. The recipe produces four wonderful, fragrant loaves of bread.

2 cups of lukewarm water (I use saved-up potato water, but plain will do.)
1 envelope dry yeast
1 tsp. sugar
1½ Tbsp. salt
2 cups milk
Additional 3 Tbsp. sugar
About 12 cups of enriched white flour
3 Tbsp. fat (butter, margarine, shortening)

Measure 1 cup of lukewarm water in a bowl. Sprinkle yeast and sugar over the water and let stand 10 minutes. Add milk, additional sugar, salt, and the remaining 1 cup of water. Add 6 cups of flour and beat with a wooden spoon until blended. Slowly, cup by cup full, add remaining flour or enough to make a smooth handling dough. Turn out on floured board and with floured hands, knead until smooth, elastic, and satiny, or about 10 minutes. Place in a large greased bowl and turn dough over so top is also greased. Cover, and let rise in warm place (80 to 85° F) until double in bulk, or about 1 hour. Punch down and let rise again until double (about 45 minutes). Punch down again. Turn

Grandma always said that kneading dough was a special time for letting your heart be happy and giving thanks.

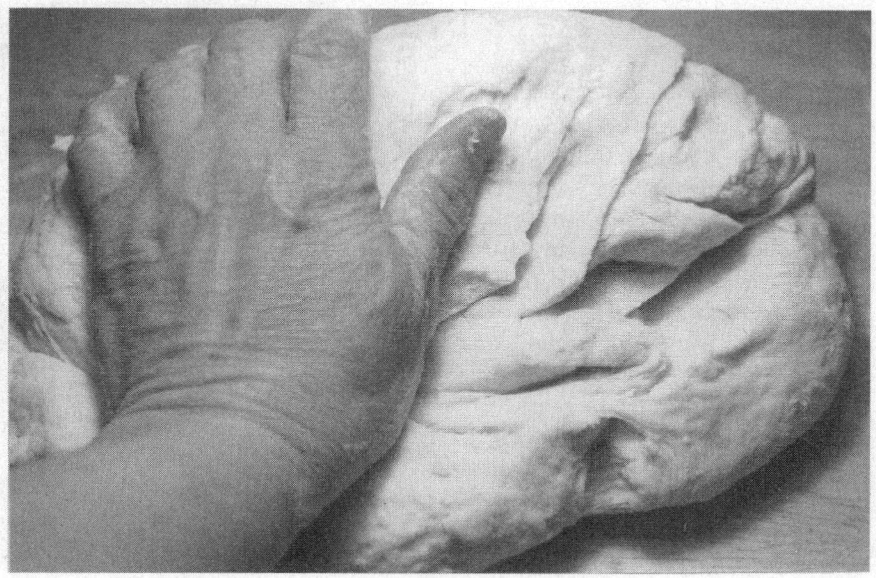

Knead dough with the heels of your hands until smooth and elastic.

When dough is well kneaded, smooth, and elastic it is placed in greased bowl to rise in warm place until double in bulk.

Here the dough has risen to double in bulk.

out on lightly floured board and divide equally into four pieces. Shape in balls, cover, and let rest 10 minutes. Mold into greased loaf pans, 8½ x 4½ x 2½ inches. Cover and let rise another hour, or until doubled in bulk. Bake at 400° F for 40 minutes or until done.

Hearty whole wheat bread

- 1 envelope active yeast
- 2 cups lukewarm potato or other vegetable water, water, or milk
- 1½ Tbsp. salt
- 4 Tbsp. dark molasses
- 3 Tbsp. melted butter
- 3 cups white flour
- 5 cups whole wheat flour

Sprinkle yeast over 1 cup of the potato water. Add salt and molasses, and let stand 10 minutes. Add butter and white flour, beating well. Add whole wheat flour, beating in until a stiff dough is formed. Turn out on floured board and knead until smooth and elastic or about 10 minutes, adding more flour if needed. Place in greased bowl, turning to grease all sides. Cover and let rise in warm place until double in bulk, or about 1 hour. Punch down. Knead again to force out air. Return to bowl and let rise a second time, until double in bulk, this time about 30 minutes. Grease two 9 x 5 x 3 inch loaf pans. Divide dough and shape into loaves. Place in pans and let rise 20 minutes. Bake at 425° F for 35 minutes or until loaves are deep golden brown.

New World super crunchy health loaf

This delicious, hearty loaf disappears faster than it comes out of the oven. Makes 3 loaves:

- 2 envelopes active yeast
- 1 tsp. salt
- 1 cup lukewarm milk
- 2 cups room temperature apple or other fruit juice or water
- ¾ cup liquid honey
- ¼ cup dark molasses
- ¼ cup vegetable oil
- 6 cups whole wheat flour
- 1 cup rye flour
- ½ cup buckwheat flour
- ½ cup oatmeal
- ¼ cup vegetable oil
- 1 cup sunflower seeds
- 3 Tbsp. flax seeds
- 3 Tbsp. wheat germ
- Optional: dab of melted butter and 2 Tbsp. oatmeal

Light German rye bread with caraway seeds

Sprinkle yeast over water. Add salt, honey, and molasses, and stir well. Let stand 10 minutes. Add oil and apple juice or water. Measure flours and oatmeal into large bowl. Beat in liquid. Sprinkle sunflower seeds, flax seeds, and wheat germ over pastry board. Turn out dough and knead until smooth and elastic. Form a ball and place in greased bowl, turning to grease all sides. Cover and let rise until double in bulk, 1 hour. Punch down and let rise again until double. Punch down and divide into 3 equal pieces. Shape into loaves and place in greased 9 x 5 x 3 inch pans. Brush with melted butter, and sprinkle with oatmeal and a few extra seeds, if you wish for decoration. Let rise 10 minutes. Bake 375° F for 50 minutes or until done.

Greek olive and feta cheese casserole bread

A mouthwatering rich square that's bursting with the exciting flavor and aroma of Greece. So good, some liken it to cake! In its homeland, this bread is often eaten with fresh sliced tomatoes that have been sprinkled with lemon juice and salt. Unlike traditional risen breads, the yeast for this recipe is added directly to the flour.

- 1 cup buckwheat flour
- 3 cups whole wheat flour
- 1 envelope dry active yeast
- 1 tsp. salt
- ¼ cup olive oil, plus more for brushing on top
- 1 cup water or as needed
- 1 cup thinly sliced black olives
- 1 Tbsp. finely chopped fresh basil (or 1 tsp. dried basil)
- 1 cup feta cheese, broken into small curds
- 1 Tbsp. olive oil

Put flours, yeast, and salt into bowl. Dribble the oil onto the flour, then add enough water to form a stiff dough. This dough should be fairly heavy and slightly sticky. Turn onto floured board and knead hard, until elastic and smooth, 15 minutes. Place dough in oiled bowl and turn to cover all sides. Cover and let rise in warm place for 2 hours. Punch down and spread into a 12 x 8-inch pan or on a cookie sheet. Top with olives, basil, and crumbled feta. Sprinkle with olive oil. Let rise 1 hour. Bake in 400° F oven for 1 hour. Cut into squares.

Variation: Greek olive and feta cheese loaf

After dough has risen, punch down and roll out to 8 x 12 square. Sprinkle with basil, olives, feta cheese, and olive oil. Roll up, jelly roll fashion, from wide side over. Pinch seams tightly to seal, and fold ends under to fit into a greased loaf pan. Let rise until double in bulk. Brush top with

Old flour sack white bread in the pans rising until double in bulk

Bake until golden and loaves sound hollow when tapped.

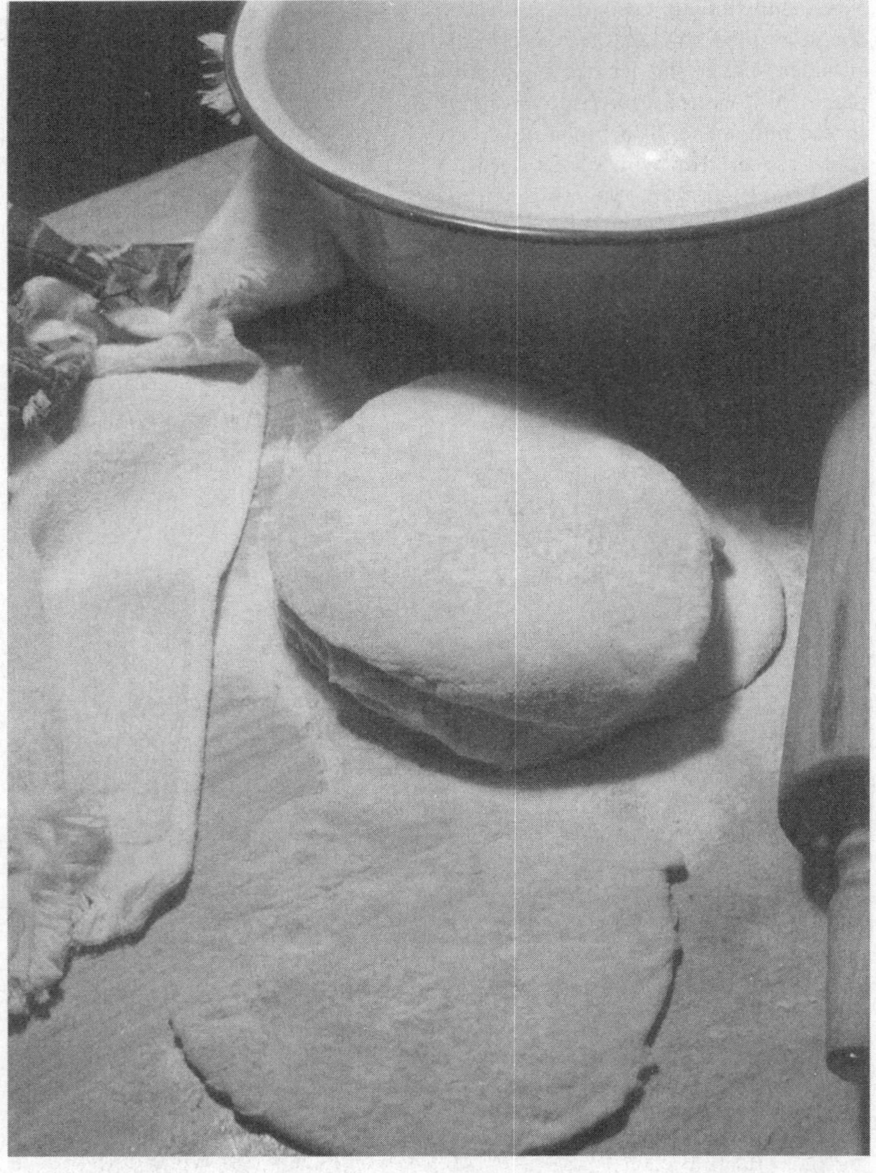

Making pita, a fun bread from the Middle East.

additional dab of olive oil and decorate with olive slices. Bake at 400° for 1 hour or until done.

Middle East pita bread

Here's an unleavened bread that kids of all ages love. Pita bread is flat, soft, and great for dipping into good things like olive oil blended with herbs and garlic. Pitas are also easy to split or fold for holding anything your heart desires. I especially like my pita bread filled with Caesar or other type of crisp salad. This recipe makes about 10 pitas.

- 4 cups white flour
- ½ tsp. salt
- 1 envelope dry active yeast
- 4 Tbsp. olive oil

Put flour in bowl, sprinkle with salt and yeast, and mix. Dribble the oil over top, then add the water, stirring well. Mix until all flour has been gathered away from sides of bowl. Turn out on floured board and knead for 15 minutes. Form a ball and place in oiled bowl. Cover and let rest 2 hours in warm place. Punch down and let rise a second time. Break off small pieces about the size of an egg and gently roll on a floured board, into a circle about the size of a saucer. Dust each round with flour as they are rolled and lay on floured surface. When all are finished, cover and let rise 25 minutes. Heat oven to 500° F. Oil a baking sheet and heat for 3 minutes. Place pitas on baking sheet and sprinkle with cold water. This helps produce their wonderful, handy hollow middles. Reduce heat to 450° F and bake 6 minutes or until they are puffed and speckled. Cool on a wire rack.

Light German rye bread with caraway seeds

From Germany comes a bread that is one of the best keepers I've yet to find. I make this bread for taking camping as it maintains freshness longer than other types, and actually improves upon aging.

- 1 package dry active yeast
- ½ cup lukewarm potato or other vegetable water or plain water
- 2 cups warmed milk
- 3 Tbsp. brown sugar
- 1 tsp. salt
- ½ cup dark molasses
- 3 Tbsp. butter
- 4 cups rye flour
- 2 cups white or whole wheat flour or half and half
- Optional: additional melted butter and caraway seeds

Sprinkle yeast over warm water and let stand 10 minutes. Add milk, sugar, salt, molasses, butter, and yeast mixture. Beat until blended. Add flour, cup by cup, fully beating after each addition. Turn out on floured board and knead 10 minutes or until smooth and elastic. Place dough in greased bowl, set in warm place, and let rise until doubled in bulk. Punch down and form into one long or two smaller loaves. Let rise again until double or about one hour. Slash top three times on an angle with sharp knife. Brush loaves with melted butter and sprinkle with caraway seeds, if you wish. Bake at 375° F for about 35 minutes or until hollow when tapped.

Healthy flax seed loaf

In recent years, flax seed has gained a lot of praise as being a number one health food good for helping to reduce cholesterol and prevent heart disease. I eat it because it tastes good and I enjoy the crunch of tiny flax seeds. This recipe makes one 9 x 5 x 3 inch loaf, but recipe can be doubled.

1 envelope dry active yeast
1 cup lukewarm milk
1 tsp. salt
3 Tbsp. molasses
2 Tbsp. melted butter
1 cup white flour
2 cups whole wheat flour
½ cup flax seeds
Melted butter and extra seeds for sprinkling on top

Sprinkle yeast over warm milk and let stand 10 minutes. Add remaining ingredients and beat until smooth and all flour has been gathered up. Turn out onto floured board and knead until smooth and elastic, about 10 minutes. Put in greased bowl and let rise in warm place until double in bulk, about 1 hour. Punch down, form into loaf, and place in greased pan. Let rise until doubled in bulk. Brush top with melted butter and sprinkle with extra seeds. Bake in 375° F oven for 50 minutes or until done.

For variety, you can add finely chopped nuts, dates, raisins, coconut, grated orange rind, or a pinch of sweet spice like nutmeg or cinnamon to the batter to create a fruity loaf that saves well. Δ

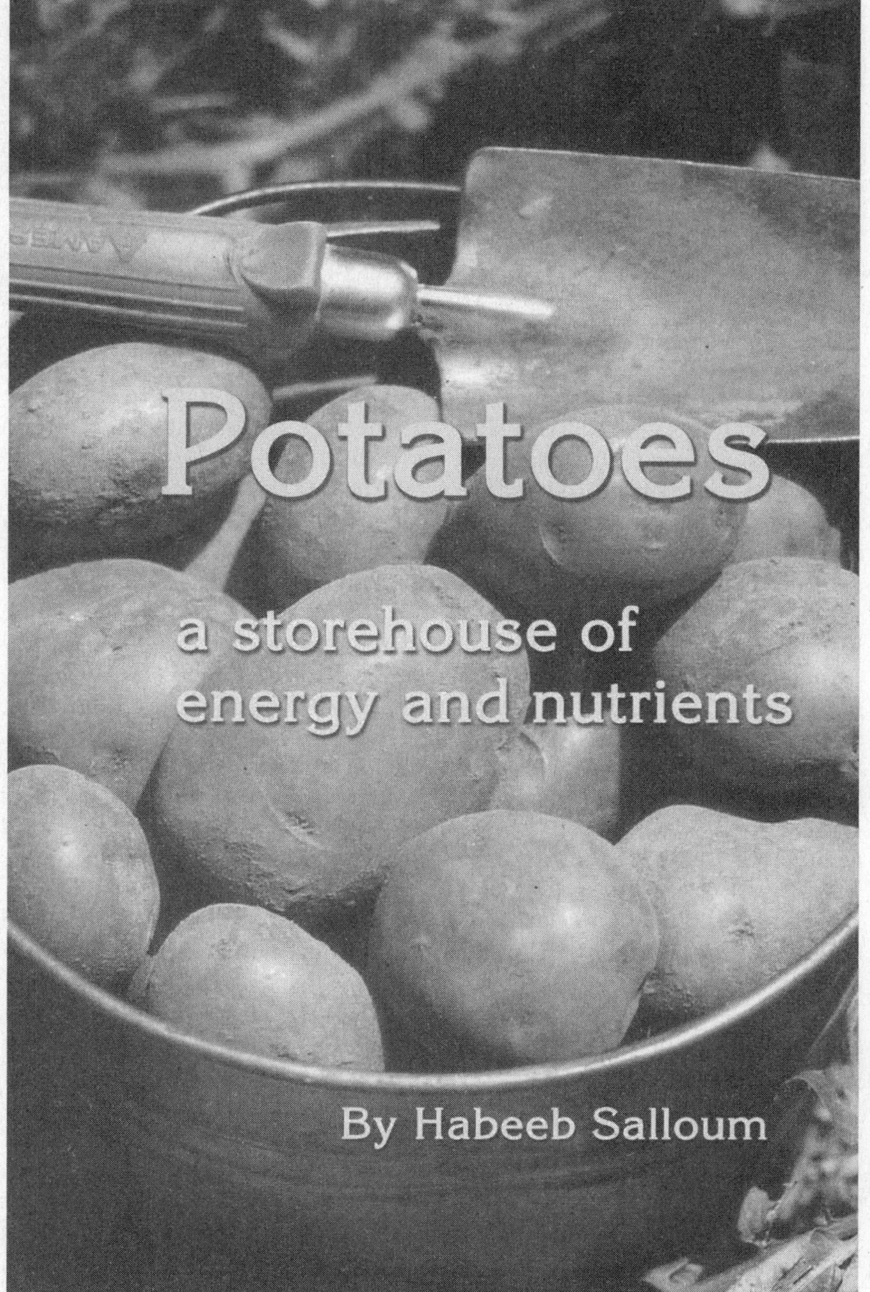

Photo credit: James O. Yeager

It was potato picking time and our whole family was at work in our garden. As my father spaded out the potatoes, my siblings and I brushed the soil off of them, then placed them in pails. Every once in a while I would stop to eat one that caught my fancy, dirt and all. Even today, I remember vividly, the delicious taste of that freshly picked potato. The potato harvest I always enjoyed, thinking of the many potato dishes my mother would prepare in the coming weeks.

Our garden's potato yield, covered with soil in our dirt cellar, would last us for almost the whole year. The dishes my mother prepared were never-ending. In soups, salads, as the main course, and for snacks, she

Potato salad

Potatoes and pine nuts

Potato and yogurt salad

would seemingly always come out with new creations. During the cold winter evenings as we sat around a red-hot stove, many a time she would barbecue sliced potatoes on top the stove for an evening snack. The cooking aroma, filling the room, whetted my appetite night after night. It was a culinary perfume that I have never forgotten.

I doubt that my mother knew when she cooked her numerous potato dishes that this vegetable was a storehouse of nutrients. Potatoes grew easily in our garden and kept for a long period of time in our dirt cellar. In the Depression years these attributes, when very little else grew, were heaven sent. Yet, even though in those harsh years we did not know the healthful qualities of the potato, this vegetable, what some call 'near perfect food,' has been valued as a nutritious edible for untold centuries.

Potatoes (Solanum tuberosum) were a staple for the Indians living in the South American Andes, its region of origin, since at least 750 B.C. The Indians developed some two hundred varieties from the original peanut size wild potato and these became the basis of their diet. Potatoes became so important in their society that they employed them to measure time. Units of time correlated to how long it took for the potato to cook.

When the Spanish Conquistadors went rampaging through the land of the Incas in the Andes looking for gold and silver, they were not aware that the potato was the true treasure of the Andes — one of the most important of all their discoveries in the Americas. This realization would come later.

A half century after arriving in Peru in 1532, the Spanish introduced this culinary treasure into Europe. They called it patata, derived from the Indian word batata, from which we get our name "potato." At first, they were not readily accepted as a food for humans. The Scots, at one time, refused to eat potatoes because they were not mentioned in the Bible. Many in Europe associated potatoes with diseases such as leprosy and rickets; others blamed them for encouraging lust. Potatoes were fed to livestock long before they became an important popular staple food in Europe.

However, all this was to change. Potatoes adapted well to the European climate and soon they became a staple food in most countries on that continent. By the end of the 17th century, they had become a vital part of the basic food supply in Ireland where people took to them with great enthusiasm. This gave birth to a saying: "There are only two things too serious to joke about: potatoes and marriage." When in the mid 19th century the potato crop in that country was destroyed by a blight, over a million people died during what became known as the "Irish Potato Famine."

Potatoes are one of the healthiest foods in the human larder. An easily-grown plant, potatoes have the ability to provide more nutritious food faster on less land than any other food crop, and in almost any habitat. They are jam-packed with fiber, minerals (chiefly potassium), proteins, the vitamins A, C and D, and complex carbohydrates — the body's main source of fuel. A medium 6-ounce potato has about 120 calories, is virtually fat free, and contains no cholesterol and only a small amount of sodium. Potatoes provide more protein and calories than any other food crop, five times more than corn, soy beans, and wheat.

The Incas, beside their food value, cherished potatoes' medical qualities. They believed that they made childbirth easier and used them to treat all types of injuries. Because of the large amount of Vitamin C potatoes contain, which is mostly lost if cooked over 15 minutes, potatoes were for centuries eaten aboard ship to prevent scurvy. Also, potatoes can help in weight-loss diets since they quickly make one feel full.

However, many of the nutrients are just under the skin, and to preserve them potatoes should be cooked unpeeled. Cooked in this way, they do not lose any of their culinary qualities. They are a superb food, being bulky, tasty, cheap, healthy and can be prepared into virtually hundreds of different dishes.

In our times, almost every country in the world grows and consumes potatoes — in many on a large scale. The chief food of the Incas has become the most popular garden produce in the world. China grows 19% of the world's supply, followed by Poland, Russia, and the U.S.A. There are hundreds of species grown throughout the globe, but only eight are commercially cultivated, all adding extra fiber, minerals, and vitamins to the daily menu.

The best potatoes, no matter which type, are fairly clean, smooth, firm, and regular in shape — producing little waste in peeling. Those that are wrinkled, have shriveled skins, soft dark areas, or gashed surfaces should be avoided. During our farming years, we ate the best potatoes after harvest time, but as the weeks slipped by the potatoes preserved by the covering soil became more and more shriveled. We did not have the luxury of the supermarkets that we have today.

Nevertheless, smooth and firm or wrinkled and dark, mother was able to produce gourmet meals from this delicious gift of the earth based on the dishes of her mother country, Syria. The following recipes include a number of her dishes, some with added spices. The others are my own creations, a few of these variations of common dishes. However, they all have their roots in the traditional dishes of the Arab world.

Potato and sumach appetizer:

This dish can be served for breakfast, as a snack, or as a side dish.

Serves 4
oil for frying
4 large potatoes, peeled, the diced into ½ inch cubes
2 Tbsp. sumach (found in Middle Eastern stores)
3 cloves garlic, crushed
½ tsp. salt
¼ tsp. pepper
¼ tsp. cumin
½ cup warm water
1 large onion, sliced

Place oil in a frying pan up to 2 inches deep, then heat. Deep fry the potato cubes until they begin to brown. Remove with a slotted spoon, then set aside to drain on paper towels. Also, retain about 4 tablespoons of the oil in frying pan, then set aside.

Combine the remaining ingredients, except onion, then set aside.

Heat remaining oil in frying pan, then sauté onion until golden brown. Set aside.

Place potato cubes on a platter, then spoon sumach mixture evenly over potato cubes. Spread onions evenly over top, then allow to stand for at least 30 minutes before serving.

Eggs and potato omelet - Bayd Ma' Batata:

Serves 4 to 6
4 Tbsp. cooking oil
5 medium potatoes, peeled and diced into very small pieces
1 cup water
1 tsp. salt
½ tsp. pepper
1/8 tsp. cayenne
5 eggs, beaten

Heat oil in a frying pan, then add potatoes, water, salt, pepper, and cayenne. Cook over medium heat until water has been absorbed by potatoes, which should be tender but still intact.

Pour eggs over the potatoes, then turn heat down to very low. Cover, cook without stirring for about 5 minutes, or until eggs are done.

Potato and yogurt salad - Salatat Batata Wa Laban:

Serves about 6
2 Tbsp. olive oil
1 large onion, chopped
4 cloves garlic, crushed
2 Tbsp. finely chopped coriander leaves
½ small hot pepper, finely chopped
¾ tsp. salt
½ tsp. pepper
4 large potatoes (about 1 lb), peeled, then diced into ½ inch cubes
1 cup plain yogurt

Heat oil in a saucepan, then sauté onion over medium heat for 8 minutes. Add garlic, coriander leaves, and hot pepper, then stir-fry for further few minutes. Add remaining ingredients, except yogurt, then barely cover with water. Bring to boil, then cover and cook over medium/low heat for 20 minutes or until potatoes are done. Place in a serving bowl and allow to cool, then stir in yogurt and serve.

Potato croquettes - 'Ajijat:

Mother often made this dish but did not use all the included spices.

Serves about 8
6 medium potatoes
6 eggs
1 large onion, finely chopped
1 small bunch parsley, stemmed and finely chopped
6 green onions, finely chopped
1 Tbsp. finely chopped mint leaves
1 tsp. salt
1 tsp. cinnamon
½ tsp. pepper
½ tsp. nutmeg
¼ tsp. cayenne
¼ tsp. dried sage
1 cup flour
oil for frying

Wash and boil potatoes, then peel and mash. Allow to cool.

Add two of the eggs, onion, parsley, green onions, mint, salt, cinnamon, pepper, nutmeg, cayenne, and sage, then thoroughly combine.

In a shallow bowl, beat remaining eggs, then set aside.

Place flour on a flat plate, then set aside.

Form potato mixture into golf-ball sized spheres, then dip in beaten eggs. Roll in the flour, then flatten into patties and place on floured tray.

Place oil in a saucepan to 2 inches deep, then heat. Fry patties until they turn golden brown, then remove with a slotted spoon. Allow to drain on paper towels, then place on a platter and serve hot.

Potato salad - Batata Mutabbala:

This Arabic version of potato salad, which mother often prepared, makes a refreshing change from the usual mayonnaise type and is perfect for picnics and barbecues.

Serves about 6
4 large potatoes, cooked, peeled, then diced into ½ inch cubes
2 eggs, hard boiled, peeled, and chopped
4 Tbsp. finely chopped green onions
4 Tbsp. finely chopped parsley
2 Tbsp. finely chopped fresh mint
4 Tbsp. olive oil
4 Tbsp. lemon juice
2 cloves garlic, crushed
1 tsp. salt
½ tsp. pepper

Place all ingredients, except oil, lemon juice, garlic, salt, and pepper in a salad bowl.

Combine oil, lemon juice, garlic, salt, and pepper, then stir into ingredients in salad bowl. Toss gently, making sure potatoes and eggs do not crumble too much, then serve chilled.

Potato stew - Yakhnit Batata:

Serves 4 to 6
4 Tbsp. olive oil
1 small sweet pepper, finely chopped
1 medium onion, finely chopped
¼ tsp. cayenne
1 Tbsp. ground cumin seeds
½ cup finely chopped coriander leaves
8 cloves garlic, crushed
6 large potatoes (about 2 lbs), peeled and chopped into large pieces
3 cups water
1 tsp. salt
1 lemon rind, finely chopped

Heat oil in a saucepan, then add sweet pepper and sauté for 5 minutes. Add remaining ingredients and bring to boil. Cover and cook over medium heat for 40 minutes or until potatoes are well done, adding more water if necessary. Serve hot.

Potato pie - Saneeyat Batata:

As in Europe, when the potato was introduced into the Arab world it quickly became a common food. This dish is one of the many Arab foods prepared with this vegetable.

Serves about 6
3 cups mashed potatoes
2 medium onions, finely chopped
3 cloves garlic, crushed
4 Tbsp. butter
3 Tbsp. flour
1 Tbsp. finely chopped coriander leaves
¾ tsp. salt
¾ tsp. cumin
½ tsp. pepper
½ tsp. ground ginger
1/8 tsp. cayenne
2 Tbsp. olive oil

Place all ingredients, except olive oil, in a mixing bowl, then thoroughly combine. Spread in a well-greased pan, then score top into diamond shapes. Drizzle on top the olive oil, then bake in a 350°F preheated oven for 35 minutes or until top turns light brown. Serve hot as the main course or as a side dish.

Stuffed potato patties - Kuftat Batata:

This dish, served with a salad and cooked rice, makes a tasty meal.

Makes 24 patties
4 heaping cups mashed potatoes
3 Tbsp. flour
2 tsp. salt
2 Tbsp. butter
2 medium onions, finely chopped
4 cloves garlic, crushed
½ cup pulverized almonds
4 Tbsp. raisins
1 tsp. cumin
½ tsp. pepper
1/8 tsp. cayenne
½ cup finely chopped coriander leaves
2 eggs, beaten
1 cup fine bread crumbs
oil for frying

Place potatoes, flour, and salt in a mixing bowl, then thoroughly combine into a dough, adding a little milk if necessary. Form into 24 balls, then set aside.

Melt butter in a frying pan, then sauté onions over medium heat for 10 minutes. Add garlic, almonds, raisins, cumin, pepper, cayenne, and coriander leaves, then stir-fry for 3 minutes. Set aside as a filling, allowing it to cool.

Place eggs on a plate and bread crumbs on another plate, then set aside.

Take potato ball in one hand, then using finger of other hand, make a well. Place 1 heaping tablespoon of filling in well, then seal and flatten to about ¾-inch thick. Continue until all balls are done.

Place oil to about 1½ inch deep in a saucepan, then heat. Turn patties over in eggs, then in bread crumbs. Deep fry until golden brown, then drain on paper towels and serve warm.

Potatoes and pine nuts - Batata ma' Snobar:

For this dish, slivered almonds may be substituted for the pine nuts.

Serves 6
3 cups mashed potatoes
½ cup finely chopped green onions
1 tsp. salt
½ tsp. pepper
¼ tsp. nutmeg
6 tablespoons olive oil
1 medium onion, finely chopped
2 cloves garlic crushed
½ cup pine nuts

Thoroughly combine potatoes, green onions, salt, pepper, nutmeg, and 3 tablespoons of the olive oil, then spread on a platter and set aside.

Heat remaining oil in a frying pan, then sauté onion and garlic over medium heat for 5 minutes. Add pine nuts, then stir-fry for another 5 minutes or until nuts begin to brown. Spread frying pan contents evenly over potatoes and serve. Δ

Ayoob on Firearms

Answering some well asked questions about personal defense

Jeff Yago, *Backwoods Home*'s energy writer, recently completed a couple of concealed carry handgun courses. The classes apparently left some questions hanging in the air, and Jeff passed along a request through Dave Duffy for those questions to be addressed in this space. Here goes.

Question 1: "What are the basic differences in handguns to help determine which is better for home defense, ease of operation (single versus double action), male or female, caliber, number of cartridges?"

The question covers a lot of ground, so the answer has to be a bit basic.

A double action revolver with swing-out cylinder is easier in terms of administrative handling (loading, unloading, checking, cleaning) than any semiautomatic pistol. This is a decisive advantage for new shooters, or those who don't spend much time maintaining their handgun skills. Many of today's auto pistols are extraordinarily reliable, but if you compare **all** revolvers with **all** "automatics," the revolvers win out in terms of certainty of firing without malfunction. Revolvers are also less maintenance intensive: they don't need constant lubrication because they don't have the long bearing surfaces that are at work within an autoloader's mechanism as it is operated.

The downside of the revolver is less firepower: in the calibers you'd want for self-defense, cartridge capacity is somewhere between five and eight. Even with a speedloader, a revolver is slower to load and reload than is the semiautomatic, with its fast-inserting cartridge magazine. Under stress, you want to shoot the revolver double action, which means a long, heavy trigger pull for every shot. Most auto pistols are "self-cocking," so at least after the first shot, and with some designs even with that first round, you have a shorter, lighter trigger pull that is easier for most people to manage when trying to shoot accurately at speed.

The semiautomatic generally holds more cartridges and is faster to reload, and can be had in models with a manual safety catch feature. This device can slow down an unauthorized person who doesn't know that particular gun, gets his hands on it, and tries to shoot it. Many cops, and some armed citizens, are alive today because the homicidal felon who got their gun away from them and tried to shoot them with it didn't know how to release the thumb safety.

Male or female? It's less about gender than about hand size and shooting experience. A home defense gun is a "pool weapon," like the shotgun in a police patrol car that's on the road for three shifts a day: multiple individuals may be resorting to the same weapon. This means that the gun's size and power have to be tailored to the smallest, least physically capable shooter who is authorized to use it. A large man can easily shoot his wife's short-stocked 20-gauge shotgun or her slim-gripped SIG P239 9mm, but she will be awkward, clumsy, and poorly prepared to defend herself with his long-stocked 12 gauge, or his fat-handled .50 caliber Desert Eagle, which also requires a long finger to properly reach the trigger.

How many cartridges? I personally like a high capacity semiautomatic for home defense, because when you grab a gun in the middle of the night there isn't always time to grab spare ammo. However, the fact is that the overwhelming majority of home defense applications of a gun are over in less than five or six shots. The revolver has a good history in defending home and hearth.

Massad Ayoob

I would recommend the .38 Special (revolver) or 9mm Luger (auto) as minimum caliber in a defensive handgun. The smaller the caliber and the heavier the gun, the lighter the recoil; the more powerful the cartridge and the lighter the gun, the harder it will "kick." The rule of thumb is that you should choose the most powerful gun that can be controlled in accurate rapid fire by the least physically capable person who is authorized to use it. The .40 and .45 caliber semiautomatic pistols aren't hard to control with proper techniques and a good level of familiarity. Larger caliber revolvers kick more and require more training and practice to control and hit with at high speed.

Question 2: "(Please discuss) basic types and calibers of ammunition, and which is better for home defense, target practice, varmints, etc."

Home defense rounds should be hollow points (HP), for the same reason that this type of ammo is universal among American police. The HP is designed to expand into a mushroom shape as it passes through flesh. This slows it down and reduces its penetration, making it unlikely that the projectile will pass through the felon's torso and go on to strike a bystander who was blocked from the shooter's position by the bulk of the criminal he shot.

Shaped like a cookie cutter at its nose, the hollow point is less likely to ricochet at a dangerous and unpredictable angle because where a round nose bullet might glance, the HP tends to bite into the surface and buries itself safely there. The expanding bullet also creates a wider wound channel that imparts more force to the intended target, helping to ensure a more rapid cessation of hostile activity. This is why HPs are better "manstoppers" than standard ammunition.

There are some exotic cartridges sold for defense, such as ultra-light projectiles designed to break up on impact at extremely high velocity. The trouble with these is that they don't always work in semiautomatic pistols, having a different pressure curve than the standard ammunition that the weapon's slide mass and spring compression ratio were developed for at the factory. They are also very expensive, and it can cost up to $600 to run the requisite 200 rounds of the "carry ammo" through the gun to be certain that it will work reliably. For this writer, that factor alone lets out the exotic self-defense loads.

For practice or training, once you know your pistol will work 100% with your chosen defense load, it's

With powerful guns, size matters. At 410 pounds, security man Marcus Kranz holds Benelli auto shotgun on target as he nails it with five rounds of full power 12 gauge buckshot in 69/100ths of one second at 7 yards. Note 3 spent shells circled, in mid-air.

much more economical to buy generic full metal jacket ammo. The more "trigger time" you deposit in the "long term muscle memory" bank, the more swift and skillful you'll be if you have to fire an accurate rescue shot in the course of an emergency.

Reloading your own ammo is a fun hobby, and fits perfectly in the self-reliance mode that runs through the whole backwoods home ethos. At the same time, generic factory produced cartridges are so cheap these days, particularly in 9mm and .38 Special, that when you figure in what your time is worth, it's often more cost effective to buy your practice ammo in bulk instead of making your own ammunition.

Consider special needs. In bear country, you want deeper penetrating bullets, and probably more powerful cartridges, than what you'd want for defense against a 200-pound erect biped. If there are poisonous snakes on the property, a revolver loaded with snake-shot cartridges for at least the first couple of chambers makes a lot of sense. There are many semiautomatic pistols that won't cycle with snake-shot loads, which tend to have too light a recoil impulse to cycle a semiautomatic pistol's slide. If the first shot at the cottonmouth misses, it's a lousy time for your handgun to jam.

Question 3: "(Give us) a few basic common sense rules and laws. For example, in most states, you cannot draw a weapon on somebody just for catching them stealing your stuff. There has to also be a bodily threat to you. Then what can you do if faced with road rage, several bullies on a dark street, or a mugger if they have not shown a gun or knife, yet you have a gun?"

This question really covers a lot of ground. You could write a book about it. Oddly enough, I did. It's called, *In the Gravest Extreme: the Role of the Firearm in Personal Protection.* Dave Duffy sells it through *Backwoods Home*, and you'll find ordering information on page 94 of this issue.

Let me offer another reference. When Dave asked me to write for *Backwoods Home* some years ago, he asked me to kick off with a series exploring when private citizens could use the lethal force of a firearm in defense of themselves, their families, and others. You can find these on the *Backwoods Home* back issue CDs, on-line (www.backwoodshome.com) with the magazine's electronically recorded back issues, and in the "Ayoob on Firearms" CD. For ordering info, see pages 96 and 97.

I'll address one point right here, though. If I find a kid stealing a bike out of my back yard, no, I'm not going to pull a gun on him. However, if I find a burglar in my home, he's definitely going to be at gunpoint. Convicted burglars I interviewed after their arrests told me that most of the time they either carried a weapon of their own, or armed themselves with something once they entered the home. Breaking and entering is a serious felony, and you have every right to take such a felon at gunpoint. You don't shoot him for breaking in or stealing, but you **prepare** to shoot him if he attacks you.

You will often hear the figure quoted that only about 7% of burglars commit their crimes armed. That's probably because only about 7% of burglars are caught red-handed at the scene. Most are arrested later when an investigation leads police to them. Their confession will typically include a statement like, "Gosh, officer, I wouldn't carry a gun when I break into a house because I'm afraid of a higher penalty if I'm caught." Yeah, right.

Queston 4: "When faced with a break-in attacker or other potential threat to your life, where do you aim, how should you stand, how should you hold the weapon? In other words, with seconds to pull out a gun, most people will not have time to think 'does the Weaver stance require my left or right foot forward?'"

Good points, Jeff, good points.

First, when you take a suspect at gunpoint, KEEP YOUR FINGER OFF THE TRIGGER! In a stressful moment like this, any number of stimuli can cause a convulsion of the trigger finger that kills an unarmed man who has just surrendered to you. Dr. Roger Enoka, the physiologist who has most authoritatively studied this phenomenon, enumerates various causes: startle reflex, postural disturbance, inter-limb response, and so on.

It's not enough to rest the finger on the edge of the trigger guard. The tight muscles of your hand will hold the finger taut there, and if you are startled, the finger can snap straight back to the trigger, unintentionally firing the gun. The trigger finger should be up on the frame of the firearm, handgun, or long gun.

At the classes we teach around the country for Lethal Force Institute (www.ayoob.com), we urge that the fingertip be in contact with the frame, pointed inward toward the gun, with the trigger finger flexed. That way, if the strong flexor muscles of the hand convulse, the finger comes across the trigger instead of straight into it, and is thus much less likely to cause an accidental discharge. It's also faster to get to the trigger if you do have to fire, if you start with the finger flexed on the frame.

For many years, I've made a point of leveling the gun at the pelvis of everyone I took at gunpoint. The main reason is that this point of aim allows you to see the suspect's hands. If you aim at his head or chest or belly, your gun and your hands block your view of his hands. Man is the tool-bearing mammal, and therefore by definition the weapon-bearing mammal. A man will kill you with his hands. Thus, the **Golden Rule of law enforcement: "Watch their hands!"**

With the gun leveled groin high, you'll be able to see in time if the suspect reaches for a weapon in his belt or in his pocket. If your gun is blocking your view of his hands, your first indication that you need to shoot will be when his bullet punches into your

Desert Eagle chambered for giant .50 Action Express cartridge is not for beginners . . .

Photo credit: Andy Vissers

. . . as handgun master David Maglio demonstrates with a test shot.

body. Talk about being behind the curve.

When a man perceives a firearm aimed at his private parts, a tremendous psychological effect is also engendered. A lot of bad guys have been shot or stabbed before, and have a lot of ego invested in having survived it. More of them have role models they met on the street or in prison who showed off the bullet scars on their torsos. This can reduce their fear of being shot in the trunk of the body. But NOTHING reduces a man's fear of being shot in the genitals. This point of aim seems to definitely get their attention, in my experience.

If you do have to fire, a shot at the pelvis is angling downward. This reduces the chance of an exiting or missing shot striking a bystander a distance behind the felon, who was blocked from your view by the criminal's body or by the tunnel vision that so often afflicts people involved in these situations. Finally, the pelvic area tends to produce dynamically "man-stopping" gunshot wounds. They tear up the lower abdominal viscera frightfully, and if the pelvis is smashed, the cross-member of skeletal support is compromised and the body almost always collapses.

Some advocate aiming the gun at the ground or floor ahead of the offender. One theory for this is that it reduces the crime of *Aggravated Assault* to that of *Brandishing a Firearm.* I say that's rubbish: it is no crime to point a gun at a felon you have caught in your home, or an armed criminal about to attack you on the street. A more reasonable argument for aiming at the ground ahead of the subject is that if your gun accidentally discharges, the shot hits the ground and not a human being who has not yet done anything to warrant his being killed or injured.

That's a good argument as far as it goes. My concern with it, however, is that criminals are predators, and predators are seasoned observers of body language. Pointing the gun at the ground instead of at him can lead him to believe, "This person doesn't dare even point the gun at me! Why should I worry that he might dare to pull the trigger?" If that happens, the critical deterrent effect of the gun can be lost. If he is emboldened sufficiently to attack, either you'll have to blow him away or you might be hurt or killed yourself, and these are not mutually exclusive outcomes. Some I have taken at gunpoint with my weapon leveled at their pelvis have fled; as a cop, I must pursue, and as a civilian you ***do not*** have the right to shoot a fleeing criminal. Most criminals taken at gunpoint have surrendered; none have yet attacked. I want to keep it that way. This is why I will personally continue to index the weapon on the opponent's pelvis when I take a person at gunpoint. The choice is yours.

As to stance, while the angled body position of the Weaver stance is still very popular, the Isosceles stance makes foot placement irrelevant. Both arms are locked straight out, putting the gun at body center, so it doesn't matter which foot is forward. The big thing you want to be thinking about when taking someone at gunpoint is increasing the distance between you and him, and perhaps getting behind cover. Always remain alert for his potential accomplices, who may enter the scenario from directly behind you or from your flank.

"House guns" should adapt to smallest and largest user. Petite Cindy, a firearms instructor, is deadly with this Beretta Storm carbine.

The fixed stock of a rifle or shotgun sized for 5'0" lady in center can be operated efficiently by males of 6'5" (left) or 6'6" (right), but not vice versa.

Question 5: "For home defense, where is the best place to keep a handgun, where is a thief most likely to look, and if you do lock it up and keep the ammunition separate like all the anti-gun lobby says, how can you get it, unlock it, load it, and do all this most likely in the dark when you hear a strange noise at the back door when home alone?"

You've got it right, Jeff. You can't jump in your car and respond to an emergency in time if you first have to open the hood and hook up its battery, and you can't unlock two cabinets and bring gun and ammo together before an intruder kicking down your door is upon you.

For me, it has boiled down to two modes. During waking hours, I simply carry the gun. On my person, it is at once always immediately accessible to me, and always inaccessible to unauthorized hands. If the lifestyle doesn't allow the handgun to be worn visibly, a compact, powerful handgun like the Ruger SP101 .357 Magnum snub-nose revolver can be worn comfortably and discreetly concealed, "24/7."

When asleep, I keep the weapon at bedside. If there are children (or adults, for that matter) in the home who are not at the level of development where they can be trusted around firearms 100%, the handgun should be in a locked security box in the bedroom, preferably a design like the *Gun Vault*, which can be released by feel in the dark by punching a simple combination into an ergonomic and easily palpable keypad. I currently live alone, so I just leave the pistol on the floor beside the bed, concealed from any intruder's view by what appears to be a casually dropped magazine.

I appreciate Jeff's questions. The fact that the questions had been left hanging in the air shouldn't be blamed on Jeff's instructors. Most concealed carry courses just aren't long enough to cover everything that needs to be covered in terms of law, tactics, ethics, weapon choices, psychological preparation, and of course skill at arms for those who might find themselves in harm's way with a gun in their hand. This is why our baseline course at Lethal Force Institute—the LFI-I class geared for armed citizens—is scheduled at 40 hours. It takes that long to cover the essentials. For information on the internet, surf to www.ayoob.com.

For the same reason, a three thousand word article isn't enough to cover it. That's why I hope readers will forgive me for referring them to the other sources available through *Backwoods Home Magazine*. Δ

Self Defense for Women — a New Year's resolution I kept

By Kelly McCarthy

Ah, those good intentions. Every year I make a list and every year I fail to keep them all. I still weigh many pounds more than I'd like to, the ability to cook gourmet food is still a dream, and the screen doors still need replacing. But some years I do achieve a couple of things.

I finally managed to allocate the five evenings necessary to complete a self-defense course for women run by our local police. Called SAFE (Sexual Assault Free & Empowered), I am told it is similar in many ways to the RAD (Rape Aggression Defense) course widely available throughout the country. Over a series of evenings the police gave us classroom lectures, taught us moves in a gym, and gave us a "real life experience" in a recreation of a typical street with storefronts and a home. They showed us how best to defend ourselves against attackers both outside and inside our homes. A useful tip such as, don't leave your cell phone downstairs at night because an intruder may cut the phone line to your house, sounds so obvious I wonder why I'd never thought of it before. The course was designed for women of all ages, all sizes, and all abilities. Very large ladies and very tiny ones were shown ways to use their size and mobility to the best advantage.

The police stressed that quite often it's your own thinking that makes you a victim. We were told that the transference of power to an assailant happens as soon as they touch you, even if the first touch isn't particularly threatening. They may just have put their hand on your shoulder.

One officer also pointed out that if someone comes up to you and says, "Come with me, I have a gun in my pocket!" your natural instinct is to go with him. In actual fact, a weapon in his pocket is not yet a threat to you. He still has to get it out. You probably still have time to slam him hard with a punch to the nose and run for it. They teach you not to think as a victim. You have to train yourself to think practically under pressure and when in fear. To think: "That gun is not pointed at me. A gun is linear; if it isn't pointed at me, it can't hit me. If I can control the barrel, I can control the fire." Or: "He's bigger than me. I have to use his weight to make him fall." And all the time you're trying to remember to breathe, to shout loudly, to attract attention. And most of all, to keep fighting.

I discovered a lot about myself in the real-life situations when the police officers (dressed in red foam from head to foot to protect themselves) attacked me. One thing I discovered is that my natural reaction to the command, "Give me your purse!" is to kick you in the privates. This is wrong apparently, as my life should be worth more to me than my purse. This is a good point and I ought to give it more consideration. Most days my purse contains a magnesium firestarter, a penknife, a small flashlight, a first aid kit, a wallet full of supermarket loyalty cards, a crumpled mass of used tissues, one credit card, and never enough cash to feed a meter. It probably isn't worth a small bruise, let alone getting killed for. If you want to learn how to fight for your life (not a purse), I strongly recommend you sign up for one of these courses. And remember, it's a great gift to give a college senior before she graduates into the big bad world out there.

The other thing I finally got round to doing in 2005 was learning about guns. I come from a non-gun culture. I knew nothing about guns. Where I used to live only the criminals were tooled up. I prefer it here. I like the idea of an armed populace. I like the idea of me being armed. Trouble is, I knew so little it was dangerous. I couldn't even tell whether a gun was loaded, or the safety was on or off. I didn't think it was safe for me to get a gun until I knew more about them. So off I went to the NRA. The course I went on was organized by *The Patrick Henry Institute's Patriette's* program, but the training was all conducted by senior firearms instructors of the National Rifle Association. (They have a special women's program if you prefer to learn with your sisters.)

Wow! The NRA is great! Their instructors don't patronize you; they just give it to you straight. Apparently they like training women, as we don't come with all the baggage that men have had since childhood. We haven't seen every bent stick as a gun. We're not obsessed with size. We are obsessed with safety. We listen.

In the NRA's *First Steps Pistol Orientation* course, I learned how to take a gun apart, to clean it, how to use the sights (aim using the front not the rear sights), how to load the magazine (often miscalled the clip), and where not to point the thing. After a four-hour introduction course, I was given an hour's one-on-one session on the NRA range with a seasoned instructor. So seasoned he used to be a sheriff. I practiced sitting down first so that I got used to the feel of the recoil (not that much on the gun used in the *Patriette's* program—which was a 9mm Glock semi-automatic) and the noise. Even with the ear protectors I was amazed at how loud small arms gunfire is. Then they let me shoot a circular target before moving on to a body-shaped target. In the final 10 minutes they controlled the target so that it would flip around from narrow to flat on, and made me fire off two shots into the torso in two seconds. In the hour I was there I fired a hundred rounds and got a really good feel for the gun and a great respect for its power. I sure hope I never have to shoot someone, but at least I learned another self defense technique. I can recommend this course to any gun-shy or gun-curious females of any age.

So what does the 2006 resolutions list hold for me? This year's number one task is to go through all my emergency supplies and list and date the perishables. I need to add up all the calories in there and make sure there are 8,000 calories per day for three months. That's based on 2,000 calories per person per day for four of us. It's a bit more than we need but stress burns extra calories. And I always over cater! It also allows us to cut rations without much pain if a situation gets worse or becomes more prolonged. What sort of emergency? Oh, you know, the usual range of nightmare scenarios. Yellowstone erupting, avian flu quarantine, WMD attack, smallpox outbreak…

Another thing on my list is important but I never get around to it, which I should because it's ultimately self-reliant. We have a well of some description in our yard. It has a rusted old pump on it. I say at least once a month that we're going to get out there and fix it up. Three years later, it's still all rusted and the nearest I got to getting a new one was looking on the internet. Your own water source is such a valuable commodity that I deserve a good spanking for not having dealt with it.

I also need to make a big checklist for an evacuation (we've been hit by a hurricane before) and put all the items on it back in the places where we expect them to be. There's nothing worse than trying to track something down in a panic. I also need to redo all my emergency documents as some have changed. I need to check the emergency bags in the car to check they're still OK and that nobody "borrowed" anything. I need to redraw the family evacuation plan to reflect recent road changes.

And added to all this, I shall continue on my quest to lose a few pounds, cook gourmet, and get the damn screen doors fixed. Δ

Flashlight! flashlight! who's got the flashlight?

By Jeffrey R. Yago, P. E., CEM

If the standard procedure for turning on your flashlight includes pounding 10 times on a table top, removing, then reinserting the same old batteries, and finally staring blankly into the unlit bulb, then perhaps it's time to rethink how well you are prepared for the next power outage or emergency.

Articles hitting the newsstands after the current rash of wild fires, hurricanes, and power outages are encouraging everyone to have an emergency pack, since outside help or evacuation may not be possible for several days. Many of my past articles have addressed emergency preparedness in great detail, and you may find it helpful to dig out some of the back issues.

All of these articles suggest that your emergency preparedness supplies include a battery-powered flashlight and extra batteries. However, there are hundreds of different flashlight types, using all sizes of batteries. Some have incandescent bulbs, some have krypton bulbs, some have LED lamps, and some have fluorescent tubes. In addition, there are flashlights designed to operate on 6-volt lantern batteries, multiple AAA, AA, C, or D cell batteries, plug-in rechargeable batteries, and mechanical motion recharging devices.

Flashlight testing

Ever wonder just how long a flashlight will operate on a set of batteries? Under normal circumstances almost any flashlight will last long enough for a given task. If the batteries are dead, you can head to the corner store to buy more. But during a real emergency, it is possible that not only your neighbors, but also everyone in your entire city or state may be without power. Your flashlights may be your only source of emergency lighting for a week or more. Even if you can find a store that is open, I assure you the flashlights and batteries were sold out days ago.

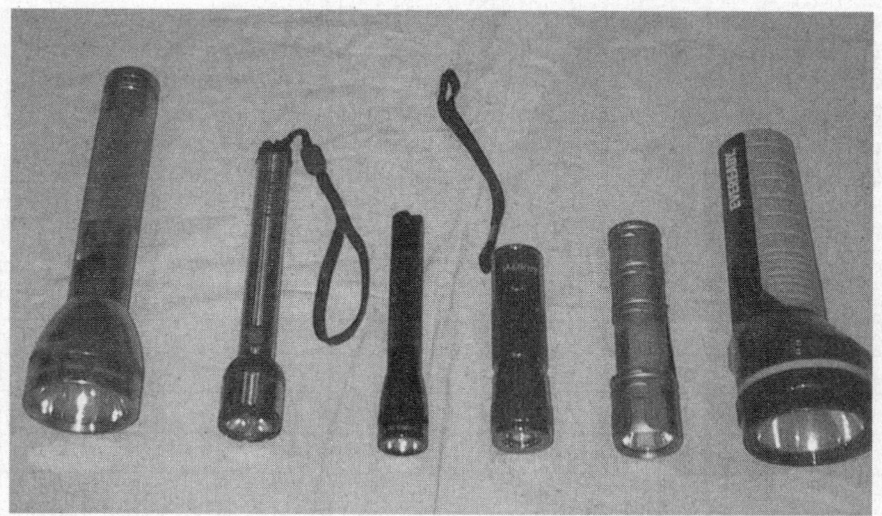

Five new technology flashlights tested against standard 2 "D" cell flashlights. (Left to right) MagLite, Garrity, Mini-MagLite, Garrity LED, Dorcy LED, and Eveready 2 "D" cell flashlight

No, shopping for real emergency battery-powered lighting does not involve looking in the discount bins for one of those $3 plastic flashlights with a slide switch. You need at least two real emergency flashlights, and expect to pay up to $20 each, plus another $20 for an extra supply of good quality batteries and a few extra bulbs. Rechargeable batteries are good for everyday use, but do not hold their charge long. This makes rechargeable batteries less effective for long-life emergency backup power, not to mention that without electricity they cannot be recharged.

I no longer buy any flashlight that uses the older style incandescent bulbs and cheap slide switch, as these never seem to work when you need them and quickly discharge their batteries. Some of the newer flashlights use a much brighter krypton bulb. These are a good choice when you need to shine a spotlight a very long distance, but they will still use up batteries faster than desirable during extended emergency conditions.

New flashlight technology

The newest generation of battery-powered flashlights use one or more light emitting diodes (LED) as the

General Electric fluorescent lantern provides room-filling light using four "D" cell batteries.

light source. Although these were fairly dim when first introduced, recent advancements have made a vast improvement in both their white color quality and brightness. Unlike all other lamps, an LED does not have a filament to burn out. It is actually a semi-conductor device like an electronic transistor, and unlike an incandescent bulb, an LED lamp has polarized positive (+) and negative (-) terminals. The theoretical life of an LED lamp is in excess of many thousands of hours of operation when used with the proper power source. In addition to long life, an LED lamp consumes battery power measured in millionths of an amp, which greatly extends how long a given set of batteries will last.

Another new type of portable battery-powered lighting is the fluorescent lantern. Due to the long tube shape of a typical fluorescent lamp, most of these battery-powered lights look like a small version of an old camping lantern, not a flashlight.

Although a battery-powered fluorescent light still uses lots of battery power to operate, they can provide really good lighting levels throughout an entire room, and are ideal to illuminate a kitchen or living room during evening meals when a flashlight would illuminate only a very limited area. I recommend having at least one battery-powered lantern to go along with any other emergency flashlights you have, and limit its use to only a few hours each evening during a power outage as they consume more power than any of the other flashlights we tested.

Unless you want to stock 10 different sizes of batteries, I suggest limiting all your battery-powered flashlights, lanterns, radios, and electronic games to just two or three basic battery sizes. This makes things much simpler when they can get complicated really fast, and limiting battery sizes allows stocking more of each. Since newer lighting and electronic technology is moving to higher voltages and smaller sizes, many of today's battery-powered devices may require three or four smaller AA or AAA batteries instead of one or two of the larger C or D size batteries typically used in older devices.

How to select a flashlight

To help demystify the process of buying a flashlight for real emergency preparedness, I recently tested five of the most popular battery-powered flashlights and lanterns currently being marketed against a standard two D cell traditional flashlight. During a lengthy power outage, you are primarily interested in finding your way around an otherwise dark house, so I have not reviewed those foot-long D cell battery-powered flashlights that can shine a spotlight a mile away. We want to illuminate a small room, not blind a deer in the next county. I would like to point out that this was a less than scientific testing process, since we are interested in the relative differences between models and not specific individual perfor-

Testing Results

MODEL	Batteries	Primary Area Diameter	Secondary Area Diameter	Foot-Candles	Run Time-Hrs
Garrity Incandescent	2 AA	16 inches	5 feet	11	10
Standard Incandescent	2 D	6 inches	6 feet	50	18
Garrity White LED	3 AAA	19 inches	6 feet	9	104
Dorcy 1-watt LED	3 AAA	5 feet	8 feet	50	80
Mini-Maglight Incandescent	2 AA	20 inches	7 feet	10	9
Maglight Krypton	2 C	26 inches	5 feet	15	8
GE Fluorescent Lantern	4 D	-----	12-ft x 20-ft room	7	41

Note: Illumination area and foot-candle readings were measured six feet from light source.

mance. Whatever flaws there were in my testing, it affected all models the same.

Since a flashlight that provides a large or very bright area of illumination may have a shorter battery life, I have included a very rough measurement of illuminated area along with light brightness. I also noted how long the particular flashlight operated on a single set of batteries. All flashlight tests started out with the same brand of good quality fresh batteries. Note that some flashlights require more batteries than other designs, which will also affect useful operating life. I am using the term "useful operating life" to mean that point at which the light output is no longer bright enough to provide an adequate lighting level, not the point when the light goes completely out.

Testing setup in photography studio shows tripod-mounted light meter and measurements of distances for flashlight under test.

Measurements being taken in totally dark room of flashlight's illuminated circle area. Each flashlight tested had a totally different illuminated area even though all were mounted the same distance to background.

Testing procedures

I set up my photography studio with an off-white flat background that covered an entire end wall. I took a light level meter that measures three different ranges of foot-candle illumination levels and mounted it in the center of this background. I then positioned a stand to hold each flashlight with the lens exactly six feet from the light meter and background. Although I could have achieved different readings at other distances, I felt this would be a good average of working distance. The measurements of the area being illuminated were taken in a totally dark room, with the flashlight under test being the only illumination. All of the flashlights produced a very bright center area, with a larger outer area that was much less bright. The outer areas still had adequate illumination for finding your way around a dark room, but only the primary center areas were bright enough to read or work by.

Final results

The table summarizes the tests of six flashlights and one fluorescent lantern. Although any of these would easily light your way down a dark stairwell or rural road, several models provided much better lighting quality and longer battery life. All of the incandescent flashlights produced a slightly yellow light, while all of the LED flashlights and the fluorescent lantern gave off a white light. The 1-watt "super bright" LED flashlight I tested by Dorcy was actually almost blinding, and provided the largest overall illumination area.

When reviewing the results of this testing, note the extremely long time all of the LED style flashlights lasted, compared to the incandescent. In fact, I called it quits after four days of continuous operation, as both LED flashlights were still providing enough light to find your way in a very dark room, but their light levels had dropped to a tiny fraction of their original illumination. The Garrity white LED was the overall winner in operating hours, and did this with only three tiny AAA batteries.

All of the flashlights illuminated a very bright round circle directly in the center of focus. However, the fluorescent lantern was able to illuminate all areas of my entire 12-foot x 20-foot studio, although no areas were illuminated as brightly as a flashlight. I strongly recommend owning at least one of these fluorescent battery lanterns. I think the traditional slide switch flashlight with two C or D cell batteries is not suitable for extended power outages due to their shorter operating life and difficulty with their switches and battery connections making good electrical contact.

All of the LED style flashlights tested had an anodized aluminum housing, a sealed push button switch, and machine-threaded parts with waterproof rubber seals. I selected these six "finalists" due to their smaller size and rugged construction, and all would make a good general purpose flashlight. My hands-down favorite was the Dorcy "Metal Gear" 1-watt LED model. The Garrity LED was my second choice, which actually lasted far longer than the Dorcy LED model due to the less bright LED. Both were small with a single LED lamp, and both required three small AAA size batteries. I really like the metal belt clip on the Dorcy, but some of you may prefer the nylon pouch with belt loop that comes with the Garrity.

The 1-watt LED Dorcy "Metal Gear" model produced a very bright center area, with a large outer area that was also fairly bright. The Garrity LED model produced a large diameter center light with very little lighted area outside this circle, which gave the appearance of a brightly focused stage spotlight.

Most of the incandescent type flashlights are focused for much greater distances than the LED types, but for compact size and excellent battery life I believe your emergency flashlights should be LED design with a gasketed, moisture-resistant, metal housing. Most flashlight manufacturers are starting to add an LED model to their product line. I liked the Dorcy 1-watt LED model so much I purchased three for myself after the testing ended. Most of the flashlights in this article are available from Lowe's, Home Depot, and Wal-Mart.

Battery considerations

During an extended power outage, you may need to operate a flashlight or fluorescent lantern for up to six hours per night, for a week or more. This is much longer than most standard flashlights are intended to operate, and could consume up to 24 batteries depending on what type and size flashlight you purchase. This is still more batteries than you normally keep on hand, so you will need to change your thinking about stocking extra batteries, and be sure to check their expiration dates every few months.

Buying the best flashlight in the world is still a waste of money if you are not willing to stock lots of spare high-quality batteries to keep it operating. The more expensive alkaline batteries will last much longer than standard batteries and are well worth the cost for your emergency preparedness. I like to vacuum-pack my emergency batteries in multiples of four, for each flashlight's battery count. A flashlight requiring three batteries will need several packs of twelve batteries per pack. This way you will not need to open more sealed packs than necessary at one time, and I keep them stored with my emergency flashlights. Do not store batteries in a freezer as some people suggest, but you do need to keep them in a cool and dry location.

Again, this was a somewhat subjective test, but should still provide a good idea of what to look for. Be sure to keep in mind the area of illumination when deciding which model is right for you, and do not be surprised if you need more than one type to meet all of your emergency lighting requirements.

(Jeff Yago is a licensed professional engineer and certified energy manager with more than 25 years experience in the energy conservation field. He is also certified by the North American Board of Certified Energy Practitioners as a licensed solar installer. He has extensive solar thermal and solar photovoltaic system design experience and has authored numerous articles and texts.) Δ

I'VE GOT THREE FLASHLIGHTS-- ONE IS LOST, ONE NEEDS BATTERIES AND ONE IS BROKEN...

(Cartoon by Jerry King)

Survival firebuilding skills

By Corcceigh Green

Firebuilding skills are essential for those who may find themselves in survival situations. As a testimony to this idea, Americans in the Gulf Coast States experienced a string of hurricanes late in 2005, two of which were devastating in their destructive force. Hurricanes Katrina and Rita left many homeless and without resources. Regardless of your thoughts on who should have responded and provided assistance to the victims of the hurricanes, these people found themselves in life-threatening situations. Should such destruction have occurred during the winter months due to avalanche, earthquake, or other disasters, we would need to immediately provide ourselves with heat and shelter.

When learning to build a fire, it helps to know something of a fire's anatomy. A fire has working parts and components that work together to perform like any other engine. In the case of fire, we are building an engine that produces heat. Heat which our lives could depend on. The first component of a fire is the coal bed. The coal bed produces the greatest amount of heat and creates an updraft of dry hot air, which is the second component of our fire. The updraft interacts with the third component of a working fire: the fuel. The fuel may be wood, paper, coal, dried buffalo chips, or anything that burns. The updraft of dry, hot air created by the coal bed flows around the fuel. This dries out and heats up the fuel to the point that the fuel releases gasses that are ignited by the heat. The fuel begins to burn down to its basic chemical composition. As it does this, it releases heat, and the gasses it releases become incandescent. We see this as flames, our fourth component. Soon the chemical composition of the fuel left in the greatest amount is carbon. At this point, the fuel has become coal and has joined the coal bed, replacing those that have lost even their carbon and burned to ash. This completes the cycle of a fire.

The makings of a fire: Tinder and kindling in the fire ring; extra kindling and starter logs set outside the fire ring; and some firewood.

By understanding the anatomy of a fire, you can see that building a coal bed is the surest way to guarantee success and maybe save your life. There are some fundamental techniques you must master to turn a spark into a coal bed and a warm fire.

First is in preparation of your fire area. More commonly known as a fire ring, this entails clearing an area of debris so that sparks cannot ignite anything and cause an out-of-control fire. Within the cleared area, place stones in a ring to contain coals and fuel. Keep in mind that you should build your shelter close to your fire, so choose the area wisely and keep the fire to a manageable size.

A fire begins as a spark. You will need something to create that spark. Most people are primarily familiar with matches as a means to accomplish that. Matches can start a fire quickly and easily under good weather conditions, but they must be sheltered and kept away from wind and rain. Matches must also have a reliable striking surface. Strike- anywhere matches can produce a spark by striking against a piece of sandstone found anywhere, but other matches must have a surface coated with potassium chlorate to produce spark and flame. When packing matches for your fire starting kit, always pack strike-anywhere matches in a weatherproof container.

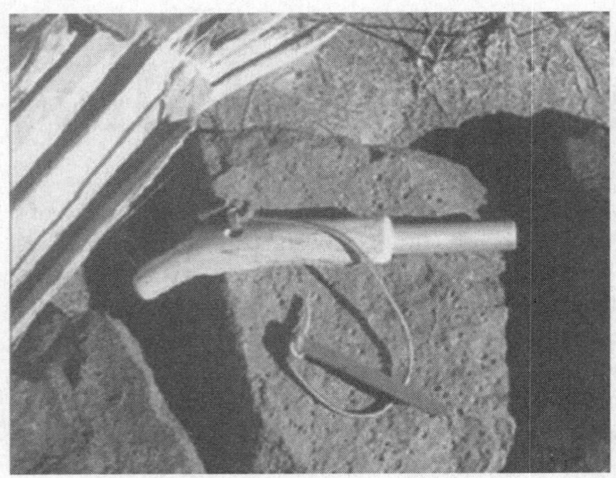

A modern flint and steel fire starter. This one sports a magnesium rod,a composite large flint rod, a deer antler handle, and a steel striker blade.

When matches are wet or used under very windy conditions, they will not work reliably. Since you may need to build a fire under the worst of conditions, it is prudent to learn other methods of striking a spark. I am never without a modern version of the old flint and steel fire starters. Most of these starters make use of modern composite flints, which provide a better spark than natural flints. They also make use of magnesium, which burns extremely hot when ignited and will catch tinder and kindling even when wet. The flint and magnesium themselves could be drenched and the water would not interfere with the flint's ability to produce spark nor the magnesium to ignite. This is because magnesium produces its own oxygen as it burns and will burn effectively even under water.

The most common magnesium/flint fire starter on the market utilizes a block of magnesium, a small flint rod, and a key chain. These fire starters cost in the $6 range. They fit in the pocket or pack quite easily. My personal fire starter utilizes a medium diameter magnesium rod, a larger composite flint rod capable of starting more fires, a handle made of deer antler that allows the user to place the flint onto the tinder while striking a spark in an ideal position and a steel striking blade that saves the blade of your knife. These cost in the $20 range. I am in the woods so often that I consider the extra advantages worth the extra bucks.

I consider the flint and magnesium fire starters more reliable than matches as they start a fire even in wet, windy conditions. There is a common misconception regarding how the flint and steel method works, which hinders many from creating a spark. The term "striking a spark" is a bit deceptive. This causes many to strike the flint with the steel in a chipping motion, which is inefficient. The correct method is to firmly rub the steel down the surface of the flint. Start with the steel at the top of the flint either toward the fire starter's handle or your hand, depending on your fire starter's design, and firmly rub the steel downward toward the tinder. This will create a shower of sparks that will land on the tinder. Place the bottom end of the flint on top of the tinder before this procedure, and you will be guaranteed that the tinder will catch a good spark.

A fuel lighter should also be carried, especially by the novice. The low-cost fuel lighters sold in grocery stores have been made safe to carry in the pack or pocket by the addition of a safety lever that must be pressed down upon "flicking" the lighter wheel to maintain the butane fuel supply to the flame. These lighters are convenient because a flame can be steadily supplied, which is more likely to dry out and ignite wet tinder and kindling. A candle stub, when sheltered from the wind and rain, will also supply a constant flame to wet tinder and kindling, but you will still need something to create a spark to light the candle.

First, place tinder in the middle of the fire ring. (Tinder is anything flammable that will catch and hold a spark.) The best tinder material is paper towels, toilet paper, newspaper, tissue paper, cotton balls soaked in petroleum jelly, char cloth, and used gun cleaning patches. Tinder material found in nature is cedar, birch and a few other tree barks, cattail pollen, goatsbeard and dandelion seed cotton, bird's nests, the pith of plants like elderberry, and dry punky wood. Of the natural materials, cedar bark works best for me, since it can be pounded with a stone to separate its fibers. The fibers are then wadded together loosely to catch a spark. When the cedar bark is ignited, it catches kindling very reliably. Should you run low on tinder in the wild, look for the above sources even while you have a fire blazing. If they are wet, keep them close to your fire to dry them out.

Next, place kindling on top of your tinder. (Kindling is fuel of a small diameter that will combust easily.) It

Tinder made from cedar bark. Pound the bark with a rock to separate fibers, pull apart, and lightly wad together. This tinder reliably lights kindling every time.

is generally any dry twig that you can gather, but not all wood is good for kindling. Cedar catches more readily than any other kindling, but it does not make great coals. Coals or embers are necessary to keep the fire going and to produce heat. Maple, Douglas fir, tamarack, and hardwoods are great for making coals. Place the cedar on the tinder in order to catch a quick, hot fire, and place the other woods on the cedar to create a quickly forming coal bed. You cannot carry much kindling with you due to bulk and weight, but it would be helpful to carry a small amount to ensure that you have some dry kindling to start a fire on a wet day.

Many people place the kindling around the tinder in a teepee fashion. I like to place the kindling on the tinder in a cross-hatch fashion. I can place the cedar closer to the tinder, then better coal-forming woods on top of the cedar. This also seems to support the starter logs more readily.

Starter logs are merely thinner versions of firewood or logs. They are much thicker than kindling, but thinner than the larger, longer-burning logs you will gather. These are faster burning, but will quickly add to the coal bed of your fire. Place the starter logs on top of your kindling before starting the fire. Because the starter logs are thinner, they dry faster and are more readily combustible, ensuring that soon you will have a roaring fire. When the fire is burning well, add the thicker firewood.

The need for a fire is most pressing under less than ideal conditions. Whatever emergency has you outside your home or turned around in the woods, most likely has brought rain, snow, and wind with it. You can survive by building a fire if you keep your head and use the following techniques:

1. Rain or snow is blowing onto your fire area: Build a reflector half way around your fire ring in the direction the wind is blowing to protect from wind and rain or snow.

2. The firewood is soaked or caked in ice: Use a hatchet to chop away the outer wood and use the drier inner wood. Use more tinder to dry out and ignite wet kindling. Scrape magnesium from your fire starter onto the tinder before lighting. Magnesium burns at 5,400 degrees and will dry the kindling quicker.

3. Your fire keeps sputtering out because of wet conditions: You need to "feed the fire." You must build up a coal bed under the wet starter logs by continually adding dry or semi-dry kindling until your starter logs have dried out and ignited. Collect wood from the upper boughs of dead trees, which will be drier. Carry some dry kindling with you to help catch wetter kindling.

4. Always carry a fire starting kit on your person. When you are hunting or camping do not leave this kit in camp. Always have it with you. The kit should include strike-anywhere matches in a weatherproof case, a magnesium/flint and steel fire starter, tinder (cedar bark, paper, used gun cleaning patches, petroleum jelly soaked cotton balls) in a weatherproof case, some dry kindling, a candle stub, a lighter, and a hatchet.

5. Carry a simple shelter-making kit that includes a military surplus weatherproof poncho in very good to excellent condition, a metalized emergency "space blanket," twine, string, or clothesline, and a knife. This is all that's necessary to build an emergency shelter. I've done so with less.

Last, but nowhere near least, is what is between your ears. Having the knowledge to build a fire under adverse conditions only gets you part way home. Now that you know the techniques to build a fire, you'll need to practice. Most people have accomplished building a fire while camping under ideal conditions. For practice under more severe conditions, try lighting a fire in your backyard the next time it rains or snows. Leave some firewood and kindling out in the weather and see what you can do with it. Survival isn't a game. It's a matter of life and death. Δ

Jordan Bothur, 6 months, of Columbia, Connecticut, goes nose to nose with newborn kid, Siouxsie. Also shown are brothers, Derek, 12, left, and Ian, 15.

How to grow POTATOES

By Alice Brantley Yeager

Potato plants need plenty of sunshine, a well drained soil, and no weed or grass interference. Ideal soil is a loose sandy loam with plenty of humus and potash content. Soil needs to have a pH of 4.8-6.5, but don't hesitate to plant them if the pH is a little higher than that. Almost any good garden soil will raise potatoes, but like anything else, potatoes have their limitations where climate and soil are concerned. Don't expect much of a crop where wet or boggy conditions prevail.

Also, the higher the pH, the more likely the tubers will be victims of scab. If the scab is not too intense, the tubers will be usable by scraping or peeling them before cooking.

If your garden, as a whole, needs liming, be sure not to apply lime within a year of planting to the area where potatoes are to be grown. Almost the same rule applies to digging in barnyard fertilizers. Those are best applied several months before potatoes are to be planted so that they may be thoroughly decomposed by planting time. Turning under a good green cover crop such as clover or other leguminous green manure crop within a few weeks of planting potatoes is very beneficial.

Timing is crucial in planting potatoes. Here in southwestern Arkansas (Zone 8), there's the old rule of planting as close as you can get to February 14. However, that definitely has to be adjusted if planting conditions are "not right"—too wet, too cold, etc. If this is your first time to plant potatoes, check with a gardening neighbor or your local County Extension Agent. They will know about the best planting time in your area.

Most local seed stores have seed potatoes available in early spring. A few will have them in the fall, too, but fall is a risky time for potatoes, as temperature is a crucial factor in raising them. An early frost can wipe out a potato patch. Potatoes do best when temperatures go down to about 53°F at night and do not soar into the upper 80s or 90s during the day.

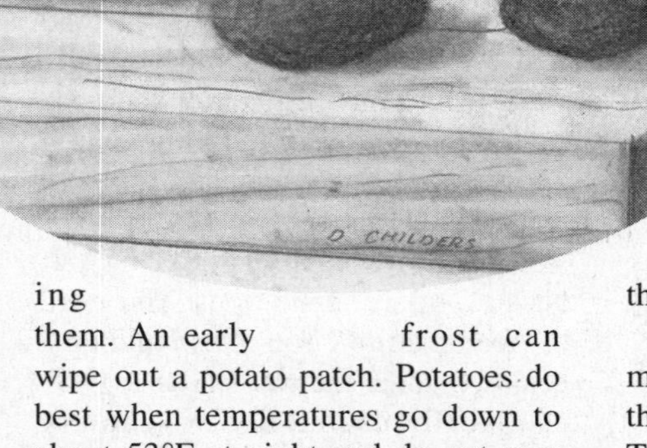

If ordered from a seed company, seed potatoes will arrive already cut and treated unless you specify whole potatoes. If purchased locally, you will probably get whole potatoes, which you will need to prepare for planting. Simply cut the potatoes in fairly large pieces, each piece containing one or two eyes. It's best not to have several eyes on a piece as too many shoots will develop, thus cutting down on the yield.

Cut the pieces a day or so in advance of planting. Spread them out on a level surface in a cool room so that the cut surfaces will dry somewhat. (A "cured" surface is more disease resistant than fresh cut.) Another good preventive against disease is to put the pieces in a bag containing some powdered sulphur; shake until all are coated and plant.

The old reliable method for planting potato pieces is to plant them in "hills." Pieces are buried eyes up, 3 to 4 inches deep, two to a hill in hills spaced about 20 to 24 inches apart. Soil should be in good condition and deeply pulverized. If clay soil is a problem, it should be improved several weeks ahead of time by adding plenty of organic material, compost, etc. Heavy soil restricts the growth of potato tubers.

Some gardeners prefer the trench method of planting, particularly if they are using commercial fertilizer. Trenches are dug about 8 inches deep and fertilizer scattered along the bottom of the trenches. Two inches of dirt are put on top of the fertilizer, and the potato pieces are placed on that about a foot apart. Roots will reach down to the fertilizer as the plants grow. Potato pieces coming into direct contact with fertilizer will "burn."

Keep plants hilled-up by drawing dirt up around the bottoms of them. Young plants can be nipped by harsh cold, so it is a good idea to put down a good organic mulch when planting, adding to it later if necessary. This also keeps soil from packing when heavy rains occur.

We like our raised-bed method for growing potatoes. With the soil in loose condition, potato pieces are placed about a foot apart on top of the soil. About 4 inches of shredded organic mulch is then distributed over the bed. Plants easily push through the mulch. More mulch is added as needed to help retain moisture and keep tubers from being exposed to the sun. This method produces a cleaner potato and one that's easy to harvest.

Plants need plenty of water to develop tubers, so don't hesitate to water thoroughly if there is a prolonged dry spell. Also, as with many other vegetables, practice crop rotation from year to year. This helps keep down diseases that may linger in the soil and assures that it is not depleted of nutrients, as happens when the same vegetables are grown in the same spot year after year.

Potatoes should be dug as soon as vines die down. Tubers may be spread in a shady place until any clinging dirt has dried. Whisk the dirt off with a soft brush in order to avoid damaging the tender skins and move them to a cool, dark, well-ventilated area for storage.

Everyone enjoys potatoes in one form or another: baked, scalloped, mashed, French fried, and so on. Potatoes are the top seller to go with our burgers. Have you ever heard of anyone ordering a favorite burger with a side order of broccoli? Δ

Sources for seed potatoes

Ronniger Potato Farm LLC, 20094 N. State Hwy 149, Powderhorn, CO 81243. 1-877-204-8704

J. W. Jung Seed Co., 335 S. High Street, Randolph, WI 53957-0001, 1-800-247-5864

R. H. Shumway's 334 W. Stroud Street, Randolph, WI 53956-1274

The science behind the potato

By George Erdosh

Potatoes are not only delicious and easy to grow, but very interesting. Here are a few facts that will help you get the most out of cooking and eating potatoes.

Green potatoes

All potatoes contain an alkaloid called solanine, and most alkaloids are poisonous in high doses. The small amount present in a normal potato is not only harmless but contributes to the potato's pleasing flavor (not unlike alkaloids in coffee beans, tea leaves, cocoa beans, or chili peppers).

Under direct sunlight or strong artificial light, the solanine concentration goes way up to toxic levels. In nature, the underground potato is not exposed to light, and solanine remains in low concentration. However, when the potato grows shallow, any part exposed to the sun turns green, indicating a high solanine concentration. Supermarket produce clerks cover potato bins when the store is closed, and potatoes are sold in dark amber-colored plastic bags to shield them from the damaging light.

Solanine usually develops within the potato skin and just under it. In these green spots, solanine may be five to 10 times the normal concentration, and the heat of cooking doesn't destroy it. Should you eat green potatoes, you will have ample warning with a burning, peppery flavor. The only solution to the cook is radical surgery. You don't have to throw away the whole potato as many cookbooks suggest. Just cut out the green parts. They, like beauty, are only skin deep.

photot credit: James O. Yeager

Kennebec potatoes

While bean, radish, and alfalfa sprouts are great additions to salads, potato sprouts are good only if you don't wish your guests to return to your dinner table ever again. Potato sprouts are also rich in solanine, even though they may not be green. Pick off the sprouts before cooking.

Another potato surgical procedure is cutting out ends that turn black. This is a chemical reaction precipitated by the heat of cooking, and its origin is not known. When you find yourself having a whole bag of potatoes with ends turning black on cooking, acidify the cooking water by adding a spoonful of cream of tartar (an acid in powder form). The acid will reduce end blacking. When other parts of potatoes besides the end turn black, the cause is bruising in rough handling.

Surface browning of the freshly cut-up potatoes (called enzymatic browning) is easy to solve. As you cut up the potatoes, drop them into water, and the harmful oxygen in the air that causes browning cannot reach the fresh-cut surface.

How potatoes cook

Potatoes cook by a chemical process called gelatinization—starch turns into gelatin.

A potato is about 78 percent water, 20 percent carbohydrates, and 2 percent protein. Most of the carbohydrate is in the form of starch granules, which are tiny, discrete, hard, elliptical-shaped grains that make up the body of the potato. They don't taste pleasant, which is why most of us don't eat potatoes raw. The starch granules gelatinize between 137 and 150 degrees. This temperature range is called the gelatinization range, and is an all-important reaction in potato cooking or baking. The compact starch granules burst open, absorb water from the surroundings, and swell up to many times their original sizes, forming a soft, moist amorphous mass.

When you stick a skewer in a still-baking potato to test for doneness and the center still feels hard, what you feel is a mass of ungelatinized starch granules that haven't yet reached the critical temperature. Once the center reaches 150 degrees, the potatoes are done and ready to serve. But to develop a brown skin and full, rich flavor, continue baking until the temperature is close to 190 degrees. You may want to stick a thin-stemmed thermometer in the potato next time you bake instead of a skewer to check for doneness.

Thanks to their high starch content, potatoes are excellent to thicken soups and stews. The starch granules on cooking burst open and escape into the surrounding liquid, swelling to many times their original size by absorbing and thickening the soup or stew. To thicken even more effectively, grate a little raw potato into the soup before cooking.

Potatoes are reasonably nutritious, but much of the nutrition is in and just under the skin. Whenever possible, leave the skin on. Vitamin B and C contents are high, and the skin is rich in dietary fibers.

Cooks place the hundreds of varieties of potatoes into two groups according to their kitchen uses:

1. The dry, fluffy, mealy types with high starch that produce the most appealing and tasty baked potatoes. These are also good choices for frying and deep-frying as they absorb less oil. They don't hold their shapes well on boiling and tend to fall apart, not a pretty sight in a potato salad. The best known in this group is the russet baking potato (also called Idaho, no matter where they are grown).

2. The waxy, moist types with lower starch content that hold up well and remain firm when boiled. They are also better as scalloped potatoes and perfect in potato salads. These waxy varieties still taste good baked, but don't get the full dry, fluffy texture that we so much appreciate in a good baked potato. The common waxy types include round white, long white, and red potatoes.

When you grow your own and want to know its starch content, either of these quick tests will separate the high-starch from the low-starch varieties:

1. Cut a potato in half and rub the two cut sides briskly against each other. If the potato has a lot of starch, you produce plenty of frothy, starchy juice.

2. Prepare a brine of 1 part salt to 11 parts water and drop a piece of potato in it. High-starch potatoes are denser and sink in the brine. Low-starch potatoes float.

Cooking tips

To boil cubed potatoes, use a small amount of salted water and drain as soon as they are tender. Overcooking makes potatoes waterlogged with pieces falling apart.

To boil potatoes in their skin, cover them in a cooking pot with well salted water and slowly bring the water to boil. Turn the heat low and gently simmer in covered pot until just tender. Depending on the size, in 30 to 45 minutes they reach tenderness without overcooking. Check the center near the end of the cooking time with a skewer or thin-stemmed thermometer. When just right, the skewer runs through easily or the thermometer reads 190 degrees. Drain and cool in cold water. Boiled potatoes are easier to skin and cut up neatly after chilling.

To bake potatoes in their jackets, don't cover them in aluminum foil. If covered, the potatoes steam instead of bake and don't develop full flavor. It is better to drizzle them with oil or smear with any solid fat. Pierce a few holes on the side with a knife to avoid explosion in the oven, and bake them in a hot 425-degree oven for about 45 minutes. Avoid the microwave oven; they are quick but don't produce good flavor.

You can use lower oven temperature for potatoes if roasting other foods, but they need longer baking time. Here is a guide:

400 degrees - 50 to 60 minutes
375 degrees - 60 to 70 minutes
350 degrees - 70 to 90 minutes
325 degrees - 90 to 110 minutes

Never use the food processor to mash potatoes. The powerful action breaks down the gelatinized potato starches, and your mashed potatoes will be a gummy mess.

Storage

Freshly harvested potatoes are rather perishable. Commercial growers put storage potatoes through a curing process, which gives them a chance to develop thicker skins and to heal bruises and cuts they receive during harvest and transportation.

You can do this if you find the right conditions. Store your potatoes for two weeks between 50 and 60 degrees at high humidity. A root cellar should be close to this environment. The ideal long-term storage temperature is between 45 and 50 degrees. Potatoes keep for as long as nine months at this temperature if the storage space is dark, and has good ventilation and high humidity. Potatoes stored all winter are still in reasonably good condition in the spring when your new crop is just tiny tubers under the new potato plants.

Never refrigerate potatoes. Refrigeration temperature of 40 degrees and lower converts some of the starch to sugar and you will have an unpleasantly sweet-tasting potato. Bringing cold potatoes back to room temperature reverts some but not all sugar into starch.

Garlic mashed potatoes:

Sautéing the garlic for a few seconds tames the power of the assertive garlic, and even people who are afraid of garlic can handle this dish. For garlic lovers, increase garlic and sauté very briefly.

1½ lbs russet cooking potatoes, peeled and cut into cubes
1 Tbsp. butter
half to one clove garlic, finely minced
½ tsp. salt
2 Tbsp. half and half or milk
2 Tbsp. parsley, chopped

1. Simmer potato cubes in enough lightly salted water to barely cover for 15 minutes. Pour into a strainer, drain, and reserve.

2. Return pot to low to medium heat, melt the butter, add the garlic, and stir constantly for a few seconds until the garlic is lightly sautéed.

3. Quickly return potatoes into the same pot with salt, half and half or milk, and parsley; heat over very low heat while mashing with potato masher. Serve immediately.

Serves four as a side dish. Δ

Ron

If you only saw the boots
You might mistake him for a cowboy
Fifty years ago
Not a bad mistake
And closer to the truth than you'd guess
The boots make him taller   no matter
He's taller than he looks   You betcha
The jeans and jacket are faded
The shirt worn and faded   bleached
By sun and washes   and something else
Under the beat up hat
His hair is grey
Over a leaned   browned face
The eyes are sharp and clear
They have seen a lot of road
And they understand   You betcha
The hands have always worked   hard
They are long and fine boned
And could have tickled ivory   or strings or
Gentler things   given the chance
The mind is quick   probably had to be
If he says it   you can bank on it   You betcha
If you only saw the boots and rig
You might miss the man   you might
But if you listen carefully for awhile
You'll hear
His heart   too big for his rig
So he shares it
When he thinks no one is watching

emet

stop breathing dirt and microbes and build a

HOME CENTRAL VACUUM SYSTEM

By David Lee

It's looking bleak. It's cold out and you've been hanging around the shanty so long you are knee deep, maybe kidney deep, in dirt, dust, and cobwebs. Your French maid is away on maternity leave. You have to find the broom and dustpan and clean the place up before it is condemned. Or you need to find your old vacuum cleaner and suck the crud away until the floors are visible again.

Problem is, the broom raises more dust than it collects. The vacuum needs a filter bag. You don't know where or if you have one, and even if you do find it, the old sucker has terminal emphysema and really deserves a dignified trip to the dump.

Is that your problem today? Do I sound like a vacuum cleaner salesman? Things have been slow this month so, yes I am. But seriously folks, vacuum cleaners are one of those great inventions that seem so good but have a dark side.

Picture a fan whirling at 3000 revolutions per minute pulling air through a flexible tube at 500 miles an hour. This means any little thing near the entrance of the tube gets mercilessly sucked through it, through the fan, and spit out the exhaust. If that was all there is to it, then it would only rearrange your dirt, so a filter is placed between the tube and the fan, and a canister holds the whole shebang in a handy unit on little wheels. Dirt collects on the filter and falls off into the canister for disposal at your convenience. That's the basic vacuum cleaner you know and love—or loathe.

There are facts that a vacuum cleaner salesman won't want to tell you. The filter needs replacing more often than anyone ever does it, plus it restricts airflow through the system at an increasing rate as the dust being pulled in plugs it up. This puts a strain on the motor, eventually killing it. Imagine yourself breathing in air through a mask while someone shovels dirt on it. It would kill you, too. By the way, that fun thing you do, putting the vacuum tube against something that stops the airflow? Don't do that anymore. It's very cruel. Vacuum cleaner motors are doomed to a short hard life as it is. This explains why people will always be around to sell vacuum cleaners.

However, that is not the really dark side. Consider for a minute that dust is actually parts of plants, people, minerals, and house pets ground into powder by the facts of life. Much of that "powder" is so small that the individual particles can pass through a vacuum cleaner filter and past the fan to be exhausted into the air in your house. It has to be this way because if the filter stopped those little specks it would almost stop the airflow since air molecules and these littlest pieces of you and yours are nearly the same size.

It gets worse. The little dusty things, called "Sub Five Micron Particles" in the vacuum filter business, tend to float in the air for a long time before settling back onto the floor to be recycled (and ground even finer) during the next vacuuming session. If you doubt this, just look at your indoor air through a sunbeam shining through a window.

I really hate to tell you the next part. Please sit down, preferably out in the fresh air on your front porch. Many of those miniscule meteorites floating around by the billions in the air of your home have living things crawling on them called microbes. Some of those microbes can make you sick. When you consider the fact that they may not have appreciated being sucked up a tube, whacked by fan blades, and flung out into space, it is conceivable they may be looking for revenge. It's just something to think about while coughing.

Okay, now you are ready for the *Central Vacuum System* sales pitch. Such a system pulls in dust, both the large and small particles, then carries it safely to the collection canister way down in the cellar where, hopefully, the installer routed the exhaust to the outdoors. With this system you breathe cleaner air and, as a bonus, there is very little noticeable noise when the machine is running. Just take the lightweight hose, plug it into one of the vacuum inlets installed on the walls of your home, and turn on your stereo. You can vacuum to Vivaldi and be happy in your work. If you are very rich and not very handy, call up the salesman and go for it. If you are not, then read on.

In 1994, the last time I passed out looking at the price, a *Central Vacuum System* installation cost about $6000 (I don't dare check now). Malevolent microbes or not, this was beyond our budget boundaries. Even with this magnificent system there were still filters to change, a canister to empty, and motors to wear out. Just the vacuum machine alone cost more than $700.

I would not be writing about this if I didn't have an alternative for you. It is the mighty *Shop Vac*, the hot rod of vacuum cleaners. These come with oversized motors and very loud exhaust. It is much too uncultured to use inside your home. Besides the noise problem, they exhaust even more fine dust than the usual petite machines. However, they can suck the paint off a refrigerator and, like any good hot rod, can be tweaked up beyond factory specs.

Here's how. Buy the most powerful *Shop Vac* you can find. The one we have is 3½ horsepower, but I've heard rumors that even more powerful ones exist. Disconnect the motor unit from the canister, take off the two filters, and remove the plastic ball inside the cage you find there. Unless you are sucking up water, it just gets in the way. Put only the foam filter back on the cage and reassemble the unit. Remove the wheels and any goo gahs not relevant to sucking. That's it! Now you have the *Enhanced Performance Hot Rod Central Vacuum System of the 21st Century.*

At this point you could set the *Shop Vac* outdoors, run a very long hose through a window and clean your house like never before. It would be crude and effective but not very elegant or convenient. Sit yourself down with a nice little tank of oxygen and I'll show you how to put this system into place.

I mentioned having the Vac outdoors, but it can't just sit there on the lawn. Pick an unobtrusive spot on the back, or "utility" wall of your house,

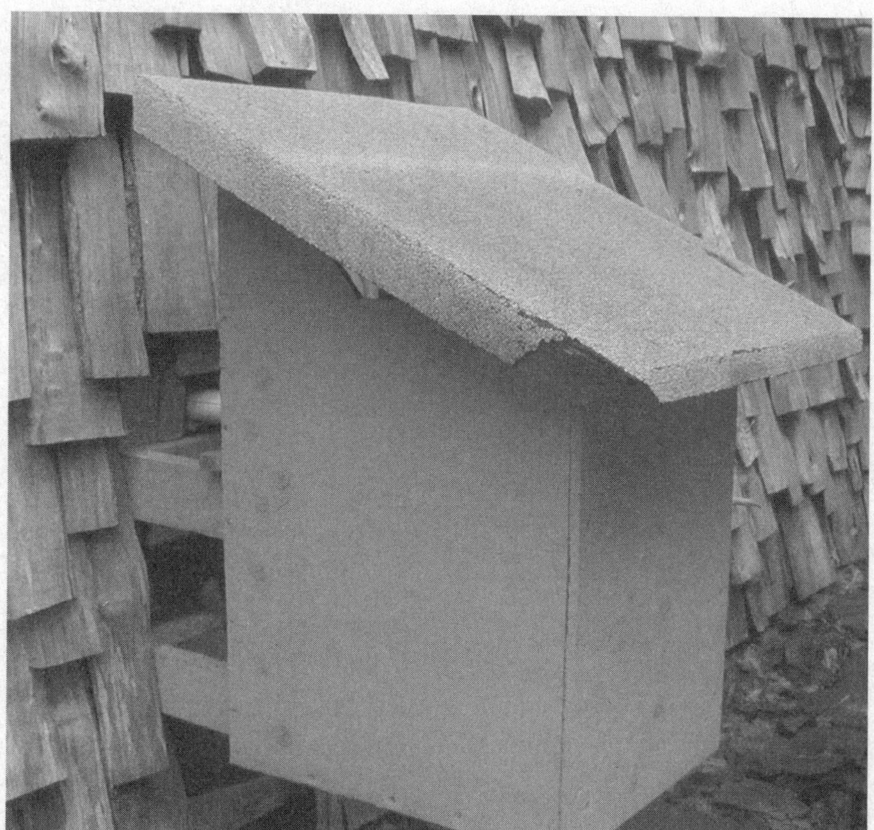

Here is our 12-year-old well worn vacuum shelter box attached to the house with a stand-off bracket. The shelter must keep rain off the vacuum machine while allowing plenty of air circulation.

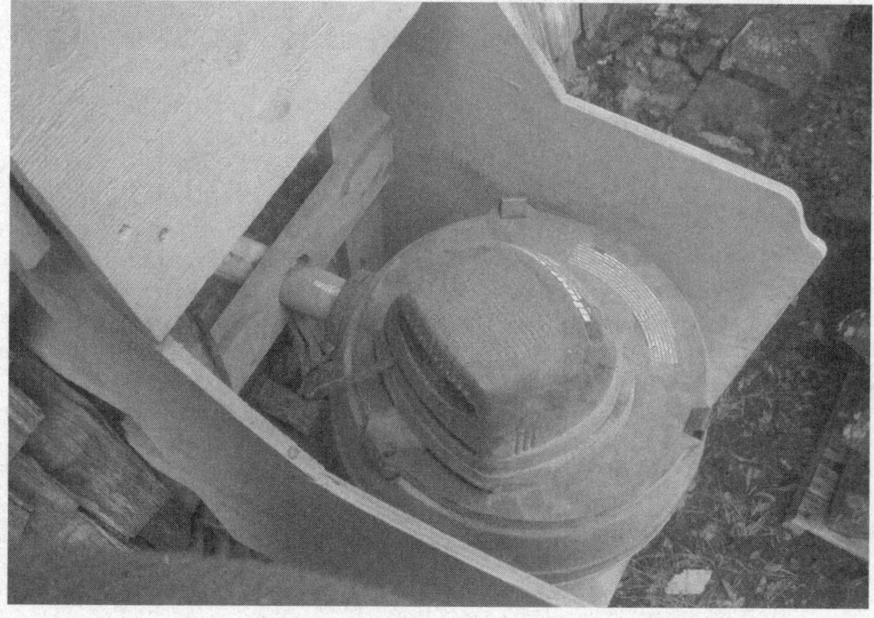

Looking down on the top of the Shop Vac with the shelter cover open to show the PVC tube in place and the copious amount of dust that would still be in our air without this system.

This shows the vacuum cleaner shelter box in the open position and the Shop Vac pulled off and disassembled for emptying. Note the PVC tube with coupling that just fits the inlet of the Shop Vac. The motor housing is kept near the shelter box and left plugged in, but the foam filter must be removed and cleaned at the same time the canister is emptied.

perhaps near the fuel oil tank, high enough up to be above the average snow line but low enough so the vacuum pipe enters the house in a suitable location. Build a housing for the Vac with plywood, 2x4s, and rolled roofing like the one in the pictures. It must shed rain but allow plenty of air circulation around the Vac. Hinge the top and front panels for easy servicing access. Attach the housing to the wall with a bracket that extends it out from the wall six inches or so. This helps with air circulation and cuts down on the amount of vibration and noise in the house.

The next step is to install vacuum tubing throughout the house. Wall inlets for this system can be as much as 60 feet apart. Our house is 60 x 36 feet and needed only one inlet located centrally on the first floor, one on the second floor, plus one in the basement. Gluing the tubes and elbows together and routing them through inconspicuous pathways is very much like installing water drain plumbing for sinks. In fact, you save money by using the very same type of 1½" Schedule 40 PVC pipe, fittings, and glue as you use for standard plumbing.

I rough-in the vacuum tubes as I build a house and hide them inside walls and between floor joists. If you missed the boat on that opportunity, you may be able to route the tubes under the first floor in the basement, up through a first-floor closet, and then to the second floor. Attach an inlet fixture directly to the pipe inside the closet and, if there is no closet or other hiding place available on the second floor, position the inlet fixture right on the floor. Just locate it where it won't be an obstruction. However, it is classier and more convenient to go to the trouble of mounting them on a wall.

At the same time you install the vacuum tubing, tape a length of 18-gage, 2-strand, insulated electric wire, called 18/2, alongside the tubes.

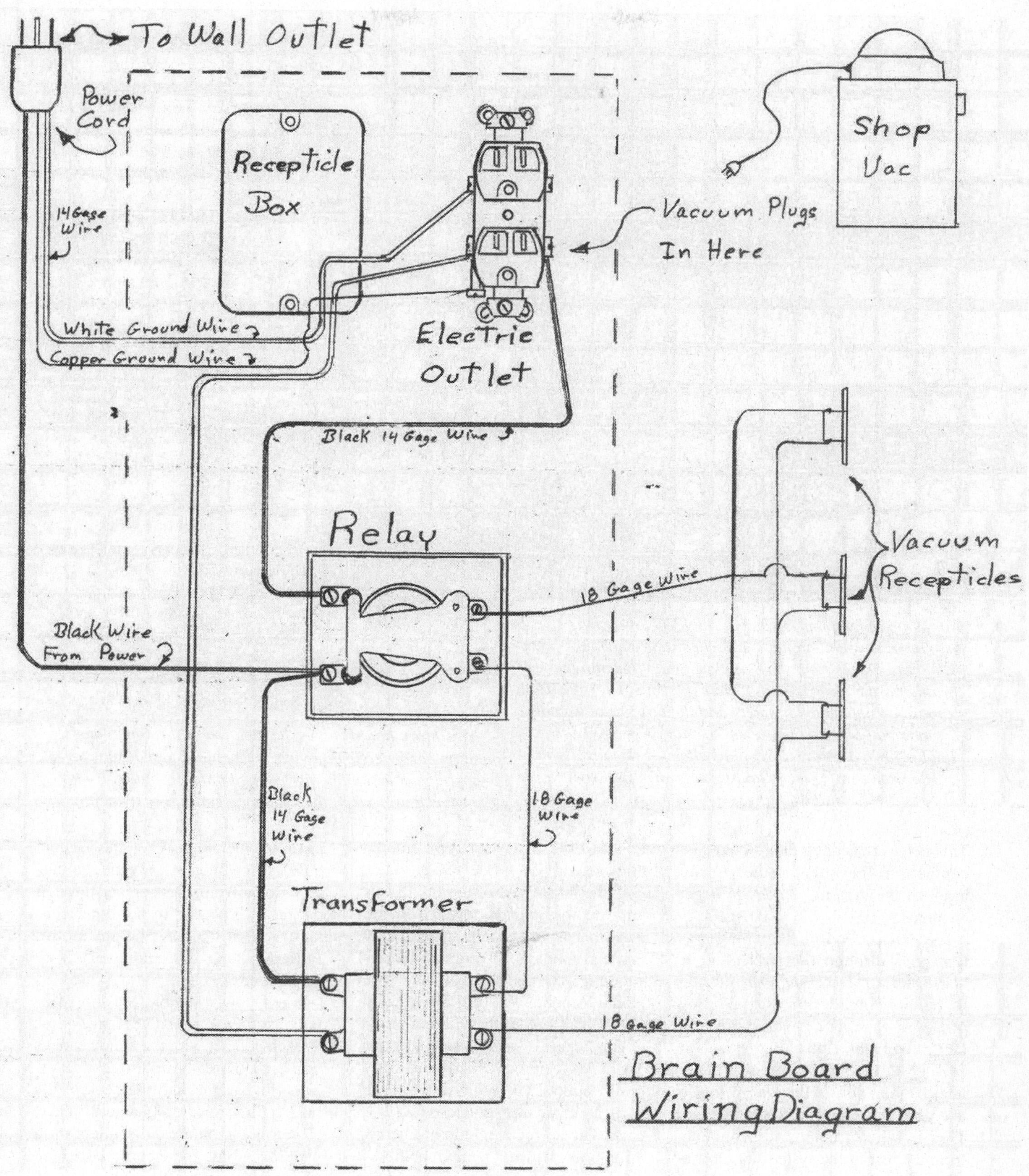

This is the latest and most improved wiring plan of the Brain Board elements of the Central Vacuum System.

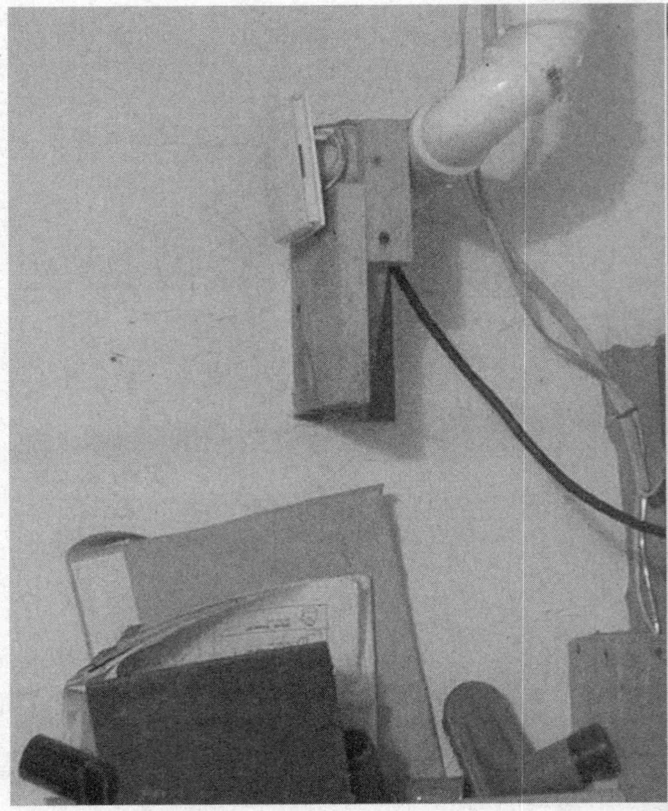

At the top of the picture you see the PVC tube where it exits the house. A vacuum inlet is attached to it. The black power cord comes from the Shop Vac and plugs into the brain board's electric outlet. Note the cover over the brain board components for safety and the box full of vacuum related parts and paperwork so they won't get lost. I opted for a direct circuit on a switch for this installation. A power cord-to-a-wall outlet as shown in the wiring diagram is less complicated.

This brain board shows the location of the components and an early version of wiring. The black tape discourages anything else from being plugged into this outlet. It only has power when the vacuum cleaner is activated.

This is for connecting the low-voltage contacts in the inlet fixtures to the brain of the system, which we'll get to soon.

The exhaust end of the tubing system goes through the wall of your house and meets the *Shop Vac* outside in its housing. I don't think they intended this, but a standard 1½" PVC coupling glued to the end of 1½" PVC pipe fits serendipitously into the inlet port of the *Shop Vac*. Do not glue the coupling into the Vac. This is where the Vac disconnects from the rest of the system for emptying, and the fit is just right for that purpose.

At the intake end of the tubing system are the inlet fixtures. You will need to buy these items from a store that carries parts for ordinary central vacuum systems. We got ours from Home Depot and a local electric supply store. Google, the internet search engine, can also help you find them. The inlet fixtures, called "automatic on-off outlets" or "utility inlets," vary a little in design and cost $10-15 each. The device is a little plastic trap door with a pipe opening behind it and two metal contacts visible in the pipe (see pictures). When the vacuum hose is plugged in, low voltage current flows from one contact through the metal hose end to the other contact, activating the vacuum motor. Pull the hose out and everything stops. It's very clever.

When you assemble the inlet fixture, attach one of the 18-gauge wires to each contact with the handy screws you find there. Standard 1½" PVC pipe slides right onto the back of the inlet fixture for you to glue in place. If you are mounting the inlets on a wall it is a little more complicated but I have faith you can figure it out.

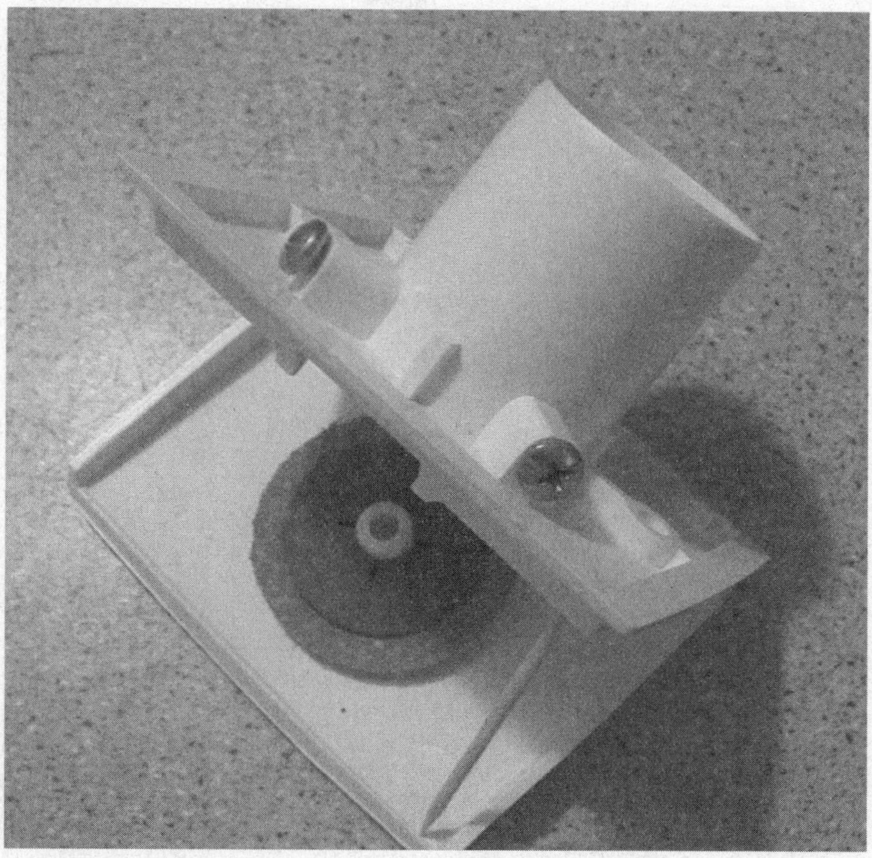

This is a vacuum wall inlet fixture held open by a toothpick to show contacts for connecting the 18/2 wires, the pipe that slides into the PVC tubing, and the weather-stripped plug on the spring-loaded door intended to prevent air leaks.

While you are shopping at the vacuum store, buy the hose for your system. We got one that is 32 feet long for about $65. Other lengths are available but 32 is the most fun. Chances are good that other equipment from your deceased vacuum cleaner such as extension wands, duster, carpet and floor brushes, and my favorite, the crevice tool, will fit the new hose. If not, encourage them to fit with duct tape.

Let's review. You have a tweaked up *Shop Vac* in a nice airy, water shedding shelter mounted on the outback wall of your house connected to a system of 1½" schedule 40 PVC tubes, accompanied by some 18/2 wires, leading to several wall or floor vacuum inlet fixtures centrally located throughout your shanty.

Next comes the brain of this system. I have included a diagram for you to peruse but I must warn you of two things. First, every time I plan one of these it comes out different because I have Nevertwicethesamia, a disorder common to inventor types. It is a curse I must live with. Second, it doesn't help that the electric parts supply industry won't produce components the same way twice in a row with the same part numbers. So I'll give you the general idea and the diagram and hope for your best.

You will need three devices: First, a common electric wall outlet, just like the ones you plug your toaster into; a cover plate for it; and a receptacle box (metal or plastic) to contain it. This one is easy.

Second, buy a relay with a 12-, 16-, 18-, or 20-volt coil. A relay is an electromagnetic switch that turns on a high voltage circuit (the vacuum motor) when a low voltage circuit (through the vacuum wall inlet contacts) is turned on. The low voltage side of the relay connects to the 18/2 circuit wires and activates the power to the *Shop Vac* when you plug the hose into the vacuum wall fixture. Do not even think about using 120 volts for this part of the system. The KGB used to wire vacuum systems with 120 to assassinate people, but even they don't do that anymore. Why there are so many "low" voltages to select from I don't know. You'll have to ask G.E. For our purpose here, stay below 20 volts to be safe. Still, it is kind of fun to try and get someone to stick their finger in the…never mind, let's move on.

Third, you need a transformer that matches the coil on the relay. If you get a 16-volt relay, buy a 16-volt transformer; for a 20-volt relay, buy a 20-volt transformer. You get the picture. The transformer reduces 120-volt power to the lower voltage needed for your system. I have seen diagrams of how this is done and still don't believe it, but it works.

In addition to the three devices, you need a three-pronged power cord and a couple of feet of 14/2 insulated copper wire, the same stuff used to wire your house. You will be mounting all this on a board about 8 inches wide and 16 inches high. Plywood or pine will do. This brain on a board is attached to the wall inside your house right next to the place where the PVC tubing goes out to the *Shop Vac*. The power cord from the *Shop Vac* must pass through the wall and plug into the electric outlet on the brain board. The cord should be long enough and the brain board close enough to leave some slack in the cord out by the *Shop Vac*. Hide the brain board behind a cover (see pictures) to keep inquiring fingers away from the wiring.

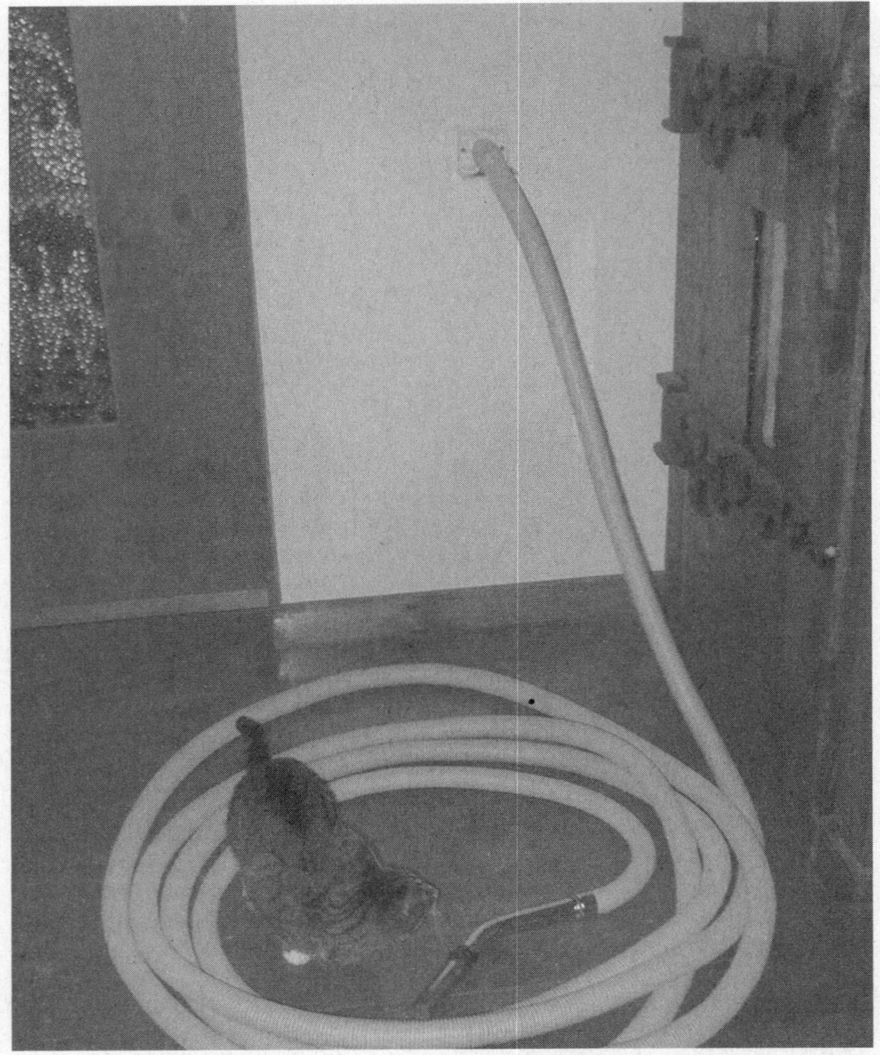

Here is the 32' hose plugged into the vacuum wall inlet quietly pulling dust and dirt out of the house. No cats were harmed during the staging of this picture.

By now you probably wish this issue of the magazine had been lost in the mail. If not, follow the text and diagram and avoid getting shocked.

If you have read this far and followed the directions, you are the proud owner of the world's most powerful *Central Vacuum System*. Congratulations. In six months or a year it will be time to empty the tank. Lift the housing cover, pull the vacuum off the PVC tube and remove the canister. Leave the motor plugged in. Empty the canister out in the woods. Take the foam filter off and knock the dust from it while you are at it. Reassemble and repeat next year.

The tools and the hose for your system should fit in the same volume of space as your dear departed vacuum cleaner…or not. We store our hose on a nice wire wall hanger we bought at the vacuum store (I was weak) and the tools are in a handy wall-hung bag with pockets (okay, very weak). All this convenience allows my wife to hate vacuuming only half as much as she did with the old machine.

The PVC parts, hose, inlet fixtures, brain board components, and miscellaneous items cost about $150. *Shop Vacs* are an interesting commodity. I bought my first one retail for $89.95. But I learned a secret. Many people who buy these beasts only use them once because they are so wild and terrifyingly loud. As a result, many of them end up in yard sales nearly new but at greatly reduced prices. Since then I have collected several of them at severely low prices.

Shop Vacs wear out just like other vacuum cleaners, maybe sooner. We have burned out three in 12 years and just started on our fourth, but for the price we pay for a replacement it is thrifty compared to the alternative. In addition, each time we find a deal on another *Shop Vac* it comes with lots of goodies like hoses, tools, and little wheels. The hoses and wands I have collected, connected together, would let us reach and clean the neighbor's house with our system, though we haven't let them know that. Since "replacement" means just changing the motor housing, I have three extra canisters (on wheels) that make handy trashcans.

Emptying the canister once or twice a year presents some interesting facts about your household. For instance, we learned that one eight-pound cat produces enough hair in one year to make a large-size felt sweater.

A rather dubious but possibly useful benefit might be enjoyed with this system. Plugging in the vacuum hose turns on the *Shop Vac* with its ferocious noise, in turn scaring the piddle out of any human, animal, bird, maybe reptile, within a hundred feet. Use this benefit prudently and never when the deliveryman is filling your oil tank.

A *Central Vacuum System* may seem like a rather ta-ta project for a modest *Backwoods Home,* but the health benefits, convenience, and tinkering challenges make it worthwhile. With the new vacuum system and a French maid you could upgrade your shanty to a Shackteau. Δ

Kids in the Kitchen

By Sharon Palmer, RD

The freeway en route to home resembles a parking lot, allowing you plenty of time to add up all of the tasks awaiting you once you walk in your front door. Let's see, there's an Everest size mountain of laundry starting to lend its perfume to the house, soccer practice for your son, your daughter's diorama book report due tomorrow, the bathrooms are screaming out for a bottle of cleanser, and that age old question, "What's for dinner?"

Why not put the kids to work and get them involved in the cooking process? The list of benefits are endless. Not only does it help you put a dent in the daily list of chores, but it teaches children the importance of learning to cook in the modern structure of today's lifestyle, when more and more people seek the fast-food joint around the corner or pick up the phone to order take-out. The U.S. Department of Labor indicates that 26.2% of single parents' food budget is dedicated to meals away from home. "Kids start expressing their interest in cooking at toddler age. This is a great time to nurture this interest. Often parents don't want the mess, but they can spend quality time with their children while they learn to cook. Down the line, parents are going to have good little helpers," says Elaine Magee, MPH, RD and author of many cooking books, including *Someone's in the Kitchen with Mommy.*

Throwing a junior apron and chef hat on your children allows them to explore the creativity found in the confines of the kitchen and introduces lifelong concepts of healthful eating patterns. By getting them into the habit of eating traditional meals that include foods from the major food groups, children need not rely on French fries and chicken fingers to fill their bellies. Child obesity is on the rise, with the National Center for Health Statistics reporting that 15% of children ages 6-19 are overweight compared with only 6% in 1976-1980. The Department of Agriculture's Center for Nutrition Policy and Promotion indicates that approximately 80% of children ages 4-9 consume diets that are classified as "poor" or "needs improvement."

When kids start cooking, there is an added bonus that they tend to actually eat what they prepare since they have a vested interest in confirming the fruits of their own labor. So you might be surprised to see them chomping on a vegetable pizza with gusto or digging into their own tossed salad with pleasure. With all of the stress of managing a family, good nutrition for the entire family is an important tool in keeping the body and mind stoked.

While Elaine Magee teaches children's cooking programs, she finds that many kids aren't getting the opportunity to cook at home. "I find that kids love to cook and that boys are just as excited, if not more so, than girls. They're not doing it at home. It's an untapped resource for busy parents," Magee says.

The benefits of spending 30 minutes around a home-cooked meal at the dinner table with the family are priceless. Children who regularly eat family meals have healthier eating habits that last a lifetime. And those precious minutes around the dining room table may be the only ones available to talk about the minutia of daily life that is so important in bracing your family in a chaotic world. A study conducted by the National Center of Addiction and Substance Abuse at Columbia University showed that the more often teens eat dinner with their family, the less likely they will smoke, drink, or use illegal drugs.

Here are some helpful tips for getting your budding chef into your kitchen.

In on the planning: Start with the basics by purchasing some children's cookbooks, visiting children's cooking websites, watching kids' cooking shows, or enrolling your child in a children's cooking program. Plenty of resources abound for young foodies. Even The Culinary Institute of America hosts a children's cooking program these days. Then you can let your child sit down and write out a weekly menu and shopping list, a fun Sunday afternoon chore. Let them pound the aisles of the grocery store, checking items off the grocery list. Now the week ahead won't look so dreary, with thoughts of English muffin pizza and vegetable soup on Monday night.

Cleanliness is a virtue: Along with cooking comes the less fun chore of cleaning, so get your child into the clean up act as well, from washing hands before the cooking process begins to scrubbing up the pots and pans afterward. Give your child a lesson on basic food sanitation. Start with an explanation that bacteria from hands, nose, and mouth can be transferred into food, and when it's left out at room temperature too long the bacteria can multiply, causing food-borne illness. Teach them how to get dishes, appliances, and counter tops squeaky clean.

Think safety: For children, the kitchen can be a dangerous place. There are plenty of opportunities for cuts, burns, shocks, and falls in this room where sharp things, electrical plugs, flames, and wet floors live. Younger children may not be ready to wield knives, but pizza wheels, egg slicers, enclosed choppers, plastic disposable knives, and blunt scissors may do the trick of cutting for them more safely. Likewise, you may want to instruct your child to let you open the oven door and stir the hot pot depending on the child's age. Teach them about safety as you go, pointing out that the stove burners may be hot even when they are turned off and that steam escapes boiling pots when lids are removed. Be sure to point all pot handles inward to avoid energetic elbows from bumping into pots and spilling the hot contents onto young chefs in training. Join in with the cooking fun by supervising and teaching them until you are confident about their newfound skills.

Pack it up: Why constrain your child to the dinner menu? Let them come up with crazy lunchbox concoctions to pack up the night before. Try out homemade granola snack mixes, banana bread, macaroni and cheese in a thermos, quesadillas, and more to beat the lunch box blues.

Dinnertime nutrition lessons: Post a copy of the food guide pyramid (www.usda.gov/cnpp/pyrabklt.pdf) on your frig and point out what foods your meal will represent on the chart. Locate the vegetables in the soup, the cheese in the pasta, and the milk in the yogurt on the chart. Try to make sure dinner provides a fruit/vegetable serving, protein serving, starch/cereal/bread serving, and a milk product serving each night. Teach your child all about food; facts like carrots are good for your eyes, and potatoes grow under the ground.

Creativity in the making: Let your child's creative spirit soar in the kitchen. Let him select colors from the vegetable bin like he chooses crayons from the crayola box to paint your dinner menu with all the shades of the rainbow. If julienne strips make her giggle, then go for it. Let her turn a broccoli spear into a tree, an orange slice into a happy face. Does he want to shape the grilled cheese sandwiches into race cars? Hand him the appropriate cookie cutter and let him speed.

Start out slow: If your child is too young or uncoordinated to master difficult cooking tasks, start out slow. Hand him a wooden spoon and ask him to stir the cornbread batter. Let her fetch ingredients, gather bowls, measure ingredients, or watch the timer. Add more advanced cooking tasks as their skill improves.

Culinary skills in the making: The kitchen is a classroom, so educate your child in the fine art of cooking. Start by letting him read the recipes and explain cooking terms like sauté, whip, peel, dice, and mince as you go. Show him the difference between cooking tools and appliances, from the purpose of a garlic press, to the operation of a potato masher.

Patience is another virtue: Remember, at the beginning it's probably easier to do the cooking yourself and kids tend to spill and behave like the untrained food service workers that they are. The end results of their food products may not appeal to you, but offer plenty of encouragement and take a deep breath when they drop the flour canister. They will eventually master their tasks.

Praise the chef: Don't be stingy with compliments. As you sit down to enjoy those precious 30 minutes, remember to tell your young culinary star how savory the green beans are and how delectable the peach cobbler is. Your child will appreciate the boost in self-esteem more than you can imagine.

Here are some favorite recipes:

Kaleidoscope fresh fruit trifle:

Kids will love layering fluffy cream, angel food cake, and colorful fruits in this tasty dessert.

12 oz. light whipped topping, thawed
8 oz. light sour cream
3.4 oz. instant vanilla pudding mix
9" angel food cake
3 kiwis, peeled and sliced
2 cups fresh strawberries, sliced
3 bananas, peeled and sliced
15 oz. can crushed pineapple, drained

In a medium bowl, fold together whipped topping, sour cream, and pudding mix. Chop the cake into large cubes. In a large trifle bowl or glass serving dish, line 1/3 of the chopped fruit. Place 1/3 cake cubes next. Then spread a layer of 1/3 of the whipped topping mix. Repeat layers twice more, using 1/3 of fruit, cake cubes, and whipped topping mix. Reserve some fruit for a garnish. Chill until serving. Makes: 12 servings.

Penne pasta with basil sundried tomato sauce and Romano cheese:

This popular pasta dish for kids features a light, fresh tomato sauce that's barely there. Make sure to let your kids take a deep whiff of the fresh basil while they are chopping it.

1½ pounds penne pasta, dried
1/3 c. olive oil
2 garlic cloves, minced
½ tsp. salt
½ tsp. black pepper
½ cup chopped fresh basil
3 ripe tomatoes, chopped finely
4 oz. Romano cheese

Cook pasta in boiling water until just tender. Meanwhile, heat olive oil in saucepan. Add garlic, salt, and pepper and sauté. Add basil and fresh tomatoes and set aside. When pasta is done, drain thoroughly and toss together with olive oil, basil, and fresh tomato mixture. Using cheese slicer, slice slivers of Romano Cheese onto each serving. Yield: 10 servings.

Parmesan garlic bread:

This easy, fun-to-assemble garlic bread will become your child's favorite mealtime accompaniment.

1 large loaf French bread
1/3 cup margarine
1 clove fresh garlic, minced
½ cup grated Parmesan cheese

Slice French bread into thick slices. Mix margarine and minced garlic. Spread bread with garlic butter, and then sprinkle with Parmesan cheese. Place slices together into loaf form. Cover with foil and bake at 400° F for 10-15 minutes until warm and toasted. Yield: 10-12 servings.

Granny's sunflower apple salad:

This tart, crunchy salad is high in fiber and flavor, starring all-time kids' favorites, apples and sunflower seeds.

2 granny smith apples, washed and cubed (leave on skins)
½ cup sunflower seeds
1 small head romaine lettuce, rinsed, dried and chopped
1 dill pickle, diced
2 tomatoes, diced
½ cup sliced cucumber
½ cup light ranch dressing

In a large salad bowl, mix apples, sunflower seeds, lettuce, pickles, tomato, and sliced cucumber. Toss in ranch dressing. Serve immediately. Makes 10 servings.

Sharon Palmer is a registered dietitian, freelance writer, children's culinary instructor, and mother of two in southern California. Δ

Creating and maintaining your own sourdough starter

By Emily Buehler

Most people know about sourdough starter—it can be used instead of yeast to make bread rise, resulting in bread with a sour flavor and a chewier texture. Bakers who use starter always save a little bit for next time. This little bit of starter is fed flour and water, and it grows into more starter, enough to use in the next batch of bread.

What is starter? And where does that first little bit come from?

Bread rises because tiny organisms in the dough are performing fermentation—absorbing sugar from the flour and processing it into gas and flavorful organic molecules. In commercially made bread, these organsims are yeasts, members of the fungus family. In starter, a population of bacteria and wild yeasts (different yeasts than those sold in the store) are thriving on a regular diet of flour and water. When this starter is put into bread dough, the bacteria and yeasts readily go to work processing the sugars in the dough; no commercial yeast is needed. In addition to the usual fermentation products, the bacteria produce acids that give the resulting bread unique flavors.

To get that first little bit of starter, a mixture of flour and water is left out. Bacteria and wild yeasts from the air move in. With regular feeding, they can become a stable population, strong enough to make bread rise. In addition, once the starter is stable, it can survive in the refrigerator and be fed only once every few weeks. Creating a starter is not a walk in the park. The bread-making bacteria struggle to gain hold; sometimes, bad bacteria take over. But the process is doable, especially if you know the pitfalls to avoid. And the reward of making bread with your very own starter is well worth the effort.

Sourdough starter is the key ingredient in sourdough bread.

Two key factors for the starter's survival are cleanliness and temperature. Make sure all your tools are clean—container, mixing spoon, measuring cups, and hands. Then rinse them, with baking soda and water—this will wash away any residue left by soap. Use your hands to rinse them, not a sponge that might have lingering soap or grease. A temperature around 70°F is ideal for starter making. In the winter, you might leave a lamp on over your starter. I once used the cabinet over a fluorescent light, which warmed up nicely when the light was on.

In addition, you will need to feed your starter every day until it becomes stable—this can take up to two weeks. Pick a time of day when you will be home.

Use a see-through container that is big enough for the starter to double in size. Marking the original height of the starter helps you monitor how much it has risen. A loose-fitting lid is important because the gas produced can cause a tight lid to burst open. A simple solution is a "lid" of plastic wrap and a rubber band. Keep the starter in the same container for the entire process—there is no reason to keep exposing it to new containers. Finally, use bottled water if your tap water contains chemicals, which can hurt the growing bacteria population.

The recipe begins with a mixture of rye flour and water. The rye flour contains additional sugars that help the bacteria get started. With rye flour, the mixture will easily rise. The feedings change gradually from rye flour to white flour—I found that a sudden change usually killed the starter. As white flour is used, the starter will rise less. Look for bubbles, a sign of life in your starter. A fruity smell is also good. Check your

Bubbles such as these are a good sign that your starter is alive.

Recipe for creating a sourdough starter

Day 1
1 cup rye flour — ½ cup water

Day 2
Do nothing

Day 3
half of the starter — ¼ cup white flour
¼ cup rye flour — ¼ cup water

Day 4
half of the starter — 3/8 cup white flour
1/8 cup rye flour — ¼ cup water

Day 5
half of the starter — 3/8 cup white flour
1/8 cup rye flour — ¼ cup water

Repeat this feeding until the starter is rising regularly. It should be nearly doubling its height. When this happens go to the "White flour feeding."

White flour feeding
half of the starter — ¼ cup water
½ cup white flour

Repeat this feeding until the starter is rising regularly, then move on to the "Dough-like starter feeding."

Dough-like starter feeding
half of the starter — ¼ cup water
7/8 cup white flour

At this point your starter should be rising and falling regularly. The cycle should take about 8-10 hours: you feed the starter, and after 8-10 hours, the starter is risen, ready to make bread or to be fed again.

starter a few times throughout the day—sometimes it rises quickly and then falls, so it might appear not to have risen at all. Once the starter is 100% white flour and rising regularly, the recipe for feeding changes to give a less watery, more dough-like starter.

To maintain the starter, keep using the "Dough-like starter feeding" recipe. Use your refrigerator to slow the rising; this way, you can feed the starter less often. After each feeding, leave it out for three hours and then refrigerate it. Most people feed their starter once a week. You can wait two to three weeks, but before you make bread, you should feed the starter and leave it out to rise. Once it is risen, then you can make bread with it. The extra feeding ensures a good population of bacteria, ready to make your bread rise. Making bread that rises is the ultimate test of success in creating a starter.

Sourdough bread:

4¼ cups white flour
¼ cup whole wheat flour
1/3 of the fully risen starter
1½ cups water
1½ tsp. salt

Make sure the flour is not packed into the measuring cup—this will make your dough hard to knead and your bread dry. Mix the flour, starter, and water with your hands until there are no dry spots. Cover the mixture and wait for 30 minutes. Add the salt and knead your dough until it is flexible—you can stretch it without ripping it. When it is fully kneaded, put it in an oiled, covered container to rise. When it is full of gas, if you have time, punch it down, fold the sides over, and let it rise again. Next, cut it into two pieces and shape them into rounds, tucking the edges under to create a smooth outer surface. Place them on a floured surface, cover them, and put them in the refrigerator. The next day, preheat your oven to 460°F. Pull the rounds out and let them keep rising. They should be full of gas when they go in the oven. Slash the tops with a serrated knife to help them open up in the oven. Use your hands to wet the surface of the loaves just before they go in the oven. Bake for 25-30 minutes. Δ

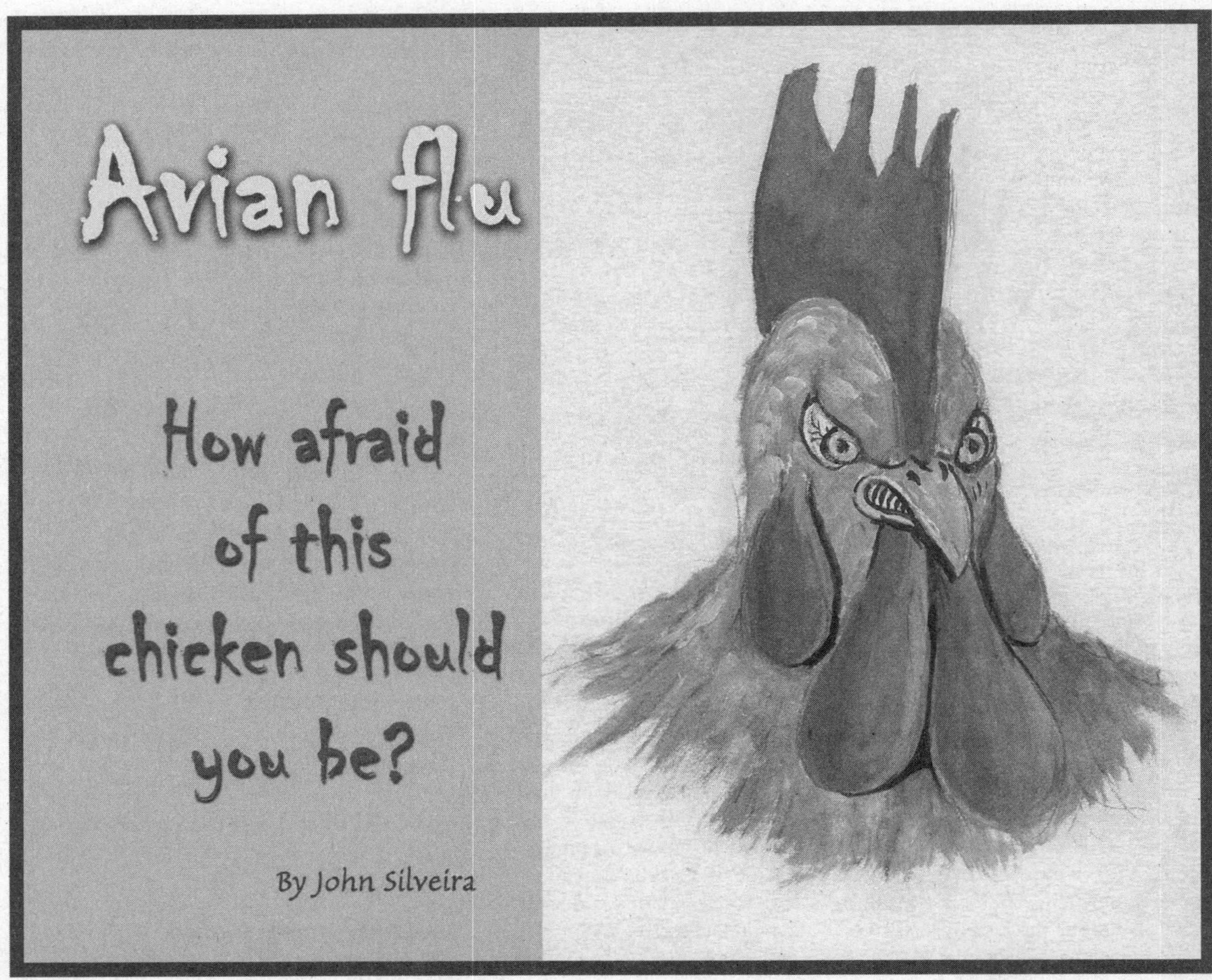

Avian flu
How afraid of this chicken should you be?
By John Silveira

There's been a lot of talk in the mass media recently about Avian flu, also known as Bird flu and the H5N1 virus, and its potential to cause the next deadly pandemic among human populations. Its prime hosts are birds. If it jumps from domestic fowl, specifically chickens and ducks, to humans in a form that is easily transmissible among humans, it could kill several hundred million people, the major news media warns us.

Even President Bush seems worried. He recently outlined a plan to spend $7.1 billion to fight a flu pandemic, including $1.2 billion to buy an effective H5N1 Avian flu vaccine. There's even talk of how to quarantine cities should the Avian flu pandemic strike America.

Tamiflu's manufacturer can't keep that antiviral flu drug on store shelves due to panic buying by an alarmed public. But is there really a reason to panic, or is this just another case of unnecessary hype by the news media?

This article tries to answer these and other questions posed by the possibility of a modern disease pandemic. It's a bit lengthy and involved because, unlike the mass media that seems interested mainly in scaring the daylights out of readers by dwelling on the sensational aspects of the story, we want to give you the whole story.

20th century pandemics

Each year there's an influenza (or flu) season that runs from about October to May. It starts, 30 to 60 million Americans come down with flu, and somewhere between 700 and 3,000 die of it. But every once in a while the flu is particularly virulent and becomes a pandemic, as it did on three occasions in the 20th century.

Many of us are old enough to remember the so-called Asian flu of 1957-58 that killed 70,000 Americans and an additional 1 to 4 million people worldwide. Eleven years later, the Hong Kong flu of 1968-69 killed 34,000 Americans and untold others around the world. It's thought the reason the '68-69 flu was not as deadly as the flu of '57-58 was because the virus that caused the pandemic in the '60s was similar enough to the virus that caused the earlier one that those who had been infected a decade before had some degree of built-in immunity to the new subtype.

But neither of these pandemics approached the doozie that was the so-called Spanish flu of 1918-19. It is against this pandemic that *all* modern pandemics are measured.

The Spanish flu killed some 500,000 to 675,000 Americans and at least 20 to 40 million (some estimates are 100 million) around the world. More people died of that flu in 18 months than died in the trenches, on both sides, during the four years of World War I. In fact, many of the war deaths of WWI were due to disease, and a large percentage of those were influenza deaths. The Spanish flu was, in part, responsible for the combatants ultimately laying down their arms in 1918, the last year of the greatest war the world had seen up to that time.

It's estimated that 28 million of the roughly 100 million Americans living in 1918 contracted the Spanish flu, and about one of every 50 of those infected died. The death rate was even higher in some other parts of the world.

In terms of sheer numbers, the Spanish flu may have been the greatest pandemic of all time. Its only rivals are the Black Death, which killed about one third of Europe's population (some 25 million people) between 1347 and 1351, and the mixture of epidemics caused by Old World diseases like small pox, yellow fever, measles, and others that swept through the native populations of the Americas starting in 1492, killing as much as 99 percent of a native population that may once have numbered more than 100 million people.

How many die each year?

The CDC reports 36,000 influenza deaths a year. This is higher than the number that occurred in 1968-69 when 34,000 died. So, why isn't *every* year a pandemic year? Because the CDC *lumps* flu deaths and pneumonia deaths together. The actual number of flu deaths is about 1,000 a year, although in a bad year it can approach 3,000. Why are the flu and pneumonia deaths lumped together? I don't know. But there are those who feel it's a scare tactic provided as a favor to drug companies so they can sell flu vaccines.

Kinds of flu viruses

There are three "types" of influenza viruses: Types A, B, and C. It is the Type A viruses, the viruses that live mostly among birds but can live in other animals, including man, that concern us.

Under Type A viruses there are at least 16 "subtypes," classified according to the proteins that make up their outer shells. The viruses that caused the Spanish flu, the Asian flu, and the Hong Kong flu were each different subtypes of the Type A virus.

Within each subtype are strains caused by mutations in a virus subtype's genes. It is the new subtypes and new strains, which are all part of the virus's natural evolution, that can lead to pandemics because our immune systems do not recognize them.

Epidemics vs. pandemics

The Centers for Disease Control (CDC) classifies influenza outbreaks into two categories. The outbreaks we usually see from year to year are referred to as "seasonal outbreaks" or "epidemics." They're caused by new subtypes and new strains of influenza viruses that already exist. Influenza "pandemics," on the other hand, are caused by virus subtypes or virus strains that are either new or haven't been seen in a long time. They are viruses for which few, if any, people have resistance.

Because of the limited or nonexistent immunity to these new viruses, the disease can infect hundreds of millions, even billions, around the world. And when the virus is also particularly virulent, as was the virus that caused the Spanish flu, it is capable of causing millions of deaths.

Though the experts may disagree on how many people are going to die from influenza in any given year, many of them feel there will eventually be another great influenza pandemic that will rival the flu pandemic of 1918-19. They just don't know when that's going to happen or how bad it's going to be. But they do have an idea of where it might start.

H5N1: the Avian flu virus

Today, there is a "new" influenza strain on the scene—the "H5N1" virus, and the disease it's causing is being called Avian flu. Many call it Bird flu because it's primarily a virus that infects birds. But it has on occasion jumped to humans. Early statistics indicate that when it does infect humans it is more than 50 percent fatal. That's a very high mortality rate; the deadly Spanish flu killed only 2 percent.

Right now, almost all of the people who have contracted it got it from handling infected birds, though a few seem to have gotten it from human-to-human contact.

Despite those few cases that may have come from human contact, it appears H5N1, in its current form, is not capable of readily spreading from one person to another. And because of that, it hasn't become what some experts feel could become the deadliest pandemic in human history.

Your immune system and mutating viruses

Why aren't we always overrun by viruses? In a sense, we are. But our immune systems generate antibodies against viruses by identifying the proteins on the virus's outer shell and developing antibodies against them. When a new flu virus invades our body, our immune system identifies it as an invader and, while we get sick with fever, sniffles, and coughs, our body learns to generate antibodies to fight it. Not only is this how the body cures itself, but the next time that *same* virus infects us, our immune system already knows how to *rapidly* generate more antibodies to kill it off before it can spread. It's the reason we won't get sick with the same type of flu more than once.

This is also why vaccines work. You have a dead virus injected into you, your body learns to recognize the proteins that make up its outer shell and, the same way it would have produced antibodies to fight a live version of the virus, it creates antibodies to destroy the dead viruses in the vaccine. Later, when live viruses of that subtype or strain *do* get into your system, your immune system immediately identifies them as something bad and knows how to quickly generate the antibodies needed to destroy them before they get a chance to successfully multiply and overwhelm your body.

That's the good news. The bad news is that viruses are always mutating — changing. Sometimes, the changes come about when one subtype of a virus exchanges its genetic material with another subtype and produces an entirely *new* virus with an outer shell of proteins our immune systems don't recognize. This is called "antigenic shift."

Viruses are also constantly undergoing what's called "antigenic drift." In this case, minor but random mutations in the virus's genetic makeup alter it over time until our immune systems, which can recognize and manufacture antibodies to combat the virus in its old form, no longer recognize the virus's new outer shell and cannot quickly respond to the "new" invader. When that happens, this "new" virus can begin to multiply and overwhelm our immune system before it can respond with new antibodies. You get sick. This can happen even if you had a case of the old virus or had been vaccinated against it. Your immune system just won't recognize it if it's changed enough.

A third way viruses can change is within the cells of animals. There is evidence that some viruses actually swap genetic material with their host's cells, the same way they can swap genetic material with each other, thereby making the animal a vehicle for the viruses' ongoing evolution. This is really another type of antigenic shift, but the important thing here is that it means that transmission of the virus from one member of that species to another member may become easier. If an influenza virus swaps genes with a human host, then when it spreads to other humans their immune systems will not recognize it until it's done its damage, including the possibility of precipitating another pandemic.

The pig factor

Another fear is that this mixing will take place not in humans, but in pigs. That's right, pigs. Pigs get the same flu viruses we do. With birds, in particular chickens, pigs, and people all closely cohabiting on farms in Asia, particularly in China, it's feared that the next great pandemic will be from a virus like H5N1 shifting or drifting in the body of a pig and jumping from there to you and me. And if it does, the new virus could carry all of the deadly attributes of the H5N1 with its astronomical mortality rate. But there's also another possible outcome, one more likely: in its altered form the virus could be a dud and not be deadly at all. How our bodies will react to these new viruses is always unpredictable, but usually we just fight them off like any other flu bug.

Why is it called the H5N1 virus?

There are many different subtypes and strains of Type A viruses. We classify the subtypes according to certain proteins on the surface of the virus. These proteins are *hemagglutinin* protein (the "H" in the subtype's designation) or the *neuraminidase* (the "N").

Hemagglutinin and neuraminidase proteins don't just provide a handy way to name the viruses; they're important to the virus because they're how it interacts with the cells in our bodies, and they're also part of the virus's outer shell that your immune system "sees" when it's trying to create antibodies to fight it.

The virus uses the hemagglutinin protein to attach itself to surface receptors on your body's cells so it can get inside them. Once there, the virus takes over the cell's genetic material and uses it to begin making copies of the pieces of itself. These pieces will later combine to make new viruses. That's how viruses have babies.

Neuraminidase is an enzyme that breaks the bonds that hold *new* viruses your cells have helped create and frees them to infect ever more cells in your body. (See sidebar, *What are viruses?*) It may, in fact, so overwhelm your system that it could kill you. In the meantime, now that you're infected, *you* will spread it to your spouse, your kids, your coworkers, and even that checker at Safeway when you hand her your money.

Other influenza viruses

Among the important influenza viruses that created pandemics in the 20th century were:

- the H1N1 virus—the killer Spanish flu virus of 1918-19
- the H2N2 virus—the Asian flu virus of 1957-58
- the H3N2 virus—the Hong Kong flu virus of 1968-69

The H2N2 and H3N2 viruses are thought to have come about after an exchange of avian and human influenza genes—a case of antigenic shift.

Though they were deadly in their day, H1N1 and H3N2 are still present in the human population. However, most people now carry some level of immunity to them. The H2N2 is not currently circulating among humans.

Another virus subtype, H1N2, appears to be a "reassortment" of genes from the H1N1 and H3N2 viruses. It's another case of antigenic shift that the medical community worries about. But in this case, the new virus produces ordinary flu symptoms and is not a virus to fear—a dud of sorts. This is what we hope happens if the H5N1 virus undergoes antigenic shift.

H5N1 in the past

Here's some good news: the H5N1 virus *isn't* new. It's been around at least since 1959 when it was first discovered—not in Asia, but in Scotland. In the 46 intervening years it has not yet shifted or drifted into a form capable of jumping from human to human, which it will have to do if it's to create a pandemic. This doesn't mean it *never* will, but it also means it's *possible* that it can't. We simply don't know enough about viruses to be able to predict what they're capable of. (Some day, with gene sequencing and computers, we will probably be able to predict much of what they do and how they'll affect us. But that's the stuff of future science.)

Misleading media news

At the time of this writing, more than half the people who get Avian flu seem to be dying of it. The major media outlets love to report this since they are in the business of dwelling on bits of dramatic news in their ongoing effort to increase viewership and readership.

However, this figure is probably misleading. The problem when dealing with any figures early on in an epidemic or pandemic is that it's likely that only the most severe cases are being identified.

When Severe Acute Respiratory Syndrome (SARS) was making headlines and scaring us to death just a few years ago, it appeared as though its mortality rate was astronomical. But, as time went by, more and more mild cases were reported and its mortality rate became more realistic.

And as time progresses, it's likely that more and more cases of Avian flu will be discovered to have been overlooked because they were mild. Once that happens, the mortality rate will be adjusted downward.

Here's more good news: There are already instances of people who are showing antibodies for H5N1 virus, proving they had been "infected," but who never showed any symptoms of having contracted flu. This is evidence there are people who are getting mild cases of the Avian flu virus without getting "sick." This may be more common than we know.

Worst case scenario

Let's say all our fears are realized and the H5N1 turns into something that is *both* highly deadly and highly contagious. How many people do the "experts" think it would kill? If it is a medium-level pandemic, some government planners in this country are saying as many as 200 million Americans could contract it, with 200,000 of them dying. Yet other "experts" say it could kill in excess of 16 million people in the United States alone.

The new U.N. coordinator for avian and human influenza, Dr. David Nabarro, originally said there could be anywhere from 5 million to 150 million deaths worldwide, though he later adjusted this to about 7½ million. But there are others who estimate that as many as *one billion* people could die worldwide.

It's a guessing game. Pick a number or make up your own; one of them is bound to be right.

Finally, here's what the CDC has to say: "Using death rates, hospitalization data, and outpatient visits, we estimated 89,000 to 207,000 deaths (in the U.S.); 314,000 to 734,000 hospitalizations; 18 to 42 million outpatient visits; and 20 to 47 million additional illnesses."

In Asia

Though the H5N1 virus was first identified among birds in Scotland, there were no reported cases of it causing sickness in humans for decades. Finally, in 1997, 2001, and 2002, H5N1 viruses jumped to people and killed some of them.

In 1997, 18 people were diagnosed in Hong Kong as having contracted it. Six of them died.

In 2003, within a family from Hong Kong that had visited southern China, two cases were identified, one resulting in death.

Since 2003 it has jumped to people several times killing at least 65 of them. Forty of those deaths occurred

What *are* viruses?

According to the old TV quiz program, *20 Questions*, the world around us fits neatly into one of three categories: animal, vegetable, or mineral. The animal kingdom is comprised of fish, and mammals—including people, birds, worms, and other things that usually move around and have to find their own food. The plant kingdom includes trees, grasses, fruits, vegetables, and other things that don't usually move around and can make their own food through photosynthesis using sunlight and carbon dioxide. In the third went all things that aren't living, like water, rocks, air, etc.

But it turns out scientists are a little more discriminating than this. They perceive life as being made up of at least five kingdoms—the two just mentioned plus three others:

- Fungi kingdom—organisms that absorb food from living and non-living things and include mushrooms, yeasts, and molds
- Protist kingdom: organisms that have single, complex cells and include amoeba and paramecium
- Moneran kingdom: organisms that have single, simple cells and include bacteria and blue-green algae.

But things get more interesting when we get to the world of viruses. Viruses are not included in any of the five kingdoms. In fact, many scientists don't even think they're alive and regard them as just inanimate chemicals with properties that mimic some aspects of life. Others see them as lying on the line between that which is alive and that which is inanimate. The problem arises because, believe it or not, scientists have yet to come up with a suitable definition of what constitutes life.

The creatures in the five established kingdoms have as attributes the ability to reproduce and eat. They reproduce by either mitosis (cell division where the resulting cells each have the same number of chromosomes, such as what happens with amoebae when they reproduce by splitting in two) or meiosis (cell division where each of the cells has half the chromosomes and, to form another individual, such as what happened when you were conceived, half of the first cell that was you came from your father's sperm and the other half came from your mother's egg).

But that flu virus that makes your nose run and gives you aching joints, and all other viruses, don't reproduce by either method. To make copies of itself, a virus hitches a ride with a new host, be it a plant or an animal. Once a virus attaches itself to a host's cell, it injects its own RNA, which takes over the functions of the cell and forces the cell to make nothing but virus parts. The cell fills up with these virus parts until it literally bursts and releases a whole bunch of new viruses, which go on to infect other cells. This can go on until the host (that could be you) dies, unless the host's immune system can create defenses that destroy the virus or defeat its ability to replicate itself. Other times, however, the virus and the host simply learn to live together in harmony.

It is this effort on the part of your body's immune system, fighting to stop the viruses from taking over its DNA manufacturing processes, that creates symptoms of disease. And, if your body's immune system overreacts, it can literally kill you.

So, here we have something that's neither living nor quite dead. Odder, yet, unlike critters in the other five kingdoms, viruses *never even have to eat*. It sounds like an unbelievable plot for a science fiction/horror film, but it's really just the world of viruses. Unless a virus has attached itself to a living cell, it appears to be nonliving.

A decent analogy for biological viruses are those things we call computer viruses. Many computer viruses do nothing more than take over a certain part of a computer's software, replicate themselves, and go on to infect the software on other computers.

Although viruses are behind infectious diseases such as HIV, flu, ebola, chicken pox, etc., the overwhelming majority of viruses are harmless and don't even affect us. They're not programmed to invade our cells. Moreover, there are other viruses that just hitch rides with us, interact with us, but never make us sick.

in Vietnam where the virus has also killed tens of millions of birds.

Late in 2004, a low pathogenic avian influenza H5N2 was discovered on a breeding duck farm in the Republic of Korea. Though the 13,000 ducks on the farm seemed otherwise healthy, the flock was destroyed. The H5N2 virus is evidence that the H5N1 may be capable of antigenic shift. But it was a dud. It has not spread to people and it wasn't harming the ducks.

In 2004, there were as many as 10 deaths attributed to the disease among several Far Eastern countries. And late in 2004, 45 tigers at a zoo in Thailand died after becoming infected with the H5N1 virus, apparently from eating raw chicken carcasses caretakers fed them. What made the report disturbing was that there was "probable horizontal transmission" among the tigers, meaning some of the tigers may have caught it from other infected tigers instead of from having eaten the chicken. However, judicious use of quarantining procedures and the subsequent cooking of the chickens used to feed them prevented any further spread of the disease.

In 2005 a man in Indonesia, along with his two daughters, died of H5N1, though none of them worked around poultry. The World Health Organization has no idea how these people became infected and says it cannot rule out the possibility that these cases were the result of human-to-human transmission.

Also, late in 2005, H5N1 was confirmed to have spread to birds in Romania, Turkey, and Russia.

There will be more reports like this in the future, but there is still no hard evidence the virus is capable of creating a pandemic among humans.

Where it will start

Earlier in this article I said we may not know when or how bad the next pandemic may be, but we know where it will probably start, and that's in Asia, specifically China.

This is the worst of all possible scenarios not only because three quarters of China's 1.3 billion people live on farms in close proximity to animals from which the virus is most likely to jump, but because of the Chinese health system. Simply put, it is both inadequate and corrupt. There are simply not enough doctors to cope with the enormous population, and because Chinese doctors, who are underpaid, often demand bribes before they'll treat patients. For these reasons, many potential victims of flu either cannot or will not see doctors or go to hospitals. This means early cases of Avian flu are likely to be missed, to be unrecognized, or they'll go unreported at a time when effective treatments and quarantining could stop its spread.

How a modern pandemic will differ from the past

In 1918-19, when the Spanish flu ran rampant through the world's population, there were no transoceanic flights. All travel, especially travel across the Atlantic and Pacific Oceans, was painfully slow by today's standards. But today, we have faster and universal air travel. People can get on a plane and cross oceans from Asia or Europe in just hours, compared to a week or more in 1918-19. And in almost any part of the world, people can and do drive between cities 1,000 miles apart in less than a day.

Increasing the danger is that people are contagious for about a week before they become symptomatic, and are contagious for about a week afterward. So, a person boarding a plane in Hong Kong or Paris may appear to be healthy while harboring the virus.

And, if a particularly virulent strain reaches our shores (or another one originates here), that person on the bus next to you may not be manifesting any symptoms while, at the same time, he's breathing on you and, guess what? You go home, you're infecting your family, and in about a

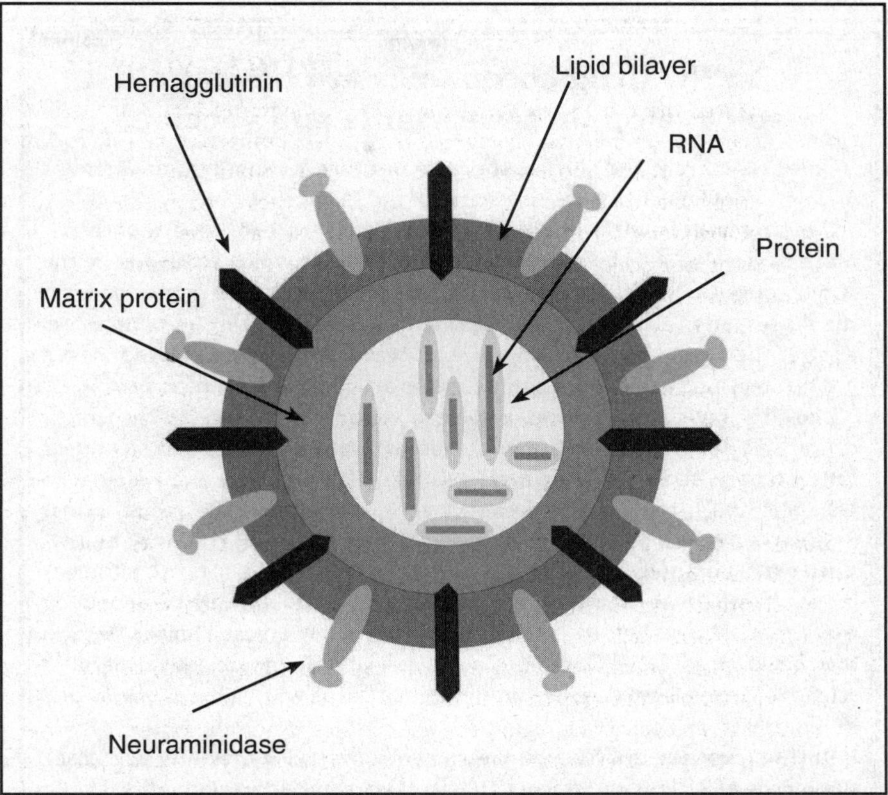

This is a stylized drawing of an influenza virus. Within the virus are exactly eight RNA strings, each encased in protein. They carry the virus's genetic makeup. The virus's outer surface contains two glycoproteins, about 500 of which are hemagglutinin (for attaching themselves to the host's cells) and about 100 of which are neuraminidase (for releasing new viruses from the host's cell after the virus has forced the host to make copies of its genes). The virus can also swap these genes with other viruses to create new subtypes, or the genes may mutate to create new viral strains our immune systems don't recognize.

> The Spanish flu is a misnomer. The disease, which began while World War I was raging in Europe, apparently started at Fort Riley, Kansas, in 1918. At the height of the pandemic, we were packing troop ships for the trip to Europe, sending loads of infected doughboys off to fight a war, and inadvertently spread the disease around the planet.

Why drug companies are hesitant to develop flu treatments and vaccines

There's a current and chronic shortage of drugs for the treatment and/or prevention of influenza. Here are some of the issues:

Getting stuck with unsold vaccine. Vaccines take nine months or more to develop. And a vaccine maker never knows which strain will be the strain going around "this" year. It's a crapshoot. But it's also money spent. If the flu season is a bust or if the vaccine maker guessed wrong, people may not get the shots, so the vaccine goes to waste. It doesn't keep, and even if it did, it may not be effective against the strain going around next year.

Liability lawsuits. Vaccines are more expensive to develop than most drugs. Vaccines are held to higher standards. We may accept that treatment for an otherwise fatal disease may have side effects. But we give vaccines to otherwise healthy people and expect zero side effects. The result is that anything perceived as a side effect often leads to lawsuits. They may be lawsuits with absolutely no basis in science. Keep in mind, a personal injury lawyer doesn't have to convince a panel of scientists, but only 12 people off the street that *he* helped hand pick. (Witness the breast implant debacle that bankrupted Dow Corning, a suit with virtually no scientific merit. In scientific circles it was a joke, but in legal circles it was hailed as some kind of moral victory.)

Patent protection. Several governments are saying they may just hijack the means of making treatments and vaccines without any indication they'd compensate the companies. If anyone thinks that's not going to inhibit the future willingness of drug companies to develop new drugs, they're not living in the real world.

week you and many in your household are sick.

In spite of this, it's still not likely to spread as rapidly and as widely as the Spanish flu because, unlike the early 20th century, today we have better treatments, better sanitation, and quarantining would be easier.

How H5N1 currently spreads

Type A viruses are called avian viruses because they reside primarily in bird populations. They have jumped to some mammals, but they are primarily a bird disease.

Millions of domestic birds in Asia have died either as a direct result of the virus or in culling when the virus is detected in domestic flocks and they are slaughtered wholesale in an effort to contain the disease.

If the virus is to reach the United States, Canada, or Mexico, it will most likely arrive through the trading of commercial poultry and the illegal trade of exotic birds.

But another problem is the spread of the viruses in wild ducks. Ducks, both wild and domestic, seem to be able to harbor many avian viruses without becoming ill. But they can still pass it on. From these asymptomatic birds the viruses can spread to other birds—and, possibly, people.

The H5N1 virus is not likely to be spread to North America by wild or migratory birds—this year. However, because of the migration patterns of some birds from Siberia, some of which cross the narrow Bering Sea to Alaska, it's thought that, beginning next summer, there may be a mixing of indigenous shore birds and migrating waterfowl from Siberia.

Infected birds, whether sick or asymptomatic, are constantly shedding the virus in their feces, saliva, and mucous. This is how it is transmitted to other birds and, apparently, to humans working with them.

Either because of trade in commercial poultry, bird smuggling, or migrating birds, it's probably just a matter of time before the virus shows up in both domestic and wild birds in North America. (However, see the sidebar, *Pandemic flu and terrorism*.)

If Avian flu arrives

For the symptoms and treatment of flu, see the sidebar titled, *Getting **and getting rid of** the flu.* If H5N1 jumps to humans, many of the symptoms will be the same as for any seasonal flu. However, with flu caused by the H5N1 virus, many of the symptoms are going to be more severe, and there are also major differences in how it attacks your body.

Unlike common cases of influenza that attack the upper respiratory syste; i.e., the bronchial tubes, nose, and throat, infection from H5N1 can go deeper into the lungs where they can do more serious damage. Victims have drowned in their own fluids, including blood, that fills their lungs. Those who survive often do so with lungs that are compromised and will be damaged for the rest of their lives.

If an actual H5N1 flu pandemic starts, avoid people who appear to have symptoms. In fact, avoid all people as much as you can. If I had children in school, I'd consider pulling them out and homeschooling them.

Over the years, *BHM* has advocated preparedness and having a preparedness kit. If you have a kit, this may be the crisis you've prepared for. If you don't, use *BHM's EPSG* book (page 66 and 99 of this issue) or some other, and start one. Minimizing your need to mix with others may save the lives of you and your family members.

I know the "health experts" are telling you not to stockpile flu drugs. If you want to be a good little boy scout, then don't. But if I had access to them, I'd quietly put some away "just

Getting *and getting rid of* the flu

How do you get flu? The flu is extremely contagious. It is most frequently spread through inhalation of air droplets that contain respiratory secretions from other infected people. These aerosols are usually spread when the person with flu coughs or sneezes. But you don't have to inhale these droplets. You can get flu handling objects contaminated by these secretions.

For the paranoid (I'm borderline) there are too many things we come into contact with that others who are infected will have touched before us:

- doorknobs
- elevator buttons
- flush handles on toilets
- the handles on paper towel dispensers in rest rooms that you touch after you've washed your hands
- money
- products at the supermarket placed on shelves by infected employees stocking the shelves, or by previous customers who handled them, then put them back
- the very air you breathe
- children who have been in contact with other children at schools, day cares, and playgrounds
- keyboards and mouses at the office or library
- hands—it's very hard not to shake hands in social situations
- utensils handled by others every time you eat in a restaurant
- a family member or friend who comes into your home infected

Flu symptoms. With the common variant of the flu, symptoms usually show up in one to four days. The most common symptoms are:

- headaches
- myalgia (muscle aches)
- joint aches
- fatigue
- sore throat
- coughing that starts out as dry and hacking but after a few days turns wet with thick mucus. It can last for two weeks or more
- in severe cases, breathing problems and pneumonia, which can be fatal
- fever, with or without chills
- nasal congestion, watery eyes, or runny nose
- conjunctivitis
- vomiting
- diarrhea

However, in the cases of flu caused by the H5N1 virus, symptoms have been more like hemorrhagic fever. Instead of symptoms in the upper respiratory tract—nose, throat, bronchial tubes—the lower lungs fill up. Autopsies reveal that the virus often destroys the lungs, and the victims literally drown in their own water and blood.

Avoiding the flu. Avoid people with the disease. Adults with flu are typically contagious for 5-7 days from fever onset. In children, they are contagious for 7-10 days and even longer (up to 4 weeks) for people with low natural defense mechanisms.

Support your immune system. Eat right, get rest, **wash your hands frequently**.

A flu vaccination can provide immunity to *some* strains of flu. But the vaccination is not 100 percent effective, nor will it protect you from all strains. The vaccines out there now are not necessarily going to protect you against Avian flu. (Do *not* get a flu vaccination if you're allergic to eggs because the vaccine is grown in eggs. Nor should you get them if you are allergic to thimerosal, a mercury-containing preservative used to preserve the vaccine.)

Treating flu. There are four drugs that will treat and/or prevent influenza: amantadine, rimantadine, zanamivir, and oseltamivir. Amantadine and rimantadine have been in use since 1976 and treat and prevent influenza induced by Type A viruses by interfering with the proteins from a channel in the virus membrane so the virus cannot replicate after it enters a cell.

The other two drugs, zanamivir (sold as Relenza) and oseltamivir (sold as Tamiflu) are a new class of antiviral drugs that interfere with the neuraminidase proteins on the outer shell of the virus, the enzyme that frees the new viruses being "born" in your body's cells. Oseltamivir, when correctly administered, can even prevent flu.

Once you have flu, none of these drugs prevent serious influenza-related complications such as bacterial or viral pneumonia. And all of these drugs have side effects such as headache, diarrhea, nausea, breathing problems, and others. Any kind of medical conditions from kidney problems to asthma to pregnancy should be discussed with a doctor before you take any of these.

Keep in mind, though, that given enough time the viruses will develop resistance to these drugs, and there is evidence that the H5N1 virus is resistant to amantadine and rimantadine.

Again, support your immune system. Get rest and increase your fluid intake. (I, for one, will eat chicken soup. It won't cure me, but I feel better and, like bananas, it is among the few things that tastes okay both when it's going down and when it's coming back up.)

There are drugs that will treat and/or prevent flu. Talk with your doctor. He or she is more apt to know what you need. But these drugs are both costly and can have disconcerting side effects. Antibiotics are useless unless they are prescribed to combat bacterial complications that your body becomes susceptible to because your body has been weakened.

Treatment of symptoms. For fever, aches, and pains take analgesics and antipyretics. These include paracetamol and ibuprofen. I take aspirin. It works wonders for me.

For runny and stuffy nose, take cold medications.

For dry cough, take something like dextromethorphan.

For productive cough, take Ambroxol, Bromhexine, Carbocisteine, or Guiafenesin.

Complications from flu. Flu very often leads to other complications. Among them are pneumonia and otitis media (inflammation of the inner ear). These are usually caused by the virus itself, but they are often the result of opportunistic bacteria. In the latter case, antibiotics may be prescribed. A rare but more serious complication is Reye's Syndrome, which is marked by delirium, seizures, stupor, coma, and even death.

Pandemic flu and terrorism

Spreading disease may not be as "romantic" a way to sacrifice yourself as blowing yourself up in the middle of a crowd, but those willing to martyr themselves for a cause may be willing to expose themselves to a disease, especially a disease that has the potential for becoming a pandemic. A terrorist could hop on the subway system of a major metropolitan city or insert himself into various professional or college sporting events, concerts, or any place that draws a large crowd.

This is not to say that terrorists currently have the capability to create pandemics. But with technological advances coming as fast as they are, it's possible it could happen in the future. For example, at the CDC in the Netherlands, scientists are trying to deliberately mix genes from the H5N1 avian virus and human flu viruses to see if the resultant viruses have the potential for creating a pandemic. This could have enormous potential in helping us to understand and control the disease. The downside is that if this technology is perfected, it may also be possible for terrorists to employ it. It could become a "poor man's atom bomb."

in case." I'm not trying to save the world; I'm trying to save me and mine.

How Avian flu is treated

The good news is that antiviral medications currently used to treat other human flu viruses appear to be effective for the treatment of Avian flu. The bad news is that these drugs are in short supply. The worse news is that, as with treatments for any diseases, the pathogens are constantly evolving so as to become immune to the treatments.

Two new drugs that can be used to treat the flu are Tamiflu, an oral medication made by the Swiss pharmaceutical company, Roche, and Relenza, made by Glaxo Wellcome, Inc., which is usually administered by inhalation. The way they work is they interfere with the virus's ability to replicate. This is important because it gives the body's immune system a chance to develop antibodies to fight the disease before the virus can reproduce enough to overwhelm it. *No* drug can cure the flu. It just slows it down until your immune system can kick in.

Right now, neither company can produce their drugs fast enough to cope with a possible pandemic. (See sidebar, *Why drug companies are hesitant to develop flu treatments and vaccines.*) But in response to the media attention being focused on Avian flu, Roche, the sole manufacturer of Tamiflu, is negotiating with four other companies to license its manufacture. However, it may be for naught. There is evidence that some viruses are evolving to become resistant to their drug and that H5N1 may be resistant to it altogether.

Lastly, here's a curious item in the news at this writing: researchers in South Korea claim kimchi, Korea's spicy fermented cabbage dish, may help treat bird flu. Scientists at Seoul National University claim to have fed an extract of kimchi to 13 infected chickens and within a week 11 of them had recovered. The researchers admitted that this was no more than anecdotal evidence, and said if kimchi did have the effects they observed, they didn't know why.

Is it true? I doubt it. It sounds like one of those quack folk cures. But it doesn't matter, I love kimchi and any excuse to eat more of it is good enough for me. And if it saves my life in the meantime? Hey!

Vaccines

Two companies have created vaccines that appear to work against the H5N1 virus, but there are two problems: If an H5N1 pandemic were to start today, there's not enough vaccine to go around. Also, neither vaccine may be effective against the virus health officials fear H5N1 may mutate into. In other words, you may get a vaccination, but if H5N1 mutates, it may be useless.

Cautious optimism

There were three influenza pandemics in the 20th century. The first was one of the greatest pandemics in human history. The way the news is being reported today, we seem poised on the brink of another.

However, though a future influenza pandemic is certainly possible, it's *not* inevitable. And, if one does occur, it's not even certain it will be caused by the H5N1 virus or one of its offshoots. H5N1 has been with us a long time without jumping species.

In fact, many experts feel that if there is another pandemic, it's more likely to come from an antigenic shift or drift of a virus no one anticipates today.

So what should we do?

First, refuse to be panicked. News outlets and government agencies thrive on creating crises where none exist. Filter sensationalized reports through your common sense.

Second, stay alert. Know what's happening in the country and the world so your common sense filter can tell you if a real pandemic emerges.

Third, and always—be prepared. We may not be able to control virus mutations, migrating birds, drug companies, or supply lines, but we can take the steps necessary to protect ourselves and our families. Have enough food, water, and other supplies to ride out a future pandemic, or any other disaster. Δ

Ask Jackie

If you have a question about rural living, send it in to Jackie Clay and she'll try to answer it. Address your letter to Ask Jackie, PO Box 712, Gold Beach, OR 97444. Questions will only be answered in this column. — Editor

84 year-old auntie never used pressure canner

My aunt (the Matriarch of our family) is 84 years old, and my garden this year has been fantastic! I asked my aunt for canning advice (Dad, her brother, was the cook and he's been gone for 20 years...) She is telling me that she never had a pressure cooker and always used a hot water bath canner. (The one I have is her sister's). She is telling me how she does string beans, peppers, squash, and corn. (and other fruits and vegetables)...Most of these are recommended in the Ball Blue Book to be pressure cooked...But how can I argue with almost 84 years of experience? Especially since I've been eating these preserves for 44 years?

Robert Stalker
Lockport, New York

Yes, yes, I know of many "aunts" just like yours. And yes, they did can for years using only a water bath canner. But yes, you can die from eating Auntie's water bath processed vegetables!

Did you get that? The dangerous bacteria that can kill you are NOT all that common, but they are around, in the soil, in the air, maybe on Auntie's hands even. All it takes is one batch of those vegetables, canned unsafely in a water bath canner, and you are very sick or DEAD. Personally, I don't want to risk it when pressure canning is SO easy and SO safe.

— Jackie

Chokecherry jelly

When I was young, my parents and siblings would come to Colorado to visit Grandma and Gramps. I remember her fresh baked bread, green chili, and always chokecherry jelly...

We have three bushes on our property. Jackie why didn't I ask grandma for her recipe? I was a lot younger then and too busy eating and not paying attention. It must be simple but I still don't have the recipe for this wonderful berry. Grandma and Mom are gone now.

I have attempted making it a couple of times, but I don't remember what berry recipe I used. The second time was a failure. It did not settle, so we used it as a syrup.

Cordelia Webb
Elizabeth, Colorado

Chokecherry jelly is one of our favorites. We love the intense cherry flavor, and the beautiful glistening purplish red clear color that makes a jar of jelly look like a rare gem, plus the fact that you can find chokecherries in so many states. We picked them in New Mexico, Michigan, Montana, and Wyoming. There are several recipes, but here's a simple good one:

Place about 2 quarts of freshly picked chokecherries into a large kettle with 3 cups of water. Simmer the cherries, then mash them with a potato masher or large spoon. Here I let the soft cherries cool, then I really squish them by hand. This releases a lot of color and flavor. It also turns your hands purple. But this is quite temporary.

Then hang the cherry pulp in a jelly bag over a large bowl overnight to drip. You will need 3 cups of chokecherry juice.

Jackie Clay

3 cups chokecherry juice
6 ½ cups sugar
1 bottle liquid fruit pectin
¼ tsp. almond extract (optional, but gives a great cherry flavor boost)

Pour juice into large kettle. Add sugar and stir well. Place over high heat and bring to a boil, stirring constantly to avoid scorching. Stir in pectin. Bring to a full rolling boil and boil hard 1 minute, stirring constantly.

Remove from heat. Skim if desired. Stir in extract. Pour into previously boiled, hot jars to within ¼" of top. Wipe jar rim. Place hot, previously simmered lid on jar and screw down ring firmly tight. Water bath for 5 minutes.

If you are a little short on chokecherries (and it takes a lot to make 3 cups juice in dry years), you can boil the chokecherries in apple juice instead of water and simply use the recipe in powdered pectin for cherry jelly. You can't tell the difference.

— Jackie

Canning green beans

I know that green beans should be the easiest things to can, but every

time I try to can them the water boils out. I leave a one-inch headspace, and I have tried cold pack and hot pack. Is there some secret that I don't know about?

Cathy Barton
Hubbard, Texas

I would seriously take your canner gauge into your local Extension office and have it checked. It sounds like you may be canning at too high a pressure. Another reason that liquid sometimes is sucked out of jars is that the person "tweaks" the pressure relief valves to let steam escape in order to return the pressure to zero. The canner must return to zero by itself, and then....and only then can you open the petcocks to release any leftover steam. Once this happens, immediately take the jars out of the canner and place them on a dry folded towel to cool. It messes things up if you leave the processed jars in the canner after processing to cool. Usually the jars seal poorly or not at all. **— *Jackie***

Boil the canning lids?

In all of Jackie's recipes for canning, she tells folks to boil the lids. On the box the lids come in it specifically says "do not boil."

Carolyn Lucas
Lapeer, Michigan

I don't know what kind of jar lids you use, but I've read three different new boxes of mine, and all say "simmer, then keep in warm water until use." My canning manuals all say to do this, as well, except this year's Ball Blue Book. It says "simmer" but do not boil. It seems that folks were letting their lids boil dry, then the seal compound on the lids failed. So "simmer" your lids at 180 degrees, then keep in the hot water, or pour boiling water over them and keep them in hot water. I will refrain from using "boiling" in the future. **— *Jackie***

Canning corn

This is my first year of growing a garden. The corn turned out exceptionally well. I was just wondering how do you can corn?

Emily Lindstrom
Hell, Michigan

Sweet corn is very easy to can. All you need to do is to shuck the corn, pick the silks off it, and slice the corn off the cob. You can buy special cutters to do this. One I use is like a saw blade, bent into a circle on two flexible metal handles you squeeze to tighten the cutting circle on the corn cob. Standing the cob on its big end, you shove the cutter down, while turning it slightly back and forth. The kernels fall right into the pan you have under the cob. I use a big turkey roaster or a large pie pan.

Of course you can simply slice the kernels off with a sharp knife, too.

Once the corn is off the cob, you can either cold pack it, which simply means packing it cold into clean canning jars to within an inch of the top, adding a tsp of salt to each jar, then pouring boiling water into the jar to within an inch of the top. It's a good idea to run a plastic or wooden spoon down around the corn to release any air pockets that might have formed.

Corn, being a low-acid food (as are all vegetables but tomatoes), MUST be processed in a pressure canner. You will process pints for 55 minutes and quarts for 90 minutes at 10 pounds pressure unless you live at an altitude over 1,000 feet. In that case, you simply increase the pounds pressure by increments depending on the altitude; see a canning manual for directions.

You can also hot pack corn. This results in a prettier, more even jar of corn; in cold packing, the corn sort of floats to the top of the jar, leaving liquid in the bottom. Same taste; it only looks different.

To hot pack, simply add water to the cut corn in a large kettle. About a cup of water for each quart of corn or a little more is right. Just heat the water and corn to a boil, then scoop out the corn and pack loosely into a clean, warm jar to within an inch of the top. Pour in enough of the water it was boiled in to cover the corn to within an inch of the top of the jar. The processing time is the same.

When the time has been reached, turn off the heat and let the canner cool until the gauge reaches zero. Then release the safety petcocks slowly and open the canner, being careful to open it away from you so that any left over steam doesn't scald your face or arms. Lift out the jars with a jar lifter and place on a dry, folded towel in a draft free area to cool. When they are cool (usually overnight), you may remove the rings and wash the jars. Test each jar to make sure the center of the lid is indented tightly. Poke it gently with a finger. There should be no give to the lid; it shouldn't pop down and up. It should remain tightly indented. Dry the jars and store in a cool, dry, dark area.

If you do not have a canning manual, pick up one at any large store or borrow a book from your library until you finish. When you can, you need a canning manual. I've been doing it for over 35 years and wouldn't think of canning without one on the table!

— *Jackie*

Recipes for well cake, and a bug spray mixture

Quite a few years ago, during home-ec class in junior high, we made a well cake consisting of cocoa, flour, sugar, water, vinegar and oil. All of the dry ingredients were placed in a 9x9 baking pan. Three wells were made, to which you would add the liquid ingredients, mix and bake. Do you have this recipe? I'm sure I've missed some ingredients. I would really appreciate any help.

I also wanted to write a response to Sally Hamilton of San Dimas,

California. Her letter (about battling bugs like ticks) to you appeared in the Sept/Oct 2005 issue. I'm sure these have been around for a while. You may have even printed them before.

Lawn Spray: 1:1

1 bar Fels-Naptha soap, grated (soaked in 1 cup water)

1 pouch chewing tobacco (soaked in 1cup water)

lemon dish soap

Listerene

Strain off the Fels-Naptha and tobacco. Put all ingredients in a pump sprayer and be bug free! I keep a grater and a bucket separate for use with this formula only.

Yard Spray

1 cup ammonia

½ cup dish soap

½ cup human urine

Mix all in a 20-gallon hose end sprayer and spray your bugs away!

I have used the former of the two recipes with great success.

Several years ago, on one of my ventures out west, I stayed at a KOA campground in South Dakota. Exploring around the area, the bugs were horrible (skeeters, gnats, flies, etc.), except at the campground. Upon talking to the owner, he told us of a "garlic juice" spray he uses. As I recall, it was rather expensive, but to him worth it in combating the critters. I'm sure a search could be done to find out more info.

Vicky Scott
Ellijay, Georgia

I have a recipe for your well cake, but I personally have not tried it. Here's hoping it is as good as the one you made in class.

Mix 1½ cups flour, 1 cup sugar, 3 Tbsp cocoa, 1 tsp. baking soda, and ½ tsp. salt in bowl. Drizzle 6 Tbsp. melted shortening over it and pour into a greased 9x9 cake pan. Make three wells across the center of the pan. Mix in a small bowl 1 Tbsp. vinegar, 1 cup cold water, and 1 tsp. vanilla. Pour evenly into wells. Bake immediately at 350 degrees for 25 minutes or until done. — ***Jackie***

Summer, winter, and herb garden hints

My husband and I are currently chomping at the bit to get out of the city.

We are busy getting all our ducks in a row before we move into the country, but a few things still have me stumped. What is the difference between a winter and a summer garden, and can you give us examples of what we may find in each? Are there certain plants that are staple to a country living?

Lastly, which herbs/spices do you find to be essential and easy to grow?

Jessica Rose Andrus
Lansing, Michigan

A winter garden contains cold-loving plants that you can grow under minimal cover such as small hoop houses, cloches, or cold frames that will produce during all but the coldest part of a cold winter or all winter in some climates. Such foods include nearly all varieties of lettuce, kale, spinach, carrots, cress, and green onions.

Your summer garden gives you a wider range of edibles. There are your main crops, such as sweet corn, broccoli, cabbage, green beans, wax beans, dry beans of all types, peppers, onions, cucumbers, squash, pumpkins, turnips, rutabagas, peas, carrots, spinach, head lettuce, etc. All of the winter garden crops can be grown in a summer garden, but prefer the cooler ends of the season.

You'll find that diversity is the key to planning your new homestead. If your aim is self-reliance, think of the kinds of foods you enjoy all year around. On the homestead, you either eat fresh from the land or enjoy foods that you put up. There don't need to be out of season foods purchased at the super market from places where they still farm using DDT.

Remember that your garden also includes perennial fruits and vegetables. Don't forget such staples as fruit trees, berry bushes, rhubarb, asparagus, Jerusalem artichokes, horseradish, and wild fruits like chokecherries.

As for your herb garden, simply include any spices you can grow in your climate that your family enjoys. Garlic, sage, many types of basil, oregano, lemon mint, catnip, and thyme are a few of our regulars.

Remember that you don't have to do it all as soon as you get to your new place. I always set out a few fruit trees and a scattering of other perennial foods, but count on doing more and more each year. The first year here, I set out five apple trees and some rhubarb, along with ten asparagus plants. This year I set out three more apples, four apricots, a pie cherry, more rhubarb, strawberries, and a few red raspberries. And next year there will be more; you get the picture. — ***Jackie***

Sending canned foods through the mail a no-no

I have a son who is in the Navy and he is missing my home cooked meals.

I was wondering if you can send cooked white beans or red beans processed in a jar, and how long it would last? He is in the states but we are in Louisiana and he is in California. I send him corn bread but I had a wild idea about sending him some cooked beans in a jar.

Julie Grivat
Loreauville, Louisiana

I have to laugh, because I sent my oldest son, Bill, some home canned chili, which was his favorite, through the mail. It must have had some rough handling between Montana and Minnesota because the seal came loose, and when he got it the chili reeked! The same year, I sent my oldest daughter some of her favorite bread and butter pickles, along with two pair of wool socks. The pickles, too, came unsealed, and Randie's wool socks ended up smelling like pickles....four washings later, too!

Now, we've moved around a bit, and hauled our pantry full of jars up dreadfully rocky mountain trails, across the country where they've been tossed into trucks and shoved around roughly. Very few ever came unsealed, but all of my mailed foods did. What does that say for the Postal Service? And United Parcel is no better.

If you want to send your son something tasty from home, better to choose homemade candy, cookies, bars, jam or jelly. The rest don't seem to make it. ***— Jackie***

Put up jelly in small batches for success

I am confused about all the different things I have read about making jelly (crabapple). Boil it too long and the pectin can be ruined and it is runny. Don't boil it enough, or add too much sugar, and it is runny. Boil it too long and it is gummy.

The spoon test never seems to work for me. I have to boil it for hours to make it glob off of the spoon like that. So I used a thermometer and boiled it to "8 degrees above boiling point in your area" according to Joy of Cooking, which is 210 degrees. It hovered at 208 for about an hour, then finally hit 210. I put it in the jars and it is runny. Is there a more foolproof way to tell when to put it in the jars without using commercial pectin?

Tania Dibbs
Basalt, Colorado

I think you are making too large a batch of jelly at a time. Jelly is one thing that must put up in smaller batches for success. Crabapples are high in pectin, so are quite easy to get the jelly to jell. And yes, the spoon test does work, if the jelly is jelled properly. Here's a simple crabapple jelly recipe you might like to try.

Chop or quarter crabapples (about 3 pounds) and add 1 cup water to each heaped quart of crabapples in large kettle. Cover and simmer fruit until quite soft. Strain through a damp jelly bag or cheesecloth bag overnight.

4 cups crabapple juice
4 cups sugar

Put crabapple juice in large kettle and add sugar. Bring to boil over high heat, stirring constantly. Cook to jelling point, where the jelly slides off a ***cool*** spoon in a sheet instead of drips. The spoon must be cool and not damp from washing it. When this point is reached, turn off the heat and quickly ladle the jelly into hot half pint or pint jars to within ¼-inch of the top of the jar. Process the jelly in a water bath canner for 10 minutes.

This makes about six half pint jars. If you want more jelly, simply make more juice. You can make lots of juice, keeping the same proportions. Then make one batch of jelly at a time using the above recipe. Do not double or triple the recipe to save time. You'll often have failures.

— Jackie

Where did the acorns go?

I live in Massachusetts and have elected to teach an after school nature class. Last year I was able to harvest a great many acorns by the school and was planning doing so with the children this year. I went to the spot where I collected and can't find any. I looked in the tree (which is very high) and don't see any up there either. Am I just too early or might we have an insect problem here?

Sarah Boynton
Hingham, Massachusetts

If there are no acorns on the tree or on the ground, either the tree is just not producing this year, which is a common occurrence in both nut and fruit trees, or you may just be too early. Squirrels and other wildlife harvest acorns, but will leave the bad ones lying on the ground. They will also usually not take every single one.

— Jackie

Make evaporated milk from goat's milk

I am a "self-taught" canner and have been putting up a variety of food for years. By the time I came along, my mother and grandmother wanted no more of canning with the exception of the occasional jams or jellies. I would like to know if there is a recipe for making evaporated milk from goat milk (naturally using a pressure canner). We currently have three milking does, and although I make a lot of cheese, there is still a surplus. I would greatly appreciate any help you can give.

Raven Smith
High Springs, Florida

You can home can milk, which turns out a lot like evaporated milk. Simply pour your strained, warm milk into clean jars to within half an inch of the top and process in a pressure canner for 10 minutes at 10 pounds pressure or in a water bath canner for 60 minutes.

Don't forget ice cream, which makes great natural smoothies and milk shakes, cream cheese, and yogurt in all kinds of fruit flavors. Our two gallon milkers scarcely can keep up with us in the summer when so many great foods are available. I, too, make lots of different cheeses. Goats are such valuable animals on the homestead! ***— Jackie***

Can I can milk bought from the store?

The reason your magazine is so appealing to us is because of the resourcefulness of your writers and subscribers.

Jim and I live in Southeast Alaska on a 1979 International school bus

Jim transformed into a livable and comfortable R.V. I cook on a wood burning cook stove that also supplies our hot water and heat. We have electricity thanks to a very fuel efficient Honda gas generator. We don't own a computer and don't have a phone service and miss neither.

Is it safe to can pasteurized milk (from the store) using the water bath method?

We buy pasteurized whole milk here at our little local store for $6 a gallon. Even at that price the cost would be economical because 10 oz. cans of store brand condensed milk is $1.29 a can.

Also, can I make and can a sweetened condensed milk using the store milk and the water bath method?

Do you have a recipe for this?

Jim and Shelly Isabell
Ketchikan, Alaska

Yes, you can home can store milk. The water bath time of 60 minutes works for pints and quarts as milk is a liquid.

Yes, I have a recipe for the sweetened condensed milk, but it is in storage right now until we get our house finished, and I can't locate that box. So sorry! ***— Jackie***

Jiggly weight canner

I recently bought an old Minomatic "jiggly weight" canner at a thrift store. It didn't include the manual, but for $12 who's complaining? I've already canned veggie soup and spaghetti sauce with it and I think it went okay. (I've eaten the results and am still alive!) I followed the general rules for pressure canning in the Ball Blue Book, but a few things were kind of unclear. How long should it take for the weight to jiggle when I put it on? I exhausted the air for 10 minutes before putting it on but after I put it on it took almost 10 minutes more to start going! There was some questionable hissing and sputtering coming from the right side and under the weight around the valve. The side stopped letting off steam when the weight started to go. Does this mean it has sealed? I started timing then. Is it supposed to take so long to seal? Lastly, how will I know when the seal needs to be replaced? Any advice would be greatly appreciated!

Confused Canner
Eggertsville, New York

There is no set time on how long it takes the weight to jiggle after you exhaust the air and put it in place. The same holds true with gauge type canners. It depends on how many jars of what type of food is in them. Don't try to hurry things or begin timing too soon. That is how people get into trouble by not processing the food long enough.

There is usually some miscellaneous hissing before things get underway. As long as it stops, you are probably alright.

The gasket needs to be replaced if it feels stiff, sort of hard, and/or steam escapes excessively and the jiggler weight doesn't jiggle or jiggles weakly. ***— Jackie***

Plastic bucket pickler

Can a 5-gallon plastic bucket be used to pickle cucumbers instead of a clay crock?

Terry Shannon
Mausten, Wisconsin

Yes, you can pickle cucumbers in a food grade plastic bucket. Personally, I don't, but I do know folks who regularly do this. ***— Jackie***

The last word

Activists on both the left and the right spotlight a broken federal government

On October 28, 2005, 400 citizens of Vermont met amid the pomp of their capitol building and voted to secede from the Union. The media, to say the least, was surprised. Those who noticed (which included *CBS News* and the *Christian Science Monitor*) treated the story as a novelty, only slightly more serious than the latest sighting of the Virgin Mary's face in a Texas taco. But the vote was the first rumble of what could become a political and cultural earthquake. And Vermont isn't the only state on the fault line. Other secessionist or state sovereignty movements are building from Hawaii to New Hampshire.

Millions of Americans perceive that the federal government is broken and might not be fixable. They view centralized power as heavy-handed, intrusive—and yet useless when it's called upon for help, as in the aftermath of Hurricane Katrina.

Right or wrong, like them or not, state sovereignty activists say, "We have a solution."

Their solution is radical local activism to restore power to citizens at the state level. They aim to make state laws that counteract federal ones. They hope to preserve local or regional cultures against homogenization. They're all aiming for their idea of freedom—although often their concepts of freedom are diverse, to say the least.

Watch them: They may be the vanguard of a much larger movement of frustrated citizens who feel helpless to achieve their aims at the federal level but who aren't willing to accept the status quo.

The Vermont meeting was a gathering of activists, not a session of the state legislature, so the secession vote has no legal force. The members of the Second Vermont Republic (SVR) consider it simply the first of many planned steps.

The SVR is "left-wing." In addition to opposing big government, it also opposes "big business, big markets, and big agriculture" and what members see as a dreary, institutional sameness being imposed on the entire world.

But secession isn't inherently left-wing. Secession is simply the separation of one political entity from another. And it's just one of a number of related ideas now being actively promoted.

Next door to Vermont, for instance, the libertarian Free State Project (FSP) aims to encourage enough activists to move to New Hampshire to permanently alter that state's politics. They want smaller government, a free-market economy, and the ability to "just say no" to the worst federal laws and bureaucratic policies. The FSP has already signed up 7,000 of a hoped-for 20,000 activists.

The FSP and the SVR arise from opposite ends of the political spectrum. They differ in tactics and goals. The FSP is not secessionist. But both groups share that key central concept: local activism to achieve aims that can't be achieved at the federal level.

Other sovereignty movements have arisen in Hawaii, Wyoming, Montana, and Alaska, among other places. The group, Christian Exodus, aims to spark an en masse move to South Carolina. There, they hope to gain control of the legislature and run state government on religious principles.

Others would like to unite Canada's western plains provinces to the USA's western mountain states, pointing out that they have more in common with each other than with their respective eastern urban centers.

Some groups, like the FSP, are determined to work within the system. Even the most radical secessionist groups hope to "go in peace." They want no trouble, just to be left alone.

"But isn't secession illegal?" some object.

Actually, probably not.

The *U.S. Constitution* is silent on secession. But the 9th and 10th amendments make it clear that states have higher authority than the federal government in all but a few specified areas. Those same amendments proclaim that the people have rights, while the central government has only limited powers delegated to it by the states and the people. In other words, since the *Constitution* doesn't say that states *can't* secede, then naturally, say the organizers of the SVR and other secessionist groups, they can.

But of course, theory and practice are two different things. The last time American states tried to act on such a claim, the federal government overpowered them, with catastrophic loss of life on both sides.

Will the Second Vermont Republic—or any other regional independence movement—succeed? The example of 1861 sets a disastrous precedent for those who want the most radical solutions. On the other hand, the former Soviet republics more recently separated from Russia without war. And historically the boundaries of countries are ever-shifting.

It's probably a long way to the first true secessionist vote. Possibly no such vote will ever be taken. But even if these projects don't achieve their ultimate aims, they do succeed in bringing activists together. They shine much-needed light on deep national problems. They get people to think "outside the box." Organizations like the SVR and the FSP could renew the cultural climate of their states and restore an independent spirit to parts of North America. That alone could be a worthy goal.

For more information:

- The Second Vermont Republic, PO Box 1093, Montpelier, VT 05601, www.vermontrepublic.org
- The Free State Project, PO Box 1684, Keene, NH 03431, 1-888-532-4604, www.freestateproject.org
- The American Secession Project, www.secessionist.us (This is a web-only listing of many secession and free state projects.)

— Claire Wolfe

Give a gift subscription...and get the 2 new anthologies FREE. See page 3.

March/April 2006
Issue #98
$4.95 US
$6.50 CAN

Backwoods Home magazine

practical ideas for self-reliant living

MONSTER QUAKE
... it won't be in California

Big Brother wants to track your livestock...see page 95.

Growing garlic
Herb gardening
All American 10/22
Emergency radio
A tire garden

www.backwoodshome.com

My view

Why you may want to get a "stress test"

Between issues I underwent triple bypass open heart surgery that saved me from a major heart attack, possibly a fatal one. It was a sudden thing. One day doctors discovered several major blockages in my coronary arteries, and two days later I was in the Cardiac Care Unit of the Rogue Valley Medical Center in Medford, Oregon, after undergoing a three-hour open heart bypass surgery to correct the life threatening blockages.

My story, and my ongoing recovery, are worth reading about because there are millions of Americans, many reading this column, who have Coronary Artery Disease (CAD) as severe as mine but who don't know it because they have no symptoms. Heart attack, which CAD leads to unless you get your arteries fixed, is the number one killer in America. With this brief column I hope to alert you walking heart time bombs out there on how to detect this killer, and stop him before he stops you.

Let me set the stage. I am 61, stay in pretty good shape because I exercise on a fairly regular basis, eat a well balanced diet that pays attention to heart and cancer-healthy foods such as fish, fruits, and vegetables, take a regimen of well-informed supplements such as heart-healthy Omega 3s and folic acid, and in general pay attention to my health and weight.

But what I hadn't considered fully when it came to my health is the importance of heredity when it comes to a healthy heart. My mother died of a heart attack at age 61, probably the same type of heart attack that was poised to kill me before my body gave me a little warning. Heredity is one of the major indicators of your susceptibility to having a heart attack, along with things like whether or not you smoke, are overweight, eat a heart-friendly diet, or have things like high cholesterol, high blood pressure, and a host of other highs that a standard blood panel will reveal. Simply getting older, like I am, is also an indicator you are at risk of a heart attack.

I typically have an annual physical, and my blood test numbers regarding cholesterol, triglycerides, HDL, LDL, and C-Reactive Protein were always very good. Only last year did I develop borderline high blood pressure, but it was so borderline I needed no medication.

Then one day about six weeks before the deadline for this issue, a mild pain, sort of like indigestion, occurred in my chest as I sat at the *BHM* editorial desk. It radiated out around my back, then into my jaw. I thought it was from paint fumes because someone was painting the walls in the next office over. I also had a pretty good headache.

It was four days later that I finally made my way to my doctor, John Delgado, three hours away in Ashland, Oregon. The pain had long since subsided and I felt terrific. He gave me an EKG, which showed nothing, and did a blood panel, which showed a slightly elevated cholesterol and a markedly elevated C-Reactive Protein, an indicator of possible heart attack, or its imminent occurrence.

Dave Duffy with brother, Hugh, after heart surgery

Off to the cardiologist he sent me, who had me take a stress test, which, by the way, is the single best non-invasive test you can take to detect CAD. It indicated a probable blockage in a coronary artery going into the left side of my heart. The cardiologist had me undergo a cardiac catheterization, which is a mildly invasive x-ray test where they put a probe up an artery in the groin and thread it up and into your heart so they can actually see any blockages. The cath test, or angiogram, showed conclusively three blockages, one a long 90% blockage. Two days later I underwent my triple bypass, a major but nowadays almost routine surgery, and am now in the midst of a 6-month, anticipated to be total, recovery.

I feel fortunate to be afforded the opportunity to *have* a long road of recovery. Many people find out they have CAD only when they experience the surprise heart attack and drop dead. That's what happened to my mother. And I had been slipping, unbeknownst to me, ever closer to that precipice until Providence, or whatever, gave me a warning of what was about to occur.

So here's the message: If you have any of the risk factors of CAD mentioned above, especially if you are getting older like me and have had a close relative—a parent or a sibling—who had CAD, ask your doctor if you could benefit from a stress test.

Most people don't like to think of themselves as having the potential of sudden heart attack. And the first reaction of most heart attack victims is to deny they are having a heart attack. But you may be one of the millions of CAD victims out there just days from a too-early death when it could be prevented in these miracle medical times. A stress test is easy; it will either alert you to a grave danger ahead, or it will give you peace of mind. ***— Dave Duffy***

Buying the right EMERGENCY RADIO

By Jeffrey R. Yago, P.E., CEM

In our last issue I addressed how to select the best battery-powered lighting for your emergency needs. Recent examples of poor emergency response during the Katrina hurricane aftermath has reinforced our belief that everyone needs to be prepared to survive on their own for a week or more before relief arrives. When selecting electronic equipment for use during emergencies that can last several weeks without electrical power, there are features an emergency radio should have that may not be realized when electrical power is available from the nearest wall outlet.

Although it is possible to use a generator or alternative energy system to power the same appliances and electronic equipment that you use when utility power is available, it is also possible an emergency power system can fail during an extended power outage due to lack of fuel or equipment failure. You may also need to relocate to higher ground or a safer shelter, leaving behind your comfortable home either temporally or permanently. This means your survival may depend on what you can carry on your back, and not what you have back at the house.

What type of radio?

In this issue I am going to address the radio devices you will need to keep in contact with the outside world during emergency conditions and the features you should look for in each. Unless you are an afternoon talk radio listener, you may not even own a portable AM radio. However, an AM radio will be the primary source for all local news, weather, and relief instructions for your town and state during civil unrest, a fast moving fire, flood, hurricane, snow storm, power outage, tornado, earthquake, chemical spill, dam break, or other disaster which can strike anyone without warning. Since television, FM radio, and VHF and UHF transmissions are "line-of-sight" due to their very short wavelengths, these signals normally can reach only 50 to 75 miles from the transmitter in hilly or mountainous areas because of the earth's curved surface.

However, AM radio transmission uses much longer low frequency wavelengths which are easily reflected from the earth's upper ionosphere. Without the disrupting effects of solar energy on this field at night, it is possible for AM radio waves to travel around the world even from relatively low power transmitters. This makes the AM radio band ideal for providing emergency information to very large geographic areas using the fewest number of radio stations.

During the 70's and 80's, the AM band was becoming a wasteland as listeners headed for the higher-quality stereo music on the FM band which was not possible on the static-prone AM band. However, with the rise in popular afternoon talk-radio, manufacturers began making higher-quality AM radios with extended range antennas and much better static-reducing filters.

As for which frequency bands you will need, if you are planning to barricade yourself in a bunker and wait for

Excellent battery-powered multi-band radios including CCRadioplus with solar option, Sony model #1CF-SW7600, and Sangean model #MMR-77 with hand crank dynamo.

the world to end, then by all means get a radio that includes the shortwave bands for listening to distant overseas broadcasts. Although this can be interesting listening, your main concern is being able to receive local and state news broadcasts, and a quality AM/FM band radio will do this just fine.

Since you may be without power and cannot operate your television, having a portable radio that can also receive the sound of non-cable television stations is also a plus, although you will need to be near these stations to receive their signals. During emergency conditions, you are primarily interested in local news and weather reports, so the sound of these local television broadcasts without the picture will do just fine.

In any city served by multiple radio stations, at least one AM station will be part of the government's emergency broadcasting system. You may have occasionally heard the testing of this system by their very obnoxious signal tones, followed by an instructional recording telling you to switch to a specific emergency station. Being able to hear these emergency broadcasts is an absolute necessity for your emergency communication needs, and this means owning a high-quality AM radio that can operate long hours on battery power.

Speaker or earphone?

Actually, I prefer a radio with both. It's nice having a small radio that includes a high quality speaker to allow others to listen at the same time. However, powering a speaker consumes more power than an earphone and can reduce battery life. It's also nice to use an earphone when you are on the move, hiking between locations, or wanting to be less conspicuous in a crowd.

I like the small "ear buds" attached to separate wires, and not single-piece headphones. Since most of my radio listening is AM band news and talk shows, I do not need earplugs in both ears as required when listening to high quality stereo music. I usually disconnect or remove one of the two ear buds which allows me to listen in on the news while still being able to hear what is going on around me.

Radio size

Being a talk radio junkie and living in a rural area, I have owned many different sizes and types of AM radios as I try to improve station reception and sound clarity.

One of my favorite AM radios is the $164 CCRadioPlus table-top model from the C. Crane Company which receives AM, FM, TV sound, shortwave, and emergency weather-alert bands. It also operates on both 120-volt AC and batteries, and has an optional solar charger when used with four rechargeable "D" size batteries. Being somewhat large, it includes a room-filling speaker and an accurate digital clock and tuner.

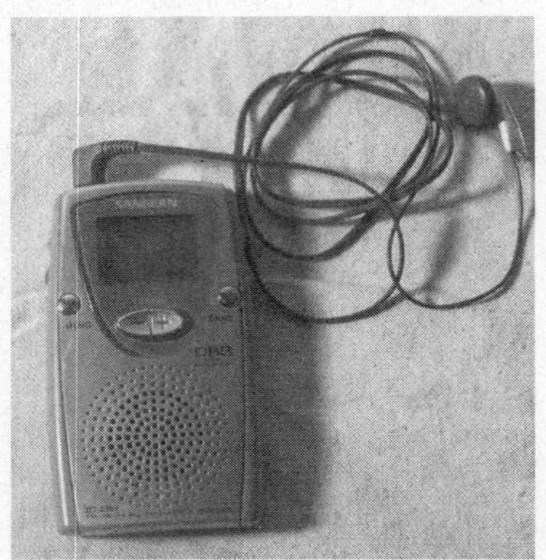

Pocket sized Sangean model #DT-210V radio with digital tuning and AM/FM/TV audio bands.

I listen to it several hours each day using the solar charger, and only need to plug it in after three days of very overcast weather conditions. The only downside I found with this model is the large size which makes it somewhat heavy and bulky if you are on the move. The C. Crane Company has just introduced a smaller "mini" model of this popular radio costing $149.00 which may be easier to handle when you need portability.

My personal favorite emergency radio is the Sangean #DT-210V shown in photo #2, although it is being replaced by a newer model #DT-300VW. This small cigarette-pack size radio easily fits in your shirt pocket, is lightweight, and includes both a quality speaker and ear buds. In addition to AM/FM bands and weather alerts, it also receives television sound, which is another good source of regional news during emergency conditions. Although a bit pricy for its small size at $79.00, it has a digital tuner not found in less expensive manual-dial radios which allows pre-programming your favorite stations for quick and accurate access. You can also find similar featured models from other manufacturers.

Battery types

In my last article which addressed selecting the right emergency flashlight, I stressed the importance of staying with only one or two battery sizes which allows stocking more of each. The last thing you need to deal with during a major emergency is a battery-operated device needing a battery size you do not have. The LED flashlights I recommended use "AA" or "AAA" size batteries, depending on manufacturer. I look for models that use the same battery sizes when shopping for emergency radios.

I have not been a past fan of mechanical wind-up radios due to their short run times, large size, and poor quality construction, but I have been pleased with the new Sangean Model MMR-77 AM/FM manual crank radio. Since it operates on both Ni-MH batteries recharged by the hand crank, and two replaceable "AA" batteries, you can operate on either power source as needed.

Although I would have preferred a digital tuner instead of a manual dial,

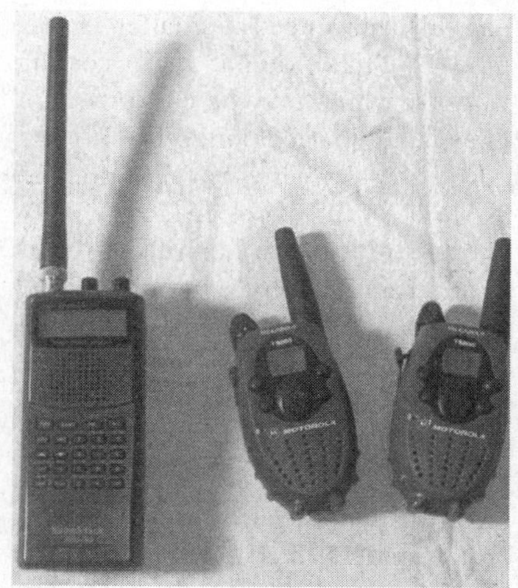

Other useful emergency radios including Radio Shack digital scanner model #PRO-89 and Motorola model #T5200 walkie-talkie.

this small radio has excellent AM reception even from distant stations. Its hand crank dynamo is also very sturdy, and the radio includes a built-in emergency light, and both internal speaker and ear buds. Although too large to fit in a shirt pocket, it can still fit in a large coat pocket and will operate about fifteen minutes for each one minute (120 turns) of the crank when using the speaker instead of the small ear buds.

The specifications indicated 30-minutes of run time for each minute of cranking, but this may be for earphone only operation. This $49.00 radio is a great for emergencies when you want a radio that can be recharged without electrical power.

Other radio needs

After you have selected your basic emergency AM radio, you may want to consider owning several special use radios. For example, more and more large budget metropolitan police departments have switched to very high-frequency (VHF) and ultra high-frequency (UHF) digital communications which are usually encrypted and skip from channel to channel making monitoring very difficult.

However, it is still possible to monitor most non-digital fire, police, and rescue communications being used by more rural community agencies with smaller operating budgets by purchasing a low-cost battery-powered scanner. Although you may have better things to do than eavesdrop on these emergency communications during normal times, you will be the first to learn what fast changing conditions are occurring in your local area during major emergencies. I have found several high quality hand-held scanners at Radio Shack that can receive fire, police, rescue, marine, and aircraft communications for under $150.00.

Although most cellular phone towers have an emergency backup generator, they do not have an unlimited supply of fuel. During an extended power outage you could eventually loose cellular phone service, especially if weather conditions prohibit refueling these generators. In addition, without electricity, most people will not be able to recharge their cell phones without a solar charger and adaptor as addressed in prior issues.

During extended emergency conditions, most families try to stay together and work as a team. For example, during the recent Katrina hurricane aftermath, many families would have one member go out in search of food or water, and to check on security conditions in their local area. For these situations, a good pair of battery-powered walkie-talkies would be invaluable when cell phone service is not operating.

Although these devices are hard on batteries, you will not need them operating except during short scouting trips, and their four to eight mile range should be more than enough coverage for local recon trips on foot. I like the small industrial Motorola models which are priced in the $100 to $150.00 per pair price range, but similar models with less range and

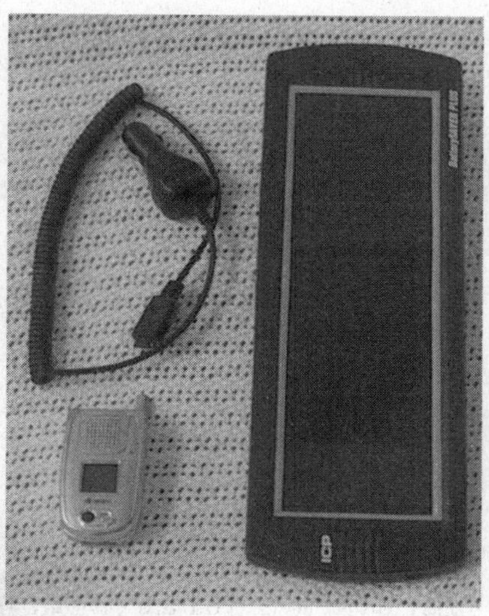

Radio Shack solar-powered cell phone charger and adapter cable.

fewer channels are available for under $75.00 per pair.

I have not forgotten CB radios as an important communication tool during emergencies. However, most are either large base station models requiring lots of power which may not be available, or mobile units permanently mounted in a car or truck which still does not meet the need for a good quality battery-powered AM band radio in the home.

By the time you read this I hope you had a Merry Christmas and happy holidays, and hopefully found one of these radios in your stocking!

(Jeff Yago is a licensed professional engineer and certified energy manager with over 25-years experience in the energy conservation field. He has extensive solar thermal and solar photovoltaic system design experience and has authored numerous articles and texts.) Δ

Replacing "butt ugly" door hinges with

BEAUTIFUL CARVED HINGES

By David Lee

Now that you are comfortable in your chair, get up, go through your house and count up all the hinges on all the doors and cabinets. Lots of them, aren't there? Between 50 and 100? Yup, that's what I got, too. Sit back down and get comfortable.

The majority of those hinges are Butt Ugly Hinges, labeled Butt Hinges in the store. They cost about six dollars a set. Any hinges that aren't ugly cost even more. Add in the expense of handles and latches and you've got four-figure hardware costs on all those doors. I can help you change all that.

There is an artful, or craft, way to deal with these components of your home. It is art if you have high self-esteem, craft if you have medium self-esteem. If you are tired of the Butt Ugliness on your doors and have some constructive amusement time available, read on. For you folks who are waiting for your new home, here is a creative project to keep idle hands busy in the interim. If you want to develop a self defense method so devastating that you may have to register with the police... well, more on that later.

Each door has different hinge requirements. Doors to the outside must have heavy-duty, durable, weather-resistant and burglar-thwarting hinges. Interior doors need strong, long-lasting hinges. Cabinets need distinctive and attractive hinges that are more delicate. And let's not forget your outbuildings. Hard wearing rustproof hinges for these structures are very expensive.

Some doors are heavy: garage, barn, and church doors, for instance. Entrance doors are fairly heavy and should be showpieces. Passage doors, cabinets, and closets are places where decorative hinges can be used to great effect. The hinges I'll show you how to build are adaptable to any doors you have because they are custom-made by you for each door, whether great strength, great beauty, or both, are desired.

What happened here? Look closely and you will see a set of four Type A hinges with cut and carved embellishments along with some colored glass. It is a very solid and rugged front door viewed from the inside of the house.

I will illustrate two methods of hinge making. I suggest you start with a simple hinge project or two to learn the details and get a feel for the nuances of making them work smoothly. After your learning projects have made you competent, I recommend that you build your hinges in sets. For instance, make all your kitchen cabinet hinges at the same time, all hinges for the doors beneath the counters in one session, all passage door hinges in one binge, all closet door hinges at one time, and so on, in order to benefit from the interchangeable parts and mass-production manufacturing methods invented by my hero, Mr. Eli Whitney, way back in about 1810...though he made rifles and cotton gins, not hinges.

I'll start with the easiest, strongest hinges, good for any size door. Let's call them Type A hinges. When you have become familiar with their construction, you can make a set in less time than it takes to drive to the hardware store and buy a set of butt uglies. These custom hinges cost at least 80% less, look mean (in a good way) and save gas money, too. I make as many as 20 of these at a time just to have some available when I get the urge to build a door. I'll describe how to make a set of these hinges; you decide how many you need.

To make hinges, you need a small drill press, a saber saw, a table saw, a screw gun, a utility knife, a small square, a pencil, a tape measure, some 16d common nails, a 9/64" or 3/32" drill bit, two vise grips or C-clamps, drywall screws, some stain, a disposable paint brush, dry socks and a 1949 Ford pickup truck. If you don't have all these things, keep reading anyway. You may be resourceful enough to get along without some of them.

Select a four-foot long piece of straight-grained 2x4 pine lumber with few knots. Split it exactly in half, lengthwise, on the table saw. Cut two 3" long pieces from each of the halves. Now you have two hinge straps that are 42" long, 1-¾" high and 1-½" wide plus four brackles that are 3" long 1-¾" high, and 1-½" wide.

I know...you have never heard of "brackles," right? Well, my research shows me that I seem to be the inventor of these kinds of hinges, so I took the liberty of giving these newly invented parts what I considered an appropriate name. If you have a better label for them, feel free to use it, but I've got copyright dibs on "brackles."

Your hinge straps and brackles have three smooth sides and one rough side where the table saw blade did its work. Pencil some X marks onto the rough sides. These will be the surfaces that contact the door and casing trim board. These pencil marks save confusion later, trust me. Look at the dimension drawing. Using a pencil, tape measure, and square, accurately pinpoint the locations of the hinge pin holes on one hinge strap and one brackle.

Study the pictures showing fixture and drill press details. Hold the

Here is a set of Type A hinges on insulated 5' x 8' workshop doors. In this example, multiple straps and brackles are stacked, using 60-penny 12" nails as hinge pins. I've used these doors for almost 12 years, and they work perfectly and keep the workshop nice and tight.

A view of garage door hinges showing details of brackle positioning, and if you look closely on the lower left, big hunky handles.

More than nine years old and still working perfectly. A plywood door on a storage shed with Type A hinges and two turnlocks. It took less than two hours to build and install.

marked hinge strap in the fixture with one hand and set it on the drill press table. With the other hand, align the drill point with the dot you made on the hinge strap and clamp the fixture to the drill press table with vice grips using your third hand. Drill the hinge strap all the way through. Take out the hinge strap and blow away the chips so the next piece will sit square in the fixture. Make sure the second and all future hinge straps are oriented in the fixture the same way as the first one. I always place the X-marked surface of each piece in contact with the inner side of the fixture. Use your left brain and understand this concept well. It cuts down on swear words later.

Notice that you have to relocate the fixture on the drill table when it comes time to drill the brackle holes because the dimensions are different. Once set up, drill all the brackles. Remember to blow away the chips and hold the parts firmly in the fixture while drilling. Your goal is to produce parts that are exactly alike and interchangeable. I usually make several extra copies of each part so, in case I reject one later, I'll have a replacement.

Go back to the drawing and see how the corners of the brackles and hinge straps are carved to a rounded shape. This is done so the door panel edge passes over the brackles and the hinge straps won't bind on the casing trim board. After you assemble one hinge to a casing board and door panel, you will understand the need to round off of these corners. Use a utility knife with heavy-duty blades for carving. There are many styles of these tools. Choose the one that is most comfortable in your hand, and change blades as needed. Later on I'll talk about carving alternatives.

The hinge pins I use 99% of the time are common bright nails, with a galvanized finish if used outdoors. For your first project, use a 16d common nail for the hinge pins and a $^{9}/_{64}$" or $^{3}/_{32}$" drill bit to make the holes the pins pass through. The pins must have a very tight fit. The rule of thumb is for the hinge pin hole to be .015" to .025" smaller than the hinge pin. This is a constant no matter what size hinges you build or size nail you use as the hinge pin. Tight hinge pins give a very steady solid feel to the working of the door and reduce long-term wear that would occur with a sloppy fit. If it makes you feel better you can lube the holes with WD-40, oil, or cheese whey, but after years of using these hinges, I haven't seen any improvement over dry holes. I think the wood sap lubricates it well enough.

While we are discussing this most interesting subject, I should mention that sooner or later your inventive self will experiment with locating pin holes a little this way or that way for different kinds of geometry to accommodate your door/hinge projects. When you want to make special hinges for some inset, offset, or upset door, feel free to design hinges that do what you need them to do. You are the boss.

Let's review. You have cut out straps and brackles, accurately located the coordinates of the hinge pin holes, drilled them straight and true in each part with the proper-sized drill, and carved round edges on the appropriate corners.

After considerable study on my own time, I find I am unable to give you a list of nail diameters and the proper-sized drill for each nail as I had intended to do. It seems every nail monger out there makes slightly different sized nails, and galvanized coatings add to the chaos. Obtaining the exact drill bit gets thorny, too, because the perfect one, in many cases, is available only to guys working at NASA. I suggest you take your nail to the oldest guy working at the hardware store, let him measure it, and find you the one closest to what you need. Remember, the hinge pin hole is .015" to .025" less than your

Hinges on a woodbox cover show added trim and slightly different geometry.

*This is a vent cover door using Type A hinges.
Note the heavy-duty locks and 3-piece carved handle.*

hinge pin/nail diameter. This is important.

Gather up all your precision made parts and the #16d nails, which will be your hinge pins, and assemble your first hinge. Set a brackle on your workbench and carefully pound a nail through the drilled hole until about ¼" of the point comes out the other side. Set the brackle on a hinge strap with the nail point started into the hinge strap hole and pound until the nail point protrudes ¼" from the hinge strap. Place the other brackle under the hinge strap, aligning the pin hole with the protruding nail head, and pound the nail all the way down. There you have it! Autograph it, date it, treasure it.

Let's check. Are the penciled X marks all on the same side of the hinge assembly? Did you think to orient the nail head to what will be the top of the hinge when it is attached to the door? Good for you. Assemble the rest of the hinge sets with the same attention to detail.

Notice in the pictures that you can make hinges with multiple straps and brackles and big hinge pins for greatly increased strength. These hinges can be scaled up to any size doors you have, giving them a rugged and durable quality you can't otherwise get, short of using bank vault doors.

You can leave your hinge sets natural, but now is the time to stain them if you wish to do so. I use any stain I can get my hands on for most utility hinge jobs. You may be fussier. Later on I will show you some options and details about this part of the operation.

Now you need to attach the hinge sets to the casing trim board on the side of the door. It is best for this board to be square edged, especially on your first hinge project. Notice on the drawing that the edges of the brackles are flush with the edge of the casing trim board. Now you will be glad you were meticulous with all that drilling you did because by lining

Here is a simple fixture made from two pieces of 2x2 scrap wood and a piece of 1/2"x 6"x 6" plywood assembled with screws and held to the table of your drill press by vise grips.

This is one of those 1000 word pictures, so look closely. The hinge strap is held in the fixture by hand, aligned, then clamped with the vise grips so the drilled hole will go straight through the center of the cross marked on the piece. Note that only the first hinge piece needs to be drawn and marked as shown here. The rest will automatically be exactly the same. Hold the piece firmly in place, drill, remove the piece, blow away the chips (very important), and repeat the process until all parts are drilled. The "brackles" are drilled using the same fixture. Thank you, Mr. Whitney.

up all your hinge sets on the casing trim board this way you automatically align all the hinge pins plumb with each other, and your door will swing straight and true, more or less, forever.

For the sample hinge set, I have indicated 3" brackle lengths. Longer ones support more weight. I usually make the length of the brackle equal to the width of the casing trim board to get the most strength from them.

Locate the two, three, or four hinge sets evenly spaced—or not—up and down the casing trim board, and attach them with 2" drywall screws from the back of the trim board. Use at least two screws in each brackle. Later, when you are making bigger hinge sets, use more screws. Make sure the screws pass through the trim board and almost through the brackle. Ideally the screw threads will pass by the hinge pin without hitting it and not protrude from the brackle. Drill pilot holes for the screws if brackle splitting occurs. Some projects will require driving the screws from the front of the hinge sets. Perhaps you have a door and casing that won't survive being taken apart, or you won't survive taking them apart. In that case, neatly predrill the screw holes to avoid splitting the hinge parts and use fancy screws. But do use screws. Nails won't last.

To keep the brackles parallel during assembly, I use a piece of 1-½" scrap wood sandwiched between the hinge unit brackles just behind the end of the hinge strap and pull it out after the screws are driven in. You will not have to do this if the hinge pins are properly fitted into the properly sized holes. I am not being critical, I'm just saying...

With the hinge sets accurately attached to the casing trim board, you are almost ready to mount the door onto the hinge straps. First check to make sure the hinges operate smoothly with no binding where the rounded end of the hinge strap must have a lit-

Type A hinges. On the left are all the parts needed, including the 60-penny 12" hinge pin. An assembled set is on the right.

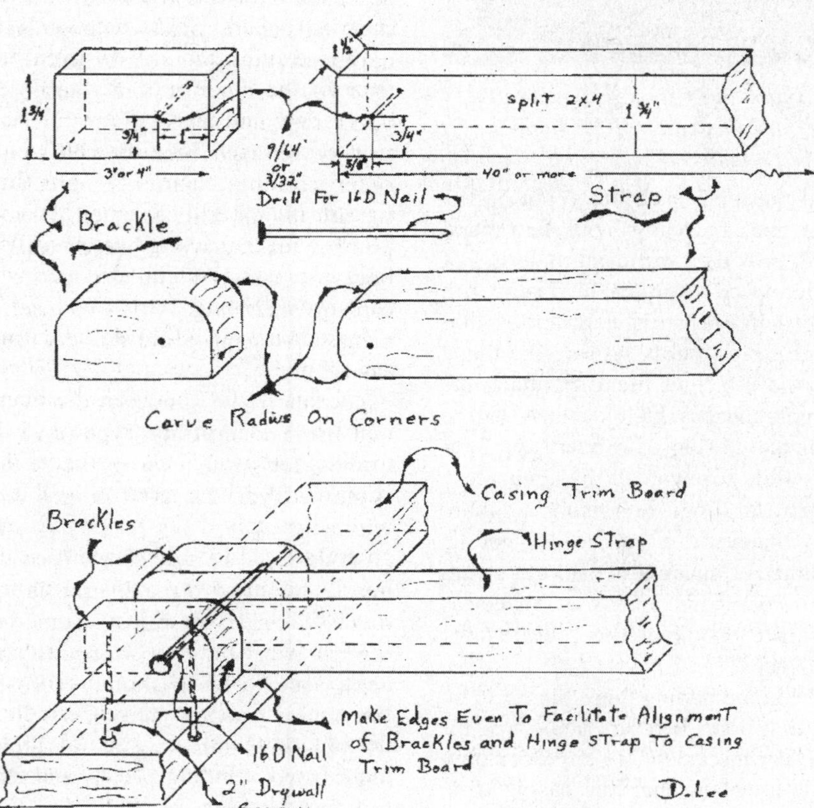

tle clearance from the casing trim board as it rotates by. If necessary, do a little more carving and touch up the stain.

The hinge straps in this sample are left long. (Well… long for most applications. I have made hinges more than 6 feet long for special doors.) Cut them to the right length, if you have decided what that is, or wait until they are mounted on the door if you want to delay the decision. Carve the tips attractively and touch up any details.

To attach the door, lay the casing trim board and hinge sets on your workbench with the X-marked surfaces of the hinges facing up. Place the door on the hinge straps, and drive screws through the door into the hinge straps. Well, it's almost that easy. Check that the hinge straps are square with the door. Leave about $^{3}/_{16}$" clearance between the door and the casing trim board, and be sure they are parallel. Use screws that don't protrude through anything to avoid exposing sharp points. Drill

Here is a close-up of a daintier version of Type A hinges on a small wall cabinet. The hinge is made from ¾" thick boards instead of 1-½" lumber. Note the one-piece carved handle.

pilot holes for the screws where necessary. Test the action of the hinges with the door attached. If the door edge contacts the corners of any brackles, fix them with the utility knife. Make sure there will be clearances where the door and floor, and door and casing trim boards come into proximity. Touch up any imperfections.

Set the door with all the goodies on it into the casing or jamb. Shim it exactly where you want it, and secure the side casing trim board to the wall with finish nails or the superior, and my favorite, drywall screws. I won't go into frivolous detail here, but add stops, latches, and the rest of the trim and take a coffee break.

The secrets to strong, long lasting hinges are these: First, very accurate locating and diameter of the hinge pin holes; second, each hinge pin on the door must be plumb with the others; third, provide a sufficient thickness of solid wood around the hinge pin where it pierces the brackles and hinge strap; fourth, be sure the hinge pins have a tight fit; fifth, attach the hinges and brackles securely to the door and casing trim board, preferably with screws; sixth, accurately attach the hinge sets using a square and whatever else you need to get the symmetry, squareness, and alignment of the door and hinges as perfect as possible. Look at the pictures for guidance.

If you are adding these hinges to an existing door, here are some tips for you. An inset door, or any door on a different plane than the casing trim, will need a spacer between the hinge strap and the door surface. Determine what the thickness of the spacer needs to be, make it, and add it to the underside of the hinge strap before assembly. Don't waste the opportunity to make an art- or craft-work of that spacer. You and your saber saw will think of something.

If you are clever, you can mount your new hinges on an old door without removing it from the casing. Just shim the old door in place with cedar shingles or some of your wife's cooking utensils. Drive out the old hinge pins (very important!), attach the new wood hinges, pull out the shims, open the door, and remove the rest of those butt ugly hinge parts.

If for any reason from the past, in the present, or off in the future, you need to take your door off the hinges, just drive out the hinge pin/nails with a suitable rod and hammer. Remounting the door is quite easy, too, compared with steel hinge sets. If you need total hinge disassembly, you can back out the screws until everything falls apart, usually without damaging anything—good to know in case you decide to restore your doors years from now.

Okay, you have been through a grueling learning experience here, and we are almost half finished. If you practice making wood hinges until it becomes easy, it could become a career. Wood Hinge Artists with sufficient self-esteem could do very well financially.

Now that I've shown you how to make mundane utility Type A wood hinges, let's move on to the really stunning Type 2 carved hinges that will make you…

Oh dear…I see that I have used up my allotment of magazine pages for this issue and have to leave some for others. We'll have to wait until the next issue to learn about seriously fine-looking carved hinges, handles, locks, jewel boxes, special techniques, secret hiding places, and that self-defense thing. Δ

Starting over 8

By Jackie Clay

Some days you wake up and start the day like a house afire. It seems like you never have the time or inclination to sit down and rest. That's the way our whole late summer and autumn have been. After finishing up with my radiation and chemotherapy treatments, I'm finally feeling like me again. As the summer progressed, I was able to do more and more.

I started off by helping David trim our goats' badly neglected feet. Dairy goats originated in rocky, desert, and mountainous country where they were herded from one grazing area to another. They ran, jumped, and climbed rocks and rough terrain, effectively wearing down their shell-like hooves. But when we put them into small corrals and pens and bed them with straw and hay, those feet grow longer and longer. Sometimes they break off by themselves, but most of the time, they continue to grow and twist. In some cases, they can permanently cripple a goat by forcing joints to absorb pressure in unnatural directions.

Goats should have their feet trimmed every six months, at least. Ours had gone more like ten months and were walking on ski-like feet.

David had never done this job before, so one bright morning we took our goat trimming shears (sharp, pointy pruning shears) out to the goat barn. All of our goats have been regularly trimmed and really don't mind. Even our big Boer buck, Rocky, and David's huge black wether, Oreo, have learned to jump up onto the

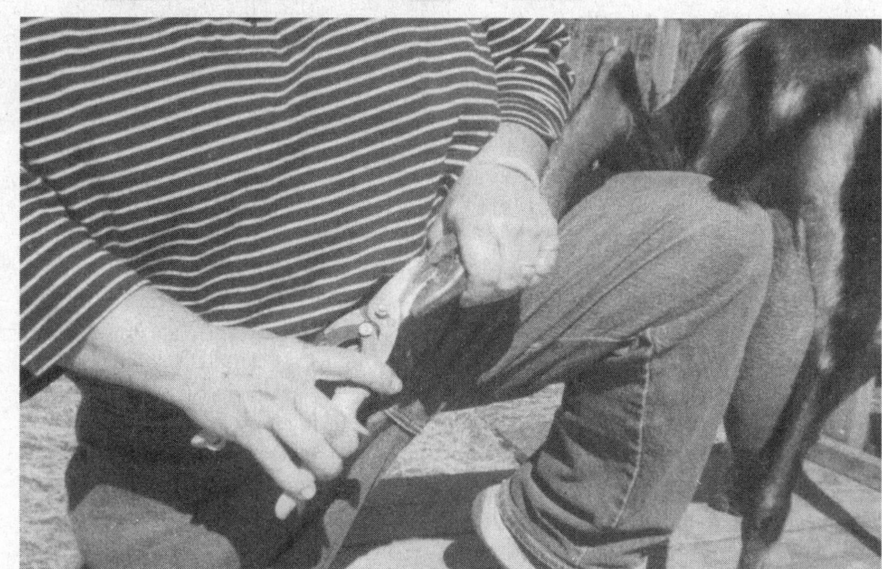

Supporting the goat's flexed leg makes trimming the feet easier on the goat.

Our Shetland ram waits for shearing day—6 months late.

milking stand to eat their feed while their pedicure is in progress.

We've learned it's easiest to trim feet on a nice day following a good rain. Walking around in the mud makes the goat's feet pliable and easy to trim.

To trim a foot, hold the leg up in a flexed position. With the trimmers pointed toward the toe, trim the excess shell off even with the bottom of the foot. If they are quite overgrown, as some of ours were, it helps to snip across the end of the toe first, then work back toward the heel.

Sometimes the heel of the foot has also grown quite long, so gently snip across that, if needed, a little at a time. This rubbery "callous" gives goats the surefootedness they are famed for, but it can get out of hand if left untrimmed.

You want the trimmed foot to look like the foot of a six-month-old kid. Nice, square, and neat. If you don't get it perfect the first time, go back in a week and take a little more off in strategic areas. We were lucky, and all our five adult goats' feet were quickly done.

That's not to say we're all caught up in the goat barn. Half of it is devoted to our small flock of Shetland sheep. These are an ancient breed of small sheep from the Shetland Islands. They are famous for their hardiness and the softness and high quality of their wool.

Unfortunately, we still have not given them their Spring shearing. That is on the list for next week. Luckily, they have a nice warm indoor stall to stay in until their wool grows back.

The house progresses

For a long while, every time I wanted to grab a hammer and start finishing work on the house, I had no energy. So the only major steps happened when our carpenter friend, Tom Richardson, came on Saturday afternoons.

I'm mudding screw heads. My hair is growing back finally. Hooray!

Windows in a log home are tricky to install. Like everything else, consideration must be given to the settling of the logs. Although they were air dried, our logs were expected to settle about 3" overall. So we couldn't cut a square in the logs and nail a window into it.

With a chainsaw, Tom cut the initial window openings to size, snug on the sides and 3" larger on top to allow for settling. Then he cut a vertical slot in each side, to receive a 2"x 2", trimmed the same height as the window, again leaving room at the top for settling. This was not nailed in, but bedded in fiberglass insulation, so that the logs can slide down this spline as they slowly settle.

This slot was outlined and rough cut with the chainsaw, then further opened up with a chisel and hammer.

Beams, before and after being sprayed with bleach. Two or three passes makes them even brighter.

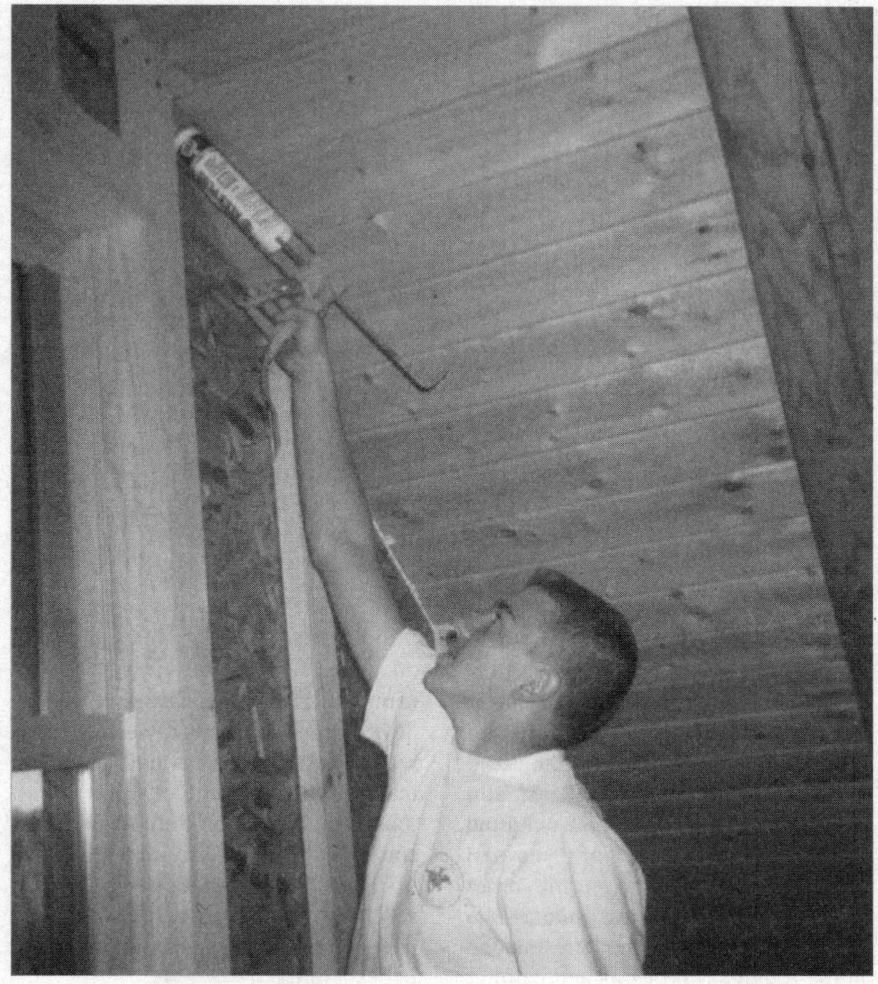

David caulks all the cracks he can find before gable ends are insulated and finished with log siding.

Once the vertical splines were both in place, the window was shoved into place and nailed to the splines. The space above the window was stuffed with fiberglass and will be covered by temporary one-inch trim until the house settles.

The sides of the windows were also stuffed with fiberglass, because caulking can retard settling. When the house has settled, they will be caulked as well.

Because setting windows and doors this way is so tiring and labor intensive, Tom would do a window or two, then hang sheetrock for the remaining hours he worked each Saturday afternoon.

I knew I was feeling better when I began to hang some smaller runs of sheetrock during the week. I also bleached the roughsawn 3"x 10" beams on the ceiling of the first floor. They'd been stacked outside for months, and many of them had weathered to a dark gray. It was a dirty, blotchy look that definitely had to go.

Back in Montana, I had cleaned up some log siding that was mildewed and weathered badly, using chlorine bleach. It had made the wood look like new. So in a hidden area, I sprayed bleach on my beams with a spray bottle. In minutes, the timber lightened right before my eyes. Another hit with the bleach and it was almost like new. I spent a couple of weeks spraying bleach on overhead beams. Some took three coats, but they all turned nice and bright.

Then I began taping and mudding the walls. I was about a day into that when a new friend of mine showed up one morning with her husband. Jeri and Jim wore old clothes and were all set to sling mud with me. Any job is more fun when you have company. We visited, taped, and spread sheetrock compound on my new walls.

We had all hung sheetrock before, but it had been a long time, and with a little helpful criticism from Tom, we learned a lot. I already knew that the sheetrock screws must be indented, but not so far that they tear through the paper. We were using too much plaster over the screws. Tom showed me how to use a larger knife and rub a little compound across the screws, then go back and level it again from a different direction, leaving very little compound on the area. This results in much less sanding in the end.

David harvests potatoes from our neglected garden.

You can't just lump sheetrock compound on a screw, then sand it down. You have to give each and every screw three separate coats, allowing each one to dry thoroughly. This was easy for me; I made one pass over every screw on a wall or two, and I was ready to rest for a while.

Then there was taping. Like the screws, we started off using way too much plaster to bed and cover the tape. This made a lumpy joint that was tough to sand. Instead, I found out that if I used a wide knife and smeared the compound across the joint, then leveled off the excess by running parallel to the joint, this left just enough to let the tape bed well. Then I cut off enough tape to span the joint, stuck one end down, and carefully ran the knife over the tape to squeeze it over the joint tightly. When this was done, I again smeared compound over the taped joint for a few feet, then went back and leveled it off, running parallel to the joint and bedding the tape into a thin layer of plaster.

Another thing I learned was to try to use factory edges next to each other at any cost. This resulted in much smoother joints, as the factory edges have a little indentation along them, allowing you to bed your tape neatly in plaster that fills it evenly.

I no sooner got the sheetrock done upstairs that I got the itch to begin painting. My son, Bill, and his wife, Kelly, gave us the left-over paint from their newly built log home, and luckily our taste in colors is similar. Almost all of the walls in their house are finished in earth tones of beige, cream, and buckskin, with wallpaper borders of moose and deer.

The stain for the logs and the spruce ceiling was a different ball game. I knew what color I wanted, but just couldn't find it anywhere. I think I looked in every paint store in northern Minnesota, only to end up finding it at our local hardware store in Cook (population 600).

All windows and doors are installed, a ramp for Mom and Dad is up, and we are dried in. Two 30' x 50' tarps on the roof finally keep the rain out.

I wanted our home to look like it had been around awhile, not just built. So I wanted the golden brown color of mellow, old pine. And I found it in a tung-oil based stain that showed the glorious grain and knots in the wood to its best advantage.

Let me tell you, it was a bear of a job to brush all those gallons of stain on the rough sawn beams and ceiling, but I've learned that you get stuff done by keeping at it, no matter how huge the job seems. The first day I got half a wall done, being careful to thin out the brush strokes and end each log in a different area so that I didn't double up on the stain and create a darkened, obvious overlapping. I also got one side of one beam and one section of ceiling stained in the living room.

I was trying to use a sponge brush, as I was instructed, and it was a miserable job. The next day, I had no more sponge brushes, as the rough wood had torn all three to pieces, and only had a cheap three-inch paint brush. Because I didn't want to drive to town, I used the brush and was pleasantly surprised at how much faster the job went. I got three sides of beams done that day, two lengths of ceiling all across the living room, a whole wall, and the leftover half wall from the day before.

A week later, the entire bathroom was stained, and all but one little strip in the kitchen. It looks fantastic. I'm so glad I finally found the right stain instead of settling for something else in desperation.

The potato patch yields

As the nights were growing colder and colder, with the aspen leaves a bright yellow, I knew it would only be a matter of time until we had to dig our potato crop. If you wait too long, any potatoes that lie close to the surface will freeze or chill badly, resulting in rotten potatoes.

So one sunny afternoon after a frosty morning, David and I went down to the potato patch with a garden fork and buckets to dig our crop. We had planted two rows of Yukon Gold potatoes under straw, and two rows of russets in the soil next to them. Unfortunately, due to our hugely busy summer schedule and my lack of energy, the russets had never been hilled. Hilling your potatoes increases the amount of potatoes in each hill as potatoes are generated from the lower stems as well as the roots; the more stems under the soil, the more potatoes you harvest. This also seems to work with the straw-covered potatoes. I usually heap more straw on the plants as they grow, and the straw compacts onto the soil. But I never got around to doing that this summer, and I wondered if we'd actually make a decent crop.

Boy, was I surprised when we turned over the first straw-covered hill and five bright gold potatoes the size of my fist rolled out onto the ground. Not all hills were so productive, but most were and we quickly filled a huge bread bowl and five-gallon plastic bucket. David jumped onto his ATV and went home for more buckets.

Again, when we started on the row of russets, I wondered if there would be any potatoes of edible size because they never got hilled and were only watered three times all dry summer. While David was gone, I stuck the fork into the hill on the far end of the row and out popped six huge potatoes. Bakers for sure and not a little potato in the hill.

Down the row we went, excited as little kids. We love to dig potatoes, and we were very happy with the four buckets and huge bowl of perfect spuds from such a neglected garden.

Putting the garden to bed

A garden is hope in earthly form. In the fall, you already are planning on next summer's crop and must get ready for it. This is a good thing for me, a cancer survivor. As soon as the potatoes were dug, David cleaned up the compost pile with our little Ford tractor.

This huge pile, which included manure from the goat barn, had composted down to half its size, but was still a considerable amount of compost to add to our new hillside garden. The soil there consists of about eight inches of rich, old woods dirt on top of gravel. It will be a great garden with a little help. The gravel and gentle hillside ensure good drainage, and the woods loam and compost we will add through the years will make it fertile and productive.

Working carefully, David scooped up the compost with the tractor bucket and spread it out to cover most of the garden's surface eight inches deep. This is about how much manure our TroyBilt tiller will till under at one time.

This spring, we bought eight-foot-long steel T posts just before the price went up. If the weather holds out long enough, we'll get those in the ground before it freezes to keep the deer out of the garden next year.

This year, they ate all the carrot tops, resulting in stunted carrots, and ate and pulled the onion tops. We quickly harvested all our onions from on top of the ground, where the deer had conveniently left them.

Luckily, the deer left alone the beans, sweet corn, potatoes, and best of all, our precious, rarest of rare, Hopi Pale Grey squash. Although small, our few vines produced six mature squash. This squash is so rare that only a handful of people raise them, and only one Canadian seed source is currently available.

Just last week I cut one in half. There were fat, mature seeds in the hollow center, and a lot of them. I sat down and carefully picked them out of the strings and laid them on a cookie sheet to air dry. By the time I finished with that one smallish squash, I had the sheet full.

We hope to be in our new house by the time winter sets in, and are working daily to make that happen. Although we will eventually be powering our home by solar panels on the roof, and heating it largely with wood, at this time we must continue to heat with propane. The time and money ran out before we could get the foam insulation, sheathing, and shingles on the roof, and the chimney built.

The Typar roof wrap was not keeping rain out of the house when it blew hard, and I knew that winter would only be worse. Not being able to afford a finished roof, I picked up two huge heavy duty construction tarps (the silver ones, not the lighter-weight blue variety) for $200, and Tom stretched them out over the roof one afternoon while we were in town. I was so surprised when we got home. It looked like an alien space ship had landed out on our point. All that silver, where a black roof had been that morning.

The next time it rained, the inside of the house was bone dry. What a relief. The roof had been leaking so badly that it was actually raining about as bad in the living room as outdoors.

Now that we have a plastic roof, using any type of temporary wood stove is not an option. Any flyaway sparks could land on the poly tarps and burn our house down!

Having a mile-long logging road for a driveway, it's sometimes hard for the propane truck to make a delivery mid-winter, so the gas company suggested that we put in a thousand gallon tank to see us through without a fill. I agreed, but now propane has gone up over $2.00 a gallon. We'll just have to fill it as we can afford it, and hope for a relatively snow-free winter. It's seems that we do everything as little as we can, and pray we have time to do more before it is needed. We call it homesteading, here in the backwoods, and we thrive on it, knowing that we owe no one for what we are creating. No one but our neighbors, friends, and family who share their work, talents, love, and encouragement with us. Without that we would have a hard time going on. Δ

Read the entire series
Starting Over
by Jackie Clay

A new use for old tires ~ a garden using tires

By Charles Sanders

There are mountains of old tires out there. Americans keep on rolling and tires keep on wearing out. Every year there is almost one scrap tire created for every man, woman, and child in the United States. In 2001 alone, Americans discarded nearly 281 million tires, weighing some 5.7 million tons. All of those old treads can provide a lot of good growing space, and we're just the folks to put them to use.

There is no appreciable risk in using recycled tires in the vegetable garden. While it is a fact that rubber tires do contain minute amounts of certain heavy metals, the compounds are tightly bonded within the actual rubber compound and do not leach into the soil. One of the ingredients in the rubber recipe is zinc. Zinc, in fact, is an essential plant element. I also expect that rubber is safer to use than treated lumber that contains copper and arsenic. Tires are durable. The very qualities that make them an environmental headache make them perfect for our uses in the garden. Once they are in place, they won't rot and will likely be there for your grandchildren to use.

Let's take a look at some ways to recycle old tires and literally reap the benefits. Gardening with recycled tires has many benefits besides those directly with the garden itself. It puts to use an article that might otherwise end up in a landfill or other disposal site. Those of us who are into "growing our own" are often on the lookout for ways to increase production with a minimum of effort. Gardening with tires presents several good ways to do just that, while at the same time helping to recycle the old treads from our automobiles and other wheeled conveyances. Stop by your local service station, recycle center, or tire retailer and ask them to save some tires for you. Currently, dealers charge $2 or more to dispose of used tires. Since they charge the consumer to take the old tires and have to pay to have them disposed of, they will likely be happy to let you have all you want. Most tire centers will have a stack of old tires out back that they will give you permission to root through.

A rubberized hotbed

As winter's icy grasp finally begins to slip, the homesteader who has not kept a little something growing all winter is surely thinking about getting a few seeds stuck into the ground. After a long winter of dried, canned, frozen, or store-bought fresh vegetables, a mess of fresh veggies would taste mighty good. One of the easiest and earliest ways to get those first lettuce and spinach salads growing is to use an old method that has been common practice around these parts for generations.

Folks around here often get those first salad greens going in a planter made from an old tire. For my own planter, I utilized the old tread from a log skidder to give me plenty of size and depth. For a project of this type, I'd recommend a fairly large one, such as a rear tire off of a farm tractor or from a log skidder like I used.

After laying the tire at the spot where I wanted it, I used a utility

Timers newly planted with spinach seed in the fall greenhouse.

knife to cut the sidewall completely out of the upper side. This was fairly easy to do, and nearly doubled the planting area available. But do it carefully, and consider using some leather gloves as protection against the knife blade.

Once I removed the sidewall, I filled the tire with some good compost on top of a six-inch layer of fresh manure and seeded my lettuce and spinach. The heat generated by the manure's decomposition helped to heat the seedbed from below. The whole thing was covered with some old storm windows obtained for the purpose by some creative scrounging. The result was a fine durable hot bed and the only cost involved was for the seed.

Use a utility knife to cut the sidewall completely out of the upper side.

Raising the roots

One of the best ways to grow vegetables, especially in cool climates, is to grow them in raised beds. Let's look at some of the benefits of raised bed gardening and how the method is a great way to use old tires:

- When the soil is elevated, it warms faster. Raised bed gardens can increase spring soil temperatures by 8 to 13° F over the adjacent soil temperatures at ground level. The black, heat-absorbing tires compound the warming effect.
- It dries out more quickly. These rubberized raised beds are helpful in improving water drainage in heavy clay soils or in low-lying areas. The soil is more exposed, and sun and wind help to dry and warm the soil more quickly.
- It provides deeper soil for root crops to develop.
- You can plant earlier in the season and get your plants off to a healthier and earlier start. This is especially true in cooler climates where spring rains often keep vegetable garden soil wet and cold. In containers such as our tires, excess moisture tends to drain away more quickly and the soil remains warmer, thus allowing for earlier planting.
- You can harvest later into the fall.
- Because of the longer growing season, you have the possibility of growing a wider range of vegetables.
- Using these beds, you can concentrate a greater number of plants in a smaller area. This will result in less weeding and greater production.
- Finally, and not insignificantly, raised bed gardening puts plants and soil back into the reach of older gardeners or others who cannot do a lot of bending as required with an ordinary garden.

In the greenhouse

Here is one way we have used tires in our own small greenhouse. Along the front wall we placed short stacks of tires and filled them with sand. The dark color of the tires serves to absorb heat, and the sand contained in each stack helps to store it. Atop each stack was placed another tire with the upper sidewall removed as already described.The top tire was then filled with compost and soil then seeded in lettuce, spinach, or whatever.

We've also found that, in the greenhouse, they make a fine planter for an extra-early or late tomato plant. Since our greenhouse. is attached to my garage and shop, I utilized an existing window opening, the woodstove in the garage, a window fan, and a timer to add heat to it. Between our tire planter, keeping a fire going in the garage—which I often do anyway—and timing the fan to turn on as the day begins to cool, we have been able to pick the last tomato off of the vine on Christmas Eve.

Jump start your tomatoes

By the same token, you can get a jump on the spring growing season by creating a mini-greenhouse, of sorts, for a few tomato plants. Once you have a stack or two of tires in place, set your tomato plants in each stack. Next, place a wire hoop or tomato cage in place around the plant. Cover the cage with clear plastic and secure it with duct tape, twine, etc. If you have them available, you can place an old windowpane over the top of this tomato tower. The combination of the black rubber tires and the clear plastic "greenhouse" will cause the plant to grow quickly.

You will need to monitor the heat and health of the young plants carefully to make sure they aren't getting too much of a good thing. Once the plant is really growing and the chance of frost is past, simply remove the plastic and allow the plant to use the wire cage to support its branches, which will soon be laden with fruit.

You can add months to your growing season using this method alone.

Tire compost bin

Used tires can also be made into a good compost bin. Begin with a half dozen or so tires as large as you can handle. Large truck tires work well. Cut the sidewalls out of both sides using the sharp utility knife. You will end up with rubber rings of tire treads. After you have several of the hoops made, place one on the spot where you want your bin to be located. Be sure to turn the soil on the spot where you place the bin. This better exposes the composting material to the bacteria, earthworms, and other compost builders. As you fill the first tire hoop, merely place another atop it and fill it. Repeat the process until you have them stacked five or six high. You can keep filling tires with garden and kitchen scraps and other compost fixin's or just start another pile.

After the compost has worked for several weeks, remove the top hoop and place it on the ground beside the original bin. Fork the top layer of composting material into this hoop. Remove the next hoop and place it atop the one on the ground and move the plant material into it. Repeat until you have the whole compost heap turned and transferred into the restacked hoops, one at a time. Note that in the process you have completely turned the working compost pile from top to bottom, perfect for producing good compost in record time. After several more weeks, the compost should be getting that good earthy smell and will be ready to use.

Potato stacks

When I was a youngster, I used a hoe to ridge up rows and rows of potatoes, pulling the soil up around the plants to help increase their yield. I have since learned of an easier way to grow potatoes that doesn't require any hoeing—just plant a vertical potato patch. If you are limited in space, then this method is especially beneficial. You can grow a nice crop of spuds in just a few tires. Here's how:

Generally, a stack of four or five tires that are progressively filled with some good compost and a couple of pounds of seed potatoes will produce around 25 pounds of potatoes. A few of these stacks can provide your winter's supply of potatoes with no problem.

To begin, pick a spot that is out of the way and perhaps out of sight where you can stack your tires. Loosen the soil just enough to allow for some drainage and place the first tire. Fill it with soil, being sure to fill the inside of the tire casing as well. Take your seed potatoes and cut them into pieces that have at least two "eyes," or sprout buds in each piece. It doesn't hurt to let each piece dry for a day or two before planting it. Plant three or four cut potato sets into the soil in the tire center. Cover the sets with enough soil to bring it level with the top of the opening.

Once the new potato plants get to be about eight inches tall, add another tire and add soil around the plants until just a couple of inches of the tops are above the soil. Repeat this process for the third and subsequent tires. As you add tires and soil to the 'tater stack, the plant stalk is covered with soil. As you do this, the existing stalk will send off roots as well as grow upward to once again find the sunlight it needs. Since you are gradually raising the soil level eight inches or so at a time, the plant is able to keep growing without suffocating. At the same time, you are creating a 24- to 36-inch tap root off of which many lateral roots will develop. Each of the lateral roots can produce additional potatoes at three or four levels instead of only one. When you water the plant, be sure that the soil is thoroughly moistened all the way down to the base of the pile.

Since the tires also act as an insulator and heat sink for your potatoes, the added warmth will stimulate the lateral roots to multiply more quickly, giving you more potatoes. To harvest your crop, wait until the top dries up and begin to remove the tires, working your way down the stack and harvesting the potatoes as you go.

Great walls of tires

Tires can even be used to create retaining walls to stabilize an earth bank. When using them for this purpose, begin by laying a level course of tires. Fill these tires completely with sand, soil, or gravel. Try to eliminate any holes or pockets in the tires that might provide a haven to vermin like mice or rats. Atop the first course of filled tires, add another row, positioning them one-quarter to one-third of the way back on the first course. This will give the wall some slope and add stability. Also, place the tires with staggered joints, that is, in bricklayer-fashion. That will add a lot of stability as well. Once several courses of these rubber building blocks are in place, the wall should be very solid and immovable.

If you choose to, remove the upper sidewall of each tire before you put it in place, and fill it with soil. Not only will it make filling the tires easier, but it will also make space available to place some ground cover plants that can grow and cover the wall. You may consider even setting strawberry plants in the spaces.

All-terrain planters

Try using old tires from riding mowers and all-terrain-vehicles (ATVs) for planters. They can be used right on the deck, porch, or patio and can hold plants such as cherry tomatoes, peppers, flowers, herbs, and other compact plants. They are smaller and therefore more portable than large tires and can fit in most any out-of-the-way spot.

Check out a tire dealer, lawn tractor dealer, or ATV dealer to locate some of the used low-pressure tires. Take one of the tires and cut the sidewall as described for the hotbed. Using a drill, bore three holes around the open end of the "bowl." Space the holes equally around the rim and drill them about a half-inch from the top edge.

You may wish to place your planters around on a low wall or rail, but you can also attach a hanger from which to suspend the planter. Using three pieces of workable wire about 26 to 28 inches long, attach one wire in each of the three holes. Bring the wires together at the top and twist about 2 to 3 inches together into a hook. That will serve as the planter hanger.

Now, cut a piece of hardware cloth to fit in the bottom of the planter. Place a thick layer of grass, moss, or even a chunk of old carpet into the bottom, on top of the hardware cloth. Fill to the top with soil, and you are ready to set your plants. These are especially handy for growing cherry tomatoes or the attractive Thai pepper plants.

Tiers of tires

Another nifty planter for small spaces can be made by stacking four tires of different sizes into a sort of pyramid. Begin with one each of the following sized tires: A farm tractor tire; a tire from a large truck; an automobile tire; and an ATV tire. Cut the sidewall out of each. Place the tractor tire where you want it and fill it with soil. Position the next largest tire, the truck tire, evenly atop the tractor tire. Fill it, too, with soil. Next, put the automobile tire in place and fill it. Finally, place the ATV tire atop the pile and fill it with soil. You will end up with a multi-layered vertical garden that is useful for strawberries, bush cucumbers, varieties of low flowers, and many other types of plants. With some imagination, you can have plants cascading down the sides of this planter.

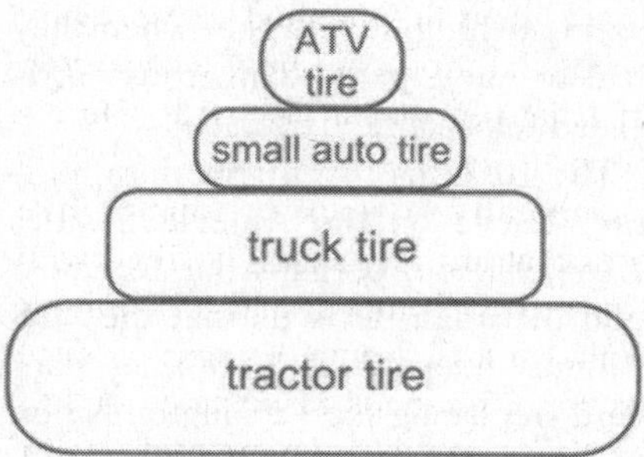

On a larger scale

If your place is a bit larger than just a plot and garden, you may find more uses for old tires. Here are just a couple of ideas:

Over in the neighboring Amish settlement, I see many horse feeders made by cutting the sidewall out of a tire off of a large payloader or other machine with wide, heavy tires. They are deep enough to hold a lot of hay, and even the largest Belgian horse cannot damage them. They would make an equally large and roomy planting bed for flowers or vegetables.

You can make a really good pasture drag by bolting some tires together and connecting them to a single beam to be pulled behind the tractor, team, or even the pickup truck or ATV. The handy homemade drag will make it much easier to break up and distribute the cowflops that accumulate in the pasture. Scattering the cowpies spreads the fertilizer they contain and prevents hot spots and clumps of pasture grass.

More uses for old tires

• Use single rows of tires and use mulch or gravel between rows. You will have easy access to all sides of your plants and will keep weeding to a minimum.

• When doing any of these projects, it's okay to use tires of different sizes. Exposed spaces can be used to tuck a plant into.

• Set blackberries, raspberries, and other brambles out in rows of tires—one plant to a tire. They will benefit from the same "raised bed" principle and will be easier to prune back and to mulch.

• If you can place a few tires in a row along a wall or garden edge, try adding a heavy wire cattle panel or simply a length of woven fence wire as a trellis for vining plants to climb. You can save a lot of space by growing beans, cucumbers, squash, gourds, and other climbers this way.

• When arranging three or four tires in a square or triangle, make use of the space between the tires instead of just mulching it. Just fill it with compost and add another plant or two. You will gain another square foot or so of good growing space.

• Go commercial. With a serious rubberized garden, it would be possible to supply every restaurant and grocery store for miles around. Organically grown fresh garden vegetables are always in demand. If you go big and create a growing patch of 50 to 100 tires, you can produce hundreds of pounds of vegetables and some good income. For example, with tomatoes selling for 50 cents a pound or more, you can make good money from your "tired" tomato patch. Starting them in the tires will help you to get them to marketable size earlier than other locally grown competition.

Using old tires is a great way to recycle. It's also a wonderful way to make the most of a small garden plot and generally increase your garden yield. Try some of these ideas, and I'm certain you'll see good results. Δ

Ayoob on Firearms

The All American Ruger 10/22 Rifle

By Massad Ayoob

The Ruger 10/22 gets its name from being a ten-shot rifle chambered for the .22 Long Rifle cartridge. It is one of the most popular firearms in history.

Steve Sanetti, the CEO of Sturm, Ruger Inc., tells me that at this writing well over four and a half million 10/22s have been produced. He is already planning the engraved milestone rifle that will be the five millionth of this model that the company has produced. It is expected to roll off the Ruger rifle production line in Newport, New Hampshire, some time late in 2006.

The Ruger 10/22 was introduced in 1964. Weighing between five and six pounds, "This rifle enjoys a fine reputation for accuracy and dependability and is considered an excellent value," notes gun expert Ned Schwing.

Ubiquitous in rural America, the 10/22 has been produced in many formats. It has been made in blue steel and stainless. It has been furnished with stocks of walnut, birch, and laminate, and all sorts of synthetics. Stock designs have included Monte Carlo, Mannlicher, competition target, and other styles... and that's just from the Ruger factory. As we shall see, the cottage industry of firearms accessories warmly embraces any gun so popular that it sells more than four million copies, and the 10/22 has been no exception.

In the last 43 years, the versatile Ruger has seen use all over the world. SWAT teams have purchased them, usually with sound suppressors, for taking out the junkyard dogs that guard drug dealers' property, and for extinguishing streetlights when they had to move in on dangerous barricaded felons after dark.

The 10/22 has even gone into military battle on the American side. Larry Wilson, perhaps our foremost gun historian, tells us that the "US Military adopted (the) 10/22 as standard (replacing the Remington Nylon 66) for selected commando issue. Navy SEALS were among the users of these arms. Specially modified 10/22s saw limited service in Southeast Asia, in the Vietnam War. Some of these special-issue arms were fitted with a device to secure the bolt closed, and some had folding stocks and other special features."

For the most part, however, the 10/22 has been a recreational firearm. It is popular with hunters. My next-door neighbor has a Class III license that authorizes him to own sound suppressors, also known as silencers. One of his favorite sporting arms is a suppressed 10/22. His idea of a pleasant Sunday morning is to get up early and sit among his groves, potting squirrels. With each shot, only a tiny "chuff" sound is heard. The neighbors are not disturbed on their day of rest. Neither are the other squirrels. A bushytail's typical reaction to a gunshot is, "Good grief, they're shooting at us!" This is followed by a rapid collective scampering out of sight. With the suppressed .22, the reaction seems to be, "Gee, Rocky fell out of the tree." And then, "chuff." Yet another in the pot. My neighbor usually has enough squirrels for a pan-fry for two well before breakfast time.

The 10/22 was the first autoloading .22 rifle to be used successfully in major shooting competitions. Its period coincided with the rise of the action shooting sports in this country. Events like the Chevy Truck Sportsmen's Challenge saw the 10/22, usually tricked out in "race" format, become the arm of choice for the rifle stage among the winners.

Massad Ayoob

They're great for exhibition trick shooting, too. The last I knew, the record for consecutive thrown targets shot out of the air with a rifle was held by an exhibition shooter of Native American descent who goes by the name "Chief AJ." The rifle he used to accomplish this feat? A Ruger 10/22, of course.

However, the overwhelming majority of these guns are plinkers. Informal target shooting devices. Fun guns. The easy-shooting rifles with which you train your kids and other new shooters in marksmanship and firearms safety.

Design features

Bill Ruger, Sr., one of history's great gun designers, began to conceptualize the 10/22 in the late 1950s. He assigned two other great firearms designers to the project, Harry Sefried and Doug McClenahan. It was they who actually handled the nuts and bolts of coalescing Bill Ruger's concept onto the drawing board, and then onto the production line.

The ten-shot .22 Long Rifle magazine that gives the gun its name is a rotary, or spool, design. "The rotary box magazine (was) inspired by one of Bill's favorites, the Savage Model 99 rifle," writes Wilson. This magazine is the heart of a simple, reliable blowback action that has earned the 10/22 its reputation for being virtually jam-free.

It's an accurate little sporting rifle. The standard 10/22 is actually more of a carbine, that being the term for a short rifle. In its standard model, the 10/22 has an 18 ½" barrel. Its rifling is 6 grooves with right-hand twist, one turn in 16".

The standard stock was obviously inspired by the M-1 carbine of World War II. Designed to replace the pistol among troops whose assignments didn't require a heavy M1 Garand battle rifle, the M-1 carbine was designed by Marsh Williams. Though its .30 caliber cartridge was puny compared to the .30-06 Springfield for which the Garand was chambered (Ruger would later manufacture a revolver that fired the .30 Carbine round), the tiny M-1 carbine was a delight to handle. The 10/22 largely duplicates that handiness in its size, shape, weight, and balance. This is one reason the 10/22 has become so popular as a "family fun gun." It is easy to handle, and to hold steady on target, even for youngsters.

Customizing the 10/22

In the world of firearms accessories, there is no rifle except perhaps the AR15 for which the shooter can find

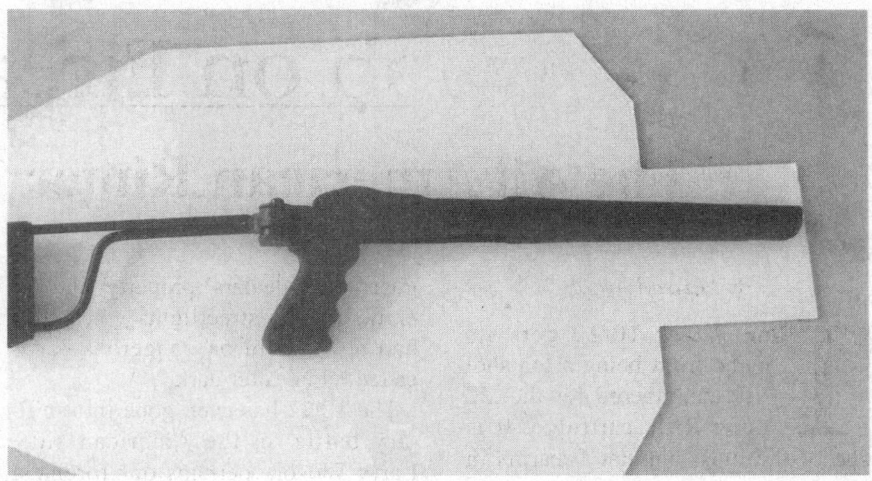

Butler Creek folding stock makes 10/22 handier for suitcase, backpack, or ATV.

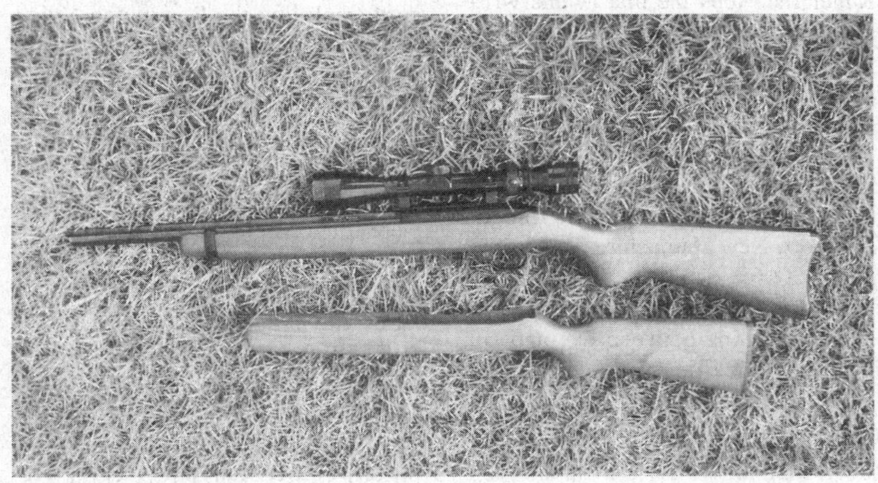

Youth stock from Brownell's, below, adapts the 10/22 for smaller shooters.

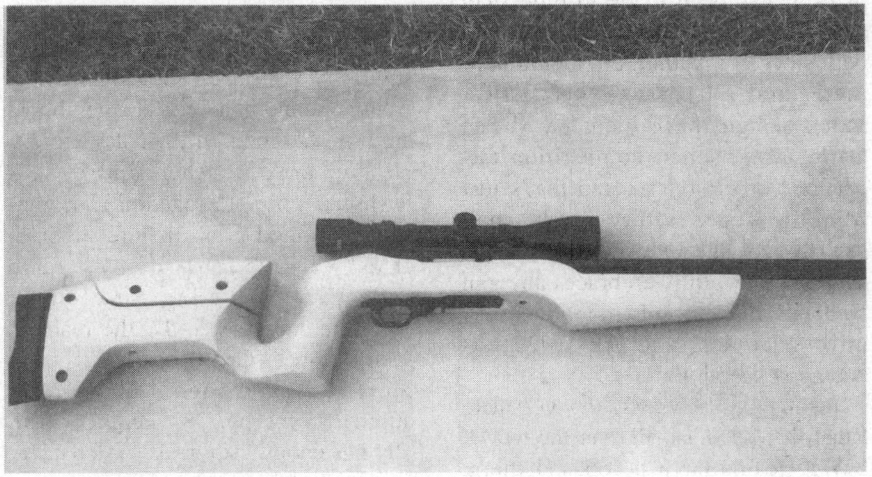

Model FAS/R22 "race gun stock" is what author chose for his Clark Custom 10/22.

Jon Strayer's 10/22 has Choate folding stock, two 10-round Ruger magazines glued together for fast "flip-over" reload. Weaver "See-thru" scope mounts allow instant choice of telescopic or iron sights.

more bells and whistles to attach. Each has its purpose for enhancing shooting performance and fun.

Sights. The typical 10/22 comes with a plain blade/bead front sight, and a flip-down rear sight of the V-notch leaf type, which is somewhat adjustable. It's OK for short range work, but this kind of gunsight just won't live up to the mechanical accuracy and shootability that is inherent in the 10/22's design.

If a low profile and super-light weight are absolutely critical and you have to stay with iron sights, a peep sight on the back of the receiver (frame) will allow most people to shoot better. Still, this is the kind of rifle that really benefits from an optical sight.

The cheapy ".22 scopes" with ¾" diameter bodies just don't do justice to the shooting potential of a 10/22. Splurge on a full size riflescope with 1" diameter. There are some good ones out there at very reasonable prices. For fast, close-range plinking, a red dot optical sight may be even better. They're more expensive, but very quick. Aimpoint, ATN Ultra, and EOTech are the brands that get my vote in a battery-operated sight of this type.

Magazines. When recreational shooting gets fast and furious, ammo runs out quickly with a semiautomatic like this, which needs only another pull of the trigger to fire the next shot. That flush-fitting 10-round magazine seems to empty awfully quick.

A lot of companies have made longer magazines for the 10/22, usually 25-rounders in the familiar "banana" shape, though some of these hold up to 50 cartridges. The two brands I'm most familiar with, and most comfortable recommending for their proven reliability, are the Butler Creek and the Ram-Line. Legal "grandfathered"

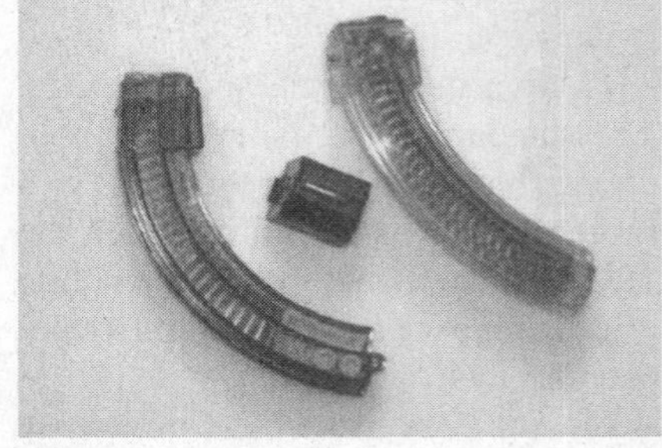

Left, 25-round Butler Creek 10/22 magazine; right, Ram-Line 50 round. Center is standard Ruger 10-round rotary magazine.

specimens of these sold for ridiculous amounts of money during the decade of Bill Clinton's useless "assault magazine ban" which, from 1994 to 2004, prevented the sale of new magazines that held more than ten cartridges. That's over now, and the higher capacity "fun" magazines are back on the market at reasonable prices.

Now, I know some traditionalists will grind their teeth at the thought of a high-capacity semiautomatic rifle for marksmanship training. "No discipline," they snap. "Kids will just blindly hose bullets downrange."

Well, not unless you let 'em. Once the new shooter has learned basic marksmanship, the next step is being

Gail Pepin's rifle with Evolution stock, ATN sight, and Ram-Line 50-round magazine. Note forward mounted sight for cross-dominant shooting.

Clark Custom "Squirrel Rifle" is more than 2" shorter overall than stock 10/22.

able to shoot accurately and repeatably. Putting multiple targets downrange—the steel disks used at the Chevy Truck Challenge, for example, or the increasingly popular "dueling tree"—teaches the tyro shooter to stay cool under pressure, stay focused on the sights, and squeeze the trigger instead of jerking it even when he feels a compelling need to fire rapidly. In that situation, I want my student to have plenty of bullets.

Another advantage of the long magazine in the 10/22 is stability. In the traditional target shooter's offhand (standing) position, the tricep is against the torso, with the rifle resting on the hand. A lot of men need to balance the rifle on their fingertips to make that work, and for kids, it's particularly hard. A longer magazine can rest its bottom on the palm of the hand in this shooting stance, for greater stability. This is one reason why, in my much younger days when I shot NRA High Power Rifle competition, I switched from the M1 Garand to the M14, the latter being available today as the Springfield Armory M1A. The projecting 20-round magazine literally gave me a palm rest for offhand shooting.

In the prone position, the bottom of a 25 round Ram-Line or Butler Creek magazine can rest on the ground. It does not seem to affect reliability, and contrary to popular myth, it will not alter the point of the bullets' impact. It does, however, steady the rifle greatly. That's particularly important to new shooters.

Before we leave this topic, Brownell's offers an extended magazine release lever that will make removal of all size magazines from the 10/22 much more convenient.

Barrels. Your 10/22 will come out of the Ruger box with all the built-in accuracy you need for small game at typical ranges, or for toppling a tin can from a fence post on the back forty. If you are the sort of serious rifleman (or riflewoman) who demands minute of angle accuracy—every shot in roughly an inch at 100 yards—your 10/22 will need to go custom.

There are numerous barrel makers out there, and many gunsmiths to install them. The 10/22 I use almost exclusively now was built for me by Kay Clark-Miculek. Best known as a firearms instructor and champion shooting woman, Kay is also a superb gunsmith. The daughter of the late, great Jim Clark, Sr., Kay works at her dad's business, Clark Custom, with her brother Jim, Jr., and their staff. Her husband, the famed master revolver shooter Jerry Miculek, uses a Clark Custom 10/22 in smallbore action rifle competition. The barrel she chose for my 10/22, which I'll discuss more later, was the Douglas brand, a full one inch in diameter, but fluted down its outer length to reduce weight and enhance rigidity. The fluting also creates more external surface for cooling air to contact the barrel than a conventional round barrel would have. It is no secret in the world of marksmanship that an overheated barrel has a deleterious effect on accuracy. This gun will indeed put five consecutive rounds of Eley

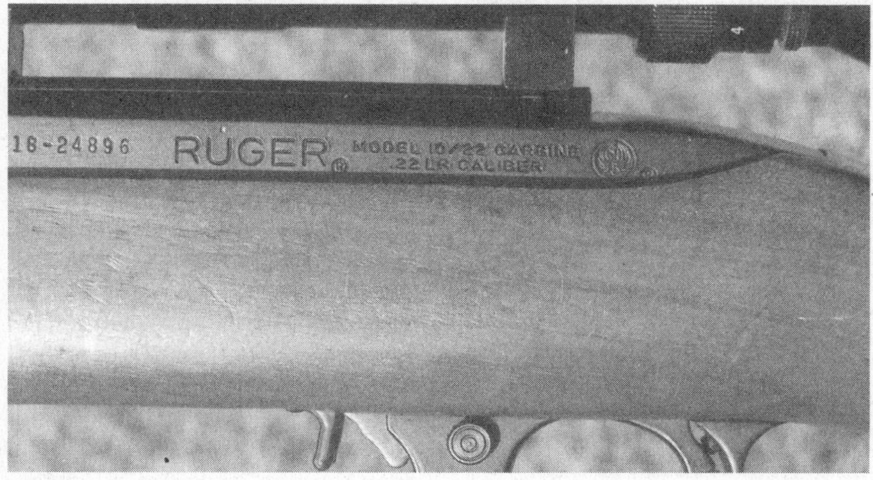

Trigger tune by Clark includes trigger stop visible at middle rear of trigger.

Match Rifle ammunition into an inch at 100 measured yards.

But there are other ways you can go with 10/22 barrels, depending on what you want to do with the gun. If, like my neighbor, you have good reason for sound suppression and you can get a "silencer" legally where you are, custom makers can install a barrel with integral suppressor. Externally, it looks like the heavy barrel of a target rifle, but when you pick it up, it's much lighter. Many sound suppressors actually make the rifle shoot tighter groups, too.

For the hiker or backpacker seeking the ultimate in portability in a reliable .22 "survival rifle," there are carbon fiber rifle barrels on the market for the 10/22. With one of those and a light synthetic stock, you can bring the 10/22 rifle down to a weight lighter than some dedicated high-power hunting handguns.

In the same vein is the Packer takedown stock from Butler Creek, now a Michaels of Oregon subsidiary. It comes with an ultra lightweight barrel and a new stock, turning your Ruger 10/22 into a neat little two-piece takedown for storage in your backpack.

Robert Stanfield with his Evolution Stock on a 10/22

The same company offers heavy target barrels, competition stocks, and a broad variety of custom components in between. For information, surf over to www.uncle-mikes.com.

The Purpose-Built Custom 10/22

There is an almost infinite variety of 10/22 formats that can be ordered by your dealer from the Ruger factory, or crafted by a custom gunsmith, or put together by shooters who are comfortable going hands-on to accessorize their own rifle. Let's take a look at just two of them.

One belongs to Gail Pepin. A petite grandmother who came to love the backwoods home lifestyle when raising her kids in a self-sufficient cabin deep in the green mountains of Tennessee, she now lives in a city for career reasons but has not given up her taste for shooting. She initially bought a stainless steel 10/22 as an all around plinker and fun gun, something to train the grandchildren with.

For Ms. Pepin, "practical" and "dowdy" don't necessarily go in the same sentence. Her shooting tastes run toward high speed, low drag, way cool Glock pistols and AR15 rifles. (Picking up the new DEA combat carbine at a display of Rock River Arms AR15s, she was heard to utter breathlessly, "Ooh…this looks good on me.")

Gail chose one of Robert Stanfield's Evolution Stock Systems (www.rbprecision.com). With four Picatinny rails—top, bottom, and either side of the fore-end—she can mount flashlights, laser sights, and what-all to her heart's content. An ATN Ultra Sight rides on top, with a crimson illuminated reticle in a cross-hair shape. She mounted the optical sight well forward, allowing some family members who are cross-dominant to aim with their left eye while shooting from the right shoulder, by simply rolling their cheek a little on the stock.

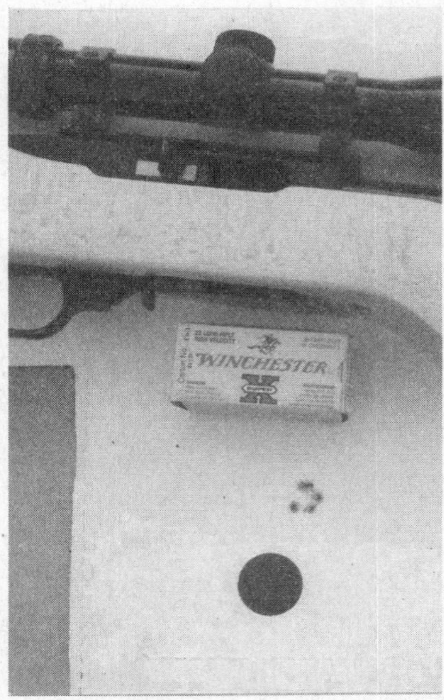

This is the kind of accuracy Clark Custom builds into a 10/22.

The ingenious Evolution Stock is adjustable for length, and this has made Gail's 10/22 much more adaptable for the grandkids of different ages. Though adaptable to kids, the stock has a solid forward heft that pleases adults as well. It comes with a removable forward pistol grip that many find an aid to aiming. All told, the Evolution Stock is an impressive little unit.

The other custom 10/22 that we'll focus on here (simply because I have it handy) is mine. Being both very nice and very affordable, 10/22s are popular merchandise prizes at big shooting matches. I won a few over the years, giving most of them to kids and keeping one for myself. This gun started as a blue steel standard model and went new in the box to Clark Custom (www.clarkcustomguns.com), where Kay Clark-Miculek turned it into the model their family shop calls "The Squirrel Rifle." The barrel, fluted 1" diameter Douglas match grade, was cut to 16-¼", barely over the legal

"This rifle is cool!" Finger off trigger, muzzle safely downrange, Samantha Sokol, 17, is delighted by her first try with Evolution-stocked 10/22 and ATN Ultra Sight.

length. This made overall length actually more than two inches shorter than that of a 10/22 you'd buy over the counter, and the result is a markedly "handier" rifle in the woods. The truncated barrel also keeps the gun from being unnecessarily muzzle heavy, yet the Douglas barrel gives enough weight where it belongs to help the gun hang dead steady when shooting from a standing position.

Kay also did the superb Clark trigger job. The result is a light, clean, crisp trigger pull that is conducive to good marksmanship. A trigger stop halts all movement after the sear releases and the shot breaks. The trigger has a very fast re-set for subsequent shots. An inexpensive 1" Tasco scope was my choice for the sight: low price, high quality, and therefore superb value. I chose a variable power magnification, 3X to 9X. The three-power setting gives you a wide field of vision that lets you track a running rabbit, while the nine-power setting lets you literally zoom in for a meat-saving head shot on that fat gray squirrel who's cautiously peering around the tree trunk to find out what you're up to. Nine-power is also the setting I use for the "club rifle matches," shot on miniature steel animal targets out to 100 yards under NRA Hunter Silhouette tournament rules. It is amply accurate for the purpose.

For years I kept the standard Ruger stock on that rifle (hell, it shot fine), but I finally decided that a custom gun that cool needed an "x-treme sports" kind of stock. I ordered a "race gun" stock from Brownell's gunsmithing supply (www.brownells.com). It was all I could ask. The radical design of this rifle stock, designated Model FAS/R22, allows multiple grasping options; it is adjustable for height to bring the eye perfectly in line to the scope every time; and it is adjustable for pull, or length from shoulder to trigger. The barrel floats completely free of the stock: an exotic look, but also one that keeps a warped wooden stock from pressing against the barrel and altering its point of aim/point of impact coordinates.

Brownell's also lists a youth stock for the 10/22. Instead of having to cut down a stock to fit your kid, just bolt on one of these. It works great for petite adult females and men with short arms, too. If you shoot your .22 outdoors a lot in deep cold, the youth stock keeps trigger and scope the right distance from a shoulder now heavily padded with winter clothing.

Erik Pepin, 12, with Evolution-stocked 10/22

SWAT cops who wear thick armor use short stocks on their M16s for the same reason. Brownell's is something of a "one-stop 10/22 shop" for a broad variety of accessories that extends far beyond stock design options.

With over 3 million produced between 1964 and 1993, sales trends indicate that the 10/22 has actually become more popular in the last several years. It's a modern classic, for many very good reasons. Δ

Take care of your knife

By John Lo Cicero

There was a time when I did not understand the value of quality, or respect for a fine tool. I received my tool education first-hand when I decided to run off and work with my uncle, a tugboat captain on the Mississippi River. You know, kind of like Tom Sawyer! I found myself in the position of a green deckhand in a world where the work was hard, back breaking, and very dangerous. There was very little romance involved other than the beauty of the river.

My first day as a brand new deckhand was not what I expected. The boat I was aboard was not exactly the *Queen Mary*. It was small and cramped, and rusty to boot. The accommodations were less than spectacular. My bunk contained a very dirty, old, smelly mattress that had a bumper crop of mold growing on it. The galley was so small it was hard to get two people in there at one time. And the roaches seemed to be the masters of that decadent chamber of gourmet delights. So as you can see, the charm and mysteries of Mark Twain's Mississippi River faded away rather quickly.

Since the space was small, our possessions were limited to those we held very dear or deemed important. Among my uncle's few possessions was a folding knife. It was always with him and one of the prettiest knives I had ever seen. It had a brass tip and dark wooden handle. My uncle noticed I was admiring his knife and asked if I had a knife of my own.

"No," I replied.

"Well, you can't be a good deckhand unless you have a knife; a good knife is your best friend out here on the water."

Well, the next time we had some free time at the fleet, I ran across the levee and found a hardware store where I bought what I thought to be a very good knife. I paid all of $2.50. That was a rather sizable amount of money to pay for an item of that nature. Also, it took most of the money I had to my name to purchase this tool that I was instructed I would need in my job.

I hurried back to the boat where my uncle was kneeling down on the bow deck splicing a deck line. I proceeded to show him my new knife and asked him what he thought of it. He took the knife from my hand and started to inspect it. He turned it one way, then another, then opened the shiny chrome-plated blade, reached into his pocket, and pulled out a one dollar bill. He wrapped the dollar around the knife handle and closed the blade on the dollar to hold it in place. He then proceeded to toss my new knife over the side into the dark, muddy Mississippi River. He turned, looking straight at me, and said, "Now you can say you threw something away that was worth something." All the while he was making an irritating little laugh.

Well needless to say, I was a little shocked and speechless at my uncle's strange behavior. "Hey, I paid $2.50 for that!" I protested. My uncle said nothing. He went to the wheel house and came back with a shiny black leather case that contained a single, stainless steel locking blade, brass tipped, dark wood handled knife—just like his own. He handed it to me and said, "You owe me $20. You take care of that knife, and it'll take care of you. Never loan it to anyone or you may not have it long. A dull knife is as dangerous as an unloaded gun."

"What do you mean?" I asked.

"Well," my uncle explained, "people take it for granted the gun is unloaded and end up shooting themselves. If you take your knife for granted and think it is sharp, it will always let you down. You'll use that knife every day you're out here on the water, so after you use it, check it and pass the blade over a stone to keep that sharp edge. Keep it clean and oil it daily. You are on the water, and that knife needs to be maintained."

At the time, in my opinion, that $20 sticker price was rather steep, considering I was making only $9 a day. But when you have to work hard for something, you value it all the more. As a result, I learned everything I could about maintaining that knife. Now I will pass on that knowledge to you.

I have seen people take a rather expensive knife to use it as a screw driver or a pry bar or for that matter even to cut wire. Did your mother ever yell at you for using her sewing scissors to cut cardboard? Well, those scissors were her tools for making those fine cuts on cloth. She did not want any raggedy edges. She valued the clean cut that truly sharp scissors made and wanted to keep them that way.

If you were to mess with a chef's knives in his kitchen, you might lose a finger or two. You'll never find real chef knives tossed in a drawer. They are usually placed carefully in a slotted wooden holder with a place for each and every individual knife. You'll never find those knives being allowed to languish at the bottom of a sink full of dirty dish water, nor even in an automatic dishwasher. Improper washing tends to destroy the integrity of the knife. The chef will always clean the blade with a wet towel, hand dry it, and place it carefully back in its holder.

Now, a hunting knife or utility knife is usually carried in a leather sheath to protect both the knife and the wearer. But one should always remove his/her knife from the leather sheath for storage because the chemicals used in making the leather are pH acidic and will lead to damage of the metals in the knife. After hunting, clean your knife as soon as possible. Blood and body fluids, especially digestive juices, have a corrosive effect on steel. Also remember, if you want to dig a hole, sharpen a stick as a digging tool. A knife was not designed as a shovel.

We have now come to the most important part of care of your expensive knife: sharpening the blade. I have to admit there are all sorts of ideas and concepts on how to perform this task. There are a ton of gadgets out there on the market one can buy to sharpen the blade. Some are good and some I feel destroy the blade. And if you talk to ten different people on the subject of how to get a great edge on the blade of your knife, each and every one will have what he believes to be the best method known to mankind.

Now, here comes the big question: What type of stone should I use? That question has been the spark of a fiery debate that still rages on. There are stones that are marketed as either "wet" or "dry." So keep the following point in mind as you shop around for that perfect stone.

- One school of thought insists that a stone should have oil, water, or saliva placed on the surface to float the metal shavings away from the stone when the blade is being sharpened.
- The other theory is that using any kind of liquid just clogs the stone with oily, gooey sludge that fills in the pores of the stone, ruining the stone forever and only polishing the blade, rather than honing it to a sharp edge.

I am not going to get myself in either side of this trick bag. The method I use works on wet or dry stones.

Place your medium-grit stone on the table in front of you. Lay the blade of your knife at about a 20-degree angle on the stone. Place your index finger on the back of the blade. Keeping the edge of the blade in contact with the stone at a 20-degree angle, drag the blade toward you with a steady, smooth, even pull. Apply medium to light pressure as you draw the blade across the stone. Then turn the blade over and repeat. If you keep the knife in the same hand, you'll need to use your thumb on the back part of the blade and push the blade away from you on this motion. Also remember it's important to keep the same angle at about 20 degrees on both sides of the blade. Go slowly and alternate forward and backward strokes. Pull to you, then flip the knife and push away. Do this several times. A dull knife will probably take a few extra strokes. A really cool trick is to mark the blade's edge with an ink marker to see if you are getting the entire blade honed correctly. If your technique is correct, all of the ink will be removed when you are finished.

Now the next question is, where do you stop? How do you know if you have a good edge? Everyone has a different idea on that as well. I have heard people say, place the edge of the blade against your lower lip. If it's cold, it's sharp. Others tell you to shave your arm, and still others say to place the blade on your thumb nail and pull the blade across it. If it cuts, it's sharp. I strongly do not recommend any of these. I personally just take a piece of paper and pull the blade lightly along and if it cuts, it is sharp enough for me. And the final step, something I always do, is to take a leather belt and flip it over so the inside of the belt is showing. I place the blade at a 20-degree angle and pull it toward me on both sides of the blade to knock off any burrs. With just a little practice, you will be as good at sharpening a knife as any old timer out there.

And by the way, I still have that stainless steel locking blade, brass tipped, dark wooden handled knife my uncle sold me 39 years ago. The black leather case fell apart and has been thrown away. But the knife survives with just a few nicks and scratches on the brass and wooden handle. The knife is still in fine shape and as serviceable as the first day I got it. Δ

The healthful hobby of herb gardening

By Linda Gabris

Nothing's more rewarding than having an herb patch to snip from whenever a sprig of something special is needed in the kitchen. Growing herbs is a fun, inexpensive hobby that can be enjoyed year-round.

A starter garden can be a simple window box or planter on the sundeck filled with mixed herbs. For more formal arrangements, herbs can be planted as ground cover, hedges along walkways, and borders around vegetable gardens. They can be worked into flower beds for added fragrance or be an entire patch of everything a creative cook's heart could ever desire.

The only thing hard about herb gardening is deciding which herbs to plant, how to start them, and picking a suitable pot or plot. Other things to consider are growing requirements like soil, water, sun, and shade.

Most herbs can be started indoors from seed. For this method, you'll need seeds, pots, and organic potting soil to fill the planters. These items can be found at nurseries or garden centers.

I prefer biodegradable fiber or peat pots as, unlike plastic or other containers, they can be set directly into ground, eliminating the need to transplant fragile young seedlings—thus reducing chances of shock.

Sow seeds following directions on seed packets regarding starting times based on zones, planting depths,

A cup of herb tea in the garden is summer's greatest joy.

Most herbs can be started indoors from seed.

watering, and other specific advice for each herb. Once started in the hobby, you can let your own plants go to seed, then gather and dry them for future plantings.

Sunrooms, sunny windowsills, gro-lights, and portable green houses can help make growing easy. Seedlings are ready to be transplanted outside when there's no longer a threat of frost.

Like houseplants, herbs can also be started by taking a slip or cutting from an established plant anytime from mid-spring onward. For this method, you'll need a herb gardening friend or neighbor willing to share.

Place the cutting in water or wet sand and keep moist for two weeks or until thread-like roots appear. If using sand, tug lightly to see if the plant has taken root. Once rooted, the slip is ready for planting. Shrubby herbs like thyme are well-suited for this method. Some semi-ripe cuttings, especially rosemary, can be planted directly into soil without pre-rooting.

Herbs can also be cultivated by uprooting a mature plant—being careful not to damage roots. Separate into sections and then transplant each portion. This is known as division method of transplanting and is suitable for chives, mint, tarragon, or any herb with sturdy roots.

The easiest way to get started, especially for those who don't have someone willing to share, is to buy seedlings from a nursery or other supplier when the time is right for planting. It is best to choose seedlings that are locally grown as they will already be acclimatized to your area.

Once danger of frost has passed, seedlings can be transplanted outside, either into larger pots with plenty of room to expand, or in ground that has been worked as you would for any garden.

Grandmother taught me not to use commercial fertilizers, but if you feel you must, ask your supplier for organic or chemical-free choices. I make my own, which are far more economical, and safer to use than store-bought products and results are every bit as good. To make your own fertilizer for your gardens, all you need is a patch of stinging nettles, which usually isn't too hard to find. Like Grandma, I encourage nettles to grow at the back of my property especially for this purpose. If you have to hunt them down in the woodlands, look for wild raspberries and stinging nettles won't be far off.

Wear gloves and a long-sleeved shirt, as they really do sting! Pick in a thinning-out fashion, and your patch will never run short. Gather an armload, put into a tub or plastic barrel, fill with water, cover and allow to brew for two weeks. Stir occasionally to help extract nutrients.

Once fermented, the potent tea is ready to use in your watering can. Nettles have a high content of nitrogen that works wonders in any garden. Since they are plentiful from early spring to late fall, the potion can

Herbal vapor baths are a good treatment for colds, headaches, and sinus congestion.

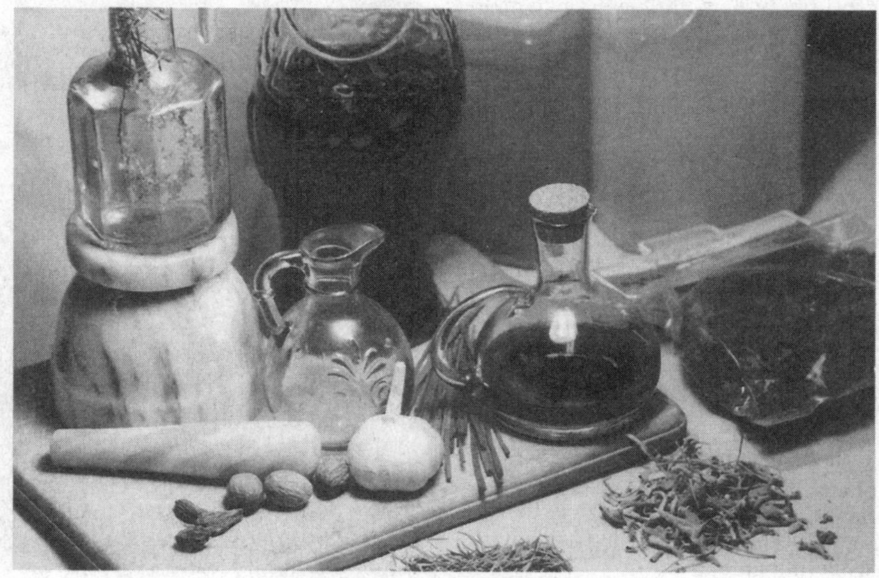

Herbal oils and vinegars

be made as needed. Other nutrient-rich weeds (or wilderness herbs as I know them), including dandelion, clover or anything that has been plucked from a chemical-free yard, can be added to the brewing pot.

Herbs are not prone to insect attacks, but if you do have a pest, the last thing you want on your edibles is poisonous substances. So steer clear of chemical-based pesticides.

If you notice trouble, usually from aphids, mix a dab of dish soap into a cup of water and add a tablespoon of powered basil, sage, rosemary, or thyme, or a mixture of these herbs, along with a pinch each of garlic powder and cayenne. Spray lightly. Amounts don't have to be exact in order to work. It just does. Traces of soap will rinse off with the next water along with the expired aphids.

If bigger pests are at work, such as cutworms, slugs, or grubs, sprinkle stove ashes around the base of the troubled plant. Once the ashes get wet, they'll leach lye into the soil, ridding the nuisances.

My favorite herbs

Following is a list of my favorite herbs, with hints for growing and putting them to good use. To get the most out of herb gardening, pay mind to Grandma's old rule of thumb. Instead of struggling all summer long trying to tame the wild, let the wild grow free—and with any luck at all, the tame will surely follow.

BASIL *Ocimum basilicum*

Native to India, Africa, and Asia, basil made its way to Western Europe in the 16th century via Oriental spice traders and to America with early settlers. Common species include sweet, cinnamon, lemon, purple, bush, and Greek.

Growing tips: Well-drained soil, full sun. Pick leaves and stems anytime for fresh use. Harvest before blooming for drying. Good plant for wintering indoors.

In cooking: Use in soups, sauces, herbal vinegars, and oils. Main ingredient in pesto sauce: Measure 1 tablespoon pine nuts, 4 tablespoons chopped basil, 5 cloves peeled garlic, and 6 tablespoons virgin olive oil into blender and puree until thick and smooth. Serve this delicious Italian-rooted sauce on pasta or use it as dipping sauce for crusty bread.

Health use: Pluck a few basil leaves and rub on exposed skin for handy bug repellent. Tea is recommended for indigestion, gas, insomnia, and anxiety. Vapor bath breaks up phylum and cold congestion.

SAGE *Salvia officinalis*

Native to the Mediterranean, the Latin name *salvia* means to save or heal. There are about 700 species. Common types are blue, golden, pineapple, dwarf, purple, Clary, and variegated.

Growing tips: Division is most reliable, thrives in well-drained sandy soil, full sun. Requires little moisture as it's prone to root rot. To keep bushy, prune in spring and after flowering in summer. Sage grows woody after 4 or 5 years, and new plants should be started by division method.

In cooking: Sage and stuffing go hand-in-hand. Use in salad dressings, herbal vinegars, oils, and breads. I especially like the lemony, camphor-like taste in soup and healing broth. Very good spice for enlivening homemade sausages and meat loaves.

Herbal oils are easy to make. Simply bruise an herb (here basil), put it in a glass bottle, and cover with olive oil to steep for two weeks.

Health use: The volatile oils and tannins in sage contain antiseptic, astringent, and cooling properties. Tea aids digestion, soothes a sore throat, and helps induce sleep. Poultices draw infection from sores. Adding sage to one's diet is said to lower blood sugar levels. A vapor bath is good for cold and sinus headache. After infused water has cooled, use to treat aching feet. Sage, like basil, is a good natural bug repellent.

THYME *Thymus vulgaris*

Native to the Mediterranean, dubbed the king of herbs. Grandmother always said, "If it needs something and you don't know what, add a pinch of thyme." Species include garden, lemon, caraway, and wooly thyme.

Growing tips: Easy to grow from seed, thyme prefers dry soil and hot sun. Over-watering causes root rot. Harvest leaves as needed. For drying, cut before flowering. Don't cut back a plant destined for wintering indoors as it will stunt growth.

In cooking: Use in stuffing, tomato, and vegetable dishes. Thyme is the prominent ingredient in bouquet garnis.

Health use: Old World herbalists used the tea to treat asthma, whooping cough, headache, cramps, colic, and a host of other ailments. Good as vapor bath for congestion and foot bath for ridding odor.

PARSLEY *Petroselinum crispum*

Native to temperate zones, its use dates all the way back to ancient Greece where it was a funeral decoration. Three common varieties are curly-leaf, flat-leaf, and parsnip or Hamburg parsley.

Growing tips: If starting from seed, hasten germination by soaking seeds 24 hours in water before planting. Needs moist soil and shade and grows best when picked often. Excellent for wintering indoors.

In cooking: One of the world's most popular garnishes for bringing color to any dish—but parsley is good for more than just sitting pretty on the plate. Rich source of vitamins, minerals, iron, calcium, and other health-giving properties. Add liberally to soups, sauces, rice, or salads. Chew a sprig to freshen breath after eating.

Health use: Add to bath water for a rejuvenating soak. Tea can be used as hair rinse for dry, itchy scalp.

SAVORY ***Satureja -hortensis*** **(summer),** ***-Montana (winter)***

Native to the Mediterranean, introduced to England by Romans during Caesar's reign, brought to America by early settlers as a fond reminder of home. There are about 30 species—two most common are summer and winter varieties.

Growing tips: Start from seed, prefers well-drained soil, full sun. Pick leaves as soon as plant is established. For drying, cut entire plant before flowering.

In cooking: The peppery taste complements lentils, beans, vegetables, casseroles, herbed loaves, vinegars, and oils.

Health use: Tea is good for treating a sore throat, and when taken cold, stops diarrhea. Vapor bath for headaches.

MARJORAM ***Origanum majorana***

Native to North Africa and Southwest Asia, in ancient times marjoram sanctified marital bliss. Common members are sweet and pot marjoram.

Growing tips: Novices might have better luck with nursery seedlings; needs well-drained soil, full sun. Pinch off leaves as needed. Cut down to 1 inch before flowering. To bring indoors for winter, pot a division.

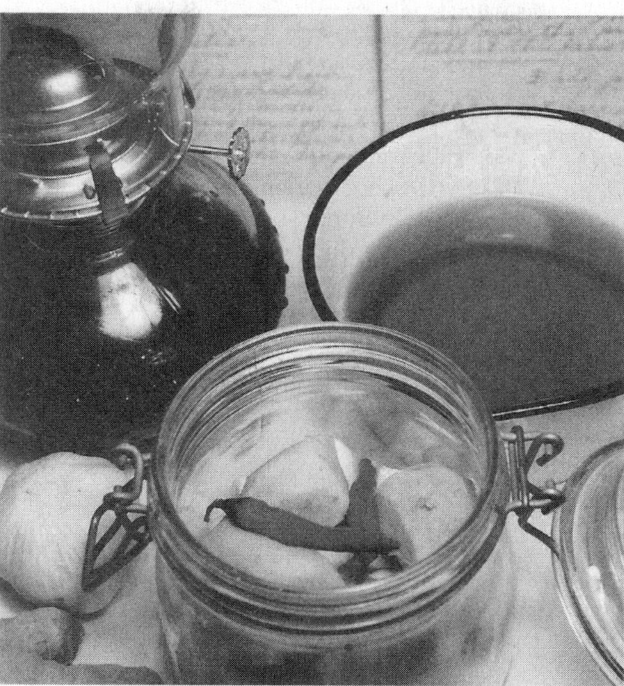

Making cold preventative medicine using a recipe from the pages of Grandma's old scribbles.

In cooking: Pizza, pasta sauces, herbal vinegars and oils, stuffing, sausages, soups, stews.

Health use: Noted antiseptic and stimulant, tea soothes a sore throat and infected mouth. Mixing fresh plant with a dab of olive oil and rubbing on aching joints relives rheumatism and arthritic pain. Good vapor bath.

OREGANO ***Origanum***

Native to the Mediterranean, its use dates to early Greek and Roman days. Trying to decipher species is difficult as it's from a very large genus.

Growing tips: Easy from seed, prefers full sun. Pinch leaves back to encourage bushiness. For drying, pick entire plant before flowering.

In cooking: The real taste of Italy in any dish, especially on pizza and pastas. Good in herbal vinegars and oils.

Health use: Herbalists recommend oregano infusions to treat indigestion, headaches, upset stomach, and cramps. Putting a generous picking of leaves into bath water helps relieve stiffness. The fragrance induces sleep, so use before bedtime. Good in herb pillows.

How to make

Herbal oil: With pestle and mortar, bruise handful of chosen herb, put into clean jar, and cover with virgin olive oil. Secure a piece of cloth over mouth of jar with a rubber band and set jar on sunny windowsill. Stir once a day for about 2 weeks. Strain into clean jar, cap.

Herbal teas: Put small handful of fresh-picked herb in teapot. Cover with boiling water and steep until desired strength is reached. Steep a bit strong when making for medicinal purposes. Tea can be made from dried herb when fresh is not available.

Herbal vinegars: Wash and scald a pretty bottle. Put in chosen herb, cover with apple cider, malt, sherry, red, or white wine vinegar, cork. Allow to infuse for about 2 weeks. Garlic, black or colored peppercorns, chilie peppers, or other seasoning can be added.

Vapor baths: Put generous picking of herbs into basin, add boiling water to cover. Drape towel over head and basin, inhale to break up congestion and ease headache. After head is cleared, use leftover infusion to soak tired feet.

Drying herbs: Simply string and hang. When moisture is gone, crush and store in spice tins or jars.

Bath bags: Place an assortment of fresh or dried herbs on a face cloth. Tie into a bundle, add to bath water for soothing aroma.

Herb pillows: Make a little square cotton pillowcase and fill with herbs. Sew up the seams and stick under your pillow at night for soothing fragrance. Δ

GROW GARLIC

and reap health benefits

By Alice Brantley Yeager
Photos by James O. Yeager

Garlic is one of our oldest herbs on record. Anyone can grow garlic without having to hover over it, hoping that it produces. That's far more than I can say about some other seasoning plants I have tried. Gardeners who can't raise garlic can't raise dust. There are many varieties of garlic and some grow better in a cool climate than a warm one, but you can bet there's one or more suited for every area. In addition to cultivated garlic, Nature has provided us with a number of wild varieties free for the gathering. There's no excuse for being unfamiliar with garlic.

Not all herbs are as universally well known as garlic. It is often mentioned in old writings, and its usage has widened over the centuries thanks to people who carried the herb from one place to another as they roamed Planet Earth. However, from way back, folks have had mixed feelings about garlic. Some have hated it with a purple passion, whereas others have declared it a cure-all. Ancient Egyptians regarded it highly—a present from the gods—and Egyptian slaves refused to work if their portions of garlic were withheld.

No one is sure where garlic originated. The Chinese have benefited from it for centuries, and the Babylonians were using garlic as far back as 3,000 B.C. No matter where it came from, ancient folks recognized garlic as an important health ally and a tasty addition to their food.

Garlic's flower stalks tower over the plants themselves. When flowers die back and plant goes into dormancy during summer, it's time to dig bulbs. Flowers are often dried and used in dried flower arrangements.

Due to garlic being easy to grow and widely distributed, it is generally known as the common man's herb. It has great value for seasoning meats, soups, cooked vegetables, salads, and so on. Eaten raw, even though its onion-like flavor is delicious, garlic is a turn off in polite society. Sadly, a raw garlic breath will not depart overnight. It takes all of two days to fade away, and that's not guaranteed. Ironically, the offending person may take comfort in the fact that garlic is loaded with health benefits.

In contrast to its obnoxious side, garlic has a valuable side. It carries a goodly amount of B and C vitamins, protein, phosphorus, and smaller amounts of other health boosters such as calcium, iron, and potassium. Garlic has long been recognized for its medicinal values, among which is the lowering of high blood pressure.

For those who take folk remedies seriously, garlic is well known as a remedy for sore throats, colds, coughs, and related illnesses. A soothing syrup is made by pouring a quart of boiling water over a pound of cleaned, sliced garlic cloves and allowing mixture to stand covered overnight. (Use stainless steel, porcelain or glass—no aluminum.) It is then strained through fine gauze or a fine stainless wire strainer to remove cloves or pieces thereof. Enough sugar, honey, or both are added to the strained liquid to make a thin syrup. This can be administered by tablespoonful as needed.

To add further to garlic's acclaimed benefits, history records that during the 17th century, when England was caught up in the Great Plague, many people who used garlic were the only ones who could minister to plague victims without contracting the disease themselves. Coming a little closer to modern times, it is said Russia once relied so heavily on the use of garlic for its soldiers that garlic became known as Russian penicillin.

There are now odorless capsules on the market for those who prefer a simple way to ingest garlic. To bolster one's confidence about no aftereffects, however, I'd ask the pharmacist for the best thing to use "just in case." Chewing fresh mint, parsley, or orange peelings is often recommended after eating salads or something that contains raw garlic.

Garlic is a perennial that, in the South, comes up in the fall from cloves left in the ground when the crop was harvested. The plant produces green strap-like leaves that remain green all winter. Extreme cold will cause mature leaves to toughen, but there always seems to be a supply of fresh tender leaves coming on to use as seasoning in case one's supply of cloves runs low. Try cooking a few chopped leaves in with potato soup. This not only has eye appeal but it enhances the flavor of the soup.

Early spring is the best overall time to plant garlic, and if there are odd spots in the garden that aren't needed to grow something else, try utilizing them to grow garlic. Such places may be next to fences or in corners. Like many other plants, garlic needs sunlight, good soil, and reasonable drainage. A dressing of well rotted compost will help, too. In other words, garlic isn't fussy about its location as long as a few simple rules are followed.

I plant garlic cloves about 2 inches deep and 6 to 7 inches apart in well-worked soil that is free of weeds. We have raised beds 4x8 feet in size, and about a half bed of garlic produces plenty of cloves for our own use. Plants will start their life cycle in early spring and, as summer approaches, will put up tall flower stalks. Foliage will die down in hot weather, and cloves are ready to be dug when plants are completely dormant. Don't wait to harvest until fall showers begin as new growth is likely to occur.

Elephant garlic has been washed of dirt and is now ready to have thin skin removed along with blemishes and tough root portions. Sliced into thin slices, it will be dehydrated until slices are crisp. Also shown are trays of sweet basil leaves ready for the drying.

A garden fork is best for digging garlic bulbs. Spades have a tendency to slice into the bulbs, damaging some of them. Letting the newly dug cloves lie in a cool shady place for 2 to 3 days will let the clinging dirt dry out, and it will be easier to brush away than fresh dirt.

We prefer to raise Elephant Garlic. It is a type of garlic that produces an exceptional crop in our Zone 8 area (southwestern Arkansas). Elephant has large bulbs and cloves and is mild tasting. We like to clean the dirt from a quantity of the cloves, put them in mesh bags, and hang them near the kitchen where they are easily accessible. They will keep for months in any dry, cool room.

Another way of keeping garlic for culinary use is to dehydrate it. I like this method of preserving garlic as a lot of garlic can be easily stored in jars in a small amount of space. Simply clean fresh cloves thoroughly and remove thin skins, root ends, and any blemishes. Slice cloves into thin slices, place on mesh drying racks, and process in an electric dehydrator at 100° to 120° F. Time required to dry garlic slices may vary according to humidity, altitude, etc. In our area, garlic slices require several hours or overnight to dry. Pieces will be crisp and break easily when ready to remove from the dehydrator. Let them cool off and immediately put them in clean, dry jars. Store in a convenient place such as a kitchen pantry.

Dried garlic does not have to be reconstituted before use. Crumble the desired amount of garlic into your casserole, stew, etc., and let it cook with the rest of the ingredients.

If you have a tried-and-true method of dehydrating, by all means stick with it. However, if you are not experienced in drying produce from your garden, I'd highly recommend buying an electric dehydrator. This method of drying cuts out a lot of guesswork and, if taken care of, an electric dehydrator will give years of service. Be sure it has a thermostat so that you do not have to be constantly checking on whatever you are drying. A good dehydrator must have a fan to aid in ventilation. Those without fans may have hot spots in them, which can lead to unevenly dried food.

Timers are okay, but they're not necessary, as you're going to check on your items from time to time anyhow, and drying times will vary.

Check out several models of dehydrators and select one that meets your needs. Let common sense be your guide as to overall size needed and cost. Frankly, I'd recommend placing a dehydrator somewhere other than the kitchen when in use. Some items, such as garlic, being dried can produce heavy odors that tend to invade the entire house. Also, there's usually some noise attached to using an electric dehydrator.

Garlic's benefits are not confined to the many delicious dishes coming out of the kitchen. It is also used in organic sprays to control insects in the garden and to discourage deer and other animals from munching on certain shrubs. We cat and dog owners often put some minced garlic in our pets' wet food to kill intestinal worms.

The many facets of garlic go on and on. If you don't have garlic growing in your garden, what are you waiting for?

Roasted garlic:

Select large garlic bulbs or clusters of attached garlic cloves. Clean and prepare as many as needed for guests, but at least one per person. Handle clusters of cloves gently to avoid too much separation.

Cut tops off of bulbs or clusters and discard or use for something else. Brush with olive oil. Sprinkle with freshly minced sweet basil leaves, rosemary or herb of your choice. (Dried herbs may be substituted if fresh ones are not available.)

Wrap each bulb or cluster in aluminum foil, and place on a cookie sheet or shallow baking pan. Bake at 350° F, for about 35-40 minutes or until soft.

Serve alongside cooked meats or vegetable dishes.

Crusty garlic bread:

- 1-pound loaf French bread
- ½ cup butter or good grade oleo, melted
- 3-4 small garlic cloves, minced
- 2 Tbsp. fresh parsley, finely chopped

French bread seems to be the preferred bread for this recipe, although other breads are good, too. Select a crusty type bread rather than a soft, sandwich type bread.

Slice French loaf lengthwise and place both halves cut-side up on a baking sheet. Combine butter and garlic and brush over cut sides of bread. Sprinkle with minced parsley. Bake in 350° F oven about 7-8 minutes and then move bread to broil 4-6 inches beneath heat until golden brown, usually about 2 minutes. Keep a close watch so as not to burn.

Cut into 2 inch slices and serve warm.

Guacamole dip:

- 1 ripe avocado, peeled, mashed, seed discarded
- 1 Tbsp. onion, minced
- ½ tsp. chili powder
- 1 small clove garlic, cleaned and minced
- 1 Tbsp. fresh lemon juice
- 1 medium ripe tomato, peeled and chopped in small pieces. (Dip tomato in boiling water just long enough to slip off skin.)

Combine all ingredients and chill in covered container (no aluminum). Serve with corn chips or veggie sticks (carrot, bell pepper, cucumber, etc.)

Companies offering several types of garlic, including Elephant Garlic:

R. H. Shumway's
334 W. Stroud St.
Randolph, WI 53956-1274

J.W. Jung Seed Co.
335 S. High St.
Randolph, WI 53957-0001

Henry Field's Seed & Nursery Co.
P.O. Box 397
Aurora, IN 47001-0397

New potatoes with garlic:

- 16-18 new potatoes, cleaned and quartered (do not peel)
- ¼ cup melted margarine
- ¼ tsp. ground black pepper
- 1 small bell pepper, chopped
- 2 medium cloves garlic, peeled and minced
- 2 Tbsp. fresh parsley, chopped fine

Boil potatoes until tender in just enough water to cover. Saute bell pepper and garlic in margarine until tender crisp and add pepper and parsley. Combine thoroughly with hot potatoes. This is a good side dish to be served with meat. Δ

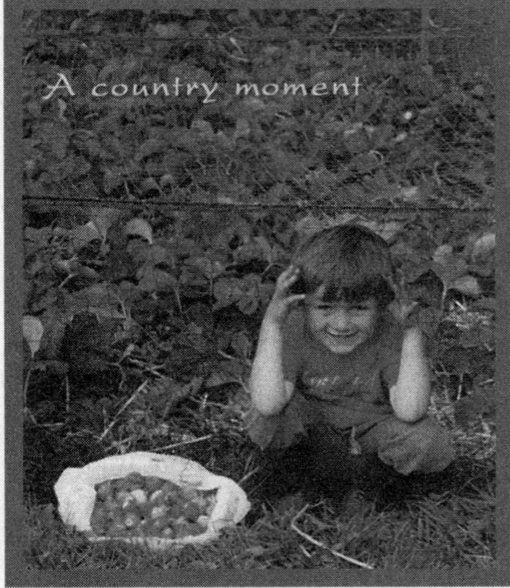

Matthew Hiscock, of Dorset, England, in his family's strawberry patch.

No-frills tomato transplants

By Raymond Nones

You're sick and tired of being ripped off by your local nursery, every spring paying through the nose for overcrowded scrawny six packs of tomato transplants. You're boiling mad, and you're not going to take it anymore! You'll grow your own—that'll teach them.

So you open a seed catalog, circle a few varieties as possible buys and then turn to the accessories page. There you find all the "necessities" for starting from seed: sterile potting and soilless starting mixtures, clay pots, plastic pots, peat pots, mini greenhouses, grow lights, electric mats, soil heating cables, plus many more items. All very nice and all also **very expensive**—gulp! What's a person to do?

Let a long time dirt-under-the-fingernails penny-pinching home gardener tell you exactly what to do. Grow them the old fashioned way as I have been doing for many years. You don't need any of that stuff.

Getting started

First, if you do not know what the last possible spring frost date is for your area, find out from your local weather service. That will be your transplanting date. Then count back six weeks; that will be your indoor seed sowing date.

Do not start earlier; overly mature seedlings will become rootbound and stunted. When transplanted outdoors, they may never fully recover. Putting plants out early also won't gain you anything. Tomatoes love hot weather, and until it comes, they'll just sit there.

The object is to have continuous progressive growth from seed right up to maturity. If for some reason your seedlings have developed flowers before transplanting time, pinch them off before setting them into the garden. This may seem contrary to logic, but if left on, the root system will not develop properly.

Let the flowers remain only if you are willing to sacrifice significant future production for the bragging rights of a few early fruits.

Planting mediums

The term "planting medium" is used to describe the substance in which seeds are started. Those available commercially are generally sterile artificial soil mixtures. They usually consist of various blends of peat moss, perlite, vermiculite, and fertilizer. Also sold are soilless mixes made up of peat moss and vermiculite, plus ground limestone and contain no true soil at all. Then there is ... well, you get the general idea. My head is starting to hurt just thinking about them.

Since the transplants are eventually going to grow in your garden soil, it makes sense to me to start them off in some of that soil. To make your own planting medium, prepare it the previous fall. Mix equal amounts of good garden soil and finished compost in large pails. Cover with plastic garbage bags to hold the moisture in. Then put in a sheltered place, a shed, garage, basement or wherever, to age over winter.

Pre-sowing preparation

About two weeks before seeding time, transfer the mix into flats. A flat is any fairly large shallow container. Some perfectly satisfactory no-cost flats are half-gallon milk cartons cut in half lengthwise, foil pie and cake pans, and empty plastic deli containers. Punch holes in the bottoms to allow for drainage.

Use a separate flat for each variety. Make sure the medium is well firmed down in the flats, spray with water, and cover with clear plastic. (Many

Once seeds germinate and are up flats should be in a south facing window where they will receive enough sun to develop.

Transplant into individual containers when seedlings have two or three well developed true leaves; plant deep right up to their seed leaves

household products come in hand-operated spray bottles. Wash one out and use.)

Then bring the flats into a well-heated room. This pre-sowing procedure is a good idea for two reasons: 1) If there are any viable weed seeds in the medium, they will sprout, and you can remove them before the tomato seeds are put in; 2) To warm everything up. **Never sow seeds in a cold medium.**

Sowing the seed

Several days before you are ready to sow, remove the plastic coverings and check the condition of the medium. Pull any weeds that may have sprouted and smooth out any dips or other irregularities. Leave uncovered. On the day of the scheduled planting date, the room temperature should be about 70-75°F. Sow the seeds in the flats by simply placing them on the surface in rows that are two inches apart. Within rows, space seed every one inch. Press them just slightly into the soil with your finger tip. Spray with the hand spray so that the mix is moist, **not soaked**. Always use tepid, not cold water. Place the flats into a clear plastic bag, or just cover with clear plastic, and keep in bright light, but not in the sun. Whenever excess condensation (some is normal) appears on the plastic, open the bag; if only covered, pull the plastic back a little to allow the moisture to evaporate.

As soon as the seeds germinate and start to show (they will be white not green), remove the flats from under the plastic and put them in a south window where they will receive direct sunlight all day. You say you don't have a south window? Then, unfortunately, you will have to carry them from window to window as the sun moves.

Once they are up, stop using the spray to water. Instead, every morning and as needed, water the soil mixture from the top very carefully with slightly warm water. Slowly pour it on and let it soak in.

Since the sunlight always comes only from one direction, turn the flats often to keep the seedlings growing straight. After sundown, move them away from the window. Night temperatures by the glass may get low enough to harm the seedlings.

A word of caution: If you have a gas range, never put them in a kitchen window; it could be their death sentence. If there is the slightest gas leak, even too small to be chemically detected, it will affect tomato leaves.

Damping off

The biggest danger to your seedlings is a soil-borne disease called "damping off." This fungus thrives in too-wet conditions. Seedlings are most susceptible for the first two weeks. After that, as the stems get bigger and harder there is less risk.

If you see plants pinched at the surface and collapsed, that is the work of the damping-off fungi. It is very important to keep the top of the soil mixture barely moist. Late in the afternoon, allow the surface to become nearly dry to guard against this disease.

As the plants grow bigger, snip off weak and spindly ones at ground level so that those remaining have more air space around them.

Putting plants into individual containers

The first two leaves on the plants are "seed leaves." They are elongated oval shaped and not true leaves. When the seedlings have developed two or three well developed true leaves, select the strongest best plants and transplant into individual containers. I use the tin cans that vegetables, soups, etc., come in. First, punch holes in the bottoms. Then to insure that the root ball comes out easy, crumple up a letter-size piece of paper and push it into the bottom of each can. Wet it down. Then fill them with the same medium that was used in the flats. Pack it down firmly.

Go to the flat and using a knife (a disposable type plastic one will do just fine) cut out a square that contains the roots and as much soil as possible around the plant. Lift out the square with the tip of the knife. Plant them deep; right up to

Since your window gets the sun from only one direction be sure to keep turning the transplants so they will grow straight.

Two picnic table benches and three lath panels are used to quickly set up a hardening off shelter capable of shielding a large number of transplants.

To remove from container, hold so that the stem is in-between your forefinger and index finger, tilt away from you and give a sharp rap on the bottom.

A cutworm collar around the stem is a necessary last step in the transplanting process.

the seed leaves. Then water by pouring it, very slowly, into the top of the container.

To prevent from wilting, keep out of the sun for a day. After that, put them back in the window. Don't forget to turn often to keep them growing straight and keep watering the soil with tepid water.

Brush tops of the plants lightly with your hand every day. Being subjecting to this slight stress will cause them to develop thicker and stockier stems.

Hardening off

Before transplants can be set out, they must be hardened off, a process to toughen them for the harsher environment of the outdoors. Introduction to outdoor conditions must be gradual.

About a week before transplanting, on a calm day when air temperature is at least 60° F, find a warm, sheltered outdoor spot. Leave the plants out for about an hour or so; then bring them in. The next day, leave them out for about two hours.

Subsequently, every morning put them out, gradually increasing outdoor time until they can stay out all day before taking them in.

On days that are cold and windy, do not put them out; it will only set them back. If the weather remains steady, by the end of the week they should be ready to be set in. A few days before the transplanting date, unless there is danger of frost, let them stay out all night.

When this hardening off process has been completed, the transplants are ready to go into the garden.

Setting them in

Even though hardened off, the plants still have to withstand the trauma of being transplanted. Bright sun could harm newly set-in plants. The best time for transplanting is on a cloudy day. But that usually is not probable. The next best time is in the late afternoon when the sun has started to decline and has lost some of its heat. This also gives them all night to adjust.

In the morning of the transplanting day, prepare the plants by pouring water into the top of their containers, little by little, until it seeps out from the bottom holes. This will help keep the root ball from breaking apart.

Measure and mark the position where the plants will go. Dig holes about twice the width and depth of their containers. Remove plants by turning the containers upside down, holding them so that the stem is in between your forefinger and index finger, and giving a sharp tap on the bottom. Usually they will pop right out. If they don't, run a knife all around the edges and try again.

Make an effort to keep the roots in your shadow. If roots are matted or have been circling the bottom of the container, unravel and position outward. If too entangled to unravel, outward root growth can be achieved by making cuts, with a knife or razor blade, vertically on the sides and horizontally across the bottom of the root ball. If these steps are not taken, sometimes the roots will just stay within that little ball and not venture out any further.

The first pair of lowest leaves should be removed before putting into the ground. Partially refill the hole so that when set-in, the remaining second set of lower leaves will be just above the soil line. To guard against soil-borne diseases, never let the leaves touch the ground. If plants are leggy, remove two or three sets of lower leaves before setting-in up to the remaining bottom leaves.

Then pack and firm soil around root ball and stem with your fingers to remove any air pockets. Leave a slight depression at the surface. Pour about a quart of water around the base of the plant. Water each plant as soon as it is set-in. Then fill the depression with dry soil.

To protect from cutworms, cut a thin strip of smooth cardboard that is about 3 inches wide and 6 inches long and form it into a circle around the stem of the plant. Hold the overlapping ends together with a paper clip and then sink into the soil about 1 inch (cereal box cardboard makes great cutworm collars).

When all plants are in, spread a layer of compost over the entire area, all around and under the plants. If the next day is clear and sunny, give them some shade to ease their adapting to the new environment. After that, keeping a consistent soil moisture is of primary importance. When the soil has thoroughly warmed up, I recommend putting down a 2- to 3-inch mulch of shredded leaves. One final word: Seed is not cheap. If you grow only open-pollinated varieties, not hybrids, they can be had for free from ripened fruits at the end of the season.

Good luck, and enjoy a bountiful crop of great tomatoes!

(Raymond Nones is a lifelong home gardener and author of the book *Modular Vegetable Gardening: The Three Module Home Vegetable Garden.*) Δ

Use common-sense when fertilizing your garden with manure

By Tom Kovach

As people who plant vegetable gardens know, adding fertilizers to the garden improves the soil and adds nutrients which in turn help boost growth of the plants. There are some risks involved though if you are using manure as a fertilizer on a vegetable garden. To make your garden safe and reduce the risks of contamination from manure use, here are some things you should take into consideration:

- Place your vegetable garden in an area that isn't affected by surface runoff from manure storage or from crop land spread with manure.
- Be careful not to contaminate your vegetable garden from wind-borne drift during the time of manure spreading.
- Always use sterilized manure, which is available at most gardening centers.
- In applying manure to a garden, use manure that is properly composted.
- Non-composted or fresh manure should be applied only in the autumn of the preceding year. In areas of cold winters, the low temperatures will destroy pathogens that are found in fresh manure.
- If you plan to apply non-composted or fresh manure in the spring, make certain that you allow four to six months of time between fertilizing and harvesting, or use on soil that is used in growing late-season vegetables.
- When you are ready to harvest your garden, remember that all produce grown in a manure-fertilized garden should be thoroughly washed in clean, cold water, and peeled, if possible, to reduce the risk of contamination. Actually all vegetables should be thoroughly washed before consumption, but it is especially important with manure-fertilized produce.
- And finally, cooking vegetables also reduces or eliminates any risk of contamination.

Manure fertilizers can really give a garden a boost. But also use safety and caution when using it. Δ

To make supplies for your garden . . . RECYCLE

By Sylvia Gist

I hate to throw anything away. Combine that with my love to grow things, and I came up with recycling stuff to get supplies for gardening. It's a win-win situation.

Growing your own food can be a wise investment. The seeds cost little compared to the value of the produce, not to mention the quality of home-grown. However, gardening can also be expensive if you buy a lot of supplies. I buy my basic gardening tools and hoses, but most of the necessities and even some of the nice-to-have things can be made easily from recyclable items or packaging materials destined for the landfill. For example, I was leafing through a seed catalog and noticed some clear plastic containers with snap-together attached lids. They looked exactly like the container in which I'd brought my leftovers home from a local restaurant. I'd saved it, as usual, but didn't know what I'd use it for. The ones in the catalog were being sold for seed-starting trays.

You'll find usable materials and items everywhere. Some you already have; others you can get from friends or neighbors who will be happy to get rid of them. Yard sales and thrift shops are other sources of possible cheap supplies. The following items can happily enjoy a second life in your gardening process.

Milk & juice cartons

Those waxy cardboard half-gallon milk cartons deserve top billing, since they have so many uses. One is seed-starting trays. In late winter or early spring, when I start seeds, I stand the carton up and cut away the side below the fold-out opening used to empty the carton (save the side for another project). The place where the box was opened will need to be taped securely.

A collection of items that can be recycled into gardening supplies

Laid on its side, it's a planting box about four inches high. I take a knife and stab and twist several holes in the bottom for drainage. (You can skip this step if you don't need drainage.) Then I fill the tray halfway (or more) full of potting soil, put in seeds, and cover with more soil. Onions and leeks can stay in such a tray until planted outdoors if you space the seeds an inch or so apart.

Get two shorter trays by cutting a milk carton in half lengthwise. This cut puts the "please open other side" on one half and the "to open" on the other half. The half where the carton was opened will have to be taped up for this second tray. These work good for starting tiny seeds you want to transplant to larger pots as soon as possible.

Want a fancy "bottom-watering" tray? Save one of those tall waxy half-gallon containers that fresh juice or other beverage comes in. They have a round spout with screw-on cap instead of the regular box opening that the milk cartons have. Then follow the steps below.

1. Stand the carton upright and remove the side below the spout with a knife.
2. Lay the carton down with open side up.
3. Insert the removed piece into the carton vertically and mark where the top of the carton comes to.
4. Cut on the line you made and install the piece to fit securely at the spout end.

This inserted piece will keep the soil from touching the spout and allow for a space behind the spout for the water to go as it flows under and through the soil.

Milk cartons make good pots, too. Mark the desired height, lay the carton down, and cut. The half-gallon size makes about a four-inch diameter pot, while the quarts and pints are about two-inch pots. The half gallons, cut about two thirds of the way up with a couple of holes punched in the bottom, usually will hold a tomato

Basil protected by mini-greenhouses

Lettuce in milk carton walls and chard (upper right) in cans

Coffee cans around cabbage

plant until it can be set in the ground. If you cut just the top off, it will accommodate a cutting that has to be stuck in quite a bit of soil. I use this whole-carton size to start my grape vine cuttings.

From the extra pieces of flat waxy carton, I cut strips across the short way to make markers measuring about three-quarter inch by four inches. I cut a point at one end to make inserting them into potting soil easier. The Sharpie extra fine point pen does a good job of writing the name of the flower or vegetable to identify what's in the pot. These work for seed trays and pots indoors.

Yet another use is to protect plants. I had so much trouble with something eating seedlings leaf-by-leaf that I began experimenting. What worked was putting a wall around the plant. One year I set out some cabbage and broccoli plants and put something around some to protect them from the elements. The ones that didn't have anything around them disappeared, while the protected ones flourished. One of my walls was a waxy half-gallon carton, top and bottom removed, cut in half to make two culverts. Set securely into the soil, it provided protection from wind and varmints for that little seedling that couldn't afford to lose many leaves.

Clear plastic jugs

The mini-greenhouse is one of my favorite uses for the heavy plastic jugs, gallon and half gallon, that juice is sold in. I cut out the bottom so that I have a sharp edge on the bottom to stick into the soil. I put these over all my small tender plants, such as basil, in May or June. If the cucumbers are up early or if I started them inside, they get these houses, which have saved them from a late frost more than once.

Gallon jugs with handles can be turned into portable waterers by punching a few small holes (you have to experiment) in the bottom. Fill

Grapevine cuttings in full-sized carton

them with water and set them beside a plant or shrub that needs slow watering.

A group of two-liter beverage bottles can be turned into a wall-o-water of sorts. Fill with water and set in a closed ring around the plant. The water will warm in the daytime and retain some heat at night. You can cover the whole thing if the temperatures fall too low.

Plastic liter bottles

These plastic beverage bottles can be turned into insect traps:

1. Cut the top part away from the bottom about a couple of inches down from the top.
2. Put appropriate bait in the bottom of the bottle.
3. Then take the top with lid removed and push it into the bottom narrow end first.
4. Put tape around the cut edge to secure it. You will have a trap that slugs, for example, can get into but not out of.

I also use these smaller bottles, top cut off and upended, to cover the tops of stakes or sticks that I need to drape netting or row cover over. It keeps the netting from slipping down or tearing. See the "sheer curtains" section later in the article.

Translucent plastic gallon jugs

These plentiful milk or water jugs can be used to dispense water to a plant. Punch a few small holes in the bottom and sink the jug into the ground a couple of inches next to the plant. Fill the jug, and the water will sink into the ground slowly. These work well with tomato plants that need a lot of water in hot weather. You know how much water you are giving each plant.

To make a jug into a hot house/plant protector, cut out the bottom of the jug. This works well for starting perennial seeds outdoors. They keep the birds from eating the seeds and the cats from digging them up. The jug can also serve as a marker so I can find that tiny plant later when the flower bed has become crowded.

I also put them to use as storage for rain water. I try to keep a few gallons for those onions and leeks I start in the house in February.

Plastic lids

The heavy plastic lids that come on margarine, frozen whipped topping, and similar containers can be turned into sturdy markers or tags to use out in the garden. Cut a tag from the plastic, write on it with a garden marker (regular permanent markers will not last), thread a brightly colored piece of yarn through it (to help you find it later in the overgrown garden), and tie it to a sturdy part of the plant. By doing this, a friend of mine is able to identify the color of an iris at digging time in July or August.

Cucumbers and squash seedlings in newspaper pots

Plastic pots

If you don't buy any of your plants at nurseries, perhaps your friends do. Sometimes they're free at garage sales. These, of course, can be scrubbed and recycled for your own plants.

Styrofoam cups

There seems to be a lot of these around when there is a gathering of people who drink coffee. The cups can be rescued and used for pots. You can punch a hole in the bottom for drainage, if desired, before adding potting soil and planting a seed or seedling. You can even write on the cup with a pen to identify the plant. Their only drawback is that they tip over easier than a pot with a larger base.

Cans

I save all sorts of cans. Some I use as scoops for potting soil and such, and others I cut out both ends and use as protective walls for seedlings. Small cans, small seedlings. Gallon coffee cans can even be used as mini greenhouses if you cut out both ends and save the plastic lid to pop onto the can on a nippy night. Remove the can when the plant can survive without it, preferably when the plant is still small enough to sustain no damage when you lift the can.

Years ago, we used cans to hold water next to the plant. We would carry water and fill each can. This may be a solution when circumstances require it.

Cardboard tubes

Tubes from toilet paper or paper towel rolls can be used to make cutworm collars. Cut the toilet paper tubes in half to get two collars or the paper towel tubes into 2- to 2½-inch lengths. To use at transplanting time, slip the tube carefully over the seedling and push the tube over the root about an inch. When you put the plant in the ground, the tube should be half above the ground and half below, which will prevent the cutworm from chewing the stem. You may have to put some soil inside the tube to stabilize the plant. I use these on all my cole crops, as the cutworms seem to be very active at transplanting time.

Newspapers

As long as they don't have toxic ink, newspapers can be used for a couple of things. You can make your own pots from newspapers without the gadget sold for the purpose. Use an empty tomato soup (2½-inch diameter pot) can or can of whatever size of pot you want.

1. For a 2-inch high 2½-inch diameter pot, cut a strip of newspaper 4 inches by 24 inches. Wrap it around the can with 2 inches extending beyond the open end.
2. Fold the hangover part over the can toward the inside so the paper is just inside the can, not pushed against the inside walls.
3. Remove the can.
4. Turn the can and reinsert the solid end of the can into the paper pot.
5. Push the bottom flat onto a counter top.

You should have a paper pot in which you can plant seeds or a seedling. With practice, making them will become easy. The pot can be set into the ground without disturbing the plant roots and will decompose faster than a peat pot. These work especially well for crops such as cucumbers, squash, and okra that I sprout indoors just to avoid inclement weather and plan to set out in the garden as soon as they get their first true leaves.

Newspapers can be laid down for weed-blocking mulch. To keep them from blowing off, you will have to secure the newspapers with some organic material. Shredded newspapers can also be used as a mulching or composting material.

Wire hangers

Wire clothes hangers can be cut to do the job of landscape staples at a fraction of the cost. Just snip off each shoulder about five inches from the point. If you make an angle cut, it will go through whatever you are tacking down easier. Plastic coated wire ones don't work as well, because the plastic can roll up as it separates from the metal. The staple can be bent somewhat as desired. Flat tops with somewhat parallel sides will reduce the tear in the fabric or whatever you are tacking. These staples also work great to keep those unruly soaker hoses in place; don't, however, pierce the hose.

Panty hose, nylons, jeans

Just using the legs of the panty hose, you can tie plants to stakes for support. You can use the whole leg or cut it into narrower strips. The stretchy hose will knot firmly, but be flexible enough for a little give, which in the wind could save the plant from snapping off. I find them handy for flowers, tomatoes, and newer grape vines. The weather is hard on them, so they will probably have to be removed after one season. To tie up a thorny plant like raspberries, it is better to use strips of denim cut from old blue jeans.

Nylon stockings, or the more common panty hose legs, can also be used as container bags to suspend manure or compost in a large bucket to make compost tea.

Sheer curtains

I was given some floor-length sheer curtains that I sewed together to make a row cover to protect my turnips, radishes, pac choi, and mesclun mix from flea beetles and root maggots in the spring and early summer. Either make the curtain large enough to amply allow for height and some anchoring, or make the plot small enough to accommodate the size of the curtain.

1. I drove two-foot stakes in the ground at intervals around the edge of my designated spot, plus put a corresponding row down the middle since I was running short rows crosswise.
2. Next I topped them with upended liter bottles with the tops cut off. This keeps the curtains from snagging.
3. Then I draped the curtains over the stakes, securing the sides and ends with a landscaping timber. Rebar will also work.

For the first time, we enjoyed turnips without maggots and pac choi without flea beetle holes in the leaves. The sheer lets in sun and rain. You just have to check periodically to see if any other critters, such as slugs, are feasting away under there.

Hoses

Hoses cost quite a bit, so I hate to just discard them when they become too worn out to deliver water properly. One of their secondhand uses came when we planted some new trees. First, a couple of feet from the tree, we put in the stakes or posts we would use to stake the new trees. Then we threaded a small rope through a short piece of hose, placed the hose part around the tree, and tied

Five gallon pickle bucket holds sand and carrots for storage.

the rope snugly to the post. The hose causes less damage to the tree trunk than does a rope or stake.

A regular garden hose is just heavy enough to hold down netting. I use a hose to go along the edge of the netting I put down to keep birds out of the strawberries and the bottom edge of netting I hung around a grapevine to keep my chickens from feasting on the unripe grapes.

I read about a fellow who used pieces of hose in his garden to simulate snakes to keep birds from digging up his just sprouted seeds. He found he had to move the "snakes" each day to make the plan work. This I haven't tried, but will if I ever have trouble with neighborhood crows in my corn patch.

Buckets

I, like most rural folks, find a use for all the buckets that come my way and even ask for them at restaurants, which sometimes give away the five-gallon variety. Smaller buckets may come with products like soap or ice cream.

Buckets are great for carrying things like produce, rocks, weeds, compost, or water. They are just as handy for storing things such as carrots in sand in the cellar. And they work great as a container in which to make manure or compost tea. The smaller buckets, around a gallon, can be used as berry buckets. Thread a belt through the handle and buckle it around the waist or hips to free your hands for picking from trees or taller bushes.

Old ironing boards

An old ironing board with a mesh grill top can be used as a portable potting bench. Set it up wherever you like and the soil will fall through. The ironing board can also be rigged into a seed-starting bench. The seed trays go on top, and a lamp with a warm light bulb is situated under the board.

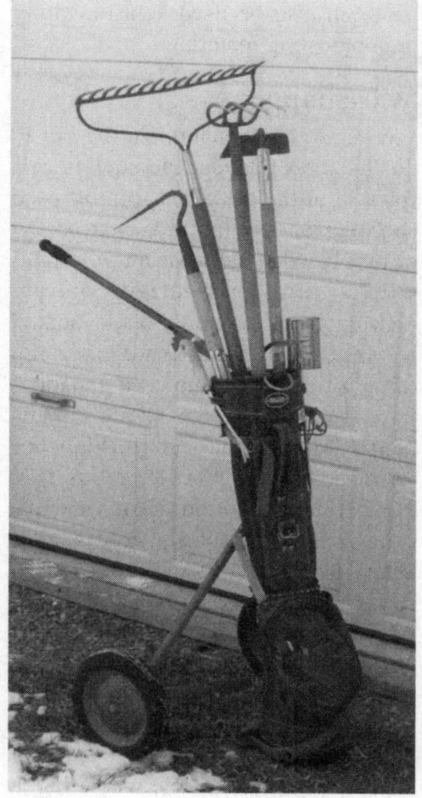

Garden tool cart

You want to keep the seeds just warm enough to sprout.

Golf bags and carts

I am not a golfer, but I have a golf bag and cart that is now a garden tool caddy. It cost me about $3 at a garage sale. The bag holds hoes, a shovel, a rake, a cultivating tool, and a trowel. Various pockets on the bag work for seed packets, string, and other small items. I can just grab the cart and wheel it to where I am working. It saves me running back to the garage for a different tool. I know where they are, and I seldom forget them in the garden any more.

Miscellaneous

Other odds and ends that I put to use include film canisters and pill bottles, which serve as storage containers for seeds that I am saving. I always label the container with the name and date.

Those small scoops that are packed in some powdered goods like laundry detergent and powdered drinks work very well for measuring concentrated pesticides and fertilizers. I just take a regular measuring spoon and use water to find the levels I need. Then I use a permanent marker to mark the line and amount on the outside of the scoop. To use, fill with concentrate to the appropriate level. I can have a separate scoop for each liquid and not worry about contamination.

When I don't have enough waterproof flats to set my pots or seed trays in, I use Styrofoam food trays and old baking pans. They aren't quite as nice, but do work.

Another item I found handy in the garden is the paper chicken feed sacks. These work extremely well for things I don't want to compost, so I bag them for the landfill. Rose bush prunings, diseased plants or shrubs, and noxious weeds about to seed are some of the things that I end up bagging this way. Feed bags are much sturdier than plastic bags.

There are so many items for which you can find a second life. For example, I didn't elaborate on the use of those pint and quart plastic containers that yogurt, sour cream, and cottage cheese come in. They make super freezer containers to store the harvest in. With a little imagination, you will think of other uses for items that are generally thrown away. You may find that you don't tell people what you are going to use some of these cast off items for; they'll think it is such a good idea that they'll be less willing to part with them.

Some of the recyclables I have mentioned can be used indefinitely, while others will last only a season. Some will get cruddy and then you can take them to recycling or the landfill. The paper products will disappear into the soil. For sure, you will have saved the landfill some by reusing, and it costs nothing to do it. Δ

Ask Jackie

If you have a question about rural living, send it in to Jackie Clay and she'll try to answer it. Address your letter to Ask Jackie, PO Box 712, Gold Beach, OR 97444. Questions will only be answered in this column. — Editor

Processing cabbage

I was reading your recipe for canning cabbage, and I am wondering, you say to process the jars for 60 minutes at 10 pounds of pressure. Now my question is are you using a pressure canner or hot water bath? And do you really mean to process for 60 minutes at 10 lbs. pressure? I'm questioning the 60 minutes.

Rozie Smith
Clarkfield, Minnesota

Yes, you must pressure can cabbage, as it is a low acid food, as are all vegetables (except tomatoes which really aren't a vegetable but a fruit…). I have two quite recent canning books which discuss canning cabbage, which isn't USDA recommended because it gets stronger when you can it. One says to process quarts for thirty minutes, and the other 60 minutes. I try to err on the side of safety and I DO process my cabbage for 60 minutes. ***— Jackie***

Black bean soup

I have searched the web for recipes for black bean soup and how to can it. While finding delicious recipes was easy, I have yet to find any ideas on how to can this tasty soup. Could you please give me some guidance on this?

Patricia Pittner
pittner@netwave2000.com

Stir up the ingredients of your soup. Boil for 30 minutes. Ladle hot soup into hot jars to within an inch of the top of the jar. Remove any air bubbles. Process quarts for 90 minutes at 10 pounds pressure unless you live at an altitude above 1,000 feet, then consult your canning manual for instructions on increasing your pressure to match your altitude. ***— Jackie***

Bubbles in tomatoes

I recently canned my garden tomatoes for the first time and for the most part it went smoothly. My only problem is that after processing (in a hot water bath), there are small air bubbles throughout some of the jars. I used a rubber spatula to get the bubbles out prior to processing, and they looked bubble-free then. My main concern is health; do I need to worry about bacteria?

Kristen Lindberg
Mamaroneck, New York

No, Kristen, you don't have to worry about small bubbles in your jars, as long as the jar is sealed properly. Press your finger on the center of each lid. (Don't do this until the jar is cooled.) When the jar is sealed, there is no give; it doesn't go down, then pop back up. If it's tight, your tomatoes are perfectly fine. The more you can, the more relaxed you'll be with it. ***— Jackie***

Canning chili with beans

I was wondering if I am able to pressure cook can chili with beans. I am only able to find recipes without beans.

Stephanie Faulks
Hilton, New York

Yes, you may home can chili with beans. I do it nearly every year, which gives us convenient, instant meals without the chemicals included in store-bought chili. Besides, mine tastes like chili, not some flavorless goopy paste.

Jackie Clay

Make up a big batch of your favorite chili, then ladle the hot chili into quart jars to within an inch of the top of the jar. Remove any air bubbles with a wooden spoon or spatula.

Process the chili in a pressure canner only, at 10 pounds pressure for 90 minutes. If you live at an altitude above 1,000 feet, consult your canning manual for instructions on increasing the pressure to correspond with your altitude. ***— Jackie***

Store-canned goods are good indefinitely

We have several cases of different vegetables that are getting close to their expiration date. Is it possible to cook these up as soups and then home can them? If so, do I hot bath can or pressure can? Would I have to cook the soup or could I just warm them and then process them? What would the expected shelf life be if stored properly? Once again thanks for everything, keep up the good work and may God continue to bless you and your family.

Steve Dunn
Batesville, Mississippi

I often cook up recipes from canned vegetables and tomato products that I get at outlet stores in number 10 cans on a great sale. This way I have quarts and pints to deal with at meal time, not gallon cans of hominy, tomato sauce, or whatever.

Don't can up recipes just because the cans have an expiration date on them. This is bogus and causes some people to actually throw away good food! Store-canned foods are like home-canned foods in this respect; once canned and properly stored, they are good almost indefinitely. True, they may lose a bit of their nutrition as this or that vitamin grows weak. But we make it up by eating plenty of home raised and wild foraged fresh food. And in a survival situation, having one can of food short of a vitamin sure beats the heck out of starving!

Yes, you can cook up soups and stews from any canned food, to re-can. You must use a pressure canner for every vegetable (except tomatoes which are a fruit....really). You must bring the food (soup or stew) up to boiling, then ladle out into hot jars. Cold or luke warm foods are not good enough. The more foods are cooked, though, the lower the nutrition.

— Jackie

Skim off the mold

I have filled a crock with cucumbers and the necessary vinegar and water and spices to make dill pickles. No mold has formed yet but my question is.... how necessary is it to skim the mold from the top? After I got them made, it occurred to me that we might be gone on a 10 day trip before they are ready to can and the mold will form on top.

Laurel Roberts
Portland, Oregon

It is quite important to skim the mold from the top of the crock as the cucumbers pickle. If you don't, you risk the pickles picking up a moldy taste and possibly spoiling. Perhaps a friend or relative would be willing to come over to your house and skim your crock periodically if you must be gone. (I'd offer them a few jars of finished pickles as a bribe!)

— Jackie

Roasting hazelnuts

Jackie, help please. A friend has these hazelnuts and we do not know if we should roast them and if so, how. Are they roasted in the shell or what?

Wilma Boulter
Vernon, B.C., Canada

To roast hazelnuts, crack the nuts and spread the meats out in a single layer on a cookie sheet. Using your lowest oven setting (usually 250 degrees), toast the nuts, stirring them a couple of times to avoid scorching. When they taste great (half the fun of roasting them), they are done. From here you can either freeze them, use them soon, or can them in half pint or pint jars. Use no liquid in the jars. Pack the hot nut meats in hot, sterile jars and place hot, previously simmered lids, which are dry, on the jars and screw down the rings firmly tight. Process in a pressure canner at 5 pounds pressure for 10 minutes. They will stay nice, without becoming rancid, for a long time.

You can also water bath can them by processing the nut meats for 30 minutes. ***— Jackie***

Slip from flowering crab tree will seldom root

How do I take a slip of a flowering crab tree and what time of the year do I do it and does a flowering crab tree have long thorns on it, or I may be getting it mixed up with a hawthorn.

Donna Macpherson
Cape Breton, Novia Scotia

A slip from a flowering crab tree will seldom root. You may, however, graft the scion onto the rootstock of another crab apple tree, flowering or not. I would go to the library and get a book that demonstrates grafting techniques, as it does take a bit of skill and knowledge for success. But it certainly can be easily learned by nearly anyone with the desire.

Once you get started, you'll want to graft a variety of trees, from nut to fruit trees. It's fun and gives you new trees at very little cost as you can often graft expensive stock onto common wild rootstock. ***— Jackie***

Vacuum packing peppers

I was wondering if you could tell me what is the best way to vacuum pack peppers from our garden and then freeze them. We'd like to use them later on in the winter to make homemade salsa. We have hot peppers, bell peppers, and sweet peppers that we are going to pick from our garden.

Karen Pyykola
Iron River, Wisconsin

With your chiles, roast them, seed them, and pack tightly to freeze. Other hot peppers, such as jalapenos and cherry peppers, simply slice, dice, and seed (or not if you like really hot peppers) and freeze. Your bell and other sweet peppers may be seeded, the stem removed and halved or diced, as you prefer before freezing. You do not have to blanch peppers before freezing. To keep them nicely separate in the bags, you can first freeze them in a single layer on a cookie sheet in the freezer, then pour into bags to vacuum pack and freeze.

— Jackie

Canning dry beans

Although I keep dry beans in my pantry, I would like to know how to can beans for those times when I am in a rush and don't have the time to spend hours cooking the dry beans so they are ready to add to chili or soup. I figure that since I can buy beans in a "tin" can at the store it should be possible using my pressure canner. Can you point me in the right direc-

tion? Also, do I need to worry about the beans becoming mushy by canning them in the pressure canner?

Lyn Ankelman
Thorsby, Alabama

You are absolutely right about the convenience of having canned beans in the pantry! And there are several ways to go here. Nearly all bean recipes may be home canned. For instance, I have in my own pantry canned baked beans, refried beans, bean soup and chili (three recipes), along with "plain" canned, previously dry beans of four varieties to be quickly used should the need or whim strike me.

And beans are really easy to put up too. Besides, it leaves them tender but not mushy. Like you said, too, it frees you from the soaking and long cooking when you are in a hurry or company drops by. Here's how to do simple canned dry beans.

Cover dry beans (or peas) with cold water and let stand over night in a cool place. Drain. Cover beans or peas with cold water two inches over the beans in a large saucepan. Bring to a boil and boil half an hour. Stir as needed. Dip out beans with slotted spoon and pack into hot canning jar to within an inch of the top. Add 1 tsp. salt to quart jars, ½ tsp. to pints, if desired. Ladle hot cooking liquid into jar to within an inch of the top. Remove any air bubbles with a small spatula or wooden stick. Wipe rim of jar clean. Place hot, previously simmered lid on jar and screw down ring firmly tight. Process pints 75 minutes, quarts 90 minutes in a pressure canner at 10 pounds pressure. If you live at an altitude above 1,000 feet, adjust the pressure to your altitude as recommended in your canning manual.

That's it. See how easy it was!

Most of your homemade bean recipes can likewise be home canned. Just keep the time the same, as beans (like meat) require a longer processing time to render safe to eat.

— Jackie

Drying garlic for long-term storage

How do you store garlic ... long-term storage.

Barbara Roer
Oak Park, Michigan

For really long term storage of garlic (and onions), the best is to dehydrate it. To do this, peel the cloves and slice them into pieces approximately ¼" thick. This may be simply slicing them in half or with larger cloves, you may end up with two or three slices. Spread them out onto your dehydrator tray or even a cookie sheet. If you have a dehydrator, dry them until they are hard and very dry. You may put your cookie sheet in the oven with only the pilot on, on a shelf over a wood stove, or even in the back of your car on a warm, sunny day until the slices are dry. Just protect from insects and dust and stir a bit to prevent sticking.

When they are dry, you can either store like that or do what I do. I have an old (salvaged from the dump) blender that I use for food processing alone. I pour in half a cup of dry slices, put a top on the blender and give it a whir. Repeat until you either have powder or coarser chunks, depending on your preference. This I dry a bit again, then store in sealed pint jars. This will keep for years provided you get the slices dry. If you don't, it will mold. ***— Jackie***

Home canning apple pie filling

I was wondering if it is possible to home can apple pie filling, and not just plain apples.

I have instructions for freezing it, but not for canning, and I have four canning books.

Also in the latest issue of Backwoods Home you said that you would be willing to send a few of your Hopi Pale Grey seeds to readers. Would you please send me a few, if you have any left, as I'm sure you've been flooded with requests.

Lee Robertson,
Webberville, Michigan

Yes, you may home can apple pie filling. Here's one recipe; you can adjust the spices to suit your taste.

12 pounds firm apples
4 cups sugar
½ cup flour
3 tsp. cinnamon
½ tsp. nutmeg
4 Tbsp. lemon juice

Peel and slice the apples. Stir in sugar, flour, and spices. When juice is making the mixture wet, stir in lemon juice and cook over a medium heat until it thickens, stirring frequently. Ladle pie filling into hot quart jars to within half an inch of the top. Wipe the rim clean. Place hot, previously simmered lid on jar and screw down ring firmly tight. Process in water bath canner for 30 minutes.

Experts today do not recommend canning this as it does contain some flour, making it remotely possible to support Botulinum bacteria which causes toxins. I have used this recipe in the past and it turned out fine. But I must add this caution or have the experts eat me alive. ***— Jackie***

A problem using gasketless canner

For years I wanted a pressure canner. I researched on the web and felt that I wanted the top of the line All American gasketless canner. My husband bought one for my birthday in March. I had never pressure canned; however, I had watched a friend do it. My first and only attempt was with spinach from my garden. I had water bath canned for years so filling the jars was no problem. When I tried to bring the canner up to pressure there seemed to be a lot of steam escaping from the "seal." There are both a dial gauge and weight. I was never sure when the steam had "exhausted" enough. It seemed to take forever and I was afraid the canner would boil dry. As we are at 3000 feet, I used the weight on 15 lbs. The dial never read higher than 12 pounds and I was never sure how much the weight should rock back and forth. I was really disappointed and seven months later I am afraid to eat the spinach or do any more canning. I really want to be successful but no one I know has a gasketless canner. I'm beginning to wish I had bought a cheaper one with a gasket. Can you help me?

Theresa Bailey
Boise, Idaho

This is not normal. Either there is a defect in the canner (unlikely) or you didn't have the lid down tight enough to the body of the canner. With your canner, you received a warrantee card and instruction booklet with a consumer helpline number. Don't be shy about calling the company. They want you to be happy with your new canner and can help you solve your problem. If your canner didn't have a number or at least an address to contact, go back to your store and ask for one. There IS help.

I have used a gasketless canner for over 30 years now and have had absolutely no problem with it. Any new endeavor is a bit frightening, but keep at it and you'll succeed.

You can also take your canner to your home extension office (usually located in the courthouse) and have them help you get started. I would call ahead to make sure someone knowledgeable is there when you arrive. This service is also free.

— Jackie

Using powdered buttermilk

I was wondering about powdered buttermilk that I recently saw in the grocery store. I don't drink milk so I never have it around, but I do like to bake, though not enough to use even a half gallon of milk or buttermilk up before it goes bad (I live alone too). I've never been happy with baking results from powdered milk; would the powdered buttermilk be better? Any tips for using it? Any suggestions for a good source? What I noticed at the store seemed to have a half inch of dust on top.

Carmen Hildebrand,
Fort Collins, Colorado

I've never had much of a problem using powdered milk, Carmen. Of course, fresh from the cow or goat is always best. I use buttermilk in a lot of recipes, although, like milk, I prefer fresh. Powdered buttermilk is nice and adds a nice rich taste to pancakes, biscuits, and many other things. You can get fresh powdered buttermilk in any large chain store, then if you wish you can freeze half of it to keep it the very freshest. But it does keep very well on your shelf for a long time.

— Jackie

Making attar from rose hips is no easy task

I recently moved into a country house that has a dozen old and very large rosebushes. Can you tell me how (or if) I can make attar from rose hips?

Stephen Botts
Burlington, North Carolina

You make attar from fragrant rose petals. And it's a long process for a very little attar. (This is the oily substance from which rose fragrance is obtained for the finest perfumes.) It takes 4-5 pounds of rose petals for an ounce of attar! And do you know how many petals there are in even one pound? You can't just dump in the whole rose flower, either; it must be petals only.

To make the attar, place your rose petals in a large glass bowl and add enough fresh water to barely cover them. Place in a sunny spot for a week until a yellowish scum floats on the surface. This is attar. Carefully skim it up with a small spoon and deposit in a small jar. It won't be much, but it will be precious.

— Jackie

Vacuum sealing seeds?

Can you vacuum seal vegetable seeds so they can be stored for a longer period of time and remain viable?

Kandis Armstrong
Colorado Springs, Colorado

I've done a little experimenting on this and I don't find that the seeds stay viable any longer than seeds that are simply put into dry, airtight jars. Most seeds, such as corn, peas, beans, squash, pumpkins, broccoli, cabbage, radish, etc. remain healthy for years under optimum storage. I once planted six beans that had come from a clay pot in an Indian ruin. The pot of beans had been carbon dated back 1,500 years! Five of the six beans germinated and grew well. Seeds store much longer than most folks give them credit for lasting.

Small seeds with thin coats, such as celery, onion, and carrot tend to last shorter storage times, but I still had carrot seeds last year that were 10 years old. I planted them in a row thickly because I thought they might not germinate well because of their age. But then they came up like the hair on a dog and I had the miserable task of thinning carrots. And that's a job I hate. I can't stand to throw away plants. **— Jackie**

MONSTER QUAKE!

It won't be in California ... but in the American heartland!

By John Silveira

Where's the scariest place to be in the lower 48 states if you're concerned about a massive earthquake that could snuff out you and everything around you in a few moments of violent shaking? Hint: It's not California!

It's in what is called the New Madrid seismic zone (NMSZ), which is in the central United States. Never heard of it? Most people haven't. The NMSZ is right in the heart of America. It weaves its way through five states: Arkansas, Tennessee, Missouri, Kentucky, and Illinois. It crosses under the Mississippi River in at least three places and beneath the Ohio River in two.

Though largely unknown to most of the world, every once in a while it stirs and reminds people it's there. Otherwise, we rarely think about it. The last earthquake of significance to take place in the NMSZ, an estimated 6.8 on the Richter scale, occurred in 1895 and is known as the Charleston, Missouri, earthquake.

But according to the United States Geological Survey (USGS), in the winter of 1811-12 at least three of the four biggest recorded earthquakes to take place in the lower 48 took place there, dead in the American heartland.

No one knows exactly how big those quakes were. Despite all the science and technology available to us, it's difficult for two seismic stations to get the same measurements on an earthquake if it happens *today*, never mind trying to estimate how large earthquakes were that took place decades before there was any meaningful way to measure them. A century after San Francisco's 1906 earthquake, there's still no consensus as to how big that one was because it, too, occurred before the first modern seismographs were built. Most estimates put it at around 7.8 while others say it *may* have been as large as an 8.25.

But many seismologists are sure that three and perhaps as many as five 8.0 or bigger earthquakes took place in the NMSZ during the winter of 1811-12. And they took place in just over seven weeks. Jared Brooks, who lived in Louisville, Kentucky, when the quakes occurred, recorded that from December 16, 1811 to March 15, 1812, he counted 1,874 shocks, eight of which were violent, 10 very severe, and 35 that were moderate. There were other reports that at least 18 of the quakes, which on the modern Richter scale would doubtlessly be classed as 6.0s or greater, were felt all the way to the Atlantic Coast, some 600 miles away.

Most of these quakes took place in a span of less than 90 days. This many earthquakes, of such severity, over so short an interval of time, have not occurred at any other time in recorded history.

Though named for a Missouri town, the actual epicenters of the quakes were in northwestern Arkansas, very near the Missouri border. But since, in that day, the closest white settlement of note, and the largest between St. Louis and Natchez, was New Madrid, the New Madrid name was pinned on them and the whole area has become known as the New Madrid seismic zone.

To understand the danger the NMSZ poses today, you should know what happened during the earthquakes that took place there from December 1811 to March of 1812, because one of the best predictors of future quakes in any area are the past quakes that occurred there.

Quakes that rocked a continent

Two centuries ago there were only 20,000 to 30,000 people living in the quarter million square miles most severely affected by the quakes. If you need an appreciation of how large an area that is, it's about equal in size to the state of Texas today. However, the total area over which damage occurred was about one million square miles, roughly one third of today's lower 48 states, and the area over which the quakes were felt was twice that, or about two thirds of those states.

The first of the quakes came without warning just after 2 a.m. on December 16, 1811. People in New Madrid were rousted from their beds. Initially, they couldn't even stand up.

> Each year anywhere from 6 to 24 earthquakes of magnitude 7.0 or greater take place somewhere in the world, with an average of about 18. One of those is likely to be of magnitude 8.0 or greater.

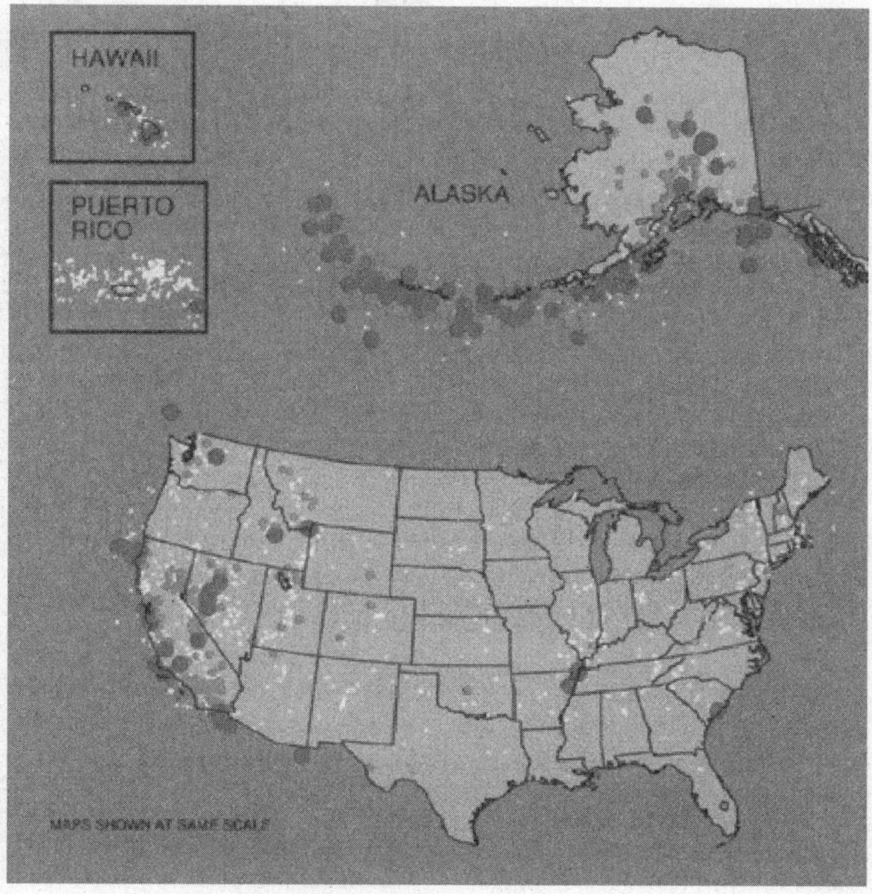

Earthquakes are a widespread hazard in the United States. Map shows magnitudes of historical earthquakes: dark, 5.5 to 7 or greater; light, 4.5 to 5.5. The U.S. Geological Survey operates instruments in many structures in the seismically active areas shown. These instruments measure how structures respond to earthquake shaking. (Photo courtesy USGS, http://quake.wr.usgs.gov/prepare/factsheets/SaferStructures/USEarthquakes.gif)

When they could, many ran from their houses.

Over an area of roughly 50,000 square miles (about equivalent to the size of the state of Alabama) the earth was uplifted in some places and sank in others. Seiches, which are like tsunamis, but on an inland body of water, rose from the Mississippi sinking boats before they raced inland. At many points the banks of the river collapsed. Parts of the river itself flowed backwards for several hours as the topography of the land beneath it was lifted as much as 25 feet in some places and sank by the same amount in others. Whole islands vanished and new ones were born. Even the river's course was permanently changed.

In other places, ponds and lakes disappeared, while a whole new 15,000-acre lake, 10 miles long and 3 miles wide, now called Reelfoot Lake, formed in Tennessee where there had been no lake before. In eastern Arkansas, Lake St. Francis, some 40 miles long and a half mile wide, was one of the many new lakes created.

The ground sank under the town of Big Prairie, in what is now the state of Arkansas, and a lake appeared in its place. Fifty miles to the north, people in the town of Little Prairie, Missouri, ran from their houses, then

An Eyewitness report

From the March 21, 1812 edition of the *Louisiana Gazette* (which was in St. Louis but was named for the Louisiana Territory which this section of the country was then called):

We are informed from a respectable source that the old road to the post of Arkansas, by Spring river, is entirely destroyed by the last violent shocks of earthquake. Chasms of great depth and considerable length cross the country in various directions, some swamps have become dry, others deep lakes, and in some places hills have disappeared.

watched as embers from damaged fireplaces and overturned stoves caught their homes on fire and burned most of the town to the ground.

The quakes continued off and on for hours, including one at dawn that was more fierce than the initial shock. Then, at around 11 a.m., an even bigger one hit.

For the next five weeks, there were one or more quakes a day. Over thousands of square miles eyewitnesses reported that during the largest of the quakes giant fissures opened and closed, sometimes spewing out water, sometimes sand, gas, or mud, and some even belched out carbonized wood before they abruptly closed up again. Some of the fissures were hundreds of feet long, 50 feet wide, and 25 feet deep. At least one was five miles long. Witnesses also reported that during the largest quakes they could actually see the ground roll in visible waves like water on the ocean.

In many places the alluvial soil, deposited over the centuries by the Mississippi, liquefied under the shaking and objects sunk into the earth like they were sitting on quicksand. Along the riverbanks entire settlements vanished into the water as the ground below them sank.

One eyewitness reported his wagon simply sank up to its axles on a dirt road that became unstable.

If widespread liquefaction were to take place in that area today, the ground in many places will behave like quicksand. Some buildings will slide off their foundations while others will simply topple over. For thousands of other buildings, sinking even a few feet will result in damage that may be best corrected by demolition.

Hundreds of square miles of forest were either toppled by the quakes or ruined because the soil was shaken from the roots of the trees. And land near the epicenter was so broken up that farming was impossible there for years.

Four hundred miles away, the quakes shook down chimneys in Cincinnati, and dislodged chimney bricks in Georgia and South Carolina. Seven hundred miles away, people in Washington, DC, were scared from their beds and ran into the streets. The quakes were felt strongly in Pennsylvania and they buckled sidewalks in Baltimore. And 1100 miles away they rang church bells in Boston.

At least three of the quakes were felt as far north as Canada and as far south as Mexico and Cuba, and east and west from the Atlantic seaboard to the Rocky Mountains.

World coming to an end

A little over five weeks later, on January 23, 1812, another huge one hit that was at least as big as those of December 16 and shook the continent again. The cycle of smaller daily quakes continued until another, an 8.0 monster, struck once more on February 7.

Lesser quakes, usually once a week but sometimes three or four times a day, continued over the next few years including two good jolts in the winter of 1815-16.

Though it ranks as one of the greatest earthquakes in history, there wasn't much property damage because there were so few people in that area in those days. There were deaths from the sinking of boats and landslides along the Mississippi River, but there was only one reported death in New Madrid itself.

Almost all the buildings there were log cabins, a type of architecture peculiarly suited to withstanding earthquakes. But the cabins did not stand for long. Damaged by the almost incessant quakes that seemed to follow, one after another, day after day, from the initial quake on December 16, through the rest of December, then through January and

An Eyewitness report

From the February 14, 1812 edition of the *Pittsburgh Gazette* this excerpt from an account by a Mr. James Fletcher, and dated January 21, was recorded. He provided eyewitness accounts of his own and others who saw fissures 8 to 10 feet wide and fountains of water that burst 12 feet into the air, the stench of sulphur filling the air, and small rivers and lakes that disappeared. The entire topography was changed, impeding travel. He wrote:

A gentleman attempting to pass from Cape Girardeau to the pass of St. Francis, found the earth so much cracked and broke, that it was impossible to get along. The course must be about 50 miles back of the Little Prairie. Others have experienced the same difficulty in getting along, and at times had to go miles out of their way to shun those chasms.

into early February, most of the cabins still standing collapsed. The last big one hit on February 7, but frequent aftershocks continued through mid-March, and sporadic aftershocks continued for another two years.

To those who lived through them, it seemed like the world was coming to an end. It's only because New Madrid was at the edge of the western frontier, and all of the states and territories that now make up America's Midwest were so thinly settled, that the quakes did not become a national disaster. If they happened again today, they would constitute the greatest disaster the United States has ever suffered. Greater than any of the great hurricanes, the great floods and fires, or any of the previous earthquakes. If it happened at the worst of times, when the Mississippi is at flood stage, it could be more destructive than *all* of the previous natural disasters combined. And here's the scary part: seismologists expect another monster there. They just don't know when it, or they, will happen.

What causes earthquakes?

Earthquakes were once thought to be the wrath of God, and Aristotle thought they were caused by winds beneath the earth's surface.

As late as the 19th century they were believed to be caused by volcanos—and sometimes they are. But today we know most earthquakes are caused because of the movement of the tectonic plates that float on the plastic layer of near-molten rock below the earth's surface.

Imagine the surface of the earth being like a soft boiled egg whose shell is rife with cracks. Some of the pieces of the shell are big while others are small. But unlike an egg, where the pieces stick to the egg, the earth's shell—the tectonic plates— floats on top of nearly molten rock deep inside the earth. In some places, the pieces float past each other like barges floating on a river, but in other places they crash head-on, with one trying to go under the other.

Earthquakes occur because all the plates, whether they're moving horizontally against each other or trying to move over and under each other, tend to "stick" along their edges. Meanwhile, the motion of the nearly molten rock beneath tries to keep them moving. When they're not moving the forces that are trying to propel them along start to accumulate. Eventually, those forces get so strong that something has to give, and the fault literally breaks, and when that energy is released, that's your earthquake. This is why some 90 percent of earthquakes take place at the edges of the plates.

However, earthquakes in the NMSZ occur in the middle of a plate, not at its edge. It's thought that these quakes are the result of faults created half a billion years ago when movements of the earth's crust tried to tear the North American plate apart. Now, new motions in the crust are compressing those ancient faults and creating the earthquakes we experience today.

A midwest quake today?

Today there are more than 11 million people living in the same quarter-million-square-mile area that suffered most severely during the quakes of 1811-12. They live in cities like Little Rock, St. Louis, Memphis, Nashville, Indianapolis, and Frankfort—all within the destructive range of a major NMSZ earthquake. And they also live in numerous smaller cities and towns, including many along the banks of the Mississippi. But in spite of the potential for calamity greater than the predicted consequences of an earthquake in California, the Midwest is unprepared for a major earthquake. Compared to California, the buildings are substandard.

According to the USGS, more earthquakes occur in the NMSZ than any other part of the United States east of the Rockies. Here are USGS estimates of seismic activity in the zone:

A quake of **4.0 or greater** occurs about every 18 months. These are usually felt but rarely cause much damage.

A quake of **5.0 or greater** occurs roughly once every 10 years. The larger of these can do considerable damage and are felt over several states.

A quake of **6.0 or greater** occurs about every 80 years. One of these will cause serious damage to masonry buildings and other buildings from St. Louis to Memphis. Estimates are that there is a 25 to 50 percent chance of one happening in the Mississippi Valley in the next 50 years. However, there are scientists who believe a quake this size is overdue and that the chances of a 6.0 or greater quake in the next 50 years exceeds 90 percent.

A quake of **7.5 or greater** occurs every 200 to 300 years, with the last one happening almost 200 years ago. There's as much as a 25 percent chance one will occur there in the next 40 years. It was a quake of this

Energy release and the Richter Scale

An increase of 1.0 on the Richter scale, e.g., from 5.0 to 6.0 or from 5.2 to 6.2 represents an increase in magnitude of 10. But the amount of energy released is actually about 31.6 times greater.

On that basis, going from 5.0 to 7.0 represents about 1,000 times more energy released and an increase of two-tenths on the scale, such as from 5.2 to 5.4 represents a doubling in the amount of energy released.

Saturated soils are soils in which the space between individual particles is completely filled with water. Much of the soil in the Mississippi Valley is saturated. Normally, such soil can support the weight of buildings, bridges, roads, dams, hillsides, etc., that rest on it. However, intense shaking from an earthquake can cause the water pressure in the soil to increase until the soil particles can move readily with respect to each other. This is called "liquefaction" and, when it occurs, the ability of the soil to support anything resting on it decreases. Buildings and bridges begin to sink into the ground or they can slide and even topple. In the photo are apartment buildings in Niigata, Japan, that toppled as the result of liquefaction of the soil beneath them during a magnitude-7.5 earthquake in 1964. Remarkably, only 28 people died. Liquefaction can also cause soil around dams to give way leading to dam collapses and flooding. It can destroy roads and airports. (Photo courtesy National Geophysical Data Center.)

magnitude that leveled much of San Francisco in 1906.

If a quake of 7.5 or greater occurs in the NMSZ today it will be felt over one half to two thirds of the lower 48 states and cause damage in 20 states. In quakes of this magnitude, ground acceleration will be so great you won't even be able to stand on your feet until it's over. The damage will be extensive.

What will the death rate and damage rates be during such a large earthquake today? It depends on how close the epicenter is, but one study concerning a major earthquake near St. Louis put the estimated number of dead as high as 4,300, with at least another 65,000 injured. More than 179,000 homes will be destroyed, one million households left without water service, and 500 highway and railroad bridges destroyed.

A quake of **8.0 or greater**, which is the size of the largest of the earthquakes of 1811-12, occurs on the average about every 400 to 1100 years. When they happen again, we can expect repeats of the phenomena that accompanied the quakes of two centuries ago. That is, fissures opening and closing in the ground, liquefaction of the soil, sinking of vast areas of ground in some places that will result in flooding, and huge areas rising at other places. Expect seiches on the river that will look and act like tsunamis.

There is evidence in the geologic record that there have been earthquakes of this magnitude in the NMSZ many times in the past. Seismologists currently feel there's a 7-10 percent chance of an earthquake this large happening in *any* given 50-year period.

Even more bad news

Additionally, earthquakes in the center of the country have an inherently greater range over which they create damage. A quake in the NMSZ will wreak its havoc over 20 times the area of a typical California quake. The reason for this is in the underlying geology of the two areas. The shock waves beneath California are more readily absorbed by the earth while those in the Midwestern states will travel further without losing energy. (*See map on the next page.*)

If a big one (7.5 or greater) does hit the NMSZ, there will be enormous damage and chaos. For example:

- Impassable roads, destroyed railway beds, river bridges gone, highway overpasses fallen
- Gas stations closed with no deliveries for awhile
- Airports closed with damaged runways
- River traffic halted with piers on the Mississippi and possibly the Ohio River destroyed
- Fires from gas and oil pipeline leaks
- Fires everywhere with emergency services taxed to the breaking point
- Water service and electricity interrupted, especially in the cities

The first seismograph, the device used to measure earthquakes, was built in Japan in the 1880s — by three Englishmen who worked at the Imperial College in Tokyo.

- Most stores closed or unable to restock their shelves
- Medical services stretched beyond the breaking point
- Hundreds or thousands killed, and tens or hundreds of thousands homeless
- Looting, much of it by people just trying to stay alive
- Lastly, no homeowners insurance to pick up the tab for damages when it's over. **Most homeowner's policies do not cover earthquake damage.** If you want coverage, you'll have to have it added on now.

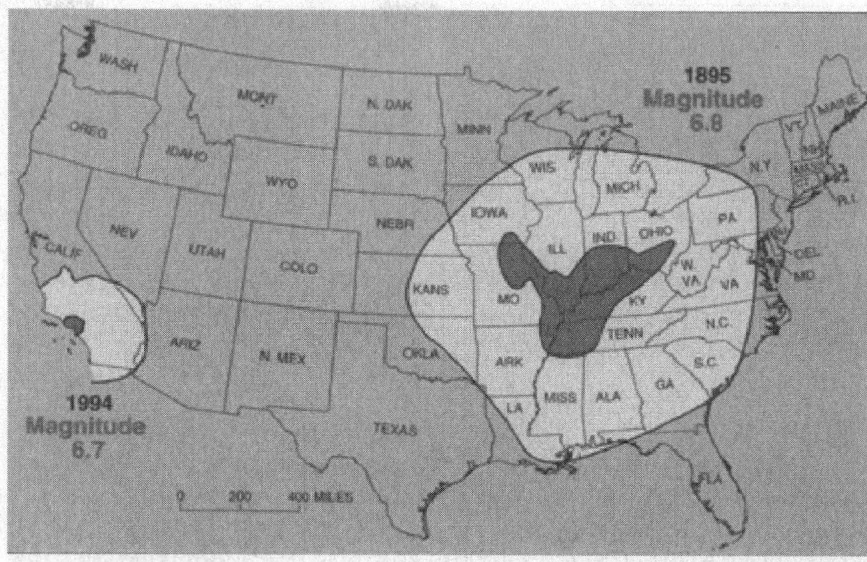

The map shows the contrast in how far ranging earthquakes are in the New Madrid seismic zone as compared to similar quakes on the West Coast. The Charleston, Missouri, quake of 1895 was similar in intensity to the Northridge, California quake of 1994, but the extent over which each of the earthquakes caused damage (dark) and over which each was felt (light) is vastly different. While the Northridge quake was felt in Nevada, Arizona, and parts of Mexico, the Charleston quake was felt over 23 states and parts of Canada. The area of damage in the New Madrid seismic zone will typically be 20 times greater than that of California because of the differences in the geology of the earth beneath the two areas. The 1811-12 New Madrid earthquakes were of even greater intensity than the 1895 quake and were felt over the entire United States east of the Rockies and well up into Canada. (Map from http://quake.wr.usgs.gov/prepare/factsheets/NewMadrid/)

If the quakes match the intensity of the 1811-12 events, and they come one after another, day after day, for several months, the problems listed above will be multiplied. If an epic quake or series of quakes hits when the Mississippi is at flood stage, levees all along the river might be destroyed. In this case the flooding will be catastrophic and as much as a quarter of Arkansas could be under water. If this happens, some predict the loss of life could go over 100,000. The economic damage will be unimaginable.

Government help?

The Federal Emergency Management Agency (FEMA) had been perceived as the first line of defense in the event of a disaster. But that agency couldn't properly respond to Hurricane Katrina even though it had days of advanced warning. Try to imagine how it will respond when there is no warning and the devastation and loss of life may be 10 to 100 times worse.

Today, to its credit, FEMA has announced that it has *no* assets. That is, it's without evacuation vehicles, emergency supplies, or medical help. What FEMA is is a coordinating agency. What this means to you is that for all practical purposes *all* practical help will be local and the first line of defense will be *you*.

And don't expect the government to pick up the tab when it's over. After any major disaster, there may be federal loans available, but that's all they'll be, loans. There may be some grant money, but it will be only to meet your basic needs, not to replace your belongings. You're better off looking into insurance coverage.

However, it's hoped that research, an increase in the public's awareness of the dangers the NMSZ poses, and better emergency preparedness can substantially decrease the losses expected to accompany a major earthquake in the central states.

To this end, in 1983 the Central United States Earthquake Consortium (CUSEC) was formed by the states of Alabama, Arkansas, Illinois, Indiana, Kentucky, Mississippi, Missouri, and Tennessee. The purpose of CUSEC is to deal with earthquake preparedness and foster study of the New Madrid seismic zone.

Their site is one of the best places to begin earthquake preparation even if you live in other earthquake-prone zones. It is one of the best earthquake preparation sites on the Web. If you don't have access to the Internet, go to your local library and check their site out.

> How close you are to the epicenter of an earthquake will determine how you feel it. If it's a rolling motion, you're probably quite far away from it. If you feel it as a jolt —well, you're there.

Earthquakes and Alaska

It's easy, when we think of earthquakes, to think "California." To many California is the earthquake center of the world, though, in reality, it's not even the earthquake center of the United States. That dubious distinction belongs to Alaska.

According to the United States Geological Survey (USGS), Alaska experiences more earthquakes each year than *all* the other 49 states combined. It averages an earthquake of magnitude 7.0 or greater just about once a year. California, on the other hand, experiences a 7.0 or greater earthquake about every 12 years or so (though there were four of them in the '90s).

Alaska also experiences bigger earthquakes. Some of the biggest in the world take place there. There were eight of magnitude 8.0 or greater, in Alaska, between 1899 and 1969. In that same time, there were *none* in any of the other 49 states (with the possible exception of the 1906 San Francisco earthquake which may or may not have been an 8.0+; it depends on who's doing the estimating). But Alaska is so large and so scarcely populated that, other than being detected by seismographs, four of those 8.0-or-greater monsters went largely unnoticed by the rest of the world.

Also, during the 20th century, three of Alaska's earthquakes were among the eight largest to take place *anywhere* in the world.

So, if you live in America and earthquakes scare you, neither Alaska nor California are where you want to live. Florida and North Dakota, on the other hand, have the fewest. But you'll never entirely get away from earthquakes no matter where you go.

Will there be a warning?

Given the current state of seismology, it's highly unlikely we'll know when the next big one is going to hit. Unlike Hurricanes Katrina and Rita, there will be no anticipatory evacuation. Everyone will be caught with their pants down. And once it hits most traffic into and out of the most devastated areas will stop for days or even weeks. What supplies are available when the quake strikes will dwindle fast. Those who make no preparations will covet your cupboards, your fuel, and your Honda generator.

If you'll recall the bridge connecting Gretna, Louisiana, to New Orleans, where authorities would not allow refugees to cross, expect a lot more of that because there will be a lot more refugees. They will not be just the urban poor as were the majority with Hurricane Katrina. They'll also be people who currently have respectable standards of living: the dentist living down the street, the office manager next door, and the cop across the alley who will not be prepared, or who will lose everything when the quaking, fires, and flooding start.

What to do when the shaking starts

When an earthquake starts, if you're indoors, stay indoors. If you're outside, stay outside. Many people are injured or killed by falling debris—chimney, gutters, broken glass, walls, etc.—just outside of buildings.

If you're indoors, take cover underneath something sturdy like a desk. Stay away from windows, mirrors, and furniture that might fall over such as overloaded bookshelves, dressers, entertainment centers, etc.

If you're outside, stay away from walls, chimneys, power lines, and trees with dangerously heavy dead limbs. Wherever you are, protect your head.

After an earthquake

Wear shoes at all times.

First thing to do is check for injuries and account for everyone you possibly can. Provide first aid when necessary.

Turn off the gas. Check for gas leaks.

Check for electrical shorts in your house.

Check for downed power lines. Mark and avoid them, particularly those outside. Even dead lines can be a hazard if, for some reason, power comes back on. Turn the electricity off.

Look for plumbing, including sewage breaks.

Inspect building damage and potential problems that can occur when there are aftershocks.

Clean up dangerous spills. This is particularly important if you are storing heating oil.

Turn on your radio and listen for instructions.

Beware of aftershocks. Structure, already weakened by the first quake, will become major hazards. And aftershocks can even exceed the power of the first shocks.

If you are driving, pull over to the side of the road, stop, and set the parking brake. Do not stop on or under an overpass or bridge. Avoid power lines, signs, trees, and other things that might collapse or fall onto your vehicle. Stay inside until the shaking is over. If a power line falls on your vehicle, stay inside until a trained person removes the hazard.

A survival kit

You should have a survival kit for all kinds of emergencies. (*BHM* has run several excellent articles on this in past issues, and our *Emergency Preparedness and Survival Guide* has detailed instructions for kits.) Make sure any survival kit is accessible. After an earthquake, things are going to be a mess. Your kit(s) should be stored in easy to find locations. You should also know the following:

• Learn your building's dangerous areas: near windows, near shelves, near bookcases, etc. Never place heavy objects such as large pictures, TVs, etc., over beds, and you should try to keep any heavy objects, including large planters, lower than the head height of the shortest family members.

• Learn the main utility shutoffs.

• Learn your building's safe areas: inside corner of building, under *sturdy* furniture, in supported doorways.

• Heavy objects such as bookcases, entertainment centers, large dressers, mirrors, cabinets, filing cabinets, etc., should be anchored to the walls. Strap your water heater to wall studs.

• As with any emergency planning, have family emergency procedures, including plans for reuniting your family.

• Post emergency telephone numbers such as doctors, hospitals, 911, etc. and make sure family members are aware of where these numbers are kept.

• Personal protection? (*See sidebar on survival kits*). Experience with Katrina was that there was looting. The further you got away from metropolitan areas, the less there was. Armed people and those who banded together did best.

• If you already own a home go to the CUSEC website and see how to inspect it. Determine if it will stand up to an earthquake. If not, and you can either afford it or you have the ability to bring it up to "earthquake code" yourself, do so. Otherwise, consider selling it. If you're in the market to buy, I'd make an earthquake inspection a criteria while selecting a place. If you're building, build with the idea that you want the roof over your head to stay where it is when the big one hits.

• Last, if you're in a seismically active zone, neither buy nor build in flood zones.

No one knows when the next earthquake or series of quakes will occur in the NMSZ or anywhere else, but history shows us that those who are prepared will fare much better than those who rely on others to help them in the aftermath. Δ

The last word

The National Animal Identification System is the bureaucrats' latest grab for power

You've always got to be on your toes these days to keep the government from making a grab for ever more power over our personal lives. And very often the power grab goes hand-in-hand with a deal the government has made with big business. They always claim it's about protecting "us." Ha, Ha! What a joke!

The latest grab for power in order to protect "us" is called the National Animal Identification System (NAIS). It's a system proposed by agribusiness and embraced by the United States Department of Agriculture (USDA) to track livestock in this country. It's supposed to help keep terrorists from intentionally infecting our food supply, and also protect us from things like avian flu, mad cow disease, and whatever else they can think of as an excuse to implement it by the target date of January, 2009—or earlier if they can continue on the fast track they are on now.

Here's how NAIS will operate. On the individual level, your home (including your name, address, telephone number, and Global Positioning Satellite coordinates) will have to be registered with the Government. Your livestock—every fish, fowl, cow, hog, sheep, pigeon, etc.—will have to be registered. Your animals may have to be electronically tagged so they can be tracked by satellite. They may also have to have blood drawn so they can be identified by their DNA. They may even have to have retinal scans. Agribusinesses, promoters of the system, will have it easier than the individual: they'll register their stock in lots, i.e, one entry covers a herd.

Who pays for all of this? The family raising a pig, cow, or flock of laying hens for its own consumption must absorb the cost of compliance themselves. Agribusiness gets to pass their costs on to the consumer.

The NAIS is also meant to increase exports, something important to agribusiness, but not so important to small farmers, homesteaders, or people like you and me. Will it actually improve agribusiness exports? Probably not. What will do that will be examining animals as they are slaughtered and going to market, like the Europeans and Japanese already do with a system they have perfected. It protects the public. If protection of the public is required, the European and Japanese systems have already shown us how to do it. The NAIS is just a power grab by big Government.

Government bureaucrats like to portray themselves as capable organizations that can ride to the rescue of ordinary folks like us in an emergency, like FEMA did—or, actually, didn't—during Hurricanes Katrina and Rita. The "national herd" concept the USDA now embraces does not bode well for those who like freedom.

The NAIS will also turn your veterinarian into a spy. He will be required to report you if you are not in compliance. And what if you do fail to comply? Enforcing compliance is one of the things not spelled out in detail yet. It's a bitter enough pill—the intrusions into our lives, the cost, the corporate welfare—without discussing penalties that will make it more difficult for average Americans to swallow. But expect enforcement to be the way bureaucrats always enforce laws: with threats of hefty fines, imprisonment, and seizure of your property. And, if cited, don't expect to be brought before a jury of your neighbors. Your freedoms will become subject to the discretion of bureaucratic tribunals, similar to the IRS courts, the DMV, zoning boards, etc.

Who actually stands to benefit from this program? Not the public. It will be agribusinesses and the high-tech companies that will provide the tracking and identification systems that will be mandated. I'm not antibusiness, but I am anti-business-in-bed-with-government. Businesses, whether they're multibillion dollar corporations or a mom-and-pop operation with a farm or laundromat, should prosper—or die—based on their ability to provide a product or service the public wants. They should not prosper because they've received government handouts or favors. NAIS is out and out welfare of the worst kind. It is a program to benefit large corporations and to expand bureaucratic power.

Who loses with NAIS? The consumer, the small farmer, the family who wants to raise a few organic hens for eggs, even the 4-H kids—yeah, even 4-H'ers will have to comply. And by increasing the burden on the small producer, the NAIS will help destroy the small producer's market, even when that market is a single family.

NAIS is not a program that was proposed by consumer groups or voters. It wasn't even run through Congress. It is, pure and simple, a naked attempt to profit and increase power on the part of both corporations and bureaucrats at the expense of small farmers and the public. It will be run by agribusiness and it will be agribusiness who makes the decisions as to what happens to small farmers and the consumers. You will not have a say.

The USDA, agribusinesses, and the tech companies involved in creating the hardware and software for this tracking system are trying to move fast on this. For them, the windfalls will be enormous, whether it's expansion of bureaucratic power or big bucks. They have much to gain by forcing it through. The small farmer, the rural family, and the consumer have much to lose.

There's still time to stop this. Call, e-mail, or write your congressman and governor to protest it. You can usually find their addresses and phone numbers in your local newspaper. Or on the Web you can go to: www.house.gov/, www.senate.gov/, or www.lib.umich.edu/govdocs/govemail.html.

Let's not let Government cancel our individual freedoms with phony programs like NAIS. **— John Silveira**

May/June 2006
Issue #99
$4.95 US
$6.50 CAN

Backwoods Home magazine

practical ideas for self-reliant living

Walden Pond
the solar version

Developing water sources
Gardening tips
Summer vegetables
Heart healthy recipes
Cold-hardy grapevines

www.backwoodshome.com

DON CHILDERS

Summer's silent heat waves —

they are deadlier than nearly all other disasters combined

By John Silveira

We all look forward to summer weather and the freedom it gives us to engage in healthy, fun outdoor activities. So it is at the risk of being labeled a doomsayer and party pooper that I point out that summer is host to the most deadly of all natural disasters — the heat wave. I see you shaking your head right now and on the verge of tossing this article aside as being unnecessarily alarmist, but read on if you want to learn about a natural phenomenon that outshines (if you'll pardon the expression) all the blizzards, tornadoes, floods, and earthquakes of the year combined.

A heat wave doesn't arrive in your neighborhood with all the sound and fury of these other ferocious storms. There is no dramatic footage on the 11 o'clock news of ruined buildings, toppled trees, or frozen deadlocked cities. It moves in slowly and silently, then just sits over an area—mute, invisible, and deadly.

In the 20-year period from 1979 to 1998, heat waves killed more Americans than hurricanes, tornadoes, earthquakes, floods, and lightning combined. With other natural disasters throughout the 20th century, the number of fatalities has generally decreased, but with heat waves the number has steadily risen. And while most other natural disasters last minutes, such as an earthquake or tornado, or pass in several hours, such as with a hurricane, heat waves last anywhere from several days to several weeks.

Some deadly heat waves from the past

Heat waves are typically underreported. What follows is just a partial list of major heat waves in the United States since 1955.

- In 1955 an eight-day heat wave killed almost 1000 people in Los Angeles.
- In 1966 246 people died because of a heat wave in St. Louis.
- In 1972 almost 900 people died as the result of a two-week heat wave in New York City.
- It is difficult to assess how many people died as a result of the heat wave that affected the Midwest in 1980. Estimates are that between 1,250 and 10,000 people died, and agricultural damage due to crop losses has been placed at $44 billion.
- In 1984 New York City saw a 35 percent rise in mortality during a heat wave, with the largest part of that increase among the elderly.
- During an 11-day heat wave in 1993, nearly 120 people died in Philadelphia.
- In 1995 there were 739 deaths attributed to a heat wave in Chicago, another 91 in Milwaukee, and more yet in other parts of the Midwest. According to Eric Klineberg, in his book, *Heat Wave: A Social Autopsy of Disaster in Chicago*, the Cook County morgue has 222 bays for bodies and typically receives about 17 per day. But three days into the heat wave of July 1995, all 222 bays were filled and there were still hundreds of bodies unstored.

During that same period, Philadelphia experienced a heat wave that lasted only two days. Yet, at least 72 deaths were attributed to it.

It's difficult to say how many deaths, during any heat wave, are attributable to the heat wave itself. People are dying everyday, and it would be easy to claim every death was caused by the heat—or that none were. The trick is to separate out the excess deaths by figuring out the average number of deaths that usually occur at that time of year and subtract that from the number that occurred during the heat wave. It is one of the ways those who figure these statistics out try to arrive at figures. After doing that, we have evidence of at least 700 deaths in Chicago, from July 11 to July 27, that were heat wave-related.

In other parts of the world the picture is even grimmer. In August of 2003, a heat wave settled on Europe killing an estimated 35,000 people including almost 15,000 in France, 7,000 in Germany, more than 4,000 each in Italy and Spain, 2,100 in Portugal, 2,000 in the United Kingdom, and 1,400 in the Netherlands.

In India it is not uncommon to lose thousands every year to heat waves.

It would seem as though heat waves should occur in those parts of the country where it gets the hottest. In general, they don't. They happen where it gets both hot *and* humid. They are also more likely to happen in urban areas than in rural areas. Urban areas have a greater amount of heat-absorbing roofs and pavement than they do cooling vegetation. These turn cities into heat islands that are as much as 10°F hotter than the surrounding countryside. Rural areas are also more likely to cool off at night while the buildings and pavement in the cities stay warm.

The combination of heat and air pollution makes heat waves even more dangerous in cities. Pollutants accumulate as the hot stagnant air over the city refuses to move, thereby adding to the distress of those already suffering from respiratory ailments.

Oral rehydration recipe

Sports drinks are fine for rehydration. They'll generally contain the salts or electrolytes needed to replace those lost during severe sweating and even dehydration brought on by excessive vomiting or diarrhea. However, they'll often be light on those salts because the salts make the drink taste lousy.

This is a recipe you can make with ingredients that, with the exception of the salt substitute (potassium chloride), are commonly found around the house. You can find the salt substitute with the "real" salt at your grocer's. Morton's is one brand to look for. Otherwise, you can substitute four ounces of orange juice or a mashed-up banana.

1 quart water
½ tsp. baking soda
½ tsp. salt
3 to 4 Tbsp. sugar
¼ tsp. salt substitute

Drink in sips. If vomiting occurs, wait a few minutes and drink some more.

(This is also a good recipe for rehydrating someone dehydrated by diarrhea.)

Who dies?

According to the Centers for Disease Control (CDC), the most likely victim of a heat wave is one who is living alone, doesn't leave home on a daily or nearly daily basis, has no access to transportation, is sick or bedridden, has few (or more likely no) social contacts, and is without air-conditioning. The victim is also most likely to be male, elderly, and black.

Barring changes in how we deal with heat waves, as the elderly population of the United States grows, we can expect the number of deaths attributable to heat waves to rise.

Property damage

Like other natural disasters, heat waves are also capable of causing property damage. Roads can be damaged by excessive heat. Asphalt softens and concrete can break because of heat expansion. During the 1980 heat wave, hundreds of miles of roads in the Midwest buckled.

Given enough heat, even train rails can distort and power lines, because their metal cores expand with heat, can sag so far that they touch the ground and short out creating power failures.

Heat waves and droughts often occur together, and with the combination of water shortages and high temperatures, agricultural losses can be astronomical. Cattle, pigs, and rabbits don't fare well in extreme heat and, in some years, tens of millions of chickens die as a direct result of heat waves.

Crop losses can also be enormous at these times. Sometimes the losses are the result of heat wave-induced droughts. But often extreme heat alone, during key stages of a plant's development, can ruin a crop.

Besides direct damage, heat waves cause inconveniences that can sometimes have deadly consequences. As more and more people obtain and use air conditioners, the drain on power companies becomes greater and greater. As a result, during heat waves the electric grid is prone to failure. To prevent a catastrophic failure over an entire geographic area, power companies may have to institute "rolling blackouts" as a way to conserve and spread energy around. But this kind of conservation can leave many without air-conditioning at critical times.

In the meantime, in many urban areas, citizens open up hydrants to cool off, causing the water system to fail in many parts of the city. This can have tragic results during fires. And, when firefighters and city crews come out to shut the hydrants off again, urban citizens have been known to drive them off by hurling stones, bricks, bottles and whatever else they can find.

Things I learned (as a kid) to keep cool

When I was a little kid living in the Fulton Heights of Medford, Massachusetts, we didn't have air conditioning. I didn't even know it existed. When it got hot, that's all there was to it. Sometimes we'd go to Wright's Pond. But we couldn't go everyday.

One day I got it in my mind that I felt cooler when the wind blew over me. But the air was still. So I tried to make my own wind by running up and down the hill in front of our house. When I ran, I felt better, but every time I stopped to rest, I just felt hotter. So, I'd run some more. Finally, our elderly neighbor, Mrs. St. Armour, came out on her front step and asked me why I was running on such a hot day. I told her the wind I was making made me feel cooler. She looked at me funny and said, "Running makes you hotter." She didn't say why. But every time I stopped, I did notice I was hotter than ever.

The cellar: The heat went on for days. Finally, even I couldn't play anymore. I spent each day in a torpor. One day I was in the house and I had to get something from the cellar. I opened the kitchen door that led down to the basement and walked into a world I didn't even know existed, a world beneath our house where the air was cool. Now I could go outside, play like a maniac until I was ready to drop, then go into the cellar and cool off.

The cow trough: The next strategy for dealing with the heat that I learned as a kid was the cow trough. I went to live with my dad and, once again, the hot weather sunk in. We had the smallest, dankest cellar you could imagine at my dad's house. It was not a place a kid wanted to hang out. So, I didn't.

But our neighbor had a watering troughs for his cattle, and one day for some reason I can't remember I sunk my arms into the water. It felt so cool that I thought about climbing in the trough, but just waited and realized something was happening. I was beginning to get cool. I was feeling better. I couldn't believe that holding just my arms in the cool water was enough to cool my whole body off. It was another lesson learned and, to this day, when I'm hot I often run my arms under cold water until I cool off.

The foot basin: The next lesson came in my teens. It was a variation on the cow trough. I was living with my Mom, again. This time she owned a three-family house in a Boston suburb and we lived on the second floor. One extremely hot day it was almost as hot in the house as it was outside. Mom had the windows closed and the shades drawn to keep out the sunlight.

She was sitting at the kitchen table wearing a light dress while she was sewing. She was barefoot and her feet were in a large pan of water.

"What are you doing?" I asked.

She looked to where I was staring under the table.

"I'm keeping cool," she said.

"Does that work?"

"Yeah," she said. "But every once in a while I throw a few ice cubes in."

I nodded. I'd learned yet another way to keep cool in hot weather.

Heat waves can even disrupt air transportation. Because the air is thinner when it's hot, airplanes lose lift, and airports have been closed for this reason. The risk is that in the thinner air, planes taking off may not have enough runway to get airborne and, as a result, may crash.

Makeup of a heat wave

The physics of heat waves is fascinating — and necessary to understand how to keep from becoming a heat wave victim.

Heat waves aren't heat alone. They're a combination of heat and humidity. Humidity, the atmosphere's moisture content, both magnifies the way we *feel* heat and changes the way our bodies react to it. The higher the humidity, the hotter the temperature feels and the harder it is for our bodies to cope with it. One hundred degrees feels hotter on a humid day in Chicago than it feels on a dry day in Tucson.

To take into account this combination of heat plus humidity, the National Weather Service (NWS) has devised a scale called "apparent temperature" or the "heat index." The concept is similar to that of wind chill, but whereas wind chill is a combination of cold *and* wind, the heat index is a combination of heat *and* the humidity. And just as wind makes a cold day seem colder, humidity makes a hot day seem hotter.

Your body's reaction

When you're active, about three-quarters of the energy your body produces is converted to heat, not motion. But this heat can't be allowed to accumulate, else it will eventually damage your internal organs, particularly your brain, much as a high fever can. It is the job of a part of the brain, called the hypothalamus, to manage your body's temperature, particularly its core temperature, and keep it in a healthy range.

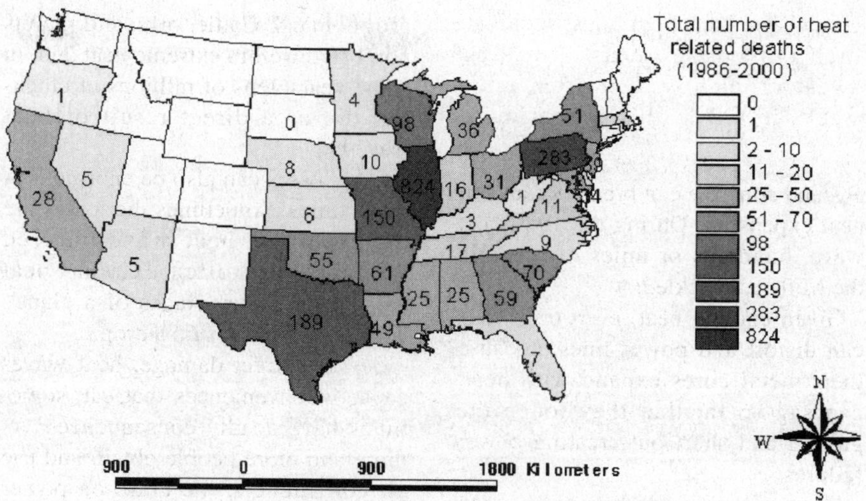

Heat wave-induced deaths in the United States from 1986 to 2000. Since there are no universally accepted reporting methods, this map may understate the number of deaths. But what should be apparent is that the greatest death tolls are not in the hottest states, like Arizona, New Mexico, and Nevada. They occur in the Midwest where the combination of heat and humidity are the worst. (Map courtesy of National Center for Atmospheric Research.)

As your body heats up, your hypothalamus directs blood vessels near the skin to expand. This carries blood away from the body's internal organs and to the skin. With it the blood carries the excess heat. Between sweating (the hypothalamus also governs how we sweat), radiation, and contact with the air around you, your skin will dissipate more than 90 percent of this excess heat.

(This is just the opposite of what your body does when faced with extreme cold. Then, your hypothalamus will instruct these same blood vessels to constrict, and blood, with its life-giving heat, is directed deeper into the body's core to keep the internal organs warm.)

The value of sweating, and heat acclimatization

On a cold or cool day, most of your body's heat is lost through convection. That is, the air flowing over your skin will carry the heat away. But on warmer days, when the air is close to or greater than your body's temperature, convection and radiation become very inefficient and your body will resort to sweating. For this, nature has equipped the average adult's body with some 2.6 million sweat glands. And the hotter your body gets, the more you will sweat.

Sweating itself does not cool you off, but sweat evaporating from your skin will. This is because the amount of energy required to turn sweat into water vapor—the *heat of vaporization*—is considerable. Every molecule of water evaporating off your body carries with it a great amount of *heat* energy.

The warmer the ambient temperature is, the faster your sweat will also evaporate. However, high humidity will impede the rate of evaporation and make it more difficult for sweating to cool you off. This is the reason you feel hotter on a humid day.

Wind will affect how your body cools. It will increase the rate of evaporation. However, if the wind is too hot it can add to your body's net gain in temperature.

If you haven't been in a hot environment in awhile, sweating will not come easy. Your body must acclimate itself to the heat. At first, it will not sweat efficiently. But after a few weeks it will learn to sweat more. Incredibly, during this time your production of sweat can increase as much as threefold.

Replacing lost salts and dealing with heat stroke

Sweating to cool off has a downside. As you sweat, you must replace

Heat Index	*General Effect of Heat Index on People in Higher Risk Groups*
80 to 89° - Caution	Fatigue possible with prolonged exposure and/or physical activity.
90 to 104° - Extreme Caution	Sunstroke, heat cramps and heat exhaustion possible with prolonged exposure and/or physical activity.
105 to 129° - Danger	Sunstroke, heat cramps or heat exhaustion likely, and heatstroke possible with prolonged exposure and/or physical activity.
130° or higher - Extreme Dangert	Heat/sunstroke highly likely with continued exposure.

Air Temp (in F)	Relative Humidity (in percent)																				
	0	5	10	15	20	25	30	35	40	45	50	55	60	65	70	75	80	85	90	95	100
140	125																				
135	120	128																			
130	117	122	131																		
125	111	116	123	131	141																
120	107	111	116	123	130	139	148														
115	103	107	111	115	120	127	135	143	151												
110	99	102	105	108	112	117	123	130	137	143	150										
105	95	97	100	102	105	109	113	118	123	129	135	142	149								
100	91	93	95	97	99	101	104	107	110	115	120	126	132	138	144						
95	87	88	90	91	93	94	96	98	101	104	107	110	114	119	124	130	136				
90	83	84	85	86	87	88	90	91	93	95	96	98	100	102	106	109	113	117	122		
85	78	79	80	81	82	83	84	85	86	87	88	89	90	91	93	95	97	99	102	105	108
80	73	74	75	76	77	77	78	79	79	80	81	81	82	83	85	86	86	87	88	89	91
75	69	69	70	71	72	72	73	73	74	74	75	75	76	76	77	77	78	78	79	79	80
70	64	64	65	65	66	66	67	67	68	68	69	69	70	70	70	70	71	71	71	71	72

Heat Index (Apparent Temperature) Chart

The Heat Index (HI) is the temperature the body feels when heat and humidity are combined. This chart shows the HI that corresponds to the actual air temperature and relative humidity. (Note: This chart is based on shady, light wind conditions. ***Exposure to direct sunlight can increase the HI by up to 15°F.****) As you can see, if the temperature is 95° in Chicago with 60% humidity, the "apparent temperature" is 114°—because of the humidity. On the other hand, if it's 100°F in Tucson with 15% humidity, it'll only feel like 97°. (Due to the nature of the HI calculation, the values may have an error of +/- 1.3F.) The NWS issues an excessive heat warning if the forecast is expected to have apparent temperatures above 105°F for more than three hours for at least two consecutive days, or if the apparent temperature is expected to reach 115°F at any point in the forecast. One of the problems with using the apparent temperature reading is that apparent temperature concept can be confusing. For example, if the forecast for Chicago is an actual temperature of 98°F with 45% relative humidity for two consecutive days, according to the NWS's calculations it is a candidate for an excessive heat warning because its apparent temperature would be about 109°F. However, if Tucson has actual temperature 109°F with 10% relative humidity for the same time frame, it falls short of an excessive heat warning because the apparent temperature would be 104°F. What can confuse people is not realizing an apparent temperature of 109°F in New York is a greater health hazard than an actual temperature of 109°F in Tucson.(Chart courtesy of NOAA.)*

not only the water you sweat away, but the salts too. For one thing, your body cannot retain water without a certain amount of salts (electrolytes) in it. You'll simply urinate it out. And without the salts you'll die of dehydration no matter how much water you drink. In fact, the more you drink, the more salts you'll lose as your body throws off the water it can't retain, and your body will heat up even more. A second problem is that if the salts in your body fall below a critical level it can lead to cramping and muscle spasms. And, of course, the heart itself is a muscle so the loss of electrolytes, particularly potassium, can lead to death.

Worse yet, as your body loses water, your blood also becomes more viscous—i.e., thicker—making it more difficult for the heart to transport blood to the skin, making it harder for your body to dissipate heat.

Severe dehydration is a major factor in heat-induced deaths. Besides circulatory problems, it can cause kidney problems and can lead to heat stroke. Heat stroke can cause permanent damage to internal organs, especially the brain. It can even cause death. The most common symptoms of heat stroke may include:

- headache
- dizziness
- hot, dry skin that is flushed but not sweaty
- high body temperature
- rapid heart beat (tachycardia)
- fatigue
- disorientation or confusion
- agitation
- hallucinations
- seizures
- loss of consciousness

It is important to treat a heat stroke victim immediately. If you suspect someone is suffering from heat stroke, get medical help as soon as possible. In the meantime, here are some first aid measures you can take:

- Get the victim to a cool place indoors or at least to available shade.
- Have the victim lie down and slightly elevate his feet.
- Remove his clothing and gently apply cool water to the skin, then fan the victim; this will enhance the water's evaporation rate and stimulate the cooling we get from sweating.
- Apply ice packs to the groin and armpits.
- Give the victim water in small doses. Sports drinks are good because they contain electrolytes—those salts the body needs. (See the oral rehydration recipe in this article.) **Do not give drinks containing alcohol or caffeine.** Both are diuretics and can make the victim's status worse.

Protecting yourself

An air conditioner can be a lifesaver in extreme heat, as long as the electricity stays on. If you're worried about losing your air conditioning during a heat wave, get a backup generator to run it. Also, the installation of something as simple as an attic fan can lower the temperature of an overheated house by as much as 15°F.

Here are the American Red Cross's recommendations for dealing with a heat wave:

- Reduce activity. Schedule vigorous activity and sports for cooler times of the day.
- Wear lightweight, tightly woven, loose-fitting clothing in light colors. Light colors *reflect* heat away from you.
- Eat less, especially proteins, which raise your metabolism.
- Drinks lots of liquids. Water and sports drinks are the drinks of choice; avoid tea, coffee, soda, and alcohol as these can lead to dehydration. If you can, mist yourself with a spray bottle to avoid becoming overheated. As the water evaporates off your body it will carry away more heat than you can imagine.
- Avoid direct sun. Sunburn can lower the skin's ability to shed heat. Wear a hat and sun glasses if you are to be in the sun.
- Spend as much time indoors as possible on very hot and humid days. If you're not acclimated to the heat, increase the time spent outdoors gradually.
- Spend more time in air-conditioned places. Personally, I found the hottest days of the year to be good times to go to a supermarket or a mall.
- If you live in a hot climate and have a chronic condition, talk to your physician about extra precautions you can take to protect yourself against heat stroke.

The earth may be going through a warming trend. Whether it's part of normal heat cycles or is man-induced, the forecast is for warmer summers, at least in the foreseeable future. With this warming trend we can expect more heat waves. Δ

Water development
springs and seeps

By Roy Martin

Water, being a requirement for life, is one of the most important considerations for the homestead. Happy is the person who has water flowing from the ground with no need for pumps or city-type water systems. Wells may provide pure, reliable, inexpensive water, but water from springs is virtually free and can have the same desirable characteristics as well water.

Springs are naturally occurring flowing water that comes out of the ground and flows onto the surface for at least a short distance. They may have very small flows of less than a gallon per minute and sink almost immediately back into the ground or they may produce many thousands of gallons per minute and flow as a river right from the spring. Most of the springs that may occur on the homestead will usually produce only a few gallons per minute or less. These are the springs that will be discussed in this article.

Seeps are essentially springs that have such low production that there is little or no water coming completely to the surface. Seeps are often identified only by moist soil during dry periods and by the growth of water-dependent plant life.

Seeps and springs can be developed to provide pure, reliable, drinking water and livestock water for the homestead. In the case of larger springs, water may even be available for irrigating the garden or a small pasture. This article will deal with springs that have flows low enough to be captured in relatively small pipes.

Identifying the water source

The homesteader who has not yet purchased property would do well to select a site that has a spring. The best possible situation is to have a spring that is at a higher elevation than where the house is located. Then gravity water can be developed that will flow to the house under pressure. After the initial costs for pipe and storage, its free water—without electricity and without depending upon any government or community body—that will usually flow for decades with just minor maintenance.

Walk or ride the entire property to look for willows, cattails, skunk cabbage, or other water-loving plants. These usually indicate the presence of water on or near the surface. If the homestead is more than just a few acres, it would be a good idea to purchase a USGS topographical map that covers your homestead. Springs that show up on the map should be checked out first and then you can mark other possible sites you have found. On small acreages a person can just remember where each site is, but on larger properties it is essential to mark each site to allow a realistic evaluation of all springs and seeps you locate.

Selection of a spring for development involves more than just finding it. There may be a lot of good springs along a hillside, but if the land below is subject to flooding and therefore unsuitable for a home site, it may be better to develop a small, less productive spring that is higher than a good place to build your home. Before moving to Colorado, I had some property in Oregon on which I wanted to build a home, so I started to look for water sources. I found a number of highly productive springs in some canyons, but none of them were high enough to provide good water pressure to the place where I wanted to build the house. I looked at areas higher on the hill and finally

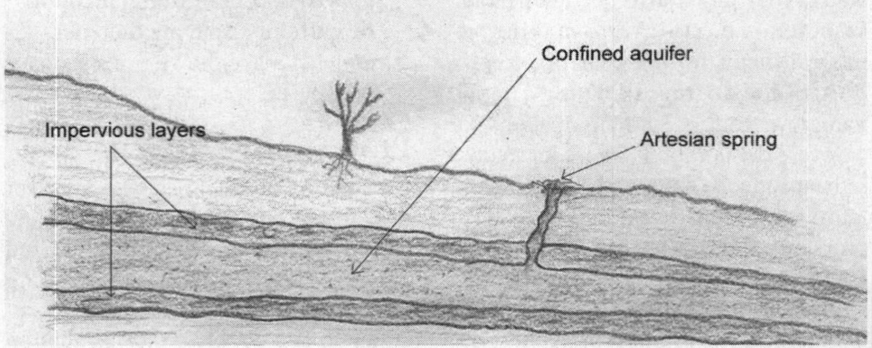

An aquifer that is under pressure because it is confined between two impervious layers results in artesian springs when there are holes in the upper confining layer. The original source of water for an artesian aquifer has to be at an elevation higher than the spring outlet.

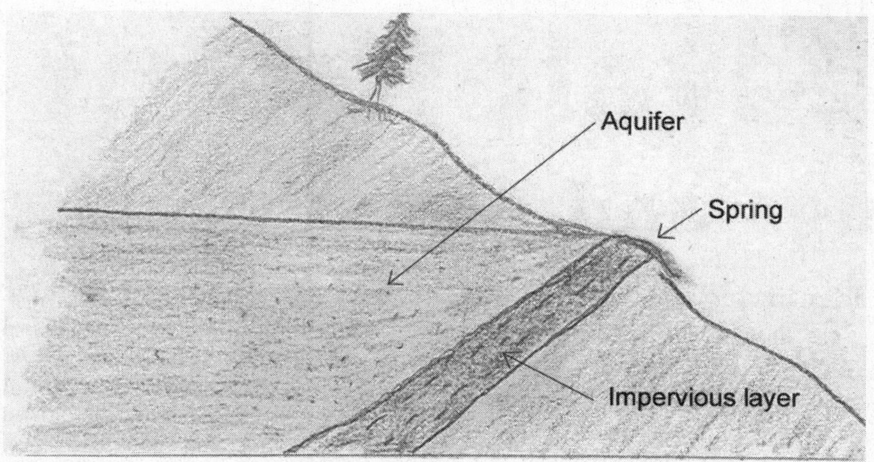

A reservoir spring is formed when the water table contacts the surface after building up behind an impervious layer of clay or rock.

found a place where there was some skunk cabbage growing, and I knew that I had located water. Oregon skunk cabbage has to have its roots in water all year long, so it is a good indicator plant. I used my shovel and dug around the skunk cabbage plants and found that water seeped into every hole I dug. Only then did I proceed with the house construction.

If no spring can be found above your existing home, or no suitable home sites are available below springs on property where you are going to build, look for good springs below the house. Even springs that are lower than your house may be a much better alternative than drilling a well and might be developed for pumping water to the house.

Types of springs

All springs are the result of water that is flowing through an aquifer (porous rock, gravel, or sand) coming up against a layer of rock or clay that forces it to come to the surface of the ground. However, there are different ways that the water is forced to the surface by the impermeable layers of rock or clay. The aquifers may be continuous over broad areas or may occur as underground streams, following narrow aquifers.

Contact springs occur where the water follows an aquifer that slopes downhill on top of a layer of impermeable rock or clay. Where the aquifer comes to the surface, the water simply runs out on top of the ground. This type of spring is the most susceptible to fluctuations in weather patterns and may dry up in drought years.

Reservoir springs are the result of water building up behind a layer of rock or clay that forms an underground dam, stopping the flow of water in the aquifer, and causing it to pond up below the ground surface. The spring is the result of water flowing over the top of the impermeable layer or through a crack or hole in it.

Artesian springs come from an aquifer that is confined between two impermeable layers of rock or clay. Water in this type of aquifer can be under pressure when the aquifer origin is elevated. This acts the same way that a water pipe coming from an elevated tank does, causing pressure. A hole in the upper confining aquifer allows water to flow to the surface. This type of spring is the least affected by variations in annual rainfall.

Hot springs are artesian springs that come from aquifers that are so deep that the water contacts rocks that are heated from the natural heat of the earth. These flow to the surface while still hot. Some hot springs have so many minerals in the water that it cannot be used for drinking or irrigation. Others have very good water with acceptable levels of dissolved minerals. If you are fortunate enough to have a hot spring, the water may be used for heating your house, greenhouses, and outbuildings. These are so rare, however, that there will be no further discussion of them in this article.

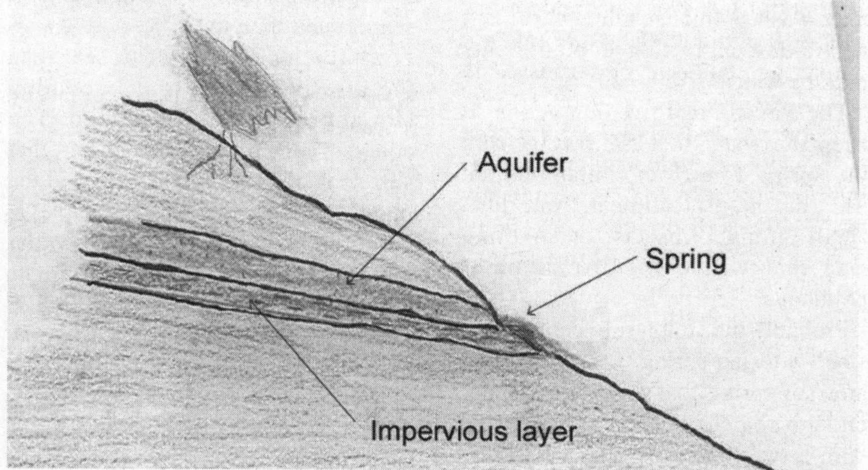

A contact spring follows an impervious layer of clay or rock until it exits to the surface. Storage in this aquifer is limited as gravity is continually pulling the water to the surface and must have a sustained source of water feeding the aquifer.

Capturing spring water

The advantage of having a spring instead of a well is that no pump is required to get the water out of the ground. There are some procedures to follow, however, to ensure that the water you get from the spring does not become polluted before it goes into the water system. Before water was piped into homes, it was usually dipped from springs in buckets out of holes that were either naturally occurring or that had been dug out to make access possible. When I was a little boy, we lived for a time in a place with no electricity or running water. We carried our water in buckets from a spring from which we dipped the water. There was a springhouse built over the spring to keep animals out of it and to provide a cool place to keep our milk and butter.

Simple capturing methods include placing a pipe into the spring, making a small dam of dirt to back up the water, and running the pipe to the house. This system, however, has the same disadvantages as dipping from a spring. The surface of the water is open to contamination from animals, leaves, dust, and from anything falling into the water. It is also exposed to runoff from surrounding areas that may wash animal manure, fertilizer, pesticides, and other contaminants into the water.

The key thing to remember is to keep the water that is flowing from the spring free from contamination. This means protecting it from dust, small animals, insects, or anything else that will carry dirt or other pollutants.

Probably the simplest to capture is a small artesian spring. I developed an artesian spring that had a flow small enough that I could get it captured with a two-inch pipe. The water was coming straight up out of a hole in some clay. I was able to push a length of PVC pipe down into the hole, and the artesian pressure pushed the water more than a foot above the ground

Springs and seeps located on a hill above a homestead can be captured to provide virtually free water. This sketch shows a spring line where the shallow water table meets the surface as it is blocked by an impervious layer of rock or clay.

surface. The pipe was first sealed by packing clay around it and then capping it with concrete. I then cut the pipe off below the level where the water had risen, glued on an elbow, and piped it to a storage tank. It was just like having pure water pumped out of the ground without the pump.

The next easiest is probably a spring that comes out of a hillside from a well-defined hole. Again, insert a pipe into the hole and then seal around the pipe. These are usually a little more difficult to seal than the artesian spring that is coming straight up out of the ground. The concrete mix usually has to be quite stiff so it will stay in place around the pipe.

Springs that arise in relatively flat land are often trampled by animals that go to the spring for water. The area is often muddy, and water may ooze out into animal tracks and other depressions in a lot of places. The main source must be located by digging to determine where the water is coming from. Often, it comes out in a relatively broad area. If the source is no more than a couple of feet in diameter, a box of some type should be placed over the spring in such a way that the water is covered where it comes out of the ground. This may be a pre-fabricated concrete box with a hole in the side for a pipe to come out; a concrete box can also be constructed on site; or it can be the bottom of a plastic barrel in which a pipe hole has been drilled and inverted over the spring. After development, this type of spring should be covered over with a thick layer of soil and/or the area around it fenced to keep livestock and large wildlife from continuing to trample it.

Contact springs and seeps often have no well-defined place where they come out of the ground. The seep I developed for my house in Oregon oozed out of the ground over a distance of about 30 feet or more. I dug a ditch all along it until I had a little trickle of water flowing down the ditch. Then I put a length of 3" perforated flexible pipe in the ditch and covered it with gravel. I connected non-perforated pipe to the lower end of the pipe in the ditch and ran it into a collection box I had made by laying a plastic barrel on its side with a hole cut into it for the pipe. At the lower end of the trench that contained the perforated pipe and gravel, I constructed a dam over which I placed black plastic. I covered the entire length of the gravel trench with black plastic sheeting and then put a couple of feet of soil over the plastic. The soil protected the plastic, and the plastic sheeting kept runoff water from entering the gravel and perforated pipe. I ran ¾" flexible polyethylene pipe from my barrel collection box to a 1200-gallon storage tank. Although that seep only provided about ¾ gallon per minute, this development provided a reliable source of water for my house, and with the large storage tank we never ran short except when a bear decided to chew up part of the polyethylene supply pipeline.

Transport and storage

Developing the spring will provide a regular supply of pure, clean water, but it is necessary to get the water from the spring to the house or other site where it will be used. Some simple spring developments, such as those that provide water for primitive campgrounds, just have spigots coming out of a storage tank at the spring, or even just a pipe coming out of the spring in the hillside so campers can get clean water in buckets. Usually, though, we want to get water under pressure to the house where it will provide the same service as water from a well and pump system or as city water, minus the chemical additives.

A storage tank is usually part of a spring water system for home use. The storage tank collects water over time so that during periods of heavy water use there will be plenty of water available. The storage tank needs to be located higher than the highest water outlet in the house. It is best to have the storage tank at least 40 feet higher than the house. This will provide almost 18 pounds (pounds per square inch, or p.s.i.) of water pressure in the house. To calculate pressure, measure the height in feet and divide by 2.3, as each pound of pressure requires 2.3 feet of elevation above the point of use. The pipeline from the storage tank to the house must be buried below the frost line to prevent freezing. I recommend using 1"-diameter schedule 40 PVC pipe. PVC plastic pipe is easy to cut, easy to join with PVC cement, and it will not corrode.

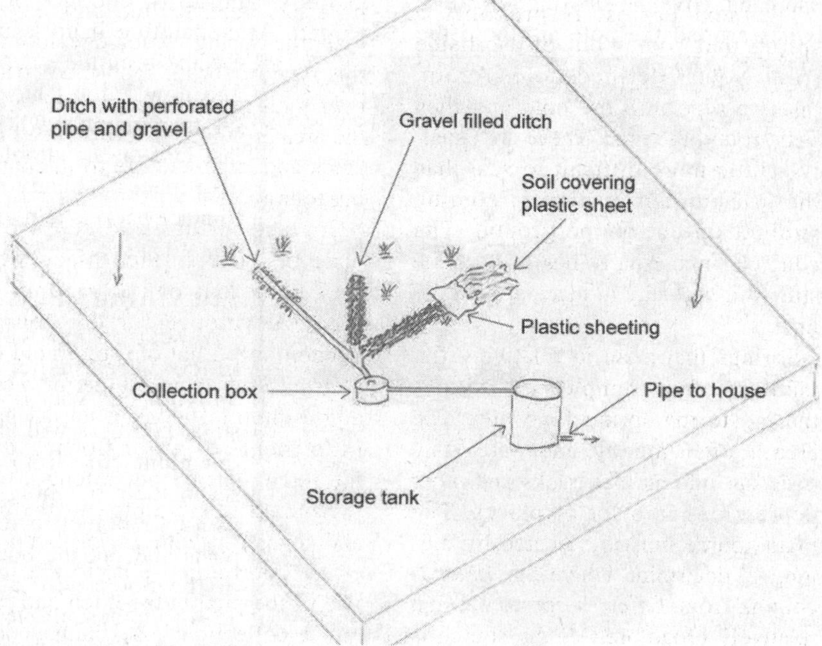

A seep may be captured with lines of perforated pipe in ditches leading to a collection box and a storage tank.

The pipeline from the spring or collection box to the storage tank may be PVC, black plastic (polyethylene), or galvanized steel. I would use the one that is cheapest (usually polyethylene or thin-wall PVC), as this water line has no pressure on it. Since it has water running continuously, it does not need to be buried below the frost line in most cases. In western Oregon, where frost is light, I just ran the polyethylene pipe on top of the ground. If avoidable, I would not do that again as bears and coyotes are often attracted by the gurgling sound of the water and might, out of curiosity, chew into the pipe. When the storage tank is full, excess water from the spring runs out an overflow. If there is enough overflow, it can be used to irrigate a garden or can go to water troughs for livestock and wildlife.

If the spring is located below the house, a pump system will need to be set up to take water from the storage tank to the house. If electricity can be taken to the storage tank, a very inexpensive centrifugal pump will pump from the tank uphill a good distance. A storage tank may be placed higher than the house to provide pressure. The pump can either fill a storage tank equipped with a float switch that turns off the pump or a pressure tank and pressure switch can be used. Where no electricity is available, a gasoline-engine-driven pump can be used to pump into a storage tank that in turn supplies the house.

In most cases the water from springs is pure and clear, and spring development can provide the home with economical, abundant, desirable water. With a little effort, even the smallest seeps and springs can be used to provide that water. Δ

Gardening tips and tricks

By Charles A. Sanders

Gardeners are an ingenious lot. Trial and error, time, study, observation, and experience all help us to come up with ideas that result in better gardens, more produce, less labor, and more enjoyment of our homesteading efforts. Over the years, I've learned several tricks that have helped us on our place. I'll present some of them here and perhaps you can benefit from my experience. Let's jump right in.

Put a board over your beets and carrots after planting. Leave it for a week or week and a half. It will keep moisture in the soil and help to sprout these slow-to-germinate seeds.

Another good way to help germinate carrot seeds is to sow radish seeds in with them. As the radishes grow and are removed, it loosens up the soil for the carrots.

Bottomless apple picker

I made a nifty apple picker from scraps around the shop. I use this easy-to-make picker every year when harvesting our apples.

I began with a length of ½" conduit. I made a cylinder of 1x2 welded wire as shown in the photo. The top of the cylinder was made with the individual wires protruding. The tip of each wire was doubled back so they would not present a sharp end. The bottom of the cylinder was left open. I attached the cylinder to the conduit using two ordinary hose clamps available at any hardware store. Now the neat part: I took an old bedsheet and cut a piece of material lengthwise and stitched up a cloth sleeve about 8-12 inches in diameter. Then the sleeve was attached to the open bottom end of the wire cylinder using some heavy lacing thread. On the cylinder itself, I bent the wires closest to the conduit inward towards the center. This will help to hook onto the stem of the apples you are picking. On the front edge of the wire cylinder, I bent the wires slightly outward. This will help herd the apples into the cylinder for picking.

To use this simple device, grasp the conduit pole and the cloth sleeve in one hand. Give the sleeve a few loose twists around the pole and hold the open end tight to the pole. Now, merely creep up on an unsuspecting apple and let the back wires hook onto the stem. Give a slight tug, perhaps with a deft twist, and the fruit will fall into the cylinder. Since the wire basket has no bottom, the apple will fall into the cloth sleeve. Its descent will be slowed by the loose twists in the sleeve. Repeat until you have several apples in the sleeve just above your hand. Now just position it over your bucket or basket and let the apples fall out of the sleeve and gently into the container. This handy device speeds up picking and prevents bruising the fruit as you harvest.

A mailbox in the garden

Mailbox in the garden

Over in the garden, it seems like I am constantly misplacing the trowel, hand fork, or other tool. I helped to solve the problem by posting an old mailbox right at the entrance of the garden. After painting it up a bit, I erected it on the gatepost, and now I don't have to try to remember where I last laid the handtools. It also makes a handy spot to place packets and sacks of garden seeds.

For vining plants

A section of woven fence wire suspended upright along your row of sugar pod peas will allow the plants to climb and reach their full height. I use a few electric fence posts and put the bottom of the fence wire about 12-18 inches above the ground. The pea vines will grow and latch onto the wire and begin their

The bottomless apple picker

Emptying apples from the bottomless apple picker

climb. The heavy wire livestock panels also work very well for this purpose. You can also do this with other vining plants such as cucumbers, gourds, and melons.

Cage your tomatoes

Good durable tomato cages can be made from five- to six-foot sections of woven fence wire. I usually put them in place just after giving the tomatoes a good hoeing, working the base of the cage into the freshly turned soil. Drive an electric fence post in as well and tie the cage to it for further support.

Tomato cages can also be made from sections of concrete reinforcement wire. Anchor them as described above, or cut the bottom wire off to make a dozen or so little spikes on the cage to shove down into the soil.

Toolshed tool cleaner

It is vital for homesteaders to keep hand tools in good condition to get proper use and long life from them. A good way to help is to keep a wooden box filled with oil-soaked sand sitting in the tool shed (this is a good use for some used motor oil). When you are done using a hoe, spade, shovel, or other such tool, merely scrape as much dirt off of it as you can (I use a small mason's trowel), then plunge it into the box a few times to further scour it clean and give it a light coating of oil. This will add years of life to your tools.

Give tool handles an oil rub

Hand-in-hand with long tool life is the following tip. If you have priced wooden handles for hand tools recently, you know that the price is outrageous and the quality of the handles has gone down. A good way to provide for long-lived handles in your tools is to try the following tip.

Give all your tools' wooden handles a good rubbing with boiled linseed oil. This compound is available from most hardware stores. (Don't try to make your own by boiling raw linseed oil; it won't work! Just ask for it by name.) Application of the oil to the wood will prolong the life of the wood, maintain its springiness, smooth the surface for splinter-free use, and even make the tool look better.

Mend a bucket, tub, or stock tank

In this day and age of plastic and throw-aways, we are not often encouraged to make repairs to something as simple as a bucket or tub. However, an important part of homesteading is to make do with what one has, to use and re-use tools and items around the homestead to get the most out of them.

A good galvanized bucket or tub is certainly handy to have around the place and each can end up seeing a nearly endless variety of uses. However, if your bucket gets a hole in it, it is obviously of lesser use. Here is a good old way to repair a bucket that is simple and that works.

Merely enlarge the hole just enough to accept a small machine screw or bolt that you have handy. Put a metal washer on the bolt, then a washer made of a piece of old inner tube or a piece of leather. Slide the bolt through the hole. Put another washer of leather or rubber on the other side, followed by another flat washer, then the nut. Tighten everything down. Many old-timers prefer the leather washer because of the fact that it will absorb a bit of the water and swell to firmly seal the hole. Many folks use rubber because they had it lying around the workshop. It seems to work well, too.

This simple repair method can be used to extend the life of what might first be looked at as a throwaway situation. I have used this quick fix on metal buckets as well as large stock watering tanks. There is no need to throw away your bucket or tub, or your money.

Pinwheels and other small tools

Wire a short piece of ½" PVC pipe to a post near your berry patch and drop the shaft of a toy dime-store pinwheel into the pipe. The wind will keep the pinwheel turning, and the pipe will allow it to turn into any available breeze. This will help to keep birds out of your blueberries, raspberries, etc.

Plastic snakes placed among the branches of your blueberry bushes will keep birds out of the bushes and away from the fruit. Be sure to tell friends and family about the toy snakes before they go berry picking!

Here is a simple tip to use whenever you are using commercial granular fertilizer while planting your garden. Don't place fertilizer directly in the row with seeds; beans, for example, will burn and they will fail to sprout. So, whenever I am preparing the soil for planting my garden, regardless of the seed types, I do the following. Lay off the rows as you normally would. Scatter your fertilizer at the desired rate down the row. Next, simply drag a short piece of chain attached to a length of binder twine or string down the row to mix the fertilizer into the soil. I use a short piece of an old log chain about a foot long and tie the ends together to the string. Then sow your seed and cover as you normally would. This simple procedure will help prevent the seed from getting burned by the fertilizer and will help insure much better germination.

A box of oily sand will help keep tools clean.

Shake those insect pests

Come garden time, we occasionally have an outbreak of Mexican bean beetles or other insect pest looking for some easy meals. We usually use Sevin® or Bonide® in the powdered form to help rid us of the critters.

A really easy way to make a garden bug duster is to use an ordinary coffee can. In the bottom of the can, make several holes using a small nail. I've found that a #2 or #4 nail will do just about right. The snap-on plastic lid makes filling the duster easy, and another lid snapped over the bottom for storage prevents spills and keeps the powder where it belongs.

Growing good plants

In the greenhouse, use small containers that you have saved. Yogurt cups, butter bowls, tin cans, egg cartons, or any other old container that can hold a bit of soil. They can all be used to transplant seedlings into or to start seeds in.

Contact your local grocery store and ask them to save the wooden crates that grapes and other soft fruits are shipped in. They are sturdy and hold about two dozen seedlings in Styrofoam cups. Depending on your store, you might be able to get three or four to eight or ten of these crates a week.

If the store sells bedding plants, garden plants, etc., in the spring, ask them to save the plastic flats that the seedlings are received in. These, too, can be recycled to save you money and re-use the plastic. If you obtain these flats, I'd first recommend dipping them in a weak bleach and water solution to clean and disinfect them. Then, just fill them with your seed-starting mix and sow your seeds directly in the flats. This system has worked very well for us for years.

If the store has a deli, or if you can contact a bakery, convenience store, dairy, etc., then you should make use of the 5-gallon plastic buckets that most of these places send to the landfills. The heavy plastic pails are food-safe, and most places will save them for you for the asking or may request a dollar or so for them. They are very sturdy and very usable. I have used them to store cleaned and processed raw wheat for years at a time, and also to store bulk grains and beans in the freezer. A small farm can never have too many buckets.

At your local pizza place, ask about the fate of the glass jars that the peppers, sauces, and other ingredients come in. These are food safe, easily

Attach webbing to your cart to help keep hand tools in place.

cleaned, and can hold large quantities of beans, pasta, rice, sugar, flour, and many other foodstuffs. The pizza maker will likely be glad to get rid of them. We like to fill these containers with pasta, kidney beans, black beans, and so on, and then store them in one of our freezers. It adds greatly to the storage life of the foods.

Paper garden mulch

To help recycle paper, contact the large users of paper in your community. Banks and large businesses go through enormous quantities of computer printer paper. Most of these places shred paper as they dispose of it and either landfill it or incinerate it. If you contact these establishments, they are often happy to allow you to pick up the bags or boxes of used paper for nothing. In some communities, organizations such as the Boy Scouts or civic organizations may already be hitting up these sources of paper. Once you've obtained your supply of shredded paper, you can either make a few cents off of it at the recycler (paper isn't bringing much at this time, although computer paper is of higher quality and pays more) or you can use it to mulch your garden plants with. The shredded paper works very well in controlling our weeds and allowing moisture to soak down to the soil. In addition, it breaks down reasonably slowly.

Since we're talking about paper recycling, try contacting those food stores and supermarkets and ask them to save some of the large boxes that paper towels and toilet tissue come in. These large cardboard boxes can be broken down and make an excellent mulch. They can be trimmed to fit between rows of vegetables and strawberries with excellent results. We often use these cut-up cardboard boxes to place beneath a layer of straw when mulching.

Cheap feed

While you are at the supermarket, you might ask the produce manager to set aside the boxes of vegetable scraps for you to pick up. When cases of vegetables are received, many of them must be trimmed and sorted prior to displaying in the produce section. These trimmings, or overripe or damaged fruits and vegetables, make superb additions to the compost pile or can be used to feed your fattening pig or chickens. The sorted lettuce and cabbage leaves can be fed to your rabbits. Some produce managers will set a box or two of trimmings out on the back loading dock for first come-first serve use.

Now, I realize that it sounds like you're going to be hitting pretty heavily on the local grocer. True, you need to be careful not to wear out your welcome. Always be friendly with the folks. They are likely members of your neighborhood and are reasonably eager to build good public relations with customers. Of course, it's likely you do business there already. Obviously, if you explain your intentions in obtaining the refuse from the store, that will help, too. Return the favor to the store folks by offering them some home-grown produce or plants for their own use. In fact, many stores will welcome the chance to sell some of your sturdy homegrown plants and produce in their store. I have sold fruits, nuts, and vegetables in our local supermarket. The produce manager, who supervised the selling of garden plants at the store, contacted me wanting some of our home-grown tomato plants for her own use. We were happy to just give her several. In any case, take the time to cultivate a relationship with the folks.

More tool holders

Back when I built my "Copy Cart," I added a couple of strips of webbing to hold some hand tools in place. You can see in the photos that they are handy for holding a variety of tools, keeping them where I can find them. I attached the webbing with small bolts and washers directly on the side panel of the cart.

Hanging baskets

We like our hot peppers. My wife uses the tiny, yet fiery, Thai peppers when she makes her infamous 911 Sauce. A few of those little peppers go a long way!

We often grow the plants in recycled hanging baskets. The plants adapt well and can soon fill a basket with pretty white blooms that soon grow to become a green globe of tiny red peppers. They make a nice accent on the porch.

Use hanging baskets for some of your vegetable plants.

These are just a few ideas of ways to utilize materials that are usually free for the asking, and just as importantly, would otherwise end up in one of our already bursting-at-the-seams landfills. Remember, just use your imagination and the materials that you have on hand. You can come up with your designs or easily improve upon my ideas. Just use what you have available. Δ

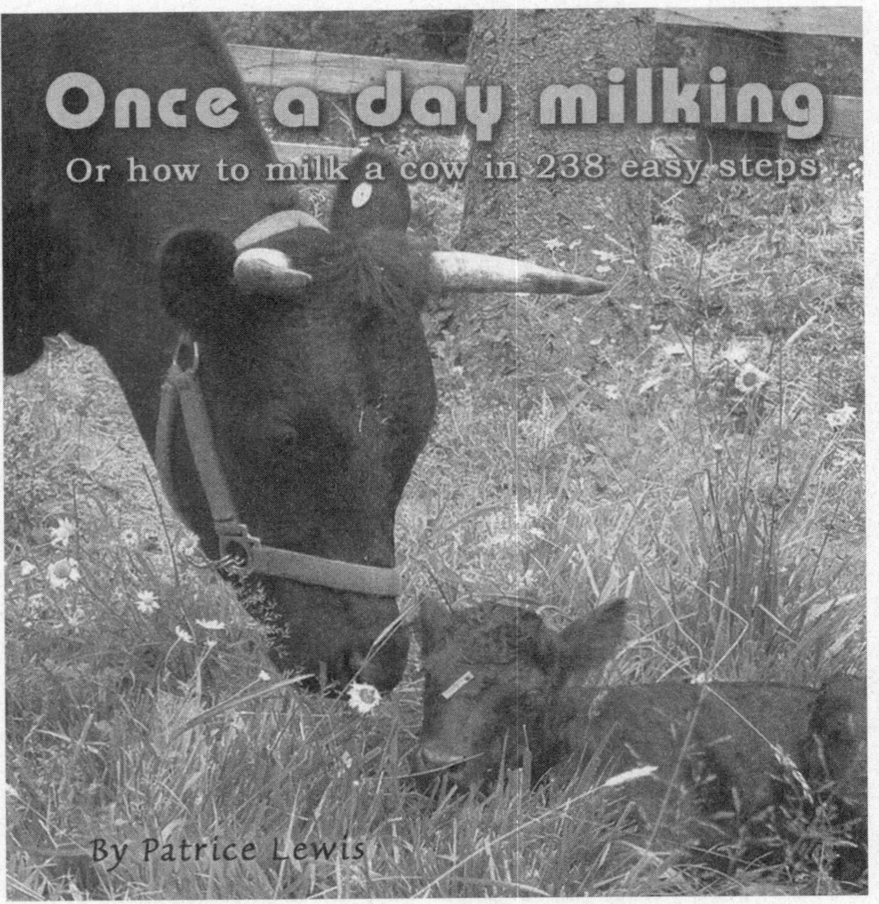

Once a day milking
Or how to milk a cow in 238 easy steps
By Patrice Lewis

It sounds bucolic, doesn't it? The simple joys of milking your own cow. Fresh milk, fresh cream, homemade cheese, butter, yogurt. What can get better than that?

But when face-to-face with a 1200-pound horned bovine behemoth, this enthusiasm might wane. While there is no doubt that milking your own cow will give you a sense of security and independence, where do you start? How do you milk a cow?

Three times in the last month I've received phone calls from people seeking advice. They wanted to milk a family cow but had no idea how to start. These people were mostly full of misinformation on what it takes to milk—how much work it is to train the cow, the difficulties in separating the calves, etc.

So, in an effort to dispel the myths and concerns, come with us on our milking adventures.

How we got started

We got our first cow and newborn calf rather unexpectedly. It was so unexpected, in fact, that the animals lived in our front yard for about two weeks until we could make other arrangements. Believe me, there is no stronger motivation to build a barnyard than to have a half-wild cow and skittish calf thrashing your lawn and leaving cow pats everywhere.

We finally were able to herd the animals to their newly-fenced (¼-acre) "corral" until we could fence the pasture. But, of course, I couldn't begin to milk the cow until I managed to separate the calf at night. So we built a calf pen and locked the calf away during the night.

After listening to the calf and cow bellow all night long with the indignity of being separated, I went with trembling heart to milk the next morning. With the cow loose—I had no way to restrain her, since she wasn't halter-trained—I put a bucket of grain in front of her and squatted down to milk.

Of course, I had no flipping idea how to milk, but after five minutes of fumbling around down there, I managed to get a few squeezes into the milking bucket.

Then the cow lifted a back leg and casually kicked the bucket over. My hard-earned three ounces soaked into the ground. Then, to add insult to injury, she finished her grain and walked away, and wouldn't let me anywhere near her udder without a bribe.

Clearly something had to be done.

Because Bossy wasn't halter-trained, I knew that trying to get her into a stanchion would be a losing proposition. So I asked my husband to build a milking stall of some sort, something I could lure her into and then lock her in place so that she couldn't get out even if she wanted to. He did this, adding it to the side of the calf pen. Then, because winter was coming and I wanted to milk while under shelter, he added a roof. One thing followed another, and over the next year he added another calf pen, a hay barn, and a passage for storing grain and the barn implements. We called it our "Winchester Mystery Barn" (for those who are familiar with the Winchester Mystery House in San Jose, California).

Once-a-day milking

I urge you to challenge your preconceived notion of how a cow "should" be milked; namely, twice a day. One woman I spoke to was stunned to learn that cows don't have to have a rigid schedule of milking. She has eight children ranging in age from three months to thirteen years, and had been resisting the idea of milking because her evenings were too full to allow for that evening chore. Once-a-day milking was more compatible with her schedule, and after our conversation she was energized to give it a try.

Once-a-day milking works for us for a number of reasons. First, it gives us all the milk we need with enough left over to make a batch of mozzarella once a week, but without giving us so much extra milk that our refrigerator overflows.

Second, I can milk whenever I want, within reason. In the summer, I'm in the barn around 5:30 in the morning, sometimes earlier. During the winter, it's more like 8 a.m. The cows don't care.

Third, I don't have to bottle-feed the calf. The cow takes care of that. This frees up our schedule in more ways than one: If we need to be away overnight, for instance, we just leave the barnyard gate open so the animals have free access to the barn. We don't confine the calves, and they just happily nurse all night long. No problem.

Since I don't have to milk the cow in the evening, my only evening chores are to call the animals into the barnyard and close the gate behind them (I've already done the barn chores, such as cleaning and filling the hay racks, earlier in the day).

Fourth, unless you are prepared to remove the calf immediately at birth and hand-raise it out of sight of the cow, you can just turn the mothering duties over to the cow herself. She's more than happy to mother her own calf. You'll have to work a bit more to halter-train the calf when he/she is older, but until then your job is simplified. This strikes me as a healthier, more wholesome arrangement for all parties involved.

All right, this sounds great. Now how do you milk a cow?

How to get started

First step: Get a cow (duh). Personally I'm fond of Dexters, (www.purebreddextercattle.org) a small Irish breed that is dual-purpose (milk and meat), and doesn't give as much milk as, say, a Jersey. This means we're not swimming in milk. Other people with large families might prefer a heavy milk-producing breed. Go with whatever works for you.

I've milked cows that are halter-trained and those that aren't. It goes without saying that halter-trained cows are easier to handle, but it's certainly possible even if the animal has no training. Of course, if your cow is completely wild and flees in terror the moment you show your face, you'll have trouble confining her to a milking stall or stanchion. Get another cow.

Putting the calf pen and milking stall side-by-side will be calming for both cow and calf.

The basic requirements for milking once a day are: (1) a calf pen, for confining the calves during the night so the cow can "accumulate" her milk for the morning; (2) a milking stall or stanchion with a grain bin or other container (i.e., a bucket in a holder); and (3) grain. Never underestimate the motivating factors of grain to get your cow to do what you want.

Train your animals to come into the barnyard at night. If your herd is scattered far and wide, you'll either have to keep your milking animals closer at hand, or you'll have to walk out into your vast holdings and lead your milking animals back every evening. We've done both.

How do you train a cow to go into a milking stall? It doesn't matter if your cow is halter-trained or not, you can train her to go in by using grain. Wave a handful of grain before her nose, then let her watch as you put it in the grain bin or bucket that you've rigged up in the milking stall. It may take the cow a few days to gird up the courage to go for the grain, but that's okay. Once she goes all the way in, don't be too hasty to lock her in and dive for the udder. Let her relax and learn that being in the milking stall is not an alarming experience.

The ideal time to train a cow is in the first two weeks after she has given birth. During those two weeks the calf should have unrestrained access to the cow, day and night, in order to provide adequate bonding and in order to provide the calf with colostrum, the immune-strengthening "first milk" the cow produces. During this time, you can train the cow to go into the stall calmly.

The first time you confine your cow in the milking stall, she may fight and kick in her efforts to get out. The stall should be narrow enough that the animal cannot turn around.

Okay, the day (or night) has come when it's time to put the calf in the calf pen. The easiest way to do this is to lure the cow inside with some

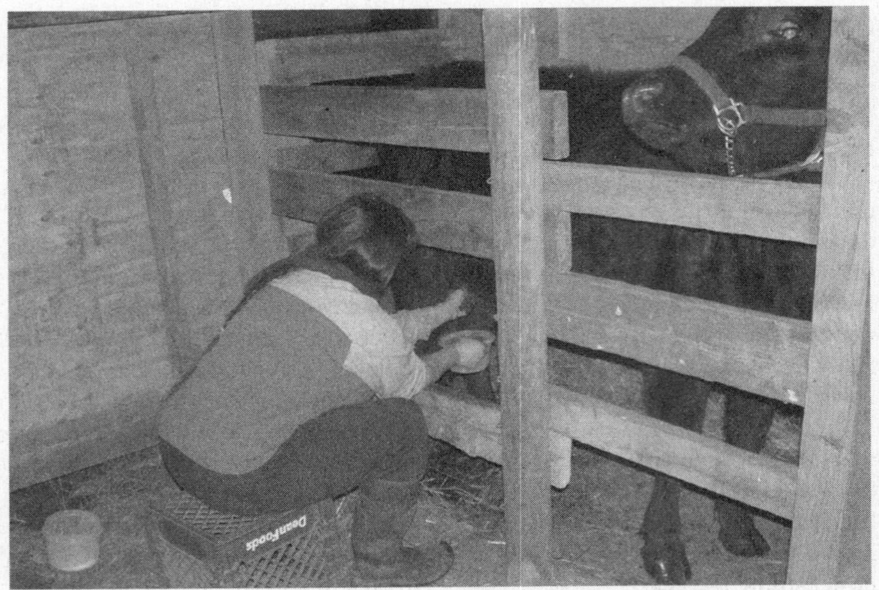

I use an old plastic crate for sitting on while milking. Notice "opening" in the stall.

grain, and the calf will follow. Have another person restrain the calf while you shove the cow back out, and lock the gate.

When you build your calf pen and milking stall, put them side-by-side. This will be calming for both cow and calf. The calf pen should allow the calves to be visible and "smellable" to the cow, but not "nursable." The animals should be able to touch noses but the calf should not be able to reach the cow's udder.

Don't be misled by the idea that if the calf is "out of sight, out of mind," then the cow will settle down quicker. Trust me, it doesn't work that way. The cow will go crazy looking for her calf if you've built the calf pen any distance away. If you put the calf pen where the cow can sniff her baby, she'll be annoyed at the separation but not frantic.

Get ready for incredible noise the first night the calf is separated from its mother. The calf will bleat and cry. The cow will bellow like crazy. Any other animals in the vicinity will bellow in sympathy. It will sound like Jurassic Park in the barn.

The next morning, with trembling heart, you will go to the barn to milk your cow. Remember, this will not go smoothly. Indeed, it may be so frustrating that you're tempted to give up. Don't.

The cow, having bellowed all night, will be in a bad mood. She will also be uncomfortable because her udder is full (plus she hates being separated from her calf). So when you first put her in the milking stall and actually have the audacity to touch her udder, she'll kick and swipe and thunder around. Don't be intimidated by the cow's restlessness and attempts to get out of the stall. Just let her thrash it out—and don't, under any circumstances, let her out before you're ready. Otherwise, the cow will learn that if she acts obnoxious, you'll get frustrated and let her loose. Bad lesson for a cow to learn. You'll be lucky to get three ounces of milk this first day. Don't worry, things will get better.

And—no matter how much your cow thrashes and kicks—never, ever hit her. Believe me, the temptation to punch your cow when she's misbehaving can be overwhelming. Resist. You never want your cow to associate anything negative while she's in the milking stall.

Be sure your milking stall is sturdy. Anything of flimsy construction will be shaken or kicked apart while your cow is getting used to being milked.

The milking stall we've built is made to reduce the likelihood that I'll be kicked. It has an "opening" through which I lean to reach the udder, but it won't enable a stray hoof to lash out and hit me in the face.

I've only been kicked once, when I tried to pick up a front hoof to see if it needed trimming. I got clocked above the left eye, an event that tumbled me backwards off the milking crate and left me with a beautiful shiner. The temptation to haul off and slug that stupid cow was strong—but I resisted. Again, don't ever hit your cow.

How long does it take a cow to learn to behave in the milking stall? I'd say two weeks maximum, and quite likely less. By that time she'll learn that the sooner she behaves, the sooner the milking will be over. She'll stand quietly (though she may bellow) and let you finish the job as quickly as possible. The moment you're done, of course, reward her for her good behavior by letting her out of the stall and opening the calf pen.

I use an old plastic crate for sitting on while milking, the kind that they use to transport dairy products to the grocery store. We found a bunch at a thrift store and find them useful for this purpose.

The milking

Put some—not lots—of grain into the grain bin in the milking stall, and lock the cow in.

Before milking, take a bowl of hot water mixed with a few drops of bleach, and an old dishcloth. Swab the udder in order to wash off any dirt or dried manure that may have adhered, paying special attention to washing the teats (I use hot water because I hate the thought of swabbing the udder with cold water, especially if it's a cold morning). Then give each teat about three good squeezes, letting the milk just fall to the ground. This gets rid of any bacteria-laden milk that may have accumulated in the teat during the night. The rest of the milk in the udder will be sterile.

The old joke says that some of the teats give chocolate milk, others give vanilla. This actually isn't too far from the truth: The first milk coming out of the udder is skim milk; the hind milk, coming out as the udder is going dry, is pure cream. So milk the udder as dry as you can, and your milk will be richer. Obviously, this won't happen the first day.

The first urge most people have when faced with a cow's udder is to pull on the teats in an effort to get the milk out. For God's sake, don't pull—squeeze.

The proper technique is to grasp the top part of the teat between the thumb and first finger and squeeze tightly. This traps the milk in the teat and it won't squish upwards as you squeeze downward. Don't be dainty or afraid that a tight squeeze will hurt the cow—it won't (you should see what the calf does!).

Now bring the rest of your fingers in, one at a time, together in a downward direction, squeezing (not pulling!) as you go. You'll be rewarded with a squirt of warm milk into your bucket.

Remember, don't pull, or you might be rewarded with a kick from an annoyed cow. (I don't know about you, but if someone tried to pull on my teat, I'd kick them, too.)

Here's another little trick I've learned: Cows kick. Most don't kick to hurt you; they "swipe" with a hind leg, as if to dislodge an irritating fly. But of course, if the milking bucket is down there, they kick the bucket, so to speak.

So I don't use a milking bucket, at least not directly under the udder. Instead, I milk one-handedly into a smaller plastic container, then empty the milk into a bucket that's well away from the cow's feet. This way, if the cow swipes and I'm not quick enough to yank the container away, I've only lost a few ounces rather than the whole morning's milking.

You might have the world's most docile animal who would never dream of swiping with a hind leg and kicking over the bucket. If so, good for you—you can merely pull your milking stool next to the cow, place the bucket directly beneath the udder, and have at it.

My cows aren't like that, so I milk with one hand at a time. The two back teats are easier to milk with my left hand, and the two front teats with my right, so I can trade off without either hand getting too tired.

And don't give up. Honestly, it gets better and easier. Right now, for instance, it takes me about two minutes to get six animals settled in the barn at night, when I open the gate to the corral (one horse, a bull, two cows, two calves). They all sort themselves into where they're supposed to go, settle down to eat the modest proportion of grain I give them, I latch the calf pen, and everyone's happy. Our routine in the morning, including milking both cows, takes less than half an hour. Everyone knows what to do, everyone is comfortable, and all is peaceful.

Remember, cows—like all livestock—are creatures of extreme habit. They do their best when their daily routine varies very little. While you don't have to be rigid in when you milk your cow in the morning (within reason), you should do your best to be rigid in what you do every morning. Cows do best when they know what to expect.

Weaning and breeding

Won't milking in the morning mean there isn't enough milk left for the calf? In a word, no.

Any (human) mother who has ever breastfed her babies knows that her milk production adjusts to the needs of the child. The more she is "milked," the more milk she produces. Breastfeeding mothers recognize the "let down" sensation while nursing their babies, after which milk flow increases.

Same with cows. As far as the cow is concerned, you are just another (less attractive) calf demanding milk from her, and her body will adjust accordingly. Frequently during the milking, you can feel the cow's udder start to fill up. Milk the udder as dry as you can.

The moment the calf is let loose, he starts to butt the cow's udder in a way that looks terrifically painful but isn't. It's the signal to the cow that she should "let down" more milk. Within moments the calf is happily nursing, getting as much milk as he needs.

Keep in mind that cows have a lactation cycle. Cows do not uniformly produce the same quantity of milk, day after day, week after week. Rather, their milk production adjusts to the needs of their calf. The amount of milk cows give also varies from day to day (I always think of days with less milk as "bad hair days" for the cows). They give less milk during their heat cycles as well.

The lactation cycle runs as a bell curve, peaking when the calf is about a month old and gradually decreasing until such time as the calf is weaned.

You should breed back your cows when the calves are about three months old, using either a bull or artificial insemination. A cow's gestation lasts about nine months and ten days. By breeding your cows when the calves are about three months old, the cows will have their calves about the same time every year. Personally, I like to breed my cows in September or October so they'll have their calves in June or July. In our climate, where spring can be cold, I like having the calves born in warmer weather, but early enough in the season that they can grow and put on body fat before the harsh winter sets in.

Don't anthropomorphize your cows. When I mentioned to my mother that cows should be bred back when the calves are three months old, she was horrified that the poor cow would be subjected to pregnancy so soon after giving birth (my mother, let it be known, had difficult pregnancies and labors). However, cows aren't people. They are happiest and calmest when they are either pregnant or have a calf to occupy them.

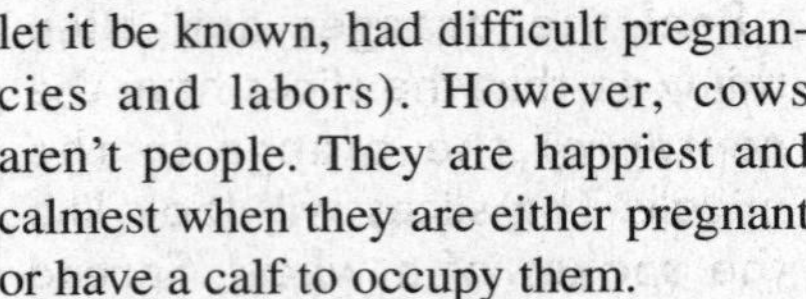

Should you wean the calf at a certain age? I was convinced you were "supposed" to do this before the cow got pregnant again; otherwise, it would stress the cow to be pregnant with a new calf while still nursing an older calf.

So we tried force-weaning our first calf by separating him from the cow. Suffice it to say it was a nightmare. In their efforts to get to each other, the cow and calf crashed through fences, gates, barn doors, and any other obstacle we could rig up. The noise was incredible. I was afraid the animals would injure themselves trying to get through the various barriers we installed. And it takes about a month, I'm told, to fully wean a calf! How on earth could we keep this up for a month?

Finally I called a cow-owning friend and asked if I could board the calf at her farm until the weaning was completed. My friend stopped me dead in my tracks with one simple question: "Why are you trying to wean the calf?"

"Well, um..." I finally stammered, "...because you're supposed to? I mean, won't it stress the cow too much to be simultaneously nursing a calf and being pregnant?"

"Well, how much stress is she under while you try to keep the calf separated?"

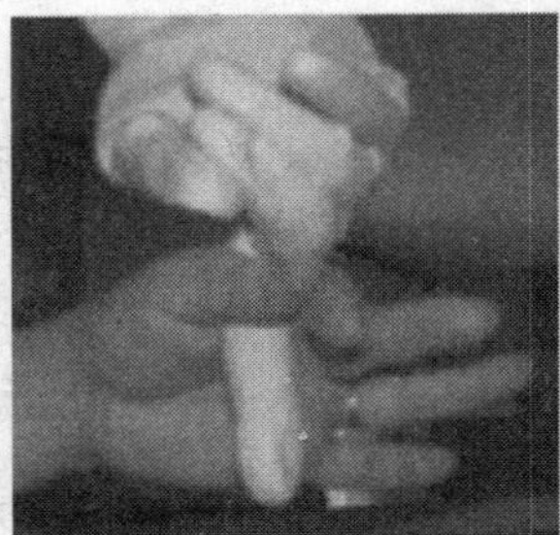
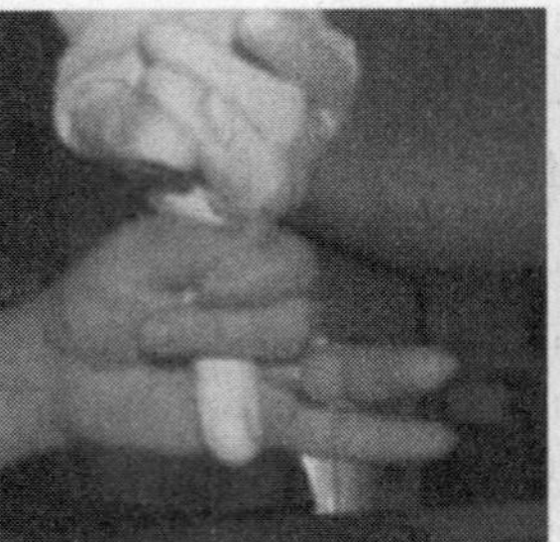
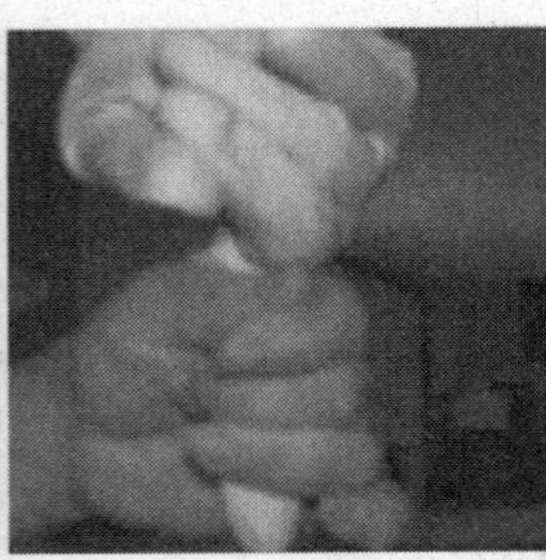

The proper technique for milking

I had to admit that they were tremendously stressed out by the procedure.

"Are you satisfied with the amount of milk you're getting from milking just in the morning?"

I admitted that I was.

"Look," my friend explained. "The cow will kick the calf off when she's ready. Don't worry, she knows what she's doing."

So trust your cow. She knows when it's best to kick the calf away in plenty of time to marshal her resources for the growing fetus. By not force-weaning your calf, you reduce the stress level for you, the cow, and the calf. Besides, I see it as a more "natural" (I hate that word) cycle for your livestock.

What to do with the milk

What do you do once you have all that milk in a bucket? If you look at it, you might be appalled by the miscellaneous straw, cow hairs, or other incidental debris. (This is why commercial dairies don't milk by hand.) Your next step is to strain the milk.

Straining is very simple. Cut up an old sheet or piece of muslin into squares large enough to line a colander. Dampen the muslin, line a colander with it, and place the colander over a clean container. Then simply pour the milk into the cloth-lined colander. What emerges is pure, clean milk.

Now, here's another trick: Put the milk, uncapped, in the freezer for one hour, before capping it and putting it in the fridge. I've found that if you have a problem with a "cow-y" odor to the milk, the freezer trick tends to eliminate it.

After about a day, enough cream will have risen to the surface that you can skim it (or, as I do, suck it off with a turkey baster). The uses for cream, of course, are endless.

Impress your friends

That's it. While this sounds complex, once you get the hang of it you'll wonder why you ever dreaded the idea of milking your cow. It goes without saying that everyone's techniques, circumstances, set-up, and styles are different. You'll settle into your own style once you get the hang of it. This information is meant to reassure you that milking your cow is do-able.

Plus you can impress the heck out of people. Recently at a writer's conference, I was introduced to an author I admire. As we shook hands, she commented on the strong grip I had. I smiled sheepishly and replied, "I milk cows." Her eyes widened, and she gasped, "You milk cows?" Turns out this woman admired the Simple Living concept but had never met anyone who actually lived it. While I was impressed to meet her, apparently she was also impressed to meet me.

So, go milk your cow. You'll amaze the heck out of your city friends. Δ

Patrice Lewis is co-founder of Don Lewis Designs (www.donlewisdesigns.com). She and her husband have been in business for thirteen years. They live on forty acres in north Idaho with their two homeschooled children, assorted livestock, and a shop which overflows into the house with depressing regularity.

Heart healthy recipes

By Ilene Duffy

I'm not a nutritionist or a medical professional, but I've gained a lot of knowledge concerning foods that are considered to be heart healthy since my husband, Dave, underwent heart bypass surgery a few months ago. I've always enjoyed preparing homemade and varied meals with lots of fresh vegetables for my family, but now I have a new determination to also make sure those fresh ingredients are prepared in a heart-healthy manner.

Dave has been reading passages to me from *The Omega Diet*, so that we can both gain a better understanding of the ways in which food is prepared in much of the Mediterranean areas. Here's a sampling of what we've learned: olive oil and canola oil give us the necessary Omega-3 fatty acids; all kinds of nuts give us protein, "good" fat, and fiber; fish should be on the menu at least twice per week; fresh fruits and vegetables...the more the better; beans, beans, the wonderful fruit—I've been putting a drained and rinsed can or two in many recipes, whether it was in the original recipe or not. We're doing our best to avoid the processed stuff as well as beef. Likewise, we're making sure we have lots of whole grains in our diet. I'm adding a scoop or so of wheat bran to many recipes, I'm using brown rice exclusively, rather than plain white rice, and I'm still working on perfecting a loaf of bread that uses more of the whole wheat flour, rather than the plain white flour. A lot of the information we're reading concerning heart-healthy foods is good news in that these foods seem to also be excellent in helping us avoid a host of other ailments such as diabetes and cancer.

The following are a few recipes that I've prepared for our family. Even though my kitchen is one of my favorite places to be, they are quick to get ready for the dinner table. Δ

Salmon patties

1 lb. pre-baked salmon
juice of ½ lemon
3-4 Tbsp. orange juice
⅓ cup bread crumbs
1 egg
2 Tbsp. canola mayonnaise
1 Tbsp. curry powder
½ small onion, finely chopped
¼ cup grated Parmesan cheese
water
ketchup, about 2 Tbsp. or so
olive oil for frying

Squeeze lemon juice and orange juice over salmon. Sprinkle with seasonings of choice. I use Mrs. Dash and curry powder. Cover the fish with aluminum foil. Bake in a 350 degree oven for about 15-20 minutes.

Crumble the fish, removing any bones, into a large bowl. Add remaining ingredients and mix by hand. Sprinkle with water if the salmon won't hold together to form patties.

Heat olive oil in pan. Form salmon into patties. Fry on both sides 'til brown.

Serving suggestions: Add a tossed salad, a can of baked beans, and some whole wheat dinner rolls. Or serve with whole wheat buns and provide lettuce and tomato to make individual sandwiches.

Sliced oranges

2 peeled oranges
dates, cut in half
walnuts or pecans

Peel the oranges and slice thinly so that the slices have the center of the orange in the middle. The slices will look like the spokes of a wheel. Spread the slices on a plate. Add the chopped dates and nuts.

This is a simple Greek dish that really looks pretty on the table and is so quick to prepare.

Crock pot turkey chili

1 medium onion, chopped
3 cloves garlic, chopped
2 tsp. cumin
⅛ tsp. cayenne pepper
1 can each drained, rinsed pinto and black beans
1 can chopped green chilies
28 oz. chicken broth
2 lb. turkey thighs, skin removed
1 cup frozen corn, thawed
2 Tbsp. flour
¼ cup water

In crock pot, mix all ingredients except turkey, corn, flour, and water. Place turkey on bean mixture.

Cover. Cook on low heat setting 8-10 hours.

Remove meat from bones and cut meat into chunks. Add turkey and corn to cooker. In bowl, mix flour and water and add to mixture. Cook 20-30 minutes more on high.

COLD-HARDY GRAPEVINES

to make homemade wine, juice, and jelly

By Gail Butler

After a day's hard work I enjoy sitting on my front porch surveying my gardens and nearby mountain peaks while relaxing and sipping a tasty glass of homemade wine. From the harvest of my cold-hardy wine grapes, I also make delicious jelly and canned juice to enjoy all winter long. Yet, when I moved from temperate Southern California to rural Zone 5 Utah seven years ago, I thought I'd have to give up these simple homemade pleasures of the vine. I believed I would have to resort to expensive, store-bought options that went against my "grow-it-yourself/make-it-yourself" grain. Then I discovered cold-hardy grapevines.

Unlike the classic vinifera grapevines I was accustomed to, cold-hardy hybrid and native species grow in cold regions that would kill off their temperate cousins. The harvest of cold-hardy varieties may be turned into delicious table wines once you invest in a few inexpensive items of equipment. In addition to winemaking, cold-hardy grapes may be used to make cordials (all varieties of grapes) and dried for raisins (Muscat varieties). Their delicious juice may be canned, frozen, sauced, or jellied.

I first experimented with a cold hardy hybrid called *Marechal Foch,* noted for its vigor and flavor. I planted this vine in 1999 in my small backyard in central Utah. In 2000, when I bought a century-old farmhouse in a nearby farming town, I dug up the grapevine and transplanted it to my large kitchen garden. The vine not only weathered transplanting to produce its first small crop of grapes in 2001, but has since become a prolific source of gallons of great wine, lovely red jelly, and tasty, naturally sweet juice. Experience has taught me that most cold-hardy grapevines thrive in all types of soil, even infertile, chalky, and stony soils. Grapevines also ignore clay and alkaline soils. As long as soil is well drained, grapevines will flourish, and once established will require little watering.

My vine prospers on the wire fence at the back of my kitchen garden. It is a vigorous grower, shielding my vegetable beds from summer's drying winds and dependably yielding tight clusters of deep purple-black grapes that ripen in early September. I make a tasty burgundy-type wine with subtle cherry undertones by leaving the skins in contact with the juice for 24 hours. If I want to make a lighter wine with characteristics and color similar to a white Merlot, I strain the skins off immediately after crushing. Grapes from this vine are so tasty that I snack on them straight off the vine, seeds and all. Most wine grapes do contain seeds, usually one seed per grape.

With the success of my *Marechal Foch* experiment, I dug up a portion of my south lawn during the fall of 2003 to install a small vineyard so I could grow other cold-hardy grape varieties. In this small four-grapevine vineyard, I planted (spring of 2004) one each of the *Cayuga* and *Traminette* strains that will eventually yield white grapes for making white wine. I also planted *Frontenac,* another vigorous red. In spring 2005 I added a *Cynthiana,* or *Norton* (also called "Cabernet of the Ozarks"). The *Cynthiana* will bring a third red variety to my collection.

I planted a second *Marechal Foch* vine along the other half of the kitchen garden fence to provide wind protection for the asparagus bed and because I want to make more of this delicious wine for gift giving and jelly making. Jelly from this vine is a beautiful, clear red, perfect for embellishing holiday cookies and adding a festive touch to rolls and biscuits.

I also added a *Golden Muscat* that will add yet another white to my repertoire. With the yield of the *Golden Muscat*, I want to experiment drying my own raisins and making champagne, sherry, and sweet vermouth. Sweet vermouth is made from white wine, but unlike dry vermouth, is flavored with a variety of herbs and spices and gets its red color from adding caramelized sugar to the wine.

Cold-hardy wine varieties

Unfortunately, if you live below the USDA winter hardiness rating of Zone 3, you won't be able to grow grapes unless you plant them along a south-facing stone or block wall and provide winter protection such as wrapping the vine to protect the wood. However, other cold-hardy fruits and berries that thrive in USDA Zones 1 and 2 may be used to make wine and mead. A few very hardy grape varieties grow in Zones 3 and 4. All types of cold-hardy grapes thrive in Zone 5 and 6.

The end product of growing, harvesting, bottling, and aging wine is a lovely glassful to sip and enjoy.

Installing a simple vineyard

My farmhouse sits on a large corner property. I wanted to install my vineyard on the south side near the house to maximize sun exposure, ensuring peak sugar production in the grapes. This meant I needed to remove a portion of the lawn.

In the autumn of 2003 I covered the portion of lawn I wanted gone with sheets of heavy vinyl left over from my attic-conversion project. Smothering a lawn is much easier than digging it out. I secured plastic sheets firmly to the ground using garden staples fashioned from old wire clothes hangers. My homemade staples were free but similar in look and function to those available at

This cluster of ripe grapes contains a small green grape that will never ripen.

garden centers and through garden catalogs.

By spring of 2004 the vinyl-covered portions of lawn were dead due to exclusion of moisture and air. Lawn shoots and roots simply dissolved back into the soil with the spring thaw. I cut away ten-foot-long by two-foot-wide strips of plastic under the vine supports where I wanted to plant my grapevines. The vinyl remaining between the vine rows was covered with homemade elm bark mulch. Vinyl here will prevent weeds from sprouting, and the bark mulch gives a tidy look to the vineyard. I outlined the outside borders of the vineyard with bricks to keep the rest of the lawn from encroaching into my new vineyard.

The exposed soil lanes beneath the vine supports allow me to grow a crop of flowers or low-growing vegetables such as bush beans.

In Europe, it is traditional to grow flowers, herbs, or root crops beneath rows of grapevines. In cooler wine-growing regions, smooth, flat river rocks are used to surface the area beneath vine supports to absorb warmth during the day and release it during cold nights. This stone paving also reduces the need for weeding in large vineyards and conserves moisture in the soil from evaporation.

The size of your home vineyard depends on how much room you have, the number and varieties of grapevines you want to grow, and how much time you have to process grapes into wine, juice, and jelly. Six varieties of wine grapes, plus one *Concord* and one *Glenora* seedless grape for eating and juice will keep me very busy fermenting, jelly-making, and canning once they all reach peak production.

A vineyard will do best if you can locate it in a high spot so that cold air cannot settle around the vines. In Europe and in the wine-growing regions in the United States, vineyards are traditionally planted on hillsides so cold air will flow downhill away from vines. Slopes also provide better water drainage.

Try to locate your vineyard in an area of maximum sun exposure and protection from wind. Planting or constructing a windbreak is a good protection strategy. Newly planted bare root vines are susceptible to freezing and drying winds until they

Finished wine bottled for storage is ready for the cellar, plus a glass for me to enjoy.

These just-harvested grapes are ready to be crushed.

develop wood. Mature vines aren't bothered much by wind.

In my small vineyard I broke most, if not all, the rules. My property is flat, and my vineyard is located on the windward side to maximize sun exposure. Also, the vines have far outstripped, in growth, the shrubs I planted as a windbreak. To add insult to injury, my two *Marechal Foch* vines in the kitchen garden are used as windbreaks. All this proves that cold-hardy wine grapes are tough and withstand more than just cold winter temperatures. Grapevines can make dandy shade spots to enjoy during summer when grown over arbors. When grown against fences they provide seasonal screens to hide bad views and provide privacy.

To create supports for my vineyard, I installed nine eight-foot-high metal fence stakes in three rows of three. These were pounded three feet into the soil for stability. Each post is five feet apart from the others in all directions. The center post of each row, as well as the center post at one end, will be planted with one vine each allowing for four vines to cover five feet of wire in either direction. Two rows of heavygauge wire were strung down all three rows and across one end, leaving the opposite end open for access.

A season's harvest of wine ferments under the kitchen counter.

Lessons learned

My first attempt at planting failed (except for the very vigorous *Frontenac*) because of the harsh winds in my area each spring.

Late frosts and winds that are both freezing and drying are factors that afford a rough start to all my new plantings, especially bare-root items. I've learned that tender, bare-root grapevines, fruit trees, and roses need protection their first season.

A five-gallon plastic bucket, sawed in half with the bottom removed, will yield two protective collars. A gallon nursery container with the bottom sawed off is also an economical solution. Either will protect young grapevines from harsh winds while allowing sufficient sun exposure. Mulch the base of a new vine in its collar with a couple handfuls of straw to help retain soil moisture and keep the roots from drying out. The collar helps the mulch to stay put.

Keeping a new vine moist but not wet is a must until it becomes well established, usually by the third season. I like to cultivate a shallow basin around the base of each vine and water thoroughly so that water soaks the soil around and below the root. By the second season, watering three or four times a month is usually all that is needed. After that, once or twice a month is usually enough depending upon conditions where you live. My *Marechal Foch* is watered only once or twice during the growing season, now that it is fully established. After the grapes begin to form, I withhold water until after harvest. This stresses the vine slightly insuring it sets more fruit with a high sugar content essential for making good wine.

Growers recommend that new vines be pruned back to two or three leaf buds at planting. Because my area suffers such harsh spring conditions, I leave as many as four or five buds. This way I usually have at least one or two that survive a Utah spring to sprout and leaf out. If a vine survives its first spring and summer season, it will generally survive winter.

In addition to leaving more buds on, I also root what I've pruned at planting time. This is how I managed to replace the deceased *Traminette*. While the bare root parent plant died its first spring, the cutting wintered over in a clay pot in front of a sunny attic window. By keeping it watered, the following spring, a dead-looking twig leafed out. This cutting was replanted the following spring in a protective collar. I've since learned that cuttings can be rooted directly in the ground. Rooting hormone is not required when starting grapevine cuttings.

While grapevines grow species-true from their own cuttings, they don't grow true from their own seeds. Seeds will readily sprout, but you may not get tasty grapes from seedlings that are allowed to mature.

Increasing vine stock from cuttings off your own established vines is a great way to save money. Having a few spare rooted cuttings provides good bartering material, too.

Grapevines are self-pollinating, and each will produce grapes true to its own variety regardless of proximity to other types.

Planting a vineyard is an investment in the future. You may have to wait as long as four years before you get enough grapes to make your first gallon of wine. A vine may produce a few small clusters its second year. These should be cut off so the plant's energy goes into roots and top growth. If a vine is especially vigorous, I may allow it to ripen its third season's grapes. There are not usually enough third-season grapes to make even a gallon of wine, but there may be enough to harvest for a batch of jelly.

By the fourth season, you will likely have enough grapes to make a gallon of wine and some jelly. Come the fifth year, you will harvest enough for

Wine varieties by zone

	White juice	Red juice
Zone 3	Elvira (N) La Crescent Prairie Star	Beta (N) Valiant (N) Frontenac Rubiana St. Croix
Zone 4 (varieties listed above plus:)	Esprit La Crosse St. Pepin	Caco (N) Concord (N) Cynthiana (N) Delaware (N) Steuben (N) Ives Landot Leon Millot Marechal Foch Swenson Red
Zone 5 (varieties listed above plus:)	Golden Muscat (N) Moore's Diamond (N) Niagara (N) Aurore Cayuga Chardonel Melody Ravat Seyval Blanc Traminette Vignoles	Alwood (N) Chancellor Chelois De Chaunac New York Muscat St. Vincent Villard Noir Vincent
Zone 6 (varieties listed above plus:)	Vidal Blanc Villard Blanc Vivant J. Riesling	Baco Chambourcin Colobel Cabernet Franc Lemberger
Zones 7 and 8 (varieties listed above plus:)	Chardonnay Gerwurztraminer Pinot Gris	Cabernet Merlot Pinot Noir Shiraz

several gallons of wine, jelly, and juice.

Homemade wine versus estate bottled

Expensive estate-bottled wines from Europe, Australia, and the U.S. are the current fashion, but this was not always so. Nearly forgotten is the rich tradition of delicious, homemade wines produced by country folk from homegrown and wild-gathered grapes.

Homemade wine, often called "folk wine," is traditionally made with simple baking yeast. In ancient times, wine was made by allowing naturally occurring wild yeast on grapes to ferment juice into wine; however, the alcohol content of the finished wine was only about 5%. While a reduced-alcohol wine can sometimes be a desirable thing, wild yeast doesn't always give a consistent or tasty product. Centuries ago, country folk experimented using bread yeast instead of depending on wild grape yeast to make their wine. They were pleased with the results, and today traditional folk wine is made with baking yeast. Many home vintners use special strains of wine yeast, but for a traditional folk product, baking yeast is preferable.

Because wine yeast is not always vigorous enough to overpower wild yeast, sulfites are used to kill wild yeast and prepare a competition-free environment. In addition, sulfites are used to treat bottles and other winemaking and bottling equipment to prevent bacterial growth.

A problem created by adding sulfites is that they are also deadly to wine yeast and once added cannot be removed. There is a delicate balance between adding enough sulfite to kill off wild yeast while still allowing wine yeast to survive to eventually ferment juice into wine.

Sulfites can cause lethal allergic reactions in people that have sensitivity to them. Too much added sulfite not only wreaks havoc with frail wine yeast, but can add a "rotten egg" taint to finished wines. Additionally, too much sulfite, if it doesn't outright kill wine yeast, can so weaken yeast that it ceases fermentation before wine attains a high enough alcohol content. A sufficiently high alcohol content prevents the growth of organisms that can make a batch of wine undrinkable. Once fermentation produces sufficient alcohol, your wine will be protected and preserved until aged and ready to drink.

Having made wine using both types of yeast, I prefer baker's yeast. I enjoy perpetuating the tradition of simply made, rustic folk wine and leaving estate-style winemaking to those that don't mind using sulfites.

Twice I have had the opportunity to serve my folk wine to purists without divulging the nature of the yeast used. One pronounced my wine "delicious," the other praised it as "eminently drinkable," and both readily accepted second and third servings. Folk-style wines are certainly less expensive to make.

I use baking yeast for several reasons:

1. Baking yeast is a traditional ingredient in folk wine since the discovery of leavened bread. Plus, I want to perpetuate my family's heritage of wine and beer making begun during Prohibition.

2. I have not been able to find that delicate balance between sulfite addition and the dying point of wine yeast with any dependable consistency. Baking yeast is vigorous enough to overcome wild yeast without the addition of sulfites.

3. Baking yeast is readily available in my area while wine yeast must be mail-ordered.

4. Wine yeast does not culture well when I've tried to make a yeast starter for long-term storage and use.

5. I always have baking yeast in some form on hand because I bake my own bread.

6. Wine I make with baking yeast is consistently successful.

7. I am very busy most of the growing season. When I make wine, I want it to be simple with as few steps, ingredients, and complications as possible.

For all of these reasons I now exclusively make all my wine with baker's yeast.

It is said that baking yeast produces a wine with an alcohol content a couple percentage points less (between 10.5 to 11%) than that produced with wine yeast (about 12.5%). I haven't been able to taste a difference in the finished product.

I grow grapes for my folk wine organically without pesticides or chemical fertilizers. To sterilize my fermenting equipment and bottles, I simply wash everything with hot water with a little added ammonia (too much ammonia may cloud glass). Rinse, rinse, rinse, then let everything cool to almost room temperature. I have not had a bacterial invasion that turns my wine sour. I like the thought that my wine is free of chemicals from growth to finished product.

Pruning grapevines

Estate-grown grapevines are severely pruned each season. Ease of harvest and sun exposure are the two main reasons. When not shaded by leaf growth, grape clusters ripen sooner and simultaneously, while developing more sugar. Vines that are not pruned ripen sun-exposed clusters first, followed by shaded clusters a week or more later. Bunches growing in shade won't always develop as much natural sugar as their sun-exposed counterparts.

I don't severely prune my grapes but do cut them back each spring to fruiting buds, usually in mid-March or early April in my area. I prune before the new buds begin to unfurl. Grapes are produced off buds from the site of the previous year's leaf growth. The older growth supporting the fruiting shoots is dark and shaggy. If buds form on this growth, rub them off. Fruiting shoots are smooth and almost the diameter of a pencil. Fruiting wood is recognizable by prominent buds located over the scars of the previous season's leaves.

A rule of thumb is that the first three buds along a fruiting cane are not very fruitful. Buds four through 13 are the most fruitful, while buds further along the cane decline in quality and quantity. Commercial growers prune the cane at this point. In a small or compact vineyard you'll want to prune a fruiting cane just past the 12th or 13th bud.

My goal in pruning my *Marechal Foch* vines is to strike a balance between maximizing grape production and allowing enough growth to protect my kitchen garden from wind. Grapevines in my new vineyard will need to be pruned a bit more compactly to only the buds of maximum fruitfulness. A few things to keep in mind regarding pruning are:

1. Excess leaf production will reduce energy going into fruiting, resulting in less fruit and smaller bunches. Over fertilizing creates excess leaf growth. Use a low nitrogen fertilizer, and use it frugally.
2. Energy going into non-fruitful and lesser fruiting buds inhibits fruit production.
3. No pruning at all results in a snarl of canes, spurs, trunks, and hard-to-reach fruit with low sugar content as well as decreased fruit production.
4. Less pruning is needed in a cold winter area to help protect wood producing next season's fruiting canes from freezing/drying winter winds.

Feeding grapevines

Grapevines do well on lean fertilizers such as leaf compost. Mix three or four parts leaf compost with one part well-rotted horse manure. If you use manure, it is important to compost it first then dilute it with rotting leaves or decomposing straw so that vine roots absorb less nitrogen. Underfertilization of vines is preferable to overdoing it. Don't fertilize your vines until the third or fourth year and then every other year after that.

When I fertilize my vines, it is with a diluted (about half the strength recommended) fish fertilizer or a rotten elm leaf mulch. Coffee grounds and tea leaves can be cultivated into the ground around vines. Small amounts of straw-rich poultry manure well distributed in nutrient-poor leaf mulch (one part manure/straw mixture to five parts leaf mulch) also works well.

When to harvest

Long before the invention of expensive gadgets for measuring peak sugar content in grapes, country folk used their taste buds to determine peak sweetness. As grapes ripen, I begin to taste them once or twice a week. When they are sweet and tasty, I set aside a dry, sunny morning to harvest them.

Some clusters will contain a few hard, green grapes that won't ripen. These immature grapes will not affect the sugar content of those you intend to crush because they will pass intact through a traditional crush to be strained out with stems, seeds, and skins. Even if crushed, a few green grapes won't affect the overall quality of the juice.

Birds are also an indicator of impending ripeness of grapes. A couple of weeks before grapes are ready for harvest, birds begin to monitor progress. While birds will eat unripe fruit, they don't prefer it. Birds begin to go after my grapes just before or at peak sugar.

I harvest the bulk of my grapes for wine and juice at peak sugar. Clusters beneath leaves that are not quite ripe are used for jelly because I have to add several cups of sugar anyway. I usually leave undersize bunches forming on less fruitful buds for the birds to enjoy. Attracting birds to your garden, even with your lovely grapes, does have the benefit of reducing insect populations. While birds enjoy nibbling in your vineyard, they also forage for insect pests, making it worthwhile to sacrifice a few grapes to greedy beaks.

Protecting the grapes from birds

I use a variety of means to protect ripening grapes from birds. Anything that will move or flap in the breeze is very effective. One of my favorite bird deterrents are free computer CDs sent by Internet service providers. I tie the CDs to fence posts and grapevines with a length of twine. With every breeze they bounce and shimmer, scaring away birds. I also use long lengths of plastic ribbon, and strips of fabric or plastic.

My least favorite prevention technique is bird netting. It's time consuming to put over the vines and difficult to remove. No matter how secure I try to make it, birds always figure out how to get under it. Also, grapes grow fast during the summer months, and fruit, leaves, and tendrils tangle in the netting.

I don't install bird-prevention measures until grape clusters color up a few weeks before harvest. Birds discover after a couple of weeks that while all the flapping of my bird prevention techniques may be unnerving, it is not harmful. My three cats also act as deterrents.

The crush

There is no way around it. Unless you are fortunate enough to have your own fruit press, the only way to crush enough grapes for several gallons of wine is to do it the old fashioned way...using your feet! This traditional method of crushing grapes separates estate-bottled wine from the time-honored tradition of making folk wine.

Grapes should be crushed right after picking to avoid attracting fruit flies. Otherwise, bacteria carried by fruit flies will turn your wine to vinegar. If you culture your own "vinegar mother," it will happily thrive on young wine you produce over and above what you intend to drink. Making your own wine vinegar in addition to your own table wine is a satisfying accomplishment.

When grape bunches are first picked, they are home to earwigs, spiders, and plant matter. I drop freshly picked clusters into five-gallon plastic buckets. By running water into the buckets and submerging the grapes, debris floats off. After removing the grapes to clean, dry buckets, they are taken into the kitchen.

The now semi-clean clusters are given a final rinse in the kitchen sink before being tossed into a washtub set on the kitchen floor on a large towel or old sheet. This particular washtub is used ONLY for crushing grapes.

Making a ritual of the crush is a tradition I've adopted from country folk. Wine harvesting and crushing in my area coincides with the completion of most of the harvesting and canning of other produce from my garden. A simple little ritual of putting on a relaxing music CD and pouring myself a glass of last year's wine makes the crushing process very enjoyable. When all is ready, I thoroughly wash and dry my feet, then tiptoe back into the kitchen wearing clean socks. While standing on clean towels surrounding the washtub, I remove the socks, step in, toast the grape harvest, and begin to gently stomp the grapes until all are crushed and juice fills the tub.

You will find that stomping grapes feels good! Grapes contain oils that are a balm and conditioning agent for the skin. The textures of slippery skins, smooth seeds, and rubbery stems will massage and soothe your soles (and soul) better than any stroll along a sandy beach. When you are finished crushing and step out of the washtub, your feet will be soothed and tingly. Keep a clean towel within reach to wipe off grape skins and juice and to dry your feet afterward.

Making wine

After the crush, your washtub contains a mixture of juice, skins, seeds, and stems. This conglomerate is called a "must" and is rife with a variety of flavor components. Juice adds the "sweet notes," while a multitude of flavor factors are found in the skins and stems. Tannins from skins and stems give complexity and dryness to a finished wine.

If you want a sweeter, more delicate wine, you'll want to strain off the skins right after crushing. To make a semi-bold red or a dry white, I remove about half the stems right after crushing. The rest of the solids and juice go into a large, plastic vat I use as a primary fermenting vessel. This vessel holds five gallons of must. Upon transferring the must to the primary fermenting vessel, the opening should be covered with a clean towel held in place with a board, an elastic band, or a fitted lid. Food-grade five-gallon buckets may be used as primary fermenting vessels and can be found behind hospitals, restaurants, schools, shelters, and nursing homes.

If you want to use dry baker's yeast to make wine, you can speed up the time it takes for dry yeast to break out of dormancy by making a "nucleus." Boil one teaspoon of sugar in a half cup of water. When this cools to skin temperature, add one teaspoon of yeast to serve approximately one gallon of juice. When the yeast bubbles up, pour the nucleus into the must. If your yeast is in the form of a starter, add one-quarter cup of active, recently fed, **room temperature** starter to each gallon of must. A starter fresh from the refrigerator or cooler will be slow to come into activity. Yeast needs to be at full vigor to combat wild yeast in the must.

To each gallon of must, I add the nucleus or starter, plus a half-cup of sugar, to jump-start the yeast population. After consuming the sugar and rapidly expanding their population, yeast will extract necessary nutrients from the sugars naturally occurring in the juice. Creating a population explosion by providing the half-cup of sugar allows baker's yeast ratios to vigorously overcome and overwhelm naturally occurring grape yeast. Although I pick my grapes at peak sweetness, I still add the half-cup additional sugar when the yeast nucleus or starter is introduced. This additional sugar won't affect the taste of the finished wine because it is consumed early on and serves only to feed the yeast and rapidly increase their population. Homemade wine may be made with or without adding additional sugar to achieve a traditional, folk product.

The day after adding yeast to your must, your developing wine will acquire a "cap." The cap is formed when skins begin to ride upon the fermenting must. The cap should be stirred down twice a day with a large clean spoon. If not, mold may begin to colonize the surface of the must, ruining your wine.

How long you leave the seeds, skins, and remaining stems in contact with the juice is up to you. With white wine, I leave the must for only eight to ten hours to increase dryness and flavor. For a sweet white wine, the skins are removed immediately.

For robust red wines, skin contact can go on as long as seven to ten days. I usually leave the must to ferment no more than one to three days to avoid the excess dryness and acidity prolonged skin contact can have on wine.

The color of rich reds, such as burgundy or cabernet-style wines, comes from several days of skin contact. A lighter red wine results from less skin contact. Contact also yields more juice, which means more wine

Grapevine sources:

Miller Nurseries
5060 West Lake Road
Canandaigua, NY 14424-8904
1-800-836-9630
www.millernurseries.com
Mostly Zone 5 grapevines with a few for Zones 3, 4, and 6.

Stark Bro's Nurseries & Orchards Co.
P.O. Box 1800
Louisiana, MO 63353
1-800-325-4180
www.starkbros.com
Mostly Zone 5 grapevines with one or two for Zone 6.

Double A Vineyards, Inc.
10277 Christy Road
Fredonia, NY 14063
716-672-8493
vine@Rakgrape.com
A huge selection of American, hybrid, and vinifera grapes for Zones 3, 4, 5, 6 and up.

The Beer Nut, Inc.
1200 S. State
Salt Lake City, UT 84111
801-531-8182, 888-825-4697
www.beernut.com
Winemaking supplies and equipment, corks, fermentation locks, yeast. Also brewing supplies and hops rhizomes.

Paradise Ranch Wines Corp.
Suite 901-525 Seymour Street
Vancouver, BC V6B 3H7
Canada
604-683-6040
info@icewines.com
Icewines and late-harvest wines

Books:

* *From Vines to Wines* by Jeff Cox, Storey Publishing, Pownal, Vermont: 1985. A great resource for in-depth information on various techniques of vine pruning, setting up a vineyard, soils, equipment. Winemaking processes outlined in this book are more complex than most home vintners are willing or need to pursue. A good research book, however.

* *Wines from a Small Vineyard, Planting to Bottling* by James Page-Roberts, Abbeville Press, New York, London, Paris: 1995.

A simpler, more user-friendly approach to growing and producing fine homemade wines.

* *Stocking Up III* by Carol Hupping and the Rodale Food Center Staff, Rodale Press, Emmaus, Pennsylvania: 1986.

Great resource for preserving the harvest. Juice and jelly recipes plus canning, freezing, and drying.

because the cell walls of the skins break down releasing additional liquid.

The next step is to strain out the solids. There are a variety of methods and equipment to do this. I opt for low-tech and cost-free. I have a large strainer I line with an old, clean dishtowel. This rests over a large bowl or cooking pot. I ladle the must and juice into the towel-lined strainer, gather up the towel edges, and twist them tighter and tighter to press out the juice. The strainer catches any solids that escape so they won't fall into just-strained juice. I repeat this step until the bowl is full of juice and all solids have been squeezed of liquid and strained out. If you want to can some juice in addition to winemaking, now is the time to set aside what you need. Cool or refrigerate juice intended for juice or jelly making for at least 24 hours to allow grape tartar to settle. Pour the juice off the tartar and make jelly using your favorite recipe.

Canned juice may be made using juice from either crushing or heat extraction. Allow the juice to sit 24 hours so tartar will settle that would otherwise muddy and affect the taste of the finished juice. Use your favorite juice recipe and proceed as you normally would or heat juice to a simmer and sweeten to taste, if needed. Pour hot juice into hot, sterile jars leaving ½-inch headroom in pints, and one inch for quarts. Place in a water or steam canner for five minutes, adding one additional minute for each 1,000 feet above sea level. Figure that seven pounds of grapes will yield about three quarts of juice. Skip the settling period of juice intended for wine production.

After the desired period of skin contact and straining, the fermenting juice/new wine is immediately poured or funneled into a secondary fermenting vessel. For my secondary fermenting vessels I use gallon glass jugs I've saved from wine or juice purchases. I also ask friends and relatives to save wine jugs for me. For the young and strong, old five-gallon glass water bottles make excellent secondary fermenting vessels and are worth looking for. However, these are heavy when full of liquid and difficult to lift up onto the sink top when the time comes to rack or bottle the wine.

Once filled, my secondary fermenting jugs are stopped with No. 6½ rubber corks fitted with water-filled fermentation locks. Rubber corks and plastic S-style fermentation locks cost about $1.00 each. If you don't have fermentation locks, you can stretch a large balloon over the neck of the jug. Gases resulting from fermentation will fill the balloon, necessitating the release of gases that might burst the balloon. Fermentation locks allow gases to escape while preventing air from getting into the wine and creating oxidation that could affect the finished wine's color and flavor.

After a few weeks, the bubbling of gases escaping through the fermentation locks slows and the water in the locks return to level instead of being pushed up one side. Sediments from spent yeast will have settled into the bottom of the jug. It's time to rack your young wine into clean jugs. This accomplishes a couple purposes. The first is that the wine will be agitated so that any remaining still viable yeast comes into contact with and consumes any remaining grape sugar, continuing the fermentation process. The second reason is the removal of wine off the sediments, or lees. Re-racking leaves behind sediment that could muddy your wine when bottling time comes. After re-racking into clean containers, re-attach the fermentation locks.

To rack my wine into clean jugs, I use a four-foot length of flexible clear plastic tubing. This can be purchased through wine suppliers, hardware stores, or pet shops. Use tubing with a diameter no less than ¼-inch. I use tubing ½-inch in diameter. One end of the tubing goes into the jug containing the wine and the other end into a clean jug. It helps to elevate the jug being emptied two or three feet above the one you are going to fill. I place the jug I want to empty on a wooden stepstool sitting on the kitchen counter. The jug I want to fill sits in the kitchen sink in case of spills. Be sure your tubing is clean of dust, old wine, and soap residue before siphoning.

I suspend one end of the tubing in the jug so it rests above the sediments. Suck gently on the other end and just before the wine gets to your mouth insert the tubing into the new jug. Once the flow has begun between the jugs, you can stop it by simply bending the tubing.

Pay attention to the dropping wine level in the jug you're emptying. Try to keep the tubing suspended above the sediments but beneath the surface of the wine. As the jug empties, I tip it gently in order to siphon out more wine before the sediments begin going into the tubing. Most of the time the sediments form a thick, sludge that won't enter the tubing until very little wine remains. I may re-rack my wine as many as three or four times over a period of months. Each racking leaves behind some unwanted sediment and stimulates any still live yeast into activity. It is important that all yeast activity ceases completely before bottling.

Anyone who has made wine will likely have the unpleasant experience of wine beginning to ferment again after final bottling. At the very least corks begin to ease out of bottles leaking wine onto the floor. At worst, the wine will burst forth leaving a widespread sticky mess. This unfortunate situation is most likely to happen if your late harvest wines are fermenting when weather turns cold. Cooler temperatures in the fermenting area cause yeast to suspend activity and may trick you into thinking fermentation is complete. Warming temperatures in spring re-activate yeast...and "Bang!" a cork will shoot across the cellar. To prevent this, locate wine that is fermenting during winter months near a source of warmth such as a wood stove or heater. During winter, my wines will cease fermenting during the night when I allow the kitchen to cool off. In the morning, they begin to bubble again as the temperature warms. The ideal is to keep the fermenting wine at a constant temperature, but my wine doesn't seem to suffer from daily warming and cooling periods.

After bottling, the finished wine is taken to the root cellar where it will age from six months to two years. Here the wine ages at a constant temperature. After final bottling, keeping wine at a constant temperature IS important.

A delightful occurrence is when a VERY SLIGHT re-fermentation recurs after bottling. A weak re-fermentation isn't likely to throw the cork from the bottle. What you do get is a slight "prickle," or effervescence, when the bottle is uncorked and the wine poured. This "almost champagne" is a real treat and will happen occasionally and accidentally.

Bottling and enjoying your homemade wine

Wait for fermentation to cease completely for several weeks before you bottle your wine for aging. I re-use wine bottles that friends and relatives save for me. Their reward for providing me with wine bottles is the gift of delicious homemade wine.

Bottling is a delightful time for this is when I sample the dregs of young wine left in the jugs on the lees when bottling is completed. This taste of young wine gives a hint of what a fully mature wine will become. Aging mellows any acidic flavor components and harmonizes a young wine's diverse flavors. While new wine will be tasty, an aged wine is ennobled making it well worth the wait.

I siphon wine from jugs into clean wine bottles using the same method I used when racking. You can also age your wine in clean jugs if you like. I always save the screw on caps for gallon jugs and if there are no sediments remaining after the last racking, I merely remove the cork and fermentation lock and screw on a cap. Don't allow your wine to age on any degree of sediment. Taste and clarity will be vastly improved if your wine is siphoned off the lees. Occasionally I will find a bit of sediment when opening a bottle of aged wine even though at bottling no sediment appeared to be present. Simply decant the wine or turn the wine bottle upright several hours before serving to allow the sediment to resettle in the bottom of the bottle.

My favorite wine bottles for aging are those with screw-on lids. If I have to use corks, I use No. 9 corks and an inexpensive corking device.

To prepare corks for insertion, boil them for ten minutes. Corks are very buoyant, so I set something heat-resistant on top so they'll sink beneath the water. Boiling the corks serves two purposes: it softens them for compression and insertion by the corking device; and it sterilizes them.

Occasionally, a cork will not insert all the way. When this happens, I use a small screwdriver whose handle is slightly smaller in diameter than the neck of a wine bottle. Resting the end of the handle on the cork, I use a hammer to firmly tap the business end of the screwdriver, thereby "nailing" the cork completely into the neck of the bottle. I sink corks slightly deeper than the top edges of the bottles' openings.

While not necessary, I like to melt a bit of paraffin to dribble onto the top of the cork. The paraffin cap helps prevent air from entering between the bottle's neck and cork and usually prevents wine from seeping out until the cork expands sufficiently to seal the bottle. Store your bottled wine on its side to keep the cork moist so it won't shrink allowing wine to escape and air to enter and oxidize the wine.

For gift giving, try melting a bit of crayon in the paraffin to color it like the wax plugs found on fancy estate-bottled wines. If you have a computer with a publishing program, you can create nice labels for your homemade wines.

To save paper and expense, I attach homemade labels only to wine that I intend for gift-giving. For bulk cellar storage, I use stick-on notes or scraps of paper held on with rubber bands. I like to include pertinent information on my labels such as grape variety, harvest date, and bottling date.

In a separate notebook, I record any variations or additions in my winemaking that yielded exceptional results as well as those that resulted in less desirable outcomes. I also include the number of rackings and their dates.

My newly bottled wine ages in the pantry for three months to be sure it won't blow any corks. After that, I move the wine into the root cellar. It's much easier to mop spilled, sticky wine out of the pantry than the root cellar where I have no water source and a lot of wooden steps to negotiate. To store my wine while it ages, I use both wire and wooden dairy crates I find discarded or purchase cheaply at yard sales. Each holds a number of wine bottles and can be stacked easily to maximize storage space.

You can create interesting blended wine by mixing wine of various grape varieties at bottling time. It is best to do this only after you've created successful wine from single varieties. Once you are successful with singles, you can mix and match to create special blends with characteristics of grapes you think would pair or combine nicely. Blend your finished new wine at bottling; don't blend raw juice.

Once in a blue moon

The Germans call it *Eiswein.* I call it "Icewine." And once in a blue moon, a rare opportunity to make this special wine occurs. Traditionally, Icewine is made from white grapes still on the vine when a hard freeze occurs. However, a vineyard in Canada that specializes in Icewine sells both red and white wines made from vinifera and cold-hardy grape varieties. Frozen grapes are picked and processed, resulting in a rare and sweet dessert wine. Germany, Canada, and cold-winter areas of the U.S. and Europe (Zones 3-5, generally, and higher zones with ideal conditions) are areas where the possibility of making Icewine exists.

For the first time in seven years, the temperature at my house dipped to 28 degrees Fahrenheit with grapes still on the vine. An unusually late harvest season and an early freeze combined to allow me to make Icewine. I processed a gallon of juice from grapes still on the vine after previous gatherings for wine, juice, and jelly.

My Icewine is still fermenting merrily in my kitchen, so I can't tell you how it will turn out. Traditionally, Icewine is thicker, richer, and sweeter than traditional wine. I'm looking forward to my first sip and sharing with friends next year.

A few final thoughts

Making your own wine is a rewarding enterprise resulting in bottles of delicious, natural wine that cost little beyond a small investment in corks, corking device, and fermentation locks. Winemaking in the folk wine tradition does not need to be the expensive, complex process depicted in many winemaking manuals. Nor do you need special wine yeast if you intend on following the time-honored tradition of making rustic country folk wine.

If you have too many grapes to process and little time to do so, you can make cordial by filling a Mason jar with clean grapes. Top off the grape-filled jar with vodka or brandy, screw on a cap, and let the mixture sit in a cupboard or pantry for several weeks. Shake the mixture occasionally. Strain off the grapes when finished, and taste your cordial. If it needs added sweetening, you can add sugar to taste. Grapes harvested at peak sugar content shouldn't need much added sugar to make a sweet cordial for after-dinner or fireside sipping.

Grape harvest time usually coincides with the end of canning and preserving the other produce from my kitchen garden and small orchard. The grape harvest and subsequent winemaking is a celebration because it marks the end of a busy season and heralds the coming season of rest when winter snow enwraps the house with a blanket of cold. One of my winter rewards is sitting in front of my wood stove sipping a glass of homemade wine while planning next year's vegetable garden. Δ

CARVED HINGES part 2

By David Lee

I had been wondering if my readers preferred serious projects or fun ones so I commissioned a poll to find out. All five of my fans answered it. Half of them liked the serious articles, half liked the fun ones, half liked everything. So...to continue keeping them all contented, this month's project is serious and fun.

Get yourselves up to speed by reviewing *Backwoods Home Magazine*'s issue #98, page 8 (included in this anthology on page 76) about how to build mild mannered wood hinges. Pay special attention to

Counter doors with foil showing through drilled and whittled holes. Note carved handles and locks.

Entry door with carved hinges and door handle, stained glass sun catchers, and small stones for decoration. Note side vents made the same way.

brackle making because these advanced hinges use the same kind.

Before actually threatening a piece of wood let's consider material and design choices. Do not use hardwood for your first hinges. It is expensive, splits too easy and is depressingly hard to carve. I make my hinges out of ¾" pine boards. Of the several thousand I have made, none has ever broken from stress or wear. If you are a wood snob and demand the luxuriousness of oak, teak, mahogany or whatever, ok, go with it, but use pine for your first efforts.

These advanced hinges require close attention to grain direction, knots and density of the wood. As you design your hinges on paper ask yourself where the weak places would be if the wood were to split along the grain. You will, of course, break this rule as regularly as I do, so later on I will advise you on this.

Knots are beautiful and enhance the charisma of your hinges. Try to arrange for them to be away from the ends or edges of your hinge parts. Knots are hard to carve (a bad thing), sometimes fall out (possibly a good thing), and they contain nice smelling sap (a good thing) that is sticky (a bad thing) but are worth the trouble. I sometimes alter a design to accommodate particularly charming knots.

Density is middling important. Softwood carves easily but dense wood wears better, especially around the hinge pin area. Pine varies in density, even within the same piece of wood. As you work with pine you will acquire a "feel" for softness and density. Let the "feel" guide you in choosing the best pieces, just like choosing a pear or a peach, or a wife.

Consider the required sturdiness of the doors you are hinging. As a general rule I use two hinges on cabinet and counter doors, three on passage doors and four on outside doors. The size of your hinges and the strength of the parts around the pin are factors in the performance of your hinges. You can add extra brackles, extra hinge arms, extra screws, supports under the hinge pins, and decorative trim as components for extra structural integrity. Fortunately you have total control over all these factors and can produce just what is needed for your projects. That is, after you practice awhile.

As you become proficient at hinge design, taking into account the uses, proportions, and weight of the door you are improving and the effect you want to create when someone uses it, you'll notice this is a form of Art. That makes you an Artist (congratulations) and perhaps creates a business opportunity. You could learn to make bodacious hinges for everything from barns to jewelry boxes.

The cost of materials for any of these hinges rarely rises above ten dollars even for a full size door with lots of goodies built into it. I cannot imagine how much custom-made wrought iron hinges would cost. Far more than ten dollars I am sure. And these hinges are much more dramatic, with a strong three-dimensional presence, and they are guaranteed not to rust. Aren't you thrilled you bought this magazine?

Let's get creative. Start with a four-hinge set for practice. Acquire some clear pine boards longer than your

On the right we see hinge parts traced on pine boards. The first cut part is used as a pattern for the rest. A saber saw is the simplest tool for cutting out the pieces. Note the saw slots, sized to tightly fit the hinge pins, in the smaller hinge parts in the lower center part of the picture. Saw slots are made on a table saw.

door width by about six inches, some shorter pieces for small parts and some 16d common nails. Using your imagination, the drawing and pictures accompanying this article, draw the long and short hinge strap shapes on paper while you are a beginner at this, or right on the wood if you are confident. I suggest you make your first hinges fairly simple until you learn the nuances involved in making them work successfully. Using your first cut piece as a template, trace out four of each strap and eight brackles. That is 16 parts. Trace out a few extras while you are at it. The extra parts allow for mistakes. Cut the parts with a saber saw and table saw.

Use the straight edge of your board as one side of your novice hinges. This allows for square and level alignment later. When you have mastered the installation of wood hinges you can alter this rule and make free-form designs. I have included pictures of various shaped hinges with this article to give you inspiration. Just

In the upper left corner are handles assembled with glue and screws, ready for carving. Below them are turnlocks drilled for pivot screws to be inserted. The two on the right have some carving started. To the right of the handles and turnlocks are hinges and brackles in various stages of construction along with my favorite carving tool, a Stanley utility knife.

Who said wood is always brown? These are some of the colors available when you learn the magic of using leather dyes as wood stain. This shows hinges, handles and lock sets assembled, carved, colored and ready to grace four doors. Note the orientation of the hinges to each other. They can be attached to the door with the straight sides up, down, aligned or opposed.

remember, the long hinge strap needs to be rigid and strong. The wood grain should run the full length of the strap. You'll see what I mean as you work.

Let's deal with the necessary technical details now. Notice the areas of the long and short hinge straps around the hinge pin slot. Use a table saw to make all the hinge straps two inches wide for a distance of three inches (minimum) from the butt end of the straps, using the straight edge of your boards as the reference surface that slides along the saw fence to control accuracy. Square off the butt end. Take a deep breath. Half the tricky technical requirements for this job are done.

The short hinge straps need a slot that tightly accommodates a 16d common nail that will be the hinge pin. Use the table saw to do this. The drawing shows slot dimensions. Note: I drew the slot out of proportion for clarity and because I can't draw that small. Moving the saw fence and controlling the height of the saw blade will achieve a tight fit for the nail. Run each and every short strap through the saw after each adjustment of the fence and blade, using the butt end as your reference surface so all parts are identical. Use a 16D nail as a guide. When the nail can be pressed into the slots with some force and does not settle in lower than the surface of the strap, you win. Got that? Square slot, round nail, tight fit. You can do this.

Ok, now you have four short hinge straps each with a slot parallel to the butt, four long hinge straps without a slot, and eight brackles. Later, when you are mass producing hinges you can save time by making several extra sets of everything. When I do cabinets I may need several dozen hinge sets so adding an extra dozen sets into the production run gives me a head start on later jobs, plus it looks cool having piles of beautiful hand-carved hinges around to impress guests.

Check the drawing. Notice the pilot holes in the long hinge strap. You may or may not need them, depending on how easily the wood you are using tends to split. Glue the short strap to the long strap as the drawing shows, using carpenters glue and 1 $^{1}/_{8}$" drywall screws driven in from the back of the long strap. Make certain the parts fit together exactly at the butt and top of each unit so everything is square, tight and right.

At this point you are going to want to put one of the 16D nails through the square hole just to actually see a round peg in a square hole. So...go ahead, get it out of your system. It should require the gentle use of a hammer. Getting the nail back out may need the use of a punch and hammer.

Now that the hinge straps are assembled, drill the hinge pin holes in the brackles with a drill press and fixture as described in the last issue. The exact size and location of the hinge pin holes vary according to the needs of your doors and casings. It's a challenge, but I know you will figure it out after reviewing the information

This is an example of colored and carved hinges I call "Swamp Vines." The hinges cross the entire width of the door plus ¾ of an inch. This gives structural support to the door and the ¾" overhang stops the door from passing into the casing. I use three or four hinges on most interior doors for strength and embellishment. Note the upper and lower turnlocks that provide ample security for tall and short people.

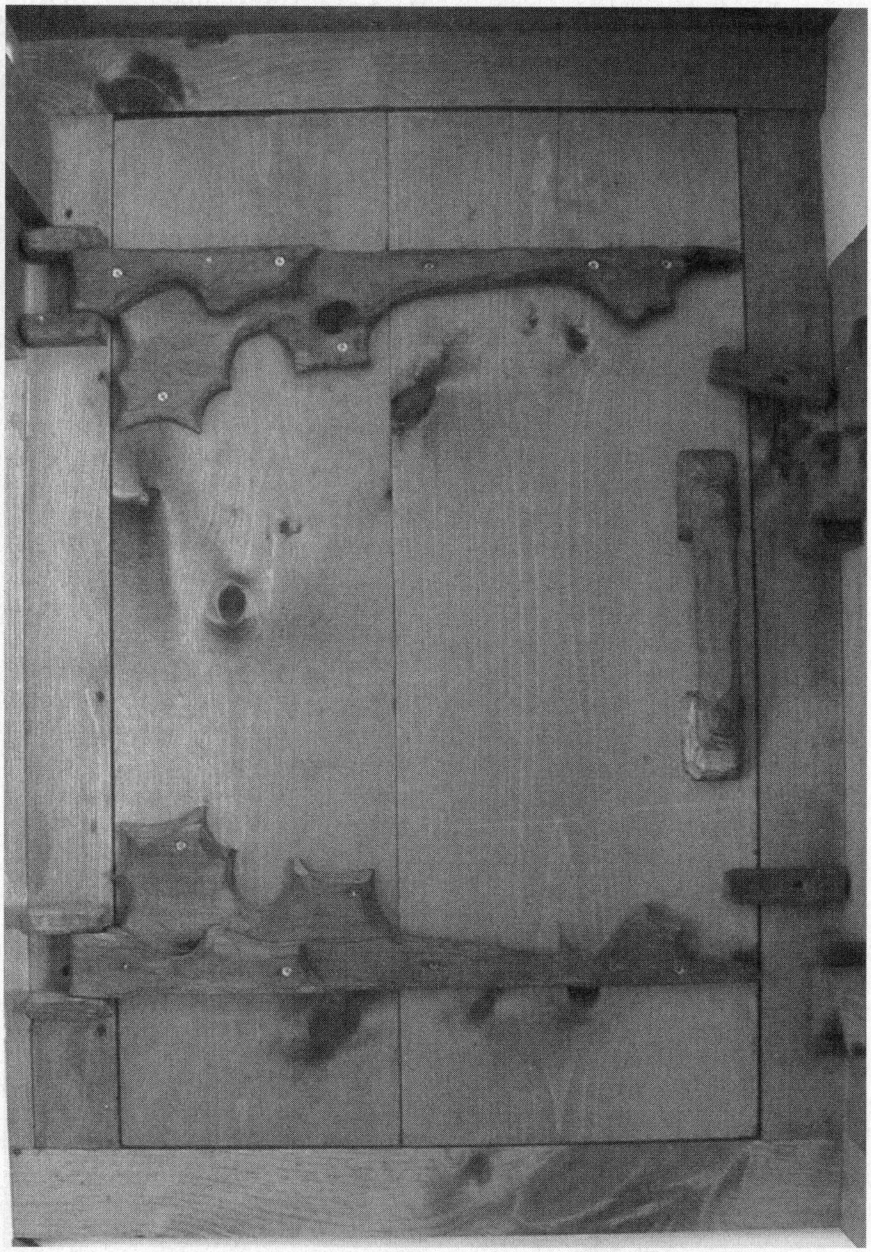

blatantly and subliminally contained in these two articles.

It is tempting to assemble all the hinge parts right now but restrain your enthusiasm for awhile because something extraordinary is about to happen. You have the opportunity to revive a lost skill and use it in a new art form.

Whittling is the lost skill. My second cousin could whittle a chain out of an apple tree branch. My grandfather whittled all the parts for his horse harnesses. In John Steinbeck's novel, *The Grapes of Wrath*, a mechanic whittled a piston for a car. And don't forget the tribute to whittlers everywhere—the famous painting of Whittler's Mother. Whittling was very important in the "old days" before Chinese imports.

Here is a vent door with dyed wood, contrasting screws, a carved handle and locks.

To whittle you need a good knife. By good I mean one that feels right in your hand. Old-fashioned ones I've seen have a four- or five-inch handle and a one-inch blade of special steel from an ancient meteorite found at Stonehenge, Grandpa said. They are still available in catalogs that specialize in old style tools. Grandpa carried his all the time. He even whittled the handle for it. However, he didn't leave it to me in his will so I had to buy a common utility knife to do my whittling and carving. You must keep

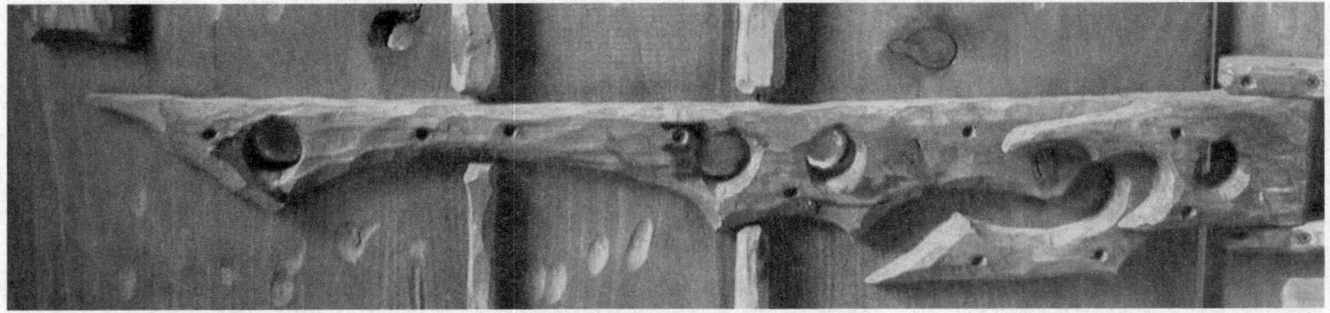

Lean, mean "Dragon Wing" hinge.

the blade of your knife wicked sharp. Swapping blades may be less quaint but it is much faster than honing a blade with a stone. Try out a few knives that appeal to you and stick with the one you like best because you are going to develop subtle hand/knife moves while whittling and changing tools could confuse your hand and blood could happen.

Look closely at the pictures and notice how all the square edges on the front side of the hinge parts have been whittled off in an eye-catching way. I keep the contours fairly simple when I turn out large numbers of hinge sets but on special occasions, say, for a front door, I get hyper-creative and do more intricate work. Find a comfortable spot and teach yourself to whittle hinge parts in your own dazzling style. As your skill increases you will get some idea of how far into the arcane art of carved hinges you are willing to go.

Ok, your whittling and carving is done and you're itching to assemble your hinges. But you must wait a little longer; there is even more art on the way.

Distressing, also known as antiquing, is an art tactic I use a lot. It makes wooden things look old real fast. I want some of my hinges to look old. I have distressed many things in my work including posts, beams, trim work, furniture, doors and, by accident once, my truck. I have tried many implements for this work but it eventually boiled down to just three: a 3/4-inch chisel with a curved blade from Japan, a hatchet from China, and a logging hook from Maine, USA.

Study your hinge parts. Got a little dirt on one? Gouge it out with the chisel and leave a dish shaped mark on the wood. Got a nail or screw head showing that can't be removed? Disguise it by indenting holes in the wood around it with the wood hook. Got areas so smooth and boring they need something? Make crisscrossing patterns with the hatchet blade, which is also good for making secret Runic symbols on your work for those in the know to discover. Of course you can and should carve your initials in everything. Try out other tools for this decorating if you have some in mind. I've heard about beating the item with a chain but that's too hostile for me.

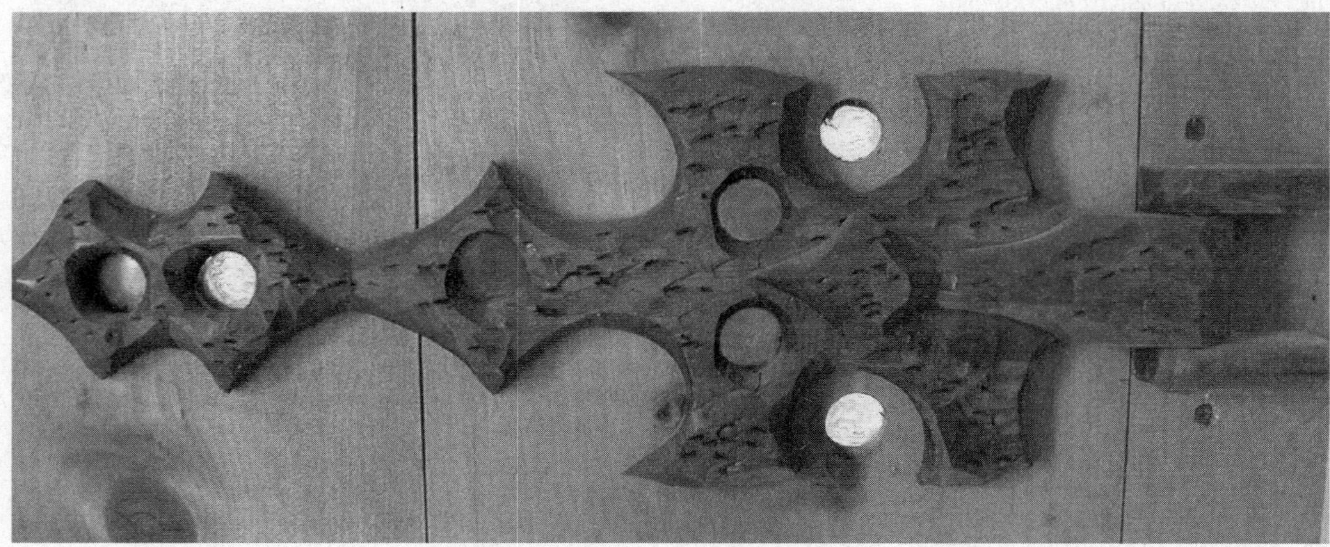

This hinge shows distressed wood surfaces and stained glass nuggets built in for cheery sunlight. Note carved edges of hinge.

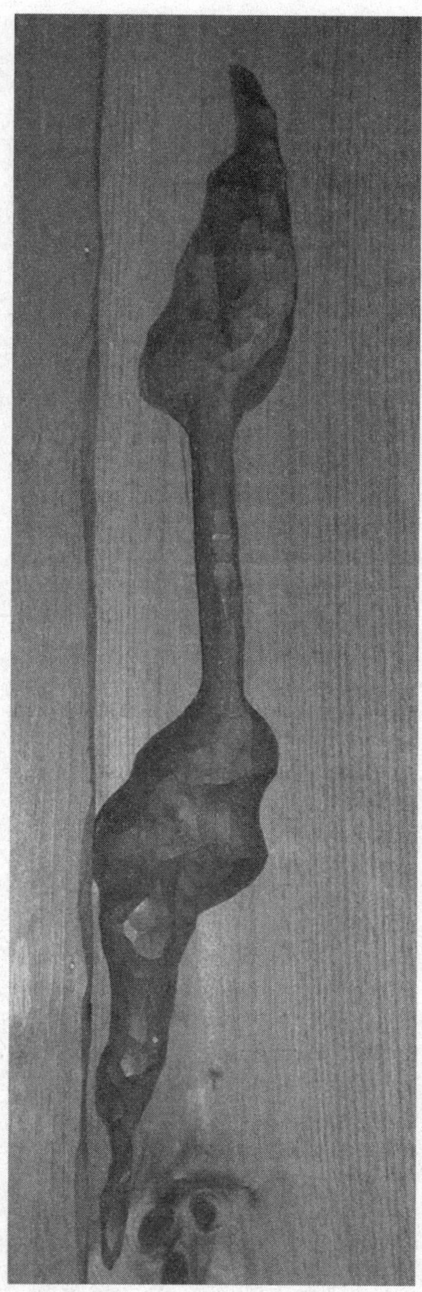

Door handle. Look closely and you can see the seams between the carved laminated parts.

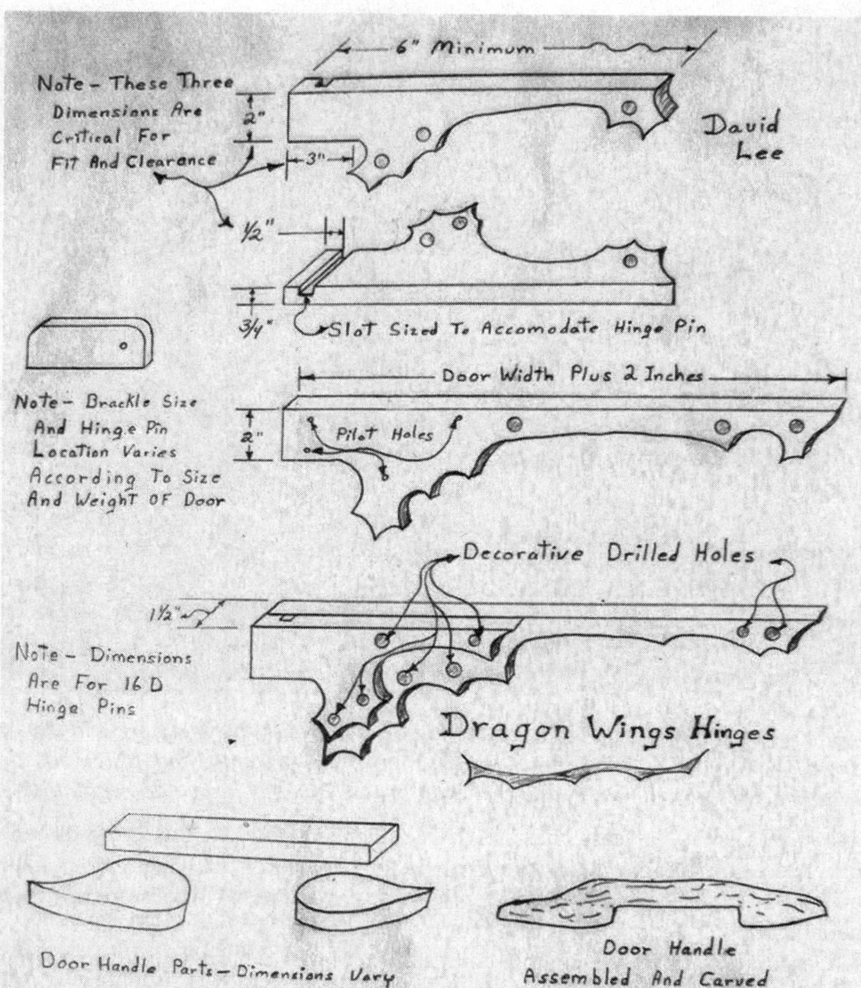

Dimension drawing

There is one more belligerent method of decoration I have only tested once and am eager to explore again. Try out a sandblaster, if you have access to one, to sculpt the hinges. It is amazing! You can bring out the grain like magic by blasting away the softer parts of the wood. All kinds of surprising things happen during this process and there are dozens of different substances you can use to blast the wood. Each will create a different effect. I got to blast one little hinge before they caught me, but sometime I would like to mount a set of hinges on a door and use the blaster to sculpt the hinges right into the wood of the door so it looks like one big piece of fantasy art!

Don't assemble those hinges yet because here is the most astounding idea you will hear this week, guaranteed!

It is time to stain your hinges. At this point in most wood working projects you would get out some version of brown stain such as we are all used to, right? Not here. Go to a leather goods store or catalog and buy leather dyes. These come in more colors than God ever intended and they soak into wood like water into a sponge. When you see the results it will make your day. The pictures in this article only give a faint idea of how beautiful dyed hinges are. My wife says they look like velvet.

Wear rubber gloves when using dye because skin, like leather, soaks up this stuff real well. Use a small paintbrush and give each piece two thorough coats, or "soakings", as I call them, and allow them to dry for a day or so. Leather dyes can fade away in sunlight so use them only on your interior hinges. A bonus is that the

Now we are talking HINGES. These Bad Boys are over five feet long and support 5' x 8' doors. Carved hinges have far more depth, texture and design possibilities than forged hinges and they won't rust. Note the carved door handles.

dye smells great. At least, the ones I have do…sort of like clean laundry on Mom's clothesline on a fall afternoon in 1956.

It is almost time to assemble the hinges. Remain calm. First I have a few ideas for you to consider for decorating your hinges. They can be done before or after mounting them on a door.

Drill ½" to about 1¾" holes through the hinge and sandwich pretty cloth material or colored foil between the door surface and the hinge so it shows through the hole.

Drill holes through the hinge and the door and use silicone glue to attach glass globs inside the holes. They will let sunlight sparkle things up a little. Whittle the edges of the holes to look nice and to allow more light through the stained glass.

Add wrought iron nails as decoration and/or to cover nail and screw heads that need to be there. Little favorite stones and trinkets make unique door decorations among the layers of wood in this three-dimensional piece of art. Check your junk drawer, there will be something in there to use.

In places where you violated the straight grained rule be prepared to glue the endangered part to the door or add a screw or nail to hold it. More likely, you will be reattaching pieces after they break and fall off. It's ok. Do what you must. I won't tell on you.

Careful whittling and the addition of certain parts to your door can disguise small hiding places for keys, weapons, through-the-door peepholes, or special devices to lock the door invisibly. Think that over as you build. I can't say more or everybody and their brother will be doing this and it won't be secret anymore.

For security on doors with outside hinges, drill a hole horizontally from the butt end of the hinge and on past the hinge pin by two or three inches, drive a tight fitting steel rod into it and disguise the hole with wood putty. This protects the hinge where it crosses the small gap between the door and casing. It prevents someone from sawing off the hinges and the person who tried would need to buy a new saw.

Ok, now you can put the hinges together and attach them to your door the same way I described in the last episode. I prefer making my own doors. Sometime I will write about that because going to all this trouble making hinges will probably tweak your appetite for building your own doors too.

As a nice touch, whittle some door handles and turn locks for your project. Handles are two blobs of scrap wood screwed and glued together with a ¾" by 1½" piece of wood 8 to 15 inches long, then carved. Look at the pictures and drawing to see some examples of handles and locks to give you the idea.

I am giving you short shrift on the door handle and lock details because making them really should be another story. In the space I have left I must warn you of the hidden danger of whittling, besides bleeding.

At some point after you have made a few dozen hinges you open a door and the knob disintegrates, or you meet someone and they collapse to the ground in pain when you shake their hand. There is no lid you cannot unscrew. You have developed uncanny new strength. This is the dreaded Whittlers Hand! It makes Whittlers a dangerous bunch. It is unavoidable. Just be aware of this new characteristic you will acquire and exploit it with care. I remember the cows cringing when Grandpa entered the barn at milking time. This is why.

I know I have only skimmed the surface of hinge making in these articles but Mr. Duffy won't let me have a whole issue, not even one time. Still, I am sure there is enough information here to keep you busy and entertained for a long time. Δ

Starting Over 9

The new house, mid-winter

By Jackie Clay

Winter is what keeps Minnesota under-populated. With more than 10,000 lakes, gorgeous forested hills of pine, maple, aspen and fir, the state would be elbow-to-elbow built up if it wasn't for its reputation for snow and cold, sometimes reaching less than 55 degrees below zero. But to tell you the truth, we actually like winter here. The snow-covered trees are gorgeous, and we feed the birds so we always hear bird-song and find new feathered folk at our feeder. The fresh snow tells a story in animal tracks each and every day that you wouldn't know about in the summer. The strike of an owl on a roosting grouse, the passing of a pair of wolves, otters playing go-slide-down-the-icy-creek, a moose crossing the trail: It's all there for us to "read."

I often go to Bob's memorial garden by the creek, in the woods down below the house. As a Vietnam veteran suffering from PTSD, he spent his life searching for peace. Stationed in Okinawa after two tours in Vietnam, he became interested in martial arts and Oriental philosophy. So after he died, we searched for a statue of the

Bob's Buddha in the winter woods

Buddha to place on a rock surrounded by flowers, where we scattered his ashes. Bill found a statue in Australia (Bob'd love that!), had it shipped, and it now sits on a huge boulder in the woods. I feed the birds down there and enjoy the serenity of the Buddha in the snow. (Neither Bob nor I is a Buddhist.) While winter is long and sometimes hard, there is always a certain peace that is soul-refreshing.

And winter keeps us indoors more often, allowing me to get more done to finish up our new log home. Yes, we did get moved in! This happened in December, just before Christmas. The first of the week I checked the propane tank of the mobile home we were "camping" in. It had been cold, and it was getting down there. So, I called the gas company. By Wednesday they hadn't shown up, and I called again. Excuses. A truck had broken down. By Friday we were REALLY getting low and so was the temperature. I called first thing that morning and was told we would get delivery "for sure." I dialed down the thermostat and waited. No truck.

Saturday morning we were down to 2%, and I knew we had to do something. The log home had 200 gallons of propane in the tank, but the basement heater could only keep the house at 60 degrees....not enough heat for my elderly parents. So when our carpenter friend, Tom, showed up to work on the house, we set about frantically moving. This entailed hooking up and moving our propane kitchen range and fridge, as well as a wall heater for Mom and Dad's bedroom.

After a night of huge rush, we got moved into the new house.

Then we had to move my parents' bed, clothing, and everything in the mobile home that would be harmed if it froze. We hurriedly boxed all of the home-canned goods in the large pantry, under the sink, and in the cupboards, plus all of Mom's store-bought canned goods—and on into the night.

We drove Mom and Dad down to the house, then continued hauling boxes. By eleven o'clock, Tom left, and we were ready for bed. Thank you so much, Tom. David slept in a chair in the basement and I slept on a mattress in the bathroom. But we were moved in, and we were WARM. Not to mention exhausted. I was beyond tired, but it felt so good to finally be home.

Hauling hay

We have goats, sheep, and three horses to feed. And because we have no barn storage, we find that feeding big round bales of hay is better than small square bales. Pound-for-pound, round bales are cheaper to buy. And because they are rolled up with a round top, they shed rain and snow moisture well. Only the "cap," or top and bottom, gets bleached and ugly. The rest is sweet and delicious to our stock. When you pile square bales up, it is very difficult to protect them adequately, even if you tarp them. You have the best luck piling them on wood pallets, then using heavy-duty tarps all the way around, fastened down with bungee cords. But sooner or later a cord breaks or comes loose and the wind rips a tarp, letting in moisture. And pretty soon, you have moldy hay.

While sheep and cattle can eat hay that has a little mold, even dusty hay is very bad for horses; they often end up with a respiratory condition that resembles emphysema in humans, called "heaves." This is very difficult to overcome and often the horse can never work hard again. Goats will frequently bloat from eating moldy hay.

So, because we have no dry hay storage area, we feed round bales. Now these bales weigh about 1,500 pounds, so you can't just roll 'em around to where you want them. Or even dump them handily out of the back of a pickup truck. We get our hay from a friend who is also a local farmer. The easy part is getting the hay loaded onto our truck. He lifts it into place with the front forks of his big tractor.

At home, we must unload it. As we have handled these huge bundles of hay for years, we've developed techniques that make the off-loading nearly as easy as getting them on to the truck. We always carry two logging chains in our old blue Chevrolet pick-up. One is 30' long and the other is 15'. One way we've unloaded rounds is to wrap the long chain around the bale, with the hooks on the cab end of the bale. (If you put the hooks on the tailgate side of the bale, when you dump the bale, the hooks end up under the 1,500 lb. bale and sometimes it is very difficult to get the chain off!)

With the tailgate either removed or unhinged and dropped down all the way, you can use a short chain or even a heavy-duty ratchet strap hooked to a stationary object and the chain around the bale to gently pull the bale back to where it is getting almost ready to fall off.

Then simply back to where you want to unload the bale, back up quickly, then apply the brakes. The bale will dump out neatly. (If the bale is rocking or you have a distance to drive, you can use the heavy-duty ratchet strap from one side of the truck, over the cab end of the bale and ratcheted down to the other side, to hold it in place safely.)

For a stationary object, we've used a tree, a boulder, and even our Suburban. Just hook securely and gently pull away slowly.

Round bales store well on their sides, with the "cap" up to shed rain. Once they are on their sides, rain and other moisture will quickly enter the bale and rot it.

We feed our horses round bales free choice. That is, they have at least one bale in their pasture at all times. If we are expecting a storm or cold weather, we quickly add another two bales. Just in case. The horses also use them as a windbreak. We don't like to be caught unprepared by a blizzard without adequate feed!

The goats and sheep don't do well with free-choice round bales as they climb on them and waste quite a bit of hay. (Goats are picky eaters and won't eat hay that has manure and urine tracked on it. Even if they were the ones that tracked it in.)

Me in the "mini pantry" in the entryway to the basement stairs

Instead of giving them free-choice round bales, we back close to the front of our goat barn and the pens, and gently drop the bale on its end. By cutting the twines and removing them, we can peel the cap off to go onto the compost pile. Then the good hay underneath can be unpeeled a little at a time with a pitchfork and fed to the sheep and goats.

Again, if you dump the hay into the pen, they will eat quite a bit and then leave the "dirty" hay. This is not only wasteful, but can be unhealthy as they can spread internal parasites among themselves. Not only is minute bits of manure tracked onto the hay unappetizing, but it may contain worm eggs.

We have made our outside pens from welded livestock panels fastened to steel fence posts. We feed our hay just outside this fence, letting the animals reach through the squares in the fence to eat. They seldom pull hay into the pen and there is little chance of manure getting into the hay. We save money, clean pens less often, and have healthier animals. Can you ask for more?

As we feed the hay, sooner or later it becomes hard to unwind as the hay toward the bottom becomes wedged under the edge of the bale. At this point, we tip the bale over, away from the hay we can't work out. This leaves a large layer of hay on the ground to feed up, as well as the nice fat, but manageable core of the bale.

The water system

Before freezing weather had come upon us, we had a crew install a septic system and also bury a water line from our well to the basement, with a T toward the goat barn. At the end of this T, a frost-free hydrant was installed. And right next to the hydrant, we moved our handy-dandy fish house. When we had first moved to the homestead, we temporarily attached this 8'x12' building to our travel trailer, using it as a living room and a place for a propane wall furnace. (Without electricity, you can't run a travel trailer furnace; there is no way to use the fan.)

But now we have moved out of the travel trailer (and mobile home), we didn't need the fish house. It would make a terrific generator shed. So, planning ahead, we had the wiring for the pump also buried in the 8'-deep trench from the well, up the side trench by the frost-free hydrant, coming out of the ground a few feet from the spot the generator shed would be.

Without grid power, we (at present) depend on intermittent generator power. So using "normal" household plumbing for our water system would not work. It isn't feasible to keep turning on the generator every time the water pressure in a pressure tank gets low.

Instead, we installed a 350-gallon poly water tank in the basement and my oldest son, Bill Spaulding, plumbed in a variable-speed 12-volt water pump. Bill works with an RV dealer and is very familiar with year-round up-scale RV living options.

So our system works like this: When we want to fill the poly storage tank, which is about once every 10 days, we turn on the faucet in the basement where the water line comes into the house from the well. At present, we have a water hose connected to it, running overhead to the tank. We turn on the generator and throw the switch for the well, and the tank fills.

At the bottom of the tank, a flexible line runs to the 12-volt pump mounted to the concrete block basement wall, then on to the toilets, and just lately, a tap near the kitchen sink. When you flush the toilet, the pump quickly fills the tank. It also provides good water pressure in the kitchen, where I have a short length of hose to fill the canning kettle I heat water with. When you shut off the tap, the pump stops. Pretty neat.

The pump is wired to a deep-cycle battery connected to a charge controller. This charges the battery while the generator is running and also keeps it from over-charging. After living a long time without running water, this is a minor miracle to me!

In fact, when Bill hooked up my toilet, we stood around and had a flushing party when the first flush took place. My ever-economical sister, Sue, complained, though: "And I had to pee! You wasted all that water!"

With running water, flushing toilets, a warm house, and ALL THAT ROOM, I feel so blessed.

As with everything here on our low-budget homestead, any and all large purchases must be planned for in advance. For instance, one month we bought two toilets and their plumbing. As Mom is in a wheelchair and Dad (94) is using a walker, we installed a toilet right next to their bed for ease of use, especially at night. The second is a "normal" toilet, although with a handicapped accessible stool, in our large bathroom.

No chimney yet, but I did find a great wood range. This summer, God willing, we'll get the chimney.

So far, we had been taking baths by heating up four canning kettles to very hot on the stove, carrying them to the tub, then carrying enough cold water from the faucet in the kitchen to make a nice hot bath. Showers are accomplished by using a battery-operated, hand-held shower with the strainer being placed in a canning kettle of hot water on the floor. It does the job, but we wanted a powerful shower. I can pee harder than the battery shower puts out.

Our next expense was a propane water heater. I shopped around and found basically the same unit for from between $290 (Menards in Duluth) to $600 at our local gas company. So I asked my son, Bill, if he could pick up a tank the next time he was coming up this way.

He got the tank and enough double-insulated B vent pipe to go up through Mom and Dad's closet corner and out through the north roof of the house. When he and David hauled the tank into the basement, I could actually feel that forthcoming pounding hot shower.

But the next night, David and I opened the faucet in the basement to fill the big poly tank and water the goats from the outside frost-free hydrant. I stood in the generator shed to throw the switch for the submersible pump in the well and popped it up. Nothing happened! We had had 20-below temperatures, and our water line had frozen.

Talk about a sinking feeling. I knew we shouldn't be driving over our water line, even though it is buried eight feet in the ground. And I knew I should heap straw over the steel well casing. But, somehow I shrugged it off and hoped it would be all right. Wrong.

Hoping for the best, we dropped a trouble light with a caged 100-watt light bulb down the casing on an extension cord. (Maybe the line was frozen where the pit-less adapter goes out through the casing to the water line. Elbows DO freeze first…) But, we only run the generator in the evenings, and so far it hasn't worked.

Okay, we like the flush toilets and the convenience of a tap to draw water for dish water. But, how could we haul water from the spring and fill the 350 poly tank so we could contin-

The old fish house (aka living room of the travel trailer) got moved down to goat pens near the new house to be used as a generator shed.

ue our present state of "civilization"? I pondered that all night and had an idea. I would buy three of those rolling garbage containers on wheels. We could bucket water in 5-gallon pails from the spring, fill the garbage cans, then back up to our ramp. With the tailgate dropped down, they would slide right off and we could roll them into the kitchen.

Luckily, we had installed a large floor grate in the kitchen, only a few feet away from the poly tank in the basement, so the warmth from the propane floor heater in the basement would radiate up into the living space.

So, David and I gave it a try. And it worked very well. With the big tank one third full, we hauled two loads of water in our three new garbage cans, filling the tank nearly full. From the kitchen grate, David would poke up the end of the garden hose we had previously filled the tank from, from the well. I stuck it into the water, and he would give a few good sucks on the other end to start the siphon. Then he stuck it into the big tank, letting the water flow. Each garbage can brought home 30 gallons (they were actually 35-gallon cans, but we slop out about 5 gallons on our rough roads).

As one can was almost empty, I would quickly kink the hose and transfer it to another can. It went very quickly and let us continue flushing until spring melts the frost out of our water line. (We kept the light down the well casing, just in case.)

In the spring, we will clear a good parking area and turn-around spot so we will not be driving on our water line next winter, and David will not plow the area above it, as he is doing now. The snow will act as insulation, and the vehicles will not compact the soil, driving frost deeper into the ground. And I will be sure to insulate the casing head where it sticks up out of the ground.

Most folks don't have this much trouble with a water line buried that deep, but because we live off grid and run water through the line much less often than "normal," it's easier for it to freeze. And it's NEVER a good idea to drive regularly over a water line.

Of course, I knew this and did not listen to ASK JACKIE! Live and learn. Or at least learn to listen to my inner voice.

The generator shed

When you live in cold country, off grid, you need to make provisions for the generator for winter. First of all, the generator needs some type of shelter to keep ice and snow off it when it's not being used. And second, generators don't start well (or hardly at all) when temperatures go below zero. Last winter, we had limped along by framing the generator on three sides with plywood and tarping the other side when it was not in use. But this was Mickey Mouse, to say the least. It resulted in the generator being frozen in the spot for weeks because the engine heated the snow, melting it into a deep puddle beneath the generator. This quickly froze once the generator was turned off. Not ideal, to say the least.

So early this winter, with our carpenter Tom's help, we dragged/carried the fish house down by the goat pen and frost-free hydrant. After leveling it and temporarily blocking it up, Tom installed a used breaker box on one wall and, later, a propane wall heater we had previously used when we used the shed as a living room.

Now, we keep the pilot only on the heater, and an hour before we want to run the generator, we simply turn up the heat. By the time we are ready to run the generator, it is warmed up toasty warm and starts on two or three pulls. This is compared to 15 or 20 hard pulls when the engine is cold and the oil is thick. To keep the generator from choking out from lack of oxygen, we open the south-facing window a few inches. Then we turn the flame down to pilot on the heater because the generator produces a lot of heat.

To make things more interesting, when it goes below about -15, the vehicles don't start. Here in Minnesota, as in other cold climates, most vehicles have a plug-in engine block heater. This effectively warms up the oil, making the vehicle start easily. Of course, we can't leave a vehicle plugged in overnight, which is the "norm." We don't run the generator that long; who could afford to?

So our system is this: Say David must leave for the bus at 6:30 a.m. I rise at 3:00 and turn up the flame on the heater in the generator shed. By 4:30, the generator is toasty, right to its heart. I start the generator with the truck previously being plugged in (so I don't have to fool around at zero dark thirty when it's cold outside). By the time the alarm rings at six o'clock, the truck is warmed up enough that it starts with little complaint. A bit complicated, but we usually only have to do this a few times during a winter.

Usually, we can just wait a few hours in the morning and the temperatures warm up to zero or above, and the vehicles start.

Throughout the winter, we have continued to work on the interior of the house. Our projects have included putting the log siding on the upstairs gable ends of David's and my bedrooms, staining that, finishing off the closet and painting the walls in Mom and Dad's bedroom, installing a tub/shower in the bathroom, and hooking up lighting fixtures in all the rooms. We have kept busy.

David plowing with our "new" truck

Our friend, Tom Richardson, working on the new green room floor

And throughout all, David has done a very good job plowing our mile-plus-long trail with the Ford F250 4x4 we bought from Bill (to replace the old, very dead Jeep we used last year). The Jeep was cheaper, but Bill's Ford is 100 times the truck. The plow is, too, being an old commercial plow that angles and throws the snow far off the trail.

We did have our problems, though. One night, David got off the bus and jumped into the truck to warm it up to plow going home. He raised the plow to leave (you should never park a truck with a snowplow on it with the plow up; it's hard on the hydraulics and springs), the lights dimmed seriously. Then when he got home, the truck killed when he tried to raise the plow. Just instantly went dead.

Instantly, I imagined all the horrible (and expensive) repairs that could be necessary. But, David called Bill and he told him to clean up the battery terminals, then re-tighten them. I helped him do this, and miracle of miracles, the truck instantly started and the plow groaned and raised normally.

A few nights later, the plow simply wouldn't raise at all, but the lights stayed on, and the truck ran fine. Another phone call to Bill (who is an automotive diagnostic technician, by the way), and he walked us through the check-ups. No taillights? Check the fuse. Yep, the fuse was blown. We were back in business.

The next night, the taillights were bright, the truck ran, but the plow wouldn't raise or even groan. Yet another call. (Bill must be getting sick of hearing from us, by now! Love ya' Bill!) We again ran through the check list, and it produced no results. Finally, David put jumper cables from the battery to the plow motor, and I tapped the motor housing smartly with a hammer, and it came to life. The brushes had just been stuck with a bit of ice. Back in business.

Now we are much smarter about the truck and plow. This is about how I learned to sweat-solder water pipes. My pipes had frozen when Bill was in diapers, and I called Dad. Over the phone 700 miles away, Dad talked me through repairing my pipes. You can learn just about anything with a good teacher.

Our new greenhouse

Well, it's March now, and I've already got some tomatoes and peppers poking up, nice and green in our kitchen window. But even that south-facing window doesn't provide enough light to keep them happy. They started leaning, looking for the sun, just about as soon as they had germinated. I bought a four-foot shop light and hung that about six inches above them. Just about instantly, they looked happier. (You don't need a gro-light to raise plants. I'm sure they are better, but I can't afford one.)

But I know how fast tomatoes grow, and we needed to meet their needs real soon. Last spring, we had built a 10'x10' greenhouse onto the mobile home. This was excellent, but it's still there, and we are here. It would be very difficult to heat that enough for growing plants while we are living down here. What to do? Put up a Mickey Mouse temporary greenhouse somewhere? Try to use the one at the mobile? We had to do something.

So, finally, we decided to build a green room attached to the south side of the new house. Tom came last Saturday, and we put up temporary treated 4'x4' corner posts, then framed the 10'x16' deck with treated 2"x8"s, then he and David quickly took the corrugated clear fiberglass down off the roof of the old greenhouse while I carried pots, planters, and other equipment out of the greenhouse.

This week, we'd like to switch the decking and begin framing the temporary roof, using the old corrugated fiberglass. We plan on putting an insulated roof over the green room, with a skylight over the living room window, then running a porch the entire length of the south side of the house. So we will use the deck, which will be permanent, but later remove the fiberglass roofing and rafters when we build the porch and roof the entire house.

By doing this, I can grow lots of plants for the garden this spring, then refinish the greenhouse for a permanent green room to allow me to grow vegetables year-round. I don't like buying out-of-season vegetables from Mexico and Chile! They still use pesticides banned (but still manufactured, by the way) in the U.S. that have been proven to be deadly additions to your diet. And besides, I refuse to pay $3 for a tomato or fresh sweet red bell pepper.

I have grown many vegetables indoors on a sun porch during the winter. I even had a nice dwarf peach tree that bore lots of gorgeous peaches, down in Sturgeon Lake, Minnesota, 20 years back. So I know it can be done, and it will make us even more self-reliant down the pike.

It is a bit frustrating to sock every nickel into the house and homestead. Even grabbing a burger at a fast food joint is sometimes out of the question; I buy nails instead. But the light is getting brighter at the end of the tunnel. So I snatch up my nails and run for the light. Δ

Buying a used mobile home

By Daniel Motz

One of the quickest, easiest, and cheapest ways to get your country home is to consider a used mobile home. Sometimes you can even find these homes free by looking in a local newspaper. But like anything else, cheaper and easier isn't always better. You have to really look at the house to make sure that you're not getting someone else's lost cause, or worse—fire hazard.

One of the things that needs careful consideration is the wiring of the mobile home. If it was built before 1978, you need to make sure that the wiring is safe. In the late 60s and through most of the 70s, mobile home manufacturers often used cheap aluminum wire and stretched it tight in order to save money. Over time and a couple of moves, this caused the wires in these houses to crack and break, causing fire risks. Examine around the fuse box for wire condition, and check service areas, such as around the water heater.

Plumbing is another issue in many trailer houses, and it's even more of a consideration if you live in a part of the country that has harsh winters. The pipes in trailers will freeze eventually, but if you take the proper steps, the amount of time you have to spend trying to reheat them can be lessened dramatically. Depending on your skill with a soldering torch or iron, you may want to consider plastic PVC piping. PVC is easy to work with and costs very little compared to the copper piping found in most mobile homes. The type of pipes you use in your house are your choice, but when winter freeze-ups happen, they should be something you're familiar with and can handle. Heat tape and space heaters are often used to keep the exposed pipes under a mobile home from freezing.

Skirting keeps the wind from blowing underneath a mobile home, and it helps keep the creepy crawlies at bay. Skirting also helps as a slight insulator against winter chill, but to add protection many people use straw or leaf bags to hold in the heat better. Another way to help the skirting hold in heat is to add foam insulation to your skirting. You will need to leave some small vents in your skirting so your furnace can suck in fresh air from below. These holes don't need to be very big, and you only need a couple of them. If you don't do this, the furnace will find other sources of fresh air, usually around windows and doors.

Other things to check include the condition of the floors. Many mobile homes use cheap particleboard as their floors. These floors often rot out from under the carpet, and should be checked often. If you have a flat-roofed home, this is going to have to be sealed again after moving because the house shifts, causing once-tight seals to become leak havens. Tarring the seams sometimes helps with leaky roofs, but other times it just isn't enough. Look for stains on the ceiling tiles to give an accurate description of the condition of the roof, but the seams should be resealed after every move.

There are a few parts of the country where zoning laws won't allow an older mobile home, and most banks won't finance an older home. So be sure you know what you're getting yourself into before buying by contacting your local zoning officials.

A good mobile home can be a great place to start or even live out your dreams of living in the backcountry easily. Their floor plans and blueprints are simple, and they can be easily adjusted to fit your family's needs. With a few simple checks, you can ensure that the mobile home you're looking at is right for you. Δ

Ayoob on Firearms

How big a gun do you need?

By Massad Ayoob

We Americans like to do things in a big way. Big houses. Big cars. Big boats. And, yes, big guns.

There are good arguments for all this, of course. The big house accommodates more guests. The same is true of large cars and boats, both of which are also more "crashworthy" if worse comes to worse. And anyone who has ever been faced with something large and dangerous at the muzzle end will tell you that a big gun is far more reassuring than a little one at such moments.

And yet, there is a strong argument for downsizing. A great many of our readers have improved their quality of life by moving from a big place in the city to a smaller home in more rural America. Smaller cars and boats are more economical, more convenient, more nimble, and often more fun to pilot. Similarly, smaller firearms are handier, more convenient, produce less fatigue when carried afield all day, and are often faster and more efficient to deploy in close quarters such as thick brush.

The first thing to consider is power level. Some situations demand more powerful guns than others. If you live in "big-bear" country, you definitely want a very powerful rifle. Most professional hunting guides would consider the 7mm Remington Magnum or .338 Winchester Magnum to be the absolute minimum caliber for facing grizzly or polar bear. If your backwoods digs are on the African continent and nasty-tempered Cape buffalo or rampaging elephants are in your backyard, you actually NEED an elephant gun in the .375 Magnum or larger class. Indeed, the game laws of most African countries specify the .375 Holland & Holland Magnum as the minimum caliber for the humane hunting of the pachyderm. Fortunately, most who read this publication have much smaller wildlife pests to contend with.

Any gun shop owner can tell you how many neophyte hunters come in asking for a .300 Magnum or 7mm Magnum rifles with which to hunt deer. Unless the country is very open and extreme long shots are the rule—in which case the flat trajectories of these powerful cartridges start to make sense—you simply don't need this power level to cleanly kill anything smaller than a large elk or a moose. Indeed, any hunting guide or conservation officer can tell you that every day, moose and elk are cleanly killed by hunters with run-of-the-mill .30-06 hunting rifles. Loaded with the proper bullet, a .30-06 or even .270 is ample for any non-dangerous game on the American continent, not to mention the common black bear.

Shotguns? I'll agree that the 12-gauge is the most versatile shell. At the same time, that's a lot of gun for some people. The legendary shotgun expert Francis E. Sell was a big fan of the less powerful 20-gauge, and found that with the right load, it was ample for ducks and geese, let alone upland birds. However, that was in the days of lead shot. The steel shot mandated long ago for waterfowl hunting (to keep spent lead out of the water and out of the bellies of living birds) does not penetrate as well as lead, and this has caused waterfowl hunters to increase their firepower.

Massad Ayoob

The small 20-gauge shell is rarely seen in duck blinds today, and the standard 12-gauge 2¾" shell, substantially more powerful than the 20, has given way to the 3" Magnum and now the 3½" Magnum, with many serious duck and goose hunters preferring the massive 10-gauge Magnum for pass shooting on the waterways. This is one area where power cannot be sacrificed, simply because of the steel shot rule.

On the other hand, lead is legal for hunting pheasants, partridge, turkey, and so on, and of course for deer in jurisdictions where the fish and wildlife laws forbid rifles and allow only shotguns for white-tail hunting. For upland birds, it's hard to argue with Sell's logic that at reasonable ranges, the lighter, faster-handling 20-gauge will get you on the rising bird more quickly than a heavier 12-gauge shotgun. "Deer slug" shotgun ammunition has improved by leaps and bounds.

Remington's all-copper sabot round has proven to be a deadly deerslayer in the 20-gauge size. Thus, with the exception of waterfowl hunting, the shotgunner's needs can be better met than ever with something smaller than the big, traditional 12-gauge.

Rifles

In the last generation, we have seen a sea change in sporting rifle configuration. When I was young, the Winchester Model 70 Featherweight and the Remington Model 600 carbine were about your only choices if you wanted a lightweight but still very accurate bolt-action hunting rifle. Today, the Featherweight is still available, and Remington's Model 7 is the best seller in this category. I've been very pleased with Ruger's equivalent, the Model 77 Compact; the sample I tested would shoot three rounds of premium-grade .243 hunting ammunition into one inch at 100 yards. Yet these delightfully accurate rifles, delivering the same power as their bigger brothers when chambered for .308 Winchester and similar cartridges, are as easy to carry all day as a much less powerful Winchester Model 94 lever action, chambered for the shorter-range .30-30 cartridge.

Often called "mountain rifles," these lightweight bolt guns have kept pace with technology developed for hikers. Lighter boots, lighter packs, lighter tents, lighter everything. Another technological parallel between the sports of riflery and hiking is improved weather resistance. Today's telescopic sights for rifles are more secure against the elements, keeping their nitrogen filler inside and reducing the likelihood of fogging. The traditional wooden stock absorbed moisture and warped, sometimes pressing against the rifle's barrel and altering point-of-bullet impact. Today, numerous space-age materials including Kevlar have largely replaced wood on working high-tech hunting rifles. They do not change dimensions with temperature or inclement weather. Rust was always the bane of sporting arms carried afield in fair weather and foul; today, stainless steel barrels and actions make rust much slower to accumulate, though stainless is by no means rustproof.

Rifle barrels tend to be shorter nowadays. A carbine, or short-barreled rifle, has historically been seen as a short-range firearm. The reason a longer barrel was equated with greater accuracy was largely that in the old times, the rifle mounted iron sights. "Sight radius"—the distance between front and rear sight—was a definite element in determining how much accuracy a rifleman could deliver downrange. The greater the distance between rear sight and front, the less aiming error there was as perceived by the human eye. The easiest way to increase this accuracy was to increase the distance between the sights, and in turn, the easiest way to do that was to lengthen the barrel, since the front sight was located just above and behind the muzzle.

Today, optical sights are more the rule than the exception. This means that the sight radius advantage of a longer rifle barrel is eliminated from the equation. In Iraq or Afghanistan, if the soldier's rifle carries the issue red dot electronic optical sight by Aimpoint, his accuracy will be exactly the same whether he is firing an M4 with a 14" barrel or an older M16 with a 20" barrel, all other things being equal.

Your precision rifleman knows that barrel length has little to do with accuracy anymore. To put the next bullet through the same hole as the first, what is important is that the barrel not change its dimensions as it heats up, and that it not vibrate differently than it did with the last shot. With this recognized, we are seeing a trend toward shorter but thicker and more rigid barrels. It is as true with the lowly .22 rimfire sporting rifles as it is with more powerful specimens.

For example, two of my favorite .22 rifles are produced by Ruger. One is the bolt action Model 77/22. Approximately the dimensions of a high-powered hunting rifle, it is an accurate gun that will put every round of match-grade .22 into an inch at a hundred yards.

The other is a Ruger 10/22 semiautomatic that has been accurized by Kay Clark-Miculek at Clark Custom Guns into what that grand old gunsmithing firm calls their Squirrel Rifle format. In addition to an excellent trigger job and some other features, Kay fitted it with a Douglas match-grade barrel. So modified, it too will put Eley Rifle Match .22 ammo into a one-inch group at a hundred paces. The Douglas barrel is thick, to dissipate heat and vibration, and would normally be altogether too unwieldy for a comfortable day of carrying in the woods, and hopelessly muzzle-heavy if trying to track a running rabbit or squirrel. However, one design element changed everything: Kay expertly fluted the barrel. The flutes, trenches milled away from the steel, run almost the length of the barrel. This reduces weight sufficiently to make the gun comfortable to carry, and give the customized rifle what I can only describe as perfect balance. The fluted match barrel is only 16¼-inches long, and the overall rifle is much shorter and handier than my standard, out-of-the box Model 77/22. For those who want this level of accuracy with something even lighter, .22 match rifle barrels made of carbon fiber are becoming all the rage among small-bore shooting enthusiasts.

The fluted barrel principle works with more powerful rifles, too. Let's look at two AR15 semiautomatic rifles, caliber .223, one of mine and one I bought for my younger daughter.

My rifle is a Colt Match Target H-BAR, an acronym that stands for

Petite Gail Pepin blasts a clay bird 20 yards off the muzzle with a Mossberg 590 shotgun, its barrel an easy-handling 20" in length.

"heavy barrel." It weighs well over eight pounds with its 20" barrel. My little girl tried it when she was 11 years old, and it was just too cumbersome and muzzle-heavy for her to aim steadily from a standing position. It's an accurate beast, though, putting every shot into an inch at a hundred yards if I use good ammunition.

For Justine's 12th birthday, I had a custom AR15 built for her. The Assault Weapons Ban was in force, and I couldn't buy a telescoping stock to fit her short arms, but I had one on a pre-ban Colt AR15 so I used that "lower," or frame, as the basis for her gun. I sent it to the custom shop at Olympic Arms in Washington. They built an "upper" for her that included a fluted match grade barrel 16¼" in length. (16" is the legal limit for rifle barrels, without a special $200 license from the Bureau of Alcohol, Tobacco, Firearms and Explosives.) The Olympic upper was in "flat-top" configuration, with a Picatinny Rail on the top of the frame that allowed wide options as to sight attachments. We chose the C-More, a top-quality red dot electronic sight that is extremely compact and weighs only a few ounces. Justine's custom AR15 came in at six pounds on the nose. It will deliver one-inch groups at 100 yards with Federal Match .223 ammunition.

Depending on the ammunition used, the .223 Remington cartridge for which most AR15s are chambered can lose a lot of its power out of a short barrel. However, most tests indicate that the wounding power of the .223 is not seriously compromised until the barrel is cut back to 14", the length of an M4 barrel. With a 16" barrel, it still seems to deliver the goods.

My daughter's rifle is dramatically lighter than mine, and distinctly shorter and faster handling. It delivers the same high level of accuracy. Being optically sighted, it loses nothing in terms of sight radius. Justine is now a tall, athletic young woman of 20 and can easily shoot my heavier rifle, but still prefers her own lighter, handier AR15. I don't blame her. It's the more practical of the two AR15s by far.

Firearms historian Gene Gangarossa, Jr., wrote *The Story of the Carbine* in the 1999 annual *Guns Illustrated*. He closed with these words: "Whenever a soldier sits in the confined spaces of an assault helicopter or in an armored personnel carrier or on horseback, or whenever a hunter stalks game at close quarters in dense brush, a short, fast-handling weapon will appeal more than a longer, clumsier one. In fact, as long as anyone needs or wants a small, lightweight shoulder arm, and is willing to sacrifice a small bit of accuracy and striking power in exchange for that handiness, the carbine will remain a favorite for military and civilian duty alike."

Shotguns

When I was a young hunter, shotgun barrels came mostly in three lengths. If you had a wide-open cylinder or improved cylinder choke swaged into your gun barrel for hunting partridge, let's say, the industry-standard length for such a barrel on a hunter's shotgun was 26". If you had a modified choke—a little bit tighter, for shooting pheasants when dogs ranging well ahead of you put up the birds—Remington and Winchester and Savage, et. al., would manufacture your shotgun with a 28" barrel. If you bought a duck gun with a full choke, the tightest constriction designed to keep the pellets together in a bird-killing pattern 40 yards away over the decoys on the water, you could expect its barrel to be 30" in length. Some waterfowl guns had "extra-full" chokes and even longer barrels, 32" or even 36".

The longer the barrel, the heavier the gun. The longer the barrel, the more the shotgun's point of balance moved forward, and the slower and "less lively" it was in your hands as you tracked a bird. The longer the barrel, the slower it was to maneuver the gun into position and poke its ponderous barrel out of the confines of a duck blind.

In those days, a hunter might own many interchangeable barrels for one shotgun. He or she would purchase, say, a Remington 870 pump gun and a 26" improved cylinder barrel for woodcock, a 28" modified tube for pheasant, and a 30" full-choke barrel for duck hunting. There might even be a 20" to 24" barrel, often complete with rifled sights, bored for the use of rifled slugs during deer season. Many hunters still follow that pattern today.

However, interchangeable choke tubes changed the face of the shotgun game many years ago. With a twist of the wrench that comes provided with the gun, the same gun and barrel are capable of the versatility that once required four shotguns, and later required four separate shotgun barrels. You'll notice that when modern hunters take advantage of this technology, they generally buy a shotgun with a shorter barrel. They appreciate the lighter weight and the faster handling.

The guns of today's turkey hunters are a good example, because turkey hunting is hugely popular nowadays. Thanks in large part to the efforts of the National Wild Turkey Federation, there are more of these stately birds living in America than ever before, including the time of the Pilgrims. It is particularly satisfying to sit down to a traditional turkey dinner at Thanksgiving or Christmas when the centerpiece is one that you have harvested from the forest yourself.

All the big makers offer designated "Turkey Guns," and most of these shotguns seem to mount a 24" barrel. The full choke is just as important with big toms as with ducks; though they're taken on the ground instead of in the air, the turkey is often encountered at distances of 40 yards, and the target is the head to spare as much meat as possible. To get maybe half a dozen #4 or #6 birdshot pellets into its head and neck at that distance, you need a tightly constricting choke. With modern shotguns, this means that you've taken fully half a foot of the length of your formerly cumbersome full-choke shotgun.

As noted in the opening paragraphs, the careful hunter who stays within his or her effective range can fill the roasting pan with wild turkey using a 20-gauge instead of the bigger 12. My favorite 20-gauge shotgun is Remington's Model 1100 gas-operated semiautomatic in its Special Field model. With straight, English-style stock and 21" barrel with interchangeable choke tubes, this remarkably soft-kicking shotgun weighs little more than six pounds. It's refreshingly handy for a day in the hunting fields, and is available in a "youth model" with shorter stock for hunters of smaller stature.

With a short 20" barrel, shooting through a window (fox outside the chicken coop, crop destroyer in the garden situation) is easy for the shooter with a 12-gauge pump gun. Rich Edington demonstrates at a shooting match.

Handguns

Advances in Titanium and Scandium frame construction, pioneered by Smith & Wesson, and polymer frame construction of semiautomatic pistols as pioneered by Heckler & Koch and popularized by Glock, have given us lighter handguns than ever before.

This is sometimes a blessing and sometimes a curse. Smith & Wesson manufactures two cases in point, the Model 340 Sc and the Model 329 PD. The 340 is an 11-ounce .357 Magnum, and the 329 is a .44 Magnum that weighs a mere 26.5 ounces. With full-power Magnum ammunition, they each deliver recoil that is nothing less than savage. This is not conducive to getting the practice you need to deliver fast, accurate hits reflexively in a danger situation.

That's not to say that you can't comfortably get a lot of power into a small handgun package. If you've kept your back issues of *Backwoods Home Magazine*, you've seen articles on two guns that deliver the same substantial power levels in approximately the same size packages, but with much less-felt "kick" because of their all-steel construction. Ruger's SP101 is a five-shot snub-nose .357 Magnum with rubbery "live-feel" grips, and is proportionally much easier to shoot swiftly and accurately than a similar but lighter revolver with the same full-power ammunition. The reason is that with all-steel construction, it weighs about 25 ounces. It's less than a pound heavier than the lightest .357 revolver, but HUGELY more "shootable."

In the Smith & Wesson .44 Magnum line, I found the super-light Model 329 very, um, interesting to shoot with full power-ammo, but just no fun at all. In the Smith & Wesson catalog, however, I head instead to the page that shows the Mountain Gun. It

Worn in the open in a uniform holster, the SIG P226 carries 16 rounds of 9mm.

has been produced in stainless as the Model 629 Mountain and in blue steel for Lew Horton Distributors as the Model 29 Mountain, and in either configuration features a tapered four-inch barrel, and radiused front edges of the cylinder. Weight is reduced noticeably over that of a standard Smith & Wesson .44 Magnum with heavy straight barrel, and the gun still weighs less than a pound more than the lightest .44 Magnum in the S&W catalog, but once again, we have an all-steel gun that is dramatically more shootable and therefore more practical overall. Yet, unlike a long-barrel hunting revolver, it is the size of some police service revolvers and something you can keep on your hip all day in a backwoods or working cattle ranch environment.

I've killed game at as far as 117 yards with a 4" barrel Smith & Wesson .44 Magnum, and find it more than adequate for my own outdoor needs. But let me refer you to far more experienced outdoorsmen than myself. Elmer Keith was perhaps the most famous hunter/gun expert of the 20th Century. He once humanely killed a deer, which had been wounded by a client he was guiding, at a range of 600 yards with his S&W .44 Magnum. His daily-carry gun was that Model 29 .44, with a 4" barrel. Keith's protégé, Ross Seyfried, wore an identical Smith .44 on his hip in his first career as a working cattleman, day in and day out. Seyfried went on to become a national pistol champion and a famous big game hunter and guide on two continents. Both stand as proof that a 4" barrel .44 Magnum revolver will "get you through the night" in the 24/7 world of the backwoods.

Now, your needs may not indicate a handgun as powerful as the .44 Magnum. You may see bears only in the zoo, and have no large livestock that might occasionally run rampant and have to be euthanized, right now, with a powerful sidearm. Rural citizens, like city dwellers, mostly keep handguns for personal defense against threats that tend to arrive on two legs instead of four. An anti-personnel sidearm doesn't need the level of "Magnum Force" that Elmer Keith needed on the day he had to shoot, from back to front, a maddened horse that was dragging him to death.

Let's say that we're looking at a .38 Special through .357 Magnum revolver, or a semiautomatic pistol in calibers ranging from 9mm Luger through .40 Smith & Wesson, .357 SIG, and up to .45 ACP. With modern ammunition, designed for the bullets to perform even at reduced velocity from short barrels, a compact sidearm doesn't handicap you with power reduction as much as it would have 20 years ago.

Let's say you've decided that a light-kicking 9mm pistol will be adequate for your needs, and that you've settled on the excellent SIG-Sauer pistol, a brand noted for quality and reliability. The largest of their standard models is the P226. This is the full-size, 16-shot service pistol used widely by members of the NYPD and the Chicago PD, and standard issue for the Navy's SEALs. NYPD issues the 124-grain +P Gold Dot hollowpoint 9mm cartridge by CCI Speer, and has found it to be satisfyingly powerful "on the street."

But maybe you'd like something a little shorter, with a smaller butt that will also bulge less under your cloth-

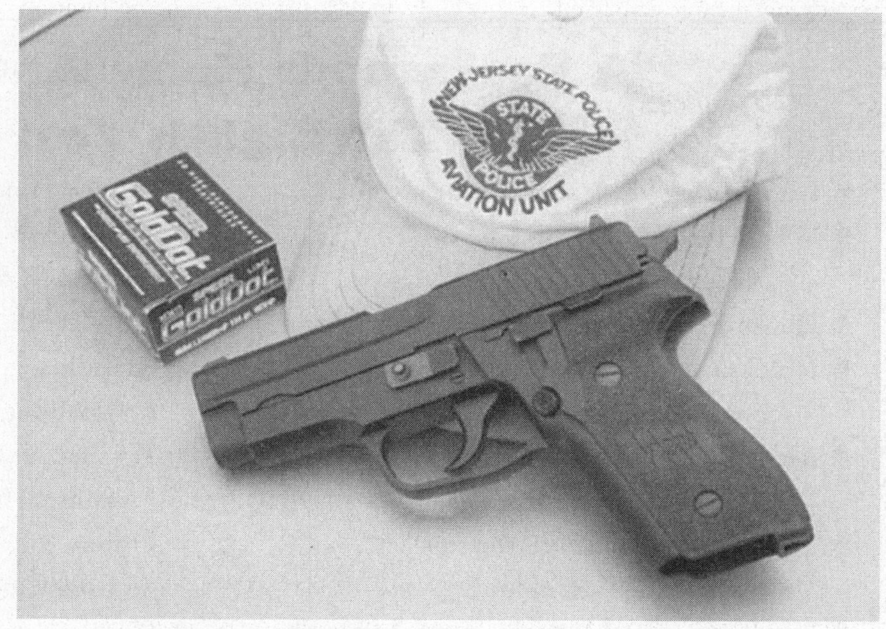

The smaller P228, equally suitable for uniform or concealment wear, carries only 2 rounds less than the P226.

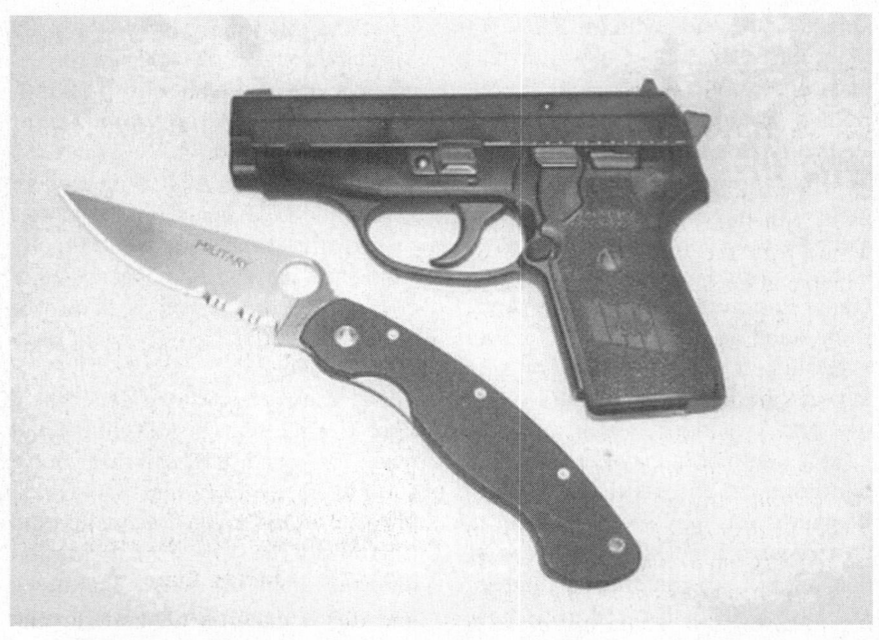

Even more compact and convenient P239 holds 9 rounds of the same ammunition, which is enough for most needs.

ing when you lawfully carry it concealed. You might go down a notch in size to the SIG P228, as recently chosen for standard issue to the troopers of the New Jersey State Police. They like that size pistol because it's compact enough for concealed carry by their troopers off duty, and by plainclothes investigators. They use the exact same 9mm ammo as NYPD, and report the same high satisfaction with its performance on the street. The P228 holds 14 cartridges.

You want something even smaller, and you don't expect to get into the high-volume running gunfights that are potential daily occurrences for city cops or state troopers alike? Consider SIG's P239. Even smaller than its above-named big brothers—SIGARMS describes the P239 as "personal size," an apt term—it is thin and flat, thanks to a slim single-stack magazine that allows a proportionally thinner grip. The price you pay for that, total cartridge capacity of nine shots, is not likely to matter in typical situations where private citizens need to employ handguns in self-defense. Yet this smallest SIG 9mm is virtually as easy to shoot well as its big brother, the P226.

Bottom line: Modern technology has allowed us to "git 'r done" with smaller, lighter, handier firearms. For working purposes, that makes it more likely that a suitable firearm will be with us when we need it, instead of left behind out of reach because it was too big and too heavy to carry. For sporting purposes, it makes the trip afield that much less tiring and proportionally more enjoyable. Δ

Ask Jackie

If you have a question about rural living, send it in to Jackie Clay and she'll try to answer it. Address your letter to Ask Jackie, PO Box 712, Gold Beach, OR 97444. Questions will only be answered in this column. — Editor

Making corn chips

Do you have a simple recipe for making corn chips?

Norman Standing-Tree Bowen
Monroe, North Carolina

We make our corn chips by mixing masa harina (corn flour available in the flour or Mexican section of larger grocery stores) with enough water to make a stiff but workable dough. Balls of this dough about the size of a golf ball are pressed in a tortilla press or on a waxed paper with a waxed paper over it, with a rolling pin. This makes a corn tortilla. Now, for chips, cut the tortilla into wedges or strips, depending on the kind of chips you want. The strips make a nice snack and the wedges are great for dipping salsa with.

With all your dough rolled out and cut up, heat cooking oil in a deep saucepan or deep fryer and when it is quite hot but not smoking, drop several pieces in to fry. The hot fat makes them puff up nicely. Move them around a bit with a long fork, so that both sides cook well.

When they are done, dip them out with a slotted spoon and drain them on a layer of paper toweling. Immediately salt them so that the salt will stick. Enjoy with your favorite salsa or salsa with cheese melted with it.

Some folks like a crunchier (although these have plenty of crunch) chip. In this case, mix half corn meal and half masa, which is finer corn flour. Mix enough boiling water with the meal to make your dough and let stand until cool enough to handle before making your balls to roll out. ***—Jackie***

Used cooking oil

Your articles over the years have been very helpful and I'm hoping you can help me yet again! I want to find a way to dispose of cooking oil in a reasonably environmentally friendly way. It is not practical for me to take it into town to a restaurant or such for recycling with their own oil. What do people in the bush do with their used cooking oil? Are there other uses for it?

Jeanne
British Columbia, Canada

First of all, you can strain your cooking oil and re-use it. While it is warm but not so hot that you will get burned, strain it through a piece of clean cloth, into a jar you can seal. Often, this oil can be used several times before you discard it. Straining removes minute (and larger) food particles that will cause off tastes in the food you cook. (Don't use this strained oil for baking or other delicate uses, but rather for frying meat, poultry and fish, for instance.)

Once your oil seems to be ready to discard, you can use it to make soap. This is getting to be a great hobby for a lot of otherwise non-homesteader types.

Soapmaking supplies can be had at most hobby stores and are available through many gardening supply houses, as well.

I also use my used cooking oil to polish the cast iron parts of my wood cooking stove. While the stove is warm, but not hot, take a folded cloth

Jackie Clay

and dip it into the oil and rub the stovetop well (when it is clean, of course). Then make a fire in the stove and let the oil cure on the top. You don't want a very hot fire or the oil will smoke like the dickens!

This works well for any other wood stove you have with a cast iron top. The iron becomes black and shiny and does not look painted as it does when you use stove blacking. It looks glistening, clean and natural.

You can also dribble a little of the used oil on your pets' food. It helps to maintain a nice shiny coat. Don't use too much, though or they may get the runs.

There are lots of other uses for this oil. Just use your imagination.

—Jackie

Canning chicken and pheasants

I'm new to canning and am looking to can chicken & pheasants in pints and quart jars could you help with pressure and time for this?

Scott Pharo
Stoughton, Wisconsin

Raw packed (bone in or not) chicken and pheasant, with hot broth or boiling water poured to within 1 inch of the top of the jar should be processed at 10 pounds pressure (unless you live at an altitude above 1,000 feet and must consult a canning manual for directions in raising your pressure if necessary), for 75 minutes for boned pints or 90 minutes for quarts or for bone-in 65 minutes for pints and 75 minutes for quarts.

For hot pack, where you can partially cooked chicken or pheasant, use the same times as above, with hot broth or boiling water (doesn't taste as good) to 1 inch of the top of the jar, as well. The pressure is the same.

—Jackie

Canning venison

I've never canned meat, so I did a "trial run" this year on a few jars of venison. I followed instructions in my "Blue Book" to brown the meat first and fill the jars with the meat, drippings, and broth. Now I find a thin layer of fat on top of the meat in the jars. Is this fat going to be rancid, and will the fat shorten the length of time the unopened jars can be stored? Do you always brown or roast meat before placing it in canning jars?

Judy Madson
Clear Lake, Iowa

The thin layer of fat on top of the meat in the jars is perfectly normal and okay. It will not become rancid and it will not shorten the length of time the meat can be stored without losing flavor or wholesomeness.

If I'm in a hurry, as when I must process a whole, large animal, such as a steer, moose or elk, I will raw pack some of the meat, just to get it put up. But over the years, I have found that the meat that has been browned packs more efficiently, looks better in the jars and, most important to me, is more tender. Raw packed meat sometimes tends to dry out somewhat as you do not put water or broth on the meat. (If you do, it can expand and force the liquid out of the jar during processing and cause the seal to fail.)

—Jackie

Seeds for chicken feed

I have a variety of banana that is cold-hardy but inedible because of its numerous seeds the size of popcorn kernels in the fruit. Can you tell me if they would make good chicken feed if ground in my grain mill?

Do you know of any other seeds of fruits that I may be throwing away that would be useful chicken feed?

Joe Pool
DeRidder, Louisiana

You can certainly feed your banana seeds to your chickens. They would eat the whole fruit, except the peel, as well. The seeds do not need to be ground. Just about any fruit seeds; orange, lemon, grapefruit, apple, grape, pear and others are relished by chickens. I keep a chicken pan on the counter. This is filled daily with "chicken scraps," which is a different container from the "dog scraps" that go to our Huskies. Chicken scraps contain crushed egg shells, potato peels, fruit peels and seeds, "old" bits of gelatin salad, salad greens, cabbage hearts, etc. The dog scraps include meat scraps (no bones), left-over pancakes, muffins, bread, soups, carrot peels, dribbles of cooking fat, etc. I may give either group left-over casseroles, mac and cheese, potato salad, stew or whatever I clean out of my fridge that is not moldy.

—Jackie

Canning tomatoes

I would like to know how long canned tomatoes last.

I opened a jar and it tasted good. But another jar went bad. How do I know how long to keep them?

Carolyn Vermeulen
Golden Valley, Arizona

Canned tomatoes should keep for years and years, provided that they were canned correctly. The jar that went bad probably had a bad seal. Just check the seal of a jar before you open it. Then if it is firmly indented in the center, look at the tomatoes. If they look okay, smell okay, they are okay to eat, regardless of age. I know I have tomatoes in my pantry that are 15 years old and I have no hesitations in serving them tomorrow. This is one of the greatest benefits of canning for long-term food storage.

The enemies of long-term tomato storage are dampness and rust. Always remove your rings after your processed jars have cooled. They do not help the seal stay sealed. But they may collect tomato residue from processing or dampness. Either will cut the shelf life of the jars, drastically.

—Jackie

Storage of canned goods

I just got a copy of the Emergency Preparedness and Survival Guide from Backwoods Home Magazine and read your chapters on food storage. I had a specific question about how long canned milk will store, but I think I should ask a more general question about storing all can goods. If the can is opened after a long period of storage and looks and smells okay, and does not taste objectionable would it generally be safe to consume? Thanks for your great articles, I get a lot of great and practical advice from them.

Tom Borchers
Springfield, Oregon

Yes, Tom, if your seal is good (indented firmly in the center), the food looks good, smells normal, it is considered safe to eat. I probably should date my own canning jars, but I don't. I can generally remember about how old a batch of food is, but not exactly. When I put my new canning on the shelves, I do take the time to pull out the oldest jars and try to stack them near the front. Then I use them first, leaving the newest produce in the back. In this way, I rotate my canned goods. But there are always some "special" foods that I kind of hoard, until I can replace them after I use a jar or two....so they get old. But we still enjoy one of the "oldies" from time to time, as a special treat.

—Jackie

Canning fresh noodles

Can you can with fresh noodles such as tortellinis? If so how? Any thing you have might help. Thank You

Tiffany Steveson
Arvada, Colorado

Yes, you can home can recipes with fresh noodles. I just make sure they are dried fairly well before I can a recipe using them. Then make the rest of the recipe up and just before you put it into the jars, add the noodles. In this way, the noodles don't turn to mush in the processing. If you go ahead and completely cook your recipe before packing it into jars, the additional cooking which happens during the processing makes the noodles fall apart and become unappetizing.

I have had great luck in home canning pasta dishes and they are certainly MUCH better than the Chef Boy-you-know-who stuff in the stores!

—Jackie

Preserving bell peppers

What are some different ways of preserving bell peppers? Could you put them in oil? I have dried some, put some in the freezer, but I would like them in jars. I have red, yellow, & green. I just cook with them a lot & freezing makes them watery. Got any ideas, let me know, please. Thanks.

Yolande Chastain
Seneca, South Carolina

I also dry sweet peppers of many different varieties. Not only do they blend well in most recipes, without reconstituting, but they taste great, as well.

You can also home can your peppers. Simply cut the stem, core and seeds out, put the peppers, whole or sliced, in a saucepan and add enough water to cover. Boil five minutes, then pack hot into hot pint canning jars. Fill the jars with the hot liquid they were boiled in up to an inch from the top of the jar. Add half a teaspoon of salt if you desire. Process at 10 pounds (unless you live at an altitude above 1,000 feet, then consult your canning manual for directions for increasing your pressure, if necessary) for 35 minutes (pints or half pints only).

You can also pickle your sweet peppers. Not only are these good to eat as a pickle, but, rinsed off, these peppers work well in many recipes too. They are crisper than are canned peppers because you do not process them so long. To pickle them, stem, core and seed the peppers. Quarter or slice, depending on your preference. Make a pickling solution of 10 c vinegar, 2 c water, 8 tsp non-iodized salt, 6 Tbsp sugar. Bring to a boil. Pack your peppers snugly into pint jars and pour the hot pickling solution over the peppers, working out any air bubbles with a wooden spoon handle. Leave ½ inch of head room in the jar. Place lid and ring on jar and process for 10 minutes at altitudes below 1,000 feet, 15 minutes for altitudes from 1,000 to 6,000 feet and 20 minutes over 6,000 feet above sea level.

To use in recipes you may want to thoroughly rinse the peppers, then use as you would raw peppers. I use these a lot in winter stir-fries and they're really good. **—Jackie**

Old pecans

I was wondering if there is anything that can be done to take out the old taste of pecans that I didn't store in the freezer soon enough. I thought perhaps freezing them might help but need some good advice. I want to save them if I can but don't want to use bad tasting pecans in baking.

Frances Watson
Springlake, Texas

Sometimes spreading the nuts out on a cookie sheet and heating them gradually in the oven, set on its lowest setting will freshen them. Unfortunately, sometimes they just are plain old rancid and cannot be saved. **—Jackie**

Pickling banana peppers

I am new at canning and last summer I grew some banana peppers and tried pickling them, but every jar I tried to pickle, came out slimy, chewy and bitter tasting. I even tried cooking them first and alum, but each time they were slimy. What did I do wrong? Help!

Stephanie Cruz
Liberal, Kansas

Boy, Stephanie, I've canned tons of peppers of all kinds, and have never had slimy or bitter ones. Try this and see if yours turn out fine next time.

Cut two small slits in each pepper. This lets the pickling solution reach all parts of the pepper. Mix 1 ½ cups salt with 4 quarts of ice water and pour over a gallon of freshly picked peppers with slits cut. Weight the peppers down with a china plate and let stand overnight in a cool place. Drain and rinse thoroughly. Combine: 2 cups water, ¼ cup sugar, 2½ quarts vinegar. Bring to a boil. Pack peppers into a hot jar and pour boiling pickling solution over the peppers to ½ inch of the top of the jar. Remove any air bubbles. Wipe rim clean. Place hot, previously simmered lid on jar and screw down ring firmly tight. Process pints for 10 minutes in a boiling water bath canner, making sure to count from the time the water returns to a full boil after adding the jars.

Good luck! **—Jackie**

The last word

"If you don't like it here, why don't you move to another country?"

That's a question I've been confronted with, more than once, when I've complained about the *PATRIOT Act*, the *RICO Act*, creeping gun control, the empowerment of the bureaucracy, the restriction of free markets, etc.

And my answer to that question is almost always, "But where would I go?"

This usually brings a smug reply along the lines of, "Anywhere, John. Just leave! Where do you want to go?"

And my response is always the same, "I want to stay here. *You're* the one who should go."

"Me?" I'm asked. "But you're the one who doesn't like this country."

That, however, is not true. I love this country. I'm deliriously happy with the way it was set up. It's the only country in all of history based on the individual and individual rights. It's the only one not founded on "the greatest good for the greatest number," "experts know best and will run your life for you," "I am royalty and you are here to serve me," or some other BS like that. There's no other place like this land of Jefferson, Adams, Mason, Monroe, and their kind, in the world or in time, and I'm trying to keep it the way it is, or at least the way it's supposed to be.

After I explain that to my listeners (assuming they let me get that far, which they often don't), I add, "You're the one who's unhappy. You're the one who should leave."

A lot of people want to terminate the conversation then and there. This is particularly true of the so-called "soccer moms." But it's also true of those who sense they're falling into a trap. However, if allowed, I continue. "There's no other country that's based on freedom. There's no other country where individual rights are not gifts from the king, the parliament, congress, the president, a dictator, a majority of your neighbors, or someone else. Even Canada's so-called *Bill of Rights* specifically says a Canadian's rights are at the discretion of Parliament. Those aren't rights; those are *privileges*. And people like you are trying to change this country into one of *those* countries. So, it's you who should move, not me. And there are plenty of places you can go. But there's nowhere for people like me, except...here.

"I don't have any choices of where I can go, but you do.

"If you want communism, there are still communist countries: North Korea, The People's Republic of China, Cuba.

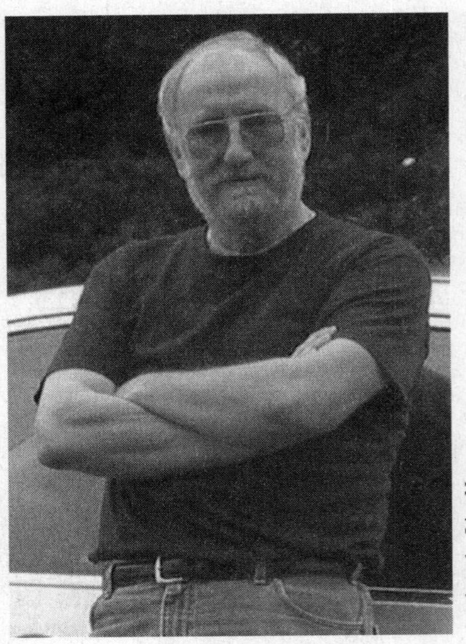

photo by Lisa Nourse

John Silveira

"If you want fascism, you can go to South America. There are plenty of countries there that will welcome you.

"If you want a theocracy, Iran may be right up your alley, or you can move to Vatican City.

"Absolute monarchy? Move to Swaziland. It's not absolute, yet, but the king needs you and will welcome you if you have ideas for making him even more powerful. And if you really want to impress him, bring your virgin daughters as gifts.

"Socialism? Go to Sweden, France, Germany—or just about anywhere else in Europe.

"Absolute democracy? Well, that's a tough one. As near as I can tell, there's only been one, and it didn't work out too well. Socrates certainly didn't like it. The majority took a vote and got him to drink hemlock. The majority could do that because there were no—what our forefathers called—'unalienable' rights.

"But unalienable rights and a constitutional government are supposed to exist here. Believe me, I'm not unhappy with the way this country was set up. I'm not unhappy with our *Constitution*. I'm not the one trying to change these things. *You* are. You're the one unhappy with the United States. What you should be doing is trying to think of what you want to change this country into, and I guarantee there's already a place just like it somewhere else in the world. Then, *please*, take your own advice, and go there. Let me stay here.

"And to prove to you what a good friend I am, let's go to your house—now. I'll help you pack your bags. *I'll even drive you to the airport.*"

If they're still listening, that's usually the point where they get insulted, make some rude comment, and walk away. And it's where I shake my head, saddened that they, like so many others today, just don't get it, or don't care if they do.

The American abolitionist Wendell Phillips said, "Eternal vigilance is the price of liberty." But there's not much to be done when there are so few of us keeping watch. Δ

— John Silveira

CENTURY CELEBRATION for our 100th issue! See the specials on pages 2 & 3.

Backwoods Home magazine

practical ideas for self-reliant living

July/Aug 2006
Issue #100
$4.95 US
$6.50 CAN

Our 100th issue!

RECIPES FOR A
HEALTHY HEART

solar getaway
healthy veggies
versatile lemons
cooking with seeds
history of medicine
solving indoor air pollution

www.backwoodshome.com

My view

If you want to take care of your health, you have to take control of your life

The other day a man called the office to thank me for writing Issue 98's page 7 editorial, in which I urged readers to get a stress test if they have symptoms or a lifestyle that could lead to a heart attack. The editorial, the caller said, saved his life because he took my advice and was now on his way into surgery to get a life-saving operation to relieve coronary artery blockage.

But that was the only call we got. That means that there are at least several hundred other readers out there who are continuing to play Russian Roulette with their lives. None of my business, I suppose; people can take whatever risks they want with their lives.

Since I had my own bypass surgery to relieve my own life-threatening coronary artery blockage, I have been eating healthier and exercising, thanks to all the health information I've learned since my surgery. In fact, I underwent six weeks of "coronary rehab exercise," which is essentially exercise monitored by an EKG machine and supervised by an instructor who also imparts information about how to take care of your heart and arteries. What surprised me during the cardiac rehab sessions was that most of my fellow exercisers, all of whom had gone through some sort of heart intervention such as bypass surgery, had very little knowledge about what to do to maintain a healthy heart. They neither understood the role of exercise nor grasped the importance of diet. And they didn't seem particularly concerned about learning. Most of them were there, as far as I could tell, because their insurance was paying for the sessions.

I don't get it! Why aren't more people interested in information that could save their lives, or at least make them live healthier? I can understand the general readership of *BHM*, at least those who haven't been whacked between the eyes yet with a heart attack or other serious illness. But what about the people who *have*, such as many of my fellow rehab exercisers? Why aren't they acting decisively when it comes to their own health? I sure am! I'm on a quest not only to stay alive, but to live to a healthy 90 or so. But the only way you can do that, short of being born lucky with a set of indestructible genes, is to learn about health and act on your own behalf.

This issue we're trying to save at least one more life by presenting articles about maintaining or improving your health, especially by eating healthy foods that are low in bad fats and sugar, high in good fats and fiber, etc. Food is your body's fuel. Eat poorly and your body won't run well, especially as you get older and the years of poor eating catch up with you in the form of clogged arteries and cancers. Eat healthy and you'll run like a Ferrari long into your 80s, unless you get unlucky.

Exercise, one of the major keys to staying healthy, can be pretty easy to come by when you live in the country. It doesn't matter what you do as long as you get your heart rate up for about 20 minutes a day. Here my three sons, Jake, Rob, and Sam, and I take a rest after getting real dirty from a couple of hours of clearing and burning brush.

Of course, there's a catch! Not only do you have to eat healthy, but you have to eat healthy portions, i.e., not too much. You don't have to be a scientist to figure out the consequences of being fat; just look around to see who is living longer and healthier. It isn't fat people. Americans live in the land of plenty of food where restaurants often compete with each other by offering supersized portions. That makes it difficult to keep a healthy weight unless you are disciplined with how much you eat. If you do eat out often, better get in the habit of asking for a doggie bag if you don't want to leave half your food on the plate.

And there's another catch to staying healthy: You have to exercise. Your heart especially loves exercise. You can demonstrate this to yourself by taking your blood pressure before and after you exercise; blood pressure drops after exercising because the arteries surrounding the heart dilate. In fact, exercise enough, as athletes do, and your heart will build extra arteries to support the increased blood flow the exercising heart demands. In other words, exercising helps create a backup blood supply for your heart.

Health is an active-participation sport. You can't just sit back and hope everything goes okay. As with other important aspects of the self-reliant life, you have to take control by first learning, then acting on your own half. This issue, and many of our past issues, contains articles that will help you do that. **— *Dave Duffy***

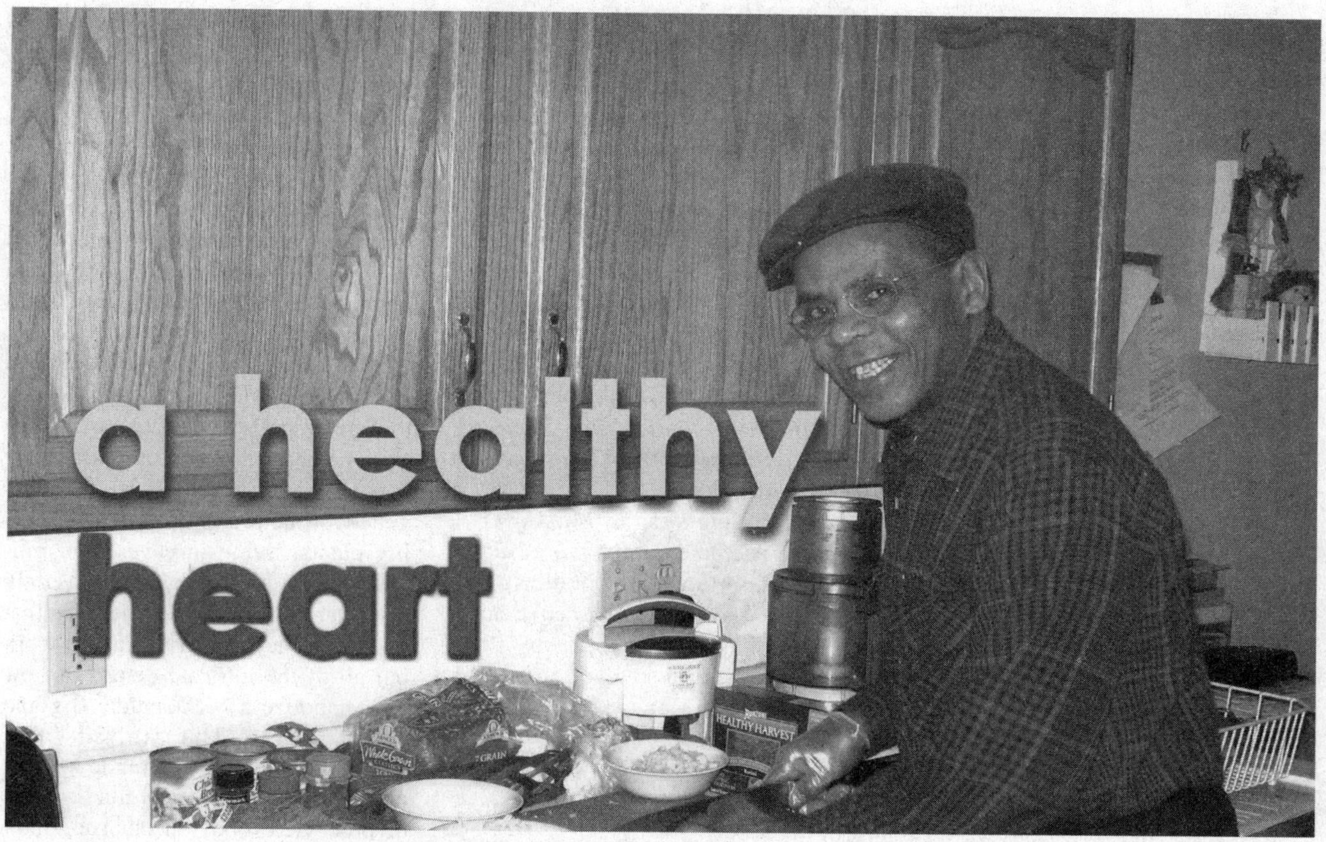

a healthy heart starts in the kitchen

By Richard Blunt

The Surgeon General of the United States recently referred to obesity as "the terror within." But who is the enemy? When we finally started paying attention to what health advocates were saying about the perils of smoking, it was easy to label the tobacco industry as a dangerous and evil assassin of innocent people. However, despite the mushrooming evidence that the regular consumption of many foods marketed at restaurants and supermarkets is the root cause of a variety of serious health problems, from heart attacks to cancer, most Americans find it difficult to label the food industry and its purveyors as evil. Instead, we blame our lack of exercise and willpower for the increase in food-related problems like obesity, diabetes, and heart disease.

Carefully controlled scientific studies show that diet-related problems are real and on the increase. But, increasing the amount of exercise we do and adopting a restricted diet regimen have not made these problems go away. Why? My personal battles against smoking cigarettes and trying to reduce food-induced high cholesterol will give you a glimpse of the reason.

I stopped smoking 20 years ago. It was difficult, but I got used to it, and today I can't tolerate even the smell of tobacco smoke. However, I also stopped eating fried clams, one of my favorite foods, 15 years ago to reduce my high cholesterol level. While eating lunch with friends and family at a seafood restaurant a few weeks ago, I found myself staring in envy at a platter of fried clams being delivered to another table. Food, even food that can potentially cause problems with your health, is *hard* to hate. The answer to solving the food-related problems that this society is experiencing will not be solved by avoiding food like it is an enemy.

Instead, we have to approach the foods we eat with knowledge. What's good for our health, and what's bad? Not only that, we need to guard against eating too much food.

Let's look at the obvious first: If we eat too much food, even if it's all healthy food, we're going to gain weight. And excess weight is associated with a variety of health problems, especially heart problems, the number one killer in America.

Food abundance clashes with our ancient genes

America is the land of plenty, for sure, and that is especially true when it comes to the production of food. We produce far more food than our population can eat. Every time we visit a supermarket, we are surrounded by this abundance. The aisles are overflowing with everything from fresh produce to highly processed foods.

This abundance, unfortunately, is in stark conflict with what humans have become used to for most of the last 40,000 years. As modern humans, we have inherited the efficiency of our Paleolithic genes. When our early ancestors planned a meal, it involved a lot more than a trip to the nearest supermarket. They routinely traveled long distances tracking wild and dangerous creatures, expended enormous physical energy killing their prey, then expended even more energy hauling their kill back home to feed others who were not able to join the hunt. With the odds for success stacked against them, the hunt often failed; when that happened, everyone often went hungry.

In the meantime, those who could not join the hunt also labored constantly to find food by foraging for nuts, fruits, berries, vegetables, and roots. Like the hunt, the effort was extreme, and the amount of calories burned in that effort was high.

Back then, obesity was likely not to have been a problem. An unreliable food supply and vigorous physical activity were key factors in preventing unhealthy weight gain.

More than likely, our ancestors were also nomads, and as seasons changed and food sources dwindled, they migrated in search of sustenance. Their travels often rewarded them with many varieties of fruits, nuts, vegetables, and game. Their receptivity to new foods added great variety to their diet and enhanced their ability to survive in changing environments.

What's a calorie?

A *dietary* calorie is a measurable unit of energy that is the result of our digestive system breaking down foods into components that our bodies can use. All foods are broken down into fats, carbohydrates, and proteins, which in turn are broken down into different and unique compounds. Fats are a dense food, containing nine calories per gram, while carbohydrates and proteins contain four calories per gram each. Balancing calories "in" with calories "out" is one way of controlling weight. Most overweight people consume more calories, daily, than their bodies can use. The unused ("unburned") calories are converted to fat by the body and held in storage for use at another time.

Scientists guess that the Paleolithic diet our ancestors ate was about 30% protein, 50% carbohydrates, and 20% fat, an eating pattern that is very close to many of the healthy food diets of today.

Our ancestors also evolved with what are now called "thrifty genes," genes that helped them survive in their uncertain world. When times were good and food was plentiful, these genes helped their bodies maximize the usable energy from the food by allowing them to store excess food as body fat. During the lean periods, their bodies shifted into survival mode and began converting the stored fats into usable calories. This reserved energy kept them going until food was available again.

Over the past 40,000 years, human DNA has changed very little. We are still genetically linked to our primitive forebears. We not only still have these "thrifty genes," but our basic genetic structure is designed for eating plants, living in caves, and running around mostly naked. It has only been during the past few decades that our genes have been forced to work out all of the intricate details of how to metabolize a McDonald's Big and Tasty, a Pizza Hut Stuffed Crust Pizza, or a Starbuck's Grande Mocha, not to mention the incredible variety of processed foods on our supermarket shelves.

Our ancient genes and modern environment have really collided in a way that has caused us many health problems. We have used developments in

Making use of healthful ingredients in his own kitchen, Richard Blunt prepares nutritious meals that appeal to the eye and the taste.

An experiment in observing obesity

As I write these sentences, I am sitting in the flight arrival area at the airport waiting for my wife and youngest son to arrive on a Delta flight from Tampa. The room fills with people retrieving their luggage about every half-hour. I have, for the past several days, been writing this article for *Backwoods Home Magazine* and I've wanted to test some of the information I've collected during the past few months.

Obesity is reported as one of the major factors in the development of heart disease, diabetes, and some types of cancer. Over and over I review numbers and percentages that claim to represent the problem of obesity as it affects men, women, and children. As disturbing as these revelations are, I have remained skeptical.

Being something of an empiricist, I decided to conduct a little experiment. I arrived at the airport two hours early to do some people watching. I have been sitting here for nearly 2½ hours observing about five to six hundred people.

If what I am witnessing here is a typical example of what is happening in America, the problem of obesity in America is understated. The number of severely overweight young children is most noticeable. I am more convinced than ever that obesity and the problems associated with it are real. However, I feel that preaching to folks about eating a balanced diet is of little value without some practical information on how to select, store, prepare, and serve healthful meals that can be *enjoyed*. Steamed asparagus on dry whole-wheat toast is healthy food, but eating food like this on a regular basis will make mealtime a sad experience, and is likely to undermine *any* diet.

agriculture, animal husbandry, mechanics, engineering, and science to produce a consistent and reliable food supply, to improve transportation of that food supply to our kitchen tables, and to make our daily job of preparing it easier. Our ancient genes are telling us to eat plenty while there's plenty of food available, but our modern society has eliminated the physical activity of obtaining that food. No wonder we're fat.

Portion sizes are also excessive in most restaurants as well as those suggested on the packages of many processed foods found on supermarket shelves.

For instance, the USDA Food Guide Pyramid recommends a diet that contains a maximum of 2,800 calories for a teen-age boy, active man, and very active woman. The animal protein recommendation for this diet is a maximum of seven ounces of meat, fish, or poultry daily. If we eat meat at both lunch and dinner, we must limit our portion size to 3½ ounces per meal. How many restaurants offer a 3 or 4-ounce steak on their menu? Their customers would laugh them out of business if they did.

And serious problems such as morbid obesity, Type 2 diabetes, and heart disease have, according to health care professionals, reached epidemic levels. These problems are steadily becoming global; i.e., as cultures become richer they are also becoming fatter.

Eating highly processed foods and "fast" foods

Abundance is not our only problem when it comes to eating. It's the availability of highly processed foods and fast foods, with their overloaded levels of fat, salt, and sugar, that is a key obstacle to eating healthy.

We are also now living in a society where fast food has become one of the defining standards for what and how much food we eat. Fast food, like the many processed foods found on supermarket shelves, contains more saturated fat, salt, and sugar than food prepared at home. And it is definitely not good for your healthy heart or any other aspect of your heatlh.

Fast-food joints (with the possible exception of places like Subway, which utilize fresh vegetables and olive oil, and offer whole grain breads as an option) make it far too easy to consume foods loaded with saturated fat, salt, and sugar. The result is that we put on weight, clog our arteries, and become diseased and die long before we should.

The supermarket takes advantage of our cravings

Unless you are a food scientist, understanding (much less even pronouncing) some of the ingredients listed on the labels of supermarket foods can be a challenge. Separating which of these foods are good for you from those that are not can be daunting.

Looking back again to our inherited genes, humans have evolved with a keen sensitivity to and liking for fat, salt, and sugar in various forms. For our ancestors, this sensitivity was a key to survival. Well aware of this, the manufactured food and fast food industry have exploited these senses by dramatically increasing the fat, salt, and sugar content in the foods they produce and serve.

Our Paleolithic genes are simply not accustomed to eating large amounts of fat, salt, and sugar on a regular basis.

Learn to read the labels on the packages of food you buy from the supermarket and try to avoid most fast foods. How much fat, salt, or sugar are in these foods? Of these three, fat is the most critical, especially for your healthy heart.

There is a difference in the types of fats we eat

On the food label of most products on the supermarket shelves is a listing of the amount of total fat, saturated fat, and trans fats contained in the product. Both saturated fat and trans fat are bad to eat. They set in motion the production of cholesterol by your liver. And cholesterol, along with the bad fats, are what primarily accumulates in your coronary arteries over the years and blocks blood flow to your heart. Eventually, this blockage can lead to a heart attack.

So avoid foods with a lot of saturated fat (read the labels). Also limit the amount of red meat and milk products (whole milk, most cheeses, ice cream) you consume because they have large amounts of saturated fat. Eat fish, skinless chicken, turkey, and veal instead, and add beans, peas, or legumes to your menu; all offer amounts of protein comparable to red meat, but without the heavy dose of saturated fat.

Butter and lard, of course, have high amounts of saturated fats, so avoid them. Margarine is no better, as it contains high amounts of trans fat. Many of your vegetable cooking oils, such as coconut oil and palm oil, also have high amounts of saturated fats.

But there are good fats out there, fats that are actually good for your heart. They are called polyunsaturated and monounsaturated fats. Unfortunately, these fats are usually not listed on the food labels of grocery store products.

Monounsaturated fats are especially good for your heart. Examples of oils high in monounsaturated fats are olive, canola, flaxseed, and peanut oils. Extra virgin olive oil makes a fine cooking oil. Also high in monounsaturated fats are many nuts, such as pistachios, cashews, pecans, hazel nuts, filberts, macadamia nuts, and peanuts.

Sautéed fresh kale and beans with miso dressing

Chicken vindaloo can be a tasty dish that fits into a healthful diet.

Monounsaturated oils have a lot of omega-3 fatty acids, which is an important fatty acid for your heart health. Oily fish, such as tuna and salmon, are also high in omega-3 fatty acids.

It would take too much room to go into all the foods you should avoid or consume, so get yourself a copy of the excellent book, *The Omega Diet*. It is an easy read and is the best source I have found to explain the difference between good fats and bad fats. You can buy used copies of the book for under $5 at eBay or amazon on the internet, or go to your local bookstore where the book is always in stock.

A few healthy guidelines for cooking at home

When we prepare meals at home, we can control the ingredients, and our food can not only taste as good, but very likely *better*, without unnecessary amounts of fat, salt, and sugar. Here are a few healthy guidelines I follow while cooking at home:

Don't limit your diet to just a few familiar foods. Try to find new favorites while eating a variety of foods.

If you don't have a garden, consider starting one. Working in a garden burns more calories than you might think, and even a small deck garden can produce most of the fresh herbs that I suggest in many of my recipes and will cost much less than the supermarket varieties.

Include plenty of whole-grain products, nuts, vegetables, and fruits in your diet. Many studies link these foods to lower rates of heart disease and cancers. Many fruits and vegetables contain soluble fiber, which can lower cholesterol and reduce your risk of heart disease.

Choose the fats in your diet carefully. Minimize saturated fats and trans fats, substituting instead polyunsaturated and monounsaturated fats. Omega-3 fatty acids (contained in fish) are especially good for you.

Moderate your use of salt. Don't omit salt from your cooking, unless instructed to do so by your doctor, but use only the amount necessary to enhance your food. Remember, if you can taste salt in your food, you've added too much.

Before you buy any processed food, get into the habit of reading the nutrition label so you can see what is really in the package.

My tools

For many years I have relied on a small but effective assortment of cast iron pans. These pans are more than 75 years old. Both my mother and my grandmother used these pans for most of their meal preparation. In past articles, I have suggested the use of cast iron in many recipes, and I will continue to do so. However, I have recently discovered that the world of nonstick pans has come forth as a standard in many professional kitchens, and for good reason. These pans offer non-stick convenience along with excellent cooking qualities. Some brands are very expensive, expensive enough to keep a cheapskate like me from buying them. Recently I purchased a 12-inch nonstick skillet with a silicone handle for only $40. To my surprise this pan's stovetop performance matches that of my cast iron pans. It features a durable nonstick surface that has made it possible for me to reduce the amount of fat in my recipes by nearly 50%. (This alone is reason enough to obtain such pans.) The pan is made by Farberware and has, in a very short time, become a workhorse in my kitchen.

Another piece of equipment I have found to be indispensable is a mini food processor. These innocent looking machines make tedious jobs like emulsifying vinaigrette dressings and mincing garlic and onions easy. I purchased my first Cuisinart Mini-Prep when I first started writing for *BHM*. I retired it last week and replaced it with a new one for a reasonable $32.

Roasted chicken and herbed potato salad with raspberry vinaigrette

Let's cook

Following are some recipes featuring familiar foods but enhanced with new flavors derived from soy miso, turmeric, saffron, and a variety of custom spice blends.

All of these recipes are delicious, nutritious, and most important, healthful and heart-friendly.

Chicken vindaloo (or hot and sour chicken)

This is an updated version of a recipe that I developed for an article that I wrote on the foods of India in issue #46 (March/April 1997). This recipe truly demonstrates the versatility of Indian cooking.

The Christian minority in the former Portuguese colony of Goa makes this dish with pork, a meat that's rarely eaten in other parts of India. In this version, I have substituted chicken for the pork, added a couple of different seasonings, and suggested serving on whole-wheat blend pasta instead of rice. This pasta is eggless and contains no cholesterol. The white Durham wheat used to make pasta is very dense and is digested more slowly than rice, which slows that insulin rush that occurs when you eat white rice of any kind. Brown rice also works well with this recipe.

Marinade ingredients:

2 Tbsp. fresh ginger, minced or grated fine
2 medium shallots, minced
2 Tbsp. dry vermouth
4 cloves fresh garlic, minced or grated fine
1 canned chipotle chili in adobo sauce, minced
3 Tbsp. malt vinegar
1 Tbsp. garam masala
1 Tbsp. chili powder

Cooking ingredients:

2 lbs. boneless and skinless chicken thighs (excess fat removed)
1⅓ cups low sodium fat-free canned or homemade chicken stock
1 oz. tamarind pulp
2 Tbsp. peanut, grape seed, or canola oil
2 cups thinly sliced yellow onions
½ tsp. kosher salt
½ tsp. cayenne pepper
1 tsp. paprika
1½ tsp. ground turmeric
1 12-oz. bag Ronzoni Healthy Harvest Wide Noodles

Method:

1. Combine the ginger, shallots, vermouth, garlic, chipotle pepper, and malt vinegar in a blender or small food processor. Process into a smooth

Seafood paella with brown rice

paste. Add the garam masala and chili powder and pulse for a couple of seconds to combine with the other ingredients. If the marinade seems to be too thick, add a little water, one tablespoon at a time.

2. Place the chicken in a zip-lock freezer bag, and add the marinade. Carefully rub each piece of chicken with the marinade. Seal the bag, and place the chicken in the refrigerator for at least one hour.

3. Place the chicken stock in a suitable-size pot and bring it to a boil over medium-high heat. Remove the stock, and add the tamarind pulp. Let the mixture soak for about 15 minutes. Strain the mixture through a strong stainless steel sieve, and then squeeze the remaining pulp to remove as much liquid as possible. Set the liquid aside, and discard the pulp.

4. Place a heavy-bottom nonstick skillet or Dutch oven over medium heat, and add one tablespoon of oil. Heat the oil until it starts to ripple, add the sliced onions and the salt. Cook the onions, stirring frequently, until they turn a light caramel brown. If the onions seem to be browning too fast, reduce the heat a little, and add a little water, one tablespoon at a time. Add the cayenne pepper, paprika, and turmeric to the onions, and continue to cook the mixture, stirring constantly, for about 20 seconds. Transfer the onion mixture to a plate and set aside.

5. Remove the chicken from the refrigerator and, using your hands, remove as much marinade from the chicken as possible and add it to the tamarind mixture.

6. Place the nonstick skillet or Dutch oven over medium-high heat. Add one tablespoon of oil, and heat until the oil starts to ripple. Add the chicken thighs, and brown them on both sides.

7. Add the tamarind mixture and the onions to the pan; bring the mixture to a boil.

8. Reduce the heat, cover the pan, and simmer slowly until the chicken is tender, about 30 to 45 minutes.

9. Place the covered pot in a warm oven for about 30 minutes.

10. Just before the chicken vindaloo is finished heating in the oven, prepare the pasta according to the directions. Serve the vindaloo over the pasta.

Makes 6 servings of approximately 400 calories each, 40 of which are from fat.

Sautéed fresh kale and beans with miso dressing

This recipe contains two of my favorite foods, fresh kale and white beans. Folks often pass on kale, a hardy green, for fear that it is bitter, hard to work with, and requires lengthy cooking. None of these beliefs are warranted. When fresh and young, kale cooks up both sweet and tender in just a matter of minutes. Recently, it has been marketed in measured bags, washed, stems removed, and chopped into one-inch pieces.

The main flavor ingredient in the dressing is miso. Miso is a savory, high-protein seasoning that has some of the flavor characteristics of soy sauce, but it's sold as a paste. Miso is made by fermenting soybeans with grains like barley and rice, along with sea salt and water, for several months. There is no equivalent for miso in the West. In Japan, it is traditional to start the day with a cup of miso soup instead of coffee. Another interesting flavor we'll use in this recipe, that can be found in the ethnic food section of most supermarkets, is mirin, a sweetened sake used in Japanese cooking. Mirin contains no fat or salt and is very low in alcohol.

When using any form of miso in a recipe, additional salt is not necessary.

Cheese miso dressing:

¼ cup white miso
2 Tbsp. natural trans fat-free peanut butter
2 Tbsp. rice vinegar
2 Tbsp. lemon juice
¼ cup water
1 Tbsp. honey
1 tsp. mirin
2 Tbsp. grated Parmesan cheese
1 Tbsp. fresh parsley, minced
½ tsp. Frank's cayenne pepper sauce or other hot sauce

1. Combine all the ingredients in a suitably sized bowl, and mix with a wire whip. Cover the mixture; refrigerate for about one hour.

Sautéed kale:

1 Tbsp. walnut oil
1 cup onion, diced
1 cup fresh sweet red pepper, seeded and julienned
3 cloves fresh garlic, minced
¼ tsp. red pepper flakes
8 cups loosely packed fresh kale cut into one-inch pieces
½ cup low-sodium vegetable stock
1 12-oz can Great Northern beans or cannelloni beans, drained and rinsed

Method:

1. Heat the oil in a 12-inch Dutch oven (or similarly sized heavy-bottom pan) over medium-high heat, until it starts to ripple. Add the onion, and cook until it starts to brown. Add the fresh red pepper; continue to cook for another minute. Add the garlic and red pepper flakes. Continue to cook, stirring constantly, until the garlic is fragrant, about 30 seconds. Add half of the kale to the pan, using tongs. Stir the greens until they start to wilt. Add the remaining greens and the broth. Increase the heat to high until the broth starts to boil. Reduce the heat, cover, and allow the mixture to simmer until the greens are just tender, about 10 minutes.

2. Remove the pan from the heat, add the beans, and gently stir until the beans are heated.

3. Serve immediately with two tablespoons of dressing.

Makes 4 servings of approximately 175 calories each, with 10 calories from fat.

Seafood paella with brown rice

Paella is one of the world's most famous rice dishes. I adopted this seafood version from my old fishing buddy, Howard. Howard spent his winters cooking in a variety of restaurants on Cape Cod in Massachusetts. When the weather warmed and the striped bass, bluefish, and black fish followed the tides, chasing smaller fish for dinner, Howard left the kitchen and became a market fisherman. He traveled from one end of the Cape to the other in his old Jeep chasing these game fish. He sold most of what he caught to local restaurants. But once in a while, during a lull in the fishing action, he would set up an ingenious portable kitchen on the beach and cook for the hungry fishermen around him. I was often one of those chosen few.

I've taken his paella recipe and increased the vegetables, reduced the salt, and substituted brown rice for the traditional white rice to make it more heart-friendly. Give it a try, and you'll see that healthy food does not have to be boring food.

Ingredients:

1 lb. raw 21 to 25-per-pound shrimp in the shell
1½ cups water
½ cup dry vermouth
3½ cups low-sodium, low-fat chicken broth
½ tsp. saffron threads, crumbled
1 bay leaf
2 tsp. olive oil
½ tsp. kosher salt
8 oz. fresh green beans, stem and ends snapped off
1 large red bell pepper, seeded and cut into ½-inch thick strips
3 Tbsp. olive oil
6 boneless, skinless chicken thighs
4 oz. Portuguese chourico sausage or Spanish chorizo (not Mexican chorizo which is an entirely different sausage)
2 cups medium grain brown rice
1 qt. warm water to soak the rice
12 littleneck or other hard-shelled clams
1 medium yellow onion, diced fine
6 cloves fresh garlic, chopped
1 tsp. Spanish paprika
1 14½-ounce can diced tomatoes, drained and chopped
2 Tbsp. fresh parsley, chopped
1 lemon cut into six wedges

Method:

1. Move an oven rack to its lowest position, and preheat the oven to 450° F.

2. Carefully peel the shrimp (remove vein if necessary). Put the shrimp in a small bowl and refrigerate.

3. In a small pan, combine the shrimp shells, water, and vermouth. Bring the mixture to a boil over medium-high heat. Reduce the heat, and simmer the mixture for 15 minutes or until the liquid is reduced to one cup. Strain the mixture. Discard the shells. Add the remaining liquid to the chicken broth along with the saffron and bay leaf. Bring the broth mixture to a simmer over medium-high heat, cover the pot, and remove it from the heat.

4. In a suitable-size bowl, combine the two teaspoons of olive oil and ½ teaspoon of salt with the green beans and red peppers. Line a cookie sheet with aluminum foil, and place the coated peppers and green beans on the cookie sheet in a single layer. Place the cookie sheet in the oven, and roast the vegetables for about 10 minutes or until the green beans start to brown and show signs of wrinkling. Transfer the beans and peppers to a plate, and set them aside. Reset the oven to 350° F.

5. Lightly sprinkle the chicken with fresh-ground black pepper. Heat one tablespoon of olive oil over medium-high heat in the paella pan, 14-inch heavy-bottomed skillet, or large Dutch oven until it starts to shimmer. Add the chicken in a single layer and cook, on one side, without moving, until the chicken is medium brown, about four or five minutes. Turn the chicken and brown the other side in the same manner. Remove the chicken to a plate and set it aside

6. Add the sausage to the now empty pan and sauté until lightly browned. Set the browned sausage aside with the chicken.

7. Soak the rice in warm water for 15 minutes, drain, and set aside.

The Blunt family salmon burger

8. While the rice is soaking, place the clams in a double boiler with a half-cup of water and steam for about 5 minutes. Remove clams and set aside. Discard any that fail to open. Steam the shrimp in the same pan. Remove the shrimp, and set them aside.

9. Add two tablespoons of olive oil to your paella pan, skillet, or Dutch oven and return it to the burner over medium heat. When the oil starts to shimmer, add the diced onion and cook, stirring frequently, until the onion begins to soften. Add the garlic, paprika, and tomato. Continue cooking the vegetables until most of the water from the tomatoes has evaporated. Add the drained rice, and stir the mixture until the rice is well coated. Stir in the infused chicken broth. Raise the temperature enough to bring the mixture to a boil. Remove the pan from the heat, cover it with aluminum foil, and place it in the oven. Cook until the rice absorbs all of the liquid, about 45 minutes.

10. When the rice has cooked, remove the pan from the oven and arrange the shrimp, clams, roasted peppers and green beans on top. Cover the pan again with the foil, and place it in the oven for about five minutes to heat the added ingredients.

11. Remove the paella from the oven, sprinkle with chopped parsley. Serve with lemon wedges.

6 servings, approximately 430 calories each, with 110 calories from fat

Roasted chicken and herbed potato salad with raspberry vinaigrette

This recipe is without a doubt one of the most popular dinner salads in the Blunt household. It is a recipe loaded with vegetables and complemented with low-fat vinaigrette that I am sure will find a place on your menu. I use walnut oil in the vinaigrette instead of olive because it adds a mellow, toasted flavor to the salad that was not possible with olive oil. Nut oils are a little pricey, so use them sparingly, and keep them in the refrigerator after opening. When buying these oils, look for the term "cold pressed" or "expeller pressed" on the label. This indicates that you are buying oil that has not been treated with chemicals or exposed to high heat during the extraction process. I will discuss oils, in detail, in future articles.

Raspberry vinaigrette:

2 garlic cloves, minced
1 shallot, minced
1 tsp. fresh thyme, minced
1 tsp. fresh basil, minced
1 tsp. fresh oregano, minced
¾ tsp. Kosher salt
½ tsp. fresh-ground black pepper
1 tsp. Dijon mustard
¼ cup raspberry vinegar
1 Tbsp. rice vinegar
⅓ cup walnut oil
⅓ cup fat-free chicken broth

Salad:

1 lb. small Yukon gold or red-skin potatoes cut in quarters
Pam or other nonstick spray
6 bone-in and skin-on half chicken breasts
½ cup coarsely chopped walnuts, toasted
8 oz. mixed greens or mesclun mix
½ Vidalia onion or other sweet onion, sliced thin
½ cup grape tomatoes

Method:

1. Combine the garlic, shallot, thyme, basil, and oregano in a small food processor or blender and pulse until blended. Add the salt, pepper, mustard, and vinegars and pulse again until blended. Add the walnut oil and chicken stock. Blend until the dressing is emulsified; i.e., has a creamy texture.

2. Preheat the oven to 450° F.

3. In a small bowl, combine three tablespoons of the vinaigrette with the potatoes. Place the potatoes, in a single layer, on a nonstick cookie sheet. Roast the potatoes for about 30 minutes or until they are slightly browned and tender. Transfer the potatoes to a plate and set aside.

4. Spray a heavy-bottom skillet with Pam or other nonstick spray. Brown the chicken breasts on both sides.

Transfer the browned chicken to the oven and roast until they reach an internal temperature of 155° F. Set the chicken aside to cool.

5. Place the walnuts on a cookie sheet and roast them in the oven until the are golden brown and fragrant, about 10 minutes.

6. Remove and discard the skin and bones from the chicken, and cut the meat into bite-size pieces.

Assembling the salad:

In a large bowl, combine the roasted potatoes and diced chicken. Toss this mixture with half of the remaining vinaigrette. Add the mixed greens and remainder of the dressing; gently toss the salad. Transfer the salad to a large platter and garnish with the toasted walnuts, sliced onion, and grape tomatoes.

6 servings with approximately 480 calories per serving, 100 calories from fat

Salmon burgers

My son, Jason, loves cheeseburgers. Every time we go out to eat, which is not very often, he orders a cheeseburger. We recently ate lunch in one of Cape Cod's most popular seafood restaurants, and he seriously considered ordering his usual fare. After reviewing the menu, he looked at me with a gleam in his eye and asked, "Dad, how are the cheeseburgers here?"

"Awful," I said. "You can't get a good cheeseburger in a restaurant that features seafood."

He sighed, reviewed the menu once more, and reluctantly ordered something else. During the two-hour ride back to Connecticut, he lamented several times about not ordering his favorite restaurant meal. After listening to this for the second time, I decided to give him my standard lecture on the dangers of saturated fat and cholesterol. I could see, in the rearview mirror, that he was trying his best not to fall asleep while I rambled on. So, I decided to take another approach.

"Look," I said, "I can make a burger substituting fish for ground beef that is as good, and probably better, than any cheeseburger you have ever eaten."

He said, "Okay, but if it is not as good, you will have to make me a big, fat, and juicy hamburger for dinner the next time you light up the grill."

I agreed, and the following recipe is the result of my effort. Jason ate two of these and probably would have tried to eat a third had there been any left. He still claims that cheeseburgers are his favorite, however...

I have served these salmon burgers twice in my household and everyone, including my super-fussy daughter, Sarah, loved them.

Salmon burger:

2 lbs. skinless Alaska sockeye salmon fillet
1 slice fresh whole wheat bread
¼ cup egg whites (from two large eggs)
1 cup onion, diced fine
½ cup cilantro leaves, chopped
2 cloves fresh garlic, minced
1 tsp. low-sodium soy sauce
2 Tbsp. eggless light canola mayonnaise or Hellmann's reduced fat or light mayonnaise
¼ tsp. grated nutmeg
1 5-ounce box of Old London Brand Mediterranean Melba toast
Pam
mayonnaise for coating the patties

Coating:

1 Tbsp. canola or Hellmann's reduced fat mayonnaise for each burger to coat
Melba toast mixture
1 tsp. chili powder

Method:

1. Preheat your oven to 450° F.

2. Put the melba toast and chili powder for the coating in a freezer bag. Use a rolling pin or other object to grind up the toast while it's in the bag. Set aside.

3. Carefully run your fingers over the salmon fillet to locate any pin bones. Remove any that you find with a pair of tweezers.

4. Chop the salmon into ¼-inch pieces with a French knife. If you feel confident enough to perform this function with a food processor, do so, but be aware that a processor can turn seafood into a sticky paste very quickly. I speak from sad experience.

5. Chop the bread fine and combine it with the slightly beaten egg whites.

6. Combine the egg mixture with onion, cilantro, garlic, soy sauce, mayonnaise, and nutmeg. Blend this mixture with a fork.

7. Divide this mixture into six 5-ounce patties, about 3 inches in diameter.

8. Place the patties on a cookie sheet lined with parchment paper. Then place the pan into the freezer for about 20 minutes, or until the patties become firm, but not frozen.

9. When the patties are chilled and firm, remove them from the freezer. Coat one side of each patty with ½ tablespoon of mayonnaise. Spread the Melba toast mixture evenly on a cookie sheet. Press the coated side of each patty into the mixture and return the patty to the freezer pan, coated side down. Repeat this step for the other side of each patty. Return the patties to the freezer for an additional 10 minutes.

Cooking and serving:

1. Remove the patties from the freezer. Spray a cookie sheet with a quick-release spray like Pam. Place the patties on the tray and bake for about 15 to 20 minutes, until they reach an internal temperature of 160° F.

2. I usually serve these to my family with a light potato or pasta salad. I top the burger with romaine lettuce, sliced tomato, and a thick slice of sweet onion.

Approximately 380 calories per serving, 45 calories from fat. Δ

Lemons
the versatile fruit

By Sharon Palmer, R.D.

The clean, pure lemon has gotten a bad rap. It has become a metaphor for getting a dud. But the lowly lemon is probably one of the most versatile fruits in the world. A single lemon seems to capture a ray of sunshine in its glorious skin. This ancient fruit is likened to two fruits in one package, as both the zesty rind and flavorful juice can be used for different purposes. Right-hand friend to celebrated chefs and old-fashioned cooks, lemons are indispensable in a number of dishes, from salads to desserts.

We've long known that lemons are packed with vitamin C and were transported by sailors on long journeys during the 18th century to ward off scurvy (vitamin C deficiency), a condition known to make their teeth fall out. Lemons have also been a standard method of flavoring foods without the addition of salt or fat. But did you know that lemons are packed with phytochemicals, plant compounds that fight heart disease and cancer?

Lemons have numerous anti-cancer properties

Lemons contain unique flavonoids, a class of phytochemicals that have antioxidant and anti-cancer properties. Liminoids, flavonoids found abundantly in lemons and citrus fruits, are compounds that impart bitterness in citrus juices and have been shown to reduce the risk of several types of cancer. And eating fresh citrus, including lemons, is one of the best ways to ward off illness and prevent disease, according to studies. Lemons are also high in fiber and beta carotenes, yet they contain no fat and a mere 15 calories. Lemons are high in vitamin C, which has been known to boost the immune system, protect against heart disease, combat cancer, and fight infection. Vitamin C is also one of the main antioxidants found in food and it travels through the body neutralizing damaging free radicals.

Lemons are also versatile flavor-enhancers, as they reduce the need for salt and fat in cooking and work as an anti-browning agent for fruits and vegetables. Unlike many fruits, lemon is a flavor on its own. Lemons can be the star of the show, as in Moroccan lemon chicken, or they can support a great dish with a small splash. Lemons can add just the right balance to a recipe by neutralizing overt flavors. Something missing in your potato salad? Try a spoonful of fresh lemon juice.

You can find lemons available year round, but your local grocery store may only stock one or two varieties. A plethora of lemons are grown across the world. Chefs have been known to value their own favorite lemon for use in their culinary strongholds.

Handy lemony tips for your kitchen

• Keep a bowl of lemons in the kitchen. Cheaper than a flower arrangement, a cache of lemons may encourage you to squeeze one into your salad dressing, over your fish, or into your marinade at a moment's notice. Added bonus: They add a fresh, clean aroma to your kitchen.

• Before squeezing lemons for juice, keep the lemons at room temperature and roll them on the countertop to release the juices.

• Add slices of lemon to your drinking water.

• Keep a mix of olive oil, fresh herbs, garlic, and lemon juice on hand for use in salad dressings, marinades, and as a dip for bread.

• Toss your used lemon rinds into the garbage disposal in order to freshen it.

• Squeeze lemon juice over sliced fruits that brown, such as apples, pears, and bananas.

• Grate lemon peel into your favorite batch of cookies, bread, muffins, or cake to add a citrusy flavor.

• Brighten the color of vegetables by squeezing lemon juice over them before they are cooked.

• Tenderize meats with lemon juice.

• Add lemon juice to rice while cooking to make it fluffier.

• Jazz up the flavor of other fresh fruits with lemon zest.

• Add julienne strips of lemon peel to stir fries and pasta dishes.

• Add lemon juice to dips, from salsa to hummus.

• Zip up the flavor of almost any pasta, potato, chicken, tuna, or egg salad with lemon juice.

• Squeeze lemon juice into your favorite soup recipe.

• Don't even think about serving seafood without plenty of lemon wedges.

• Try lemon juice or grated lemon peel in your risotto.

• Blend lemon juice into yogurt for a healthy fruit salad dressing.

• Keep a pitcher of fresh lemonade in your refrigerator for a refreshing beverage.

Remember, when life gives you lemons—grate, squeeze, grind, and slice them up to add zest to your foods and life.

Lemon varieties

- *Avon* This variety first grown in Florida produces heavy crops of fruit perfectly suited for frozen concentrate.
- *Baboon* Originated in Brazil, this intensely yellow lemon has a flavor more similar to lime.
- *Bearss* Also known as the "Sicily," this lemon is similar to the "Lisbon." The fruit is large and the peel is rich in oil.
- *Berna* This medium-sized fruit is Spain's most important lemon.
- *Eureka* This is the leading variety commercially and for home planting in the U.S. It is well adapted for growing in California. The fruit has a high juice content and high acid level.
- *Femminello* One of the oldest Italian lemons, it accounts for almost 75% of Italy's lemon production. This medium-sized fruit is tart with a high acid level.
- *Genoa* Very similar to Eureka, this lemon was introduced to California from Genoa, Italy.
- *Interdonato* Grown in Italy and Turkey, this is often the earliest lemon of the season. It has low juice content and is mildly bitter.
- *Lamas* Popular in Turkey, this lemon is stored in caves.
- *Lapithkiotiki* The main lemon of Cyprus, this lemon is similar to the Eureka.
- *Lemonade* This lemon has a pale yellow skin with a grapefruit-like flavor.
- *Lisbon* This lemon originated in Portugal and eventually made its way to California about 1849. The fruit is very close to the Eureka, but it surpasses it in California.
- *Meyer* A popular home plant in California, this hybrid is thought to be the offspring of a lemon and orange. The fruit looks like a small orange and the pulp is light, yellow-orange.
- *Nepali Oblong* This lemon, grown commercially in India, looks like a citron and is very juicy with medium acidity.
- *Otaheite Lemon* This unique lemon is sometimes ranked as a separate species. It is commonly used as an indoor ornamental plant and produces deep yellow, spherical small fruits.
- *Perrine* A hybrid of the Mexican lime and the "Genoa" lemon, this pale yellow lemon is juicy with a slight lime flavor.
- *Pink Lemonade* This medium-size fruit boasts a striped rind when it is immature. The juicy, tart flesh is pinkish.
- *Primofiori* This lemon with a smooth, thin rind is the first to mature during the season in Spain.
- *Sweet Lemon* This is a general name for low-acid lemons or limettas. They are usually grown in the Mediterranean region and India.
- *Villafranca* This lemon is similar to the Eureka and was the leading lemon in Florida for years.
- *Volkamer* This small, round lemon is light orange in color and low in acid level. It is thought to be a hybrid of a lemon and sour orange.

Parsley salad, lemon vinaigrette

1 shallot, minced
1 tsp. finely grated lemon zest
2 Tbsp. Lemon Vinegar or seasoned rice vinegar
1 garlic clove, minced
½ tsp. Dijon mustard
¼ tsp. salt
pinch of freshly ground black pepper
¼ cup Lemon Olive Oil or olive oil
6 cups loosely packed fresh flat-leaf parsley leaves (about 2 bunches)
6 cups loosely packed fresh curly parsley leaves (about 2 bunches)

Whisk together the shallot, zest, vinegar, garlic, mustard, salt, and pepper in a small bowl. Whisking constantly, slowly add the lemon oil in a thin stream, and whisk until the vinaigrette is emulsified.

Just before serving, toss the parsley with the dressing in a large bowl, arrange on a chilled serving platter or salad plates, and serve immediately. Serves 6 to 8.

Lemon scallop ceviche

1 pound tiny bay scallops
1 sweet red onion, finely diced
1 yellow bell pepper, seeded and finely diced
zest of 1 lemon, removed with a vegetable peeler
1 cup fresh lemon juice (about 4 large lemons)
1 cup loosely packed cilantro leaves
3 Tbsp. Lemon Olive Oil or olive oil
1 to 3 jalapeno chilies, seeded and minced
1 to 2 garlic cloves, mashed to a paste with ½ tsp. salt
¼ tsp. ground coriander
radicchio leaves for serving, optional

Stir together all of the ingredients except the radicchio in a large bowl. Refrigerate, covered, for at least 4 hours, or until the scallops are opaque throughout and firm, or up to 24 hours.

Just before serving, taste and add more salt, if necessary. Serve the ceviche chilled on radicchio leaves, if desired. Serves 4 to 6.

Peaches and berries with rose water and lemon

1/3 cup sugar
4 strips lemon zest, removed with a vegetable peeler
1 Tbsp. fresh lemon juice
pinch of salt
4 firm ripe peaches, peeled and sliced
1 or 2 tsp. rose water (or orange flower water)
¼ tsp. pure vanilla extract
1 cup mixed fresh ripe berries

Bring 1 cup cool water, the sugar, zest, lemon juice, and salt to a boil in a small saucepan over high heat. Remove the pan from the heat and let stand for 2 minutes. Add the peaches and let stand for 10 minutes. Add the rose water to taste and the vanilla. Let the mixture come to room temperature.

Stir in the berries. Chill, covered, for at least 1 hour and up to 4 hours before serving. Serves 4.

Lemon vinegar

1 cup seasoned rice vinegar
2 Tbsp. finely grated lemon zest

Place the vinegar and the zest in a glass jar. Let stand at room temperature for at least 1 week, shaking occasionally.

Pour the vinegar through a strainer and discard the zest. Transfer to a jar and store, tightly covered, at room temperature. Makes 1 cup.

Lemon oil

1 cup extra virgin olive oil, olive oil, grapeseed oil, or other vegetable oil
2 Tbsp. finely grated lemon zest

Place the oil and the zest in a glass jar. Let stand at room temperature for at least 2 weeks, shaking occasionally.

Pour the oil through a strainer and discard the zest. Transfer to a jar and store, tightly covered, at room temperature. Makes 1 cup.

NOTE: Recipes are compliments of Lori Longbotham, author of *Lemon Zest* and *Luscious Lemon Desserts*.

(Sharon Palmer is a registered dietitian and freelance food and nutrition journalist in Southern California.) Δ

A brief history of HEALTH AND MEDICINE

FROM WITCH DOCTORS TO COMPUTERS

By John Silveira

As little as a century ago, the average life span in the United States was 49 years. Today it is 77. Fifty years ago, the average life span in India or China was 40. Today it's in the mid-60s. Increases in medical knowledge and surgical procedures play a role in this increased longevity, but not the major role.

Sanitation and nutrition

The increase comes mainly from surviving birth and childhood. The fact is, in societies with low life expectancies, the biggest reason they are low is because of deaths during childhood.

In fact, a person born in Greece 2,000 years ago had a fairly good chance of making it to old age if he or she could simply *survive* childhood.

What's brought about this leap in longevity? The greatest advances have been in sanitation and nutrition. Improvements in medicine are a distant third. Granted, if you have a disease, you could die without treatment. But, in general, sanitation alone is the greatest contributor to today's longer life spans. If you're 80 years old, the most important thing to maintaining your health may be medical science. But if you're a newborn, the most important things to *making it to 80* are good sanitation and nutrition.

The need for sanitation is so great that the sewer should rank as one of the great inventions of civilization. The greatness of Rome probably rests more on its engineering feats; i.e., the building of aqueducts to bring clean water to its cities, and the building of sewers to take away waste—as well as its ability to build and maintain its ubiquitous roads—than it did on its formidable army.

In Western civilization today, we take for granted the clean water coming from our taps and the sewer systems and trash trucks that carry away our waste. But, they have done more to improve our health than all the doctors, nurses, and hospitals combined. It may be difficult to comprehend that the garbage man, the sewer worker, the farmer, and the grocer are more important to your health than the highly paid doctor, but it's true. The leap in life spans has not been a medical leap, but a leap in public sanitation and nutrition.

Sanitation includes the control of vermin. The Black Death that swept Europe, killing at least a quarter of its population and perhaps as many as a third, could not have been nearly so devastating if people of that time had simply controlled the rats. It was the fleas on the rats that transmitted the deadly disease.

Sanitation has also brought about the eradication of many diseases. Epidemics of yellow fever and malaria used to sweep portions of this country until the draining of swamps and invention of pesticides brought about the control of the mosquitoes that transmitted the diseases.

Still, medical science is important, and has added to our overall health and well-being. And while I could get a job fairly easily picking up garbage or working on a sewer line, I could not make it as a doctor without investing a lot of time and money in an extensive education.

Besides, writing about the history of medical science is much more interesting than the history of water pipes, sewage treatment, and trash removal. Medical history has occupied some of the best minds the human race has ever produced, and it is the stuff of gripping drama.

Early man practiced health care and medicine

It's safe to say you don't have anything if you don't have your health, and it appears as if humans, since before the dawn of civilization, have been obsessed with their health and how to preserve it. And there's actual evidence that this is true.

It may be difficult to comprehend that the garbage man, the sewer worker, the farmer, and the grocer are more important to your health than the highly paid doctor, but it's true.

Although it's silly to say conclusively what cave art or the figurines found at archaeological digs meant to the prehistoric people who made them, they suggest those ancient people believed in spirits and supernatural forces that affected the real world around them. And if we extrapolate from what we know of the beliefs of primitive people living today, and their uses of amulets, ceremonies, and spells, we can infer with virtual certainty that similar beliefs existed among our prehistoric ancestors. And just as with both modern and primitive people alive today, it is also easy to imagine that among the concerns of our long-ago forebears was their health, their well-being, their lives, and their deaths.

Health care and medicine may seem like modern inventions, but we know they were practiced in prehistoric times, even if what was practiced back then may seem strange to us today.

There is evidence of medical treatments among ancient peoples. Archaeologists have found everything from mended bones that had been broken and set, to evidence of care of the elderly who suffered some of the diseases that afflict us even today, such as debilitating arthritis.

Ancient Incas performed invasive brain surgery

There is even evidence of surgical practices found in the fossil record. Trepanned skulls have been discovered in many places in the world, but particularly among the ancient Incas of South America. And what was this trepanning of a skull? It was a procedure in which holes were drilled through the skull to reach the brain. Why they performed this surgery we don't know. But, whatever their intentions, they performed it often—and successfully. In an ancient world that could have known nothing about microbes and not nearly as much about human anatomy, we know now people survived this radical procedure because many of the skulls archaeologists have found show complete healing around the wounds. So these people lived for years after the surgery was performed.

Medicine suffers setback at hands of the Church

Also, many of the drugs we use today, such as digitalis, morphine, and aspirin come from plants we know ancient people used to treat illnesses and injuries. And there were other drugs as well. But an entire pharmacopoeia of drugs that naturally occur in plants and minerals was lost to Europeans when, in the Middle Ages, the Church deemed many of the women who practiced this kind of medicine to be witches. Some were executed, others simply ceased to practice. But much of the knowledge that had been passed on from mother to daughter for centuries ceased to exist and is only being rediscovered today.

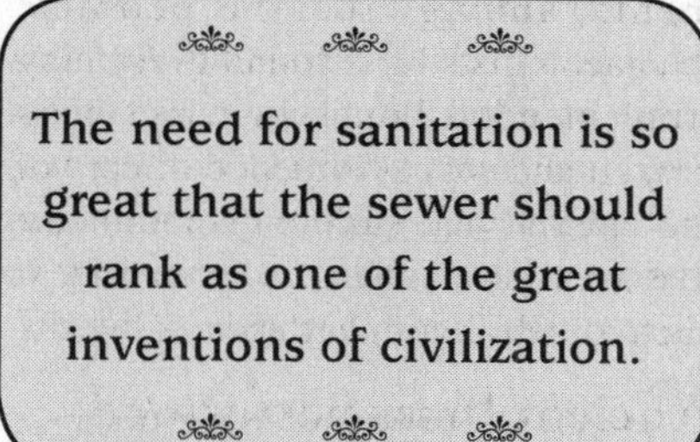
The need for sanitation is so great that the sewer should rank as one of the great inventions of civilization.

Once the use of herbal and mineral cures was outlawed by the Church, European medical practices became more primitive than that of prehistoric man and the primitive tribes that live today in South America and Papua New Guinea. For in witch-hunting Europe, there was little done to care for the ill other than to make them comfortable and to pray over them.

This is not to say that what was lost with these women were some kinds of miracle drug or supercures. Many of the "treatments" they used probably had no effect at all. But some were doubtless things we'd like to take a look at today and may have value that modern medical science could exploit.

We don't usually know what may have made the ancients try or settle on any particular treatments for a particular malady. They are likely to have depended on several things: Traditions, superstitions, trying something and because the patient recovered—whether it was coincidence or not. But there was no scientific research per se, as the *scientific method* with its insistence on reproducibility of results and peer review had not yet been invented. So medicine was largely a hit-and-miss proposition.

But even hit-or-miss can get results. Many of the discoveries, drugs, and medical equipment we have today are based on serendipitous and chance discoveries. Among these are penicillin, the pace maker, and even x-rays.

What follows is an abbreviated history of health and medicine that may help you understand how medical science got to where it is today and where it may be heading in the future.

It's been a long and winding road with many dead ends and reversals of direction. But it is a road humanity has taken because of our obsession with improving and maintaining our health.

The earliest medicine

Religion, health, and healing were almost always mixed together in the ancient world. We know from reading ancient Egyptian hieroglyphs that various gods were thought to be responsible for different parts of the body, and that evil and unseen spirits were believed to be responsible for illnesses. There's evidence that there were medicines, including opium and cannabis, used to treat pain, and ointments and lotions that were used to treat other diseases. But they were not usually used for curing. That was thought to come through prayer.

The ancient Egyptians

Because the ancient Egyptians knew how to remove various internal organs before mummifying the dead, it's clear they also had a pretty good idea of human anatomy. But they did not use that knowledge for the treatment of diseases since disease was thought to be the result of supernatural forces and the gods.

However, they were not without medical practice. Among the earliest advances in medicine were their treatments of injuries. While it certainly wasn't clear, until recently, what causes diseases such as measles, plague, smallpox, and other microbe-caused illnesses, or why someone could just drop dead of a stroke or heart attack, cuts and broken bones suffered in day-to-day living or on the battlefield *were* treatable, even if the treatments were primitive by modern standards and even if they often failed.

Following the ancient Egyptians, the ancient Greeks also believed in many gods and thought they had influence on the day-to-day affairs of men. But the Greeks had something else that would ultimately transform all of civilization. They were inventing *science*. That is, they looked for natural ways to explain the universe around them instead of supernatural explanations. Among these men was Hippocrates, who lived from about 460 to 377 BC, and is sometimes regarded as the father of modern medicine.

The four humors of the Greek, Hippocrates

While many others still believed illnesses were visited on men by the gods, Hippocrates thought there were more natural explanations, including what he regarded as the four *humors*. The humors included blood, phlegm, black bile, and yellow bile. Illness, he thought, resulted when the humors were out of balance, and it was the physician's responsibility to treat a patient and get these humors back in balance.

For example, fever was thought to be the result of an excess of yellow bile and the treatment was to increase yellow bile's opposite, which was phlegm, which is associated with water. So the "doctor" would prescribe cool baths. On the other hand, when a common cold manifested itself with excessive phlegm, the prescription was to bundle the patient up, as warmth was associated with blood, the opposite of phlegm.

We may laugh at this, today, but it was an attempt to take the treatment of illnesses out of the world of magic, mystery, and religion and rationalize it. And, even today, the treatments Hippocrates might have prescribed often make sense. It's his reasoning

During the years of the Bubonic Plague, cats—one of the effective means of controlling the rats that were spreading the disease—were almost nonexistent in Europe. This was because cats were being exterminated. They were considered demonic animals and thought to keep company with witches.

modern medicine finds fault with, not necessarily what he prescribed. But his teachings were carried to Rome and held sway in Western civilization well into recent times.

While modern medical practice no longer believes in "unbalanced humors" being the cause of bad health, today we still practice one thing that may not have originated with Hippocrates and the Greeks, but was codified by them. That's the *medical examination* where the doctor takes case histories and makes diagnoses before prescribing treatment. Again, it was an attempt to rationalize the universe and to find cause and effect, particularly in medicine.

Treating the gladiators and the Roman legions

Following Hippocrates by several centuries was another Greek named Galen (129 to 199 AD), who travelled to Rome where he treated professional gladiators who were wounded in the arena.

Since it was illegal to dissect the dead, Galen dissected many animals and discovered many surgical techniques that were taught to other doctors to further the treatment of gladiatorial wounds. These treatments were later extended to treat wounds suffered on the battlefield by members of the Roman army.

But the Romans made an even greater contribution to general health. Without understanding germs or even realizing their existence, they did understand the link between health and hygiene. To maintain public health, they built aqueducts to carry fresh water and sewer systems to carry away waste. And as I said earlier, this probably did more to keep the Roman Empire strong than its army.

The Dark Ages and the rise of the Arab world

Following the fall of the Roman Empire, Europe fell into what has often been called the Dark Ages, when much that had been learned in Egypt, Greece, and Rome was lost to the Europeans. But the discoveries of the Greeks and Romans were not entirely lost. Many of their texts were carried off to the Arab world, which became the center of science and learning until the Renaissance.

The Arabs further developed Greek and Roman medical practices and created hospitals where surgery was performed and pharmaceuticals were dispensed. For centuries, the Arab world would not only remain the repository of scientific, medical, and mathematical knowledge, but they would add to it. It wasn't until the Renaissance that Europe became aware of this legacy.

Around 1030 A.D, the Arab physician, Avicenna, produced a five-volume tome whose title translates as *Laws of Medicine*. It detailed the formulation of drugs, diagnosis of disorders, general medicine, and therapies. When it was finally translated into Latin, it influenced the development of medicine in Europe for centuries to come.

But until that time, in Europe medicine was still dominated by religion. Illness was considered to be punishment from God, and the cure was to pray for forgiveness. Hospitals were founded in monasteries and doctors, as they were, were usually priests or religious scholars, and treatment consisted of making the patients comfortable and praying over them.

The roads open to modern medicine; e.g., the herbal remedies and such that had been developed since prehistoric times, were considered witchcraft and banned.

When the Black Death (most likely Bubonic Plague) raged through Europe killing as many as 25 million people, effective treatment was nonexistent. Since the plague was considered punishment from God, there was no attempt at hygiene, quarantine, or rodent control, which is necessary to control the fleas that spread the disease.

While many others still believed illnesses were visited on men by the gods, Hippocrates thought there were more natural explanations.

However, surgery was still performed for wounds such as those suffered on the battlefield. The setting of broken bones, the amputation of severely damaged limbs, replacing dislocations, and the binding of open wounds were relatively common. Opium was sometimes available as an anaesthetic, and wounds were often cleaned with wine in an attempt to prevent infections, although the cause of infections was still unknown because no one yet knew microbes existed.

Beginning in Italy, Europe began to awaken from the Dark Ages, and intellectuals began to rediscover the works of the ancient Greeks and Romans that had been preserved by the Arabs. The Renaissance was born. Men rediscovered Greek and Roman art, mathematics, and science, including their practice of medicine. And the invention of moveable type brought about mass publication and relatively inexpensive books. This promoted the spread of education, particularly in the natural sciences. A revolution in how Europeans thought was underway.

Renaissance discovers the heart is just a pump

During the Renaissance, major strides were made as doctors such as Andreas Vesalius and the brilliant Leonardo Da Vinci dissected human cadavers and recorded what they observed in detailed drawings. However, the ancient Greek theory that illnesses were cause by imbalances in the four humors still prevailed.

One of the great breakthroughs in medical science occurred when the English physician, William Harvey, made the astounding discovery that the heart is no more than a pump and that the system of blood vessels that are found throughout the body are the conduits through which the blood flows. Furthermore, he discovered that the blood was restricted to flowing in one direction, being regulated by a series of valves that prevent the backflow of blood.

This is so obvious today that it's hard to appreciate the impact this discovery had on medical science. No one knew why the blood circulated through the body, but the discovery that it did was a quantum leap in our understanding of how the body works.

During this time, European doctors built on what they learned from studying Arabic writings, while European explorers travelled the entire globe and returned home with new drugs aboriginal people in foreign lands used in the treatment of diseases. Some, like quinine, which is used to treat malaria, are still used today.

The first vaccinations

Smallpox has been a great killer of humanity since ancient times. The disease had no cure. Those afflicted with it had to let it run its course. While many died, those who survived were often dreadfully scarred, but immune from another attack of smallpox.

Then, in 1796, William Jenner discovered that inoculating someone with the pus from a cowpox pustule made the subject immune to the deadly disease smallpox.

It was not the first time *vaccination* had been used. The Turks used the pus from victims who had contracted milder versions of smallpox to do the same thing, though the method sometimes backfired when the patient developed severe cases of smallpox and died. Lady Mary Wortley Montagu had already introduced this Turkish type of vaccination to England 75 years earlier.

But Jenner noticed something no one else had apparently seen, that those who contracted cowpox, a disease similar to smallpox—but which occurred in cows and usually caused mild infections in humans—rarely caught the dreaded smallpox. He made the logical leap that if you intentionally infected someone with cowpox, you could make them immune to smallpox.

No one knew why the blood circulated through the body, but the discovery that it did was a quantum leap in our understanding of how the body works.

The way he tested his theory would be unacceptable today. He deliberately infected an eight-year-old boy with cowpox pus. After the boy developed a mild case of the disease and recovered, Jenner infected him with the deadly smallpox pus. As Jenner expected, the boy proved immune to the disease.

Jenner's discovery was met with skepticism, and it was more than half a century before his method of smallpox immunization became standard all over Britain.

Despite his discovery, neither Jenner nor anyone else knew what in the pus caused the disease nor what occurred in the body to make one immune. But, once the concept of vaccination was discovered, it would eventually be tried for other diseases.

Today, we use weakened or dead bacteria or viruses of some deadly diseases to inoculate people so their immune systems will "learn" to develop antibodies against those diseases. Then, when a viable microbe invades the body, the body's immune system can rapidly develop antibodies that overwhelm the invader before it can get a foothold in our bodies. That is how vaccinations work: They train the body to rapidly create antibodies to specific microbes before the microbes can overwhelm it.

Diseases against which vaccinations would later be discovered include measles, mumps, influenza, polio, rubella, and yellow fever.

Louis Pasteur discovers germs source of diseases

The next great discovery in medicine began with the French chemist Louis Pasteur and germ theory. Pasteur didn't develop germ theory, but he did provide the first scientific evidence that was correct, and his studies led to advances in both sanitation and nutrition.

His novel experiments with flasks containing broths in which all the microorganisms were killed by heat showed that the broth would remain unspoiled unless and until new microbes were introduced. This discovery led to what would become the *pasteurization* of various foods.

From his experiments he also deduced that microorganisms were the source of many diseases, and he proposed that by inhibiting their entry into the human body, diseases could be prevented. This led to the concept of sterilization in hospitals and to better sanitation practices everywhere.

Following on the discovery of vaccination that had worked with smallpox, Pasteur would discover, though serendipitously, immunization techniques for chicken cholera and the deadly diseases, anthrax and rabies.

Though he wasn't a physician, it could be argued that modern scientific medicine really begins with Pasteur; much that came after him builds on his work.

Hospital sanitation

Up to the 19th century, no thought was given to sanitary practices, even during surgery. A doctor treating an open wound or performing a surgical procedure might have come to the operating theater just after wiping down his horse, and without washing his hands.

The Hungarian-Austrian physician, Ignaz Semmelweis, found that if medical personnel simply washed their hands before treating other patients, the incidence of puerperal fever could be dramatically reduced.

In the 19th century, Joseph Lister advocated the sterilization of surgical instruments to prevent septicemia. The first chemical he used was carbolic acid. The acid was even sprayed all around the operating theater. The use of this kind of sanitation alone resulted in a reduction in the mortality rate from infection that followed surgery from 60% to 4%, an astounding reduction at that time.

The concept of sanitation in medicine began to spread. History's most famous nurse, Florence Nightingale, tended wounded soldiers during the Crimean War and realized that most of the wounded died of infections they got in the hospitals rather than from the wounds themselves. Using this knowledge, she insisted on sanitation, which dropped the number of deaths dramatically. And on her return to England in 1857, she revolutionized both nursing and how hospitals were kept sanitary.

Today, sterilization procedures are practiced not only in hospitals but in doctors' and dentists' offices around the world.

The development of modern anesthetics

Because of the lack of anesthetics, surgical operations used to be conducted with speed to minimize the pain and movements of the patients. Amputations could take place in seconds. But with the invention of effective anesthetics, surgeons could take their time, be more deliberate, and conduct more involved surgical procedures.

The very first anesthetics date back into prehistory. Hypnotism and acupuncture have been used, and applying ice to an area that was to be worked on was known to dull the nerves. Hyperventilation, the kind used today in Lamaze births, can change how we sense pain and was sometimes used in surgery.

Various herbs, some which go back to prehistory, were also used. These included opiates, cannabis, cocaine, alcohol, and mandrake.

But it wasn't until the 19th century that the first "chemical" anesthetics were used. These included ether, chloroform, and nitrous oxide. And the first practitioners were usually not physicians, but dentists.

Eventually, new anesthetics would be developed until, by the beginning of the 21st century, there are numerous agents for anesthetizing, including local anesthetics for dentistry and ophthalmology. Anesthesiology has now become a medical specialty in itself. The result of modern anesthetics has been better surgical procedures with more comfort to the patient.

Diagnostic equipment

Thousands of tools have been invented to advance the progress of medical care. Worth mentioning are the stethoscope, invented in France in 1816, the sphygmomanometer (for measuring blood pressure), invented by the Austrian physician Samuel Siegfried Karl Ritter von Basch in 1881, and even the medical thermometer, invented in 1867 by the English physician, Thomas Allbutt. All of these seem so common today as to almost seem unimportant. But all are critical to modern healthcare.

Up to the 19th century, no thought was given to sanitary practices, even during surgery.

The discovery of x-rays was an accident. The German physicist, Wilhelm Roentgen, stumbled on them while studying a new invention called a Crooke's tube. Once he realized he could use them to see the body's internal structure, he saw their use as a diagnostic tool in medicine. Though dangerous if misused, they came to be used not only to view the body's interior, but as a treatment for diseases such as cancer.

By the end of the 20th century, the x-ray machine would inspire other tools that would often replace it. Among these are Magnetic Resonance Imaging (MRI).

Antibiotics

One of the incredible discoveries of the 20th century was modern antibiotics. Living as we do in an ocean of microbes, it's amazing that we live at all. And, occasionally, when some of those microbes get a foothold in our bodies, unless our immune systems can fight them off, we can get very ill and even die.

One of the best things you can personally do to maintain your health is to wash your hands frequently.

What antibiotics actually do is assist our immune systems. They don't wipe out a disease. They kill enough of the microbes, or inhibit their ability to reproduce enough, so your body's immune system can do its job. It's your immune system that has to finally kill off *all* the invaders.

The very first antibiotics date back into prehistory, and we know from their writings that both the ancient Greeks and ancient Chinese used various molds to treat infections. However, what they didn't know or have the means to do was to distill the active components from the molds to concentrate them or to produce them artificially. That would have to wait until the 20th century.

In 1928, the English physician, Alexander Fleming, discovered that the mold *Penicillium notatum* could destroy various bacteria. By the early 1940s, the Russian scientist, Ernst Chain, and the Australian scientist, Howard Florey, both of whom had emigrated to England, would work together to isolate the active ingredient. It would be used to treat many diseases and, when available, it produced miracles on the battlefields of World War II.

The problem was that is was only available in small quantities. But in 1948 an American, Andrew Moyer, would be granted a patent for mass producing it.

Other manufactured antibiotics would follow until there is now a myriad of them, many specific to combatting a narrow range of microbes.

What does the future hold for medicine?

Just in the last 50 years medical inventions and discoveries have come fast and furious. Part of the reason for the increase has been a greater number of talented people studying the subjects. Part, of course, is because of the greater wealth in the world. But mostly it's because new discoveries are being built on previous discoveries—sometimes discoveries in other sciences, as medical x-rays were built on a discovery in physics. But there have been more advances in medicine in just the last few decades than there were in *all* the thousands of years that came before.

Nowadays, heart-lung machines can keep patients alive during critical surgery, dialysis machines can keep them alive while awaiting kidney transplants, hearing aids and cochlea implants can restore hearing, and though they're so common we may not think of them this way, eyeglasses have for several centuries been a remarkable invention that corrected poor eyesight.

In 1956, the forerunner of the pacemaker, the device used to regulate heartbeat, was serendipitously invented by Wilson Greatbatch, and four years later the first one was implanted into a human.

In 1967, the world's first coronary bypass was performed in the United States by the Argentine doctor, René Favaloro.

Between the pacemaker and coronary bypass procedure, deaths due to heart disease have been reduced by an amazing 50 percent in this country.

Also in 1967, the South African doctor, Christian Barnard, performed the world's first human heart transplant.

Today, the use of miniaturized tools, miniature cameras, lasers, and computer-guided surgical tools are making possible treatments and surgical procedures undreamed of just a few years ago.

What's the future of health and medicine? Its history has been a bumpy, winding road. Science does not progress in an orderly fashion. Those who expect it to are doomed to disappointment. This is especially true in medical science.

In the future, nanotechnology and its promise of tools smaller than the body's cells, may allow a doctor to inject a patient with thousands of microscopic machines that will allow computer-guided surgical techniques that can be performed at the cellular level and remove obstructions in the circulatory system or attack and destroy cancer cells one at a time while leaving the surrounding tissue intact.

In the same way, there's the hope of future drugs that will target specific illnesses or specific organs in the body while leaving the rest of your body untouched.

There have been more advances in medicine in just the last few decades than there were in *all* the thousands of years that came before.

Even as I write this, scientists are talking about cloning an individual's internal organs for transplants. Cloned organs will make tissue rejection a thing of the past. And computers will see wider use as diagnostic tools.

Today, when you go to a doctor, he'll interview you and get your symptoms, just as Hippocrates did more than 2400 years ago. You may tell him you have a headache and fever and you feel nauseous and have diarrhea. But there are a lot of illnesses that can produce those symptoms. A competent doctor will then lead you with more questions. If he's knowledgeable, he may be familiar with your disease and get right to a diagnosis and treatment. But we've all heard stories of misdiagnosed patients, some who tragically die when they could have been saved if their malady was diagnosed properly and treated in time.

Now, imagine if a doctor could enter your symptoms into a database that contained all the diseases that could manifest these symptoms. And, since more than one disease can cause the same symptoms, the software provides the doctor with more questions to ask. Conceivably, the computer's software could lead to more and more questions to ask until it either narrows it down to one thing or to a group of diseases with suggestions for tests that could narrow it down further. Misdiagnoses would become fewer and perhaps even a thing of the past.

Studying our genes and battling future diseases

In 2001, two groups announced they had completed mapping the human genome and that all 20,000 to 25,000 genes in human DNA had been mapped.

With ongoing work, as the mysteries of our DNA are unlocked, and the genetic basis for some diseases are revealed, new treatments and cures will be developed. With a patient's entire genetic sequence known, it will be possible to accurately predict his response to a given drug or how he will react to other substances in his environment. In fact, it will be possible to predict what diseases are latent in our genes, such as a predisposition to heart disease or certain cancers. It will also be possible to create tailored treatments based on the patient's DNA or even determine what lifestyle adjustments he should make to protect himself from many diseases.

What else can we expect in the future? The end of illness and disease? The end of aging? Immortality?

Immortality can never happen. No one can live forever. Actuaries once calculated that if we could all live our entire lives as teenagers, the average life span would be a little under 800 years because death would still come as the result of accident, suicide, and murder.

Actuaries once calculated that if we could all live our entire lives as teenagers, the average life span would be a little under 800 years because death would still come as the result of accident, suicide, and murder.

But, remember the line by comedian Steven Wright who said, "I intend to live forever—so far, so good." So there's hope.

Dark pictures are being painted of supermicrobes that are resistant to today's drugs, and it's almost a fait accompli that they're going to be causing pestilence in the near future. Yet, no one knows what new drugs are going to be discovered. Nor even what new treatments may come down the pike. For example, it's conceivable that scientists will find ways to harness one set of microbes and turn them against another. For even at the microbial level, there are bacteria and viruses preying on each other. The world of microbes has its own predators and prey, and life there is every bit as vicious and savage as life on the Serengeti Plain of Africa. In fact, it's probably even more so. It's conceivable that scientists will one day be able to harness that. Have a virus? There may be another virus or a microbe that feeds on it without regards to you, and a simple treatment may rid your body of the offending virus or at least bring it down to a level that your immune system can deal with.

They may even be able to create microbes that attack specific cancers or eat the plaque off the walls of your arteries.

The road from witch doctors to high-tech health has been long and arduous. And it's not over. Though we know much about what it takes to improve or maintain good health, there is more to learn. What's sad is that many of the things an individual can do for himself or herself are within reach, but people simply won't do them. This includes eating right, getting exercise, getting periodic checkups, losing weight, quitting smoking, not abusing drugs including alcohol, driving safely, practicing safe sex, etc.

Many of the improvements you can bring to your health can be done cheaply, free, or even at a profit (such as the money you save when you quit smoking). And they are all things you can do without a doctor's prescription.

As I said earlier, if you had to say what have been the most important developments in promoting and maintaining your health, it would be sanitation and good nutrition. And, thankfully, these are two aspects of your life you have a lot of say in, and you don't need a prescription or a doctor's approval to pursue them.

Want to get started today? Radio personality and writer, Dr. Dean Edell, has stressed that one of the best things you can personally do to maintain your health is to wash your hands frequently. Again, sanitation. It's easy, it's cheap, and it's safe. Go do it. Δ

More good reading:

The Coming American Dictatorship

By John Silveira

Starting Over

By Jackie Clay

part ten

Spring is here! Glorious spring is here, and our water line thawed out! After being without running water from our well to our basement storage tank and the frost-free hydrant by the goat barn, we had thawing. Our snow went very early this year. It's been gone for over a month and the frost followed by only two weeks, but our deep-in-the-ground water line took an extra two weeks after the frost had gone to thaw out. I had been trying the well switch every day for a few seconds and always the same; nothing but a hum as the pump kicked on way down in the well. But on April 22, our carpenter friend, Tom Richardson, showed up and was getting ready to work on the new green room addition to the house. As he would be cutting lumber with a circular saw, I went out to the generator shed and started the generator. Out of habit and wishful thinking, I flipped up the pump switch, glancing out the window to the open frost-free hydrant. Water began flowing happily out of the spout.

I ran out into the driveway and yelled for David and Tom. (I think they figured I'd finally gone off the deep end.) Then we all chatted happi-

The new "temporary" greenhouse

ly, watching the hose fill up the goat water tank. It was so good to watch that clear water flow. Of course, we then quickly topped off the 350 gallon poly storage tank in the basement of the house and all had a good drink of ice water from the hose. Not wanting it to stop, I also connected the hose to the horse watering tank down in the pasture and filled that, as well. For me, it was a major miracle. (And a reminder not to drive on the water line this winter and to thoroughly insulate the steel well casing that sticks up out of the ground.)

The greenhouse emerges

Our first spring project was to get the temporary greenhouse built onto the south side of the new log house. I desperately needed it done so I could transplant my spindly tomato and pepper plants from inside the house. Although I had installed a four-foot shop light to give them more light than a kitchen window would provide, we simply did not run the generator long enough to give the plants as much light as they craved. We had torn down the old greenhouse from the mobile home, and Tom refit it to the larger dimensions available on the new house. Where it had been 10'x10', now it is 10'x16'. It took one Saturday afternoon to deck the surface, using screws and the treated 5/4 decking. There was a lot of cutting to fit so that we didn't waste any material. (Tom is great at that. We only ended up with a few very small waste scraps too small to reuse.)

The floor was screwed down to treated 2x8s, which were hung in rafter hangers for extra support. As this will be a permanent deck, but built on temporary pillars, we got it as level as possible with the snow still going off. In the future, we will be using used power poles for porch supports and rafters, as the green room and porch will extend across the full south side of the house.

Detail of roof construction in the greenhouse: Rafters, purlins, corrugated wood support pieces, and fiberglass roofing sheets

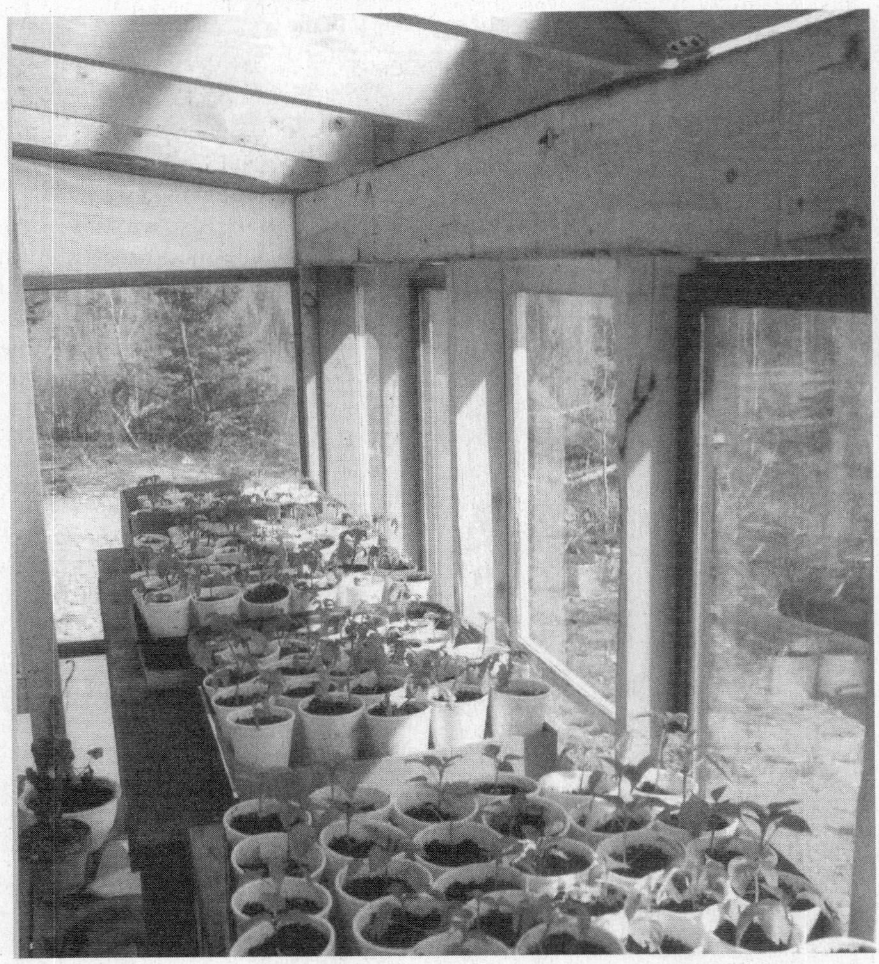

Hundreds of transplanted tomato and pepper plants thrive in the greenhouse.

Eventually, the green room will have insulated windows (reject double-pane patio doors Tom salvaged from another job), along with insulation in the roof, and crawl space underneath. So we are making another "temporary" greenhouse to get by with until it gets rebuilt, this time for the last time.

The reason we are going "temporary" now is that we still have the silver tarps on the roof and can't take the time to place the heavy pole rafters and supports for the finished roof; the temporary roof is the corrugated fiberglass paneling from the old greenhouse, hung on 2x6 rafters with 2x4 purlins, installed under the house roof to shed water easily.

After decking the greenhouse, the next Saturday afternoon was spent hanging rafters, screwing down purlins and the thin corrugated wooden support strips for the lightweight roofing, then screwing down the roofing. As the old roofing was longer than the roofing we needed, Tom reversed a blade in his circular saw and we were able to easily cut two pieces of roofing at a time. Nice and smooth. I had visions of splitting fiberglass flying around everywhere, but it cut very nicely.

To strengthen small fruit trees, pinch off the blooms.

I cut the panels and handed them up through the rafters to Tom and David, who were positioning them and screwing them down. There are a few holes that didn't line up, and leak when it rains, but I am going up there and filling them with dabs of silicone sealer. That does a great job and lasts for years.

Before it was very late, Tom managed to frame and hang a few of the old windows on the south side (also leftovers from other jobs). It looked pretty darned good. Then on Sunday afternoon, David and I went to work and hung more windows on the east and west ends of the greenhouse. Two of these were windows that opened, having screens for ventilation on hot days. Then we screwed blocks over the openings at the eaves and finished up by hanging doubled 6-mil plastic over the odds and ends openings that we had no windows to fit. Not gorgeous, but certainly functional.

The very next day, we moved the homemade tables and benches down from the mobile home and installed them in the new greenhouse. Finishing up with a large dollar-store thermometer, we moved the plants into their new home.

Of course, although the daytime temperatures out there were in the 70s, the night temperatures fluctuated down into the 20s without heat. So I carefully carried in the plants each evening, just to make sure none froze after all that work.

But, those sorry plants sure needed help; they were so leggy. So, I went to work and began transplanting. I've found that my plants do best when transplanted into large Styrofoam cups (also dollar store). I set to work filling them with potting soil, then burying them so that only the strong, straight top showed at the top. Tomatoes will grow roots all along the buried stem, making the leggy plants stronger, and peppers don't mind a bit being planted deeply.

I used a tablespoon for a transplanting trowel, carefully handling the plants only by the leaves. You can easily damage the stem of the young plant by squeezing it with your fingers. This can even kill the plant. Even if you pull off a leaf, no lasting damage is done.

The only problem with using the Styrofoam cups is that they are tippy when full. To solve this problem, I cut down cardboard banana boxes that I get goat scraps in from our local supermarket. These boxes are heavy and have handles on the ends, which I carefully leave. The only problem is that the boxes have a large ventilation hole in the bottom. To solve this, I simply cut strips of leftover cardboard to lay over the holes.

Then, as I transplanted, I put each cup into the box, filling it snugly. When I have to move a box of plants, it is simple and safe to do. (And I'm glad to find another use for those boxes.)

When I finished, I had more than 100 tomato plants of 13 varieties. I was amazed, as I thought I was a little short of tomatoes. Of course, I'll give some to my son Bill and his wife, a few to Tom, the carpenter, and trade a few with friends for a few different varieties. And I came out with about 60 peppers of seven different kinds.

Two weeks later, every single one of those plants is thriving and getting very strong and lusty. They love their new home. I can't wait to get them moved out into the garden, in their snug Wall'o Waters. The temperatures are okay now, lows getting only into the mid 20s, but I don't have the garden ready yet.

Mom and Dad have both had hospital stays in April, due to the flu and pheumonia, so I was more than a little busy and couldn't garden when I wanted to.

David picks up rocks in the big garden.

Canning pork loin and chicken breast

But while I had to be in the house more than I wanted, it did give me time to stock up on my meat. Our local supermarket was selling some very good whole boneless pork loin and chicken breast at a huge savings, so I bought as much as I thought I could handle canning.

These were very easy to can. I simply boiled a batch of breasts or a cut-in-half pork loin, with seasoned water, in a very large stock pot until the meat was about half cooked. This let it shrink and become firm enough to cut if needed and fit nicely into the jars. The chicken breasts, I packed whole into wide-mouth pint jars. Leftover pieces, I diced into half pints. Then the jars were filled to within an inch of the top of the jars with the hot broth they were boiled in.

I processed the hot-packed chicken at 10 pounds pressure in my pressure canner, in pints and half pints for 75 minutes, and it turned out absolutely wonderful.

The pork loin was sliced or diced, depending on the part of the loin I was working with. The nicest meat was simply sliced about half an inch thick and slid carefully into pint and quart jars. Some was diced and packed into pint jars to use for casseroles and barbecue pork. All was covered with the hot broth that the meat was boiled in, to within an inch of the top of the jars.

This was canned in a pressure canner at 10 pounds pressure for 75 minutes (pints) and 90 minutes (quarts).

I put up 12 pounds of boneless chicken breast and three whole boneless pork loins in two afternoons, giving us meat for more than 56 meals. Well worth the effort, I'd say.

During Mom and Dad's recovery at the hospital, I also had my bi-monthly xrays and lab work to make sure my cancer was gone. It's been a year since I began treatment for the pea-sized lump on my elbow, which turned out to be a rare Merkel Cell Carcinoma, and I am very happy to report that everything came back absolutely normal.

Getting the garden ready

Now, with all those plants growing so nicely in the greenhouse, it was time for me to get busy and get the garden ready to go. And, with the weather being so fantastic for the time of year, I wanted to get some of the earliest crops in, like peas, carrots, turnips, onions, and lettuce. Because my oldest son, Bill, had vastly enlarged the garden with his crawler last summer, removing many tree stumps, logs, and large rocks, the whole thing needed lots of work to get ready for planting.

I had planned to get my large hoop house up this spring, but because of Mom and Dad's illness, that just won't happen. I'll use other methods of protecting my tender crops until next year.

Because my large garden is on a gentle slope next to the house, it is basically a slope of gravel and rock; not the best soil, but it's what we've got. Last fall, David hauled the compost pile (rotted goat and chicken manure and straw) onto the garden with our little Ford tractor and loader. It was spread quite well, but there were still humps and piles here and there. And brush roots. Oh my.

As the garden now measures about 100'x100', there's lots of fixin' that needs to be done. David brought the garden trailer down to the garden with his ATV, and we picked rocks all afternoon. Then I tilled, unearthing many more. So while David picked those rocks, I began to pick up, pull up, and dig up tree and brush roots. Some of them were 10 feet long. And if I had not pulled them, they would have suckered little sprouts all over the garden.

I'm very sure we didn't get all the big rocks or roots. But this is an ongoing process, and we will be at it for years. Our garden in Montana was also carved out of virgin slope, under like conditions. And when we left, it was a pretty darned good piece of ground. It is amazing at how much improvement a lot of work and rotted manure can make on a less than perfect garden. The trick in all gardening is perseverance. If you quit or "put up with bad conditions," you lose.

Once we got the upper side of the garden worked up quite well, I hooked our furrowing attachment onto the TroyBilt. I had found a terrific sale on two-year-old, very large roots of Jersey Giant asparagus. All of the Jersey asparagus varieties are pretty much "all-male" plants. The female asparagus plants are the ones that produce the little red berries. And they are generally less productive as table asparagus, as they put much of their energy into reproduction. With the all-male hybrids, you get bigger, fatter, and more asparagus. Last year I planted a dozen Mary Washington (plain, common garden asparagus) down on the edges of our paths, as tame "wild" asparagus. It's growing, but I wanted more asparagus and more easily accessible to the kitchen. As asparagus is one of our favorite crops, I bought two packs of 10 roots each. (We ended up with three "free" roots, to boot.)

Planting asparagus is a bit different than many crops. The best way is to dig a trench along the row, about 8" to 10" deep. Spreading the roots out as much as possible, I laid the roots into the trench about a foot and a half apart. I have a pile of two-year-old, very black rotted compost that I forked onto the plants, covering each one by about two inches of the compost. Then, in between the plants, I forked some of the year-old rotted manure to provide fertilizer and keep down any sprouting weeds.

As the asparagus grows, I'll keep covering it, just like you'd do hilling potatoes. This buries the roots deeply, but encourages plant growth.

On the near end of each trench, I planted rhubarb that I transplanted from the gravel slope. It wasn't getting enough water or care, and I know that it'll be much happier down in the main garden. Especially since I dug in several forkfuls of well-rotted manure around each plant.

I like as many perennial plants around the place as possible. They just keep getting better each and every year. Rhubarb and strawberries yield the first tame fruit on a new homestead, so are much cherished. But I have also planted "slower" fruits.

Two years ago, my parents and sister gave me five apple trees (Harlson and Harlred) for my birthday, and we planted these in what will eventually be our orchard/chicken yard. Last year, I planted a hardy pie cherry, a Minnesota apricot (Moonglo), a Honeycrisp and Fireside apple, along with Manchurian apricots and Nanking cherries, a hardy bush cherry.

On checking my baby trees this spring, I've (maybe) lost only one apple tree. Everything else is popping out leaves and even a few flowers. David and I just planted an Alderman plum, which is now flowering. But on the littlest trees, I'll pinch the blossoms off so the trees will put all their energy into growing and developing strong roots. It's hard, but will pay in the long run.

I was worried about the trees I planted last spring. Because of all the running to the hospital, I didn't get the trunks covered with screen or fencing around the trees. Voles, mice, and rabbits will girdle the lower trunk of young trees, often right under the snow. This nearly always kills the trees. I had it happen years ago with more than 20 young apple trees, so I learned my hard lesson. And, deer love to munch on the twigs, bark, and upper branches of the sweet young trees. I lucked out. The trees sailed

My on-sale asparagus roots were huge. I spread the roots to place in the furrows, then place the asparagus roots in the trench. After covering the plants with black compost, I fill in between with one-year-old rotted manure.

through the winter without becoming lunch for our wild neighbors.

With all the newly planted fruit, which should begin bearing a little this year or next, we also have so much wild fruit around: Red raspberries, blueberries, chokecherries, and wild plums. I feel blessed. My new basement pantry is all ready to receive this summer's bounty.

Disbudding our baby goats' horns

We had two single goat births on the homestead, earlier this spring. They were both very nice baby bucks. We raise Nubian-Boer crossbreds. The Nubians are colorful, elegant big milkers with cute, floppy big ears. But they tend to be like race horses, tall and narrow. We wanted more size and meat ability, so for years we have been crossing Nubians with Boer meat goats and have been happy with the results. The does milk about three quarts to more than a gallon a day of very good tasting milk. And the bucks and wethers are very large and quickly put on bulk. Chevon (goat meat) is very good, being consumed, worldwide, much more than is beef. And when you have limited refrigeration and no freezer, you can handle the meat that comes off a goat, where 800 pounds of beef is just too much to handle in many cases.

All of my goats are hornless. They were not born that way, but disbudded soon after birth. No, that is not what nature intended, but nature didn't intend that goats be penned up and milked twice a day. Horns on goats may be "protection," but I have seen our old hornless Nubian doe run a big coyote all the way across our acre of pasture. Goats have a big attitude and don't generally have predator trouble, unless they are on a tether chain and stake or in a small pen. Then it is usually a dog that will be the culprit, rather than a wild animal.

Horns are just trouble on a homestead goat. They get stuck in fences, mangers and ropes, even their own collars, sometimes resulting in strangulation and death. Does sometimes break the legs of their own kids by butting at them and catching a kid's leg in the V between the horns. And the horns are a definite danger to the person handling and milking them. Goats don't mean to hurt you with them, but by turning their head quickly, they can bang your face, twist your fingers, and otherwise do harm. Especially to children who are not so observant and careful when handling them.

Our Nubian/Boer goats milk well and are big. David's pet wether, Oreo, towers over me on his hind feet, standing 6½ feet.

It's a major surgery to remove the horns from an adult goat, but very easy to do with kids. At about three days of age, we disbud them. This involves using an electric disbudding iron, available at most goat supply houses for around $50. I heat the iron to coppery red, then while David holds the kid on his lap securely, I apply the hot iron to first one horn bud, rocking it slowly in a circular motion for even disbudding, then the other bud. I hold the iron on each horn bud for about seven seconds; just enough to burn a good even light-colored ring completely around each horn.

Then I go back and see if the edge of the iron will flip off the burned scab on the tip of the bud. It usually does, and I repeat the process on each one, for a little less time. Yes, the kid does yell, but not as much as you'd think. And then it's over.

I apply a handful of snow on each bud, then give the kid a bottle or let it back in with its mother. It happily drinks and seems to forget all about the process. They don't fear you and don't seem to feel in pain. And you have just saved their life or injury to a person you love. I don't like doing it. It stinks of burning hair, and I hate to hear the kids bawl. But it really is necessary. If you can't afford an iron, go into partnership with a friend and help each other disbud. It goes easier with two people, anyway.

But, you can do it alone. Build a kid holding box. This is a narrow plywood box, just wide enough for the kid's standing body to fit in. The top is hinged at the back and there's a notch in the front just big enough to let his head and neck stick out. There is a small, semi-circular shelf just below the notch for his chin to rest on. So once in, the kid can't move around much. You can sit on the box and hold his head down with one hand and use the disbudding iron with the other. It goes quite nicely this way. You can make a box yourself or buy one.

A goat supply house that I use a lot for everything from disbudding irons to cheese making supplies is Hoegger Supply Company, P.O. Box 331, Fayetteville, Georgia 30214 or www.thegoatstore.com.

Planting wildflowers

As spring is here full-force, many of the daffodil, crocus, and grape hyacinth bulbs that I planted last fall and the year before are popping up and blooming. It's always such a thrill when the first cheerful crocus opens and sings to the morning sun.

I like to bring beauty to everywhere, so I am constantly planting bulbs and flowers, often in unexpected places. Right now, Bob's memorial garden is coming alive with flowers and birdsong. Besides the flowers, I have bird feeders and houses in several places, so the mornings ring with song. (And the birds also help keep the insect pests out of my garden, so attracting them serves a two-fold purpose.)

Of course, we have many wildflowers here on the homestead, but I always pop in a few more. It seems that I can't get enough flowers; I like something blooming all the time. It encourages your soul.

I'm planting daylilies (you can also eat daylily buds), which come back every year, bigger and stronger, requiring minimal care. And I'm planting lots of wildflower seeds in the disturbed area around our building site. One spot, especially, cried out for help. That is the large denuded area where the septic drain field lies. Major ugly. So I ordered inexpensive wildflower seeds from Wildseed Farms, 425 Wildflower Hills, P.O. Box 3000, Fredricksburg, Texas 78624-3000 or www.wildseedfarms.com. With a crank-type seeder, I mixed fine seed-starting medium with the mixed seeds and walked back and forth on the bare, loose soil. It had been raining, so the soil was just waiting for the seeds.

Then, after the seeds were spread evenly, I gently ran the ATV back and forth on the area, packing the seeds into the damp ground. A more accepted way is to gently till the soil an inch deep, then seed, then roll the area or walk on it to press the seeds into the ground. But on our gravel pit soil, that would be about impossible without major work. I'm sure that unorthodox method will work fine.

Luckily it will rain off and on all week. But I have a hose and sprinkler out there if it should stop. New seeds must be kept damp (not soggy) while germinating and beginning to grow. That ugly spot will soon be a glowing haven for hummingbirds and butterflies—not to mention me. Δ

drinks and desserts to help you beat the heat

By Linda Gabris

Summer fun and cold treats go hand-in-hand, but keeping up with demand can be demanding, especially when relying on expensive store-bought items to quench big thirsts all summer long.

But relax, for even though the heat is on, there's no need to sweat it. All you have to do to keep your cool is get out the blender and whip up a batch of something super delicious to chill out with.

Making hot weather quenchers is a fun, easy, and economical way to ensure that your family is keeping cool with healthy choices. And the real fun is letting your creative juices flow freely—being as versatile as fruits and vegetables of the season allow.

The best thing about making your own drinks and icy treats is the fact that it allows one to control or eliminate unhealthy additives like artificial flavorings, colorings, and preservatives as well as sugar and salt content.

Fruit and vegetable juices are miraculous cleansers for flushing impurities from the body, and the best way to cash in on their goodness is by juicing. Juices are loaded with vitamins, minerals, enzymes, and other easily absorbed nutrients that are vital to good health and well-being.

So for some juicy fun, start twirling with the recipes below.

Versatile veggie cocktail

Here's a homemade version of the commercial drink known as V8. When tomatoes are hanging heavy on the vine, this is a tasty way to use them up. Some folks stew the tomatoes before processing. I don't. If tomatoes aren't in season, you can use home or store-bought canned tomatoes or tomato juice as a base, and the thickness will reflect your choice. Some like it thick, some thin. Use as much or as little of the other vegetables as you wish. Makes 3 quarts.

2 quarts tomatoes, fresh or canned
boiled water
vegetables—celery, onion, cucumber, garlic, sweet peppers, carrots (carrots are naturally sweet so use them instead of sugar to get desired sweetness), garden radishes, horseradish, or Oriental white radish

Puree tomatoes and vegetables in batches until smooth, using water or juice to achieve desired thickness. Mix well. Strain to remove celery threads and tomato skins, if necessary. Season with pepper, salt if your diet allows, hot sauce, or anything your heart desires. Serve over ice.

Healthful variations: If you want to sneak an extra dose of good health into the pitcher, toss some green or red cabbage leaves or heart into the blender. Cabbage juice is good for the digestive tract, helping to prevent stomach ailments. Broccoli and cauliflower stalks that normally get discarded add extra kick and, like cabbage, are real system flushers. Beets add earthy flavor and are a powerful liver detoxifier. Watercress acts as a blood builder, dill neutralizes stomach acid, and basil, aside from having the power to draw sweetness from tomatoes, is said to bring good fortune. All add exciting zip to the drink.

Versatile veggie cocktail—a good glass of juice to begin the day with

Tutti-frutti shake

No rules here. Mix and match fruits, berries, and juices for endless, exciting variety. The version in the picture calls for enough orange pulp and juice to puree strawberries into a thick luscious shake that is served over crushed ice with a fat straw. For another day try peaches with raspberries, grapes with pears, melon with blueberries, or grapefruit with kiwi. Add a squirt of lemon or lime juice for zip, a dab of grated ginger root for zap, and sweeten with honey or maple syrup if you wish. Puree using as much pure fruit juice of choice as needed, until desired consistency is reached. Serve over ice or blend with ice until slushy.

Indian barley water

Here's an ancient recipe for barley water that flaunts the invigorating taste of India. It was passed down to me from a Kathputli doll puppeteer who vouched that the frothy drink soothed the worst of parched throats. And it does.

Simmer ½ cup barley in 2 cups water for 5 minutes. Strain into blender. Save barley for another purpose (I enjoy its texture in green salads). Add 2 cups boiled water to barley juice along with juice of one lemon or lime, 8 basil or mint leaves, and honey to sweeten. Whirl until frothy. Serve over ice. A nip of gin does justice to this fine drink.

Nutritious strawberry orange yogurt pops

This recipe is so easy and versatile; no two pops ever have to be the same.

- 1 quart pure orange juice with pulp
- 2 cups fresh or frozen, wild or tame, strawberries
- ¼ cup honey or sugar
- 1 cup of soy yogurt

Puree strawberries with juice until smooth. Add yogurt and blend. Pour into molds and freeze. Yields 16 to 18 pops.

Variations: Substitute homemade or pure unsweetened apple, pineapple, grape, cranberry, cherry, or other juice in place of orange and raspberries, blueberries, blackberries, or another pick instead of strawberries to create an endless array of exciting possibilities.

Yummy grape and mandarin toadstools

I freeze these in little tin ramekins that look like mushroom caps, thus their name. You can freeze them in anything you wish, call them anything you will, and they'll still be a hit.

- 2 cups grapes pureed with 1 cup of water (or 3 cups pure grape juice). Some strain; I don't.
- purple grapes make purple toadstools, white grapes make orangey-colored pops.
- 1 cup canned mandarins or tangerines

Puree mandarins with juice until smooth. Pour into molds. When slushy, insert sticks, then continue freezing.

Peach creamsicles

- ¼ cup soft or silken tofu
- 1 cup soy milk
- 3 juicy fresh peeled peaches or 2 cups canned peaches with juice
- honey or maple syrup to sweeten

Puree ingredients in blender until smooth. Pour into molds; freeze. Makes 12-14.

Variations: Instead of peaches, use apricots, pears, mangos, or whatever tickles your fancy.

Melon snowballs

Here's the simplest treat, hard to beat. Let the kids make them as often as they wish. Use in place of ice cubes for keeping other drinks cold. All you need is watermelon, honeydew, or cantaloupe (or for exciting color, some of each) and toothpicks.

Using melon scooper, scoop out balls and insert a toothpick in each one. Freeze until solid, then store in covered container.

Raspberry shrub

Here's Grandma's recipe for raspberry shrub. In the olden days, this was known as pop.

- 4 cups raspberries
- 1 cup apple cider vinegar
- sugar or honey

Pour vinegar over berries in a jar. Cover and let draw at room temperature for 3 days. Force through cheesecloth, discarding seeds. Add ¾ cup sugar or honey to each cup of juice. Simmer 15 minutes. Cool and bottle. For shrub, mix 1 part syrup with 3 parts water or soda and serve over ice, stirring until fizzy.

Homemade citrus bitters

Original recipes for ancient bitters call for exotic ingredients like myrrh, saffron, angelica, and other things not common in most pantries. But you can make simple citrus bitters out of easier to obtain items.

One tablespoon of bitters blended with soda makes a pleasant aperitif,

Barley water from India: A healthful, refreshing drink that's easy and economical to make

Making your own frozen pops allows you to control or eliminate unhealthy additives like artificial preservatives, flavoring, or coloring as well as sugar and salt content.

stimulating the appetite, and when sipped after meals, helps aid digestion and eliminate gas. Bitters should not be given to children, due to alcohol content.

½ cup dried orange, grapefruit, or lemon rind (before juicing citrus fruit, grate off rind and dry in airy place until crispy)
1 Tbsp. of cardamom seeds, caraway seeds, coriander seeds and pinch of ground nutmeg
4 Tbsp. sugar
2 cups vodka

Put spices in bottle, cover with vodka, cap. Infuse for 2 weeks.

Strain and rebottle liquid. Empty catchings into saucepan; add ½ cup water and sugar. Simmer 10 minutes. Cool, strain, and add to vodka. Cork. Let stand two weeks before using.

Fruity summer desserts

Nothing takes the heat off a hot weather meal like a cool dessert, and what could be better than serving up an elegant fruity creation that's delightfully refreshing and super healthy to boot.

When I was a kid I never heard tell of—let alone sampled—many of the fascinating fruits like mango, kiwi, and fresh pineapple that one sees in the produce departments of grocery stores today. As a matter of fact, a Christmas treat of oranges, an occasional tin of pineapple, and lemons that grandmother always pointed out as being dear, was the most exotic fruits we ever indulged in.

Today I am grateful for the endless array of fresh worldly fruits that are readily available and easy on my budget. And even though I still heed grandma's old advice about an apple a day keeping the doctor away, along with my daily dose of apples, I try to cash in on the healthy benefits of other fruits as well. Below are a few of my favorite summer desserts that are light as a feather and cool as the breeze.

NOTE: To reap the healthy benefits of any exotic fruits, make sure you buy organically grown, as some third world countries still use unhealthy chemical fertilizers, herbicides, and pesticides.

All recipes below make about 6 servings.

Mango sherbet

The first time I sunk my teeth into a juicy, tangy mango I fell in love with the taste. But even better is the fact they're loaded with vitamins and are a rich natural source of beta-carotene, which is an effective antioxidant that helps ward off body invaders, as well as dishing up healthy amounts of amino and glutamine acids.

Mangos are rich in iron, and in India, their land of origin, the blood

Melon snow balls: A simple treat that's hard to beat. Just scoop, stick, and freeze for a mouthful of icy goodness.

building fruit is called upon to stop bleeding, strengthen the heart, and improve memory. Mangos contain potassium and magnesium, the latter being a noted muscle relaxant, so after a day of frolicking in the sun, a bowl of icy mango sherbet is bound to rid kinks.

4 mangoes, peeled, and seeded
2 ½ cups of water
1 cup sugar or honey

Using blender or food processor, puree mangoes and put into a bowl. Set aside.

Put water and sugar into small pan and bring to a boil. Reduce heat and simmer 5 minutes. Cool.

Whisk syrup into puree.

Pour mixture into freezer trays or flat dishes and freeze about 2 hours.

Empty partially set sherbet into plastic container and whisk, breaking up ice crystals.

Leave in container and return to freezer.

About 10 minutes before serving, take out of freezer and let soften enough to scoop.

Orange and kiwi loaf

A glistening, mouthwatering slice of jellied orange and kiwi loaf is a brisk dessert to chill out with. Everyone knows that oranges are bursting with vitamin C and other good things, but one might be pleasantly surprised to discover that the quaint little kiwi is one of the most nutrient-dense fruits available and holds its own for boosting good health.

Recent studies have indicated that eating two or three kiwi fruit a day does the heart a world of good. It helps thin blood and reduces clotting by lowering fat in the blood stream, without upsetting healthy cholesterol levels—working in much the same way as a recommended daily dose of aspirin.

This is an ideal vegan recipe as you can use agar-agar, a stabilizing agent made from seaweed, instead of traditional gelatin, which is derived from animal matter.

Agar-agar has been widely used in Asian countries for centuries as natural treatment for constipation. Herbalists claim it keeps the system regular, making it an ideal ingredient in a meal ender.

1 ½ cups fresh squeezed orange juice
½ cup water
½ cup sugar
2 tsp. agar-agar
3 kiwi fruit, peeled, sliced thinly

In saucepan, bring orange juice and water to a rolling boil. Add sugar and stir until dissolved. Remove from heat. Sprinkle with agar-agar and whisk until dissolved. Wet down a 3 cup loaf pan or desired mold with water and pour in mixture. Leave in refrigerator to jell, about 4 hours. Dip pan in hot water for a second to loosen. Unmold onto serving plate and decorate with thinly sliced kiwi. Serve extra kiwi on the side.

Pineapple ice

Pineapples, like oranges, are rich in vitamin C making them a noted antioxidant and immune system booster. They belong to the bromeliad family and contain high amounts of an enzyme known as bromelain that is a powerful anti-inflammatory, helping the body to naturally heal itself.

Eating pineapples helps relieve pain of rheumatoid arthritis and reduces swelling and tenderness of sprains as well as helping to prevent mouth diseases like gingivitis and periodontal disease, which have been linked to more serious ailments, including stroke and diabetes.

Bromelain helps break down amino acids and is said to be good for indigestion, making it an ideal meal topper. When indulging in pineapple strictly for good health, choose fresh fruit over canned as valuable brome-

Mango sherbet—a fruity summer dessert that's loaded with vitamins. It's a rich source of beta-carotene, an effective antioxidant that wards off body invaders.

Jellied orange and kiwi loaf—a wonderful cool summer dessert that's bursting with good health

lain is destroyed by heat during the canning process.

1 fresh pineapple
1 lime
1 ⅔ cups water
¾ cup sugar (or honey)

Halve pineapple lengthwise, leaving leaves intact. Using sharp knife, carefully remove flesh from the shell. Save shells in fridge for serving dishes for the ice, if you wish.

Peel lime, remove pith, and quarter. Puree pineapple chunks and lime in blender or food processor. Set aside.

Bring water and sugar to a boil and cook into a thin syrup, about 10 minutes. Cool, then whisk into pineapple puree.

Pour into freezer trays or flat containers and let freeze until partially set.

Using whisk, break up to remove ice crystals. Do this several times during the freezing process.

Before serving, take a big fork and break up the mixture to make it look like crushed pineapple.

Fill shells with the ice or serve in tall sherbet glasses.

Pineapple ice—one of the fruitiest, coolest desserts of summer

Glorious grape ring

Here's a tantalizing dessert that's fit for formal.

Purple and black grapes get their lustrous color from a healthy compound known as flavonoids, which gives all "blue" fruits including blueberries their coloring. In recent years, flavonoids have gained a reputation as helping to reduce heart disease by thinning the blood, thus reducing the risk of clots.

White and green grapes go down in history as helping to cure high blood pressure. Juice extracted from grapes, especially from dark grapes, helps fight breast, liver, and colon cancers.

1 pint of homemade or organic grape juice (white juice produces a clear jell, purple juice a darker creation)
3 teaspoons agar-agar (or 1 tablespoon or envelope of powered gelatin)
2 tablespoons lemon juice
1 cup white or green seedless grapes split in half
1 cup purple or black seedless grapes split in half
¼ cup mixed grapes left whole for decorating
1 tablespoon powdered sugar

Put ¼ cup of hot juice in small bowl and sprinkle with agar-agar or gelatin. Let stand 5 minutes.

Stir in remaining juice.

Spoon enough of the juice into a chilled 2 pint mould and swirl to coat all sides. Let set in fridge 10 minutes.

Arrange one third of the split grapes in the mold and cover with ⅓ of the juice. Let set until gelled.

Repeat twice then refrigerate until firmly jelled, about 4 hours.

Dip the mould in hot water for a second before emptying onto serving plate. Decorate the crown with whole grapes that have been 'frosted' by shaking in bag with the powdered sugar. Δ

Ask Jackie

If you have a question about rural living, send it in to Jackie Clay and she'll try to answer it. Address your letter to Ask Jackie, PO Box 712, Gold Beach, OR 97444. Questions will only be answered in this column. — Editor

Using a pressure cooker as a pressure canner

Can you use a pressure "cooker" as a pressure "canner?"

Roy Sherman
Modesto, California

I'm sure some folks get by doing this, but I would not advise it. First of all, the pressure cooker does not have a rack to keep the jars off the bottom of the pot, as does a pressure canner. Second, the cooker is much too small for any serious canning. And finally, the pressure cooker is built for cooking in mind, not canning and I have doubts as to whether it would hold exact pressures for the length of time necessary for processing home canned foods safely. ***— Jackie***

Seed varieties

Can you tell me the variety of seeds you plant?

Wilma J. Turner
Springfield, Kentucky

Sure, Wilma. Now this list is never ALL I plant, as I always experiment and grow a wide variety of experimental crops to see if maybe I like them better or to see how they will do where I am living. Here goes:

For garden peas, I usually plant Alderman or Tall Telephone and Green Arrow, as they are the most productive peas that I've grown. They are also very tasty, too.

The carrots I plant are Kuroda. They are a very large carrot that takes not-so-perfect soil and is quite early to harvest. They're also sweet and tender.

For onions, I choose Copra for storage and Alisa Craig for large sweet non-storage onions. Copra is hard as a rock and lasts well into spring.

I usually plant Dragon Tongue, Provider, and Top Crop bush beans and also bush yellow Romano and Nugget wax for their taste and productivity.

For dry beans, I plant a variety of mostly early Native American beans such as Dog, Arikara, Hopi Black, and Shalako.

My pole beans vary from year to year, but I always grow Cherokee Trail of Tears, which is a purple (turns green on cooking), very productive and tasty bean. It is black seeded and also makes good dry beans.

For sweet corn, I grow Kandy Kwik, which is a hybrid, but when I had a longer growing season, I grew True Gold (open pollinated) so I could save seeds from it. I have also grown Santo Domingo Blue for roasting ears and also flour corn. This year I am planting Painted Mountain, which is 90 days till dry. It is a very beautiful "Indian Corn," developed in modern times by a seedsman looking for an early dry corn. Looks promising.

My watermelons are usually Blacktail Mountain and an early strain of Moon and Stars, but I also have grown Hopi Yellow and other Native melons that I really liked.

Muskmelons that work for me consistently are Alaska and Uncle E. Like the watermelons, I usually also grow a Native melon as well, as the taste is always superior.

Jackie Clay

For squash, I grow Gold Bar yellow zucchini, Hopi Pale Grey (winter squash), Early Butternut or Long Island Cheese if I'm feeling lucky (it's a 105-day maturity and needs a good summer here in the north).

I usually grow either Howden or Rouge Vif D'Etampes pumpkin.

My tomatoes vary greatly. This year I have something like 16 different varieties. I love to experiment. But my old standbys are Oregon Spring, Early Cascade, Early Goliath, Stupice, and Principe Borghese (a small tomato for drying). All of these are dependable and extremely tasty, too.

Peppers are another thing I'm nuts about, this year growing at least a dozen different varieties. But I usually always grow Big Early, Giant Marconi, Senorita (a mild jalapeno), Big Chile, and Chimayo.

Goliath and Packman work the best for me in the broccoli department, and Early Snowball gives us plenty of cauliflower.

I usually grow Summer Dance and Climbing Japanese cukes because I like to trellis the cukes and have nice slim, long ones to make lots of pickles.

Of course, I grow lots of other things such as herbs, flowers, and assorted veggies, but this will give you a good idea of what you'll find in our garden. I do try to save my own seeds, so I usually only grow one variety of each species of vegetable unless I can separate the plantings by enough space so they will not cross. Some vegetables, such as beans, require little separation, but others, such as corn, requires as much as a mile to ensure pure seed.

Some of the catalogs I order from often are Native Seeds/SEARCH, 526 N. 4th Ave., Tucson, AZ 85705 or www.nativeseeds.org; Baker Creek Heirloom Seeds, 2278 Baker Creek Rd., Mansfield, MO 65704 or www.rareseeds.com; Seed Savers Exchange, 3094 North Winn Road, Decorah, IA 52101 or www.seedsavers.org; and Seed Dreams, P.O. Box 106, Port Townsend, WA 98368. These catalogs carry open pollinated, old traditional, and Native varieties. ***—Jackie***

Weevils in rice

I love brown rice and have used it almost exclusively for many years. But lately I have had a major problem of finding weevils in my air-tight metal rice canister. Three times I have sorted and sifted the entire canister tossing weevils and dark grains. Each time I open the canister, more weevils are there. Short of storing the rice in the freezer, do you have any suggestions? The thought of throwing out several pounds of rice really goes against the grain—no pun intended.

Margaret Anderson
Birmingham, Alabama

I hate to tell you this, Margaret, but your rice probably has eggs in it that keep hatching weevils. These weevils are the larvae of pantry or maize moths, which lay their eggs in cereal, rice, flour, cornmeal, etc. I would dump the rice, wash the container, then check other foods in your pantry that attract these pests. You'll often notice "webs" in the top part of containers before you'll actually see "bugs." Sometimes it takes quite a bit of doing to get rid of them.

Several gardening supply catalogs carry pantry moth traps, which work very well and effectively rid your home of these wasteful insects. Gardens Alive!, 5100 Schenley Place, Lawrenceburg, IN 47025 or www.GardensAlive.com; and Territorial Seed Company, P.O. Box 158, Cottage Grove, OR 97424-0061 or www.territorialseed.com both carry these traps.

In the future, be very careful not to buy any dry food that has "flour" sifting out of holes or tears in the bag; these containers are easily infested with moths. ***—Jackie***

Sterilizing jars

What is the proper way to sterilize jars? After washing in soapy water, my grandmother just rinsed them in bleach water. I boil the water, but that's such a hassle. My friend says just run the jars in the dishwasher. Once they've been sterilized, how long can they sit before they are no longer sterile? After boiling them, I turn them upside down in the dish drainer and cover with a flour-sack towel. I usually need to add more water to the canner and bring it to a boil for processing. It may take me another 15-30 minutes before I have all the jars filled and ready to go into the canner. (OK I'm very slow!) Anyway, I've always wondered if I should do as my grandmother did and just leave the jars in the hot bleach water until I was ready to use them. I don't have a dishwasher, but it would give me one more reason to get one if that would get the jars sterile.

Charlene Nelson
Casselton, North Dakota

To sterilize canning jars, simmer them in a boiling water bath canner for 10 minutes. Then keep them in that hot water until you are ready to use them. Take them out of the water, one jar at a time, turn upside down briefly to drain the water out, then right side up for a few seconds while you prepare to fill them. The heat will adequately dry the jar. This is simple and also keeps the jars hot, preventing any cracks while you fill them with hot foods. (A cool jar filled with a hot food will sometimes crack.)

Fill the jars, then place the filled jars on a folded dry towel until all are filled. Then refill your canner, if necessary, and bring it up to very hot again, and put the jars in. There! You're ready to go; with sterile, filled jars. ***—Jackie***

Beef jerky without salt

I am looking for a way to make beef jerky without salt, as I retain water when I use salt.

Can the meat be dried by smoking with the ingredients for jerky minus salt? This meat will be frozen after it is dried and smoked.

Several people tell me it is dangerous to do it this way. I need your opinion. I have 20 pounds of good beef for curing.

Robert Kager
Mt. Vernon, Washington

No, it is not dangerous to make jerky without salt. Indians hung strips of meat over smoky low fires to dry it for centuries. Another possibility is to marinate the thin strips of meat with spices and brown sugar and use your dehydrator or oven on low temperature to dehydrate the meat. It is a good idea when making "modern" jerky (not rock hard and crispy dried) to freeze or at least refrigerate it to prevent it from molding. Today we like our jerky quite a bit more tender and flexible than the old timey pioneer jerky. — ***Jackie***

Rose hips

Rose hips, vitamin C, how? When ripe they have a lot of dried fluff and 4 seeds in them. How does one use them to get the vitamin C?

I've tried holding carrots over to replant to seed, but it looks like wild carrot. Do they revert back? I've not had luck holding a bit back and replanting to get seed. How can I make it work?

Alwilda Crouch
Breckenridge, Michigan

Most folks use rose hips as tea to access the vitamin C. To do this, harvest the hips when they are full, red or orange, and shiny. With scissors, snip off the stem and blossom end. Small hips you can simply dry whole, but larger ones dry better if you snip them in half. Dry them that way, never minding about the seeds. When you want to make tea out of them, simmer a heaping tablespoonful of dried hips in a cup of water. The longer you let the hips steep in the water, the stronger the tea. Rose hips really lack flavor, so you'll probably want to add perhaps lemon and honey, cinnamon, or herbs of your choice. When the tea is done to your taste, strain it, and it's ready to drink.

As for your carrots, just be sure you are holding over non-hybrid (open pollinated) varieties. It sounds like you may be using hybrid carrots. But remember that in the second year, the carrot does look wild and the root gets all hairy and tough. The seed heads and leaves extend higher than the compact carrot tops we're used to seeing in the garden. Carrots are really quite easy to save seed from, but for the fact that you must over-winter the carrot root with an inch or so of the top left on, then replant it early in the spring in order to get seed. — ***Jackie***

Sealing dried foods in jars

How do you seal a jar with dried foods in it like peas or bananas? Are they fine not sealed?

Do you know how to can homemade peanut butter?

Dezarae Graham
Indian Valley, Idaho

I keep my dried foods such as peas and banana chips in gallon glass jars with screw-down wide-mouthed lids. They will keep this way, nearly forever, providing they are kept dry.

You can home can homemade peanut butter in wide-mouthed pint jars. Pack it well, with no air bubbles, to within an inch of the top of the jar. Wipe the jar rim clean and place a hot, previously simmered lid on the jar and screw down the ring firmly tight. Process the jars one hour in a hot water bath canner. — ***Jackie***

Vine borers

We enjoy your column, although we can't understand why so many people run away from using a pressure canner. It is not only the safe, right way but also the easiest.

We have gardened and canned together for 33 years (planning garden #34 now). We pressure can all types of fruits and vegetables. We would like to can water to keep for emergency use, but haven't tried it yet. We do have a question for you, though. Like you, we have a favorite squash. Ours is the Blue Hubbard. We plant it, it grows fine, blooms, and sets on fruit and then the borers get at the vine at the base, and eventually cut through the vine. I've tried Sevin Dust, which helps a little. Any suggestions?

Jim and Linda Knight
Evansdale, Iowa

The common treatment for squash borers is to cut into the vine when you notice the hole and wilting in the area, and remove the borer. Then bury the vine in that spot to prevent disease and help the vine heal.

I have had better luck by injecting about 7ccs of Bt in the area where the borer is active. This nearly instantly kills him as he continues to eat, ingesting the fatal Bt, that is, fatal to caterpillars and other pest larva only...not YOU! I also spray my squash vines weekly during "borer" season with a rotenone solution. This is a natural solution and I feel much better about using it, rather than Sevin. — ***Jackie***

Wax in honey

I found a large Mason jar of honey that a beekeeper gave to me years ago with about 2 inches of honey in it. I put the jar in the microwave to melt the honey, so I could pour it into another jar...everything melted, and the honeycomb is melted into the honey. It has not "set up" yet, but is it okay to eat it this way?

Rebecca Covalt
Albuquerque, New Mexico

Yes, you can eat the melted honeycomb, with the honey. We used to pack honey in the combs and of course, we always ended up eating some of the comb, with the honey. And we're still here to talk about it. Actually, I kind of like the taste of the honeycomb, myself! — ***Jackie***

Sugarless bread

My husband has type 2 diabetes and I need a recipe for bread using whole wheat unbleached flour, NO SUGAR. This is the only grain he can have. I am really at a loss. At this point NO pasta, cereals, rice, any kind of grain other than whole wheat.

Donna J Brannam
Wilson Creek, Washington

Here is one sugar-free recipe for whole wheat bread:

European Whole Wheat Loaves:

Put 2½ cups warm water into a large warm bowl. Add 2 Tbsp. dry yeast and stir gently. Let soften. Mix in 3-4 cups whole wheat flour and mix well, making a heavy batter. Cover and place in a warm place and let rise for an hour or so. Now add 3-4 more cups of flour, one cup at a time, mixing well, until a nice ball is formed that is NOT sticky, but not stiff, either. Return to bowl and let rise again until nearly double. Divide the dough in half and place in greased tin or on a greased cookie pan. Slice top of loaf about half an inch deep, either lengthwise or several slashes, crosswise. Cover again and let rise. Bake at 350 degrees until golden brown and hollow sounding when thumped with finger. This will be about an hour. Remove from pan and let cool (if you can stand waiting!).

— Jackie

Reusing canning seals

I have a question about the seal on my canning lids. On several of the lids that I used with the hot water bath, the seals sealed perfectly, but when I removed them they look "NEW." The food or jam is fine. Have you ever reused a canning seal?

Cybele Connor
Hammonton, New Jersey

I would not use a "used" lid on anything canned in a pressure canner (i.e. vegetables, meat, poultry or combinations thereof). In an emergency, I HAVE used "used but pristine" lids for such things as jelly, pickles, preserves; foods that will mold if the seal fails, not grow deadly bacteria. Of course, it is not a good idea to re-use lids. All canning manuals will tell you this. And I would NEVER reuse a lid that I had to pry off with a can opener as it dents the lid and damages the seal.

Any lids that I have reused, I have simmered for several minutes to ensure that the gasket material on the lid is nice and soft. A good compromise is to reuse the lids, but as lids on jars of dehydrated foods, seeds or spices. In this way, you reuse the lid, putting it to good use. But you are not depending on it to keep your home canned food fresh, tasty, and safe.

— Jackie

Growing coffee

I am slowly becoming self-sufficient as far as food preservation is concerned but I still have one major vice, coffee! I drink several cups a day and cannot imagine doing otherwise. Of course, I have to purchase it from the store and that distresses me. I see coffee plants advertised in seed catalogs, but could I actually produce "real" coffee from them? I live in agricultural zone 6.

Also, any recipes or tips on creating an emergency back-up grain-based hot beverage (chicory, etc.?)

Perè Walsh
Dugspur, Virginia

Yes, you can produce coffee from indoor or greenhouse-grown coffee plants. But you would not grow enough to satisfy your craving. Sorry. I'm "addicted" to Mountain Dew. (Hey, everyone has bad habits!) And if emergency times hit, I'll just suck up and go cold turkey. You might try drinking tea and see if that will satisfy you in a pinch. Tea stores longer than coffee does, without any rancid taste.

Yes, you can use roasted grain coffee substitutes (such as Postum). You can make your own version by roasting 4 cups wheat bran, a cup of cornmeal, mixed with a half cup of molasses. Stir it well, place on a cookie sheet, and bake at under 200° in your oven until it is crisp. Then when it is cool, crush it through your meat grinder to give it an even appearance.

Or you can make dandelion root coffee. Dig the roots in the spring before blooming or in the fall for the best taste. Wash the dirt off them, place on a cookie sheet in the oven, and roast as above until they are dry. Then, roast at 375° for about 15 minutes until they are coffee colored when you snap a root and look at the insides. Cool, then run through your meat grinder a couple of times, and it will look like coffee. You will use about 1 tsp. per cup of "coffee."

And then there is chicory root coffee. Wash the roots and roast at a low temperature until very dry and nice smelling. Grind and store in an airtight container. Boil your "coffee" water and put 1 tsp. of ground chicory root in it, and let it steep.

With these alternate coffee substitutes, you'll have to experiment and see how you like your personal cup. You may want more or less ground "coffee." Or, you may want to use creamer or honey. Experiment and enjoy. (Just remember that these alternative coffees do not contain caffeine, which makes it not as satisfying to some). ***— Jackie***

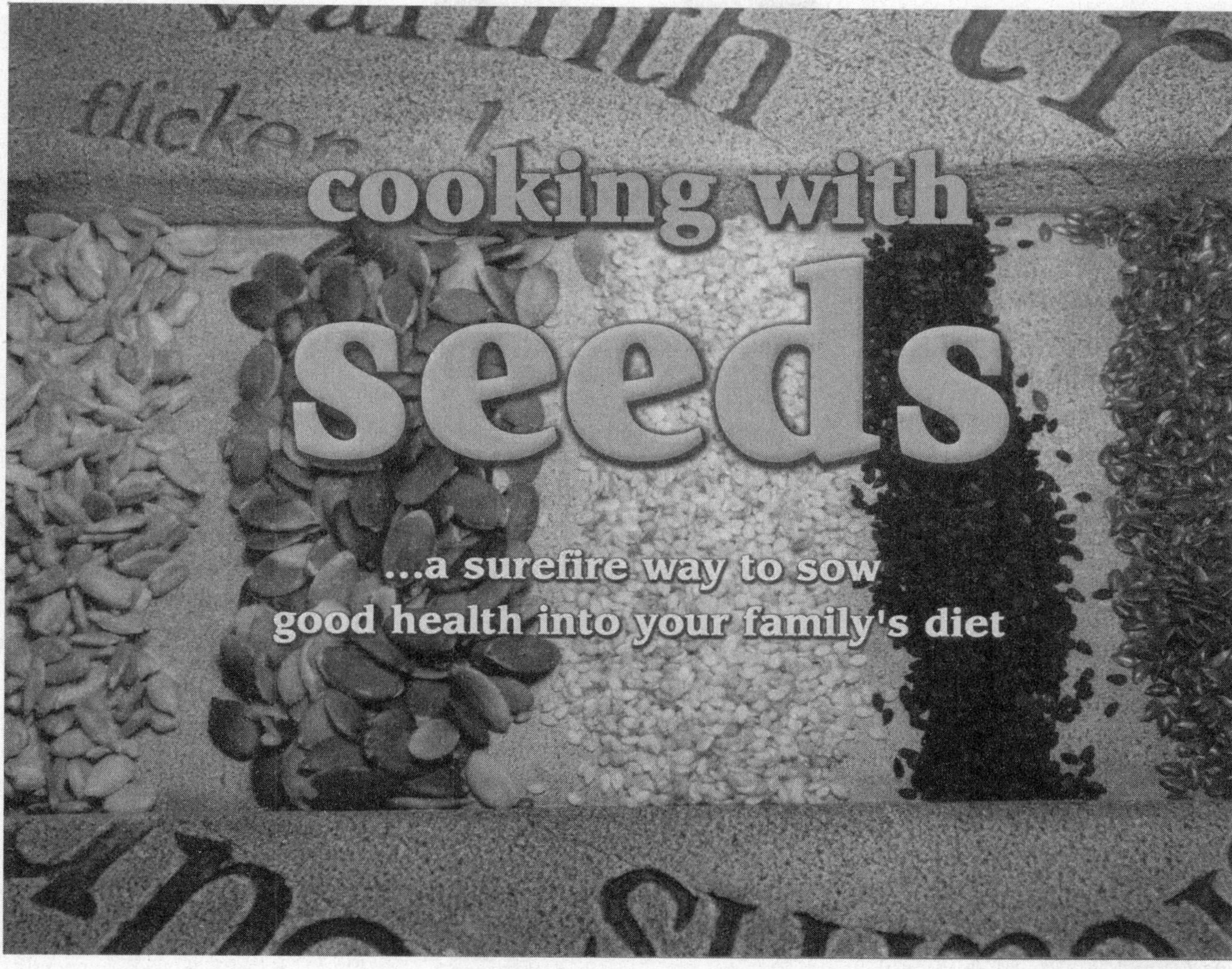

cooking with seeds

...a surefire way to sow good health into your family's diet

By Linda Gabris

Even though it sounds a little seedy, planting an array of tasty seeds in your daily cooking is an economical way to sneak an extra dose of good health into your family's diet without fuss or muss.

Nutritious seeds add delicious flavor and interesting texture to most any dish and are fun to experiment with. For the best of health, buy organically grown seeds.

Flaxseed

Cultivation of flax can be traced as far back as ancient Babylonian civilization where it was used as food and medicine as well as to make linen cloth; and throughout history flaxseed has held its ground as an important worldwide staple.

Herbalists use flaxseed as a remedy for stomach ailments and nervous disorders and as poultices for drawing infections from wounds.

My Grandmother, who sprinkled flaxseeds into the porridge pot every morning, has it noted in her doctoring journals that a daily dose keeps the system regular by flushing impurities from the body. She also has it written that flaxseed is good treatment for pimples, blackheads, psoriasis, eczema, and other skin problems.

Using flaxseeds in cooking is a tasty way to increase dietary fiber, vitamins, and minerals, but the best news is that flax is a number one source for Omega 1 and 3 essential fatty acids known as good fats.

Recent medical studies have indicated that North American diets are deficient in essential fatty acids, and one proven way to fill the Omega bill is by including flax in the diet.

According to research, Omega-rich flaxseed helps prevent coronary heart disease by reducing cholesterol, blood pressure, and plaque buildup. Flax not only promotes healthy cholesterol levels, but also aids digestion.

Since flaxseeds absorb about eight times their weight in water, they can be useful in weight-loss programs as their high-fiber content helps satisfy

Recent medical studies have indicated that North American diets are deficient in essential fatty acids. Adding whole flaxseeds or flax ground into flour to your baking helps fill the Omega bill.

Pumpkin seeds are bursting with pep, and in China are a symbol of fruitfulness.

the appetite sensibly while increasing fat-burning power.

Flaxseeds contain more than two dozen identifiable cancer-preventative compounds that ward off and fight various cancers including breast and prostate cancer.

They are an abundant source of lignans—a type of insoluble fiber that is useful treatment for menstrual cramps and symptoms of menopause.

The fatty acids in flaxseeds lubricate the joints, reducing inflammation and relieving arthritic pain. Studies have shown that folks with flax in their diet have better immune systems than those without, and some claim it helps calm migraine headaches.

Flaxseeds have a nutty flavor and can be eaten raw as in the days of early Greeks and Romans. Be sure to chew well to get out all the nutrients before they pass through.

They are excellent when sprinkled on salads, pastas, rice, cereals, cooked vegetables, baked potatoes, or used as thickening for soups and stews. They can be used whole to add nutrition and crunch to breads, rolls, cookies, and other baked goods. If you're not looking for crunch, flaxseeds can be ground into flour and added to traditional flours to increase nutritional value.

Ground flaxseeds are a suitable substitute for eggs in baking recipes, making them popular with vegetarians or those who are allergic to eggs. One tablespoon ground seed mixed with three tablespoons of water equals one egg. Allow to stand for a few minutes to plump before adding to batter.

Because of their high content of beneficial oil, flaxseeds can be used to cut down on butter, shortening, or other fat in many recipes. Use one cup of ground seed to replace one-third cup of fat. The finished product may be somewhat moister and heavier in texture but much healthier on the table. This nifty trick is especially good for muffin and cookie recipes.

Even though flaxseed oil is fairly expensive, you can still cash in on its goodness by hunting down a bottle at a health food store and using it very sparingly. Unlike traditional kitchen oils, flaxseed oil is not intended for general cooking purposes, but can be used as a dietary supplement.

Try using a dab of flaxseed oil in place of, or mixing it in part with, other oils in salad dressings. Lightly brush it on cooked vegetables instead of melted butter, cheese, or other sauces. Brush over fruit wedges and sprinkle with ground cinnamon for an easy dessert or make super protein shakes for breakfast by adding a teaspoonful to the glass for a boost of energy. When used in this fashion, a small bottle will go a long way toward promoting good health and well being.

Sesame seeds

Like flax, sesame seeds are deeply rooted in history. The Assyrians believed that sesame wine instilled great strength and wisdom.

Babylonians used it for food, medicine, and cosmetic preparations, while in 8th-century China, seeds were eaten and used medicinally. Oil was burned as lamp fuel, creating soot prized by ancient Chinese calligraphic artists.

An Egyptian tomb depicts a baker sprinkling sesame seeds on bread, proving that the practice is as old as the hills.

In India, sesame oil has been used for centuries as a ceremonial anointment and the seeds called upon for treatment of piles as well as being a common kitchen condiment.

Brought to America by West African slaves in the 17th and 18th centuries, *benne,* as they are known in their native tongue, quickly took root in Southern cooking.

Today sesame seeds and oil are popular throughout the world, and one of the most traditional uses for sesame is in the making of tahini, a smooth creamy paste that is the basis for *hummus*, a wonderful Middle Eastern dip that's delicious and healthy to boot (see recipe included).

In the olden days, herbalists used sesame seeds to expel worms from the intestinal tract. An Old World common cure for toothache and sore throat was to boil sesame seeds in water until all the oil was released, then used as gargle. I find that gargling with pure sesame oil works wonders at soothing sore throat and mouth. Do not swallow the oil as it will be contaminated with germs that have accumulated while swishing.

Modern herbalists recommend sesame to relieve constipation, aid digestion, and circulate blood. Sesame oil is often taken with medication to help distribute drugs evenly through the system.

They are a rich source of vitamins, minerals, and protein and contain an abundance of calcium, making them a good choice for building strong bones, teeth, and nails.

Because of their high vitamin E content, sesame oil works wonders at healing chronic skin diseases and soothing sunburn. A dab around the eyes at night prevents wrinkles, and a cotton swab dipped in warmed oil removes earwax. An old Chinese remedy for bug bites and burns calls for a simple paste of crushed seeds and water to be applied to the affected area.

Raw seeds are milder in taste than toasted ones, and some say they are more nutritious as heating may destroy some of the enzymes. Although they are nutritionally equal, in Asian kitchens black seeds are more prized than white.

To cash in on their goodness, try sprinkling raw or toasted seeds over steamed vegetables in place of butter or sauces. Add them to cookies, muffins, and other baked goods for nutritional bonus. Raw vegetables and fruits are delicious when squirted with lemon or orange juice then dipped into sesame seeds that have been seasoned with fine herbs like dill or chives or ground cinnamon.

To toast seeds, spread on cookie sheet and toast in oven at 350° F until golden. Do not roast until dark brown as protein will be lost in the process.

Sesame oil can be used sparingly to instill the wonderful taste and aroma of the Orient in any dish including stir-fries, soups, noodles, and rice.

One of my favorite recipes using sesame seeds is for Dukkah—a delightful spice mixture that is a meal in itself, which comes from the Middle East (see recipe included).

Pumpkin seeds

"Peter, Peter, pumpkin eater, had a wife and couldn't keep her..." probably because he was too darn quick for her to keep up with!

Pumpkin seeds are bursting with pep, and in China they are a symbol of fruitfulness.

Pumpkin seeds add delicious crunch to breads and other baked goods, not to mention nutritional boost.

In folk medicine, pumpkin seeds have been used for centuries as preventive medicine and treatment for prostate disorders, and only in more recent years has the medical world taken a closer look at the beneficial effects of pumpkin seeds on the male system.

Modern-day research has shown that pumpkin seeds, which are a natural diuretic, contain a native plant hormone that is very beneficial to male hormone production. Seeds are reputed as having a regenerative, invigorative, and vitalizing influence. In countries like the Balkans and Eastern Europe, where seeds have been a common pocket snack for centuries, prostate problems are less prominent than in countries where the good word has not yet taken root.

Aside from being a readily available medicinal treat for men, herbalists recommend pumpkin seeds for bladder and urinary disorders, and Grandma claimed that pumpkin seeds were "good for the blood and soul."

Pumpkin seeds are richer in iron than any other seed and are loaded with phosphorus. The best way to cash in on the goodness of pumpkin seeds is to carry a pocketful and enjoy whenever you need a nibble. A handful of pumpkins seeds a day is the most delightful way I know to boost vitamin and calcium intake.

Pumpkin and sunflower seeds are delicious, affordable trail treats to boost energy while backpacking or hiking, but when eating from the shell and using public trails, be courteous and carry out the waste rather than litter the walks with unsightly discards. My motto is, "one pocket for in, one pocket for out," a simple lesson for teaching kids to pack out what they pack in.

To produce nutty breads, add raw pumpkin seeds to the dough, and for extra goodness, brush tops of loaves with oil and sprinkle generously with seeds before baking. They are delicious in cookies and muffins, add exciting crunch to cereal or porridge, and are a pleasant surprise in salads and yogurt.

Sunflower seeds

Sunflower usage dates back to the Incas, who worshiped the sun and the flower. North American Indians cultivated the plant from wild seed and made use of every part: the leaves as animal fodder; petals for dye; and seeds for food and oil.

In Russia, the plant is a major crop used for everything from food and fodder to lamp fuel and fertilizer. In the Old World, the leaves were used to treat malaria, and in China, fabrics are made from stock fiber.

Grandma's old remedy for sore throat and bronchitis calls for equal parts crushed seeds and honey, along with a couple sprigs of mint, to be simmered in enough water to cover for an hour. The mixture is then strained, bottled, and taken by the teaspoonful. It tastes good and works!

Sunflower seeds are a source of phosphorus, magnesium, iron, calcium, potassium, and vitamin E. They also contain trace minerals, zinc, copper, and carotene, no doubt why Grandma claimed they were good for the eyes.

Use sunflower seeds in place of bacon bits on salads. Instead of using all meat in loaves and casseroles, substitute a portion of the meat with seeds. They're economical and downright good. Add them to cookies, muffins, or breads. One of my favorite desserts is a bowl of tart applesauce crowned with crunchy sunflower seeds and a sprinkle of nutmeg.

Like flaxseed oil, sunflower seed oil is highly nutritious, and the good news is, it is affordable and intended for healthy cooking purposes. Sunflower oil is an excellent source of unsaturated fatty acids. Using the oil in place of other oil and fats for cooking and baking can help lower cholesterol deposits in the blood.

To plant some good health into your family's diet, try the fun, easy recipes below.

Easiest-ever hummus:

2 cups cooked or canned chickpeas (if using canned, drain and rinse under cold running water)
juice of 1 lemon
5 ounces of tahini paste
4 cloves of peeled garlic
2 tsp. ground cumin
2 Tbsp. sunflower or traditional olive oil
sea salt and black pepper to taste

Put all ingredients in blender and puree until smooth, using a little water or cooking juice from the beans if needed. Serve with pita, crackers, or as vegetable dip. Serves 4 to 6.

Sesame and coriander dukkah:

Dukkah ("doo-kah") is a spicy Middle Eastern creation that is made up of toasted nuts and seeds, herbs, and spices of choice. It is wonderfully

Sesame and coriander dukkah makes a wonderful picnic food. When stored in an airtight container, dukkah saves indefinitely.

versatile and can be made to suit any taste to a T.

The mixture—which is always dry—is served with pita (see recipe below) or other type of unleavened or flatbread bread and oil. In its homeland, it is sold on the street in little paper cups as a carry-away snack simply eaten with the fingers.

The first time I sampled sesame and coriander dukkah (*simsim wa kuzbari*) I fell in love with it. It makes an exotic, almost romantic, patio lunch and is a delightful picnic food, being spoil-proof and super easy to tote.

The secret to making perfect dukkah is in the grinding of the nuts and seeds. They should be processed fine in order to release all their flavor but not pulverized, as you do not want them to turn oily. So, whiz lightly when making dukkah. Have fun and experiment for no two dukkahs ever have to be the same.

When tightly capped, it saves very well, and the recipe below makes a big batch—about 12 to 16 servings. Keep it handy for a healthy quick snack or impromptu meal.

12 ounces sesame seeds
5 ounces coriander seeds
4 ounces coarsely chopped and lightly roasted hazelnuts
sea salt and coarsely ground black pepper to taste

Toast sesame seeds under oven broiler until just lightly golden, then set aside.

Spread coriander seeds on baking sheet and toast until flavor and aroma are released, about 2-3 minutes. Using a spice grinder or pestle and mortar, crush until fine.

In blender, lightly whiz hazelnuts. Add sesame seeds and coriander and twirl quickly for about a second; any longer and the nuts and seeds will turn oily. Add sea salt and pepper to taste. Recipe can be halved if you wish.

Flaxseed in the porridge bowl is the tastiest and easiest way to sneak a dose of good health onto the table.

To serve: Pour a little flaxseed oil, sunflower oil, or traditional virgin olive oil into a little bowl or onto a flat plate. In another dish, pour out some dukkah. Dip an ear of pita into oil then dunk into dukkah.

A few other ways to plant seeds into your daily diet:

• In the cereal bowl. Seeds are wonderfully nutritious when added to the porridge pot, but you can also cash in on their goodness by sprinkling them onto any kind of dry cereal, such as corn flakes, to add zip and zap. Try toasted sesame, sunflower, pumpkin, or flax in the cereal bowl. It's great.

• Seedy jello. When jello is partially set, stir in some seeds for a very unique treat. Kids love it.

• On sandwiches. Sprinkle sandwiches with seeds for enlivening crunch. A light spread of butter, mustard, or mayo helps hold the seeds in place. Great with deli meats, adds enlivening crunch to egg salad, and turns plain old jelly and jam into something worth talking about.

• In soups and salads. Better than croutons cause they don't lose their crunch.

• On ice cream. You'd be surprised at how interesting a bowl of ice cream becomes when sprinkled with crunchy, chewy seeds.

• Seedy little snacks. Need just a little snack to take the edge off hunger pains? In a big jar, mix up all your favorite seeds. Add a few raisins, if you wish. Maybe even a scoop of chocolate chips, nuts, or shredded coconut. Shake well. A little pinch whenever you need it takes the sneak right out of snacking. Δ

Indoor air pollution SOLVED

By David Lee

Winterizing your home saves heat and money, and it keeps you very cozy—actually, too cozy if the air becomes polluted. People really need to breathe fresh air on a regular basis. Changing the air in your home regularly, even during the winter months, is a good practice. You will be healthier for doing it, even if you do waste a little heat. It would be a good thing to get outside and breathe the real stuff as often as possible, too.

In this article I will show a better venting system for your home than regular windows can provide. I will also give advice on how to eliminate some sources of air pollution, especially for those of you who use wood heat.

Long, long ago in a state far away, while working on my first building project, I needed to install a window that would accomplish the usual window functions of letting air into the house and allowing me to enjoy the nice view available. I was a newbie builder who knew no better, so I went to the retail window store, told them what I needed, and had my first experience with sticker shock. A single 4'x4' window with sidelights and screens was—I'll always remember—$129.95. This in a time when a hamburger, fries, and shake cost 65 cents!

Some thinking on the subject of air and light coming into a home gave me the chance to design my first vents and, more importantly, develop a windows and vents theory for home building, which is: Put big uncluttered windows where the views are and vents where the air circulates best. These are often not one and the same locations.

The walls of your house are there to separate you from the outdoors, protect your privacy, and keep you comfortable in your own personal nest, all snug and comfortable. Ordinary windows limit those attributes. They don't insulate as well as a good wall, privacy is lessened, security is an issue, and they annoyingly require routine cleaning and maintenance.

Aesthetically, they are a compromise, too. Your view is broken up into two sections, one of which is covered by a screen that restricts it even further. Often the parts are further divided into a whole mess of small panes trying to replicate windows used during a time when they burned witches. And sooner or later they leak water, air, or both.

The ventilation aspect of these windows is their best feature; that is, if the screen is intact and they are not stuck shut by dried paint, swelling, warping, or permanently closed with a nail driven through it by someone hoping to keep out burglars. In fact, the burglary service industry has produced special tools that turn most windows into convenient entryways.

I like to use double-paned factory-made tempered-glass panels that are permanently built into the wall. They are sealed against water and air, give the maximum view, are not excessively expensive, come in most any size, are easy to clean, and relatively uncomplicated to replace if necessary. They also come with special features such as low emissivity glass, and several color tints are available. They allow a designer to plan a home that is better oriented to its surroundings than one designed only to look symmetrical on a blueprint with a window every six feet. That solves

This unit has two double-paned windows flanking a vent.

the light and view benefits of windows.

Now let's consider the venting needs of a home. A vent is a hole in the wall that allows air to move in and out of your building. A screen over the hole keeps bugs out. A cover or door over it stops airflow when you want the inside atmosphere to be different from the outside. That's the basic functional vent.

Let's take it up a notch and build a nice ¾" pine lumber casing and trim parts instead of just making a hole. Check the drawing for the parts, and I will guide you through the construction. On the outside of the building is a "picture" frame built with screws (because, most times, screws are superior to nails). Stapled to the backside of this frame is a piece of screen with mesh fine enough to keep out insects.

I make screen frames that rest against the outer perimeter of the casing and are held in place with hook-and-eye sets. It is easy to attach or detach the framed screen from inside the house right through the casing. If the screen gets damaged, just unhook the frame, rip off the old screen, staple on the new, and hook it back into place. This method lets you to do nice neat repairs if needed. And, at times, it is good to have easy, unimpeded passage through a wall. The detachable framed screen can be wrapped in 6-mil plastic during winter to give extra weather protection.

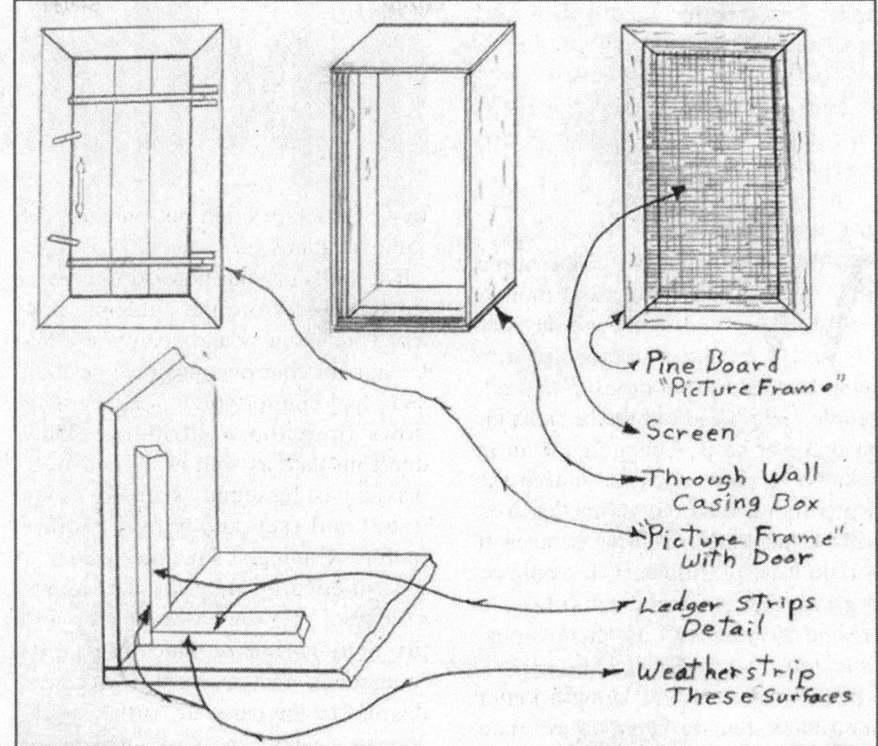

Vent unit details

Vent unit showing plastic-wrapped detachable screen held in place with hook-and-eye set (one of four). Note ledger strip with weather strip foam tape.

A four-sided casing box passes through the siding, sheathing, studs, and drywall as precisely as possible and is securely held in place with screws. Seal any spaces around the box with fiberglass insulation or builders' foam.

For the interior treatment make another "picture" frame fitted around a wood door with some nice wooden hinges and two turnlocks, as shown in the drawing and pictures.

The interior frame is attached to the casing box with screws or finish nails and to the wall studs behind the drywall, creating a solid structural connection of everything involved. The hinges of the door are attached to the "picture" frame with screws. Check issues #98 and #99 of *Backwoods Home Magazine* for how to make and use wooden hinges.

Notice in the drawing and pictures that ledger strips are added to the inner edges of the casing box. The vent door contacts the ledger strips.

These ledger strips should be weather-stripped. I prefer using ¼" thick x ¾" wide open-cell foam tape for this. It holds up well, crushes easily to form a nice airtight seal, and is easy to replace.

The ledger strips should be glued and screwed into place. The lip (or ledge) they provide will discourage any stray rainwater that blows through the screen from passing into the house, so the joint where they meet the casing needs to be leak-proof. They also add strength to the casing.

You can paint or stain your vents' woodwork. I recommend stain along with the application of a sealer such as Thompson Weather Seal every year or so.

Most of my vent doors are composed of a painted panel of plywood facing the outside that is glued and screwed to stained pine boards facing the living quarters. Along with sturdy wooden hinges and simple turnlocks, this makes a very rugged, weatherproof, secure, easy-to-use vent unit for all seasons.

I have not given dimensions for these vent units because they can be just about any size. Using the window and vent theory, install vents on a home where natural breezes tend to be forceful. Vents are almost as good as having an air conditioner. A breeze blowing through a strategically located, properly sized vent easily circulates air through one room and often works for several connected rooms. Be aware of the need for another vent (or two or three) on the opposite side of the room or house for the breeze to escape and continue on its way.

When planning vent sizes, take fire safety into consideration. I make most of my vents to fit between wall studs that are usually on 24" centers, giving me a vent with a 21" wide opening. I generally make the vertical opening 36" to 45" high. About 80% of the people I know could escape through a hole that size.

Burglary prevention shelves built into a vent unit with two shifty characters considering breaking and exiting.

A 21"x36" screened vent with residents practicing a fire drill.

I find making vent doors with a layer of plywood two feet or less by four feet or less makes best use of a 4'x8' piece of plywood and gives me a good efficient vent. I try to design at least one of this size vent unit in every room for a fire escape and, of course, ventilation.

My second favorite size vent is 10" or 12" wide x 70" high, more or less. I use these on each side of large windows and doors. When two of these tall narrow vents flank a big window, the view is unobstructed and plenty of air comes through. A 1½" wooden dowel on brackets above the window/vent unit can support sweep-aside floor to (almost) ceiling curtains. You will have fresh air and a view during the day, privacy at night.

Tall side vents next to an outside door means you will not need a screen door. Your security is assured because you can keep the door closed and locked while letting breezes through, day or night. You can converse with people approaching your door without compromising your safety. The vents are too narrow for access and you can enhance that feature by building shelves in the vent cavity between the screen and vent door. The shelves make a nice place to set small plants in summer.

Another popular vent size I employ measures 10" or 12" wide x 16" high. In winter when your home is closed up tight and fresh air is less available, you can do yourself a very healthy service by closing the door to your bedroom at night, shutting off the heat to the room and opening two of these small vents located as near your lungs as possible. The vents allow clean outside air to flow gently toward you during all the hours you are asleep. You also save heat by keeping the bedroom cool and make better use of those cozy blankets and the flannel nightcap you received last Christmas.

I install one of these little vent units in bathrooms right beside the toilet. They are easy to open and close, and venting in this area is a good idea.

Another good place for strategic venting is on the wall behind your cooking surface. I know powered smoke vents are popular, but this is a

This shows a screened vent with a glass panel and wood hinges above the tub. Fresh air while bathing is a good thing.

A good place for a small vent unit is within easy reach of the throne.

good, inexpensive, energy saving alternative.

Let's review. Make a four-sided casing box that fits through your wall with a screened frame attached to the casing with hook-and-eye sets accessible from indoors. Add a frame around a hinged door and secure it to the interior edges of the casing box. Also screw or nail the interior frame to the wall studs through the drywall so nothing moves but the door, which rests against weather-stripped ledger strips. I am not quite sure if "ledger strips" is in the building term dictionary, so if you don't understand what they are, just check the drawing.

Now that you know how to build vent units of any size and plenty of them, let's explore their other benefits.

Say you have enough vents installed to make you feel like you are actually living in the great outdoors. You may begin to worry about burglars popping through those screens and stealing your TV.

Go walk around the outside of your home and pretend you are a burglar with breaking and entering intentions. Certain vents will stand out as optimal entry points. Build a set of shelves in the space between the screen and the door in these units. I attach mine with just four screws so they come out for easy cleaning. Display things on the shelves that will make lots of noise if they hit the floor. I suggest pretty glassware, though my wife disagrees.

Doing this accomplishes two things: First it makes the vent appear too complicated and noisy to break through; second, the shelves will give the burglar a subliminal impression of jail bars. Both are good deterrents to crime.

You could build shelves in all your large vent units, but you must balance the fire escape safety factor with the burglary prevention strategy. It's a hard decision. At least when the vent doors are closed and locked, they are much safer than closed and locked regular windows.

Earlier I mentioned wrapping detachable screens with plastic for cold weather. If you live where winter is seriously frigid, you can greatly increase the R-factor of your vents by putting R-19 or R-21 (or even thicker) fiberglass batt insulation inside a common plastic garbage bag, then stuffing it in the cavity between the screen and door of your vent unit. Custom-make these for each vent. Cut the batts to fit in the space without being too loose, but don't crush them either. This makes your vent units as resistant to heat loss as your insulated wall, maybe even more so. No regular window can approach this kind of performance. You can understand why I haven't considered buying regular window sets for many years.

Various sized, strategically located, easily operated vents installed in your home make you healthy, wealthy (well…maybe not that), wise and less sleepy during hibernation season.

A prime reason for adequate venting is because many people use woodstoves to heat their homes, and smoke in the living space is a problem.

There are two main reasons for this. First is because the stove has openings, cracks, loose-fitting doors, or perforated chimney pipe where smoke leaks.

The second, more likely, reason is because the chimney does not sustain a strong updraft. If it is working properly, a few small crevices in the stove will not leak. The draft should actually pull air into the stove rather than let smoke escape. The draft works best during the hottest part of the burn cycle. However, when the fire slows down, the smoke is not driven up the chimney forcefully and will find other exits from the stove or pipe. Worse yet, what escapes is more than smoke. A variety of unpleasant gases, not as obvious as smoke, can escape into your living quarters from a leaky stove. These problems can be fixed.

Small vents on each side of the bed for fresh air while sleeping

First, seal the stove. Many woodstoves can be disassembled and put back together using furnace cement to seal parts and seams together as good as new. Furnace cement comes in a small container and has a putty-like texture. You apply it with a small spatula or other, similar, tool. It is also available in a caulking-gun-sized tube for even easier application. But if your stove has seen too many heating seasons and successful reconditioning is risky, consider buying a new or good-quality used stove.

Here is a couch with small vents on each end. The curtain turns this into guest sleeping quarters, sometimes preferred more than a bedroom.

Use quality stovepipe fitted tightly into the chimney. Some furnace cement applied here will help assure this joint will not leak smoke into the living quarters. It is a good idea to connect the stovepipe sections together (and to the stove if possible) with two or three self-drilling sheet metal screws through each overlapping joint. Space the screws evenly around the joint and through both layers of metal. It is easy to do this using a regular electric drill with a #2 Phillips head bit. Making the stovepipe a single strong unit prevents leaks if the pipe gets jostled or if it the joints slide apart during heating and cooling cycles.

Stovepipe does not last as long as your stove. Even galvanized stovepipe rusts after a few seasons. Rusted pinholes in the stovepipe allow smoke and gasses to get into your home. Inspect your pipes closely and change them if you have any doubts. It is good insurance.

This is a 21"x60" screened vent with an added louver panel to deflect rain.

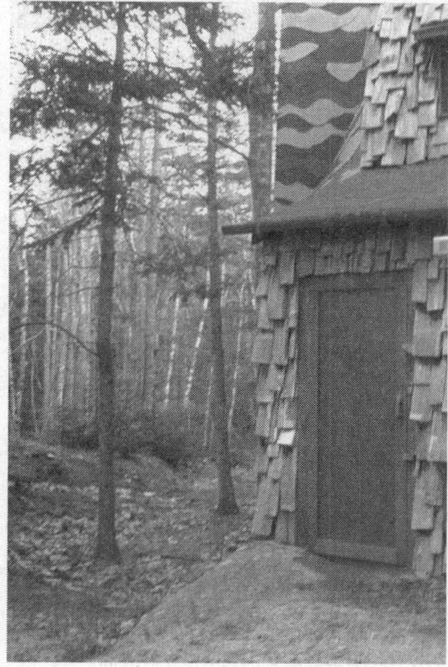

An attached shed encloses a hot air oil furnace. The small vent to the right of the purple door lets in plenty of air for combustion. Note the power venter just under the roof edge. A furnace located this way separates combustion air from air to be heated and limits furnace noise.

The second, even more important, way to keep smoke out of your home during the heating season uses a specialized vent made just for the stove.

Your fire needs lots of fresh air, something on the order of three times room volume per hour. That is a lot. A stove trying to pull its combustion air from inside your buttoned-up-for-winter home is like you trying to suck something through a straw that has been pinched shut.

To correct this problem, install a vent on the outside wall of your home to bring outside air directly to the air inlet on your stove. Make a through-the-wall vent as described earlier. A 6"x6" screened opening is good for most applications. Use 6" stovepipe and elbows to get the fresh air from the screened opening to the air inlet on the stove. Keep the distance as short and neat as possible. Be as diligent about the construction of this pipe as you did the chimney stovepipe.

Some stoves need a handmade sheet metal piece to get that last connection right and tight. Some have a three or four inch round inlet that accommodates your stovepipe. A 6" pipe adapted down to a 3" or 4" inlet is ok. The more air made available to the stove for combustion the better.

Installing this special vent will keep your home warm longer between firings because the stove won't be using the heated air in your house for combustion and sending it up the chimney. More importantly, if the draft in the chimney slows down and becomes a back draft (sometimes called down draft), the smoke and gases will exit through this vent rather than into your home.

By attaching this fresh air vent to the stove, smoke is less likely to come out the stove door opening when you add wood. If it does, make a way to close the air inlet while you fuel the stove. A common damper from the hardware store installed in the inlet pipe will work. Closing the damper forces the fire to pull air through the open door rather than let smoke drift out. Be sure to fully open the inlet vent damper again when the stove door is closed.

I am assuming your chimney has been inspected and is in reasonably good condition. If cleaning it won't help and a new one is called for, check *The Art of Chimney Building* in *Backwoods Home Magazine*'s issue #91, page 8, for more in-depth information.

Oil and gas furnaces have a similar habit of using inside air for combustion, and they can suffer an occasional back draft, too. It may be caused by age, wear, dirty filters, or neglected tune-ups. I do not recommend bringing outside air through a duct to the combustion air inlet section of these machines already installed in your home. Correctly installed commercial home furnaces have provisions for combustion air, usually an open window in your basement. Not the best solution, but it's the rule. Be sure to keep up the maintenance on them.

When I build a home, I like to install the oil or gas furnace outside the living quarters in a ventilated shed attached to the house. Air ducts are routed from the house to the air inlet of the circulation fan housing. More ducts are added to carry warmed air from the furnace plenum to the distribution ducts inside the house.

The goal is the same as the woodstove's fresh-air duct project. Separate the air in your home from air used for combustion by the furnace and allow outside air to supply the combustion chamber needs of your heating device. Locating a gas or oil furnace outside the living quarters provides the extra bonus of diminished noise.

Winter is about over here in New England and soon we can open all the vents for summer and once again feel like we live in the great outdoors, minus the bugs. It will be great. Δ

Ayoob on Firearms

Centennial of the All-American .30-06

By Massad Ayoob

In the long love affair between America and the rifle, there has never been an interlude quite as intensive as the epoch of the .30-06. This cartridge celebrated its 100th anniversary in 2006. It is still going strong, a favorite of hunters and shooters. It was the primary military small-arm caliber of the United States Army for more that half a century. The *Speer Reloading Manual* noted many years ago, "No other smokeless powder rifle cartridge has achieved the popularity and wide use of the .30-06. It has been used with great success by big game hunters and target shooters for almost three quarters of a century. The U.S. and many other nations have used it as a standard rifle and machine gun cartridge."

Designed with a view to replacing the Krag rifle and its .30-40 round after the Spanish-American War, this cartridge actually began as the .30-03, with a 220-grain bullet loaded to a velocity of 2300 feet per second. New developments in European small arms and ballistics, however, quickly convinced the U.S. military's ordnance experts to go to a lighter, faster bullet, loaded into a slightly shorter cartridge casing. The new round was accordingly tweaked, and the result was the .30 caliber U.S. cartridge of 1906, hence the designation of ".30-06." It had been designed for the Springfield bolt-action military rifle of 1903 (thus, the "30-03" designation for its original cartridge), and the new load was officially known thereafter as the .30-06 Springfield.

This was the cartridge that America brought to World War I, the Springfield rifle augmented with the Enfield 1917 model. Both were rugged bolt-action guns that could quickly be reloaded through the top of their mechanism with five-round "stripper clips." The same cartridge would be used for the magnificent BAR, the Browning Automatic Rifle, which hit the field at the very end of WWI and did noble service for the United States in the Second World War. Alongside the BAR in the Pacific and European Theaters alike was the fabulous M1 Garand, an eight-shot semiautomatic rifle, which gave American infantry a deadly edge against the slower bolt-action Mausers of the Germans and Arisakas of the Japanese. The .30-06 would march through Korea, too, as the standard U.S. cartridge, before giving way in the late 1950s to the M14 rifle and its 7.62mm NATO round, which in essence was simply a shortened .30-06. The 7.62mm NATO military round is known in sporting circles as the .308 Winchester.

The .30-06 round was in service as late as the Vietnam war. Carlos Hathcock, the famously deadly Marine sniper, used .30-06 there before being forced to switch to a .308.

Though the M1 Garand and the BAR are now relegated to the museums as far as the U.S. military is concerned, back on the home front the .30-06 remains the most widely used sporting cartridge in the country. For as long as this writer has been alive, the .30-06 has been the most popular center-fire rifle cartridge in this country.

There are good reasons why, and as the cartridge celebrates its centennial in 2006, it is worth reviewing those reasons.

Massad Ayoob

All manner of exotic, high-velocity, fat-bodied cartridges crowd the hunting fields and the outdoor magazines today. But talk to conservation officers and ask them what round is used to bring down the most deer in the jurisdictions where they work. The answer you'll hear will very likely be, "thirty-ought-six." Try to get a box of .338 WSM (Winchester Super Magnum) at the little rural general store with the gasoline pump out front. They'll try not to laugh in your face. But if they sell ammunition at all, you can be sure they'll have some .30-06 in stock.

In its century-long march across the pages of American history, the ought-six has made a slew of friends. Some of them were famous. The .30-06 was probably the choice of more Presidents than any other rifle in history. Theodore Roosevelt took one to

Africa, a beautiful sporting version of the Springfield. Harry Truman was issued a .30-06, like every other doughboy in the trenches of World War I. (He also carried a 1917 model .45 revolver in that conflict—no new-fangled automatic for the practical Harry!) There are pictures of Franklin Delano Roosevelt as a young man, wearing a leather shooting coat and preparing to shoot a rifle match with a Springfield .30-06. Jack Kennedy and George Bush alike would have qualified with the Springfield and maybe the Garand during the basic training that began their World War II service. Lyndon Johnson was as likely to have a .30-06 as anything else in the front seat with him as he drove guests across the plains of his LBJ Ranch, looking for deer to shoot from the front seat of his open-top Lincoln Continental.

America's gun experts all took the ought-six to their bosoms. The late, great Jack O'Connor was most famous for his advocacy of the .270 Winchester cartridge and the 7mm Mauser round, but some of his favorite hunting rifles were chambered for the .30-06. Elmer Keith considered the .30-06 altogether too light for elk or moose, but allowed it was suitable for smaller critters, and shot many a match with the cartridge. It was also one of the favored cartridges of William B. Ruger, perhaps the most acclaimed sporting arms designer of recent times.

Henry Stebbins was one of the top all-around gun experts of the mid-20th Century. He had much to say about the .30-06 cartridge in his classic book *Rifles: A Modern Encyclopedia*. Stebbins wrote, "Up to the limit of its killing power, which is considerable, the .30-06 is still our best all-round cartridge. Few smaller sizes handle round bullets so accurately, and at the other extreme, 250 grains is a respectable weight-in a long bullet like a .30—for any American big game."

Versatility is one of the key reasons for the .30-06's popularity in rural America. A well-off sportsman may have a battery of 20 different rifles for hunting 20 different combinations of quarry and terrain...the homesteader or full-time outdoorsman may be limited by finances, logistics, or "keep things simple" philosophy to one rifle for all purposes. Those who reload their ammunition have a bullet weight range of 100 grains (light recoil loads for informal target shooting or "plinking") through those big 250-grain custom loads that Stebbins was talking about. In factory-produced ammunition, the range is from 110-grain bullets for varmint hunting to heavily constructed 220-grain projectiles suitable for bear, moose, and much of Africa's large plains game.

When I hunted in the Republic of South Africa and in Southwest Africa (now Namibia), I noticed that many of the indigenous big-game hunters chose the .30-06 as their "light" rifle for plains animals such as kudu, gemsbok, and other giant antelope. While some considered the cartridge a little light for critters that big, the Afrikaaners had learned over generations that with 220-grain bullets with round, soft, noses, the .30-06 would reliably shoot deep enough into big soft-skinned animals to put them down. Many of them felt it was suitable for lion as well.

A ballistic patriarchy

The .30-06, in 100 years, became the father of many other cartridges. "Neck it down" (that is, narrow the forward part of its taper to hold a smaller, lighter projectile that can go faster at similar internal pressures) and you have the almost equally timeless .270 Winchester. Neck it down further, to a mere quarter inch of bullet diameter, and you have the .25-06, a favorite for small American pronghorn antelope. Widen its case mouth to hold a fatter bullet, and you have the .35 Whelen, a big game cartridge beloved by the cognoscenti for decades.

Shorten the .30-06, and you have the .308 Winchester/7.62mm NATO, today the odds-on choice of military

Power range

To understand the versatility factor that has made the .30-06 so greatly and enduringly popular, we need to look at some ballistics tables. The following are the bullet weights and velocities of the most common .30-06 cartridges. All use a bullet that is .30 caliber, or to be more specific, .308" in diameter.

Bullet weight	Velocity at muzzle	Energy at muzzle
55 grain	4080 feet per second	1412 foot-pounds
110 grain	3370 feet per second	2770 foot-pounds
150 grain	2970 feet per second	2930 foot-pounds
165 grain	2800 feet per second	2872 foot-pounds
180 grain	2700 feet per second	2910 foot-pounds
220 grain	2410 feet per second	2830 foot-pounds

The 55-grain bullet was actually .22 caliber, .224" in diameter, contained inside a plastic sabot and introduced by Remington as the .30-06 Accelerator in the late 1970s. Its intent was to broaden the .30-06's versatility even further, and this it did, but I and others who tested it at the time found its accuracy to be mediocre at best, and the Accelerator has not become all that popular.

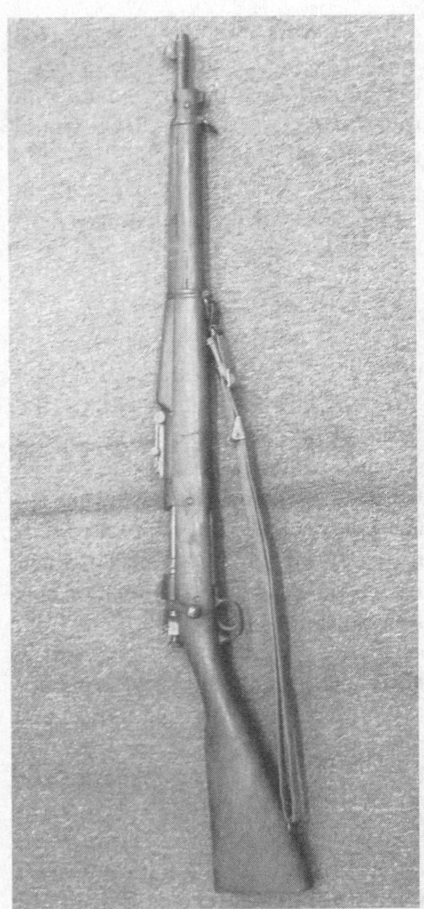

The gun that started it all: The 1903 Springfield service rifle, caliber .30-06.

snipers and the precision riflemen on police SWAT teams. Take that cartridge in turn: neck it down, and you have the popular .243 Winchester, or neck it up to create the promising if unpopular .358 Winchester.

The above are not the only ballistic developments that can trace their lineage to the .30-06 cartridge.

As Frank C. Barnes noted in his authoritative text *Cartridges of the World*, the key to both the popularity and the versatility of this cartridge is the user's ability to select the particular loading of the cartridge that is right for the job at hand. Said Barnes, "The .30-06 is undoubtedly the most flexible, useful, all-round big-game cartridge available to the American hunter. For many years it has been the standard by which all other big-game cartridges have been measured. To say that a cartridge is in the .30-06 class means it is suitable for any game in North America. The secret of success when using this cartridge is to be sure and select the right bullet for

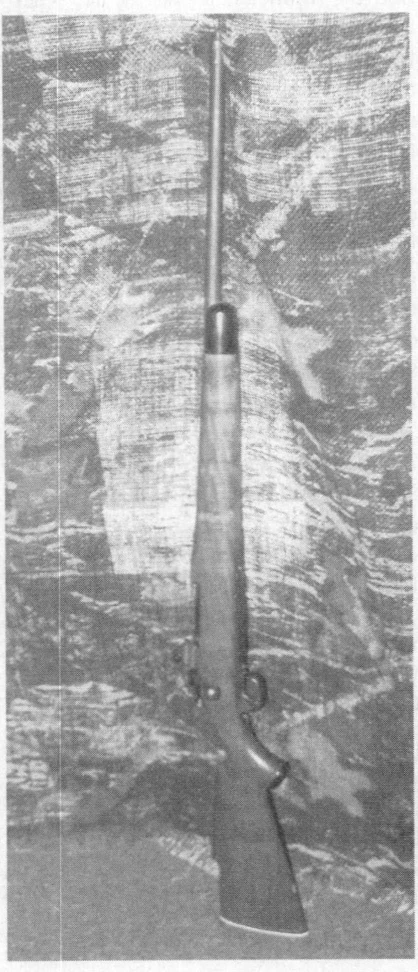

A 1903 Springfield A3 sporter, still at work after all these decades. Caliber, of course, is .30-06.

the game and hunting conditions at hand. The lighter bullets...should only be used for varmint hunting. While these bullets can be driven at impressive velocities, starting out at over 3000 fps (feet per second), they are made to expand rapidly on small animals and will not penetrate properly on large game. For deer, antelope, goat, sheep, black or brown bear, under most hunting conditions, the 150 or 165-grain bullet is proper. For heavier game, such as elk, moose, or the big brown bear, the 180, 200 or 220-grain bullet is the best choice.... As a matter of fact, the .30-06 will give a good account on all but the heaviest or most dangerous African or Asiatic species under average hunting conditions. The 220-grain bullet is generally recommended for African game, although the 180-grain also has a good reputation there. With the proper bullet, this cartridge can be

Author's favorite .30-06 these days is this Ruger Model 77. It will hold every shot in less than an inch at 100 yards.

adapted to any game or hunting situation in North or South America, whether in the mountains, plains, woods or jungle. Few other cartridges can claim equal versatility."

Most ammunition manufacturers gear their 180-grain bullets for heavier animals, putting stronger copper jackets on them so the bullets expand more slowly and therefore penetrate deeper.

Over the years, I came to the conclusion that the thinner jackets on the faster 150-grain bullets made them ideally suitable for smaller and medium-size whitetail deer. The 165-grain bullet is, like the 150-grain, particularly accurate in most .30-06 rifles, and the 165-grain is the bullet weight I'd choose for all-around use in a .30-06.

The .30-06 has become all the more versatile in the last few years with two new trends. One is Hornady Ammunition's Light Magnum ammo series, which offers .30-06 loads at higher than usual velocities for the variety of bullet weights available. Another is the proliferation across the brand lines of premium ammunition that uses high-tech bullets like the Nosler Ballistic Tip, the Winchester Ballistic Silvertip, and more. Sport shooters once had to "roll their own" to get that level of specialized performance. Now, in .30-06 among other calibers, it's available over-the-counter.

Other side of versatility

When a backwoods person hefts a .30-06, one side of its versatility is the cartridge it fires. The other is the kind of rifle that fires it. Over the years, every type of popular rifle mechanism has been adapted to fire the .30-06 cartridge.

Semiautomatic rifles. At the beginning of WWI, the timeless M1 designed by John Garand and the unique Johnson rifle purchased in small quantities by the US Marine Corps, proved that this high-powered

A small sampling of the .30-06's diversity. From left, Remington 55-grain Accelerator (note plastic sabot around bullet), 150-grain soft point deer load, 165-grain soft-point elk load.

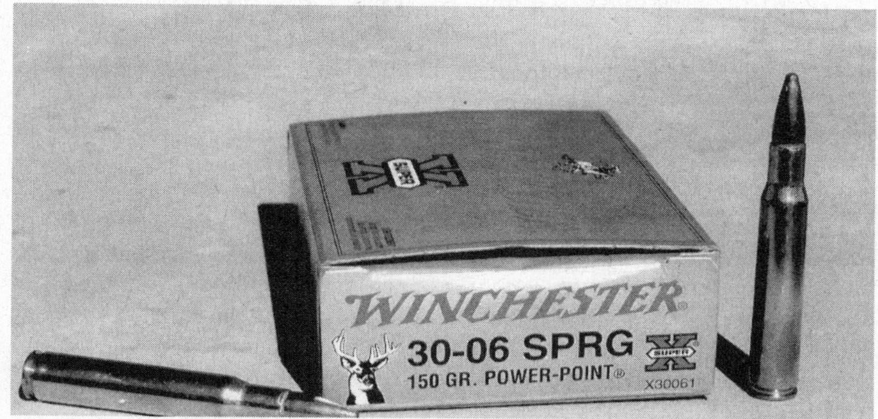

For his deer hunting needs, author finds standard-grade 150-grain softnose .30-06 all that's needed.

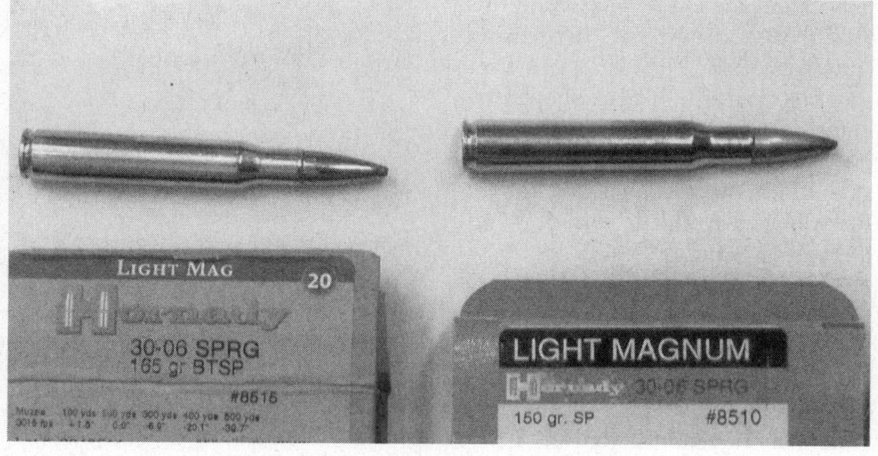

Hornady's introduction of Light Magnum .30-06 made the cartridge more versatile than ever.

Dog-leg bolt handle, rabbit-ear rear-sight protector made the 1917 Enfield .30-06 a butt-ugly critter, but it served America nobly in WWI alongside the Springfield. The Enfield was the rifle issued to hero Alvin York.

cartridge could work in a self-loading mechanism. When GIs came home en masse after the victory, they had an appreciation for rifles that could fire as fast as they could pull the trigger, and a demand arose for sporting .30-06 autoloaders.

Remington was the first to answer that demand, and their version has been the most popular forever after. Introduced in 1955, the five-shot Model 740 was an instant success. It was soon upgraded into the Model 742 and the Model Four, and has remained hugely popular—particularly where deer are hunted in heavy timber at close range—ever since.

Browning followed with another gun called the BAR, and while this model also stood for "Browning Automatic Rifle," it was a sleek five-shot sporting arm of exquisite craftsmanship and high natural accuracy potential, and a far cry from the splendid battle machine that fought for America from the end of WWI through Vietnam.

The M1 Garand of "the best generation" is now produced in a civilian version by Springfield Armory in Geneseo, Illinois. Military surplus Garands can be had by law-abiding American citizens through the CMP (Civilian Marksmanship Program) headquartered at Camp Perry near Port Clinton, Ohio. The .30-06 that kept the Free World free lives on.

Slide-action rifles. Curiously, while Americans created and took to their collective heart the slide-action shotgun, the same design of rifle has never been hugely popular. Again, it was Remington who made it possible, with their Model 760 pump gun introduced at mid-20th Century. In varied models, including the designations 76 and 7600, the Remington pump was the favorite of the famous Vermont deer hunting family, the Benoits, and at one time was issued by the FBI because of its commonality of handling with the slide-action Remington 870 police shotgun. .30-06 has always been one of the most popular calibers for the Remington pump rifle, perhaps the single most popular.

Lever-action rifles. Winchester produced their distinctive Model 1895 lever-action rifle in caliber .30-06, though there were gun experts then and now who felt that the design was too fragile for such a high-pressure cartridge. They may have been right, because the concept never caught on.

Single-shot rifles. Obsolete by every practical and logical standard, the single-shot hunting rifle survives today because of moral standards and esthetic standards. The esthetic standard: just look at them! They are beautifully balanced, by the test of the eye and the test of the hands alike. The moral standard: Some hunters think it best to handicap themselves by giving themselves only one shot at the quarry.

Many fine single-shot hunting rifles are produced today, virtually all available in caliber .30-06. The most popular is the Ruger.

Bolt-action rifles. Here we find the natural home, the ancestral home, the once and future home of the .30-06 caliber rifle. The Springfield Model 1903 was bolt action, of course, and

Maximum versatility: Ruger Model 77, 3-9X variable-power telescopic sight, and Federal Premium 165-grain .30-06 ammunition.

so was the Enfield of 1917. .30-06 was the most popular caliber for Winchester's defining bolt-action sporting rifle, the Model 54, and in 1936 when Winchester introduced their classic Model 70, it became far and away the best selling caliber for that model. (Ironically, this same year that celebrates the centennial of the .30-06 cartridge would have been the 70th anniversary of the Model 70, but the Winchester plant in Connecticut closed its historic doors in March of 2006.)

The Model 70 was known as "the rifleman's rifle." It was the choice of master shooters, rifle champions, and great hunters from the aforementioned Jack O'Connor to the also previously mentioned Carlos Hathcock, who used a Model 70 .30-06 to set the first stage of his deadly record as a Marine sniper in Vietnam before being issued a Remington bolt-action in .308.

That Remington was based on a sporting rifle known stateside as the Model 700, perhaps the single best-selling .30-06 today. Exquisitely accurate, deliciously smooth, and with a trigger pull that any trained marksman can appreciate, the Remington 700 is one of our classic hunting rifles in any caliber, and definitely one of the classic .30-06s.

Ruger's Model 77 series are exquisite bolt-action sporting rifles. Accurate. Smooth. Traditional in style. And eminently shootable.

The Savage Model 110 and its descendants are high-value guns, historically delivering low bid price with exquisite accuracy. The Savage was also the first mass-produced bolt-action rifle to be manufactured in a left-handed version.

The list goes on. BSA in England, Musgrave of South Africa, Steyr of Austria, and countless more, as well as virtually every custom and semi-custom rifle maker in the U.S., have produced fine bolt-action .30-06 rifles.

The future of the .30-06

Like Shakespeare's Julius Caesar, the .30-06 once "bestrode (its) narrow world like a Colossus." Today, there are many more cartridges available with higher velocity, heavier bullets, and flatter trajectories than hunters had access to during the ought-six's heyday. For a good half-century, the .30-06 absolutely ruled the National High Power Rifle Championships of the United States. Then the .308 Winchester took over in the winners' circle, and today, custom-made rifles in the pipsqueak .223 caliber are the ones that win at the Nationals. You only see the .30-06 now in the specialty matches for "period guns," and special events for M1 Garands.

The military's switch almost half a century ago to the .308 was predicted at the time to sound the death knell for the .30-06. Those bells have remained silent. While the .308 has become hugely popular, the .30-06 has not declined that much by comparison. Its longer cartridge casing allows a wider range of bullet weight and velocity combinations. That range is 110-grain to 220-grain in .30-06 factory ammunition, but only 125-grain to 200-grain in .308 factory ammo.

When I was young, cheap military surplus .30-06 practice ammo was available in abundance. When a gun club I belonged to offered members up to a thousand rounds of GI ought-six ammo for a penny a cartridge, I bought the limit and then went out and bought a .30-06 to shoot it in. I still own the rifle, a Steyr Professional that would reliably put three shots into three quarters of an inch at 100 yards all day, if I held its Burris telescopic sight sufficiently steady. That ammo is long gone, but I still have the rifle. Back in the early '90s—shooting match-grade Federal brand—that Steyr put me into the Top Ten of the Buckmasters international hunting rifle competition. It's in the will for the kids, and not for sale… one of literally millions of fine .30-06 rifles that have performed so well when the chips were down that they earned their way into their owners' hearts and became family heirlooms.

That cheap ammo is no longer a reason to choose a .30-06 over, say, a .270; the ought-six surplus ammunition is a thing of the past, and modern generic low-price ammo is no cheaper for .30-06 than for other calibers. Still, if you are going to have only one rifle, the .30-06 makes an excellent case for itself.

I'm right-handed, but I like the idea of having a left-handed rifle accessible, both to loan to southpaw friends and in case I sustain an injury that forces me to switch sides. My lefty bolt gun is a Savage Model 110, and because it would indeed be my only rifle if I was in that situation, I made sure to order it in caliber .30-06.

When I got divorced and moved from city to countryside, I had to leave most of my gun collection in storage to retrieve later, and took with me only the firearms I was most likely to need. The only bolt-action sporting rifle to make the cut was a pet Ruger 77 with 3-to-9X variable power telescopic sight. Its caliber? .30-06, of course.

The .30-06 rifle is an American icon. It earned its longevity through its ability to accomplish hard work and deliver practical performance on demand. Its 100th birthday is a fitting thing to celebrate in tandem with the 100th issue of *Backwoods Home Magazine*. Δ

The last word

Confident liberals vs. whiny conservatives?

I read a piece on the Net the other day about what kind of kids grow up to be liberals and which grow up to be conservatives. The article begins with a quote from the *Toronto Star*: "Remember the whiny, insecure kid in nursery school, the one who always thought everyone was out to get him, and was always running to the teacher with complaints? Chances are he grew up to be a conservative... The confident, resilient, self-reliant kids mostly grew up to be liberals."

This conclusion was based on a study conducted by Jack Block, a University of California, Berkeley, professor who followed about 100 children over several decades. According to the *Star*, Block theorizes that insecure kids look for "reassurance provided by tradition and authority, and find it in conservative politics." While "The more confident kids are eager to explore alternatives to the way things are, and find liberal politics more congenial."

The beauty of such conclusions, reached "scientifically," is that liberals don't have to defend them because Block has shown that liberals are well adjusted, while those who disagree with their politics are suspected to be somewhat immature and paranoid.

Let's put aside my doubts about the conclusions of the "study" since it was conducted by a professor with a liberal track record at UC Berkeley, a bastion of liberal politics, in a town where over 90 percent of the vote in elections goes to liberal candidates and causes.

Let's ask: If the conclusions of the study are valid, what do they mean? Do they mean it was confident, resilient, self-reliant kids who grew up to create Big Government? And is this imposing your will on others, some Orwellian way to provide a new definition of "self-reliance"?

Let's also consider what liberals have accomplished. They have confidently forced what's "good" for you onto you—whether you like it or not, and they have put in place a system of penalties with which to punish you if you think you're free enough *not* to comply with their social engineering.

Let's face it, it wasn't conservatives of either party (yes, Virginia, there used to be conservative Democrats) that came up with the income tax or Social Security. It was liberals who put the freedom-depleting bureaucracies out of reach of the voters—and even the legislators. It's liberals who want to disarm the law-abiding public, and it is they who deny property rights. It's liberals who turned our money into fiat currency. It's they who keep inventing new "civil" rights that aren't gifts from God or nature, but have to be supplied to you by government—at the expense of someone else. It was liberals who pushed for laws saying parents are incapable of caring for and guiding their children on sex and pregnancy matters and that those functions should be handed over to the monolithic state and faceless bureaucrats. It's liberals who want to micromanage your life.

Photo by Lisa Nourse

John Silveira

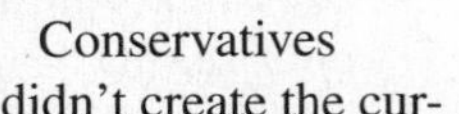

Conservatives didn't create the current education system that has failed and is still failing, and it's not they who claim it can be fixed by throwing ever-increasing amounts of *your* money at it—after the last several rounds of money thrown at it failed to repair it. And it's not conservatives who think little kids who make guns *with their fingers* should be suspended from school. (Yes, if you've missed it, that's actually happened.)

The list of liberal "accomplishments" could go on for pages. But there would be precious little that reflects confidence in the American people or promotes self-reliance.

I say, if it's self-reliant little kids who grow up to be liberals intent on grabbing our freedoms, give me the whiny, snively-nosed little freedom lovers any day. Yes, I'll admit, it's we conservatives who want the authority of the Constitution back and want controls put on government.

Liberals are confident, that's for sure. They're confident that you're an idiot who isn't self-reliant and can't take care of yourself. They grew up with a feeling that everything is relative and that includes the *Constitution* and the *Bill of Rights*. They know what's best for you. And the irony is, their solutions to society's problems are *never* self-reliant solutions. They're the Big Government solutions that *they've* created.

If the "whiny" kids who supposedly grew up to be conservatives are asking for anything, it's to be left alone and—irony of ironies—be *allowed* to be self-reliant. But there they are, those "confident" and "self-reliant" liberal kids, wanting to disrupt their lives with their bureaucratic rules and threats of force.

Of course, the truth is, the attributes these "researchers" were talking about are not confidence and self-reliance. They confused those attributes with arrogance and bullying. Because, even back then, that's what they were doing. The fact is, the guys who ran the study are idiots.

— John Silveira

Backwoods Home magazine

practical ideas for self-reliant living

Sept/Oct 2006
Issue #101
$4.95 US
$6.50 CAN

Preparing to build your new home

MAKING BIODIESEL
HOMEMADE PICKLES
PICKING CHANTERELLES
RAISING QUAIL
FRONTIER HANDGUNS

FREE books
See page 2

www.backwoodshome.com

DON CHILDERS

My view

The Government gorilla in our home

Dave Duffy

The other week, Vince, a contractor who does occasional work for me, was arrested for slapping his 14-year-old daughter on the behind when she talked back to her mother using abusive and obscene language. Vince left a mark on his daughter's behind, enough for the local child welfare bureaucrats to accuse him of child abuse and demand he leave his home so his children would be safe. Or, they warned, he would go to jail immediately.

Vince protested that the mark he left was inadvertent and that his daughter needed a father's discipline because she was beginning to hang out with unsavory kids who were experimenting with drugs. Vince's pleas were dismissed and he was banished to an old trailer in the backyard of his home. The triumphant daughter became even more abusive to her mom, then ran away from home. She began using drugs and subsequently became pregnant.

The welfare agency made little effort to help the daughter, but the Government prosecuted Vince. He was convicted, fined, and ordered to undergo 15 months of anger management training. Vince, by the way, had no previous history of child abuse or any criminal record. His daughter is still a runaway, but Vince is not allowed near her.

Vince's predicament is not an isolated case. Many of you reading this story no doubt viewed the TV documentary of a few weeks ago in which a TV camera crew followed a child welfare worker into a home where the father was accused of child abuse. The father, like Vince, had slapped his 14-year-old daughter, this time across the face because she, too, was out of control. This father also left a mark on his child—a bruise on the face.

Like Vince, the TV father protested that his daughter needed a father's discipline now more than ever. The welfare worker dismissed his pleas and said she had consulted with her supervisor by phone and the supervisor agreed with her that all his children had to be removed from the home to protect them. The man had two other younger children.

The father and mother were astonished, and they pleaded with the welfare worker not to remove their children from their home. The TV camera occasionally caught sight of a uniformed police officer who stood silently by as the drama unfolded. He was obviously the power—the Government—behind the welfare worker who had decided to remove the children. Eventually, the father beseeched the welfare worker through his tears: "Don't take my children; put me in jail instead."

To no avail! Even as one child, about three years old, clung to the father and cried, "I want to stay with Daddy," the third child was awakened from his sleep from a bedroom upstairs. The welfare worker took the children.

The TV documentary followed the family for two years. The children were put in foster care for three months before being allowed back home. The parents eventually divorced, citing the invasion by the child welfare agency into their home as "the beginning of the end."

The documentary made no attempt to take sides with either the family or the child welfare agency, but just recorded what was happening. Call me prejudiced, but I sided with the family. I was sickened by the display of omnipotent Government bureaucratic power that seemed bent on destroying the family to save the children from a father's discipline. No wonder the parents divorced.

The program closed with a commentator stating that the debate continues as to whether Government does more harm than good when it takes a child from the home to protect it. I can't imagine many viewers went away from that program thinking that the Government did any good.

At his court hearing, my friend Vince asked the judge, "May I speak point blank or should I watch what I say?"

"You may speak point blank," the judge said.

"This system," Vince said, with his voice beginning to shake, " is totally f___d up. I'm all for protecting children from abuse, but my daughter needs guidance. You're tying my hands and threatening me with jail if I go near her. What the f__k is going on?"

"Court adjourned!" the judge said and got up and left.

Court adjourned! Sounds like the pronouncement I would expect from a misguided, out-of-control Government that has given power to a gigantic and misguided, out-of-control welfare bureaucracy. We've let a big gorilla into our home to protect our children. How will we ever get it out?

— *Dave Duffy*

Homesite preparation and foundation

By David Lee

I read how-to-do-it homebuilding books and magazines all the time. They cover most projects you can do on your home from the foundation on up, and some of the centerfolds are really hot. However, actual do-it-yourself site preparation and home foundation building information is a bit sparse. This is because very few of us own the necessary tools—bulldozers, for example, or backhoes, excavators, and the big trucks used to tow them around. If you do own such things, then you would be excavating sites and building foundations all the time to pay for the machines and their upkeep. And that is a big reason why you do not see much encouragement for you having anything to do with foundation building and site improvement as practiced these days.

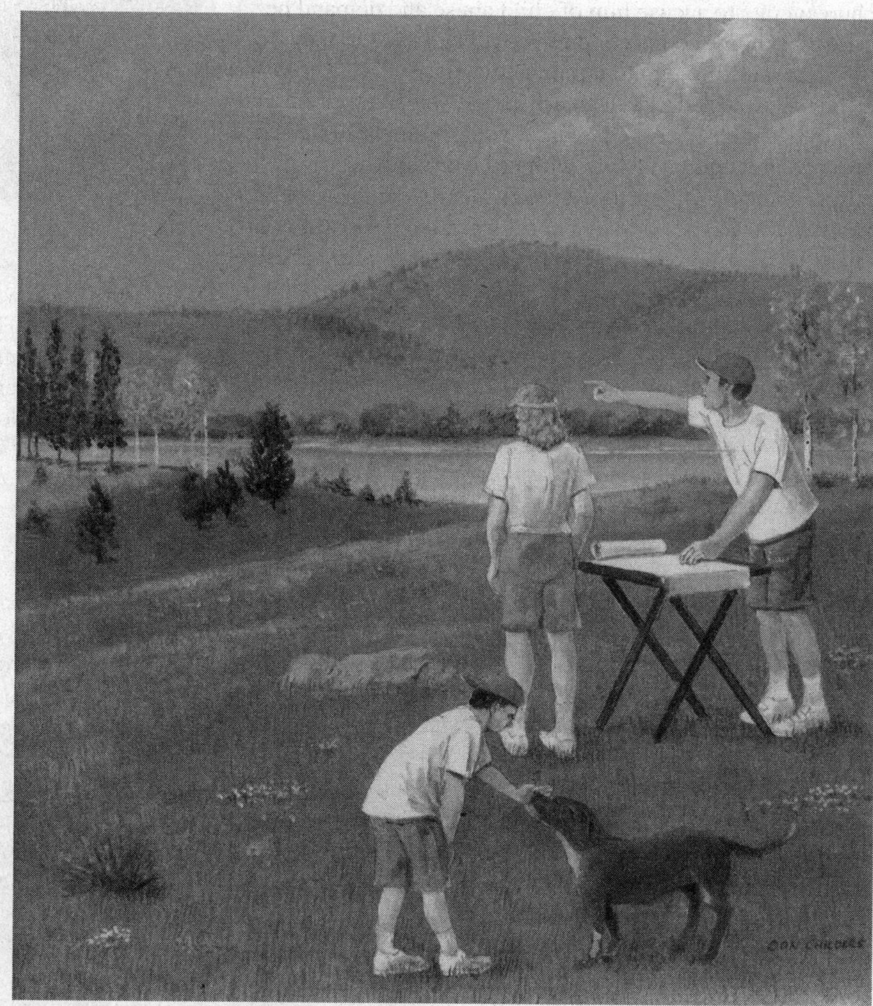

Doing this work has been relegated to professional contractors in nearly all new home construction. When you think about site work and foundations, the big holes needed, the shear tonnage of materials involved, and the skills of the machine operators, masons, carpenters, and laborers needed, it is no wonder such thoughts can generate nightmares.

When planning a home, I want it to be in a beautiful setting. I spend lots of time and considerable money finding the right lot, just as you would. Suppose you find such a place and it has attributes such as special trees, wild flowers, shrubs, mossy rocks, ledges, pleasing contours, or other endearing features you want to preserve.

However, your house lot must have certain land-altering installations. These include a driveway, a well and water line, a septic system, and the home's foundation. These all require disturbing the land. By carefully planning when, how, and by whom all these systems are carried out, you can save a lot of money, time, and angst. You can also minimize the need for the majority of the dinosaur-sized machines used on most building projects and have your home on that beautiful lot just the way you envisioned it in the first place. You can manage this if you take control of the situation and do the work and planning necessary to make it happen the right way.

Turning your precious house lot over to a contractor is like inviting the Green Bay Packers into your living room for a spot of tea right after a big win while they are still suited up and celebrating. It will be exciting, noisy, destructive, and expensive.

All the vegetation, roots, and topsoil in a half-acre, or larger, area are annihilated, bulldozed, and trucked away or worse, smooshed and pushed up into ugly heaps. A huge hole is dug and the dirt piled far enough away so the big machines have stomping room.

The building path

That's awful scary. There is a kinder, gentler way. Let's back up to the time just after you had the real estate closing on your little slice of heaven and consider a different approach. You and your significant other have found the perfect spot for your storybook cottage, and it is time to make the dream home come true. Before visiting your friendly banker for a building loan, go to your favorite hardware store and buy some good limb loppers and work gloves, a five-tine pitch fork and lawn rake, perhaps a nice hatchet, a roll of plastic ribbon in a pretty color, and a chainsaw.

Pack a picnic lunch, go to your land, and spend quality time marking out the driveway, precise house footprint, and (with a cooperative soil engineer you have hired) the septic system location with sticks and ribbons. Try to keep these areas on a confined, continuous path. In other words, the driveway leads right up to the house site and the septic system is right behind the house. Let's call this the Building Path. The distance of the Building Path from the street to the back of the septic system for the house shown in the pictures accompanying this article was about 240 feet.

During the next few days cut away just enough trees and brush to clear the Building Path. The driveway should be about 15 feet wide. The house site should be cleared with about a 10-foot working perimeter around it. If you consulted a soil engineer, he will have given you a map showing where the parts of the septic system go and flagged their locations. You should clear all that plus a 20-foot perimeter around it. Later this will be your back lawn and/or garden. Taking that into consideration, the work will seem more worthwhile.

I am giving you the procedure I used for my last house site because it had all the hardest problems to solve. You may have different conditions. I once did site preparation on an old farm field with clay subsoil and it was so easy that I actually gained weight doing it. All I had to do was mow it with a riding lawn mower a few times

Here is a site that deserves careful preparation to preserve its beauty.

With the slash of a dozer blade, your site could look like this.

Trim limbs, cut wood, pile brush, repeat. This is quite satisfying and healthy work.

The trees have become firewood, the brush has been burned. Stumps will be pulled and trucked away.

while munching cookies. Sometimes you need only ditches dug to connect water and sewer lines and a dab of gravel for the driveway. Lucky you. But read on and commiserate with the rest of us.

Take your time clearing the Building Path on your lot. Cut the trees into firewood (perhaps fence posts and rails) and pile it out of the way where it will season and be ready for use later. Burn, chip, or mulch the limbs and brush. Chainsaw, limb loppers, pitchfork, my old battleaxe, a big plastic lawn rake, gloves, and fire are all I use for this work. Any rocks I can move get piled out of the way for landscaping or stonework later. After awhile you should have a parked-out site with only tree stumps sticking up on your Building Path. Have another picnic lunch to celebrate.

Now it is time to hire your contractor. This fellow is going to install your septic system and do a few other jobs. Most systems require the construction of a gravel path wide enough so big-wheeled vehicles can get to the system location with leach field materials and the concrete septic tank. Doing this properly requires digging out and trucking away the stumps, dirt, and roots along the path the trucks need to pass, then laying down a gravel bed. Clever you have planned it so the stumping, scraping, and graveling along the Building Path provides you with a basic driveway and a partially prepared foundation site at the same time.

When you are getting estimates for your septic system, tell the contractor you want a little extra gravel in the driveway and a little neater scraping at the house site, where you have thoughtfully placed ribbon-decorated stakes marking the locations. It will cost a bit extra but saves great gobs of money later.

You now have another matter to decide. The final covering over the leach field of your new septic system is negotiable. It can be simple mulch, but if you want a lawn out there, you might want reasonably good topsoil put in place. If you want a garden, then a thicker layer of really good soil is the stuff to get. Specify this to your contractor. Again, it costs a little more but saves in the long term and this is the very best time to put it in place.

Another backhoe job is installing a culvert pipe under the driveway next to the town road or street. Most towns require it. Some give you the culvert pipe; most don't. Some driveways don't need one but, if it is necessary, now is the best time to have it put in. Check with the highway department in your area.

If you are a skillful planner, you will have this same contractor dig the ditch for your water line, even though the well comes later. You should have the water line parts there in advance and get all this stuff buried while there is a backhoe on site. More on this project in a little while.

The contractor will likely be happy to do these extra things for you. The time you spent clearing has made his job easier. The extra gravel makes a

Driveway has been scraped and the gravel path to the septic system is in progress.

The driveway has been graveled and the stonework for the foundation is started. The septic system is behind the foundation and ready for service. Not obvious in the picture, but the well has been drilled.

firmer footing for his trucks. Extra leach field cover means more profit for him and he probably has a yacht payment due soon. Stress the fact that you would appreciate his keeping within the boundaries of your Building Path, avoiding the rest of the lot.

Be on site every minute that work is being done, but don't be annoying. Use your time to collect all the stones that turn up and put them on your collection piles for later. Stay safely out of the way. If the contractor needs anything from you, he will ask. Other than that, just say nice things about his backhoe once in awhile.

If the job gets done neatly, it is a good idea to shock the contractor by adding a gratuity to the check. Later on, you will need delivery of a few loads of something or other, and this goodwill gesture will earn you better service. He may know the good and not-so-good reputations of other contracting businesses, too. This is useful gossip to be aware of because the next contractor you need is a well driller.

The well

The well is best drilled right beside the driveway to make access easier for the big well drilling rigs and to avoid messy additional land clearing. Pay attention to local rules about distances between the well and septic system. In our area, the separation must be at least 100 feet. If your local water witch dowser says the well must be in some other location, then...you are on your own.

Here is a good plan for the water line project. Enclose the water line (usually 1-inch black plastic) inside a seamless 4-inch flexible plastic drainpipe. Alongside the water pipe, you will need some 10/4 electric wire for the water pump. The well driller will install the water pump, along with its wires and other equipment, inside the well and make the water line connection, using a special adapter, through the well casing. If you have the water pipe and wiring from the house site already buried almost to the wellhead, it makes the job easier and will save you money, labor, and ditch-digging costs later. The 10/4 wires should be as long as the 4-inch flex-pipe plus 5 feet extra on the wellhead end and a minimum of 10 or more feet extra on the house end. The water pipe should have about 2 feet extra on the wellhead end and 10 feet or more extra on the house end.

The septic system with lots of fill and interesting components being installed. The leach field, covered with the right soils, can be a garden, lawn, or returned to natural growth.

The wellhead end of your 4-inch flexible pipe, along with its contents, should be very near the spot where the well is to be drilled and wrapped in heavy plastic to keep everything clean, dry, and protected during the drilling. The other end should also be wrapped and extend into the house footprint. Leave each end of this assembly exposed a couple of feet for accessibility. The rest of the flex-pipe gets buried right beside the driveway, but not under it. If it ever becomes necessary to dig it up, you will know right where it is. The depth of the ditch will vary according to frost expectations and soil conditions.

Here is another good idea. When I assemble a water line and power wires inside the 4-inch flexible pipe, I add in at least two lengths of 12/3 electric wire in addition to the water pipe and pump wires. These come in handy later for installing lights and an electric outlet in a well house built over the wellhead. A well house protects the wellhead, is a good location for driveway lighting, and provides a place for a convenient exterior electric outlet (see the pictures with this article).

If your waterline cannot be installed deep enough to be safe from freezing, there are remedies you can put in place during site preparation. Some protection is provided by the air space in the 4-inch flex-pipe, but you can add a jacket of foam pipe insulation,

These behemoths filled the driveway but did no damage to the surrounding landscape.

available at home center stores, in a size that fits on your water line.

Thermostatically controlled heaters that are taped against the water line and prevent freezing are available. I attach two of them to the water pipe. One is wired and working, the other is saved for back up. These devices don't last forever and adding an extra one now saves a big dig for replacement on some future day.

Here is one more tip. Include a length of ¼-inch nylon rope in the 4-inch flexible pipe. If, in the future, another wire or something needs to be added to the contents, the rope will let you tow it through.

After the well driller is done and the water pipe and wires are connected from the well pump, up the casing, and all the way to the house footprint, it is time to seal the 4-inch flexible pipe where it meets the well casing. Use builder's foam to prevent any water from getting into the pipe. Shoot foam into the 4-inch pipe a few inches around the pipe and the junction of the water line and well casing. When you are done, a nice big blob of foam should thoroughly encase the whole mess, but with the wires for the well pump and the extra 12/3 wires sticking out. What the heck, use up the whole can. Seal the other end of the 4-inch pipe with foam, too, as insurance against water infiltration.

Now finish filling the area around the wellhead with dirt, letting the extra wires stick up out of the ground, accessible for later. The vulnerable connections at the wellhead are protected from damage, water seepage, and freezing but if, God forbid, it becomes necessary to get to the goodies, the foam is easy to dislodge and replace.

Time to review. You searched out and bought your precious lot, consulted a soils engineer, got a septic system permit, and marked out and diligently hand cleared the driveway, house site, and septic system area except for the stumps. You saved the useable wood and made a bonfire with the brush. You got estimates and hired a contractor to install the septic system, gravel the driveway, add a culvert, and remove the topsoil and roots on your Building Path while you collected all the stones you could lift. The contractor also dug and refilled the water line ditch, burying the 4-inch plastic flex-pipe stuffed with water line, 10/4 electric wires,

Well drillers hard at work. Note large rocks put in place for the foundation by the kindly contractor who did the septic system and driveway work.

Well house over the wellhead contains yard lights controlled by a motion sensor and an outside electric outlet. The waterline is buried along the side of the driveway. This is my style, many others could be built. A well house built tall enough can be the connection location of electric power from the grid.

two lengths of 12/3 electric wire for later, freeze protection of foam insulation or heater lines, and perhaps a rope and some telephone and other wires, while you were at it, which you had all assembled and ready beforehand.

The well driller came the next day (that's a joke), drilled the well, installed the pump with its related equipment, and connected the water line and power wires you had waiting for him. You sealed the wellhead connections with a gob of builder's foam and neatly finished filling the area to ground level. You went over the whole Building Path with the lawn rake, marking out your future lawn and making the driveway edges blend neatly with the natural landscape, and began contemplating the next job, which is: Electric service.

Electricity

When contractors build a home, they need electricity. Some bring generators to the site, but most have a temporary electric service installed until regular service can be connected to the home's permanent meter and service entrance.

A temporary service consists of a pole, service wire, a meter, a breaker panel, and several GFCI (ground fault circuit interrupter) protected electrical outlets. This system costs hundreds of dollars to set up. Later on, it costs hundreds of dollars to remove it and transfer the electric power lines to the home when it is ready. Let's do this a better way, add a couple benefits, save money, save labor, and provide an important property improvement all at the same time with a job you can mostly do yourself.

Remember the well house to be built over the wellhead that I mentioned earlier? If you build that well house, say 12 to 16 feet tall, it could be the electric service connection point to your lot. It eliminates the need for a pole (temporary or permanent) and the very unattractive installation of meter and wires scabbed onto the side of your house, as is unfortunately typical. The well house, which I think we could now call a tower, would have the permanent meter mounted on it, a service disconnect inside for connecting the power to the new home when it is ready, and a couple of electrical outlets available for construction tools. From this tower you could, later on, supply power to future outbuildings. Building this little architectural delight costs less than setting up temporary power and you can do most of it yourself, saving time and work. The main power wires for the house that go from the tower to the new home are buried at the same time as the water line.

Underground power lines are a classy enhancement to any new home, and you will be arranging it in advance. Installing lines underground from the tower to the house is regulated by the power company, as is the proper installation of the meter and service entrance equipment, so I recommend you hire an electrician to guide you during that part of the project.

You may not be able to bury the power lines in the same ditch as the water line, though they could go in a parallel or extra-wide ditch, accommodating the requirements for each project. It would be another job for the contractor who does your other site work for you, but still a good money and time saving thing to do early. Note: Without too much begging, you can get a little book from most power companies with drawings and information about proper installation of electric service equipment on your property. It's a jewel. Acquire one.

Close up of back side of the well house shows "secret door" partly open. Note that foundation leaves the ground accessible for digging up wellhead to water line connections if necessary.

Here is the result of careful lot planning using minimum machinery and maximum owner labor. The lot retains the wooded beauty and most of the beautiful features it had before building. The septic system provides a lawn out back and the driveway is just the right length. The wellhead and other options are in the well house on the left. Trees left in place give welcome shade.

The well house tower should be a strong, solid building with a heavy foundation that is structurally up to the demands put on it by the strain of power wires coming from the street. It should be pleasing to the eye, too. It could look like the one in the pictures or maybe a lighthouse, a minaret, or a street light on steroids. If you need two ditches for the utility hook ups, how about building two towers? One on either side of the driveway as gate towers would be impressive. You can probably think of more options to include in your tower if you put your mind to it. This is a project with lots of practical and aesthetic potential; my favorite kind.

Having the driveway paved is one more possibility that may be available for improving your site. We once bought a lot in a subdivision that was about to have the street paved. We got a price that was about one third the cost of what it would have been to have the contractor come and pave just our driveway. And the pavement blends seamlessly into the street. We bought into the subdivision very early, and this was one of the advantages available as it was being developed. It is something you should be aware of if you want a subdivision lot.

Now that you have brought your lot up to park-like beauty and you are contemplating the next step, stop awhile and have another picnic to celebrate. As you enjoy yourselves, look over what you have accomplished. You have a beautiful home site with a well, driveway, septic system, and electric service all ready for building. You have also improved the value of your lot beyond the amount of money you have invested.

Business opportunity?

What if (my wife cringes when I say this) you sell your lot, take the profit, and do this again? The work was healthy and kind of satisfying, wasn't it? And what you learned would make the next project better and proceed faster.

You could buy a piece of land and create two improved home sites simultaneously. Sell one and keep one, or this could become a business. After doing one project, you are going to learn a great quantity of valuable, practical knowledge. You will have made friendly contacts with the contractors you need. You will know how to do the bureaucracy dance. You have learned how to search for and recognize good land and building lots. You will have experienced real estate closings.

For a husband-and-wife team, this could be a satisfying, interesting business. Between, sometimes during, house-building projects, my wife and I have developed lots and once developed a four-lot subdivision that will bear our names in the county records office in perpetuity. It's not at the Donald Trump level of property development, but we are getting there. Think it over.

This article should give you plenty of ideas for developing a new home site or adding amenities to your present homestead. I've condensed the details to some extent for brevity, but you will learn a lot from the real estate people, contractors, and maybe even the bureaucrats you meet as you gain experience. This project is not for wimps. It is sometimes physically hard and it requires thinking, thoughtful planning, and people management talents, but gives you an opportunity to save money, learn new skills, get a better home site, and maybe even start a business.

If you get to work now, by the next issue you could have your lot prepared for part two of this article: Building your own foundation. Δ

Water development Wells for the homestead

By Roy Martin

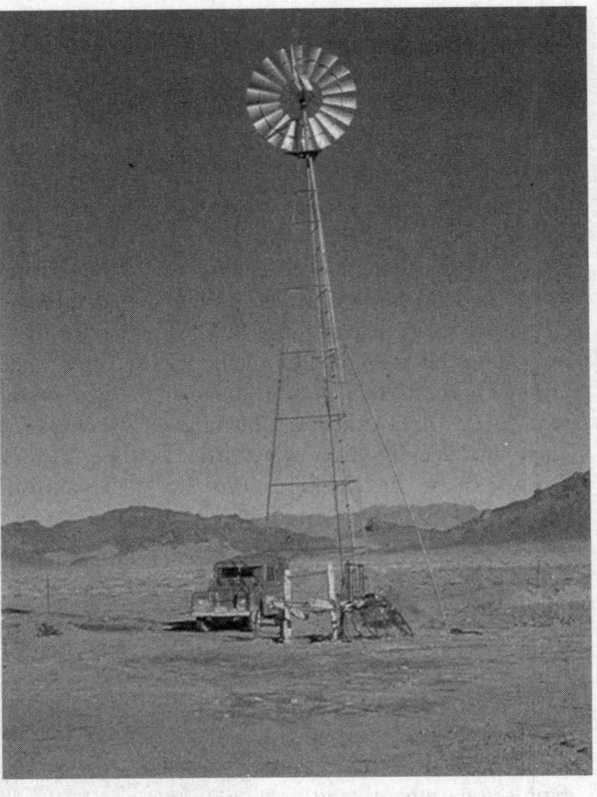

A windmill pumps water from a well in this semi-arid area.

It seems amazing, but virtually all of the inhabitable land on the earth has fresh water under the surface. Even many of the extreme deserts have aquifers containing large amounts of water. Some of the countries in North Africa have tapped aquifers under the Sahara Desert and developed rich agricultural areas and piped fresh water to the cities. The depth of an aquifer under the surface varies greatly, and sometimes there are several layers of aquifers. In the area where I live in the plains of Colorado, there are at least three aquifers where water occurs in layers of sand and gravel separated by layers of shale. The water table (the top surface of the water in the aquifer) from which we draw water for our home lies about 50 feet below the surface and is resting on a layer of shale that is more than 70 feet thick. Below that shale are two or more aquifers that are, at least in some places, hundreds of feet thick and that can produce very large flows of water.

I know of a few places where water is so deep that it is impractical to drill and pump water. In some areas of southwestern Colorado, farms had to haul water for domestic use until a reclamation project dammed a nearby river and constructed canals, taking water to the farms. In other areas, people have to drill wells more than 1,000 feet deep before getting acceptable quantities and quality of water. Areas with these problems are rare, however, and water is usually available within 100 feet or less and often within just a few feet of the surface.

The use of wells to provide water in areas where surface water is not available is as old as the history of man. There are many references in the Bible to the construction and use of wells. Abraham dug wells in Canaan to water his flocks, and his grandson, Jacob, also constructed wells in the area. These allowed access to grazing areas that would not have been useable without wells to access the ground water for domestic livestock.

I greatly prefer to have springs to develop that will provide gravity pressure to my home and garden, but this is not always possible, and in most areas it is necessary to access the groundwater below the surface. This necessitates finding the water and making a hole that will connect the surface and the water table and then providing a way to get the water to the surface so that it can be used.

Selecting a good site for your well

In some areas the water table is quite uniform, and wells can be placed almost anywhere. The selection of the site for the well is only a matter of convenience for access to the home and garden. Many areas, however, have aquifers that are not uniform, and a person must pay close attention to the geology of the area. This is particularly true in areas that are basically granite or basalt. These areas often have solid rock not far below the surface. Water can be found only in valleys and depressions where sands and gravels have been washed over eons of time, and these sands and gravels collect and hold water that runs off of surrounding areas. Wells in these areas will access the water held in these aquifers.

Other likely sites are below the openings of canyons or valleys. Water will run below the surface out of the canyons even if there is no aboveground stream. Wells placed below the mouth of canyons will have a higher chance of success than those that are just along the base of hills or mountains where there is not a canyon mouth. Look carefully at the landscape and decide where water would likely run on the surface, and the chance of finding groundwater is greatly increased.

Probably the most difficult places to find groundwater are those where an arid or semi-arid climate combine with a granite or basalt-based geology. If the homestead has no valleys or depressions where sand and gravel have accumulated to depths such that they form aquifers, the only chance for finding groundwater is to locate cracks in the rock where water collects. Wells in these sites often produce relatively small amounts of water.

Homesteads on sand or gravel alluvial deposits (water-deposited material) or coarse sedimentary rock formations have the best chance of easy access to groundwater. The reason is that these formations are porous, allowing water to flow between the particles. In many areas where these formations are found, wells can be placed almost anywhere, and water will be found.

Dowsing

Any discussion about selecting well sites would not be complete without discussing dowsing or witching for water. This is a method of finding groundwater by holding a forked stick or a metal rod in the hands to locate water by feeling or watching movement of the instrument. People seem to either firmly believe in the effectiveness of dowsing or they completely dismiss it as just foolish folklore. I guess I fall more in the former area than in the latter since I had some wells located by dowsing and they were completely successful. When living in southwestern Colorado, my brother and I were developing our homestead, and we had dug a well by hand and had found water at about 18 feet.

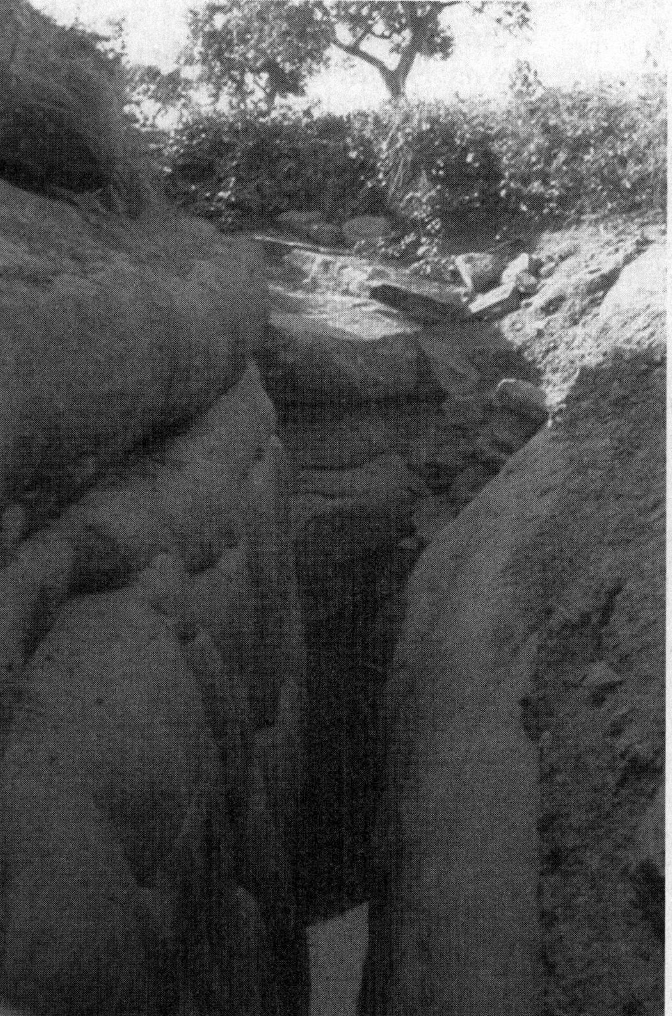

Well dug in the crack in a rocky plateau in Africa

We then learned that a friend of ours claimed that he could dowse for water, so when we were ready for the second well we asked him to locate a site. He took a stick and when it dipped at a particular place, then held a radio antenna from an old car and it wiggled back and forth, he said that the water was less than 15 feet down. By that time we were able to afford a backhoe to dig a hole and we found abundant water at 15 feet.

When our neighbor saw what had happened, he asked if our friend would check out his place. He had a well he had used for more than 40 years that would go dry every winter; he wanted a more reliable well. My friend checked the area around the neighbor's house and found that an underground stream went within 30 feet of the old well. He, too, had his well dug with a backhoe and had reliable and abundant water from that time on.

My friend would never accept payment for his dowsing as he said it was a gift, and he felt that it would not be right to charge for it. My advice would be to find someone who has had good experience in finding producing wells and who does not accept payment for the dowsing.

As to how they do it, some feel that there are electromagnetic waves produced by the underground water and some people are able to sense those signals. I would say that it is certainly in the mind of the dowser, since there are a variety of materials used for the dowsing instrument. Some will use only a green, forked willow stick while others use brass welding rods or car antennas. I think it works, but you can make up your own mind. If you believe in it, try it; if not, just locate your well the best you can from studying the lay of the land.

With the site selected, the next step is to decide the best way to put in the well, or you may have selected the site to meet the requirements of the type of well you plan to construct.

Wells that are commercially drilled

Most people living in the country go to a local well driller to have the well drilled, cased, and the pump installed. This is by far the easiest way to have a well done and is also by far the most expensive. The well driller will be familiar with the local aquifers and will likely know if the place you have selected for your well will have a good chance of producing adequate water. He will also be able to drill the well, install the casing, and put in a submersible pump in a day or two. This has a lot of advantages if you have the money and want the well in and operating quickly and without any fuss. It also means parting with anywhere from a couple thousand to many thousands of dollars.

Modern commercial well drillers use truck-mounted rotary drills that have a collar on the drill head that allows the use of compressed air, water, or a mix of water and bentonite clay to carry the cuttings out of the drilled hole. Drill stem pipe sections are commonly about 20 feet long and are lifted in place by a power winch. Drill bits used depend upon the type of material that has to be penetrated in drilling into the aquifer. They may be just a simple chisel welded to a short piece of pipe to drill through sand and clay to a diamond impregnated roller bit to bite through the hardest rock.

The commercial driller is generally paid by the foot, so there may be a tendency to drill deeper than may be absolutely necessary. If you are paying $20 per foot or more, you probably won't want the driller to go through two or three shallower aquifers to end up in one that is several hundred feet deep. If you just depend upon the driller, you may end up with a very deep well without knowing anything different. Be sure to ask around to see what wells in the area are like. Find out about well depths, where existing wells are drilled, what the water quality is, and who put the wells in. Compare all of these with your site to see what you can expect and how much it will cost. Talk to the driller about stopping at the first reliable source of water instead of going deeper.

Hand-dug wells

Wells that are dug by hand are the real wells! Not that I want to dig any more wells myself, but these were the first wells and they are still important producers of water throughout the world. People see the need for water in a particular place for home, livestock or gardens, they start digging, and sooner or later they usually end up with water. I have seen wells that were dug among the rocks of a rugged plateau in Africa that provided water for the hand irrigation of onions, the main cash crop of the people of the area; and I saw wells in Iran that had ramps dug down in tunnels to the water to allow access to nomadic sheep herds. There are dug wells that reach down more than 250 feet and others that only required digging a few feet below the surface. But, each of these wells provides essential water, and that water was obtained by the labor of shoveling out a hole to reach the water table.

Most hand-dug wells are less than 50 feet deep. Deeper wells become a real problem due to the need for good ventilation and the task of pulling the dirt and rock out from that deep in the ground. When I worked in Iran in the mid-1970s, a very deep, hand-dug well was pointed out to me, and it was said that two men died from poisonous gasses while digging the well. It may have been that they dug into a pocket of methane or carbon dioxide or they may have just depleted the oxygen because of the lack of ventilation. There were some very deep wells in Africa in the southern edge of the Sahara Desert where I watched as the local herders used donkeys and camels to pull buckets made of old tires from the depths of the wells. These were emptied into hollow log watering troughs. I measured the ropes at one well that were more than 80 meters long. That is well over 250 feet down. While I was at one such well, one of the herders dropped his rope through the wooden pulley, and they had to lower a boy down on a bucket to retrieve the lost rope and bucket.

There is a well in Greensburg, Kansas, that is billed as "World's Largest Hand-Dug Well." This well was constructed in the late 1880s and is 109 feet deep and 32 feet in diameter (Greensburg Chamber of Commerce, www.bigwell.org). It may not actually be the world's largest, but it certainly ranks up near the top.

Wells usually require some sort of casing or shoring inside the hole to prevent the sides from caving in.

Construction of hand-dug wells requires just a few simple tools.

An ancient hand-dug well still provides livestock water in the Middle East.

Most hand-dug wells are dug in material that is self-supporting while being dug and then lined with material that will hold the sides and prevent future cave-ins, but I have seen many wells that were never lined. One such well was the one we dug when I was in my early teens. My dad confirmed the location of water by using a posthole auger that he kept extending with pieces of pipe until he brought up dripping-wet sand from 18 feet below the surface. (Since then, I have wondered why he didn't just put a pipe down that hole and use it for the well.) We then dug our way down to the aquifer, and it provided house water and water for irrigating the garden for years. We did have to clean out sand in the bottom of the well every couple of years.

Casing was traditionally done with mortared stone or bricks, but in some cases wood was used. Wood, however, had to be maintained regularly or it would rot away and the well would cave in. I have seen a number of wells that had log cribbing near the surface and then no lining the rest of the way because the surface soil was sandy and loose and the remaining depth was in a more solid material. Casing, when made of brick or stone, was usually started at the bottom after the well was dug as far into the water-bearing formation as possible. The masonry would be only partially cemented so there would be plenty of spaces for infiltration of the water. Then, above the water level, it would be constructed with mortar filling the gaps just as in the construction of any masonry wall.

In very loose soils, especially sands, it is necessary to case the well as it is being dug. This is most easily done using short sections of concrete pipe, at least three feet in diameter. As the dirt is removed from inside a section of pipe that is standing on end, the pipe will sink down the hole, providing a lining for the well. Additional sections of pipe can be added as the well is dug deeper so that the entire depth will be lined by concrete pipe when the digging is finished.

The process of digging the well involves the use of a short-handled shovel (and in hard digging, a pick), a rope and bucket, a tripod, and a pulley. This is really low-tech and can be done by any two people with the persistence to continue the process until water is reached. One person can begin the digging process, but as soon as a depth is reached where it is difficult to throw out the dirt with a shovel, another person is needed to lift it out of the hole with the bucket. The hole needs to be wide enough to allow the digger to bend over to remove soil from the bottom of the hole and to place it in the bucket for

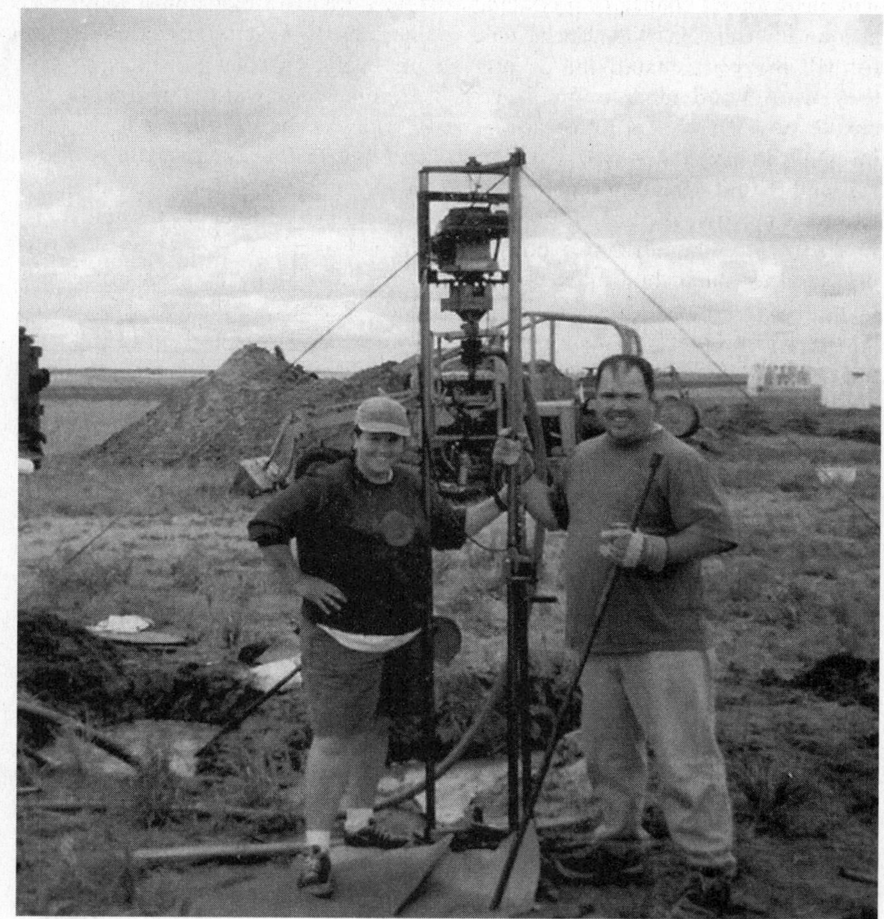

Miniature rotary drilling rig

removal. I have seen wells as narrow as three feet or so and others that must have been six feet in diameter. To me, the wisest choice would be to dig as narrow a well as possible while still being able to work. It takes a lot of effort to remove each bucket of dirt, and the smaller the hole the fewer buckets of dirt. For this same reason, wells are generally round in cross-section since that shape requires the removal of the least amount of dirt for the diameter of the hole. Square, oval, or any other shape would work as well for removing water from the ground, but I see few cases where those shapes would be better than round. Some old wells were square for the simple reason that they used wood planks for casing and it was easier to fasten the planks in a square.

This hand-dug well has a protective wall around it.

When the hole is deep enough to require the use of a bucket to lift out the dirt, a tripod is erected over the hole. This can be constructed of four-inch diameter poles or 4"x 4" boards. These should be long enough so the top of the tripod will be about eight feet high when erected. The ones I have seen have been tied together with rope. A pulley, through which a rope has been threaded, is tied to the top of the tripod, and the tripod is placed over the hole. This allows the person on top of the ground to lower a bucket tied to the end of the rope into the hole where it is filled with dirt. It can then be pulled to the top to empty the material and returned for another load. Another option is a homemade windlass, but I like the tripod and pulley because it is easier to pull the bucket away from the mouth of the well to make a spoils pile.

The well digger should always wear a hardhat while in the hole. A slip by the person operating the rope and pulley may send dirt or rocks down the hole, causing no little discomfort to the one below. I can remember having dirt and gravel rain down on my head many times, and a larger rock falling could have caused some injury. The thing I remember best from being the one digging in the bottom of the well after hitting water was how cold the mud and water was when it slopped from the bucket on its way up out of the hole. It seemed that my brother who was on the rope could not lift the bucket out smoothly enough to prevent it from slopping out some of the water. Well digging is not a clean, pleasant job but it is very satisfying to reach the water and then to be able to pump or dip water from a well of your own making.

When the water table is reached, you will be digging while standing in water. It is desirable to dig on down into the water as far as possible to make sure you have enough water for your needs. If your area has distinct wet and dry seasons, it is best to dig the well during the dry season or plan to dig it deeper if the water table recedes. In some irrigated areas of the West, wells tend to have more water during the summer growing season since the irrigation water from the farms percolates down into the ground, contributing to the ground water and raising the level of the water table.

After you are satisfied that you have dug into the water-bearing formation as far as is practical, it is necessary to line the well to keep the dirt from caving in and to keep foreign objects and small critters out of the water. In one well that my brother and I dug, we used cobbles removed in the well-digging process to build a stone well lining. Below the top of the water table, we left a lot of small holes when we mortared the rocks together so water could flow freely into the well. Above the water table we made a solid wall of rocks and mortar. Bricks, concrete blocks, or pre-cast concrete culvert pipe also make acceptable well lining. I had one friend who even lowered a galvanized culvert pipe into the well to line it. He had drilled holes in the lower end to allow water to percolate into the well. Of course, if the well has not been dug clear to the bottom of the aquifer; that is, it is not resting on a layer of solid rock or clay, a lot of water will enter the well from the bottom, but I think it is best to leave holes for the water to come into the sides of the well to allow it to refill quickly as water is pumped from it.

Sealing the top of the well is also important. Surface runoff can potentially carry all sorts of undesirable pollutants into the well. The lining of the well should extend slightly above the ground surface and a tight cover placed on it. The cover can be made of concrete if it is removable or if it has a manhole in it with a tight cover. Access to the well for cleaning or repair is essential. A heavy plank cover could be used as long as it is well sealed and has a tight fit on the well lining. A plank top would also have to be treated to prevent rot. A rotten well cover is extremely dangerous as someone may fall through and into the well. When I was a boy, we had a well that was unlined and it just had a box-like structure sitting on the ground as a cover. One time the water began to smell bad, and my dad thought it was time to check the well and clean it out. When we cleaned out the bottom of the well and checked the contents of the water, we found a somewhat decayed snake that had somehow wiggled its way through a hole and had fallen into the well. I don't know why it didn't make us sick. We did seal off the top of the well better and I don't remember any problems after that.

Hand-dug wells are not easy to construct and are not suitable in all locations, but in the right place will provide water to the homestead with a minimum of investment.

Drilling wells with miniature rotary drills

There are small rotary drills that operate almost like the large, truck-mounted rigs. One made by Deep Rock Drilling, the Hydra-Drill, uses a small mast that rests on the ground, a vertical shaft engine much like a small lawnmower engine, a coupler that allows a stream of water to be directed down hollow drill stem, and a pump to circulate water into the hole to float out soil and rock cuttings. A similar one, the RockMaster, is made by the Hydra Tek Company. These are very small units with drill stem sections of ¾ inch pipe that are just 5 feet long, compared to commercial drills that have drill stems that are usually 20 feet long.

These miniature rigs are normally rated to drill as deep as 200 feet, although rigs can be ordered for deeper drilling. I have drilled to 170 feet with the regular Hydra-Drill. I used one for a project in Pakistan where I had a local man operating the drill and we were able to drill two wells in sandstone. The biggest problem there was the lack of available spare parts, and when we had problems with the drill engine, we were not able to repair it. My son, daughter, and I drilled several wells in Colorado with one, and our biggest problem was that when drilling in sand, we had problems with the sides of the hole caving in before we could insert the well casing. The small pump that came with the rig wore out after about four wells, and we had to use another pump that we had. Even allowing for the few problems, I would recommend these miniature drilling rigs where it is not practical to use cheaper methods. The most cost-effective way to use these small rigs is to find other people who want to drill their own wells, go together on the purchase, drill the required wells, and then sell the used rig. This spreads out the purchase cost so the cost-per-well is reasonable. The purchase of one of these rigs just to put in one well would likely not be economical.

The Hydra-Drill is easy to assemble, following the instructions. We found that it was much more steady when we stabilized it with three guy wires fastened at the top of the mast and secured to stakes in the ground. You will need to dig two connected pits next to the drilling rig; one to pump water from and the other to settle out the cuttings that float up with the water that circulate through the hole. We found that two to four 55-gallon barrels of water were generally sufficient for one day's drilling. Water is placed in the pump hole and the pump outlet connected to the water collar on the drill. As the drill stem rotates, the collar allows water to enter the drill stem as the stem rotates. The water goes down the drill stem, out through the drill bit, and back up the hole outside of the drill stem to the surface. A small channel will need to be dug from the top of the drill hole to the settling pit. Most of the cuttings from the hole will settle out, and the water will run through a connecting channel into the pump water pit to be re-circulated through the system.

Water will carry the cuttings to the surface, and the walls of the hole will remain intact long enough to allow the insertion of the well casing in most soils. In very sandy soils, however, the sides of the hole will collapse during drilling and may even trap the drill bit and drill stem, making it difficult or even impossible to remove from the hole. To prevent this problem, it is necessary to add bentonite clay, called drilling mud, to the water. This can be purchased from drilling suppliers. In very sandy soil, such as on my place in the high plains of Colorado, the dry, powdered clay needs to be added to the circulation water until it is soupy. I made the mixture about the thickness of tomato soup. The clay/water mixture does two things: It holds the walls of the hole during drilling because it is thicker and provides support to keep the walls from caving it; and it also penetrates into the walls of the hole making a light cementing action so the well casing can be inserted after the hole is drilled and the circulation water is gone.

Simple drill bits are fastened to the first section of drill stem used to begin drilling the hole. The bit used in drilling through soil is a small piece of hard steel plate welded across the bottom of a pipe coupling, making a rotating spade that loosens the soil and allows it to be washed to the surface by the circulating water. A similar bit blade is used for clay, although the piece of steel plate is cut to divide the end in two and each side is bent in the direction of rotation. It is sharpened so it makes a knife action to cut into the clay and to shave it off, again letting the pieces of clay to be washed to the surface. Cutting through rock can be accomplished by adding carbide granules to the soil bit, providing hard, sharp pieces that will grind through the rock. The carbide can be purchased from the drilling rig company. Core samples may also be taken from rock by adding the carbide to a pipe coupler without any cross piece attached to it. It will cut a circular hole in the rock, leaving the core to be lifted up with the bit.

Carbide is added to the drill bits by heating the bit to a glowing red and dipping it into the carbide granules. I used my acetylene cutting torch, but the bits could also be heated in a forge or even in a very hot fire or with a good propane torch.

One challenge in using a rotary drill that uses circulating water to carry the cutting out of the well is determining when the water table is reached. Usually, when an aquifer is intercepted by the drilling, the circulation water will either be lost down the hole or much less will come up than is being pumped down the drill hole so the level of water in the pump pit rapidly decreases. This loss of circulation water is caused because it flows into the aquifer since that formation allows water to flow through its gravel or coarse sand. Another sign is the water becoming less muddy or is much colder than the water being pumped down the hole because water from the aquifer comes up with the circulation water.

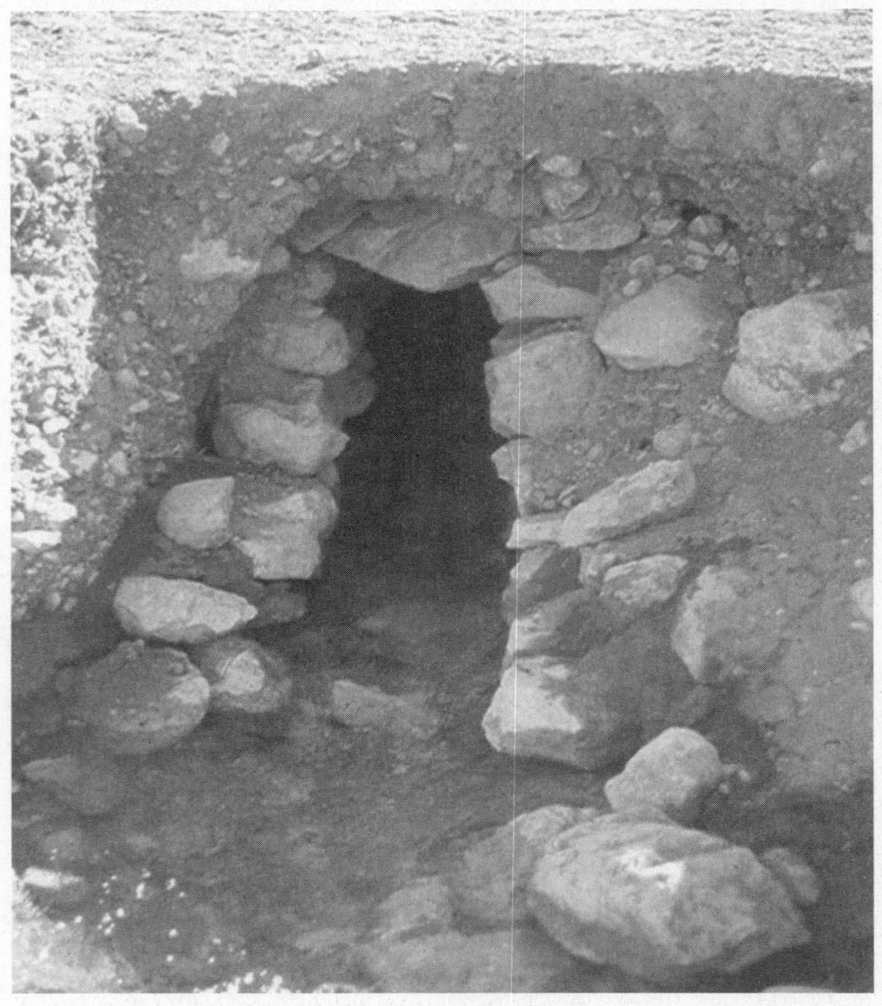

Water flowing from the mouth of a qanat tunnel.

A small pilot hole is normally drilled with the miniature rotary drilling rig. After the aquifer is found and the hole drilled well into it, the hole has to be enlarged to accommodate a drill casing and either a submersible pump or a pump cylinder. Progressively larger drill bits may be drilled down the pilot hole to accomplish this. When I drilled in our very sandy soil, I found by trial and error that we had fewer problems with caving of the walls by welding a pilot hole bit to the bottom of a six-inch bit that is normally used for enlarging the hole after drilling a pilot hole. Since our soil is nearly pure sand only a few feet below the surface, we had no problem loosening the soil. Our biggest problem was the caving walls. We overcame that problem by using drilling mud and by making just one pass to minimize disturbance of the walls.

After the hole is drilled into an aquifer, it is necessary to insert a well screen. This is a piece of well casing with thin slits cut in it through which water can pass but which screens out sand and gravel. The best casing is four-inch PVC pipe, glued together as it is lowered into the hole. In some areas, local regulations require that top 20 or so feet of the casing be steel pipe.

Miniature rotary drilling rigs provide a very effective and efficient way to drill moderately deep wells if you need a few wells drilled. The cost of the drilling rig is about the same or slightly more than the cost of having a well commercially drilled in most areas, so it is probably not worth your while to purchase one unless you need more than one or two wells or if you can share the cost among others who want to drill their own wells.

Driven point wells

This is the easiest way to get a well, but is limited to only certain locations. The "well point," "driven point," or "sand point" is a section of heavy pipe (of various sizes but is commonly two or three inches in diameter) to which is fastened a section of well screen and a point. It is driven into the ground where there is a shallow water table and suitable soil. It will not work in large gravel or rock or in areas where the soil is very hard.

The well point has a driving cap that will protect the threads and provide a surface to take the impacts that drive the point into the ground. As the point is driven down, additional sections of pipe are added and the driving cap placed on the added section. This can be continued until the point is driven well into the aquifer. This essentially produces a cased well in one easy step.

Driving can be done with a sledgehammer, but a platform is required from which to begin driving as each section of pipe is added. I use 5-foot sections of pipe. The tailgate of a pickup will usually work as a driving platform. As the pipe is driven down a ways, it can be driven on down to the ground surface while standing on the ground. A person can also make a simple pile driver using a heavy weight suspended with a rope and pulley using a tripod. The weight can be lifted by the rope and pulley and then released to pound in the well point. A fishing weight on the end of a string can be used to determine the depth of water in the well as the point is driven into the water table.

If the water table is less than about 20 feet down, the casing can also serve as the pipe from which the water is pumped. A hand pump or electric pump may be plumbed directly on top of the pipe that has been driven into the ground with the well point. At deeper than about 20 feet, it will be necessary to have a well point and pipe that is large enough to allow the insertion of a submersible pump, a jet pump Venturi, or a pump cylinder down below the water table.

An aerial view of a qanat in Iran.

Cable/percussion wells

Most of the commercial drilling rigs around when I was a kid were the cable/percussion type. This involved the use of a truck-mounted power winch, a tower or tripod from which a pulley was suspended, and a heavy weight with a tube of the desired diameter of the well. The cable was threaded through the pulley and the weighted bit fastened to the end of the cable. It was essentially a pile driver with no piling. The winch would pull the cable up to the pulley and release it, allowing it to fall to the earth. A small amount of water would be poured down the hole so the cuttings from the weighted bits would make a mud slurry. After several drops of the bit, a heavy tube would replace the bit on the cable and it would be lowered into the hole. It would be filled with the mud, lifted to the surface, emptied, and the process begun again. This would be repeated until the hole was as deep as desired and then the well casing was inserted. This process took much longer than the modern rotary drill rigs.

There are now small percussion drilling rigs that work much the same as the old truck-mounted rigs. A small power-winch rig constructed by the Consallen company in the U.K. is designed for use in developing countries where a trained crew can use it to drill wells in numerous villages. It is considered to be intermediate technology, between dug wells or simpler hand-operated rigs, and the large commercial rigs used mostly in the more developed countries.

A small, hand-operated percussion rig has been designed by Well Spring Africa (www.wellspringafrica.org) to be constructed with simple materials and to be used by villagers in the lesser-developed world. They indicated a cost of about $200 to construct their drilling rig. A CD with simple construction directions and a video of this machine being used is available from this nonprofit organization for

$5, plus shipping. I think this might be a machine that would be useful for homesteaders wanting to drill their own wells, although I have not yet tried the system.

An advantage of all percussion drilling is that there is no mistaking when the water table is reached. Since little drilling water is used, it is easy to determine when drilling has intercepted the water table.

Horizontal wells

Horizontal wells are basically man-made springs in which an aquifer that is located on a hill or slope is intercepted by drilling horizontally into it. This allows the water to flow from the ground by gravity.

The ancient Persians developed a primitive but effective type of horizontal well called a qanat. The interior of Iran (Persia) is arid and semi-arid plateau country consisting of basins and mountain ranges similar to the topography of Nevada. The mountains collect rain and snow that recharge aquifers that are near enough to the ground surface to be reached by hand-dug wells. The qanat diggers would dig down to the aquifer up slope from the area where the water would be used. This initial shaft is referred to as the "mother well." After water was reached, the diggers would begin a tunnel toward the village area where the water would be used for irrigation and domestic purposes. Periodically, additional vertical shafts would be dug to remove the spoils from the horizontal tunnel and to provide ventilation for the diggers. If sandy or gravelly areas were intercepted where the water would be lost by percolation, an oval sleeve made of sections of baked clay would be inserted to keep the water flowing through the tunnel. Thousands of these qanats still exist in Iran and throughout the Middle East and North Africa, providing abundant quantities of flowing water to villages and towns. I am not suggesting this as a realistic solution to the modern homesteader, however. Many qanats are miles in length and some took families of qanat diggers multiple generations to complete.

Modern horizontal wells are constructed with drilling rigs that allow drilling horizontally to intercept an aquifer. They were originally designed to de-water road cuts to help prevent landslides caused by excess water in the formations through which a road is being constructed. The principle has been adapted to obtain water for livestock and human use.

After reaching water with horizontal drilling, concrete mix slurry is pumped into the casing/drill stem to seal the pipe into place. A smaller drill is inserted into the casing and the concrete is pierced, allowing water to flow from the pipe. A valve is attached to the pipe to control flow, and one has a well that is producing water without a pump. The water can then be piped down slope to the point of use.

In the high plateau country of the southwestern United States, there are areas where sandstone aquifers are exposed, resulting in walls of "weeping sandstone." I was able to hand-drill a horizontal well into one of these sandstone walls in northern Arizona, using a hammer and hand drill. By the time I was into the wall about five or six feet, I had a flow from the hole of about one gallon per minute. A pipe was then inserted into the hole to provide a flow of water that could be stored in a tank for home, livestock, or garden use.

The most common sites for horizontal wells are seeps or places where vegetation and rock formations indicated subterranean moisture coming from an aquifer near the surface. Deep Rock Drilling Company makes a horizontal well adapter for their Hydra-Drill. There are also companies that make larger horizontal drill rigs. Horizontal wells, where suitable sites are available, can provide sealed, sanitary flows of water that require no pumping to the home or other sites where water is required.

Pumps

All wells, except horizontal wells, require a means to bring the water to the surface where it may be used. In olden times, and in many more primitive societies today, ropes and buckets were used to lift water. Today many types of pumps are available to aid in bringing water from the water table to the surface. In general, these can be divided into two classes: Piston-type pumps and centrifugal or turbine-type pumps.

Piston pumps use a cylinder with an enclosed piston and valves to enable a positive displacement of water, pulling water into the piston through a valve and pushing it out through another valve (one valve often located in the piston itself). The cylinder may be located in the water or above the water level. Centrifugal pumps have a rapidly rotating wheel with fins (an impeller) that "flings" the water outward, where it goes through an opening leading to a pipe. This outward movement of water creates a partial vacuum that then "pulls" water in through an opening at the center of the wheel. A turbine pump (such as most submersible electric pumps) consists of a series of wheels that spin very rapidly, creating enough pressure to push the water through hundreds of feet of pipe to the surface. "Jet" pumps are centrifugal pumps that use the pressure of the water from the pump, directing it through a Venturi tube (the jet) that in turn creates a partial vacuum, drawing water from the well.

Piston pumps are the best type for hand operation since there is positive displacement of the water and great speed is not required to create the pressure needed for lifting water. A shallow-well hand pump may be a simple, old-fashioned, pitcher pump that has the cylinder and piston attached to the handle in the pump itself or a deep-well pump that has the cylinder and piston below or just above the water table attached to the handle by a long rod that fits inside of the supply pipe that brings the water from the pump cylinder to the ground surface.

Centrifugal and turbine pumps are only useful if you have a dependable supply of electricity or a fuel operated engine since high speed rotation is required to make these pumps work. Submersible electric pumps can be operated by power from the grid, solar power, or fuel-powered generators. They can be purchased for use with 120 volt AC, 240 volt AC, or 12 and 24 DC voltages.

I like the convenience of a submersible pump system since it is not subject to freezing, is in the water so there is no priming problem, and it can be set up with either a pressure tank or a float-valve storage tank system. Having said that, I also have a hand pump that requires only muscle-power and is something that I can easily repair when it breaks down. It is always there on standby in case something happens.

Shallow-well versus deep-well pumps: To differentiate between these two broad classifications of pumps, one needs to understand the principle behind lifting water with a pump. Gravity is the actual force behind it all. The atmosphere around and above us has weight, being attracted by gravity. The height of the atmosphere above us determines the amount of pressure exerted by the atmosphere. At sea level there is the maximum amount of atmosphere (with the exception of a few below-sea level places) above the earth and the greatest pressure, while high in the mountains there is less atmosphere and less atmospheric pressure. When a partial vacuum is created (such as that created in the cylinder or impeller chamber) in a pump, atmospheric pressure pushes water into the intake and through the pump.

Because there is a limit to the amount of water the atmospheric pressure can push (or, as we usually think of it, the amount the pump can suck), the pump can be only a limited distance above the level of the water table. Theoretically, a pump placed at the ground surface should be able to lift the water from more than 30 feet deep. As a practical rule-of-thumb, you can count on a lift of less than 25 feet because of loss of efficiency and because of elevations above sea level. A hand pitcher pump, then, can be used if the water is within about 20 feet or so of the ground surface. A water table deeper than that will require a "deep-well" piston pump. The cylinder from this pump will be placed below the water surface and will be activated through a rod connected to the pump handle.

Well sanitation

Groundwater is generally free of disease organisms and pollutants because of the filtering effect of the soil. It is important, however, to keep the water in the aquifer clean. When a well is constructed, a connection is made between the ground surface and the aquifer through which pollutants can enter. In many parts of the world, well pollution is the cause of a majority of disease problems. When there is no closure at the top of the well and dirty buckets and ropes are thrown down into the water, there is a very great chance for the water to become polluted.

The first step in well sanitation is protecting the water from exposure to pollution. All wells should have a sealed cover, and the area around the well should slope away in all directions so rainwater will run away from the well. Hand-dug wells can have a concrete cap poured that will fit tightly when placed over the mouth of the well, or a cap with a manhole in it may be poured in place, sealing the well. Drilled wells should have slurry of Portland cement (regular cement powder without sand or gravel) poured around the top 15 feet or so of the casing to seal around the casing. This will keep surface runoff from going down the hole outside the casing.

After digging or drilling a well and after casing it, plain chlorine bleach (hypochlorite solution without perfume) should be dumped in the well to kill microorganisms that got in during the construction process. Then water should be pumped until there is no chlorine smell to the water. Collect a quart jar or bottle of the water and have it tested to make sure it is free of disease-causing bacteria. In areas of intensive agriculture, well water should also be tested for nitrates. Near mining or industry, have it tested for other pollutants known to be associated with the particular operations.

After initial sanitizing, wells usually need no further water treatment. I use a particulate filter on my system because fine sand seems to always work its way into the water pipes. In a few areas there is so much dissolved mineral in the ground water that well water needs to have filters especially designed to remove things such as iron and sulfur.

Legal issues

Finally, one must consider legal issues surrounding construction and use of wells. Since regulations vary from state to state, I will not try to cover all of the various regulations. In some states, construction and use of wells for use in the home is exempt from regulations. Oregon, for example, considers such wells exempt, but requires well permits for irrigation. Colorado, on the other hand, requires permits for any well and charges $600 just for the permit to construct a well. Check with local regulations to make sure that you comply with the law. Δ

Starting Over part eleven

By Jackie Clay

I'm looking out the upstairs bedroom window where my desk is. The green is SO intense. The poplar trees are in full leaf now and their bright, shiny green contrasts with the darker green of the pine and balsam, dancing with the soft blue green of the white spruce. The beaver ponds are dark, reflecting the woods around them. Somewhere to the west, a loon cries its weird laugh as it flies to one of the dozens of lakes in the area. Welcome, summer in the north woods.

I needed an evening like tonight. Last week we lost Dad, 94, who lived at home with us. After a long bout with recurrent pneumonia and being in the hospital for two weeks, he just stopped breathing. Just three weeks ago, he'd been laughing and enjoying the day as my son, Bill, came up bringing a battery-powered golf cart, giving Mom and Dad rides all around the homestead. Dad had a hard time walking with a walker and Mom is in a wheelchair, so neither of them get around outside as much as they'd like. Both enjoyed their rides very much. I try to remember that day, and many, many in the past that we shared. But, it's hard, especially after losing my husband of 14 years, Bob, just a year and a half ago.

The garden

In the middle of May, we finally got the garden worked up and most of the serious rocks and roots picked out. So, we began to put in the garden. I laugh when people tell me they planted their garden "yesterday." It takes me weeks.

First to go in are the cold-weather crops. These are crops that not only survive a freeze or frost, but seem to like this kind of weather. Because my pantry has gotten too low for my liking, I wanted a large-enough garden so I could seriously restock it this summer and fall. But, because it's a new garden, carved out of a patch of small trees and heavy brush, I couldn't make it as large as I would have liked this spring. It's about 50'x75', with room to enlarge it (with lots of work) to double that size in the future. But, this year's garden is still much smaller than I really need to grow everything I want to. Therefore, I had to be creative in laying out things.

First to go in were the onions and carrots. The onions I planted in a three-foot-wide bed, placing the

Work on half the roof is half finished.
Note roof brackets and planks for ease of working and safety.

onion sets three inches apart all ways. In the same space that I could have planted 50 sets in a single row, I planted 200 sets. On the end of the onion bed went the carrots. But, like the onions, I needed more carrots than one row would allow…and all I had room for was that one row. So I planted a 20-foot row, placing a light planting of radishes in the row to mark it and also make it a double row; two crops grown in one row. Then, I moved over four inches and planted another row of carrots, giving me two rows in a little more space than one row took. (Carrots also do well in a wide-bed planting, but our soil is just too rough yet. In a year or two, I'll plant even more carrots in a smaller space, using a well-worked wide bed.)

After the carrots and onions were in, I planted two 40-foot rows of Yukon Gold potatoes, then a 20-foot row of a potato my grandfather grew in the Gallatin Valley of Montana, Bliss Triumph. This is a solid, white-meat red potato that is very good for all uses and stores well into the spring. Another 20 feet of row went into Ozette, a fingerling potato grown by Native Americans in the northwest. I grew it by accident, back when we lived on the farm in Sturgeon Lake, Minnesota, and I'll always remember how much we loved its taste and unique texture; almost waxy.

Between the Yukon Gold and other potatoes, I left a spot for a row of bush beans. I was planning on planting a row of Provider bush beans and want to save seed for next year. Beans should have 20 feet or more between varieties to avoid cross-pollination when you save seed. That spot was perfect.

But, it was too early to plant beans; we were expecting at least a couple of frosts before the weather settled to safer spring-like weather. Instead, I planted squash, pumpkin, melons, watermelon, and cucumber seeds in Styrofoam cups in the greenhouse. I can get a big jump on these crops by starting plants inside and transplanting them when the soil warms up. Not only do I gain a month of growing season for these longer-season crops, but the plants can be gently set out in warm weather, and they take off like shooting stars. I plant these only four or five weeks ahead of the time I want to set them out. If the vines get too large, the plants never seem to do well in the garden.

I also planted cabbage, broccoli, and cauliflower plants that we had grown in the new greenhouse.

The tomatoes are ready to leave the greenhouse.

Cukes, melons, and squash pop up; starting inside gives me a full extra month of growing season.

And, I set out 34 tomato and 22 pepper plants, a dozen at a time. Wait! Too early to plant beans, but I'm setting out tomatoes and peppers? Hah! I planted them in my gardening partners, Wall'o Waters. I had experienced 18° F weather for several nights, with a foot of new snow, back in Montana, and knew for a fact that not only do these little plastic tipis protect the plants, but actually make them thrive and grow quickly into stocky, well-rooted plants.

So my son, David, and I took turns filling the cells of the Wall'o Waters with water. (It is a little hard on your back after a few.) We would set the plant in deeply, then place a five-gallon bucket over it, upside-down. Then the Wall'o Water would go on. One of us sat on another upside-down bucket and held each cell open to receive the garden hose and the other would stand and place the running hose into each cell. This way, the tomatoes went in quite quickly. (All except the night that David was away. I turned on the weather radio just before dark and was shocked to hear the "F" word: Frost warning! And I had plant-

End of week one: All tomatoes and peppers are planted.

ed a dozen tomatoes and a dozen peppers without the Wall'o Waters, figuring on doing it in the morning when I had help.)

I grabbed a flashlight, ran out and turned on garden hoses, then started the generator, switched on the pump, and ran down to the garden. I filled six Wall'o Waters before my back started screaming. But, the moon had come out full and cold into a starry, clear sky. There was a definite chill in the air; frost was sure to come. I couldn't stop. So I squirmed around, filled plastic, got wet, cold, and miserable, but kept filling Walls. Finally there were only two plants left uncovered. I just couldn't bear to do another one, so I set the two buckets upside-down over each plant, figuring that would surely protect them.

I turned off the water and went in the house, shivering, to a hot bath.

Week three: Look at these babies grow.

In the morning, there was not only frost on everything, but ice a half an inch thick on the water tub for the goat pen. Ice!

When I later checked the garden, all the plants in the Wall'o Waters were fine and dandy. But, the two under the buckets were black and dead as a doornail.

Luckily, I had dozens of plants left in the greenhouse, so I pulled them up and replanted them, along with more the next day. (One of those plants was a Silvery Fir Tree tomato, and it started growing from the root, right in the edge of the onion bed, where I threw it. Now, five weeks later, it's nearly as tall as the plant I replaced it with. I don't have the heart to kill it, so it's growing with the onions).

By the time we got all the tomatoes and peppers planted, it was time to seed in the beans and corn. I planted seven fairly short (15') rows of sweet corn, each with 10 Tom Thumb popcorn seeds at the north end of the row, making two adjacent blocks of corn. Corn grows best in blocks of rows, instead of one or two long rows. This ensures complete pollination. If the ears are not pollinated well, they do not fill out to the tip or else fill out poorly all along the ear.

The reason that I can grow popcorn and sweet corn in the same garden, right next to each other, is that the popcorn is an 85-day corn and the sweet corn is a 62-day corn. They will pollinate at different times, therefore ensuring that they don't cross. This crossing would make impure seed and might affect the taste of the sweet corn.

Corn requires a great deal of space between varieties when you are saving seed, and some types of sweet corn require isolation for the best taste. It is generally accepted that you need at least 200 feet between types of corn to keep relatively pure seed; a mile for truly pure seed.

If I'm in a hurry to get the corn to sprout, I'll soak it overnight in warm

Eek, frost warning! Everything tender got covered—and saved.

Mom and Bill enjoy the garden.

water, then plant it the next morning. This year, I was afraid of another frost, so I just planted it in the warm soil; we were having daytime temperatures in the 70s, so I knew it would come up well without soaking. (Never plant corn in cool soil. Let the soil warm up, even if it means waiting a week or more. Most corn seed does not germinate well in cold soil and will just sit there and rot.)

After the corn, I planted my bush green and yellow wax beans, then my three choices of pole beans for this year: Cherokee Trail of Tears; Brejo; and Chinese Red Noodle bean. I did not put the wire up for them to climb on yet. I prefer to do this just before the beans begin to climb so I can place it well.

By the time the beans were up, I figured we were about done with frost, so I pulled the Wall'o Waters off the first row of tomatoes. The tomatoes were already popping a foot out of the top. So, I pulled the protectors off carefully and staked the tomatoes. I will admit that when you first pull the Wall'o Waters off the plants, they look terrible; all long and floppy. But, I've learned that they have put down excellent roots, and with about 10 days of being staked, they look dramatically better.

I also planted a row of cukes, assorted squash, pumpkin, melon, and watermelon plants. The daytime temperatures were in the high 80s and with water, the garden was booming.

But, that afternoon I noticed that the clouds were clearing off and the temperature was falling. No, no way! But I turned on the weather radio. It began with a frost warning. Oh crap.

Screaming for David, I headed for the garden, carrying all the tarps I could hold. He madly jumped on his four- wheeler and dashed for the mobile home, where we had another stash of tarps. Luckily, our friend Tom had pulled the huge tarp off of half of the house roof and begun to finish it so we had that tarp as well. For an hour, David, Tom, and I covered plants, being very careful not to mash them down. It looked like a war zone. But, when the moon came up into a clear-as-a-bell sky, all but a short bit of one bush bean row was covered.

"Yeah, right," I grumped. "All that, and it probably won't freeze."

But, it did. If we hadn't covered the garden, it would have frozen. The only thing we lost was that piece of uncovered bean row. And that was quickly replanted. You really need to pay attention to the weather here in the northland.

We removed the tarps and laid them all around the edges of the garden, just in case another freeze popped up. In addition, they would act as a deer barrier to help keep the pests out of the garden until we could take the time to get it fenced.

I spent time every day staking the tomatoes. The strongest, tallest stakes are on the indeterminate (vining) tomatoes. These continue to grow and grow, setting fruit until frost. But, I also stake my determinate tomatoes. These are shorter growing, stop growing, and set fruit. I stake them for protection against strong wind and breaking off when they are heavy with fruit.

To stake tomatoes, simply drive in a sharpened stake near the plant. I use everything from the 1"x1" stickers that held our sawmill lumber apart in the stacks, letting them air dry, to pipe and tomato cages from the dump. With soft yarn, strips of cloth, or anything that will not cut into the vines, I tie the plant to the stake. Usually, I begin tying at about a foot or so up the plant, and as the plant grows, I tie the main branches to the stake.

I found several part rolls of concrete reinforcing wire at the dump and brought it home to make tomato cages. This works very well, and the wide wire squares are easy to pick through. I just haven't had the time to make 'em yet. Oh well, maybe next year. It doesn't pay to get nuts about such things.

To make these cages, I unroll enough wire to make a cage about two feet in diameter. Then, with bolt cutters or wire cutters, I cut off the wire, leaving long wires on my new cage. I roll the wire into a circle and use the wire ends to bend back, fastening the cage together securely. After this is done, I snip off the bottom wire, leaving all those sharp wires pointing downward. Then I go back and cut off three, leave one, cut off three, leave one, all around the circle. This leaves me with several sharp wires to push into the soil, holding the new tomato cage in place. This cage is set down over a lightly staked young plant. Then, as it grows, I reach my hand through the wire, guiding the growing vines out through the wire here and there.

Making tomato cages is a great winter project. I hope to use my toasty basement to manufacture many cages this year. (Last year I forgot to get the wire in, and it got buried in the deep snow. Now, *where* is that wire?) In the fall here in Minnesota, you'd better make sure all your tools are picked

David and Tom tearing off the silver tarp on the house roof

up or you won't see them until April. Snow sometimes comes early and stays late.

The house gets a roof

Well, half a roof, anyway.

Because our new log house is a pay-as-you-go building, I can afford to do only one project at a time. (You'll remember we spent last winter with no insulation in the roof and only two large construction-grade tarps on it, in place of roofing.) This did work very well and we were more than satisfied with the results. David's and my bedrooms are upstairs, and I'll admit that we had frost on the rafters and every nail head of the gable-end log siding when it was cold. Some nights it was cool in the bedrooms, but I can truthfully say I was never cold in bed; better than the place where we lived in New Mexico.

But, knowing that the tarps were not going to work as a long-term fix, I began saving money early in the year. Not trusting myself, I cashed my small income tax return check and handed it to Tom, in advance for the roofing job, then did the same with two more checks. Finally the weather was nice, and half of the house roof was paid for in advance. I like that; no worrying about paying for it later. (Sort of a reverse credit card purchase.)

So, one fine afternoon, Tom showed up with his huge red Ford truck, loaded down with scaffolding. And he began setting it up. I'm such a chicken about heights, I was glad he had strong planks to walk back and forth on the whole length of the house.

In the morning, the dogs started barking, and David and I stepped outside. A big truck was coming. Our roof was arriving. Sure, it was piles of lumber, Typar, boxes, and shingles, but it was our roof. How exciting! And, it was going to be on before any serious rain came.

The following morning, Tom arrived in a cloud of dust and rapidly unloaded tools, safety harness, and rope for David, and our new roof was underway. Because I wanted the log rafters and beautiful knotty pine tongue-and-groove 2"x6" roof boards to show in the upstairs bedrooms, the insulation had to go outside, on top of the roof. And because we live in a climate that is pretty cold in the winter, Tom (a roofing specialist by trade as well as a fantastic cabinet maker) opted for a cold roof. This type of roof keeps the warmth in the house in the winter, yet lets cold air vent on top of the insulation, keeping condensation outdoors and not beading on the wood.

I was not familiar with this type of roof construction, so it was interesting to learn the whys and wherefores. Basically, this is how it went:

First David was fitted into a safety harness and roped to a fitting fastened to a log rafter. Then, he and Tom began tearing off the 1"x4" strips that held down our huge silver roof tarp.

Roof framed in

The day was warm, and that plastic tarp was slippery. Tom installed brackets and planks for ease of working, but they still had to be careful, especially at the edges of the roof, where it dropped more than 25 feet.

After the tarp was down and folded up, Tom cut 2"x6"s to run from eave to the ridge peak, doubling them on the outside (leaving a small space between). Then, another 2"x6" was spiked on parallel to those, over two feet. This space was left uninsulated to keep the cold overhang cold and allow air to flow through it. Then, another 2"x6" was spiked horizontally from one vertical to the one on the opposite end of the house. This was to support the four inches of extruded foam insulation. Tom hauled out his hole saw and drilled a hole at either end in the vertical 2"x6" to let the cold air from the uninsulated roof over the overhang circulate into the spaces above the insulation. Then, 2"x6" blocks were cut from scrap lumber to support the horizontal 2"x6" firmly.

The stiff, light extruded foam board then went on. Quite a trick in the wind. I thought David was going to learn parasailing that day. After that was in place, 2"x4"s were laid, 16" on center, from the blocks at the eaves to the peak. These would hold the roof sheathing off the insulation board, allowing cool air to circulate over it, carrying off moisture.

On top of these, they nailed the OSB sheathing using long ringed pole barn nails, which went down through the OSB, the 2"x4"s, and the four inches of insulation board, anchoring firmly in the log rafters or 2"x6" roof boards.

Tom and David stretched a sheet of ice shield across the roof and stapled it down tightly. This is to protect the roof in case of ice dams, which can form on the eaves or valleys of a house from melting water trickling down to where it is colder and freezing. Subsequent melting can be forced uphill, under the shingles. The chances of this happening on our cold roof are very small, but we used the ice guard, just to be sure.

David and Tom sheathing roof. (Notice shirt stuffed in septic vent. Peeuee!)

Once the first sheet was in place, the starting row of shingles was nailed in place. This is a narrow band of shingle material, cut with adhesive on both top and bottom side to ensure a tight seal. It went all along the bottom of the roof and along both ends.

Then our beautiful antique green shingles started going on. How exciting. (Of course it was even better because we had gotten a great deal on "last year's" shingles.) But, I really did like the color, and I liked it even better on *our* house.

After a few rows of shingles went on, another row of ice shield was stapled tightly in place, overlapping the one below. Then more shingles. When Tom got almost to the top of the row of ice shield, he stretched a roll of Typar underlayment, overlapping the row of ice shield, and stapled that tightly. Tom likes Typar better than tarpaper. It breathes better (less

Tom stretching ice shield straight and tight

chance of condensation), it is tougher (less prone to ripping during installation), and it is lighter. In this manner, the rest of the roof was laid.

In one day, we went from ugly silver whale tarp to half the roof half shingled. It was amazing. Through all this, I acted as a go-fer, handing up supplies, retrieving dropped nails, running to town for more nails, and so forth. Once the OSB was in place, Tom wanted no one on the roof with him. He said it was safer that way, with no one to watch out for. Seemed to work for him.

I was glad that Dad lived to see the finished roof go on. He was always asking how it was coming: Was Tom shingling yet? How did it look? We brought him outside to see it the next morning, and he was extremely pleased with our new roof.

Now, I am in the process of saving for the south side of the roof. This is harder for me to wait for, after seeing how gorgeous the north side turned out. But, the south side will be more expensive because we are putting in two six-foot dormers, one for each bedroom. Tom said he could do one dormer and half of the roof for one "job," and then do the other when I could afford it. Thanks, Tom.

Tom is laying the starter row for shingles.

Bill taking Dad for a good ride around the homestead

Today he showed up unexpectedly, between jobs, and moved his scaffolding around to the west end of the house. I had saved enough to buy 200 lineal feet of 10" half-log siding, and tomorrow we will begin putting it up in the gable end (pointy end!) of the house. I'm doing the west end first, for that is the direction our bad weather usually comes from.

So, while he set up scaffolding, I hauled out a gallon of stain and began staining the house logs. I had planned to stain the log siding before it went up, for ease of handling. But, my son, Bill, was out and suggested that I wait a couple of months to let the siding age. He said he'd done just what I had planned on doing, and the color didn't match his logs at all. They had weathered and the siding hadn't. (Yes, he cleaned and pressure washed his logs before staining, so the color was "new," but it didn't matter.) On the other end of his house he waited, and the color matched very well.

I guess I won't be staining the siding before I put it up. I'd rather learn from someone else's mistakes; I make enough of my own.

Somehow, I came up with a bum knee. For awhile it was so painful that I could hardly walk. I was so glad that Bill left the little golf cart for me to take Mom around the place. For awhile, it took *me* around the place. (By the way, I love that little rechargeable cart. No gas, no fumes, quiet, and it took me over the miles I walk every day.) Climbing ladders was definitely out, but today I managed to climb the pipe scaffolding and ungracefully clamber up onto the plank walkway. The knee is getting better, but I used an elastic knee brace, just to give it a little help.

One thing I've learned is to just keep going. No matter what. It's easy to fall into a pity bag when it seems like everything is smacking you in the face. But, if you can manage to put one foot in front of you (even if you have to use a golf cart) and keep going, things will work out. Just when I was pretty darned low, I got a nice letter in the mail, then David showed me a dozen electric green tree frogs taking a dip in our goats' watering trough one night. It's the little things like that, or seeing the first green tomatoes in the garden or the first tendrils on the cucumber vines. It brings a little smile to your soul and gives you the courage to go on. Δ

Ayoob on Firearms

Frontier style handguns for the modern backwoods home

By Massad Ayoob

The year was 1873. Samuel Colt had invented the revolver—or at least introduced it to America—in 1836. The Colt Navy .36 and Army .44 cap-n'-ball revolvers had been the primary handguns of the Civil War, and had proven themselves the dominant cavalry weapons of that conflict. Smith & Wesson had leapt ahead of Colt's Patent Firearms with the Rollin White patent for the self-contained cartridge. That patent had now run out, and Colt was not going to let its arch rival take over the market. Colt now offered the world a new revolver. Sam Colt had passed away, and one William Mason was the new gun's designer.

Colt called it the Model P. It was quickly adopted by the United States Army and became the Single Action Army, or SAA in gun-enthusiast shorthand. In caliber .44-40, Colt called it the Frontier Six-Shooter.

The world at large came to know it as "the Peacemaker."

If you grew up in the 1950s and '60s, and ever played "cowboys," you probably had a Mattel Fanner 50-cap pistol that was cloned from the Peacemaker. Pausing briefly for WWI, Colt produced the original gun from 1873 until the beginning of WWII. After the second great conflict, the company determined that the design was obsolete and not in demand, and let it die. But, in the early- to mid-1950s, a spate of TV Westerns featuring the Colt six-shooter brought a new surge of interest. A young entrepreneur named Bill Ruger, who had started a gun company in Connecticut in 1949, decided in 1953 to bring out a copy of the famed "cowboy gun" in .22 caliber, and called it the Single-Six. It was followed by the Blackhawk in .357 Magnum (1955) and .44 Magnum (1956). A new company called Great Western was formed exclusively to create copies of the old Peacemaker in the mid-'50s, and it was, in fact, a Great Western .45 that James Arness is said to have wielded as Marshal Matt Dillon on the classic TV series *Gunsmoke*.

Colt woke up and started making them again, in what gun collectors would call a Second Generation. Colt made the SAA in various forms off and on through the rest of the 20th Century and through the present third generation, currently produced at Colt's Custom Shop with a hefty price tag. In recent years, the sport of Cowboy Action Shooting truly rejuvenated these old-time six-guns. Italian companies like Armi San Marcos and Uberti began duplicating these and many other firearms of the old frontier, at reasonable prices. Today, the market is full of them.

An original Colt is still a pricey thing, and you can expect to pay well into four figures for an original First Generation Colt like the Frontier .44-40 I got for $150 along with a Colt Police Positive revolver thrown into the deal by the seller back in the 1960s. They are excellent investments. The best news is, there are many fine clones available for reasonable prices. These include Ruger's Vaquero series, recently downsized from its heavy .44 Magnum frame to a more manageable "original Colt" size; the very nice Beretta Stampede revolvers manufactured with superior quality control since Beretta's purchase of Uberti a few years ago; and the latest low-priced, high-quality bargain, the Gaucho series from Taurus of Brazil.

Massad Ayoob

The allure of the Peacemaker

These revolvers are gate-loading single actions, and as such were obsolete before the 19th Century turned into the 20th. "Gate-loading" means that cartridges are inserted one by one through a cut-away exposed by a flip-out gate at the right rear of the cylinder. Live cartridges or spent casings are ejected through the same portal, with a finger-pushed ejector rod mounted in a housing offset on the right side of the gun's barrel.

Single action means that the hammer has to be manually cocked with one or the other thumb before the trigger will fire a shot, and this has to be done for each and every shot. A fast "cowboy shooter," holding the gun and working the trigger with the dominant hand and cocking the hammer with the support hand thumb in a two-hand hold, can shoot one of these

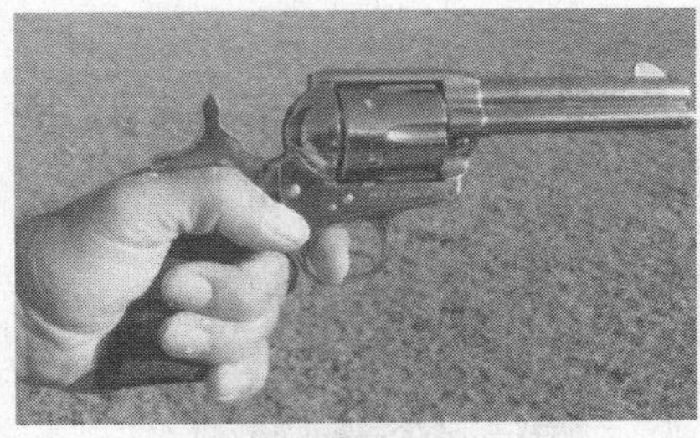

This is the intuitive way to hold a single action, with all three grasping fingers in front of the grip. It softens recoil but slows rate of fire because...

...it causes the gun to roll up in the hand at the shot. If you can handle the recoil and want a fast follow-up shot...

...hold the cowboy-style revolver this way, with little finger tucked under butt, and...

...when fired, whole arm rises with gun, but gun stays in position relative to hand, allowing faster thumb-cocking to the next shot without having to re-grasp.

old-time revolvers as fast as a modern double-action revolver, which needs only a pull of the trigger for each shot. When firing one-handed, though—the way half or more emergencies requiring reactive use of a handgun end up happening, it seems—the single action just can't keep up with a modern double action.

Since the 1890s, Colt and S&W and similar double-action revolvers have had swing-out cylinders from which all six spent casings can be ejected with a single push of an ejector rod. With the cylinder swung out of the gun, all six cartridges can be reloaded at once in a double-action revolver if the shooter has a speedloader or a moon-clip device to hold all the cartridges together in a single unit.

Let's put the difference in reloading time into perspective. Plucking cartridges one by one out of belt loops or dump pouches, cops from the 1930s onward were able to meet a demanding standard that the FBI developed during that period: Draw, fire six shots double action, reload, and fire six more, all in 25 seconds from seven yards, the distance FBI had established was the average for gunfights back then. This became much easier in the 1970s when speedloaders—which had actually existed in the late 1800s—became popular among police and armed citizens. Give me a good double-action revolver and full moon clips or Safariland Comp III speedloaders, and on a good day I can do that drill in only six seconds. And if that seems fast, consider this: The record, held by Jerry Miculek, is 2.99 seconds for those same 12 shots, all hits, with a Smith & Wesson Model 625 .45 revolver, reloading with a "moon clip" that holds all six cartridges together.

By contrast, today or at any other time period, it took a true master shooter to make the 25-second time with a single-action, gate-loading Peacemaker or equivalent. That's how long it took to punch each spent casing out of the cylinder and reload each of the six chambers one at a time.

But today, you still see single-action frontier-style revolvers worn by traditionally minded people ranging from working cowboys to ordinary folks who just like living in the back country.

Part of it is tradition.

But there is more than tradition at work there...

The backwoods rationale of using the single action

There are several rationales for using the single action in the backwoods. The least of these, but still on the radar screen, is the fact that the large frame models are more rugged with heavy handloads than double actions. Back in the 1950s, the great outdoorsman and gun expert Elmer Keith wrote that he had determined the Ruger single-action Super Blackhawk to be a stronger .44 Magnum than the only double action then available in the caliber, Smith & Wesson's Model 29. The first .454 Casull revolver, a crushingly powerful weapon, was the superbly crafted five-shot Freedom Arms, a gun designed faithfully in the single-action, gate-loading Peacemaker style.

A more important reason for some was cost. A friend of mine who won many honors on the Alaska State Patrol calls the Ruger Super Blackhawk "the official Alaskan handgun." People who go fishing or hiking in bear country there are in truly deadly danger from the big brown bruins, and when the .44 Magnum came out in 1956, the double-action Smith & Wesson cost in the $120 range, but the Ruger single action had a $96 price tag. To this day, the top quality single action is less expensive than the equivalent quality double action, most brands for most brands.

I would submit that there is a much better and much more practical and tactical reason why so many people who live in rural America choose a single action as their "backwoods gun." They are not particularly concerned about self defense against human predators, and should that come up, they are not terribly disadvantaged in having a powerful, reliable revolver at hand that only holds a few rounds. Most man-against-man gunfights are over with less than six rounds fired, anyway.

No, it's because even today, the modern backwoods dweller rides horses. Rides snowmobiles. Rides all-terrain vehicles. And that person may have to fire the handgun from that moving platform to save his or her life.

And, when you've had to fire a single action revolver from a moving platform such as that, ***it is not going to fire a second time by accident***. It can't ***possibly*** fire again until you ***intentionally*** thumb its hammer back to prepare it for the next shot.

Let's think about it. You are the typical horseman, whose mount is not accustomed to gunfire. Suddenly, that fox that has been at the henhouse comes into sight, or you see a feral dog chasing your livestock. The handgun comes out of your holster. You take a sight picture, you press the trigger, and...

Ruger's New Vaquero .45 is a faithful replica of the original Peacemaker externally, but with much sturdier and more modern (and safer) internal mechanism. It is also far more affordable.

BANG!

Depending on the caliber, the handgun's report explodes not terribly far from your horse's ear, at something between 100 and 140 literally deafening decibels.

Is the horse likely to shy? Oh, yes.

You have one hand on the reins and one hand on the gun. As the horse rears violently, throwing you off balance and destabilizing you, your non-dominant hand desperately convulses on the reins. You have just fired a shot an instant before, so the trigger finger of your dominant hand is on the trigger of the handgun.

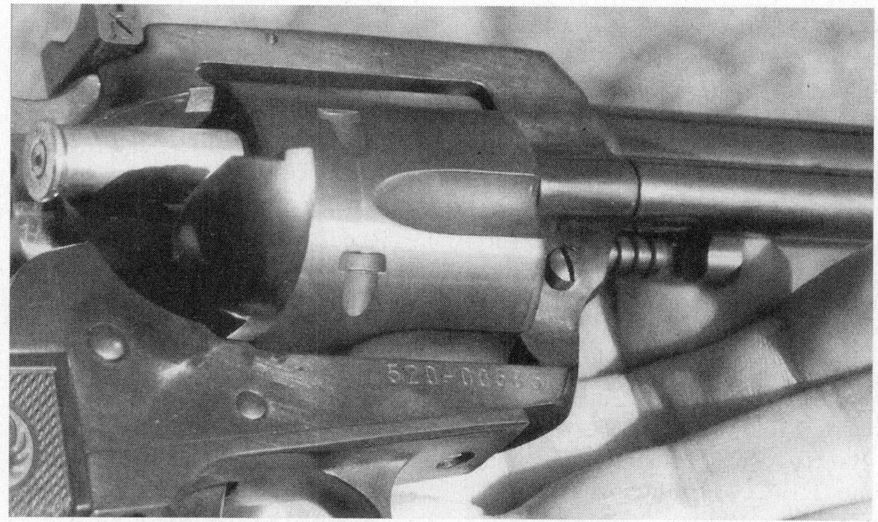

Unloading the "peacemaker" style single action. Finger pushes rod (A), inside ejector housing (B), forcing spent casing (C), out of cartridge port (D), with loading gate (E) open

Physiologist Roger Enoka long ago scientifically determined how certain natural human movements under stress cause accidental discharges of guns in hand. There is interlimb response: As one hand closes on something, the other hand closes sympathetically, and...BANG. There is postural disturbance: As we start to lose our balance, we move convulsively to regain it, and our muscles sympathetically tighten, and ... BANG. There is startle response: Something startles us and makes us jump or convulse. The gun is in the hand; the finger is on the trigger; the flexor muscles that close the fingers are stronger than the extensor muscles that open those fingers, and...BANG.

It is very likely to happen with a self-cocking semiautomatic pistol. Even if the trigger has come forward on a double-action revolver or semiautomatic pistol that might take 12 or more pounds to activate, the average human hand can close its fingers with far more pressure than that, and a person who is in shape can exert the equivalent of their body weight on the hand dynamometer, or hand-strength

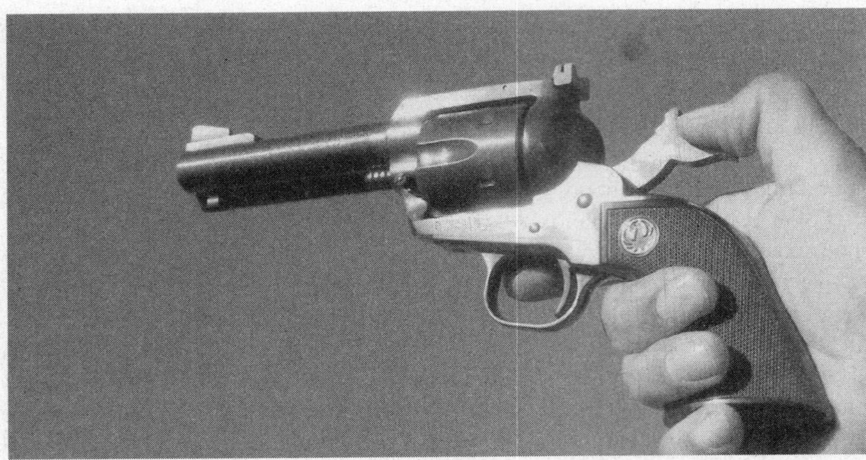

Thumb must cock the hammer for every shot with a single-action revolver like this Ruger Blackhawk

*If you want to be **really** traditional, use a muzzle-loading black powder six-shooter, like this modern Ruger New Army in .45 caliber.*

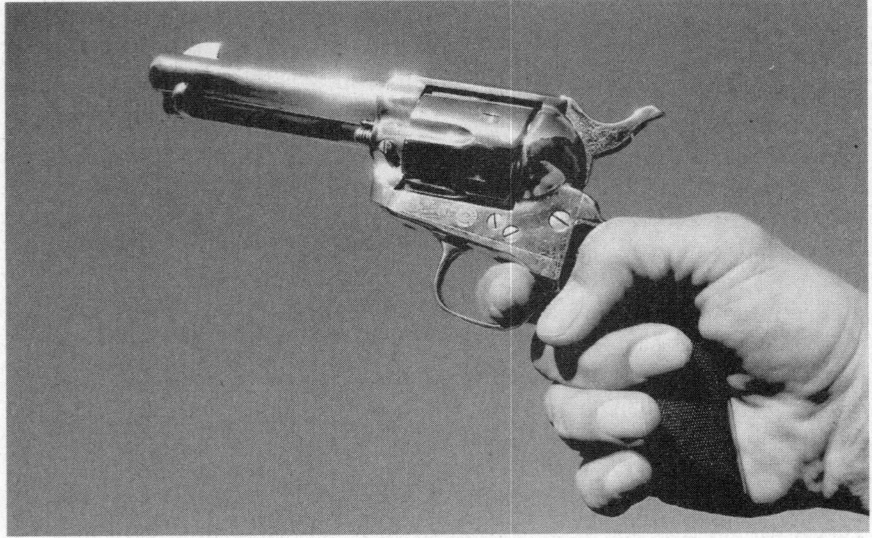

Once this Gaucho .357 Magnum has been fired, as shown, it can't fire again until hammer is deliberately cocked. This can prevent accidental shots on horseback or if thrown from mount with gun in hand.

gauge. Autoloader or double-action revolver, in that situation, you will hear...BANG.

But with a single-action, frontier-style Peacemaker or equivalent revolver, you will hear...nothing. Because the gun's design is such that it ***cannot*** fire until the thumb has performed the deliberate movement of cocking the hammer again.

Does this sound far-fetched? If it does, you haven't talked with some of the backwoods people I've talked with. I know men who have had to shoot snakes and such from horseback. Even when the horse is supposedly "broken to gunfire"—that is, trained not to rear up and panic at the sound of a shot—none of that training encompasses getting the horse used to the thing that may have triggered the shot. In other words, you can train a horse to ignore gunfire. You cannot train the horse to ignore the striking rattlesnake or the lunging mountain lion that has caused you to draw and fire your gun in the field instead of in training.

Is it far-fetched to think someone might have to fire from a moving snowmobile, mountain bike, or ATV? Perhaps. But then, I have not been chased by a pack of wild dogs while astride a bike, a horse, or a snowmobile. For those who have had that experience and have had to fire to protect their lives, a gun that won't "go off by accident" as they struggle to regain control of their "mount" doesn't seem far-fetched anymore.

How to shoot a single-action revolver

The first thing you need to know about single action revolvers is, ***don't carry them with a live round under the hammer***. Load the six-shooter with five cartridges and leave that last empty chamber under the down-at-rest hammer and the firing pin.

For a century, Americans understood this. You didn't leave a live round under the hammer of a single-action revolver because it could go off if dropped or struck. Historians say that happened once to Wyatt Earp. Where does that leave the rest of us "lesser gunfighters?" Don't leave a standard-shift car parked on a hill in neutral without the parking brake engaged, don't put a live round under the hammer of the single-action revolver you carry, don't eat the yellow snow. These were good, logical rules of life, well understood by people who had common sense.

Unfortunately, as the 20th century wore on, common sense became less than a common trait. People forgot the old wisdom and the old ways. Stupid people killed and crippled themselves and others when they dropped their six-guns that were loaded with all six shots and the predictable and terrible BANG! was heard. Gun companies were sued.

Led by Ruger, the gunmakers who produced single-action revolvers came up with floating firing pin designs that used a transfer bar mechanism and allowed modern SAAs to be carried safely with all six chambers loaded. The problem that followed was one of habit: If we got used to carrying ***one*** single action with a live round under the hammer, we realized, we could transmit that habit to others.

Thus, it has become the mark of the firearms professional that ***any*** single-action revolver is to be carried with an empty chamber under the hammer. Engineers may consider it redundant safety practice. Anyone with common sense calls it "the belt and suspenders approach." Firearms professionals call it "the rule."

My gun safes at the moment contain two old-style Colts that would discharge if dropped on the hammer with a live round under the firing pin, and one—Colt's much more recent Cowboy model—that won't. They also contain Beretta/Uberti, Ruger, and Taurus single actions that are mechanically drop-safe with all six chambers loaded. In my hands, all of those revolvers will be carried with an empty chamber under the hammer. End of story, end of safety lecture.

Now, let's talk about shooting this kind of handgun, and shooting it well.

If you can get both hands on the gun, use the dominant hand on the grip-frame and the dominant index finger on the trigger, and the thumb of the support hand to cock the hammer. This is far faster and more efficient than asking one hand to do all the work and the other to just go along for the ride.

You want to have a firm hold on these guns. They have a slow lock time. In firearms parlance, "lock time" is what elapses between when the trigger pull is completed and the firing pin starts to move forward, and when the cartridge in the firing chamber actually discharges. As the photos show, these guns had big, heavy old hammers to be sure they had enough impact to light off the percussion caps of the muzzle loaders and then the early-generation primers of the old black powder cartridges the Model P was originally designed for in 1873. Those hammers come down with a ***clank*** that can actually move the gun if it isn't held firmly, not the click of the lighter hammers of more modern double-action revolvers. The heavier the impact of the falling hammer, the more disturbance to aim. This is why Peacemaker-style revolvers—even Colt's Bisley model, named after the famed international shooting range not far from London, England: Bisley Camp—was obsolete as far as target shooters were concerned very early in the 20th century.

If you look at the accompanying photos, you'll see what has become known as the "plow handle" grip shape of the frontier-style single-action revolver. It was designed to mitigate the discomfort of recoil by letting the gun "roll up in the hand" when the shot went off. They do this very well, and it has made generations of heavy revolver shooters more comfortable in terms of "kick" with single-action .44 Magnums instead of double-action versions. However, it also slows down recovery time between shots because the gun has to be repositioned in the hand before the next shot.

Author practices for "gunfighter" class at a Cowboy Action Match, which requires a revolver in each hand fired alternately. Taurus Gaucho .45 in right hand has just fired and hit the steel plate at right (note hammer down), while .38 caliber counterpart in left hand is about to be fired (hammer still cocked).

In my mid-teens, shooting my modern Ruger Blackhawk .44 Magnum and my antique Colt .44-40 Frontier Six-Shooter, I figured out that if I curled my little finger under the butt of the gun, it wouldn't roll up in my hand. The recoil pattern didn't hurt me that much more, it just changed to where the whole arm lifted in recoil instead of the gun lifting in the hand. However, the relationship of gun to hand remained constant, and allowed

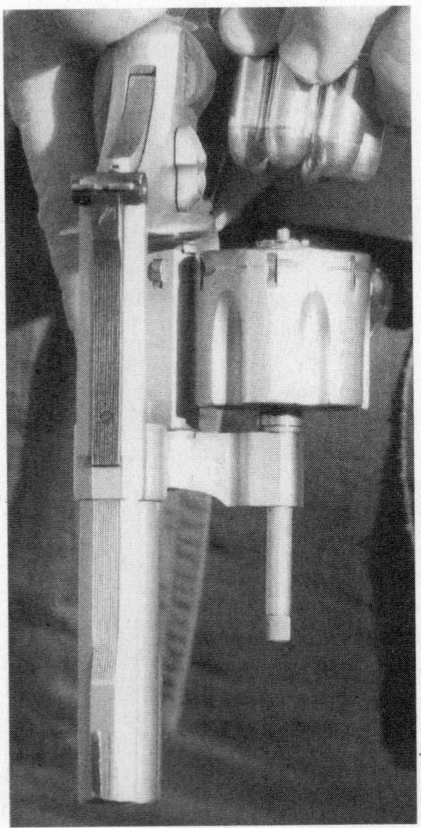

No single-action revolver will ever be as fast as this double action Smith & Wesson Model 625. It needs only a pull of the trigger to fire each shot, and it can be reloaded with six .45 rounds at once using a moon clip as shown.

me to get back on target and thumb-cock that Peacemaker-style revolver for the next shot much more quickly.

I was pretty proud of myself for figuring it out, until I read Elmer Keith's classic book *Sixguns* that was written in the early 1950s and showed the exact same technique. Turns out that Elmer learned it from the old cowboys he knew in his own youth in the early 20th Century...and ***they*** had learned it in the 19th. All I had done was re-invent the wheel.

Know how to safely load and unload your "cowboy-style" revolver. With that gate-loading system, only one chamber at a time is visible to the operator of the gun. It requires your immediate and total attention. Slowly rotate the cylinder around ***twice***, six plus six, to make ***sure*** that every single chamber is empty.

When you are loading, to guarantee that an empty chamber comes up under the hammer when you're done, with most single actions you want to follow the protocol developed in the American West in the last quarter of the 19th Century, the original heyday of this gun. It goes like this:

Load one cartridge. Rotate the cylinder past the loading gate until an empty chamber has gone by. Then load four more. This should bring the one empty chamber up under the hammer. Then lower the hammer on that empty chamber. With the hammer all the way down on that empty "launch tube," the action is locked and a loaded chamber can't rotate up "by itself." The old cowboys called the protocol "load one, skip one, load four."

Always double check visually! Looking in through the side of the gun—use a flashlight, if you're manipulating the revolver in the dark—you'll be able to see the space between the rear of the cylinder and the back part of the frame in which it sits, which is called the cylinder window. You will see the rims of the cartridges in five of the chambers, and you should be able to see the empty space, indeed the empty rear of the chamber, at the back of the cylinder under the hammer. If you are absolutely certain that you are seeing this, then things are as they should be, and you are safe.

To free up the cylinder to make it rotate so you can load and unload, the original Colt SAA and most of the clones require the hammer to be drawn back to the half-cock notch. Modern Ruger revolvers, the so-called New Models, free up the cylinder when the loading gate is opened and the hammer is down in its "at rest" position.

Do you really want a single-action revolver?

Let me be plain here. I've discovered in three and a half decades of writing that if you say something positive about something, you are seen as endorsing and recommending what you wrote about. That ain't necessarily so, and that's true here.

I live in a rural area these days. I don't carry single-action revolvers. I carry modern semiautomatic pistols and double-action revolvers.

I ***use*** single-action revolvers. Sometimes for hunting. Sometimes for cowboy competition matches. Sometimes just for the fun of shooting them.

I do not ***recommend*** single-action revolvers for everyday carry, except for the rural person who is constantly on horseback and may have to fire from the saddle. In that situation, and only there, I think the single action may have a place as a constant-carry sidearm. If the "mission profile" of your handgun is geared more toward self-protection, you are better off with something more modern. Slow loading/unloading/reloading time, slow pace of sustained fire if shooting one hand only, and difficulty of quickly and safely checking loaded versus unloaded status all militate against the old cowboy-style gun, and show you why it has so long been considered obsolete by those who go in harm's way.

What I am saying is, if you're more concerned about a mountain lion or a rattlesnake when you're on horseback than a carjacker when you're on the road, the single action may have an advantage for you if you carry it carefully and safely, the traditional way.

And if you are careful and responsible, and the old ways just feel better for you, and you just feel more comfortable when armed with a single action revolver, you know what?

You'll get no argument from me. Δ

Make your own biodiesel for 80¢ per gallon

By Jeffrey R. Yago, P.E., CEM

My Ford F-250 diesel crew-cab pickup did not cause me to become interested in making my own bio-diesel fuel. No, the final straw was when I filled up its 48-gallon fuel tank at a cost of $150 that made me decide to find out what this bio-diesel commotion was all about!

I think it took longer for me to consider bio-fuel than most; as all I ever heard or read about bio-diesel was coming from the save-the-earth crowd driving around in old diesel school buses, plastered over with "flower power" and faded "stop global warming" bumper stickers—indicators which call for immediate purging from my memory. Actually, a family friend named Jack Jones who owns multiple diesel vehicles asked me one day if I knew how to make bio-diesel fuel, and this started me on a quest.

Regardless of who the early promoters were, making your own fuel to power diesel trucks, farm tractors, and back-up generators is a perfect fit for anyone living off-grid or on a farm. Not only is diesel fuel easy to make, but it requires very little equipment to get started. Like all hobbies that can turn into an obsession, it is certainly possible to refine the process with more expensive equipment later, so I will start with the basics.

Where to start

You will need a local and continuous supply of discarded cooking oil, and without it, you are just wasting your time. This means you need to make friends with the managers of nearby fast-food restaurants.

All bio-diesel-making processes start with discarded waste vegetable oil (WVO) from commercial deep fryers, and may include lard and other kitchen grease. In most cases, this waste cooking oil is dumped out at the end of each day into temporary storage tanks behind the restaurants.

Many different sizes and shapes of chemical tanks are available to make bio-diesel. (Photo courtesy of Utah Bio-Diesel Supply)

Currently, most fast-food locations pay somebody to remove this discarded oil each week along with the other restaurant wastes. However, as the popularity of bio-diesel becomes more mainstream, we will soon be protecting our own sources and fighting over who gets there first each week! Since you cannot just back up to a 500-pound tank of liquid waste oil and dump it into a bucket, you will need a 50 to 100-gallon tank in your truck bed or on a small trailer. You will also need a battery-powered fuel pump; but not to worry, all these items are easy to find, and I will list suppliers of all equipment discussed at the end of this article.

I have stressed that you must find a source of waste vegetable oil first. If you have to drive 100 miles into a city to locate a fast-food restaurant, you may be using more fuel collecting waste oil than you can manufacture, so keep this in mind.

Chemical process

I am not going into a detailed description of the actual chemical process that takes place, as you will easily learn this when you get more involved. Because it's so easy to make bio-diesel fuel, the Internet and do-it-yourself magazines are full of advertisements for kits that are fairly inexpensive and will make it much easier for you to get started. Once you have actually started producing your own diesel fuel, there are fuel test kits, fuel filters, and other devices you can purchase to improve the quality and consistency of your fuel making.

Regardless of whose fuel-making kit you buy (and there are plenty of them), it takes four things to make bio-diesel: Waste vegetable oil, methanol (racing fuel), sodium hydroxide (household lye), and water. No matter how simple or complex the process you choose, these are an absolute must.

Safety issues

Before you head out in the backyard and drop a can of drain opener (lye) and your son's model airplane fuel (methanol) into a coffee can full of cooking oil, a few safety cautions are in order. Due to the minimum equipment required to make bio-diesel, it is certainly possible to build your own processor from scratch. However, how these very reactive chemicals are mixed together and their handling during this mixing presents some serious safety concerns.

First, methanol is extremely flammable, but unlike most other flammable liquids, it does not have a visible flame when it burns. You may have watched high-performance sports car racing when a member of the pit crew suddenly started rolling on the ground for no apparent reason. These cars are fueled by methanol, and fuel spills are common during fast pit stops, which sometimes results in a crew member getting severe burns even though you see no flames or smoke. Once it is mixed with lye, the resulting sodium methoxide will burn anywhere it touches bare skin. In addition, you will not realize you are being burned, as it immediately kills all nerve endings.

If you have ever used common household lye to open clogged drains or make soap, you know lye is also very dangerous to your skin and gets extremely hot when poured into water. Lye will also quickly corrode aluminum, tin pans, zinc coatings, and most paints, so use only glass, stainless steel, or chemical-grade polyethylene containers when handling these caustic chemicals.

A final warning: Sodium methoxide (mixture of methanol and lye) vapors are extremely dangerous to breathe, so your fuel-making work area should be well ventilated (preferably an outside shed). Have a fire extinguisher and a nearby water hose constantly discharging fresh water into a bucket during the actual mixing process.

Bio-diesel making kits

Although there are endless possible piping and tank designs, I have found that most of the bio-diesel making kits can be divided into two general categories, and where you live and the quality of the fuel desired can have a lot to do with which process you use.

At the very basic level is the no-heating process that consists of two tanks, usually having funnel-shaped bottoms. Almost all of these advertised kits will make an average of 40 to 44 gallons of diesel fuel per cycle, so the larger tank will be about 60 gallons in size. This tank will hold the waste cooking oil at the start of the process.

Mounted next to the larger tank is a much smaller tank, usually about 15 gallons, which will hold the methanol (racing fuel) and sodium hydroxide (household lye) mixture. The actual amount of these two chemicals that will be pumped into the waste vegetable oil tank after they are mixed depends on the quality and water content of the cooking oil being used. As a general guide, you will require about 20% of methanol-to-waste-oil by volume, which averages about 8 gallons per 40 gallons of vegetable oil. This chemical reaction will also generate approximately 5 gallons of glycerin per cycle, which will form at the bottom of the mixing tank after the 24-hour reaction time. Since glycerin is bio-degradable, it is usually drained off and discarded.

Waste vegetable oil will contain food particles and various levels of moisture that need to be removed before starting. Most suspended solids can be removed by first passing the used oil through a strainer as you fill the mixing tank. Mixing lye with vegetable oil and water makes excellent soap, so too much water in the waste vegetable oil and your diesel fuel may turn out to be really good liquid soap.

To reduce the effects of colder ambient air temperature and improve moisture removal, some bio-diesel kits use a glass-lined electric hot-water heater for the mixing tank. The tank is modified by adding different piping and valve connections to the original hot, cold, and drain openings. This makes an excellent way to heat up the waste oil to 130° F before starting, which helps evaporate any remaining moisture in the waste oil.

Bio-diesel kits that do not involve heating the oil first to remove the moisture may work better in warm climates, as I cannot imagine trying to do this in a Wisconsin barn in February. However, the no-heat kits do produce bio-diesel if you follow the directions and avoid letting the mixture get too cold during the mixing and reacting process. Some kits include tank insulation blankets to retain the heat produced by the chemical reaction.

Although the non-heating bio-diesel kits can produce quality bio-diesel fuel, I personally think the heating process may introduce a higher level of quality control and reduces the chance for unwanted soaps and excess glycerin to be produced. However, each system and tank type has advantages and disadvantages that need to be considered.

Buying the chemicals

Methanol is a popular fuel for automotive racing, and high-performance engine shops and racetracks are a good place to purchase small quantities. Petroleum distributors usually sell methanol in larger 30 and 55-gallon drums if you can afford to buy this much at one time. Do not be surprised if you get a visit from the local sheriff, as this is also the primary ingredient for methamphetamine ("meth") labs manufacturing illegal drugs. Make sure they know who you are and what you are going to do with the methanol.

It is also a good idea to discuss your methanol storage plans with your

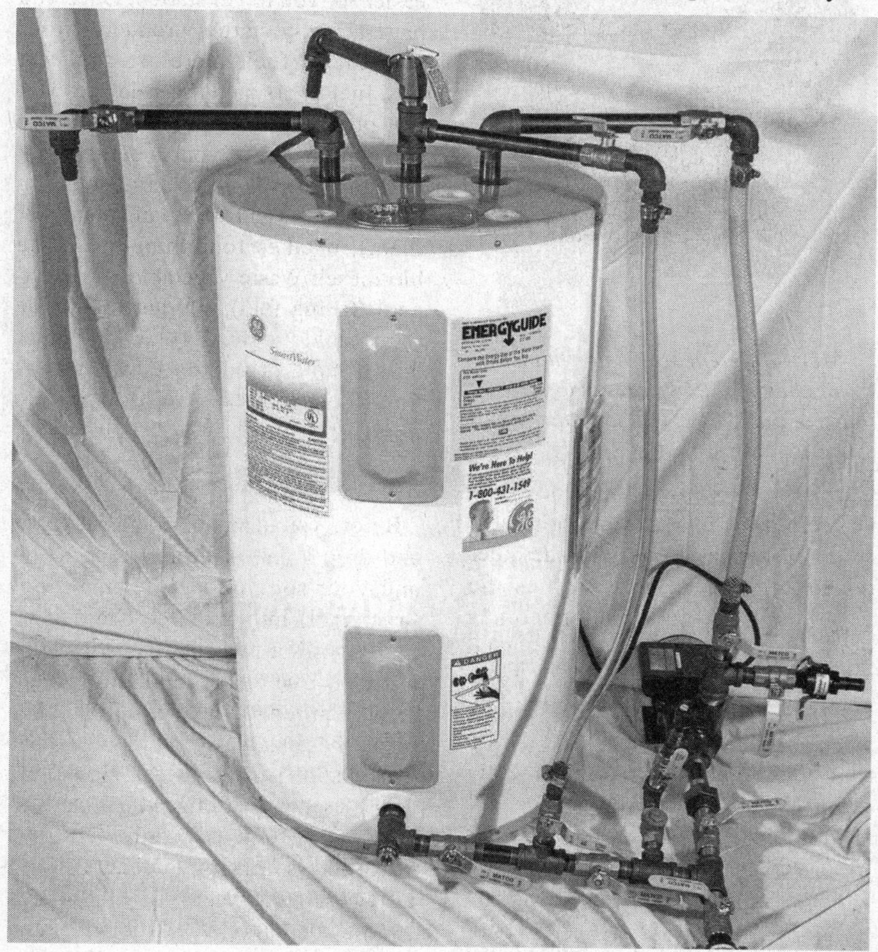

Basic bio-diesel making kit using residential hot water heater. (Photo courtesy of Utah Bio-Diesel Supply)

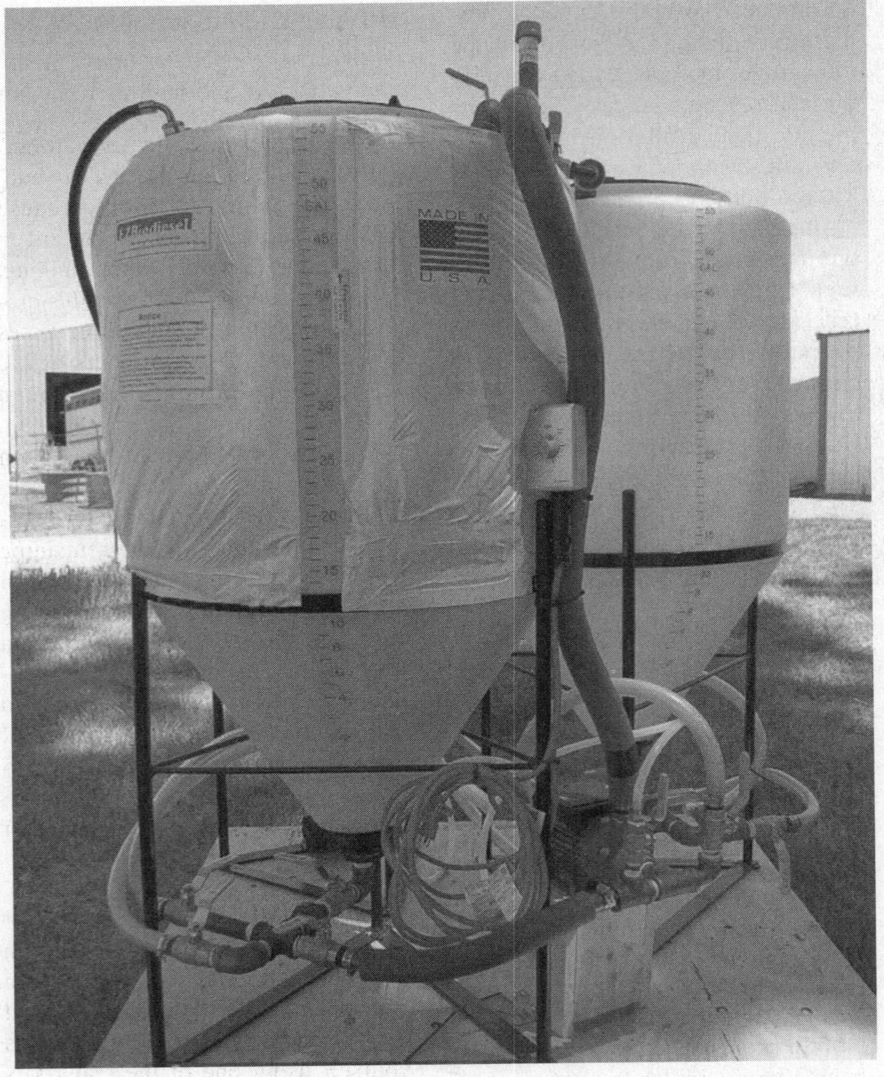

Non-heating bio-diesel making kit.
(Photo courtesy of Summit Enterprises, LLC and EZ Bio-diesel)

county's fire marshal, as volunteer firefighters do not expect to find drums full of highly toxic and potentially explosive chemicals when called to fight a fire in an old barn or garage. Most fire marshals will appreciate you considering the safety of their volunteers who will be the first to respond if you have a very bad day.

Since you will use very little lye per batch of bio-diesel, your local grocery store will be your best source. Also, by buying lye in small sealed cans, there is much less chance of moisture reducing its effectiveness after it has been opened several times.

Mixing the ingredients

Regardless of whether you will be using a water heater-type mixing tank or polyethylene funnel-bottomed mixing tank, the mixture of Methanol and lye in the smaller tank will be transferred into the larger mixing tank already containing the waste oil. Most bio-diesel kits include at least one explosive-proof electric pump prepiped to a series of manual ball-valves that allow using a single pump to fill the tanks, mix the liquids in the tanks, and drain the tanks, depending on which valves are opened or closed.

The actual testing, measuring, and mixing takes about one hour. Then you allow the chemical process to take place, which takes 24 hours. Most kits include a dial-timer to shut off the mixing pump at the proper time, so you do not need to stand around and wait. Unwanted glycerin will settle at the bottom of the mixing tank during this time, then be drained and discarded.

Titration

As mentioned earlier, although very little will be needed, the actual amount of lye required will be slightly different for each batch of used cooking oil. If you add more than the required amount of lye, your mixing tank could end up filled with gel-type soap. If you use too little lye, only part of the cooking oil will convert into bio-diesel, with a large layer of glycerin settling to the bottom of the mixing tank.

Since determining how much lye to use is so critical, most bio-diesel kits include a PH test kit for the waste oil, like those used to test pool water before adding chemicals. However, the testing of waste oil is slightly more detailed, as it uses a process called "titration." This test requires samples to be accurately measured and mixed according to specific instructions before the resulting sample is tested for PH level. Entering the test results on a mixing chart gives the exact weight of lye this particular batch of used cooking oil will require to fully convert to bio-diesel. As a general guideline, most used cooking oil will require abut six to seven grams of lye for each liter of used cooking oil.

Vegetable oil will not combine directly with Methanol, so the lye serves as a catalyst for this chemical reaction, and the amount required is critical to the success of the final product. This is why the titration test is so important before starting every new batch.

Bio-diesel kit (Photo courtesy of Home Bio-diesel Kits)

Water wash

I realize my initial warnings described how any water in the used cooking oil will cause the lye to produce soap, so why do we need to add water, especially to fuel? I had a hard time with this one myself when I first started. This water is added after the mixing of the used oil, methanol, and lye has taken place and the bio-diesel fuel has been created.

The purpose for adding water at this final stage is to remove any remaining waste products. Regardless of how good you have measured and mixed, there will always be some unwanted "trash" that needs to be removed from the final product, including left-over lye, glycerin, soap, and unprocessed methanol. All of these waste products are water soluble and can be easily removed from the bio-diesel fuel with a water wash. However, this does not mean turning the water hose full blast into the mixing tank. If you have ever taken a jar half-full of any oil, added water, and vigorously shook it, you ended up with a milky foam mixture that was almost impossible to separate into the original two layers of oil and water.

The water-spray wash process involves tiny "misting" spray nozzles located in the top of the mixing tank that gently introduces water down onto the surface of the oil in very tiny droplets without causing any physical mixing with the oil. After a few hours, this water mist will migrate down through the bio-diesel fuel and absorb the waste products before settling to the tank bottom where it is manually drained off.

More sophisticated processes use a bubble-wash similar to an aquarium aerator. A tank is slowly filled 1/3 full of water and 2/3 full of finished bio-diesel fuel without mixing. A small air pump sends air down to the bottom of this tank through a tube ending with an aquarium "air stone," which produces lots of tiny air bubbles. The rising air bubbles cause unwanted contaminants in the oil to dissolve in the water without mixing. The water is drained off, and this process is repeated at least three times over a period of several hours before all the contaminants have been removed.

After the wash process has been completed, the finished bio-diesel fuel is allowed to stand again overnight, giving time for any remaining water to settle to the tank bottom where it is drained off. The piping valves are then reversed and the pump transfers the final product to a 55-gallon oil drum for storage until ready to use. Some kits include a special 5-micron fuel filter on this delivery line to remove any remaining particles that could harm injectors or other diesel engine parts.

Conclusions

Although this has been more of an overview, it should give you a basic understanding of how bio-diesel fuel is made and how easy you can do this yourself using one of the many kits available. Most basic kits start around

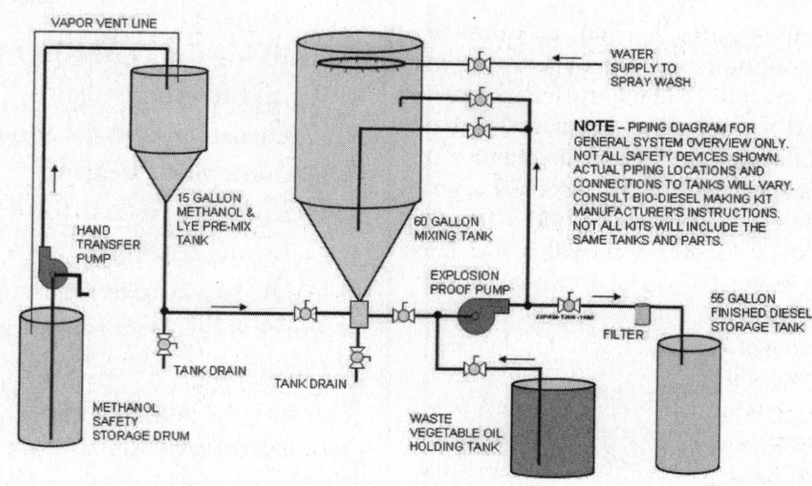

Sources of Free Biodiesel Making Information

Non-profit bio-diesel community web site: www.biodieselcommunity.org

Bio-diesel discussion forum: www.biodiesel.infopop.cc/eve/

Free photos of home-made bio-diesel systems: www.biodieselpictures.com

Mike Pelly, advocate of bio-diesel with practical advice for the novice: www.journeytoforever.org

Sources for Quality Biodiesel Kits and Equipment

Utah Bio-diesel Supply:
www.utahbiodieselsupply.com
fax only: 801-660-4054

Bio-diesel Warehouse:
www.diyfuel.com
3-6 Simm Lane
Newtown, CT 06470
203-426-1876

Home Bio-Diesel Kits:
www.homebiodieselkits.com
P.O. Box 5515
Bella Vista, AR 72714
800-679-1398
9:00 am to 7:00 pm Mon.-Fri.

B100 Supply, LLC:
www.b100supply.com
P.O. Box 1184
Woodstock, GA 30188
678-528-1899

Bio-diesel Solutions:
www.biodieselsolutions.com
1395 Greg St., Suite 102
Sparks, NV 89431
877-358-6400

EZ Bio-diesel:
www.ezbiodiesel.com
Summit Enterprises, LLC
1848 J Road
Fruita, CO 81521
970-858-0673
9:00 am to 6:00 pm Mon.-Fri.

$1,800 for those using the non-heated tank process, and $2,900 for kits using more commercial-quality components. I also found several sources that sell the plumbing packages containing only the explosive-proof pump and pre-piped valve assembly for under $1,000, which you can easily connect to your own electric hot water tank that you can buy locally.

Regardless of which kit you decide to purchase, or which level of sophistication your process will involve, please follow all safety instructions and wear proper protective eyewear, chemical-resistant gloves, respirator, and splash-proof clothing. Work only in a well-ventilated area. You should also know that transporting and storing methanol is extremely hazardous, and the National Fire Code only allows two 5-gallon cans to be stored in a single residential location. There have been homes burned down in the past from people involved in automotive and go-cart racing who carelessly stored a 55-gallon drum of methanol in their attached garage.

The following web links have some excellent free information on bio-diesel making. The Bio-diesel Community website and the Bio-diesel Discussion Forum have extensive free information and photographs describing each phase of the bio-diesel making process, including: Chemistry, testing, mixing, washing, and filtering. The bio-diesel equipment suppliers also listed below have everything from individual pipe fittings to complete kits. Be sure to check all of the links for more information.

(Jeff Yago is a licensed professional engineer and certified energy manager with more than 25 years experience in the energy conservation field. He has extensive solar thermal and solar photovoltaic system design experience and has authored numerous energy and off-grid articles and texts.) Δ

Build a 6,500-gallon concrete water tank for $1500

By Dorothy Ainsworth

When I bought 10 dry barren "affordable" acres back in 1981 I got what I paid for: No electricity, no septic system, no well, and no water. What I *did* get was a long narrow rectangle carpeted with star thistle and poison oak, situated on the southern face of a hill (500'x1320'). Buying bare land was a big gamble, but I wanted my own piece of dirt so badly, I could taste it—if only I had some water to wash it down with. Thanks to the local well driller and good ol' Mother Nature, I got that drink of water. I lucked out and struck it rich with a 50 GPM well at a depth of 150 feet for $3,000.

The next steps were basic. I procured the appropriate permits, built a pump house around the well casing, set a power pole, wired in an electrical box and meter, and called the inspector.

When all my lifelines were hooked up, I installed a submersible pump from Sears by following the do-it-yourself instructions, and to my amazement, when I turned on the control box, water spewed right up out of the pipe! Now I could get serious about improving the property. I'd start with a water storage tank because I believe "you are only as secure as your water supply."

To take advantage of gravity for water-on-demand, the logical place to put a holding tank was at the top of the hill, with the well at the bottom. I called a backhoe man to dig a 3' deep trench ¼-mile long and level a spot at the top end for a 12'x12'x6' concrete tank (6500-gallon capacity).

Floor forms and gravel base

The 2hp submerged pump in the well would fill the tank via an 1½" PVC pipe buried in the trench. When the tank was full, I'd use the same pipe to gravity feed water to supply all my household and irrigation needs. Every 60 feet down the line, I would put a 1" PVC riser sticking up out of the main pipe and cap it with a non-siphoning valve for irrigation. I would later put in 1" PVC pipes underground off of that main line as needed to supply my various structures as I built them.

Bill tamping the first wall pour

With a holding tank I would have the security of a week's or month's supply of water at a time (depending on the season) if the electricity went off for any reason. A stored supply would also save the pump motor from having to cycle on and off whenever a faucet was turned on. My storage tank would fill up in about 4 hours, then the pump would rest, and the well would replenish itself. It sounded like a good plan, so I got busy hauling gravel. I would need tons of it!

I found a source for cheap crushed gravel (¾ minus, meaning no rocks bigger than ¾"), but, again you get what you pay for—I had to load it myself. I hauled a yard or two a day in my pickup until I stockpiled enough to build the tank. I had it down to a science: Each load took 300 shovels full. When the tires were flattened "just so," I knew that that amount of too much was just enough. I'd creep home, front end floating, turn into my driveway, and step on it full throttle to get a run at the hill, fishtailing all the way to the top. (I had no roads yet.) Poor old "Bessie," my 1971 ½-ton Ford pickup, has endured cruel and unusual punishment for 20 years, hauling a hundred 1-ton loads of gravel for roads and 780 logs for houses, but she's still going strong.

It took two weeks of shoveling rock to have enough for the job, but loading and unloading the truck 20 times was just the half of it! Each of those 6,000 shovels full of gravel would have to be lifted again—either thrown on the ground to level the pad, or heaved into a cement mixer with sand and cement and water, then dumped and tamped into forms. I looked forward to the day when the "cruel gruel" would be entombed forever.

The floor

I had no electricity on top of the hill, so I borrowed a cement mixer and a gas-powered generator from a neighbor. He was a Bill-of-all-trades who also did everything the hard way to save money. I paid him what I could to help me with the general layout of the tank site, which consisted of setting up batter boards and making sure everything was plumb, level, and square. I covered the large pad where the tank would sit with about 8" of gravel. Then we built the forms out of 2"x8" lumber, set the 2" PVC drain pipe in place, and poured the 8" thick floor in two grueling days (32 mixers full = 4 cubic yards). We used a garden rake and a shovel to evenly

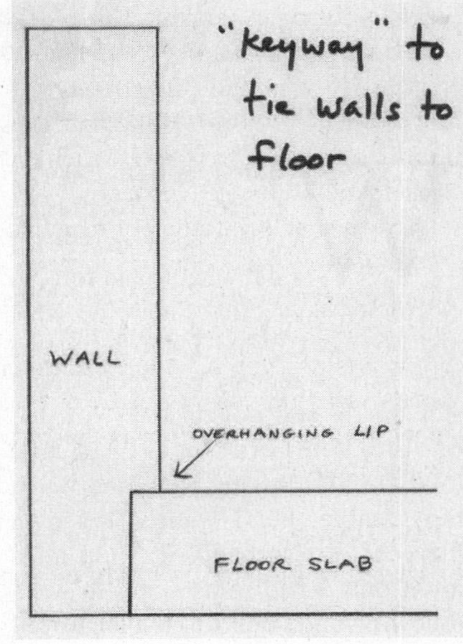

distribute the mix around and work it into every corner. Together we dragged a 2"x6" on edge across the surface of the wet concrete floor using the tops of the forms as guides—a procedure called "screeding." Bill advised me to use no rebar in the slab because it would be filled with water inside and sitting on wet ground outside, and the rebar would eventually rust, leaving voids that would weaken the concrete. Right or wrong, I had no experience to question him, so that's how we did it.

Before the floor set up as hard as a rock, we roughed up the sides of the slab and a 2" wide strip around the top perimeter to serve as a keyway (an overhanging lip) to help tie the vertical walls to the floor. We used 5/8" plywood nailed to 2"x4" frames for the 8" thick walls. I sprayed the sheets of plywood with petroleum oil (using a garden sprayer) so they wouldn't stick to the concrete when it was time for removing and repositioning them.

We secured vertical rebar at 2' intervals inside the wall cavities. Bill helped me with the floor, but then he had to go to another job, so I carried on solo. A cubic yard and a half of concrete was all I was physically capable of shoveling, pouring, distributing, and tamping in 12 hours. I let each daily pour set up, then moved the forms up and raised the cement mixer platform and piles of ingredients to the new level. Bill stopped by on his way home from work each day to help me lift the heavy stuff.

A series of separate pours meant "cold joints"—the lines of demarcation between pours. If the preceding surface is roughed up while the concrete is still "green," the next layer bonds just fine. It's not as ideal as a monolithic pour, but it was the only doable method for me.

The recipe

There are three basic mixtures that are commonly used for concrete con-

Set up for the first wall pour

Rough on the outside, but Thorosealed and smooth on the inside

Troweling on the Thoroseal

Roofing the tank with shingles

struction, from strongest to strong enough. They differ in the ratio of the three basic ingredients: Cement, sand, and stone. How they are proportioned makes a huge difference in strength and durability. The more cement used, the stronger (richer) the mix, with 1:2:4 being a happy medium for most projects. The less water you can use in relation to the dry ingredients and still maintain a workable consistency, the stronger the mix. A runny mix is weak.

The consistency of fresh mixed concrete should feel like oatmeal cookie batter—but don't lick your fingers. The trick is to not touch the mix at all with bare hands, but for a novice, that's easier said than done because it's tempting to catch the drips and smear them around.

Because Portland cement has abrasive silica and caustic lime in it, I ended up with no fingerprints at all until the "tread" grew back. It would have been a good time to take up a life of crime, but I stayed on the straight and narrow—and plumb.

When you make a batch of concrete, the sum total of the ingredients mixed together will result in a much smaller volume than the separate components—kind of like what happens to that mountain of flour when you make a loaf of bread, or when you can't believe you just used a ½-gallon of ice cream to make only two decent-sized milkshakes.

Bill advised me to use a 1:3:5 mix: 1 heaping shovel of cement to 3 of sand, and 5 of gravel. For me, that mixture would be economical for my budget and yet strong enough for my particular application: a heavy foundation and thick retaining walls. Because the tank would be sitting on impenetrable hard rock, I knew it would have to be back-filled to bury it partially underground, which would also help equalize the pressure on the walls. (Water weight pushes out; wall of dirt pushes in.) Backfilling would also keep the water cool in the summer.

Calculating what you need

Using some simple math, I estimated the walls would take 8 cubic yards. Here's how: Multiply length (12') x height (6') x thickness (¾ of a foot = .75) x 4 walls and divide by 27 because there are 27 cubic feet in one cubic yard.

The walls

The growling gyrating cement mixer held 1/8 cubic yard (approximately 3.5 cubic feet) at a time, gobbling up 2 shovels of cement, 6 shovels of sand, 10 shovels of gravel. I worked as fast as I could slinging them in, counting and alternating the ingredients very carefully, while constantly adding the water with a measuring bucket (about 4 gallons).

When the batter was "just right," I shut off the motor, swung the cement mixer around on its axis and dumped the load into the forms, then tamped, tamped, and tamped with the business end of a short shovel. I also tapped the sides of the forms with a hammer to vibrate the concrete into every nook and cranny. On the fifth and final pour, I set a pipe through the wall near the top to make an overflow hole. I would later run a 1½" polypipe through that hole and out to my pond.

Each daily pour amounted to 12 mixers full, which totaled 24 shovels of cement, 72 shovels of sand, 120 shovels of gravel, and 48 gallons of water. I guzzled another 10 gallons of water and dumped even more on my head. It took five days of working from daybreak to backbreak to complete the walls. The whole project had to be a marathon because concrete sets up fast in extreme heat, and time

Conservation tips

When you live on well water and have to pump every drop, here are some astonishing figures to consider:

A running faucet uses 3-5 gallons a minute.

A running faucet while you brush your teeth can use 5 gallons.

A running faucet while you do dishes can use 30 gallons.

Washers use 30-60 gallons for each cycle. Wait till you have a full load of clothes before doing the laundry.

A long shower can use 50 gallons. You'll know it was too long when you run out of hot water. You'll know it was way too long when you run out of *cold* water.

Gabled roof on tank inside

was running out on my week vacation from waitressing.

Needless to say, I put my fitness center membership on hold for a while. *Sixteen Tons* by Tennessee Ernie Ford was my theme song for the week, although the tank ended up weighing 24 tons. Blistered hands on Monday had turned into lobster claws by Friday.

The roof

On top of the last pour, I dragged a short 2"x6" on edge across the 8" wide wet surfaces to smooth them out. I then set four 2"x4" pressure-treated sill plates in the concrete and leveled them with a long level by tamping and wiggling them into place around the outside perimeter, making sure the corners were squared.

They would be an integral part of the roof construction, providing a wood surface to build a short stem wall on. The "pony wall" would be screened for cross-ventilation, rather than covered with plywood. I built a gabled roof on the tank, with the rafter tails secured to the top plate of the stem wall. (See photos)

When the job was done (floor AND walls), I had used approximately 55 sacks of Portland cement, 6 cubic yards of sand, 10 cubic yards of gravel, and about 400 gallons of water. Not exactly like building Hoover Dam, but it felt like it.

I kept the concrete slab and walls wet while they were curing by spraying everything down with a hose, including myself, as often as possible. I had a hose hooked up to the inlet/outlet pipe in the floor of the tank so water was handy.

Note: This mandatory procedure should go on for at least a week when working in hot weather.

Sealing the tank

I think the reason my tank has held up so well for 23 years now, in spite of the 1:3:5 "poorman's mix" I used, is because I coated the inside of the tank with a cohesive sealer called "Thoroseal."

Thoroseal is a Portland-cement-based coating that, when mixed with a milky-looking catalyst called Acryl 60, fills and seals voids and waterproofs the concrete. It prevents any water seepage from leaking into fissures where it might freeze and expand and crack the concrete. It also resists hydrostatic pressure (as inside a water tank) and is non-toxic in potable water tanks. It can be brushed on, but Bill advised me to trowel it on about ¼" thick for an impenetrable bond. It took a lot of elbow grease applying it in smooth swipes on the entire inside surface of the tank, but it covered up all those rough cold-joint seams and made it look as smooth and beautiful as a baby-elephant's butt.

I don't claim to be an expert on the subject of concrete tank building. We built the tank during possibly the hottest July in history, so my memory of the details may be a little off due to sunstroke. All I know is that I built it under Bill's tutelage, and it has stood the test of time.

When I look up the hill and see the water-level flag sticking up out of the tank's roof and dancing in the breeze, it helps to quench my thirst for security and self-sufficiency.

Back in the summer of 1983, the finished tank with its shingled roof cost me a total of $750 to build, including the lumber and plywood used for the forms.

One little access door to the inside of the tank

The odd couple

Today's average prices

Ingredients to make the concrete:

80 lb. bag of Portland cement = $2.50

Cubic yard of "construction sand" = $15

Cubic yard of crushed gravel (¾ minus or pea gravel) = $10.

Note: You can buy construction-grade sand and gravel already mixed in the ratio you want at any large rental equipment yard or your local sand and gravel supplier for about $32/yd. or $350 for a 10-yard dump truck full, delivered to your site. That sure beats the way I did it. Having the raw ingredients delivered would have been heaven instead of "the other place!"

Framing and roofing lumber:

2x8s = .70/ft.

2x6s = .50/ft.

2x4s = .35/ft.

5/8" CDX plywood for roof = $18/sheet

Roof: I recommend composition roofing (cheap) or metal roofing (fireproof). I used cedar shingles back then, but now I would choose metal roofing and also divert the annual rainfall via rain gutters into the tank to supplement the supply.

Total materials it takes for a 6500-gallon tank:

55 bags cement = $140

5 yds. sand = $75

10 yds. gravel = $100

2 yds. gravel under pad = $20

Forms: (40) 2x4 x12s = $168

(8) 2x8x12s = $67

(12) sheets of 5/8" plywood = $216

Stem-wall: (12) 2x4x12s = $50

Roof: (20) 2x6x8s = $112

(12) sheets of 5/8" plywood = $0 (I recycled the same plywood I used for the forms)

Assorted screws and nails and drain hardware: About $50

Thoroseal: (10) 50-lb. bags to cover 500 sq. ft.= $250

Acryl 60: 5 gallons = $125

Composition roofing to cover the 200-sq. ft. roof = about $50

Labor cost = your energy (a renewable resource)

Strong back = fringe benefit

Optional cost of labor if you treat yourself to pizza and beer to celebrate when the job is done = $20

The same tank today adds up to $1,500; still not bad for a permanent 6500-gallon water tank. I say "permanent," but now I have my doubts after overhearing an old timer at the hardware story drawling to another old timer: "There are two kinds of concrete—concrete that's cracked, and concrete that's gonna crack." Then they cackled and wheezed.

Closing thoughts

Any able-bodied person can mix and pour concrete. Building the forms to contain and shape it is the easiest and most elementary carpentry going. So, even though my cave-woman ordeal with concrete might sound difficult, don't be intimidated by the "stuff." It's malleable and infallible. My style is to overbuild everything; it needn't be yours. If you have a little extra cash and aren't in a big hurry, working creatively with small batches of concrete mixed in a wheelbarrow can be downright fun! Δ

(Editor's Note: You might be interested in a companion article that Dorothy wrote for our November/December 2004 Issue #90. Entitled, "Water pumping windmills," Dorothy includes an historical background of windmills, explains how they work, their uses, windmill installation and maintenance, and more. It is available in *A Backwoods Home Anthology, The Fifteenth Year*.)

Homemade pickles and relishes

...a wonderful way to turn autumn harvest into winter treasure

By Linda Gabris

When I was a kid, my grandparents had one of the biggest gardens in the countryside and, come autumn, there was nothing I enjoyed more than helping Grandma "put up" bushels of canned goods to stock the cellar shelves for winter use.

Of course, in those days, putting food by—or canning—was an important way of life for we seldom went to town in wintertime to shop for groceries. Every fall, Grandma and I did up enough mouthwatering goodies to carry us all the way through to the next year's harvest.

Even though today, unlike grandma, I have easy access to year-round shopping, I still take great pleasure, pride, and comfort in doing up my own preserves and condiments, like pickles and relishes, from the bounty of my backyard garden.

To me, there is no greater joy than breaking open a sparkling jar of something from the cellar and boasting that, "Yes, indeed, it's homemade!" And, the good news is, there's no need to fret if you don't have a garden or if your veggie patch didn't produce enough surplus crop for canning as you can get reasonable buys on seasonal produce at local farmer's markets, roadside fruit and vegetable stands, or even in grocery stores to fill your sealers for winter.

As far as home-canning goes, the rules have changed some since my younger days. Canning jars have been updated, and home canners today have a set of basic rules laid down by experts that we can follow to help ensure that food is canned safely and does not go bad.

The antique sealers that my grandmother used (known as bailed or lightning jars) with glass lids, rubber rings, and wire clamps are no longer recommended and have been replaced by modern, self-sealing jars loosely referred to as Mason jars.

In the olden days, Mason referred to the name of the maker who invented the first jars with handy screw-on caps, rather than bails that were patented in 1858. The Mason jar became so popular that it went down in history as both a commercial and household name.

For safety's sake, health officials today advise home canners to use modern Mason-style jars that are fitted each season with new self-sealing lids and screw on bands.

Mason-type jars are made of heavy glass that can take heat under pressure without breaking. Using unapproved jars or those that commercial food has been purchased in (and yes, I know firsthand that some old timers have done just that) are apt to break under pressure and should never be used for processing food at home.

First and foremost, make sure that your jars are free of nicks and have been fitted with new seals each season as the sealing compound loses its muscle after use. You can reuse the screw-on bands so long as they are not bent or rusted.

Jars must be sterilized before filling. Wash in hot sudsy water and then scald. Put jars in a large kettle of water, making sure that they are covered well. Heat to boiling, then boil 15 minutes. Hold jars in hot water until ready to fill with food.

Process the seals according to the manufacturer's directions on the box. Most brands are submerged in hot water to soften sealing compound, but not boiled as this can damage the seal. Since manufacturers' directions may vary, read and follow directions carefully.

Use only top-quality ingredients. Let's face it, if you make dill pickles out of sandy, wilted cukes, you can bet your bottom dollar that your pickles will be gritty and lacking in crispness.

Same goes for making corn relish out of moldy ears of corn. The finished product will not be blue-ribbon worthy. Harvest your vegetables when they are at a prime for picking—on canning morning—wash thoroughly, then hold in icy cold water.

For long-term storage, you must heat process ALL home-canned foods either by boiling water bath or in a pressure canner. High-acid foods such as the pickles and relishes in the recipes below—which have large amounts of acid added in the form of vinegar—can be safely processed in a boiling water bath.

Even though my Grandma processed all her foods the old fashioned way in a boiling water bath, this practice for low-acid foods such as vegetables being done up without the aid of vinegar—example canned peas, beans, asparagus—is not recommended today. These types of low-acid foods must be processed in a pressure canner for safekeeping.

The recipes below are well suited for processing in the boiling water fashion. Because the temperature in the jars of food being processed by the boiling water bath never exceeds 212° F, it is suitable only for such strong-acid foods as pickles and other vinegared things. The bath does three important things: Kills bacteria, yeast, and molds that cannot live at such a temperature; drives out air in the food that can cause spoilage; and seals the jars.

In order for the bath to work properly, the jars must be kept completely submerged at least 2" underwater and the water kept at a full rolling boil for the exact times indicated. Take note that cooking time of the recipe is NOT counted as part of the processing time. To thoroughly destroy all microorganisms that can cause food to go bad, the food must be heated to proven temperatures as stated in time-honored recipes.

Any lidded kettle that is deep enough to accommodate the size of jars being processed and that can be fitted with a wire or mesh bottom that will hold jars slightly off the bottom, will suffice as a boiling-bath canner although there are large, enamel kettles specially built for the purpose. They can be bought cheaply at hardware stores and come with perforated or wire mesh racks that keep jars off the bottom of the kettle so water can circulate properly.

Before starting, you should round up all needed equipment. Along with boiling bath kettle, ample jars and new seals, you will need a large earthen, glass or stainless bowl for soaking and a large, heavy-bottomed kettle for precooking food. And fill your tea kettle with water and keep it whistling throughout your canning session as you will need readily boiling water.

Bring out your alarm clock or kitchen timer to ensure proper timing. Round up a ladle, a measuring cup, jar-lifter, and spatula, and you're ready to roll.

A precious trove of homemade pickles and relishes ready to be stored in the cellar for winter use.

How to use the boiling water bath

Put the bath kettle with rack in place on a large stove burner. Fill with water to the halfway mark, and start heating.

Prepare food as stated below:

Fill hot, sterilized jars leaving 1" headspace with prepared food.

Wipe jar rims with clean dishcloth that's been dipped in hot water.

Follow manufacturer's directions for preparing and adjusting lids. When all jars have been filled, lower into hot water.

Add enough boiling water to cover at least 2 inches above the tops of jars.

Put the lid on the kettle and, when water comes back to an even boil, begin timing, adding boiling water if needed to keep covered. When time is up, remove jars and allow to cool undisturbed for 24 hours, keeping upright.

Remove screw bands and check the seals. A properly sealed lid will curve downward. If jar is not properly sealed, it must be stored in the fridge and treated as an already opened jar.

You can replace the bands lightly or store the jars without bands.

Label and store canned foods in a cool, dark place.

Grandma's old-fashioned garlic-style dills:

Here's a pickle recipe that's hard to beat. Select uniformly sized, firm, fresh cucumbers. Grandma always said, "pick cukes in the morning and

Grandma's old-fashioned kosher-style garlic dills

pickle before lunch if you want a really super pickle." This recipe can be halved, doubled, or tripled depending on the size of your crop. Let these pickles age for at least 3 weeks before cracking open a jar. Makes 8 quarts.

- 8 pounds pickling cucumbers
- a large pan that holds enough water and ice to cover cukes (Grandma soaked hers in fresh-drawn ice-cold well water)
- 8 sprigs fresh dill
- 32 cloves whole peeled garlic
- 8 Tbsp. pickling salt
- 8 tsp. mixed pickling spice
- 8 cups white vinegar
- 8 cups water

Wash cucumbers and scrub lightly with vegetable brush to remove sand. Rinse under cold running water. Put cucumbers in large bowl and cover with water. Add ice and let stand for an hour if fresh picked. If cucumbers are older than a couple of hours from picking, let stand for at least 4 hours to firm up, adding ice as needed or keep in fridge underwater.

Make pickling liquid by mixing vinegar and water in large kettle and bringing to boil. Reduce heat and hold simmering while filling jars.

Remove jars from water. Place 1 sprig of dill, 4 cloves garlic, 1 tablespoon pickling salt, and 1 teaspoon pickling spice into each jar.

Pack cucumbers, standing upright. Add pickling liquid to cover, leaving headspace. If more liquid is needed, mix equal parts vinegar and water and bring to a boil.

Using spatula, remove air bubbles. Follow directions above for proceeding with boiling water bath. Process 15 minutes.

Spicy dilled carrots:

Great color and crunch for any pickle platter. Make one jar of super long sticks to use as cocktail stirrers. Makes 8 quarts.

- 7 pounds carrots
- 6 cups white vinegar
- 2 cups water
- 1 cup sugar
- ½ cup pickling salt
- 16 cloves garlic
- 8 sprigs dill
- 8 hot peppers (or 8 pinches of hot dried chili peppers)
- 2 Tbsp. pickling spice

Scrub carrots. Cut into desired-size sticks. Drop into icy water until all carrots are prepared.

Mix vinegar, water, sugar, and salt and bring to boil. Keep hot.

Put 2 cloves garlic, 1 sprig of dill, 1 hot pepper, or pinch of chili pepper and ¼ teaspoon pickling spice into each hot jar. Pack carrot sticks to within ¾" of rim. Add boiling brine to cover.

Spicy dilled carrots—A canned treat that's hard to beat

Aunt Mernie's mustard pickles

Remove air bubbles. Proceed as above for boiling water bath. Process 15 minutes.

Aunt Mernie's chunky mustard pickles:

The saying goes that Aunt Mernie got the recipe from Grandma, but over the years—after adding a pinch of this and a pinch of that—she perfected the pickles to the point where Grandma had to ask for the recipe back. Makes about 5 quarts or about 10 pint-sized jars.

2 quarts sliced cukes
(Grandma used chunks of peeled yellow, seeded garden cucumbers. Aunt Mernie used unpeeled pickling cukes cut into fours; perhaps that's why her pickles were so much more gourmet)
2 cups sliced onions (for gourmet use baby or pearl onions)
1 cauliflower, cut into small flowerets
2 sweet red peppers, cut into chunks
½ cup pickling salt
2 cups vinegar
1 cup water
3 cups sugar
2 tsp. celery seed
pinch each of ginger and curry powder
2 Tbsp. mustard powder
1 Tbsp. turmeric
¾ cup flour
1 cup water

Place cucumbers and onions in large bowl. Sprinkle with salt. Let stand one hour. While soaking, steam the cauliflower and peppers until barely tender. Drain.

Corn nugget relish in the kettle

Drain cucumbers and onions. Rinse under cold running water. Add cooked vegetables and mix well.

Place vinegar, water, and sugar in pot and heat to boiling. Whisk dry ingredients with water until smooth and slowly blend into vinegar mix, cooking until thick and smooth. Add vegetables and bring to a rolling boil.

Ladle into jars. Proceed as above for boiling water bath, processing 20 minutes.

Corn nugget relish:

So pretty, so good. In our house we use corn relish in place of salsa for dipping and dunking everything from nachos to celery sticks. Makes 3 quarts or 6 pint-sized jars.

6 cups fresh corn, cut off the cob
1 cup chopped onion
2 cups chopped sweet red peppers
1 cup sugar
1 tsp. salt
1 tsp. pepper
1 tsp. mustard seed
1 tsp. celery salt
2 cups cider vinegar
3 Tbsp. mustard powder
1 Tbsp. turmeric
½ cup flour
½ cup cold water

Put first 9 ingredients into kettle and mix well. Bring to boil. Lower heat and simmer for 1 hour, stirring often.

Combine mustard powder, turmeric, flour, and water in bowl and mix until smooth.

Slowly blend into corn mixture, stirring until thick. Cook until bubbles break surface for 3 minutes, stirring constantly.

Ladle into hot jars. Process pint jars 10 minutes and quart sealers 15 minutes. Δ

The enchanting CHANTERELLE

GOURMET GOODIES FREE FROM THE FOREST

By Devon Winter

They're prized by the world's top chefs. They're served in the most elegant restaurants. You'll pay a pretty penny for them at farmers' markets. Yet they're abundant and often free for the taking in forests all over the world. Even a newcomer can gather them easily after only a few minutes instruction.

I'm talking about Chanterelle mushrooms. You can pluck these golden gems in the hills of California or the ancient *wald* of Germany. They grow in the steamy spring woods of Missouri and the foggy fall forests of the Pacific Northwest.

The Chanterelle is distinctive and beautiful. It's a great target for novice mushroom hunters, because it's both easy to identify and rewarding to the tongue. If you become a serious Chanterelle hunter, you might even make money from your gatherings.

What is a Chanterelle?

The Chanterelle is an edible fungus of the genus *Cantharellus*. There are many Chanterelle species, but the most common and easy to identify are *C. cibarius* (the yellow Chanterelle) and *C. formosus* (the Pacific Golden Chanterelle).

These two are so much alike that only recently did scientists decide the Pacific Golden was a separate species. (See photo captions for more about Chanterelle species.)

The Chanterelle is lovely to look at, delicate in flavor, and goes well with "lite" meats like chicken. It also makes excellent soups and appetizers. You can happily toss Chanterelles onto a fresh green salad or a pizza.

Taste a raw Chanterelle and initially you'll perceive a firm, moist, fibrous texture, but merely a slight flavor. After a moment, though, your throat will feel "peppery"—a sensation that might linger for several minutes. To me, the overall impression is almost radish-like, though the texture is softer.

When cooked, Chanterelles lose their pepperiness, but add a pleasantly delicate flavor and texture to any dish, from an omlette to a side of rice.

Where and when do you find them?

Chanterelles grow in a symbiotic relationship with living trees. They gather moisture and minerals to feed the trees, and in return, trees offer the mushrooms food in the form of photosynthesized carbohydrates.

Because of that intricate relationship, Chanterelles are almost impossible to cultivate and are not yet commercially grown (although researchers are trying).

In many parts of the world, including California and the mid-Atlantic coast, they grow around the base of

Photo by Pamela Kaminski ~ www.pamelasmushrooms.com

This photo displays the lovely trumpet-like or goblet-like form that gives the Chanterelle its name. This specimen is C. lateritius, *the smooth Chanterelle, found on the east coast. Chanterelles found in Washington and Oregon usually have more pronounced gills, but they share the same basic shape and color.*

Photo by Pamela Kaminski ~ www.pamelasmushrooms.com

The distinctive underside of the classic Chanterelle, C. cibarius. *This mature specimen has the typical wavy edge and the pronounced gills typical of Chanterelles in the drippy Pacific "North Wet." Notice the way the stem widens and flows outward; the chanterelle does not have a separate cap.*

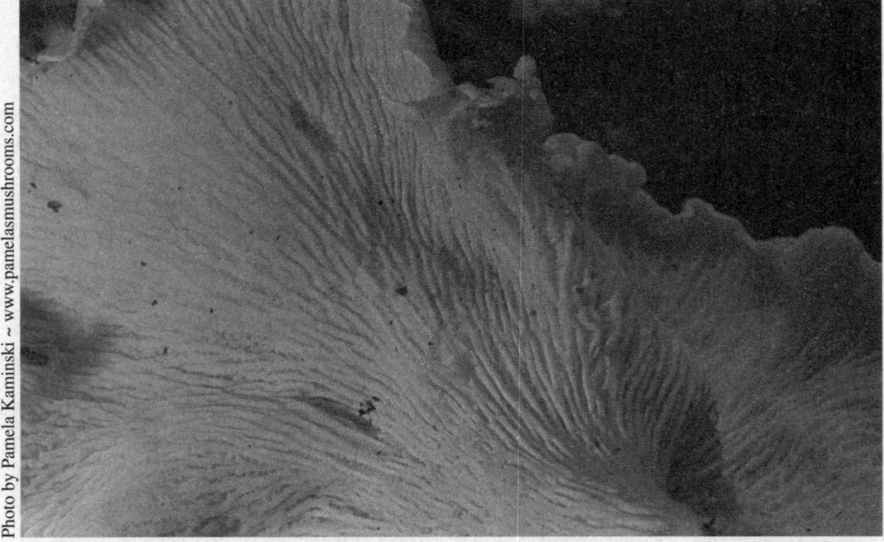

Photo by Pamela Kaminski ~ www.pamelasmushrooms.com

The underside and elegant curling edge typical of the Chanterelle. The gills you see here are the mushroom's spore-producing surface. This example is C. lateritius, *whose gills are less pronounced than those of some other Chanterelle species.*

oak trees. In the Pacific Northwest, they favor Douglas-fir and western hemlock forests. But wherever you seek them, you'll always find them around the base of living trees.

They like mature trees. But my own personal best gathering ground has been in a 20- or 25-year-old tree farm that's overdue for thinning. They love the darkness there, the undisturbed ground, and the lack of competition from greenery.

Chanterelles are a spring or early summer crop in the southeast and many parts of California. Look for them after rainstorms in late May or June. In the forests of Saskatchewan, Chanterelles may appear in the late spring and grow throughout the summer. In the Pacific Northwest, they're a fall crop—popping up after the rainy season arrives and sharing their bounty until the first frost.

What do you look for?

Before you hunt any mushrooms, know what you're doing. If you're new, go out with an experienced person the first time.

Also, know whether it's okay to gather in a given area. In some parks, mushrooming might be forbidden. In other places, you might need a permit or an okay from a property owner. Where I live, you simply go out onto logging company lands and begin.

First, as you scan the forest floor, look for bright, wholesome gold or yellow dots near the bases of trees. Think of the most beautiful, classic golden retriever dog you've ever seen. That's the color. (And these little goldens are well worth retrieving.)

The shape of a mature Chanterelle has been described as a funnel, a goblet, or a trumpet. It does not have a separate stem and cap, but a graceful, almost seamless curve in which the stem broadens and unfurls to become the cap.

They are so goblet-like that sometimes you'll find a fully formed Chanterelle holding a shot-glass full of rainwater. Normally, though, the top splits as it unfurls, so water runs off. The edges of mature Chanterelles are also wavy or curvy.

Immature Chanterelles appear to have a round cap, but when you pluck them and examine the underside, you'll see that it's not a true cap, but simply hasn't finished unfurling yet.

Chanterelles may be smaller than your thumb, or when full grown, as large as your fist. They have a matte surface. The underside reveals fine gills, either the same color as the cap or slightly lighter, that begin below the point where the outward curve starts. The gills, the spore-producing portion of the mushroom, may be pronounced, as in *C. cibarius*. Or they may be smoother, depending on the species and the growing conditions. Wet conditions tend to produce a more pronounced gill. Tear a Chanterelle open and the flesh inside is pure white, firm, and shreds easily.

Another sure identifier: Pluck a Chanterelle and hold it to your nose. The aroma is similar to that of an apricot—the stronger the aroma, the stronger the flavor.

How to tell Chanterelles from similar mushrooms

In general, a Chanterelle is *not* brown, weak yellow, white, or red. There are exceptions to this rule, definitely. But when first exploring the world of Chanterelles, think *bright* gold or yellow.

Photo by Pamela Kaminski ~ www.pamelasmushrooms.com

This is C. lateritius, *the smooth Chanterelle, typically found in oak forests in the American east. But this photo gives an excellent idea of what the novice Chanterelle hunter should look for anywhere—a golden, matte-colored, wavy-topped fungus growing in the dark, moist environment of the forest floor.*

Safe mushroom hunting

The old saying goes, "There are old mushroom hunters and there are bold mushroom hunters. But there are no old, bold mushroom hunters." Although yellow and golden Chanterelles are among the easiest edible fungi to identify, and although they have no deadly imitators, a first-time hunter should still think smart. Make your first hunt with a trusted, experienced person.

If you don't already know such a person, consider contacting a local club of the North American Mycological Association, an organization for amateur and professional mushroom hunters. This group has clubs all over the continent.

North American Mycological Association
6615 Tudor Ct.
Gladstone, OR 97027-1032
503-657-7358
www.namyco.org

A Chanterelle is *not* slick or shiny. A Chanterelle does *not* have a pointy cap, extremely deep gills, a spindly stem, or a distinct, separate cap. A Chanterelle does *not* grow directly on wood (again, there are exceptions for some rare and distinct Chanterelle species, but our little "golden retrievers" grow only in moist forest soil).

The two most common Chanterelle look-alikes are the false Chanterelle—which won't hurt you, but makes a disappointing dinner—and the Jack-O-Lantern. The Jack-O-Lantern will make you sick but won't kill you. The Jack-O-Lantern is pretty easy to distinguish, though. Its cap is more brown, it has deeper gills, and it does grow directly on wood. It's also bioluminescent—that is, it glows in the dark. A Chanterelle *never* glows in the dark.

Within 10 minutes of beginning my first Chanterelle hunt, I'd made a rule that's never led me astray: If I have to ask myself, "Is that a Chanterelle?" then it's *not* a Chanterelle. Real Chanterelles practically jump off the forest floor at you, once you know what to look for.

How to harvest

Harvesting is simple. Gently tug the mushroom out of the ground, rocking or twisting as necessary. Don't cut a chanterelle out of the ground with a knife, as this may lead to infection in the remaining stem and might damage the hidden understructure on which the next crop of mushrooms will grow.

Feel free to take both mature examples and small ones (which many people find more tasty). But don't over harvest. Leave some small mushrooms and leave the ground as undisturbed as possible. Nature will reward you with more mushrooms in the future.

Once you've captured your golden gem, use a sharp knife to slice off the end of its stem. Then leave the end in the woods.

Place your "catch" in a basket. Carrying in a woven basket is good for the mushrooms you've picked as it helps keep them from getting mushy. But it's even better for future mushroom harvests. With each step you take, your basket sheds spores that might turn into future Chanterelle patches.

You can also tote your harvest in a paper bag lined with paper towels to absorb extra moisture. Real Chanterelle aficionados say never to use a plastic container. But in practice, people use plastic bags and buckets all the time. Just don't keep your Chanterelles in plastic very long. Empty them onto a towel once you return home.

Photo by Larry Evans ~ www.fungaljungal.org

These are young Chanterelles whose caps haven't yet unfurled into the distinctive wavy shape. At this stage, they are more firm, and many people say more tasty than when mature. Lift a Chanterelle of any age to your nose and enjoy the apricot aroma.

How to clean and store

Tend to your mushrooms as soon as you get them into your kitchen. If you've sliced off the stem ends while in the woods, your cleaning job will be relatively easy. Just lightly brush off the dirt and debris with a paper towel or soft cloth. You can also use a small brush to get dirt out of the gills and curves, but you'll be scrubbing off the surface of the mushroom at the same time.

Don't wash Chanterelles unless you absolutely must—and in that case it's best to do it right before cooking.

To store fresh: Place them in a paper bag in the veggie-keeper compartment of your refrigerator. They'll be good for 7-10 days.

To freeze: Most people prefer to saute their Chanterelles before freezing. Just place a tiny bit of oil or butter in the pan, quarter the mushrooms, and stir for a few minutes over medium heat. (Chanterelles have so much moisture that with just a starter drop of oil they'll "dry saute" themselves in their own water.) You can freeze them in their cooking liquid, discard the liquid, or separate the liquid and use it in soups.

If you saute them with butter and onions before freezing, you have a ready-made appetizer or soup ingredient; just defrost, add wine or stock and spices—and *voila!*

You can freeze without sauteeing, as long as you do it in small, meal-sized containers. If you use large containers, the Chanterelles' high moisture content will cause them to clump into one indivisible mass. HINT: Since chanterelles tend to get rubbery or mushy when preserved, freeze only young, firm specimens.

To can: I don't like canned mushrooms, so here I'll pass along the word of a third-party expert. According to the web site: *Wild About Mushrooms* (www.mssf.org/cookbook/chanterelle.html):

Photo by Larry Evans ~ www.fungaljungal.org

The camera lens cap gives you a good idea of the size of a typical mature Chanterelle. Young (but very tasty!) Chanterelles may be smaller than the tip of your thumb. Conversely, in Northwest rainforests, hunters have found examples as large as a fully spread hand.

"To can Chanterelles, clean them thoroughly and cut them in big chunks and steam for 20 minutes. Place the pieces in small [sterilized] canning jars and cover them with the liquid from the steaming vessel or boiling water to make up the difference. Add ½ teaspoon salt and ½ teaspoon vinegar. Finally, sterilize them for 40 minutes in a pressure cooker at 10 pounds pressure."

You can also pickle your Chanterelles using any standard pickle recipe, adjusting the seasonings to suit the very delicate flavor of the mushroom.

To dry: Quarter your Chanterelles and lay them in the open air. Cover lightly with cheesecloth if insects are a problem. Then store them in a lidless container that allows them to breathe a bit. When it's time to serve, just soak in water for an hour or two. NOTE: Dried Chanterelles always retain a slightly leathery texture. Once dried, they might be suitable as an ingredient in a soup or stew, but not in a stand-alone mushroom dish.

A tip for dividing your Chanterelles: You can slice them with a knife, as you would any mushroom. But try this instead: Hold a Chanterelle by its top, push your thumbs into the center of the cap, and simply tear lengthwise. You can tear into pieces as large or as small as you need. Much easier and faster than slicing.

Chanterelles are extremely versatile. Here's a sampling of very easy recipes.

Chanterelle casserole:

Serve this as a side dish or as a sauce over chicken or pasta.

1 pound Chanterelles, cut in halves or quarters
1 onion, chopped
¼ cup chicken broth
½ cup cream
salt and pepper to taste

Pre-heat oven to 350 degrees. Spread the mushrooms in the bottom of a baking dish. Spread the onions over them, cover the dish, and bake for 20 minutes. Remove from oven, stir, and add broth, cream, and seasonings. Bake another 15 minutes. Try not to boil the cream.

Serve garnished with fresh parsley. Serves 4.

Chanterelle and wild rice soup:

The textures of this soup are almost as good as the flavors.

1 Tbsp. olive oil
1 onion, finely chopped
1 pound Chanterelles, shredded
½ cup white wine
2 cups chicken or vegetable stock
1½ cups evaporated milk
1 cup cooked wild rice (or blend of brown & wild rices)
ground black pepper to taste

Heat oil over medium heat. Add onions and mushrooms and saute. Gradually add wine. Add stock and bring to a boil. Reduce heat and simmer for 10 minutes. Add cooked rice, evaporated milk, and pepper, and simmer until heated through. Serves 4.

Beefless Chanterelle stroganoff:

Here's a quick and easy recipe that will also let a preparedness buff use a few stored ingredients.

¾ cup beef-flavored TVP
1 medium onion (or equivalent in dried onion flakes)
3 cups Chanterelle slices
3 Tbsp. butter or oil
salt and pepper to taste
½ tsp. basil
a grating of nutmeg
¼ cup dry white wine
1 cup sour cream

Hydrate the TVP with boiling water and set aside. In a skillet, saute mushrooms and onion in butter. Add the salt, pepper, nutmeg, and basil. Drain any excess water from the TVP. Add the TVP to the mushroom/onion mix. When thoroughly heated, add the wine and sour cream. Heat until these final ingredients are warmed, then serve over green egg noodles. Serves 2-3.

Chanterelles and hazelnuts in Madeira:

As an appetizer, this adaptation of a recipe from a famous Northwest restaurant will dazzle your taste buds. Or you can ladle it over chicken or mix it with hearty rice blends.

5 Tbsp. butter
salt and pepper to taste
1 hearty dash of Tabasco sauce
1 tsp. Worcestershire sauce
1 tsp. green onions or dried onion flakes
1 Tbsp. minced garlic
2-3 Tbsp. hazelnuts (or pecans), finely chopped
2 cups Chanterelles, quartered
½ cup Madeira wine

On high heat, melt butter in a saucepan. While butter is melting, add salt and pepper, Tabasco, Worcestershire, onion, and garlic. Once this mixture is bubbling, saute the mushrooms and nuts. As the toasty aroma arises, gradually add the wine, still cooking on high. Cook a few more minutes until the sauce reduces slightly. Then serve garnished with fresh parsley. Serves 2.

Chanterelle salad:

Here's a quick, light summer lunch or healthy starter dish.

Mix green leaf and red leaf lettuce in a bowl. Top with:

raw, quartered Chanterelles
raw, unsalted sunflower nuts
vine-ripened tomatoes, sliced
finely chopped slices of your favorite cheese
croutons or a sprinkling of Italian-flavored bread crumbs

Serve with oil & vinegar or a light vinaigrette dressing. Serves as many as you prepare for. Δ

Raising quail

a home grown delicacy

By Allen Easterly

Raising quail is inexpensive, easy, provides very healthy low-fat white meat, and supplies the fertilizer you need for your home garden. The moderate start-up costs for raising quail are well worth it. A simple 8x8-foot open-sided pole building is fine to start with. You can also use an empty corner in an existing outbuilding. Wall in the upper half to keep strong winter winds away. Sturdy wire should be applied over the bottom half to help keep pets and predators at bay. There are a lot of wild critters, including snakes, that like to snack on quail and their tasty eggs. At eye level on each side of the building, hang a 30x30x14" grow-off pen built with ½x1" mesh wire. At the end of the building at waist height, construct a simple frame to hold a brooder, breeder pen, and incubator for the quail. Keeping the birds off the ground helps reduce the chance of parasite infestation or disease. It also makes cleaning up after the birds quicker and easier. You are almost ready to begin production.

A source for chicks or hatching eggs might be your local feed store. If not, there are several mail order companies that can provide eggs, chicks, equipment, and the supplies you need. The Japanese or Coturnix quail are the fastest growing and reproducing birds. After just 16 days in the incubator, your initial egg purchase should provide at least a 50-percent hatch rate. Feed the baby birds a game bird starter mix for the first four weeks and a game bird grower mix for the next two weeks. For a small operation, select the best nine females and three males from the hatchlings as breeders and move them to the breeding pen. The remaining hatchlings are now old enough to butcher for the dining table. Maintain a three-to-one female-to-male breeder ratio for the best egg fertility. At this age, the breeders can start laying eggs. Begin feeding them a game bird breeder mix that contains the higher calcium needed for healthy egg shell production. Keep the breeders under 16 hours of light daily, and they will begin to lay eggs. Maintaining the same number of hours under lights will keep your Coturnix quail laying eggs throughout the year.

Under prime conditions, each female bird will lay about 300 eggs each year. When your breeders are laying eggs consistently, collect hatching eggs daily. Keep the eggs in a cool dark place until they are ready for the incubator. Collect eggs for 10 consecutive days, then set the batch of eggs in the incubator at 99½° F. Maintain humidity levels identified with your incubator instructions. Eggs should always be kept pointy end down and need to be turned twice daily to keep the yolk centered inside the eggshell. You can do this manually or with the use of an automatic turner. Once hatched, transfer the chicks to a pre-warmed 100° F brooder. Each week, drop the temperature in the brooder by five degrees. At four weeks old, the young quail can be moved from the brooder to one of the grow-off pens. At six weeks old, the birds are ready to be processed for the dinner table. The eggs, while small, are also considered a delicacy.

Quail poop is like brown gold for your garden. It's low on odor and isn't very messy to deal with. Shovel up your excess quail manure each

Coturnix quail

week and move it to a garden manure bin to age until it breaks down before using it on plants. It is high in nitrogen, and when fresh, it can burn plants. In the heat of the summer, if the manure does emit much odor, a light covering of lime will eliminate it and sweeten the pile.

Low in fat and high in protein, the all-white-meat quail is served as a delicacy in many fine restaurants. You can enjoy dining on this nutritious bird from your own home-grown stock with surprisingly little effort. Quail eggs are also a delicious delicacy served in many professional kitchens. It takes about three Coturnix quail eggs to equal one small chicken egg.

An average six-ounce skinless quail contains about 123 calories, 40 percent of the recommended daily allowance (RDA) of protein, 50 percent niacin, 30 percent vitamin B6, and 28 percent of iron. The same bird has only 1.2 grams of saturated fat, 1.2 grams monounsaturated fat, 1.1 grams polyunsaturated fat, and 64 grams of cholesterol.

Whether you choose to pluck or skin your birds is a matter of personal preference. The skin has very little fat, unlike most commercial birds raised for maximum weight gain. When plucking, be careful not to tear the skin, as it is very thin. The skin does provide a suitable protective covering that prevents the meat from drying during cooking, so there are advantages to plucking. However, when cleaning a large number of birds for the home dining table, you might find it more efficient to skin the birds. It is far less time-consuming, and your fingers won't be worn out after cleaning a flock.

Euthanize your birds by quickly removing the head. Using a pair of kitchen shears, remove the wings and feet. You can then pluck the birds if you desire. To skin the birds, dunk them in a sink of cold water for a few minutes to cool the skins. This helps keep the feathers attached to the skin when it is removed and loosens the skin from the body. After the birds are plucked or the skin is removed, use your shears to split the bird lengthwise up the back. Remove the innards. If you have access to an outdoor hose, a blast of water into the body cavity will quickly remove any residual particles. The birds are now ready to be wrapped and frozen, or canned for future use.

Your first dozen breeder birds will provide you with hundreds of quail and thousands of eggs during the

Typical quail-rearing setup with breeding pen, brooder, incubator (white box), and grow-off pen

Starter Coturnix quail breeding flock in breeding pen

Sources for quail hatching eggs and equipment:

★ GQF Manufacturing Company
P.O. Box 1552
Savannah, GA 31402-1552
Phone 912-236-0651
Fax 912-234-9978
sales@gqfmfg.com
www.gqfmfg.com/

★ Stromberg's Chicks
P.O. Box 400
Pine River, MN 56474
Phone 218-587-2222
Orders only 1-800-720-1134
Fax 218-587-4230
info@strombergschickens.com
www.strombergschickens.com

year. Replacing your breeder stock annually maintains peak production.

The cost of feed and supplies is minimal considering all the meat and eggs you get for your efforts.

Batter-fried quail:

12 quail
3 cups water
1 Tbsp. salt
1 cup pancake or biscuit mix
2 tsp. onion powder
2 tsp. seasoned salt
¼ tsp. seasoned pepper
2 envelopes instant chicken broth
vegetable oil

Cover quail with salted water. Chill at least one hour. Combine remaining ingredients in a paper bag. Remove quail from water, and shake in bag of mix. Fry in hot oil only until golden brown. Serves 6.

Grilled quail:

2 quail (skin on) per person
lemon juice
salt and pepper to taste
butter
breadcrumbs

Sprinkle quail with lemon juice; salt and pepper. Dip in melted butter and roll in breadcrumbs. Grill about 5-6 minutes on each side.

Baked pineapple quail:

8 whole quail (skin on)
1 can (20 oz.) sliced pineapple (drain and reserve juice)
2 tsp. Worcestershire sauce
2 tsp. Dijon mustard
1 tsp. dried rosemary
1 Tbsp. cornstarch
1 small thinly sliced lemon
salt and pepper to taste

Preheat oven to 400° F. Arrange quail, breast-side down, in a shallow baking dish. Blend pineapple juice, Worcestershire sauce, mustard, rosemary, and cornstarch. Pour pineapple juice mixture over quail. Bake uncovered for 20 minutes. Turn quail breast-side up and arrange pineapple and lemon slices over quail. Baste with sauce and bake until quail are fork tender, 15-30 minutes longer. Salt and pepper sauce to taste and serve over quail. Serves 4.

Drunken quail:

6 quail
6 Tbsp. butter
3 Tbsp. flour
2 cups chicken broth
½ cup sherry
salt and pepper to taste
3 ounces chopped mushrooms
6 ounces long grain wild rice (cooked)

Brown quail in butter. Remove birds to baking dish. Add flour to butter. Stir well. Slowly add broth, sherry, and seasonings. Blend thoroughly. Add mushrooms, and pour over quail. Cover and bake at 350° for 1 hour. Serve over rice. Serves 6.

Stuffed quail:

4 quail (skin on)
dressing (see below)
salt and pepper to taste
4 Tbsp. vegetable oil
flour
1 cup chicken broth or hot water

Stuff birds lightly with dressing; salt and pepper. Place birds in a deep saucepan with vegetable oil. Cook until well browned, reduce heat, and cook slowly for 20-30 minutes. Make gravy of drippings thickened with flour, and add the chicken broth or hot water. Serves 2-4.

Dressing:

1½ cups dry bread crumbs
1½ cups of finely chopped celery
half finely cut onion
1/3 tsp. poultry seasoning
1 egg (or 3 or 4 quail eggs)
1/3 tsp. dried savory
1/3 tsp. salt
¼ tsp. powdered rosemary
1/3 cup broth or water

Combine all ingredients and mix well. Stuffs 6-8 birds.

Home-pickled eggs:

5 dozen peeled hard-boiled eggs
pickling solution:
2 pints white vinegar
1 pint water (less for tangy eggs)
2 Tbsp. salt
1 medium chopped onion
1 ounce pickling spice (2 ounces for spicy eggs)

Bring pickling solution to a boil and simmer for a few minutes. Let cool and strain. Place eggs in sterilized quart canning jar. Cover eggs with cooled solution. For best flavor, let eggs soak in solution in the refrigerator for at least three days.

Hard-boiled quail eggs:

Place 2-5 dozen eggs in cool water with a pinch of salt and bring to a boil. Hard boil 5 minutes, stirring frequently to prevent yolks from settling to one side. Plunge into cold water until cool enough to handle. Eggs peel easier if one week old before cooking. Place in cold water or refrigerator until very cold before peeling. Peel by rolling egg on hard surface to loosen shell. Shells can also be dissolved by placing in full-strength vinegar for about 12 hours, agitating every several hours. This leaves the egg enclosed in the membrane.

Serving suggestions: Dip in sea salt; coat with lemon mayonnaise then serve on salad; dip in favorite salad dressing; heat in cheese sauce; sprinkle with cheese and brown under broiler; heat in curry sauce and serve with rice.

Brine eggs:

hard-boiled quail eggs in shell
brine solution: 2 ounces salt per pint of water

Place eggs in sterilized canning jar with shells still on and cover with brine solution.

Allen Easterly is a freelance writer living a near self-sufficient lifestyle in Stafford, Virginia. He can be reached via www.writesolution.biz. Δ

Ask Jackie

> If you have a question about rural living, send it in to Jackie Clay and she'll try to answer it. Address your letter to Ask Jackie, PO Box 712, Gold Beach, OR 97444. Questions will only be answered in this column. — Editor

Stems on mulberries

I avidly read everything you write and enjoy it very much.

I have just recently made my transition from a more urban lifestyle to one more rural and I am loving it so far. I expect that the advice you offer to your various readers will benefit me almost daily as well, and for that I thank you very much.

Upon my arrival at my new home, I discovered, much to my delight, a mature and heavily fruited mulberry tree in the front yard. I have basically jumped in with both feet and figured out how to make some very lovely jam with the fruit.

My question is in regard to the stems of the berries and whether or not they must be removed in the process of preparing the fruit? I have spent hours snipping the stems off of each and every berry before preparing the fruit for cooking. It seems like a waste of time. However, my concern is whether the presence of the stems will affect the flavor of the jam adversely, which is why I don't "risk" leaving the stems on the berries.

O. M. Gillen
Los Lunas, New Mexico

Congratulations! Both on your new homestead and your mulberry tree. You do need to stem the mulberries to make whole-berry jam. But the good news is that you don't need to snip the stems off. Simply use your thumb and first fingernails to pinch off the stem. If you mash the berry a little, that's okay. You'll find that this goes much quicker. If you're not set on whole-berry jam, you can mash the berries and simmer them a little until they're soft and then press them gently through a sieve. This lets the "meat" go through, but not the stems and other coarse berry parts. The jam tastes the same, but the procedure goes much faster if you're making a lot of jam.

If you made the jam including the stems, the taste would be the same, but there would be some coarseness to the jam some may find unappetizing. — ***Jackie***

Jam not setting

I have a situation where I am trying to make strawberry preserves or jam. I have tried both ways. The first time I made jam, followed the directions explicitly on the box of Ball liquid pectin, and it didn't set up. The second time, I used powdered Sure-Jell, but didn't smash the berries. It didn't set up either. Is there any way to save it? I don't know what I've done wrong.

CMorris1456@aol.com

Did the jam not set right away? This is normal. Many times strawberry jam does not set for a few days. I hope you kept the jam! If it doesn't set, no big loss. You'll love it over pancakes, waffles, or as a dip for your French toast. It's also great on ice cream, or drizzled over vanilla pudding or frozen yogurt.

If you follow the directions on your pectin product, you will get strawberry jam that sets; it just doesn't always set up right away.

To be sure your jam sets, you can skip the pectin method and use the old-fashioned method, using only

Jackie Clay

strawberries and sugar. It takes more strawberries and sugar, and takes longer to cook, but it will set, right before your eyes. This is how to do it:

Strawberry jam:

> 2 quarts ripe strawberries
> 6 cups sugar

Wash strawberries and remove stems. Mash them well with a potato masher. Combine strawberries and sugar in a large kettle. Slowly bring to a boil, stirring until sugar dissolves. Raise heat and boil rapidly, stirring frequently, or it will scorch. As it thickens, stir more often. When it reaches the jelling point, a clean spoonful of the hot jam will slide in a sheet off the side of a spoon, instead of drip off in drops. When this point is reached, ladle hot jam into hot jars, leaving ¼" of headroom. Process 15 minutes in a boiling water bath.

Good luck. In jam making, there are no failures, just a few times the jam doesn't set. — ***Jackie***

Keeping potatoes in lime

We have just dug our potatoes and a friend tells me that she puts her potatoes in a wooden cow trough and rolls them in lime from the feed store to "keep" the potatoes. When she wants potatoes to cook she goes to the barn and gets a bucketful, rinses off the lime, and cooks the potatoes. Is using lime in this manner safe, and have you ever tried it?

Brenda Coneley
Madisonville, Texas

This is one that I've never heard of before. I'm sure someone taught your neighbor this method. But simply keeping dry potatoes in a dark, cool place, they'll keep for the entire winter without all the extra fuss and work. ***— Jackie***

Crickets in the garden

I've got crickets in the garden. I can hear them, but can't find them. My cucumbers come up, new leaves get nibbled, and it makes me mad. Do crickets eat the new garden veggies, or is it another pest? What can I do to get rid of the little buggers?

Ilene Duffy
Gold Beach, Oregon

I have always had plenty of common crickets in my gardens and have never had them attack anything. If there are lots of little holes in the leaves, the culprit is probably a host of tiny flea beetles. If you look real close, you can see "grains" like black pepper hopping off the plants as you approach.

If there are suddenly NO leaves, your raider may be a rabbit. They love new melon, squash, and cuke leaves.

I've found that if you dust damp leaves with rotenone or pyrethrin powder (made from a type of daisy), this will not only kill any insect pest eating your leaves, but will make them taste yucky and the rabbits and other little varmints, including deer, will leave 'em alone. When the vines get bigger, they get picky, and most pests leave them alone.

Covering the row with Remay or other protectant row fabric will also stop insects, such as grasshoppers, as well as small furry varmints. It will do little to protect them from flea beetles, as they are living close to the soil and will be enclosed in the fabric with the plants. ***— Jackie***

Groundhog damage

My green and yellow bean plants have had their leaves chewed off by a groundhog, along with my cauliflower and broccoli. I have just bare stalk left on all plants.

Will the leaves grow back and the plants survive? Or should I just pull them all out and start new?

Kim Rigney
Stoney Point, Ontario

Most of the time, the plants will regenerate leaves after being chewed. My own beans and some cucumber vines have been eaten down by "helpful" deer this spring. The ones that were eaten down a week ago already show tiny new leaves sprouting from the stems. The broccoli and cauliflower are a little more touchy. You might want to get right down and check them thoroughly. If there is little stalk left, I'd plant a new plant a few inches away from the old one. If both grow, you can gently replant the new one to another location in the garden. But if the old one dies, you are still in business.

This method will also work for corn or beans that have been chewed off. Simply make another row an inch from the old plants. If the old ones don't recover, the new ones will take off and fill the row, albeit crooked in spots. But in a few weeks you won't be able to tell, anyway. ***— Jackie***

Blossom end rot

I live in an apartment and I have two tomato plants.

They were green and full of fruits, but lately the leaves are turning yellow and drying out. The fruits are turning nice and red but the bottom part of them is getting rotten. I was watering them once a day and I'm using moisture control soil by Miracle Gro.

Can you tell me why the leaves are turning yellow and drying out and why the fruits are getting rotten in the bottom?

Am I watering them too much or too little? I know they are getting plenty of sun. My apartment faces east, so I get sun from sunrise till about 2 or 3 p.m.

Thanks for helping me to save my tomatoes.

Steve
pokerbaz1@yahoo.com

I think you are watering them too little. The rotten spot on the bottom of the ripe tomato is called blossom end rot and it is frequently caused by the plants getting too little water. A big tomato plant that is producing fruit uses a LOT of water in a day. You want the soil moist but not wet, drying out just a little between waterings. I would pick all the tomatoes that show blossom end rot to let the tomato plant put its energy into sound fruit. Water regularly and more thoroughly and I think you'll soon be harvesting nice red, ripe tomatoes.

— Jackie

Canning jars

Thank you so much for all of your information on canning over the years. Your article has been helpful.

Whenever I find canning jars at yard sales, I look for Ball/Kerr with no chips or cracks. Recently my husband's grandma gave us five boxes of glass jars. While many of them are "recent," there are some that look like quart canning jars, but I am leery. Some actually have Ball printed very small on the bottom, while others have a number stamped on them. The threads looked like they were canning jars, too. My mother-in-law thought there was a universal number you could go by, but wasn't sure. They look pressure-canning grade, but I won't chance it unless I know for sure. Please note there were obvious jars that were mayo, pickles, and commercial jelly jars. Thank you for any info you can give.

Trina McMillen
Gresham, Oregon

I'm not as fussy about my canning jars as some folks are. I can in any sound jar that will accept a standard canning lid and ring, allowing it to be screwed down firmly tight. And I include mayonnaise jars, too. I've successfully canned foods requiring pressure canning like meat, corn, and beans in these jars and have had no more breakage than when I used big-name jars. One thing I have done to make sure I have less breakage is to always warm up the canner before I place hot jars into them. In the past, I didn't do this and found that I frequently had a jar or two break out the bottom from the old cold-hot conflict. Since I began doing this, I have had very few jars break.

Sounds like you made quite a haul. Good for you. ***— Jackie***

Canning unusual items and storing honey

After searching past issues, I found most of the answers to my questions on canning "unusual items." I do, however, have questions on cheese. I'm a fairly new canner and need more specific instructions.

Also the ground hamburger, once it's browned, drained, and in the jars, do you add a liquid or just can it "dry" like the walnuts?

Could you suggest a book or write an article on other items most people wouldn't think to can?

Last question, I have honey in one-quart plastic jugs from the manufacturer. I'm worried about the honey picking up odors from the basement or chemicals leaching from the plastic after long-term storage (15-20 years). Should I transfer to Mason jars?

I love this magazine and everyone's willingness to share their wealth of knowledge.

Lisa Kujawa
Macy, Indiana

I home-can cheese by cutting it into one-inch cubes and placing it into wide-mouth pint jars in a roaster half filled with boiling water. As the cubes melt, I add more, stirring as needed. When the jar is filled to within ½" of the top, I wipe the jar rim clean and place a hot, previously simmered ring on the jar and tighten it firmly tight. The jars are then processed in a boiling water bath for 40 minutes.

To use the cheese, again heat the jar, barely melting the outside cheese, using a double boiler-type arrangement. Then, with a table knife, gently slide it around the cheese and dump it out onto a plate. It's like you'd do with Jello. Let the cheese set in a cold place to "regroup", then slice or grate and use.

I've found that the cheese may get a little stronger with long storage, but still remains good.

To can browned hamburger, simply brown the hamburger, then add a little water and let it simmer slightly. Then dip the hamburger out and pack it into pint jars to within 1" of the top. Add the hot broth to cover the hamburger also to 1" of the top of the jar, seal, and process for 75 minutes (pints) or 90 minutes (quarts) at 10 pounds pressure, unless you live at an altitude above 1,000 feet. Then consult your canning manual for instructions in adjusting your pressure to match your altitude, if necessary.

I don't like plastic. I can taste plastic in foods stored in it, whether it is milk, flour, or honey. Some folks think I'm nuts, but I really can, and if I can taste it, I figure that isn't a good thing. I store all my long-term foods in either glass or metal cans and have been happy with the results. Just pour your honey into sterile Mason jars and seal them. I've never had honey "go bad." ***— Jackie***

Preserving peppers

We like to can pickles (dill) with cayenne peppers packed inside for extra flavor. What is the best way to preserve the peppers if they ripen before the cukes? Or maybe even for the next year, if possible?

KC and Jane Carter
Poplar Bluff, Missouri

I've never had hot peppers ripen before the cukes do. Most cayenne and other hot peppers don't get ripe for at least 80 days and cukes seldom require more than 60 days to reach pickling stage; many sooner.

But, if your peppers DO get ripe before the cukes are ready, I would dry them. To do this, simply spread them out in a single row on a screen in a hot, dry place. They will be dry in a couple of days. If the humidity is high, you might want to dry them in your oven with only the pilot light on or another DRY, warm place (attic, in a closed car, etc.). When crunchy dry, like leaves, you can store them in a glass jar forever (or until your cukes are ready). ***— Jackie***

Making wine vinegar

Can you tell me how to make wine vinegar? I make all kinds of fruit wines, though I have never made grape wine, which I hope to change soon. Now, my next question is if you use the other fruit wines, do they taste good when done? Also, is it hard to make cider vinegar?

Zeldon Linn
Umatilla, Oregon

I can tell you how to make wine vinegar, but as I'm not a drinker, I don't make wine and therefore don't make wine vinegar. However, a friend does, and here's how she does it:

Pour your wine into a crock and cover it with a clean tea towel to keep out unwanted critters and dust. First, you'll notice the wine will go flat (taste it by spoonfuls), then after a longer time, it will start to become vinegary. Taste it until it seems stout enough to suit your taste. Use reasonably soon or it will become very acidic. You can dilute it with water if it does.

The old-fashioned way to make cider vinegar is to mix a gallon of good cider with a quart of molasses and put it into a crock. Cover with a clean tea towel and let set. Check periodically. First, it will be "hard cider," then eventually begin to taste vinegary. If it gets past the acidity you want, dilute it with clear water.

Like winemaking, vinegar making takes a little practice. But it is definitely a homestead skill that is quite easy to learn.

Remember that you want about a 6% acidic acid content in your vinegar for pickling. If your vinegar seems less than "store-bought" strength, let it work longer.

— Jackie

Making whitewash

Can you give me a durable formula for making up one's own whitewash?

Jim Herbert
Tenino, Washington

There are a whole lot of formulas for making whitewash, and probably most of them are good. One that has worked for me for whitewashing the inside of my barn and chicken coop is:

Boil ¾ lb. of rice and ½ lb. sugar in 7 pints water until the rice has dissolved. Remove from heat and add 1 pint raw skimmed milk. Then mix in hydrated lime, a little at a time, until the consistency is like paint. Apply soon, keeping the mix stirred as you work. **— Jackie**

Preserving avocados

I have a cousin in Texas who called me wanting to know if you can freeze or can avocados.

Lottie (Jane) Rogers
Albertville, Alabama

You can freeze avocado puree for future use in guacamole or sweets. To do this, simply peel, seed, and mash ripe avocados. To each quart of puree, add 1 Tbsp. lemon juice. Pack into a freezer container, leaving ½" of headroom. Seal and freeze. **— Jackie**

Canning milk

We also live in northern Minnesota. We moved to the country 3 years ago. Best thing we could have ever done. I started canning goat milk last year and was very happy with the outcome. It is great to be able to make bread in the winter with it and not have to buy. I have always had good luck canning it until today. My oldest milk was only 5 days old, but when my milk came out of the pressure canner, 3 jars were bubbling like mad and looked different (the 4 jars that looked normal were from the morning milking). As they cooled, it looked like the milk had curdled and whey was on top of the jar. Any idea what happened? I wonder if I should throw the milk to the chickens or save it and hope it will be okay.

Lori Gallagher
Culver, Minnesota

It sounds like perhaps your pressure got up a little high or you slipped and processed the milk just a little too long. When pressure-canned milk does this, it often "curdles," as you described. Personally, I'd just use the milk in a casserole, providing of course that the jars are sealed and the milk smells okay when you open the jars. I don't think it's much of a problem, other than appearance.

— Jackie

Canning grapefruit

I was wondering if you have ever heard of canning fresh picked grapefruit. I have a new home in SW Florida and I have Ruby red grapefruits and would love to can them. Can you help with this?

Chris Vest
Punta Gorda, Florida

Yes. Actually, grapefruit sections are very easy to can. The hardest part is sectioning the grapefruits. First, section each grapefruit, removing any seeds. Prepare a thin syrup (4 cups water or juice mixed with 2 cups of sugar or honey). Fill hot jars with sections, leaving ½" of headroom. Add boiling thin syrup, leaving ½" of headroom. Cap. Process in a boiling water bath for 10 minutes for either pints or quarts.

(With grapefruit being very juicy, it is usually best to use the "left over" grapefruit juice to make your syrup, as the taste of the finished product is better.) It's great you have your own. Lucky you! **— Jackie**

No fuss, no muss, One-pan grouse supper

By Linda Gabris

Next best thing to spending a thrilling day on an upland trail is sitting down to a grouse supper, and here's a versatile dish that's fast, easy, and delicious to boot.

Since it only needs one pan for preparing, the recipe is ideal for making in camp. And if eaten right out of the pan when dining solo, cleanup is almost as easy as licking the pot!

On bountiful hunts when you've bagged enough grouse for taking home and sharing, this one-pan meal deal is a great way to show off your birds.

The basic recipe calls for typical camp staples like onions, potatoes, and carrots, but you can use whatever veggies, whether fresh or canned, that you normally tote. A few shaggy manes, puffballs, or other edible mushrooms from the field add delightful flavor to the dish, but only if you are sure of your pick.

When making the dish at home, going from good to gourmet is as simple as adding a sprig of fresh herbs like basil or sage, a handful of button mushrooms, some baby turnip, and a splash of white wine near the end of cooking.

No matter how you cook it, the secret to a super grouse supper lays in the field dressing of the bird. Whether you dress out the whole bird or practice the breasting method, the chore must be done immediately upon shooting as innards can cause delicate meat to sour quickly. As law requires for identification, don't forget to leave one wing (or both if you'd rather) attached until the bird lands on the chopping block.

A few extra potatoes and even one bird can serve two in style.

Below is the "one-man" one-pan camp special. The recipe can be doubled or tripled as luck will have it, and since it's just as good the second time around, you can cook up two meals in one shot.

1 grouse
4 Tbsp. flour
1½ Tbsp. camp fat (butter, oil, lard or drippings)
1 or 2 cloves minced garlic or pinch of garlic powder (if you don't have any in camp add it to your list for next time around as garlic and grouse go great together)
1 chopped onion
1 cup water
1 or 2 cubed potatoes
1 cut up carrot (or some of whatever kind of camp veggie you tote)
seasoned salt
pepper

De-bone the grouse breast by running a sharp knife down each side of the breastbone while working meat away from bone. Cut breast meat into 1-inch cubes and leave legs whole, if using. Discard the back.

Dredge meat in flour. Heat fat until sizzling, then add grouse and sauté until golden. Add garlic and onion and fry until soft.

Slowly add water, stirring until thick and smooth.

Add remaining ingredients. Reduce heat, cover, and simmer until potatoes are tender, about 5 minutes.

Taste and adjust seasoning. Serve with bread, bun, or biscuit for getting up the rich gravy. Δ

The last word

The land of the unfree

It's official! The numbers are in once again! For I-don't-know-how-many-years-running, the United States, this so-called "land of the free," is imprisoning more people, in both absolute numbers and percentage of its population, than any other country in the world. Russia? China? Cuba? Zimbabwe? Vietnam? We put more people in the calaboose than any of them. And it's not vast numbers of illegal aliens pouring over our borders we're incarcerating. It's not terrorists. It's us. We're locking each other up in record numbers. This shouldn't come as any surprise because all the figures that support what I'm saying come straight from our own justice department. Yet it *is* a surprise to most people I talk with.

What's amazing is that some 80 percent of those in prison are there because of what they do to themselves. They're not murderers, rapists, child molesters, or robbers. They're not purveyors of death, mayhem, plunder, and destruction. They're simply people who are doing what they want with their own bodies. During Prohibition, it was a bottle of whiskey that could put you in the clink. Today, it's "Light up a joint and go to the Big House." In fact, take out the murderers, child molesters, rapists, and robbers, and leave nothing but the consensual criminals, and we'd still have more people in prison than any other country.

It's insane how we Americans are bent on regulating each others' behavior. Witness seat belt laws (yes, you should drive with your seat belt on, but having cops pulling you over to enforce it?), drug laws, licensing laws, zoning laws, eminent domain abuses, blue laws, "free speech zones;" the list goes on *ad nauseum*. We think of ourselves as free, but we are simply the most regulated society in history. And we have more *new* rules, laws, and regulations pouring out of our legislatures and bureaucracies every year than any other country *ever*. We just can't get over this uniquely American obsession of outlawing each other's behavior—and fining or jailing those who don't comply or conform.

And get this: We also have record numbers of people whose livelihoods now depend on ensuring others are deprived of their liberty. Get rid of victimless crimes and you'd have to lay off tens of thousands of cops and start shutting down prisons, and most lawyers would have to find a productive line of work. Even drug kingpins would have to start flipping burgers when the prices of their drugs crash because they're not "regulated" by government prohibition. So, we're not only bent on jailing those whose behavior we disapprove of, there are millions of Americans with *economic reasons* for keeping other Americans unfree, disenfranchised, and locked up. Because paying off mortgages, funding IRAs, and making car payments depend on the system as it stands, there is zero possibility that the problems all these regulations are supposed to be solving will ever go away. Worse, if they did go away, do you *really* think the regulators will clean out their desks and go home? They won't. They'll create new laws, new reasons to throw you, your family, your friends, and your neighbors in prison. Little Johnny needs braces, so off you go to the dungeon. Imprisoning each other is now as American as apple pie.

And, by the way, if the price of "illegal" drugs drops to that of a six pack of beer, drug users will no longer have to burgle, rob, or assault to get money to feed their habits. They'll be able to afford to buy them while they're flipping burgers alongside the erstwhile drug kingpins. So, even the rate of violent crime will drop. That is, there'll be even *fewer* people in prison for *violent* crimes than there are now.

Despite the fact that this country was founded on the concept of natural or God-given rights, in other words, rights no man could take away, we have come to the belief that with a simple majority vote we can and *should* be able to deprive anyone of his or her rights.

Decades ago I read a statement by a historian who said that long after the fall of the Roman Empire, people still pridefully regarded themselves as Romans. He wrote they just didn't know or care to admit that Rome had become a victim of its own excesses and decadence and that the Empire was gone—and so was Rome.

In the same vein, we are no longer the Land of the Free. Those days are gone. Yet, we still boast of it as if all those freedoms we were once ensured still exist. And we still kid ourselves about them. There are people who still buy the line that the reason for 9/11 was that the terrorists hate us for our freedoms and our democracy. Folks, that had zero to do with it. Most of our freedoms were seriously eroded or long gone well before that tragic day. And it wasn't because of terrorists. We've been taking them away from ourselves. Yes, a country founded on the concept of individual freedom, and supposedly governed by one of the greatest documents ever written, now blithely ignores both its heritage and its *Constitution*—including its *Bill of Rights*.

I'll bet that the last time most people read any part of the *Constitution* was as a kid, for a school assignment, and not as an adult when it would now mean something to them. And, having read it way back then, they're not going to read it again. Not now. And because of that, they have no idea what the limits are that are supposed to be placed on our government; they have no idea what their freedoms are.

So, next year, I expect even more Americans to be imprisoned by their fellow countrymen. I expect more laws on the books at federal, state, and local levels. I expect more of our behaviors to be regulated. I expect more cops, lawyers, prison guards, and prisons. I expect more idiots will still be calling this "The Land of the Free." Like the Romans of old, we're not smart enough to see that those days are long gone.

— John Silveira

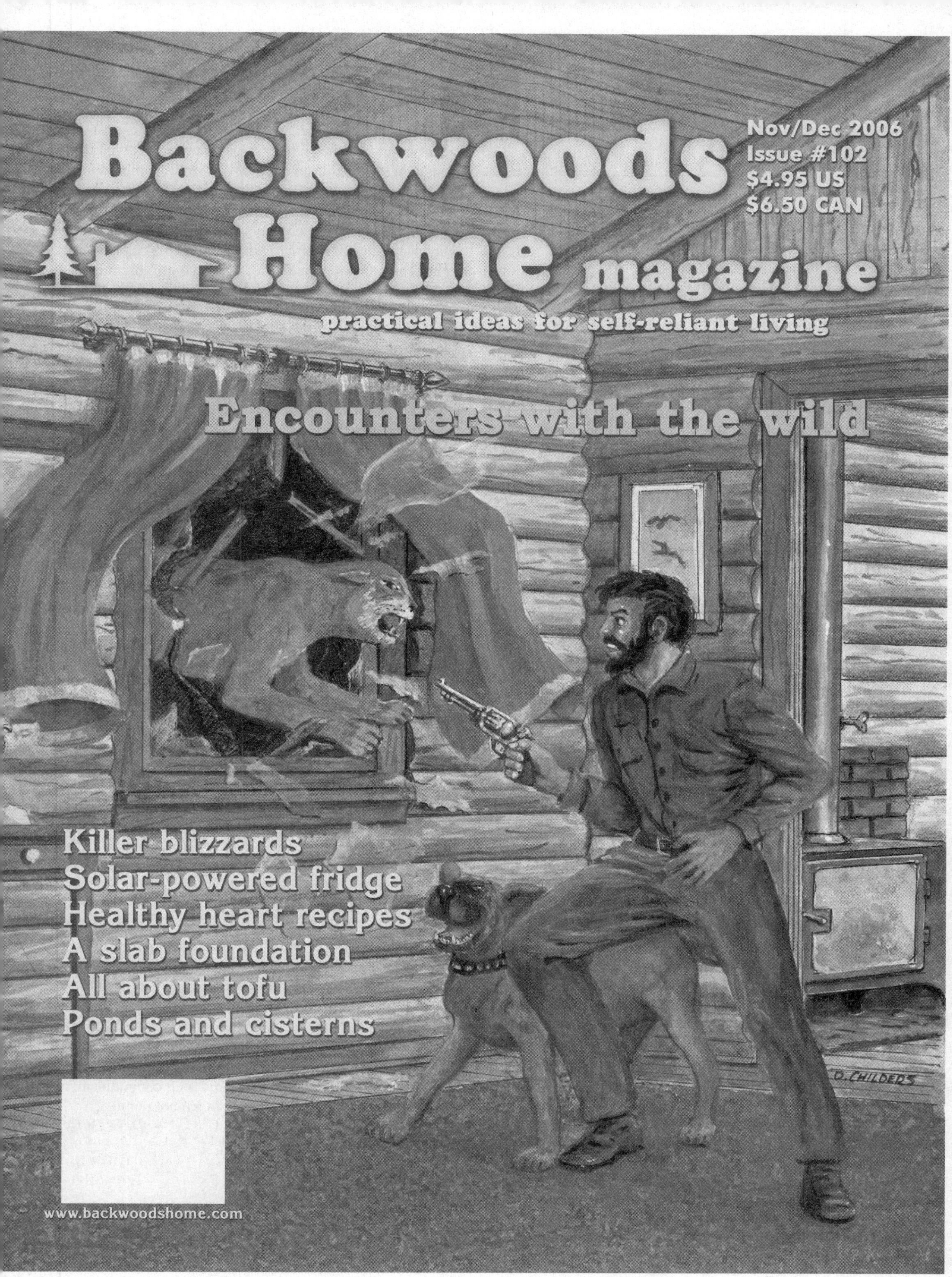

Backwoods Home magazine

practical ideas for self-reliant living

Nov/Dec 2006
Issue #102
$4.95 US
$6.50 CAN

Encounters with the wild

Killer blizzards
Solar-powered fridge
Healthy heart recipes
A slab foundation
All about tofu
Ponds and cisterns

D. CHILDERS

www.backwoodshome.com

My view

Which wars work best? The ones we fight or the ones we avoid?

History is supposed to teach us the lessons of wars past so we won't blunder into stupid wars in the present. Since I have mixed feelings about our War against Terrorism and our war in Iraq, I thought I'd review the wars America has fought in my lifetime, as well as the ones we avoided. Maybe it will paint a path for America to follow now.

I was born one year before the end of World War II, which history calls "the good war" because it saved Europe and possibly the world from the tyranny of the Nazis. We lost 400,000 dead, the world lost 60 million dead, European and Japanese civilizations were nearly destroyed, and Soviet Communism, a system at least as murderous as the Nazis, emerged from the war a superpower. But we forced American-style democracy on Germany and Japan, and after they got over the bitterness of defeat, they prospered under democracy and became allies of America. America was the only real victor in that war. Our homeland had not been devastated by bombs, and we emerged as the most powerful nation in the world.

The Korean Conflict raged while I was a boy. That war ended in stalemate after 50,000 Americans died, but our side, South Korea, went on to prosper under American-style democracy while the other side, North Korea, undergoes famines and starvation to this day under a regime that sells arms to the highest bidder and is working to develop a nuclear bomb that the buyer will no doubt aim at America. We still have to maintain an army in South Korea.

Then came Vietnam. My college friends were among the 50,000 Americans killed there, but after public pressure from back home, America abruptly left and ushered in a blood letting in Southeast Asia that killed millions of civilians in Vietnam and Cambodia. Vietnam is the war we seldom talk about today because it accomplished nothing but the destruction of the cream of America's youth. Today, as before the war, Vietnam does not openly threaten America.

Most recently we've had America's two wars against Iraq, both spectacularly successful militarily. We had to fight the first war because Iraq invaded Kuwait and threatened our oil supply, a fuel we probably should have made ourselves independent of a long time ago. We fought the second one because we thought Iraq was trying to develop a nuclear bomb that could possibly be sold to terrorists. This last contention is vehemently debated now by politicians running for office. But we are in Iraq nevertheless, with more than 2,000 Americans dead and no end in sight.

Along with Iraq, we have our ongoing War against Terrorism, launched when radical Islamists brought down the twin towers in New York. We killed or captured much of Al Qaeda, main sponsor of the radical Islamists, after invading Afghanistan. Now the War on Terrorism and the war in Iraq have sort of combined, with a civil war among Shia and Sunni Arabs thrown in, and with Syria and Iran and others fanning the flames. It's become a big mess.

Here's the wars we didn't fight in my lifetime:

We never fought the Soviet Union, the most dangerous enemy of America in my lifetime. We would have won because we had better technology than them, but many of our cities would have fallen to nuclear bombs. As capitalists, we understood that communism was an unsound economic system, so we wisely pursued a policy of "mutually assured destruction," keeping the Soviets at bay until the inevitable happened. It was the wisest war we never fought. The Soviet Union is now a bunch of separate countries, sort of third worldish, and no longer a threat to us.

We also never fought the Red Chinese. This communist system was never strong enough to pose as serious a threat as the Soviets, and as the Soviets stumbled under their own bad economic policy, the Chinese cracked its doors open to the West to see if it could avoid the same fate. Luckily, that much-maligned former president, Richard Nixon, seized the opportunity and extended America's hand. China is now the workshop of the world, prosperous, and less and less communist every day. It is simply evolving out of its tyrannical former self and into a prosperous capitalist society. The fact that it remains communist and godless does not seem too relevant anymore. This is the second wisest war we never fought.

So in light of all these past wars and avoided wars, what can be deduced to guide us today?

Obviously, the wars we avoided worked out best. No one got killed, civilizations were not devastated, and America was triumphant. That was because American-style capitalism was allowed to do its thing. Our system is simply better than anyone else's. The Soviet Union learned that too late, but China learned it just in time.

All the real wars had disappointing results. Even World War II, which I don't think America could have avoided, ended up empowering the communists for half a century.

Our current wars don't look promising in light of history. Sure, we can defeat any enemy in the short-term, but history says that for success in the long-term we need to convert the enemy to American-style capitalism so they, too, can prosper. I don't know how we are going to do that. I don't think anyone does. But just as it did with communism, I think it will make Islamic jihadism a moot point.

— Dave Duffy

the healthy kitchen

Good spoons knives food

By Richard Blunt

Despite being omnivores endowed with the ability to eat nearly everything, we humans are very selective about what we consider acceptable food. A close look at the culinary habits of people in any region of this planet will reveal that a mere handful of the edible plants and animals form the core of the cuisine. This is in part due to the advent of agriculture and its influence on human development. Currently, humans cultivate only about 600 plant species and 50 animals out of edible varieties that number in the thousands. The actual selection varies depending on where you live.

We even resist any changes or deviations in our selection. It's an innate response for us to distrust foods we perceive as strange, often fearing that they offer us some harm or discomfort. We do this even when our health and longevity will benefit from a change in the type and amount of food that we consume.

A heart healthy diet doesn't have to be drab and boring. It can include meals like this tasty and filling garden mushroom and vegetable lasagna.

This is the small garden I plant in front of my house every spring. This year I grew basil, thyme, oregano, rosemary, dill, mint, and cilantro. Not only can you save money harvesting from your own garden, but once you discover the flavor boost garden-fresh herbs give all foods, you'll cook with them as often as possible.

Think back, if you dare, to your last experience with the flu, serious cold, or any other condition that produces fever and/or stomach upset. Often, during periods such as this, the last thing you can envision is eating food of any kind, even though a cup of broth, a dish of jello, or a cup of tea would, if nothing else, help you to feel better by replacing nutrients your body needs to rebuild itself. And even though a well-prepared cup of hot, homemade beef, chicken, or vegetable broth would be both nutritious and good tasting, you'll reject it.

While managing kitchens that prepared and served food to patients in hospitals, nursing homes, and retirement communities, I was often witness to the powerful healing potential of well-prepared food served in appropriate portions to folks with a wide variety of medical problems. For patients and residents in these facilities, food can, and often is, a vital element for accelerating healing and lifting the spirits. Monitoring the quality of the food served to patients and residents is considered a critical and mandatory function. In this setting, food that is prepared incorrectly or presented in an unattractive manner is almost always rejected. When the body is already weakened by illness or age, a negative experience at any given meal will often make matters worse.

Let's bring this scenario closer to home. Consider being advised by your doctor that your bad cholesterol, the Low-Density Lipoprotein (LDL), has gone through the roof, and your weight is way out of the normal range for your age and height. You are also told (as if you didn't already know) that food is the culprit. You must make drastic changes in your eating habits to prevent serious health problems.

Does this mean that you are doomed to a dietary hell of raw carrot and celery stick salads and steamed asparagus on dry whole wheat toast? No, but we all need to develop an eating pattern that provides, in sufficient quantity, the healthful food we need and reduces the consumption of foods that can cause health problems. And, it is not necessary to be a culinary master, nutritionist, or registered dietitian to accomplish this goal.

Surprisingly, the list of foods to avoid is much smaller than the list to embrace. Fats, sugar, salt, and carbohydrates do not really deserve the killer image in which they are cast. Eating any food in excess can cause health problems.

For instance, all fats deliver the same number of calories. If your goal is to lose weight, substituting olive oil for butter is not enough. Reducing your intake of *all* fats must be considered.

Also, the proper use of salt in cooking will eliminate the need for the salt shaker at the table.

And you should also realize that adding two teaspoons of sugar to your morning coffee is not necessarily a problem when you consider that more than half of the sugar ingested in this country comes hidden in many processed items sitting on supermarket shelves. What is important is limiting our intake of *all* sugars which, according to The World Health Organization, should be 10 percent or less of our total daily calories (about 10 teaspoons). The way I see it, the two teaspoons of sugar that go into your morning coffee are not a problem. The unseen sugar in a can of soda or a bottle of ketchup could be, simply because it's more difficult to calculate the intake of sugar from these sources.

The road to developing and implementing an overall healthier lifestyle, in which diet plays a substantial role was, in very simple terms, mapped 47 years ago by the noted cardiologist Ancel Keys. His advice:

"Don't get fat; if you are fat, reduce. Favor fresh vegetables and fruits. Avoid the heavy use of salt and refined sugar. Get plenty of exercise and outdoor recreation. See your doctor regularly and do not worry."

I will add to his recommendations: *Eat less junk food.*

The impact of eating an occasional hamburger, a few french fries, and a can of soda as part of an otherwise healthful diet is going to be small or nonexistent. But we should not make it a habit. What matters most is our habitual eating pattern. As a general rule, eat less (especially of foods containing saturated fat), exercise more, and eat lots of fruits and vegetables.

My kitchen

I believe one of the essential keys to adopting a healthful eating regimen is setting up a healthy kitchen and stocking it with food items that suit the individual and diverse culinary preferences of your family. You cannot impose a diet that people are going to reject as foreign to their tastes, because it will fail.

In the last article I mentioned two kitchen utensils that have become standards in my kitchen: A selection of affordable nonstick cookware and the Cuisinart Mini-Prep food processor.

Good measuring spoons

Last month while making a cake for a group of my wife Tricia's special students as a reward for class achievement, I discovered that two pieces from my favorite set of measuring spoons were missing. So I rushed to Wal-Mart to buy a new set.

I am not one that believes in or practices the imprecision of eyeballing ingredients, especially when baking. My Wal-Mart set was cheap and got me through my perceived emergency, but I was not satisfied with how they performed. The plastic handles were hard to hold and the spoons were of the shallow design that allow easy spillage when measuring liquids. So I logged onto Amazon.com, my favorite kitchen equipment supplier, to look for something better. What I found was a set of heavy-gauge, stainless steel measuring implements. The set included four measuring cups in ¼, ⅓, ½ and 1-cup sizes, and a set of deep-bowl measuring spoons in ⅛, ¼, ½ and 1-teaspoon sizes along with a 1-tablespoon measure. The measuring spoons have a unique and clever design—a bend at the end of the handle that allows the spoon to sit upright on its own. The set also comes with a lifetime warranty. This set is for anyone who does as much cooking as I do and is inconvenienced by the performance of faulty equipment.

The set is made by Cuisipro and costs about $30. If you don't need the measuring cups, you can buy the spoons for about $11.

When I outline the flavor-enhancing value of herbs and spices in the next article, a real emphasis on accurate measurement will be essential to achieving success, and a quality set of measuring tools will prove to be indispensable.

Crucial kitchen knives

Like most folks, I believe the greatest cook who ever lived was my mother. She was very meticulous when it came to buying and caring for her kitchen utensils, especially her knives. At a young age, she taught me the value of owning a high-quality set of kitchen knives as well as how to care for them.

She owned four high-carbon steel knives that she bought on sale in 1960 at one of Boston's best known knife retailers. These knives are still used in my kitchen today. Her complete knife set included a 10-inch cook's knife, a small paring knife with a 4-inch blade, a straight back boning knife with a 6-inch blade, and a nonserrated slicing knife with a 12-inch blade. Her favorite was the cook's knife. While using this knife, she would often stop working and remind me that, "This is the most important tool in this kitchen."

To keep her knives razor sharp, she used a whetstone and a butcher's steel. To prevent her knives from staining, she carefully washed and dried them after each use. The knife set pictured contains knives made of high-carbon stainless steel, a hard

This set is the workhorse of my kitchen, and if I travel to visit friends or family, my knives go with me. I never know when they will ask me to prepare a meal.

metal that, once sharpened, will stay sharp during repeated uses. Unlike my mother's knives, they do not stain. This set is the workhorse of my kitchen and if I travel to visit friends or family, my knives go with me. I never know when they will ask me to prepare a meal.

The straight back boning knife is invaluable for sliding between bones and under silver skin (that shiny stuff you see that's connective tissue) on beef, pork, and lamb. The 10-inch cook's knife has a long, gently sloping curvature, which is necessary to achieve the necessary rocking motion when mincing and chopping.

Restoring a knife's edge

The butcher's steel is not a sharpening tool. It's main function is to straighten the knife edge when it becomes feathered. "Your blade is feathered," is industry-speak for describing a knife edge that has become slightly bent from repeated use. If the knife you are using is a quality blade made from high carbon stainless steel, and seems to be losing its edge, the usual cause is feathering.

The butcher's steel will restore the edge. Safe and effective use of it is simple:

1. Place a kitchen towel on a cutting board to prevent the steel from slipping. Position the steel perpendicular on the towel (i.e., with the handle "up" so you can grasp it with your noncutting hand). Firmly grasp the knife in your cutting hand, and place the heel of the knife (the area near the knife's handle) against the steel. Hold the blade at a 20° angle against the steel.
2. While maintaining the 20° angle, use a light pressure, and slide the blade down the steel while pulling the knife toward you at a rate so that the tip of the blade has passed over the steel completely when you get to the bottom.
3. Repeat the same motion on the other side of the blade. Four or five strokes on each side should return the edge to its original sharpness. If it doesn't, the knife has lost its edge and must be sharpened. If you are not practiced in knife sharpening techniques, I recommend having a professional do it. Many supermarkets will sharpen knives for free. They use an industrial-grade electric sharpener that removes some metal from the blade with each sharpening. If this really concerns you, I suggest you buy a good diamond-dust sharpening stone and practice sharpening your own knives. I will include some knife sharpening tips in the next ***"the healthy kitchen"*** article.

Well, it's time to do some cooking. The following recipes were developed with a substantial contribution from a small garden that I plant in front of my house every spring. During the spring, summer, and fall months, I save a lot of money by planting a variety of herbs, salad greens, and vegetables. This year my garden contained basil, thyme, oregano, rosemary, dill, mint, and cilantro.

These herbs share space with two varieties of tomato, a bed of carrots, two varieties of chili peppers, and a small bed of mesclun salad mix. This fall I will plant a hardy fall and winter salad mix.

Once you have discovered the incredible flavor boost that garden-fresh herbs give all foods, you will look forward to cooking with them as often as possible. I will discuss herbs and spices in considerable detail in a future article.

Chili

Chili is one of those one-dish comfort foods that I can't imagine living without. I fell in love with chili after reading Frank Tolbert's book, *A Bowl of Red*, in 1968, two years after it was published. Unfortunately, some of the best chilies are made using lots of saturated fat and red meat. Not exactly heart healthy food. So, for the past several years I have been experimenting with different chili formulas, some of which are meatless and others that contain meat.

In the Mediterranean, meat is often incorporated into recipes as a flavor and texture enhancer. In her book *Mediterranean Cooking*, Paula Wolfert includes several couscous recipes in which meat plays such a role. These recipes are loaded with vegetables and grain. Meats like beef, pork, lamb, and chicken are used as condiments to add balance, taste, and texture.

With this in mind, I set out to develop a chili recipe using this format. The following low-fat recipe uses some ingredients that are not chili fare, but my recipe review committee, after eating chili three times, gave it a unanimous thumbs up. Try it. I assure you that it is long on real chili flavor and delivers a lingering chili pepper warmth that satisfies.

I use both fresh and dried poblano chilies, a combination that contributes a fresh, lively taste that can only be attained with fresh peppers, along with deep, rich flavor found in dried peppers. I added anchovies and Parmesan cheese rinds to replace the rich taste that is associated with animal fat. I buy Parmesan cheese rinds at the deli counter in a local supermarket. These rinds are simply cheese that has hardened during the aging process. They are packed with flavor and can be used as a flavor booster in any soup or stew. They are also cheap, about $2 a pound. The rest of the Parmesan wheel sells for about $13 a pound, and the flavor is the same.

The baking chocolate I use is optional, but it adds "depth" to the flavor of the recipe. It's worth a try.

Ingredients:

- 2 fresh poblano peppers, peeled, seeded, and deveined
- 2 dried poblano (a.k.a. ancho) peppers, seeds and veins removed
- 4 ears fresh corn (remove the kernels, discard the cobs) or 12 ounces of frozen corn
- 3 anchovy fillets, chopped fine
- 1 canned chipotle pepper in adobo, chopped fine
- 2 Tbsp. cumin seeds, toasted and ground
- 1 Tbsp. coriander seeds, toasted and ground
- 1 bay leaf
- 1 tsp. dried oregano
- 1 Tbsp. chili powder
- 1 Tbsp. peanut oil
- 1 lb. boneless top round steak with all visible fat removed, cut into ½-inch pieces
- 2 cups yellow onion, chopped
- 6 cloves fresh garlic, minced
- 1 28-ounce can diced tomatoes, with juice
- 3 Tbsp. tomato paste
- 12 ounces of fresh apple cider (preferred) or unsweetened apple juice
- 1 14-ounce can reduced sodium vegetable stock
- 2 pieces Parmesan cheese rinds, approximately two ounces
- ½ ounce bitter-sweet baking chocolate (optional)
- 1 15-ounce can pinto beans, drained and rinsed
- 1 15-ounce can black beans, drained and rinsed
- salt and freshly ground black pepper to taste

Method:

1. Set your oven to broil and adjust one of the shelves to the middle position. Remove the stems from the fresh poblano chilies by cutting around the base of the stem with a paring knife. Cut the chilies in half, from stem to tip, and remove the pulp and seeds. Arrange the seeded peppers on a foil-lined cookie sheet, skin side up, and place them under the broiler until they are evenly browned and blistered. Remove them from the oven and place them in a plastic bag. Seal the bag and let the peppers steam for about 15 or 20 minutes. While the fresh peppers are steaming, set the oven to bake at a temperature of 400° F. Set the dried peppers on a foil-lined cookie sheet and roast them in the oven until they are lightly browned. Take them out and set them aside to cool for a few minutes. You can now peel the skin from the roasted fresh peppers with little effort. Dice these peeled peppers and set them aside in a small bowl. Remove the stems and seeds from the dried peppers, break them into small pieces, and set them aside in the bowl with the fresh roasted peppers.

2. If you are using fresh corn, remove the kernels from the cob using a paring knife. Set the corn kernels aside. Chop the anchovies and the chipotle peppers and set them aside in the same bowl containing the fresh peppers.

3. Toast the cumin and coriander seeds in a small nonstick skillet over medium heat until they become fragrant. Set them aside to cool. Once cooled, grind them to powder and combine them with the bay leaf, oregano, and chili powder. Set this mixture aside.

Though heart healthy, this chili dish has all the flavor characteristics you expect in a hearty, one-dish meal.

4. Heat one tablespoon of oil in a large nonstick Dutch oven or other suitable size heavy-bottom pot until it starts to ripple. Add the diced beef and sauté until the beef starts to brown. Add the onions and continue cooking until the onions soften and turn translucent. Add the garlic and cook for about 30 seconds or until the garlic becomes fragrant.

5. Add the diced tomatoes with their juice, tomato paste, cider, and vegetable stock to the Dutch oven. Bring this mixture to a simmer over medi-

The tough review committee at the Blunt home consists of my three children, Michael, age 16, Sarah, 20, and Jason, 18. The other critic is my wife, Trish.

um heat, stirring frequently to prevent sticking and scorching. Reduce the heat to a point where the chili is at a slow simmer. Add the seasonings, peppers, corn, anchovies, spice mixture, and Parmesan cheese rinds. Continue simmering over low heat for about an hour or until the beef is tender.

6. When the chili is ready, gently fold in the drained and rinsed beans. Adjust the seasoning by adding salt and freshly ground black pepper to taste.

Makes 8 to 10 servings with about 380 calories and 8 grams of fat per serving.

Note: Easy with the salt. Remember, the main function of salt is to enhance flavor. If you can taste the salt in your cooking, you've added too much.

Garden mushroom and vegetable lasagna

This recipe is a salute to the treasures of my home garden and the flavorful fresh vegetables and herbs that it delivers every growing season.

Be sure to use Italian fontina in this recipe; it has a rich buttery taste and melts beautifully, helping the various layers of this lasagna hold together. The portobello mushrooms are a favorite when I need a flavor substitute for meat. If cholesterol is not a problem, you can substitute one large egg for the egg substitute. The egg serves only as a binding agent for the ricotta cheese mixture. The Barilla no-boil lasagna noodles are great for this recipe because they are not as thick and dense as the traditional noodles. They cook to a perfect tenderness in this recipe.

Ingredients:

approximately 6 portobello mushrooms (with 4 to 6-inch heads), rinsed well and drained
1 Tbsp. olive oil
2 cups fresh zucchini, seeds and pulp removed, cut into ¼-inch slices on the bias
15 ounces low-fat ricotta cheese
¼ cup egg substitute (or one large egg)
2 Tbsp. low-sodium chicken stock
2 Tbsp. fat-free yogurt
2 large shallots, minced
4 garlic cloves, minced
¼ cup fresh parsley, minced
1 Tbsp. fresh thyme, minced
½ tsp. dried oregano
9 sheets no-boil Barilla lasagna
1½ cups homemade or canned marinara sauce
¼ cup coarsely chopped fresh basil leaves
½ cup shredded Parmesan cheese
1½ cups shredded Italian fontina cheese (about 5 ounces)
¼ cup shredded Parmesan cheese (this is separate from the Parmesan cheese above)
1/3 cup sun-dried tomatoes
3 vine ripened tomatoes, sliced about 1/3 inch thick
1 tsp. dried Italian seasoning
1/3 cup pale dry sherry

Method:

1. Adjust an oven rack to the middle position and preheat the oven to 400° F. Cut each of the portobello mushrooms in half, position the cut side of each mushroom half down on the cutting board and cut them into ½-inch slices. Place the cut mushrooms into a suitable size bowl. Add one tablespoon of extra virgin olive and gently toss to coat the mushrooms. Place the coated mushrooms in a single layer on a cookie sheet and roast in the oven until they start to shrivel and most of their liquid is gone, about 15 minutes. Set them aside to cool. Remove the stem from each zucchini and cut each of the squash in half on the vertical. Using a teaspoon, gently remove the seed pulp from the middle of each half. Slice each half into ¼ inch thick slices. Lightly coat a cookie sheet with a nonstick spray, distribute the zucchini slices in a single layer, and roast the squash for about 10 minutes or until it begins to soften. Sautéing the squash in a 10-inch nonstick pan, coated with a nonstick spray, also works well.

2. In a suitable size bowl, combine the next nine ingredients and gently blend them together with a wooden spoon or rubber spatula.

3. Coat a 9x13-inch baking dish with nonstick spray. Arrange three no-boil lasagna noodles in the baking dish, according to the directions on the box. Spread half of the seasoned ricotta cheese mixture over the noodles. Evenly spread the mushrooms and zucchini over the cheese mixture. Top with three more sheets of lasagna noodles. Spread the marinara sauce over the noodles. Distribute the fresh basil over the sauce. Sprinkle ½ cup of shredded Parmesan cheese and one cup of the fontina cheese over the sauce. Top with the last three sheets of lasagna noodles. Spread the remaining spiced ricotta cheese mixture over the noodles and top with the sun-dried tomatoes. Lay the fresh tomato slices over this and evenly spread the remaining ½ cup of Fontina and ¼ cup of shredded Parmesan cheese. Finally, sprinkle the dried Italian seasoning on top.

4. Evenly pour the dry sherry over the lasagna. Tightly cover the dish with a piece of aluminum foil and bake in the oven at 400° F for one hour. After removing the lasagna from the oven, let it rest for at least 20 minutes before serving.

Makes 12 servings with approximately 260 calories and 10 grams of fat per serving.

Latin-style chicken & rice (Arroz con pollo)

This is the full-flavored cousin of American-style chicken and rice. In Latin countries, this is a basic comfort food. I use a medium-grain brown rice that I have only been able to find in an Asian supermarket in nearby Hartford, Connecticut. Unlike many other brown rice varieties, it does not rupture or curl when cooked in a casserole like this one. The poblano peppers that I use are grown in Oxnard, California. The flavor and texture of these peppers is the same as those grown in many parts of Mexico. If you can't find fresh poblanos, you can substitute a green bell pepper. It's not a *great* substitution, but it works.

Marinade ingredients:

1 tsp. ground coriander powder
½ tsp. ground cumin seed
1 tsp. chili powder
½ tsp. ground cinnamon
1 small garlic clove, minced very fine
1 tsp. dried oregano
1 Tbsp. olive oil
1 tsp. lime juice

Main ingredients:

8 bone-in, skinless chicken thighs, excess fat removed
1 fresh poblano pepper
1 tsp. olive oil
2 cups Asian medium brown rice or basmati brown rice
1 medium onion, diced medium
1 fresh garlic clove, minced
1 tsp. ground turmeric
1 chipotle pepper in adobo, minced
2½ cups reduced-sodium chicken stock
1 8-oz. can tomato sauce
1/3 cup green olives pitted and halved
1 Tbsp. capers
½ cup jarred roasted red peppers, diced medium
1 tsp. extra virgin olive oil
1tsp. white balsamic vinegar
2 Tbsp. fresh cilantro, chopped
salt and fresh ground black pepper to taste

This Latin-style chicken and rice dish is the full-flavored cousin of American-style chicken and rice.

Method:

1. Combine the marinade ingredients in a small bowl. Combine the marinade and the skinned and defatted chicken thighs in a large zip lock freezer bag, and place them in the refrigerator for one hour. Preheat the oven to 450° F. Remove the thighs from the marinade and place them on a cookie sheet coated with nonstick spray. Place the tray in the oven, and bake the chicken for 20 minutes or until the chicken starts to brown on the surface. It is not necessary to cook the chicken completely at this point. When cooked to the desired degree, remove the chicken from the oven and set it aside.

2. Remove the stem and seeds from the pepper; cut the pepper the long way and roast the pepper in a dry heavy-bottom pan over medium-high heat until the skin is blistered. Place the pepper in a plastic bag for about 15 minutes to steam. Remove the pepper from the bag, peel off the skin, then dice and set the diced pepper aside.

3. Heat one teaspoon of oil in a 10-inch, nonstick sauté pan, add the raw rice and cook, stirring frequently until the rice is a light brown. Add the onion and garlic and continue cooking for another minute until the onion and garlic become fragrant. Remove the pan from the heat and stir in the ground turmeric and chipotle pepper. Set the mixture aside.

4. Combine the chicken stock, tomato sauce, green olives, and capers in a 10-inch Dutch oven over medium high heat and bring the mixture to a slow simmer. Add the rice mixture and partially cooked chicken. Cover, reduce the heat and cook the rice for about 25 minutes or until the chicken is cooked completely. Remove the chicken from the pot and set it aside to cool enough so that meat can be separated from the bone. Continue cooking the rice over low heat until all of the liquid is absorbed.

There is a place for lamb in a heart healthy kitchen. These tasty lamb kabobs are made with American lamb with all the fat removed. You can see how big the meat and vegetables should be cut to fit perfectly on the skewers.

5. While the rice is cooking, remove the bones from the chicken. Break each thigh into four or five medium pieces. In a suitable size bowl, gently toss the pulled chicken meat with roasted peppers, olive oil, vinegar, and cilantro. When the rice is completely cooked, gently fold the chicken mixture into the rice and cover the pot for about 5 minutes to reheat the chicken. Adjust the seasoning with a little salt and pepper. Serve immediately.

Makes about 5 to 6 servings of approximately 285 calories and 9 grams of fat per serving.

BBQ vegetable and lamb kabobs

For folks who live by the grill, as the Blunt family does, meat is an essential offering. When meat is on our outdoor BBQ menu, lamb is a favorite. I always buy American lamb because it is less gamey than its Australian or New Zealand counterparts. I usually buy a whole bone-in leg with the butt end removed and bone it myself. This gives me enough meat to use with a long list of recipes, from Mediterranean couscous to Middle Eastern Bulgar salads and, of course, barbecue.

The sometimes gamey flavor in lamb comes from the fat. Removing as much fat as possible not only makes this delightful meat healthier, it also tastes better. Check the photos if you are wondering about the size of the cut vegetables. You can also ask the butcher at most supermarkets to cut the lamb chunks from the large leg muscle and wrap the rest for you to take home and freeze. Don't worry, there is definite role for lamb in a heart healthy kitchen. More recipes will follow.

Main ingredients:

- 2 lbs. lamb leg, cut into 1½ to 2-inch chunks
- 1 fresh pineapple, trimmed, cored, and cut into two-inch chunks
- 1 medium green pepper, cut into one-inch pieces
- 1 medium red pepper, cut into one-inch pieces
- 1 large red onion, cut into pieces

Marinade ingredients:

- 3 cloves finely minced garlic
- 1 tsp. ground cumin
- ½ tsp. dried marjoram
- 1 Tbsp. toasted sesame seeds
- 1 Tbsp. pure vanilla extract
- 4 Tbsp. cranberry juice
- 2 Tbsp. walnut or extra virgin olive oil
- ½ tsp. Kosher salt
- 1 tsp. fresh ground black pepper

Method:

1. Combine the marinade ingredients in a suitable size stainless steel or glass bowl. Add the diced lamb and toss to coat evenly. Cover and refrigerate until fully seasoned, at least 4 hours or up to 24 hours.

2. When you are ready to start cooking, fire up the grill. I fill my large Weber chimney with charcoal, about four pounds.

3. Using 12-inch metal skewers, I construct each kabob as follows: Thread each skewer with a piece of pineapple, a stack of onion, a chunk of lamb, and one piece of each kind of pepper. Repeat the sequence three times. (The photo shows that.)

4. Grill the kabobs uncovered until the meat is browned and cooked to medium or medium rare, depending on your preference. Turn the kabobs every minute or so to cook all sides evenly. Serve immediately.

6 servings of 300 calories and 11 grams fat per serving.

Brown rice salad

Here is a salad that is a perfect complement to grilled lamb and vegetables. It is enhanced with a lively balsamic vinegar dressing that adds balance to the full flavor of lamb.

This recipe really demonstrates that low-fat, high-fiber food need not be dull and flavorless. You will notice I use regular olive oil to cook the rice and extra virgin olive oil in the dressing. Extra virgin olive oil is expensive and has a fruit flavor that, I feel, is

This brown rice salad demonstrates that low-fat, high-fiber food need not be dull and flavorless.

diminished with the level of heat that is required to sauté the rice. I will, however, use it to sauté vegetables at a lower heat range.

Ingredients:

1½ cups Basmati brown rice
1 tsp. olive oil
1 garlic clove, minced
1 large shallot, minced
3 cups reduced-sodium canned or homemade vegetable stock

Dressing ingredients:

2 Tbsp. extra virgin olive oil
2 Tbsp. white balsamic vinegar
½ cup Italian broad leaf parsley, minced
¼ cup fresh cilantro, minced
2 Tbsp. fresh mint, minced

Topping ingredients:

2/3 cup dried cranberries
½ cup toasted pistachio nuts

Method:

1. Soak the rice in four cups of warm water for about 20 minutes. Drain the rice and rinse in cold water. Drain the rice again in a wire mesh strainer.

2. While the rice is draining, heat the olive oil in a nonstick 10-inch skillet over medium-high heat until it ripples. Do not allow it to reach the smoking point. If it does, discard it, wash the pan, and start over. The smoke from overheated vegetable oil is toxic and a known carcinogen.

3. Shake the rice to remove any remaining water and add the rice to the hot pan. Cook the rice, stirring frequently until it begins to brown. Add the minced garlic and shallot and cook for about another minute or until the garlic becomes fragrant.

4. Combine the rice and vegetable stock in a two-quart sauce pan and bring it to a gentle boil. Reduce the heat, cover the pot, and continue cooking the rice at slow simmer until all the stock is absorbed, about 40 to 45 minutes. Uncover the rice, transfer it to a suitable size bowl and set it aside to cool for about 20 minutes.

5. While the rice is cooling, prepare the dressing by combining those ingredients and tossing gently. Add the dressing to the rice and mix gently with a wooden spoon or rubber spatula.

6. You can serve this salad warm or cold. Just before serving, sprinkle the nuts and cranberries on top.

8 servings of 225 calories and 7 grams of fat per serving.

Well, it seems that developing a heart healthy kitchen isn't at all dull and lacking of culinary excitement. Please read Dr. Willett's book. When it comes to down-to-earth nutritional advice supported by solid research, I am convinced that you can't do better. Let me know what you think. Δ

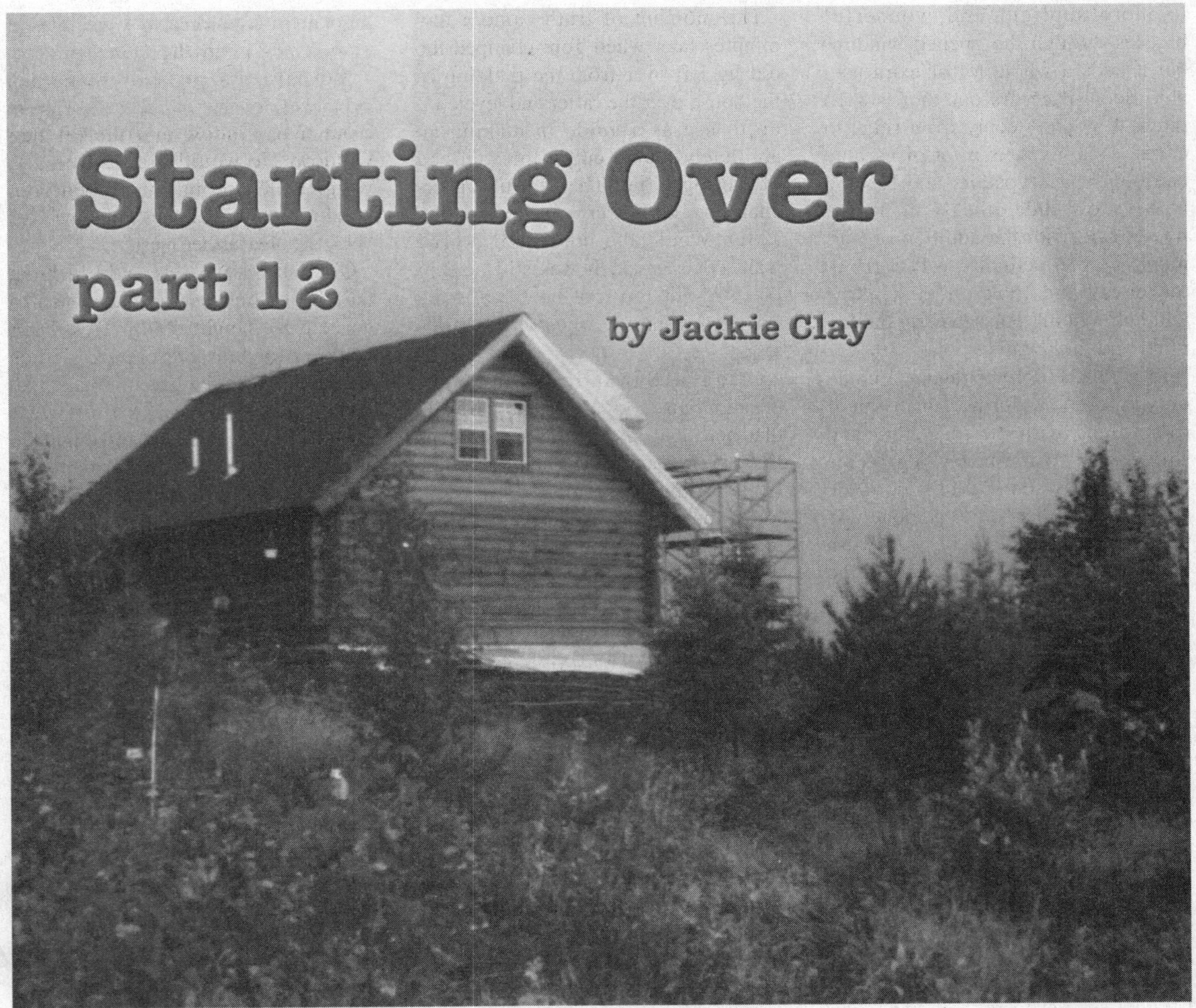

Starting Over part 12

by Jackie Clay

How fast the summer has gone! Already the leaves are turning yellow on the popple trees around us. And just last night, I heard a big flock of geese honk by, right outside of my upstairs bedroom window. I could hear the beat of their wings, they were so close. Beautiful, but telling me it's time to get ready for winter. As if that hasn't been happening all summer. Here in the northland, you begin getting ready for winter in May.

But, we're so much more ready than we were last fall, when we were still living in that old mobile home, building on our log home every spare second. Where last fall we had only the ugly but serviceable silver construction tarp over our 2x6 roof boards (no insulation; couldn't afford it), we now have three-fourths of our house roofed and insulated. Because we pay as we go, our carpenter friend, Tom Richardson, has been doing our roofing by pieces. A bit peculiar, when most folks simply go to their bank and get a construction loan. But as our place is paid for, I do not want to get into debt. There are just too many things that can interfere with being able to meet those loan payments. Things you never could have thought of. Like my husband, Bob, dying last spring, then two months later my brush with cancer. Yep, I'd rather know that every board and log over my head at night is paid for in full.

The rest of the roof becomes a reality

Where the first half of our house roof went on so fast it seemed impossible, the second is dragging along. This is because on the south-facing side of the roof we are installing two very large dormers with large double-hung windows. Not only does this let in more sunlight and wonderful breezes through the opened window, but it adds a whole lot of extra useable floor space. As our roof is a 10 pitch, it slopes steeply from ridge to eaves. This gives us a lot of useable bedroom space upstairs and lets the heavy snow slide quickly off of the house. But, with the addition of dormers, we can actually walk right to the eaves and look out a window without bonking our heads on the log rafter and roof boards.

To build the dormer (again, I could only afford the dormer in my bedroom along with the insulation and shingles up to the beginning of the dormer on my son, David's, dormer), the first thing that had to be done was to remove "old ugly," the well-worn silver tarp covering the roof. On the south side the tarp took a harder hit because of the sunlight. It was much more brittle and worn; it cannot be reused to cover hay as our tarp from the north side was. Because it would take several days to cut the dormer in, build it and make it weather tight, David and Tom did not take it entirely off. Instead, it was thrown back and used as a tent each night, just in case it would rain. Ha, ha! We have had a severe drought all summer, so I thought we should leave the roof open and MAKE it rain.

Once the roof was exposed, standing on his scaffold, Tom used his circular saw to cut the roof boards over the log rafter on either side of the new dormer opening. As we will be reusing the expensive tongue and groove 2x6s, Tom was very careful not to damage them in removal. Starting at the eaves, he pried them off of the center log rafter, which was going to be removed. As he took boards off, David pulled the nails and handed them to me to stack down in the basement. All of a sudden, we had a great open-air view of the small beaver pond and the woods. (Was that a rain cloud over to the west?)

The moment of truth came a few minutes later when Tom clamped the old jig left over from the building of the house over the rafter and leveled it up to use as a guide in making an absolutely plumb cut in the wall end of the log rafter. Then, firing up his chainsaw, he bravely cut through the rafter. Would the house fall down? Nah, not a creak. It was still held in place by the top roof boards and the lag screws into the opposing log rafter.

Using a Sawsall, he then cut through those log screws and the nails that held it to the boards—very gently—while David and I held the rafter from falling. It creaked as it came loose, but the wall end was against the wall and the top end was still on the ridge pole.

Getting on a ladder, Tom got his shoulder under the top end and David worked the bottom end, and they slowly wiggled it out of place and eased it to the floor. Hooray, it didn't drop through the floor into the kitchen!

Mom hadn't been upstairs in months, so David and I pulled/pushed her wheelchair up the stairs so she could see what all the commotion was about. She ooohed and ahhed and immensely enjoyed the view from the huge hole. (Since that time, David went down with the chainsaw and removed a few trees so we have a much better view of the beaver pond from that window and the kitchen window. He would grab a tree and wiggle it. Standing in my bedroom window, I would shout "That one!" or "No, the one farther west!"

Okay, here we were, with a huge hole in the house. And David had to go help the neighbor hay. He'd been working for him all summer, and as the saying goes, he had to "make hay while the sun shines." So, off went David. Tom said confidently that he and I could frame the dormer wall and set it up. "It'll only weigh about 800 pounds." So what that if it fell on through the hole, it'd end up down 20 feet? But, Tom is a confident person.

Taking careful measurements, he framed the dormer wall on the floor of my bedroom, with the bed squashed firmly against the north wall. The only problem was that the overhang of two feet on each side meant that the wall would be about four feet wider than the hole we would need to tip it out of. I shut up, helped, and figured that if it fell out and we didn't get killed, I guessed we could build another one.

David pulls nails so we can reuse the boards as Tom pulls them off.

Tom readies to shingle the second section of roof. Notice weather-watch ice shield only on lower part where porch roof will be next spring.

He got it framed and sheeted, leaving an opening in the top for the log rafter that would be cut to make a functioning ridge pole (also attractive) for the dormer rafters. When sheeted with OSB, that puppy was heavy. The moment of truth arrived, and we grabbed a couple of four-foot 2x4s and started working it up. As it went up, Tom heaved first one overhang corner out, crawling out the window hole to drag it into place. In the meantime, I held the wall and made sure that the 2x4s were secure, bracing it fairly well in place. It reminded me of a huge rat trap, and I was the rat.

Once the first corner was outside, we heaved and heaved to twist the second overhang out so the wall would end up upright. First, we got it too high and the sill plate hung up on the butt of the rafter he had cut. Then we got it pried loose from there, and it didn't want to drop down into place. But finally, with the help of a crowbar, it slipped snugly into place and didn't fall out the opening.

A few spikes later, we stopped for a break and a couple of cold Mountain Dews.

Then, with a double header of 2x8 over the window and extra vertical framing on each side of the window opening, Tom framed the open space over the window, leaving a hole for the ridge pole to fit into. It would rest on top of the house's ridge pole and be supported by the framing on the wall side.

So here we are; still no David, and it's time to hoist the new ridge pole. But it went pretty good, actually. Tom slid the wall end through the wall opening while I held the other end, balanced on the ladder. That end couldn't fall down, anyway! Then we swapped positions, and I held the log while he wiggled and dragged it into place on top of the ridge pole. It fit, and it looked great. A few very large spikes and it was captured for eternity.

He finished framing the dormer in the second day. It would have taken me a week, with all of the compound cuts involved. (Gee, those sure look like rain clouds over west.) That evening, David was back home. (They saw those clouds, too.) He helped Tom batten down the hatches, dragging the tattered, worn old silver tarp up and over the new dormer. It was framed, but not sheeted. Definitely not watertight.

But we were lucky. We desperately wanted rain, but I didn't want a foot of water in the house, and that old tarp was not waterproof at this stage.

The next day, we sheeted the roof of the dormer and started in on the main roof. Work went slowly at this point, as there were so many compound measurements and cuts for all the material, along with more flashing along the edges of the dormer where it met the main roof. Without adequate flashing underneath the shingles, the roof will eventually leak.

Mom enjoys the view from the dormer-to-be.

Our old homestead ranch house in New Mexico had this problem. Someone had roofed over the old shake roof with corrugated sheet metal roofing and had not bothered to put in flashing in the valleys. Every time it rained, we discovered new leaks. We constantly fixed what we could, but were never happy with the underlying construction mistakes.

It took nearly two weeks to get that part of the roof finished, including the dormer. The dormer took about a week, then the next week went into finishing off the insulated roof. Tom also cut holes in the roof for our vent pipe for the drain on the kitchen sink and the tub that we'll put in the dormer of my bedroom. (A very nice *BHM* reader wrote and offered me his used, but in great shape, Metalbestos chimney for my wood kitchen range. Thank you so much!)

We didn't shingle down to the eaves this time because next spring I want to add a full porch on the south side of the house, 16' of which will be a year-round green room so I can grow food for the table and not have to pay $3.99 for a pound of fresh and very tasteless tomatoes or green peppers. This strip of the roof was covered with Typar and then Weather Watch ice shield and left until we build again next spring.

Right now, I'm regrouping financially until I can get enough to finish up the roof with the dormer in David's bedroom and the remaining insulation/shingles. It looks like construction will be starting soon.

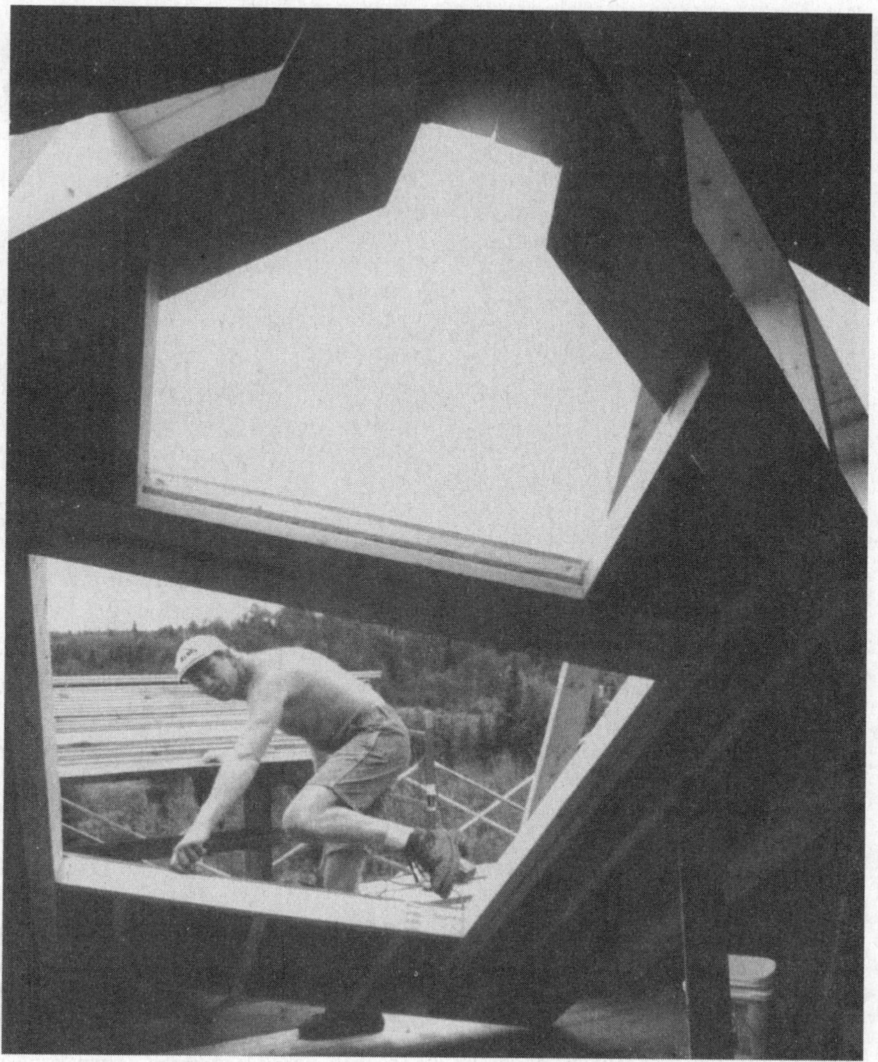

The dormer wall going up. That baby's 10' high and weighs 800 pounds!

The garden is attacked

About the time I was patting myself on the back for how great the garden looked, we started having trouble. Rows of beans were being chopped down. Corn came up missing. Terrorists? Well, in a way. They had four legs and soft brown eyes. Bambi and company decided my garden looked like a deer restaurant. I was in the process of fencing it. We had had deer in it last year, but they didn't bother it until late fall, after most everything had been harvested. Not so lucky this year, though.

I had bought 8' steel T-posts, before they went up in price, along with a 100' roll of six-foot 2"x4" welded wire fencing. We had cleared a strip of brush (the garden is going to be enlarged this fall) and unrolled the wire. But David began working as soon as school was out, and with me being only 5' 2", I can't reach up to pound 8' posts from the ground. So it hadn't gotten done. I had figured on fencing one side at a time.

Well, the deer didn't come in from that side; they didn't want to wade over the down fence. It was propped up on small trees. So, they came in from the creek side instead. I carried steel posts down there and then went for the step ladder. My bum knee was much better, but climbing was not very fun. I stood up one post at a time, slid the driver on, and while clutching the ladder with my toes, I pounded posts. I did two at a crack, then went to sit down on the garden bench.

I did the corners first, then stretched out a piece of lightweight electric fence wire tightly to mark my line so

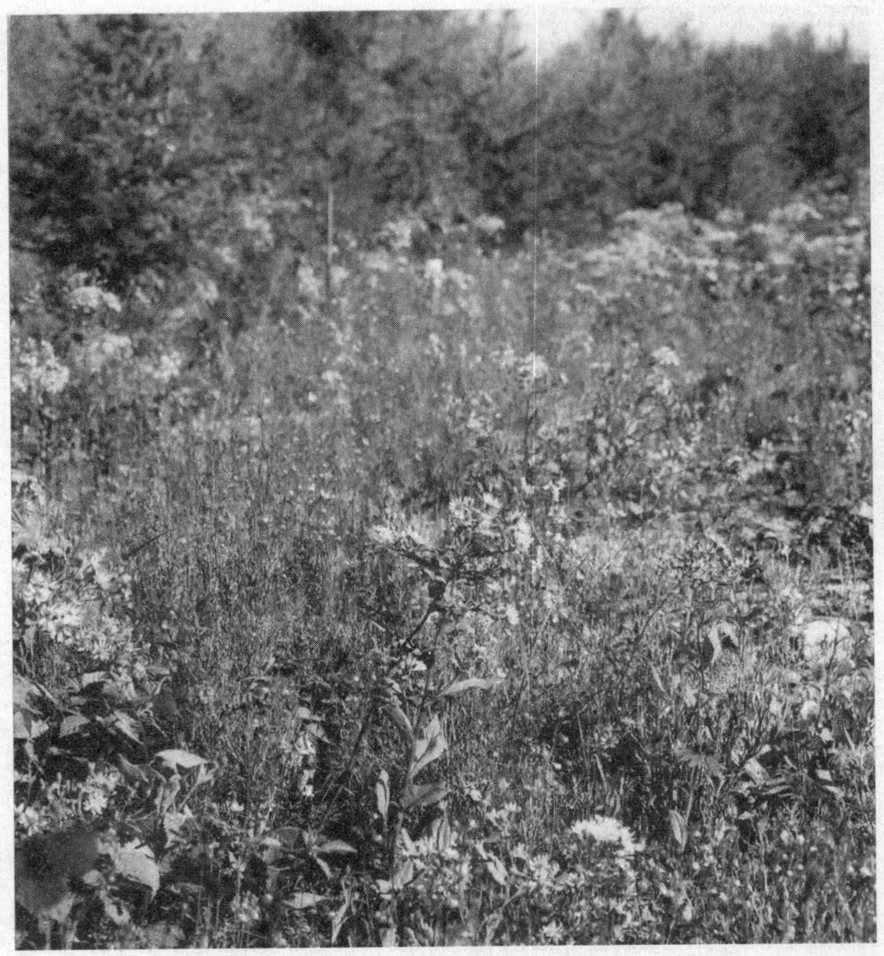

My wildflower garden starts blooming.
Would you believe it's the septic drainfield?

the fence would end up straight. I got the posts in, but because of the roofing expense, I couldn't afford to buy 6' fence rolls. I had some 4' welded fencing left over from another project, so I used that. I figured it would help until I could afford better. And maybe they'd stay out for awhile.

Yeah, right. They walked around it and again munched down my regrowing crops. And started in on my first green tomatoes, just like apples. So, I drove more posts on that side of the garden and put up more 4' fence. And I tried a few natural spray/sprinkle-on deterrents to try and buy time until I got the garden totally fenced. I used hot pepper spray, rotten egg-type sprays, and blood meal. They all worked. Until I watered. Then it was free lunch again. And at $12.99 a bottle and a 100'x75' garden, I was going broke doing something that wasn't working.

And, don't tell me I should have used predator urine. In Montana, we let our wolf-malamute hybrid run in the garden during the winter and early spring. The deer never minded his pee. I don't figure they'd care about bottled coyote pee, either. By the way, I've tried "marking" the edges of my gardens with my own urine, as I've read some folks have had success with that. All I got was briar scratches all over my hind end. And, all I could think of was, "Sure, now is when the neighbors will come calling!"

To make a long story short, I ended up fencing the entire garden, first with 4' wire, which was easy for a single person applying the fence. Then, I added another 3' of wire on top of that, to raise the height. Yes, the deer did jump over the 4' fence, but it took them just long enough for me to come up with enough money to buy more fence.

As soon as I totally got it fenced better than 6' high, I stopped having midnight callers in the garden. Midday, too. One day before I was done, I went down to water and a big fat doe was standing in my sweet corn. I asked her politely what she was doing in my garden and I'll swear she said, "Your garden? I thought it was my garden!"

I yelled, and she skipped off. With sweet corn breath blowing back on me.

The deer quit, then the ground squirrels started. And the little buggers fit nicely through the 2" spaces in the fence. The marauders I'm talking about are Richardson's Ground Squirrels. They are grayish, long-bodied gophers with a long hairy tail. They look kind of like a mongoose. And they have cheek pockets like a chipmunk. Boy, can they stuff a lot of your garden in those cheeks, too.

Now I love all animals, but I declared war on the ground squirrels. First I tried leaving out grain to see if I could bargain with them. I'd give them grain, if they'd leave my melons alone. I did, and they ate holes in every watermelon that began ripening. Enough is enough. I got out the .22. I figured if I shot a couple of them, the rest would become frightened and go back to the brush. Ha.

I ended up shooting one or two a day, but after awhile, there is only an occasional ground squirrel and they are content to eat the grain I leave out to bargain with the chipmunks, who also enjoy my garden. They like to eat my tomatoes.

My first crop of cukes and summer squash fill my market basket.

Every tomato that began ripening was eaten into. But that was easy to deal with; I just picked all the lower tomatoes just before they were ripe. They ripen fine in the house. I leave a few runty ones for the chipmunks, along with the grain, and we are all happy. I can't bring myself to shoot chipmunks; they're just too cute, and they were Bob's favorite critter.

Canning, canning, and more canning

This spring, I started all of my cucumbers, melons, and squash in our temporary greenhouse, and I was not disappointed with the results. To protect my precious Hopi Pale Grey squash seedlings, I covered them with a 4'x4' mini-hoop house made of leftover 2x4s and ¾" PVC pipe. I had deer eat my squash and pumpkin vines before, and I was not going to have that happen with the Hopis.

In short climates, it is just about necessary to start these long-season vining crops indoors to get a substantial crop. So, I had planted little vines 6" tall in their spaces in the garden. And they took off like wildfire. Luckily, with our water line being reworked when it was dug in last fall, our little submersible pump now puts out about 14 gallons per minute, compared to the tiny 3 gallons last year. So we were easily able to run lots of water on the garden during our long, very dry summer. And those vine crops especially liked it.

Because our garden is still small for my needs, I planted my carrots and bush beans in double rows, eight inches apart. That worked wonderfully and I'll never plant single rows again. Likewise, I pounded in steel posts on either end of my cucumber row and tied rolled stock fence from the dump on them. I had planned to trellis the cukes, so had ordered Japanese Climbing Cukes and Summer Dance, both straight, very long cucumbers that climb. Now climbing cucumbers do climb, but as they grow you have to gently pick up the growing end and poke it through the fence, higher and higher. The vines have strong tendrils that hold it in place very quickly and the vines will then support huge crops of foot-long cukes.

And, it wasn't too many weeks into summer when I got my first "small" picking from those vines. I pick into a Vietnamese market basket because it holds lots, and I can balance it on my head to make carrying heavy loads easy. The bottom is soft on the head and when I get to the yard, I can rinse the vegetables at the hose. The excess water drains out due to the relatively loose weave.

My basket was nearly full of nice long cukes, so I set about making our favorite Bread and Butter pickles. These are sweet, crisp, and fast and easy to can. Because of our move from Montana in the dead of winter,

The first canning corn of the year. Three ears filled a pint jar.

my pickles had all gotten frozen and gone soft, so I lost them all. Having a big shelf full of pickles of all different sorts was looking so good.

Here's how I do my quick Bread and Butters, in case you want to try them.

Bread and Butter pickles

- 14 long slim cucumbers (or more short slim ones)
- 3 medium large onions
- 1 green bell pepper
- 1 red bell pepper
- 5 cups sugar
- 5 cups vinegar
- 1 Tbsp. mixed pickling spice with NO hot dried pepper
- 1 Tbsp. whole cloves
- 1½ tsp. turmeric
- 1 tsp. celery seed

Slice washed cucumbers, discarding stem and blossom end, then slice remaining vegetables and cut into bite-sized pieces. Mix well and put into large pan (I use a turkey roaster). Sprinkle with ½ cup pickling salt and pour ice-cold water on to cover pickles. Let stand overnight.

In the morning, drain well. In large pot, mix spices, sugar, and vinegar. I do not use a spice bag because I like the extra spiciness of leaving the whole spices in the pickles that I can. Bring mixture to a boil. Then pour over vegetables and bring to a boil. JUST bring it to a boil. If you boil the pickles, they will get soft.

Pack hot into pint jars, removing any air bubbles. Pour liquid over them to within ½" of the top of the jar. Don't over-pack the pickles. Process for just 5 minutes in a boiling water bath. Have the water bath boiling when you put the pickle jars in it so the processing will go quickly. You don't want limp pickles.

That's it. When they are cool, check the seals, remove the rings, wash off the jars if they are sticky, and store in a cool, dark place. If you store in the light, they will lose their green color and become softer.

We love these pickles at most all meals. That's why they are called Bread and Butter pickles, because you eat them at meals like bread and butter. When I was a kid, I wouldn't eat them. I thought Mom had made them using bread and butter. In pickles? No way would I touch them.

But, then, our adopted son from India thought Americans made hot dogs from ground-up dogs. And he asked me while he was munching happily on his second hot dog, too.

Along with the Bread and Butter pickles, I made a few batches of quick dills, as the crop got heavier and heavier. I don't have time for brining them in a crock. And my quick dills taste just about as good, without all the days of skimming scum. Here's that recipe, too. Like the Bread and Butter pickles, they're very easy, fast, and tasty, too.

David hauls railroad ties with our old moving dolly. (Framed flower beds in background.)

Quick dill pickles

- 18 lbs. small pickling cucumbers or the same longer ones to slice
- 9 cups water
- 6 cups vinegar
- ½ cup salt
- ½ cup sugar
- 2 Tbsp. mixed pickling spices
- 1/3 cup mustard seed
- 7 cloves garlic (optional)
- 7 small dried pods of hot red pepper
- fresh dill heads

Wash cucumbers well, removing blossom end if necessary. You may slice, halve, or quarter the cukes if they are larger. Put in large pan (I use the turkey roaster) and sprinkle with salt; cover with ice-cold water. Let stand overnight. Drain and rinse cucumbers.

In a large pot, combine vinegar, 9 cups water, salt, sugar, and the mixed spices tied in a spice bag, or not, as you prefer. Heat to boiling. Keep hot.

Place a head of dill in the bottom of each jar, then pack drained cukes in jar to nearly ½" of top. Place another head of dill on the top and also ½ clove of garlic (or more) and half a pod of hot red pepper (optional). Pour boiling pickling liquid over pickles. Put lid on jar and screw band tight. Process 20 minutes in boiling water bath (10 minutes if you have used slices). Makes 7 quarts or 14 pints, approximately.

Along with the cukes, soon the green beans and corn were starting to produce. I had only room for a small patch of sweet corn (I planted an early Kandy Kwik this year) and then the deer had eaten the rows down to stumps at least three times. So, of course, I had little hopes to even get a couple of meals from it, let alone enough to can. But with the water and a good side-dressing of manure, that corn rebounded with energy. Finally, I saw ears with the tassels beginning to brown on the ends; a sure sign of maturity.

I squeezed an ear and found it nice and firmly plump. Then, carefully, I peeled a husk back and peeked in at the corn. Nice, shiny, fat yellow kernels peeped back at me. I picked enough for a meal for us, then looked up and down the rows.

Maybe, just maybe, I could can a small batch tomorrow? Would there be enough? I started picking in the morning and picked and picked. Soon, my market basket was full to overflowing, and I had picked only two rows.

Carrying it up to the round plastic table we have in the yard for outside food-processing chores, I began to husk corn. Behind me, I heard the fence creaking as all eight of our goats stood up, hungrily watching me. They knew I would give them the leftovers.

That table works so well for all kinds of work. Just the week before, our good friends, Jeri and Jim Bonnette, came over and helped us butcher five of our huge meat chickens. We used the table for plucking and dressing the birds, and it was so easy to use a garbage can for the waste, hose the table clean between birds, and be able to stand out in the open, not worrying about making a mess.

Likewise, when I pull carrots, I stop at the table, rinse them with the hose, then cut off the tops and root ends, giving them to the goats before I even take them into the house. Less mess in the house, and the goats sure like the extra treats.

I have one of those round, saw blade-type corn cutters I use for large batches of corn. It cuts real well, but I always end up cutting my left hand, as I hold the corn with that hand on the board and twist the cutter down over the cob with the other. I'm too frugal, I guess; I always cut down too far sooner or later and get myself. So on those little batches, I cut the corn off by standing it on end and using a sharp knife.

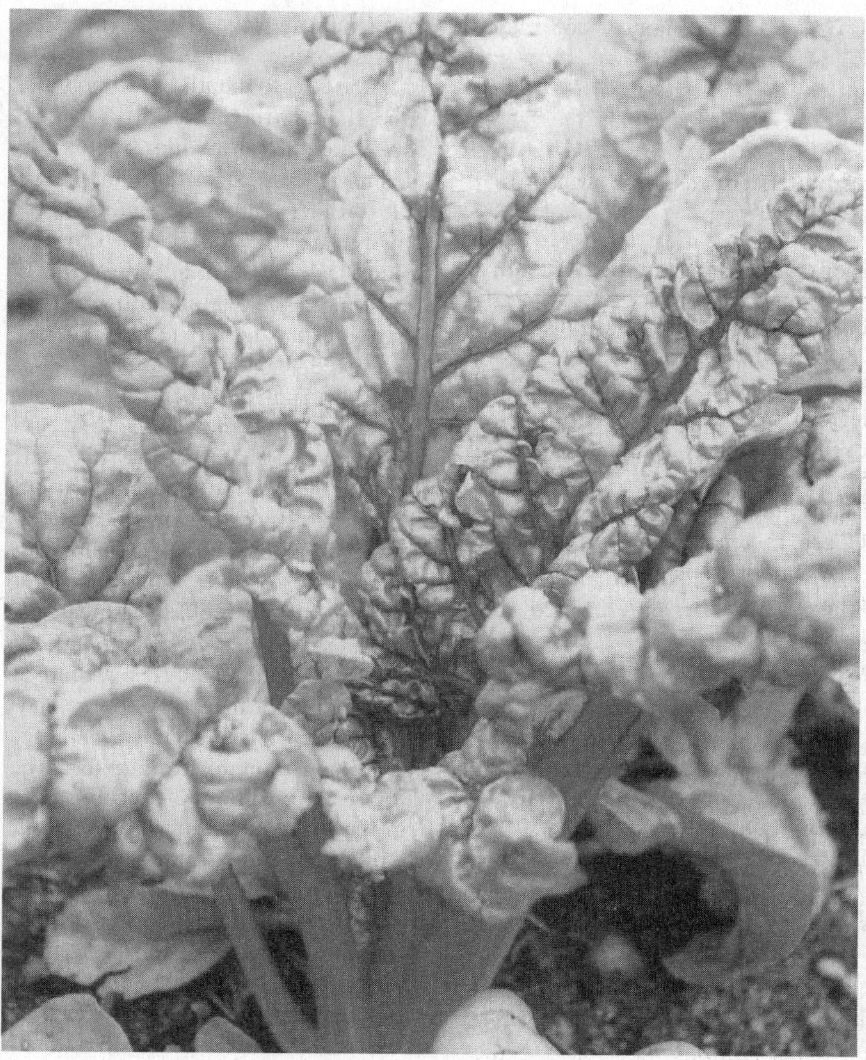

Swiss chard, "Bright Lights," lights up our garden.

I pack the raw corn into pint jars to within an inch of the top, add a teaspoon of salt, and pour boiling water over the corn to within an inch of the top of the jar. It's that easy. Pints of corn are processed in the pressure canner for 55 minutes and quarts for 85 minutes at 10 pounds pressure (unless you live above 1,000 feet and must adjust your pressure accordingly; check your canning manual for directions).

Our family was getting so sick of "store" corn. It's always too mature, too tough, and has no taste. We had been living out of the pantry for 3 years, and my sweet corn had gotten down to two quarts and two pints, even with me hoarding it. Once you taste home-canned, home-grown sweet corn, you're spoiled for life. I have to laugh when folks ask me, "Why don't you just buy cans of corn at the store and not go through all that work?" Some people just don't know any better, I guess.

It's like telling me I should eat chuck roast instead of prime T-bone steak. No, thank you.

The yard gets a facelift

After more than two years of living on a raw gravel ridge, I was just itching to make our front yard a yard, not a parking lot. It is solid gravel, with tons of large stones; impossible to pick rocks to make a nice yard or flower beds.

Our friends, Jeri and Jim, asked David to come over and help them haul railroad ties out to their new garden. They garden exclusively in raised beds made of truck tires and railroad ties, and they needed more garden. So David went over and helped make beds. They are 24' long and about 4' wide.

Then, they ordered a big dump truck full of screened black dirt to fill them. I watched as the beds progressed, when I came to pick up David and bring him to work. And the wheels began clicking in my head. Jim had gotten a big truck load of the ties for a "great deal" and had often offered me all the ties I wanted. So far I had waited, not knowing just what I wanted to do with them.

Last fall, another friend, Joe, came over to see if I would like some black dirt that the county had dug out of a ditch near his place. He told them to dump all they had "over by his garage" so he and his wife could have a little garden. He was away, and they dumped and dumped and dumped; all day long with several trucks. When they came home, there was a mountain range of black dirt out there, and he couldn't get in his garage.

Joe knew we had a tractor with a loader on it, and he had an old, beater dump truck. So David went over and they hauled four big loads of black dirt over to our front lawn-to-be. Then his truck broke down and winter closed in with an ice storm. He could get in his garage, but didn't have much room.

In the spring, he asked if we would still like more black dirt. He only wanted enough to work up for a garden and there was still tons there. So I called our friend, Dale Rinne, who I knew had a track hoe and big dump truck. Dale had hauled many loads of rock and gravel on our mile-long drive and was always quick, cheerful, and very fair.

Three days later, Joe had a nice level garden spot, and we had five more loads of black dirt on our yard, spread out fairly well. Dale also dug out our walk-out basement approach and even made me a large hole that will be a fish pond one day. As he also sold screened black dirt, I bought 10 yards from him, and he dumped it right in the yard where it would be handy for our beds.

So, here we were with nice black dirt on our rocky yard, and the offer of free railroad ties. What could I do? We built raised beds for flowers and herbs along the sides of the yard to hold back the woods and brush and make a place for our flowers that had been lacking for all this time. (By the way, if you are planning to use railroad ties for your vegetable garden, be aware that used ties are creosoted, but after years the creosote is leached and weakened. Enough is left to smell and protect them from rotting, but not enough to cause gardeners much concern. I have used them for years for raised beds and foundations for chicken houses and goat sheds.)

I dragged a heavy oak pallet over the area we would be making the yard with our riding lawn mower/garden tractor, then we began laying out our beds. As an experienced bed-maker, David placed the ties, using our faithful moving dolly to haul them. Our beds along the north are 16' long and 4' wide. We cut ties in half to make the short ends, then spiked them together using 10" pole barn nails.

We left an 8' open space between beds in the event the propane tank needed replacing in the future. The gas man wouldn't like to back over a railroad-tie raised bed with his tank trailer. In this space, we just mounded a gentle hill of dirt without the ties.

On the end of the second north bed, I made an 8'x8' square with a 4'x4' square laid on top of the black dirt that filled the lower square. I had been envying my son, Bill, and his wife, Kelly's, circular strawberry tier garden, but I couldn't afford the cost. So we made our own version, and I love it. Two years ago, I had planted Ft. Laramie strawberries down on a flat area below where our house now sits. But the deer had kept them trimmed, and they had only a few berries because I didn't water or care for them very well.

So I took a bucket down there and dug up 24 plants. They were nice and healthy, despite the deer munching, but they like it so much more in a well-watered raised bed. I carefully picked all grass out of the roots so I didn't plant grass (the #1 enemy of a strawberry patch) in my new bed, along with the strawberry plants. I dug down deep enough so the long, rank roots would comfortably fit with the crown just at soil level. (If you plant the crown too deeply, the plant will not do well and if you plant it so the roots show at all, the plant will die.)

Then, I watered the bed well, stood back, and smiled.

In the other beds, I've planted iris, fancy daylilies, sage, chives, and peonies. Mom is all excited about the new beds and has ordered fall bulbs, more lilies, peonies, and other perennials, so our garden will soon be full. I've always had lots of flowers. Some folks say it's a waste to plant things you can't eat. I believe that they're wrong. Where food satisfies your body, flowers feed your soul. Δ

Ayoob on Firearms

When wild animals invade your homestead

By Massad Ayoob

The flash from the amateur camera makes the mountain lion's eyes glow above the gaping blackness of its open maw as it crashes through a window in Colorado. Millions of people saw this iconic image on aol.com/news, one that reminds us of how fragile the wall is that separates that domestic creature *Homo sapiens* from the predatory wielders of fang and claw.

The readers of *Backwoods Home* choose to live not only close to nature, but in its very heart. This brings many satisfactions. But it also brings some dangers.

The recent movie, *Snakes on a Plane,* probably had a particular resonance with country folk who had woken up with a poisonous "snake in the house," or occasionally, "snake in the bed." There are true stories of human beings facing the bear on the back porch, the mountain lion on the hiking or cycling trail, and so on. Some of these stories have had very tragic endings.

Everyday happening? No.

Everyday possibility? If you live in the backwoods…YES!

You deal with everyday possibilities the way you deal with everyday happenings. Preparation. Equipping yourself. Being alert. Being ready to respond…hopefully, with something a little more potent than a camera.

Buck's story

Buck is a six-year-old Bull Mastiff who weighs 110 pounds and lives in rural Suwannee County, Florida, with a couple who retired from careers in emergency public service a little the worse for wear, but still fully cognizant of the responsibility to remain alert to any possible danger. Horses share the idyllic retirement property with Mike and Kathy Larney. So do their little grandchildren. So do dogs like Buck.

Suwannee County is coyote territory. A couple of years ago, Mike and

Kathy were on an extended visit elsewhere and a friend was house-sitting for them when she heard a ruckus near the front porch. A young German Shepherd puppy was sleeping there that night, under the watchful and protective eye of Buck, when a pack of coyotes crept up, apparently drawn to the sounds made by the puppy.

Coyotes can be vicious things. They take down and kill and eat animals larger than themselves. A human child is literally easy meat for them. Small dogs and cats are seen by coyotes as tasty treats.

The housesitter got to the door in time to see Buck chasing two coyotes out around the house and toward the woods in back. By the time she reached a phone and a gun, the big dog had already been ambushed by the rest of the pack. Looking out the back window through the dim light, the housesitter saw one and then another wiry canine form flung through the air. She made her emergency call.

By the time she got outside, it was over. Buck was limping back, covered with severe bite wounds, which would require 40-some stitches and drains in his chest and legs. The surviving members of the pack had fled, but two of their number were not going anywhere.

Buck, the Bull Mastiff, today. He has healed from the injuries he sustained when he drove a pack of six coyotes from his home, killing two.

They found the dead coyotes there at morning light; two of them. Blood trails indicated that Buck had inflicted damage on more, who were smart enough to run away while their bodies still worked. Buck had torn the throats out of two of the coyotes, and in his rage when their cohorts fled, had disemboweled them. Buck has massive jaws, which, with his jowls drawn back, resemble something out of the movie *Predator*.

The puppy, the original target of the coyote pack, was unharmed.

Buck is not a vicious dog. He is a loving animal, friendly to guests, and enormously protective of Mike and Kathy's little grandchildren. On the night of the attack, this great beast was outside keeping watch on the little one of his kind the way sheepdogs guard the flock. The coyotes infiltrated, with lethal intent.

Buck did what he was not only trained, but bred, to do.

He stopped them. Decisively. Faster than emergency services could respond to a rural homestead. Faster even than a human inside could access a loaded firearm and go out after the deadly interlopers.

There is a lesson here. True, the dog will not always be able to do it by itself. The housesitter felt badly that her gun wasn't closer to hand. She thought that if she could have reached it sooner, she might have kept Buck from being torn up by the coyotes.

But the gun wasn't close enough. By the time she heard the commotion, she—inside—would have been able to do no more than avenge a dead puppy, if she'd had only the gun.

Buck was close enough, and that meant he was able to interdict in time to keep his ward completely from harm.

Which is why, from the time of cavemen with domesticated wolves that "came to the tribe's campfires," dogs have served as super-efficient sentinels for humans.

A snake in the grass

I had a recent personal experience that reinforced the good sense of having a protective dog as part of the rural household. These days, I divide my time between a rural home in Florida and the state of New Hampshire, where I lived most of my life and still work as a part-time cop. At the southern digs, I had rescued an abandoned puppy and was taking care of her until I could find her a good home. Since she was an outdoor dog who spent most of her time on my backyard range, I named her LadySmith, the Range Puppy.

A Catahoula hound, LadySmith comes from a breed developed in Louisiana for hunting wild hogs. She showed early her tendency to guard the homestead and to alert to any potentially hostile wildlife. One night, I was walking some friends out to their car when the puppy went on point and began barking at something in the grass just ahead of us. I pulled out my ever-present SureFire flashlight and found myself looking into the open, cottony mouth of a decidedly poisonous water moccasin.

I was wearing a Glock 31 pistol, and it seemed to come into my hand by itself, and soon the snake's decapitated body lay writhing its last. The G31 is chambered for the .357 SIG cartridge, and the Gold Dot ammunition it was loaded with sends a jacketed hollow-point bullet out of the barrel at almost 1400 feet per second. There was no splash of blood and brain matter when the bullet hit the business end of the snake, the way you see the special effects in movies. Its head was just suddenly…gone.

Since then, I've been able to place LadySmith with a wonderful young couple in New Hampshire who will be at home to take care of her and love her more than I will. I hope they appreciate her as much as I did the night she saved me and my guests from the bite of a snake sufficiently venomous to make adults very sick and to kill little children.

I was glad I had the dog.

I was also glad I had the pistol.

Glock 31 and Gold Dot .357 SIG ammo author used to kill a venomous cottonmouth outside his front door. This pistol holds 16 cartridges. Some states still limit owners to 10-round magazine capacity.

The rationale of the sidearm

A majority of rural people in America have firearms readily accessible in their homes. Sometimes, they keep them propped in a corner near the door or hung over the mantel. Sometimes they keep them in the working pickup truck or even racked on the snowmobile or the ATV. And, sometimes, they keep them on their person.

There is a reason why the classic image of the cowboy includes a gun strapped to the hip. That image has very little to do with range wars, feuds, or gunfights. It had a lot more to do with the fact that a cowpuncher on the frontier was constantly working around large animals like horses and beef critters that could easily trample him to death if they were having an "off day." Elmer Keith, perhaps the greatest gun expert of the 20th century, began his life as a cowboy and learned much from men who had lived in the Old West. He learned from them to carry a powerful revolver all the time.

That practice saved his life many times over. Once, a handgun was the only thing that kept a maddened horse from dragging Keith to death when his foot was caught in the stirrup and he was down on the ground on his back. Another time, it kept him from being trampled to death by a crazed steer. On a third occasion, it allowed him to kill a rattlesnake before the rattlesnake could kill him.

A .357 Magnum revolver will do for cougars and mad dogs and has been used to kill large bears. Top, six-shot Ruger GP100 service revolver; below, five-shot Ruger SP101 concealment revolver.

"Sidearm" ain't that tough a word. "Side." "Arm." The arm is at your side. That way it's always within reach, no matter how unexpected the emergency. And whenever it's on your body, it's out of reach of unauthorized hands. That's an element of "gun safety."

Until the day in the early 1980s when the stroke took him down, Elmer Keith always carried a heavy, powerful revolver at his hip. From about 1956 on, that revolver was a Smith & Wesson .44 Magnum with a four-inch barrel. It was a gun and a cartridge he helped design. It was a weapon too harsh in recoil for an average person to handle effectively, but for a practiced shooter like Keith, it delivered the power of a deer rifle readily available and within reach at all times.

But if large bears are not part of the local problem, you can get by with something less than a .44 Magnum. From its introduction in 1935 to the .44 Magnum's coming in 1956, the most powerful available handgun was the .357 Magnum. Today, revolvers in this caliber are produced in compact sizes that make them easy to carry in a holster or even concealed in a pocket, 24/7. For that purpose, it's tough to beat the little five-shot Ruger

SP101, a small-frame revolver that has the accuracy of a target pistol if you do your part, and enough power to solve the kind of problems that mountain lions can bring through a window. As I write this, sitting at a computer in a rural setting, the gun holstered on my hip is a Ruger .357 Magnum.

Powerful semiautomatic pistols have taken over from once-traditional revolvers in the police sector. I've met genuine cowboys who are more likely to carry a .45 automatic on the open range (not just the shooting range) than any revolver. The conservation officers of Pennsylvania recently switched from the six-shot Smith & Wesson .357 Magnum revolver to the sixteen-shot Glock 31 pistol chambered for the .357 SIG cartridge. This is the same pistol I used to shoot that cottonmouth, and I can't blame the Pennsylvania wardens for liking it. It's lighter to carry, easier to shoot due to lighter recoil, and powerful enough for the job. If you have to face the same half-dozen coyotes that Buck the Bull Mastiff faced, six targets and six bullets leave awfully little margin for error. And, with a five-shot revolver, well, let's just say it never hurts to have a bit of a buffer zone.

When animal friends turn bad

Elmer Keith found himself less likely to get killed by wild mountain lions and bears than by domestic cattle and horses. The wild critters only rarely come to visit your homestead. The large, powerful livestock live there all the time, and don't have Valium or Dr. Phil to calm them when they experience hostile moments.

The same has proven true throughout America, from cities to suburbs to boondocks. Many reading this have seen the videotape shot by a TV news crew of a vicious dog chasing a young African-American boy. At the last moment, the child is saved from a horrible mangling by a police officer who draws his pistol and, necessarily, euthanizes the dog on camera.

In another incident, an out-of-control canine set upon a little girl. Her brother, a young teenager, grabbed a .22 rifle from the house and killed the animal before it could kill his little sister. A .22 is less powerful than what one would normally want for an emergency of this magnitude, but the brave young man made it work. His sibling suffered scars, but her brother saved her from being killed or crippled.

A friend of mine lived in rural New Hampshire and found his homestead plagued by savage dogs owned by neighbors "down the road." The night came when two of those big, mean animals attacked his wife as she smoked a cigarette on the veranda outside the house. He heard her scream as she ran for the kitchen door.

He snatched up a Colt .45 automatic pistol as he sprinted toward the sound. He and his wife passed each other in the doorway, the dogs close behind her. He brought up the pistol, indexed it on the threat, and opened fire. Moments later, both dogs were down and dead from his accurately aimed, rapidly fired hollow-point bullets. His wife, a slender and beautiful woman who would have been no match for two dogs each almost her own size, was unharmed. The police department quickly determined that his action was totally justifiable.

In a given year, you are more likely to be killed or crippled by canine teeth than by the fangs of a bear or a cougar. Sometimes, the animal that attacks is one that you brought into the home with you, and it simply snapped. Heaven knows, people have been killed by other people they've brought into their homes with the best of intentions. Why should animals be any different?

If there is a theme in all these stories, it is this: A gun that is locked in a cabinet, unloaded, and separate from ammunition that is locked in another location, is unlikely to do much good in an emergency. There simply won't be time to bring all the components together when danger strikes hard and fast.

Ruger Mini-14 Ranch Rifle rests in a corner of a rural home. Firing chamber is empty; magazine holds up to 20 rounds. Check local laws for legal magazine capacities.

And the same is true when the danger doesn't slither or walk on four feet.

Two-legged dangers

The fact is, home invasion by feral humans is a greater danger than will ever come padding in on us atop four paws, if we look at the statistics. The Clutters were a rural family. They died in their midwestern farmhouse at the hands of the two vicious little b------- whom Truman Capote glorified in his book, *In Cold Blood*. The Clutter home, as I recall, contained firearms, but they were kept stored away for sporting purposes. They were not accessible to members of the family when they needed them for defense of their own lives.

I know a cop in California, retired now, who puts his gun on when he gets up in the morning and takes it off when he goes to bed at night. When he sleeps, his Glock is within reach at his bedside.

There is a reason for this. He worked in an area that, for some of his career, led the nation in murder rate. He responded frequently to the tragic aftermaths of home invasions. He discovered that they happened quickly. The victims were raped, or beaten, or murdered faster than they could have run to another part of the house, spun a dial on a gun safe, and then loaded a firearm with which to protect themselves. He realized early on that the only chance when the door came crashing in would be to have a gun within reach at the very moment of the first alert to deadly danger that had breached the walls of the home.

People who believe in moonbeams and butterflies think that's paranoid. I don't. I've seen some of what that retired detective has seen. I do what he does. My gun goes on in the morning, doesn't come off until bedtime, and stays accessible at bedside between the dark and the daylight.

It's always accessible, like the fire extinguishers in my home and in my car. I don't know when I'll need them, but I know that if and when I do need them, I'll need them desperately, and I'll need them RIGHT NOW. That's why they're always accessible.

The defensive firearm is directly analogous to the fire extinguisher. Each is a piece of emergency rescue equipment whose job is to save human life. I don't know when I'll need them. I do know that if and when I do need them, I'll need access to them immediately, so I keep them around all the time.

The good news is that when human aggressors are confronted with guns in the hands of good people, they either surrender or turn and run most of the time. I was a cop in one small town where a rural home on the edge of a river was invaded by a psycho who grabbed the woman of the household. Hearing her screams, her husband grabbed a small pistol and came to her aid. The intruder backed away at gunpoint like a vampire cringing before a crucifix, and when the now-freed woman ran to a bedroom and brought her husband a 12-gauge shotgun to reinforce his side of the argument, the intruder ran like the dog he was. I was the first responding officer, and I didn't get there until it was over.

I was damned glad it was an armed household.

Sometimes, of course, human home invaders aren't smart enough to know what is good for them. One of my students was a nice lady in Michigan who was awakened in the night by a man climbing through a window in her home. She drew down on him with the Smith & Wesson .38 Special revolver she kept accessible at her bedside and made a statement to the effect that if he continued the felony he was committing, he would be shot.

He snarled at her, "You don't have the balls to shoot me, bitch!"

BANG!

End of story.

Ruger 50th anniversary model Blackhawk .44 Magnum revolver is powerful enough to kill giant bears, but requires training and practice time to master due to recoil commensurate with its high power level.

Bottom line

It isn't always mountain lions. Within a year of the Colorado incident, there was a highly publicized case of a deer crashing through a window and into a home in heartland America. The man of the house wound up grappling with the animal hand-to-hand for an agonizingly long time before he finally managed to break its neck. By then, he had been pretty well torn up and had suffered a painful groin injury.

Thinking of that case, and the Colorado mountain lion, I keep flashing back to Elmer Keith. He might or might not have spilled his coffee before he got his ever-present Smith & Wesson .44 out of its ever-present hip holster and "tamed" the intruding beast. If he photographed it, it would be after it was dead on the floor.

As noted earlier, a cougar coming in your home is not an everyday occurrence. But, all things considered, if that happens when my grandchild is in line of sight of the predator, I would very much like to have the latest incarnation of Elmer Keith babysitting.

With Buck the Bull Mastiff backing him up. Δ

In the Gravest Extreme
By Massad Ayoob

Killer Blizzards

understanding them could save your life

By John Silveira

Winter storms and blizzards can occur any time from late fall to early spring, and in some northerly regions or high elevation they can happen all the way into April.

What is a blizzard and how does it differ from a typical winter storm?

The National Weather Service (NWS) defines a blizzard as having the following conditions that persist for more than three hours:

- A lot of snow either falling *or* being blown around
- Winds of 35 miles per hour (mph) or greater
- Visibility below ¼ mile

If snow has stopped falling but persistent winds continue to blow snow around, reducing visibility, the conditions are sometimes referred to as a *ground blizzard.*

How blizzards form

Three things are needed to create a blizzard:

- Cold air (below freezing)
- Moisture in the air
- Warm, rising air

Cold air. There must be one weather system in which the air must be cold enough at high altitudes for snow to form and cold enough near the ground to keep it from melting before it hits the ground. If only the upper air is warm, the storm will start out as rain and may turn into sleet. Sleet is somewhat reminiscent of hail. On the other hand, it may fall as rain and become "freezing rain" as it hits the cold earth and other surfaces and freezes. Freezing rain makes for particularly hazardous driving conditions. (See driving article by Don Fallick in Issue #26, which is in *A Backwoods Home Anthology, The Fifth Year.*)

If the upper air is cold and air near the surface is warm, what begins as snow at high altitudes will become rain before it reaches the ground.

Moisture in the air. The way blizzards form is when warm wind blows over a large body of water, such as the ocean, and picks up moisture. So, there must also be a weather system with warm air. This is how Nor'easters develop as warm air over the Gulf or the Atlantic gets saturated with moisture and moves north where it will run into a cold-weather system.

It has to be *warm* air simply because warm air holds more water vapor than cold air. In fact, if it gets too cold, snow won't form at all because the cold air will not hold enough moisture. It is from this that many old-timers came up with the phrase, "It's too cold to snow."

Warm air rising. While warm air is required to hold the moisture that goes into making snow, it's also needed because warm air rises and where it rises over the cold air, a *front* is formed. It is at the front where the moisture-laden air turns to snow. As the moisture in the air condenses, it also releases an incredible amount of energy. Part of this energy is turned into wind, and without wind we won't have a blizzard.

The fiercest winter storms and blizzards occur in the "Snowbelt," which stretches from Minnesota to New England. But, they also occur outside this zone with devastating consequences simply because more southerly parts of the country are less prepared for heavy snowfalls.

If you live in a Gulf Coast state and get a heavy snowfall, you may think you just had a blizzard. In all likelihood, you didn't. However, the Southeast and the Gulf states, though unaccustomed to snow and freezing conditions, are not immune to winter storms. When these storms sweep though the South, local municipalities may find themselves unprepared, as they usually do not have equipment for either snow removal or for salting or sanding the roads.

Also, though blizzards seem more often to be phenomena in the eastern states, blizzards and bad winters also occur in the West. It was an early winter blizzard and severe winter that led to the legendary trapping of the Donner Party near today's Truckee, California.

Can we prevent blizzards? Like all weather phenomena, there is little we can do with current technology to prevent or even moderate blizzards.

In the meantime, even if there is global warming, blizzards are likely to remain a part of our future. In fact, they may even become worse because as the air over the Atlantic and the Gulf of Mexico warms up, it'll carry even more moist air north than it does now. And when it collides with late-season cold fronts hovering over the Great Plains and Canada, even bigger blizzards are likely to occur.

The effects of blizzards

Blizzards are not new. However, to the first Europeans who settled this continent, they were. They knew snow when they left Europe, but they had rarely, if ever, seen anything like the winter weather they discovered in the New World.

If we look at historical blizzards, several things become apparent. Until late in the 20th century, blizzards could come as complete surprises. Major cities were often isolated from the outside world as both communications and transportation broke down in the face of heavy snowfall, fierce winds, and freezing temperatures. People caught off guard were stranded away from home, some away from any kind of shelter. People died as a direct result of the storms.

Because of the presence of warm air that frequently precedes blizzards, the weather can sometimes seem unseasonably warm before a storm strikes and people get lured out into the outdoors wearing less than they should. It's the reason that during the Armistice Day blizzard of 1940, so many hunters died. They had simply gone out underdressed into the path of one of the worst storms ever to hit the Midwest.

As time has passed, some things have changed, but some have remained the same. With each passing year, because of satellites and improvements in computer technology, weather forecasting has become better. So, the storms have become more predictable—though the severity of an encroaching storm is not always obvious.

Communications continue to improve, and with today's wireless communications, people are more apt to be able to stay in touch with loved ones, rescuers, and the outside world

An impromptu lean-to, coupled with a fire and a reflecting wall, will never have all the comforts of home, but it may be enough to keep you alive.

even if away from home, and even if other lines of communication are down.

On the other hand, improvements in transportation seem to make it more likely many people will be stranded away from home. Sometimes, they will be stranded at jobs, sometimes they will be snowbound on roads while making a bid to make it home, and sometimes people will try to make grocery runs at the last moment thinking they can make the round-trip in no time at all, unaware of just how *fast* a blizzard can come up and strand them.

Records of blizzards go back to the days of the earliest settlements in North America, including "The Great Snow of 1717," which was really a series of four snow storms that occurred between February 27 and March 7. And one of the most notable, the "Blizzard of 1899," created record low temperatures from New Orleans to New England, some of which stand today. It would be 94 years before a storm comparable to that one wracked the country, and that was the Blizzard of 1993, the so-called "Storm of the Century," which we *will* talk about.

Let's look at five historic blizzards and see what happened to the people who endured them, and see what can be learned from them.

Historic blizzards

The blizzard of 1888, sometimes called the Great White Hurricane (March 11-14, 1888). This is the blizzard against which *all* other blizzards in the United States are measured. It has become a legend in the annals of winter history.

For almost everyone who endured it, the greatest blizzard on record came without warning. There were no satellite photos as there are today to see it developing or to warn the cities in its path when it began to move. And, when it hit, no one knew how bad it was going to get until it was over.

It was March, the weather was warm for that time of year, frequently rising into the 50s.

And this is our first lesson about blizzards: They can come in what seems like beautiful spring-like weather and catch even the most self-reliant people by surprise.

On the 11th of March it began to rain heavily. On the 12th, a Monday, the rain turned to snow as temperatures plummeted and the wind picked up. The combination of falling and drifting snow started to choke the Northeast.

There have been storms with heavier snowfall, and there have been storms that have been colder, but the Great White Hurricane was a combination of bad weather conditions not seen before nor in the 118 years since.

The storm spread over an area from Washington, D.C. to Maine and brought the nation's capital, along with the cities of New York, Philadelphia, and Boston, to their knees. Businesses closed, fire stations closed, and hospitals were inaccessible. More that 200 ships ran aground in the gale-force winds and whiteout conditions with a loss of more than 100 seamen, and there were at least 300 other deaths directly attributable to the storm.

That particular combination of events couldn't happen today. But in 1888, people afraid of losing their jobs went out into the storm that Monday morning, and many of them died later in the day trying to get home.

In rural areas, people who left that morning were stranded away from their homes for as much as two weeks as families and friends, bewildered by the catastrophe, had no idea what had become of them.

Measured snowfalls were up to 50 inches in New England and 40 inches in New York and New Jersey, and

Greatest snowfalls in North America

	Place	Date	Inches
24 hours	Silver Lake, CO	April 14–15, 1921	76
1 month	Tamarack, CA	Jan. 1911	390
1 storm	Mt. Shasta Ski Bowl, CA	Feb. 13–19, 1959	189
1 season	Mount Baker, WA	1998–1999	1,140
1 city	Buffalo, NY	1976-1977	199

Courtesy U.S. Army Corps of Engineers, Engineer Topographic Laboratories

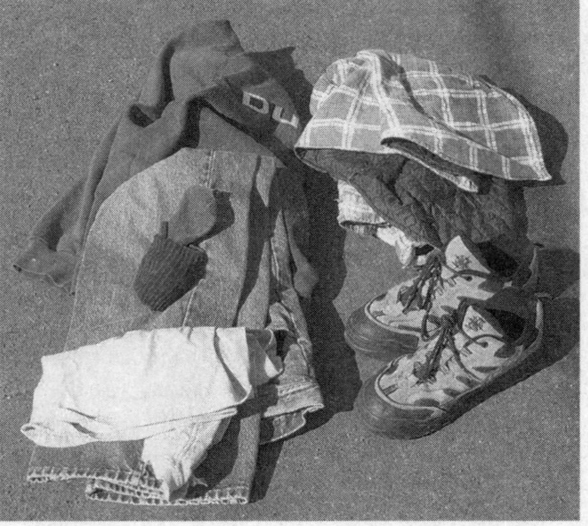

Among clothing items I carry in my vehicle year-round, are (clockwise from upper left) a "hoodie," some quilted shirts, a spare set of old but still wearable shoes, a clean shirt, socks, and jeans. Spare underwear is good, too, but I didn't want to photograph them.

An advantage of the German military surplus entrenching tool is that it can be opened at a 90° angle to expose a pick that is handy for digging or breaking through crusty snow.

severe winds created snowdrifts that were as much as 50 feet deep.

The only means of electronic communication at the time were the telegraph and telephone. When those lines went down, which they did under the weight of accumulating snow and ice buildup, that entire part of the country was out of touch with the rest of the world for days.

Not only were streets and roads blocked, but drifting snow actually rose high enough in some places to block the elevated trains. The transportation crisis created in New York City led to the decision to build that city's subway system.

Armistice Day Storm (November 11-12, 1940). Fifty-two years after the Great White Hurricane, another deadly blizzard of epic proportions hit. This one was in the Midwest.

Like the 1888 storm, the weather preceding the blizzard had been unseasonably warm. In fact, gardens were still producing in the orth country well into October. It was a beautiful fall, the kind you like to savor.

Then, on Armistice Day (now called Veterans Day), November 11, 1940, with temperatures still in the 60s, a storm moved into the Midwest from over the Rockies. It had started in the Pacific Northwest, and, when it arrived in Minnesota it met warmer, wet air that had been travelling north through the midwestern states from the Gulf of Mexico. Along with that was a cold front that was moving down from Canada. The three weather fronts were about to collide.

Duck hunters, out to enjoy the great fall weather, found themselves in some of the best hunting in memory as ducks flooded into the Mississippi Valley. Survivors said shots could be heard from all directions as hunters were bent on easily filling their limit. What they didn't and couldn't know was that the ducks were fleeing the storm that would soon create a life-and-death struggle for hundreds of hunters and thousands of others as well.

Then it began to rain. Unconcerned, the hunters stayed out. Soon, the rain turned into sleet...then snow. Then, with the rising winds, the conditions for a blizzard were set, and hundreds of hunters realized, all too late, they were trapped—and poorly clothed for what was to come.

In the meantime, as occurred in the 1888 storm, telephone and telegraph lines were soon downed, putting many towns out of touch with the outside world. Almost every road across several states was closed as snow piled up faster than any highway department could remove it.

With any blizzard today, this can still happen: You can expect power lines to fall and roads to be blocked.

Meanwhile, because of whiteout conditions, an engineer driving a freight train missed a track-side signal, and he was unaware that the track he was on was also being used by an oncoming passenger train. So, instead of pulling into a siding, he lumbered on into a disaster—and his own death—as the two steam locomotives collided in a head-on wreck.

Winds as high as 80 miles per hour created snowdrifts of more than 20 feet. Other trains on other tracks were slowed down by the deepening snow until finally almost all rail traffic in the northern Midwest ground to a halt, and they were snowbound with their crews and passengers.

Farmers who had left their rural farms for a day of shopping and provisioning in the nearby towns found themselves unable to get home for days.

The storm created a 1,000-mile swath of death and destruction though the Mississippi Valley and sunk boats on Lake Michigan, where at least 66 sailors died.

At least 80 other people died because of the storm, most of them the unprepared hunters who had left home without adequate clothing that morning and were stranded in the outdoors with no means to keep themselves warm.

One young hunter, who may otherwise have died of exposure, found a novel way to keep himself warm: He started running. He ran around and around a tree on the island where he'd been stranded. He ran, and ran, and ran. When rescuers reached him the following morning, there was a well-worn path in the snow around the tree, but he was otherwise healthy and safe.

Economic losses from the blizzard were difficult to assess, but they included thousands of cattle and more than a million Thanksgiving turkeys that were being groomed for the upcoming holiday.

The Blizzard of 1978 (February 6-7, 1978). There were two blizzards in 1978, one in New England, the other in the Midwest.

The New England storm was the more severe. It was the result of three air masses, one moving in from Pennsylvania, a second from Georgia, and a third from over the Atlantic. The storms converged over Connecticut, Rhode Island, and Massachusetts, forming one huge storm.

This new storm packed winds of 65 miles per hour. Unlike the typical

Nor'easters that hit New England and pass through in 6 to 12 hours, this one stalled before a high-pressure area that hovered in Canada, and for 36 straight hours it poured its snow onto and tore the states with its high winds. It was even accompanied by unusual winter thunderstorms.

Despite the steady improvements in weather forecasting, the severity of this storm still caught many New Englanders by surprise.

Once again, people were stranded away from their homes. Some died in their cars from carbon monoxide inhalation, unaware that snow blocked their exhaust pipes as they idled their engines in an attempt to keep warm.

Transportation broke down as some roads were buried, and many became difficult or even impossible to plow because of the abandoned vehicles. Other roads became difficult to plow simply because they ran out of spaces to push the snow. In Boston, with no place else to put it, the snow was often loaded into trucks and dumped directly into Boston Harbor.

When it was over, more than 3,500 cars were found abandoned on major roads and highways, and countless others were found abandoned on side streets.

People who found themselves trapped in their homes were lucky. Many others found themselves trapped at work and were unable to reach their homes. Some couldn't even leave the buildings they were in because snow drifts as deep as 15 feet blocked the exits.

How bad was the storm as compared to other storms? For the first time in years, New York City schools were closed. Ordinarily opened in even the most severe weather conditions (remember, the breakdown in transportation during the blizzard of 1888 was one of the reasons the New York City subway was built), the blizzard of 1978 succeeded in closing them. And one of the only means of transportation, such as getting the ill to hospitals, was the use of snowmobiles on the city's snow-choked streets.

Among the tools I have in my vehicle are (clockwise from upper right) two military surplus ground mats that can insulate you from the ground, plastic trash bags, blankets, gloves, fire starter sticks (one package is opened to show what they look like), two butane lighters, a military entrenching tool with the sleeve that fits over the shovel blade, and a flashlight.

Superstorm of 1993—also dubbed the "Storm of the Century" (March 12-15, 1993). This is an example of a storm they saw coming. Yet, despite all the advances in meteorology and the use of satellite photos, the fact that the meteorologists saw the storm as it was developing, days in advance, wasn't enough to prevent it from being catastrophic. Nor was it enough to keep people from getting stranded.

What the meteorologists saw was an extremely low-pressure weather system loaded with moisture as it moved north from the Gulf of Mexico. This warm, wet front was on a course to collide with an arctic high-pressure cold-weather system moving in from the Great Plains. That cold-weather system was being forced further south than it ordinarily would have been for that time of year by the jet stream. Meteorologists say such an event happens only once in 500 years.

When the two fronts met, they created perfect conditions for a blizzard.

Beginning March 12, snow fell from as far south as Alabama, and north to New York. (Remember, March 12 was the exact day the snow started to fall, 105 years before, during the Great White Hurricane.) As snow accumulated, winds picked up, temperatures fell, and fully one-third of the country was affected as roads became impassable and literally millions along the Atlantic seaboard and further inland lost power. Because airports couldn't plow the snow off runways fast enough, a quarter of all the air traffic in the United States was disrupted for the next two days.

Fully 26 states and eastern Canada were affected. In the South, where heavy snowfalls are so rare that it makes no sense for municipalities to make heavy investments in snow removal equipment, transportation broke down. In the North, despite winter preparedness, automobiles and trucks were, once again, abandoned on major thoroughfares, people were stranded away from their homes, and power outages left people cold and in the dark.

Because of record snowfalls, roofs on factories not designed to withstand accumulations of standing snow, collapsed, as did the decks and porches of many homes.

Extreme low temperatures for that part of the year followed the snowfall. Records were set in more than 70 locations in the East on March 14, and 75 more record lows were set on the 15th. Wind gusts of 144 miles per hour were recorded on Mount Washington in New Hampshire.

Though meteorologists say this type of storm can only happen once every 500 years, no one really knows.

Still, this was not the worst blizzard of record, by any standards. Yet, some 300 people died.

What is there to learn from such a storm? If you hear one coming, don't go out, don't drive, stay home, keep warm, and wait it out.

Blizzard of 1996 (January 6-12, 1996). To New Englanders, the storm of record in the 20th century is the Blizzard of '78. And other parts of the country may feel other storms were greater in their area. But for the amount of snow that fell over so wide an area, nothing beats the Blizzard of '96.

In fact, from a meteorological standpoint, this wasn't a blizzard at all. It was actually three separate storms that lay siege to the eastern United States from January 6 through the 12th. High winds, freezing temperatures, and massive snowfall combined to shut down much of the Middle Atlantic States. More than a foot of snow fell in parts of Ohio, while two-foot and two-and a half-foot accumulations were common all along the seaboard from Virginia to Boston.

Many roads, though plowed, were quickly closed again by drifting snow driven by the winds.

The federal government was virtually closed down. In some counties, as many as 50 percent of the residential neighborhoods lay unplowed for days, and for a week after the storms many people found themselves on streets that had not yet seen a snowplow.

To compound the problems, after the three storms passed, temperatures shot up causing massive snow melts that resulted in flooding.

This storm killed at least 50 people.

Preparing for a blizzard

According to the United States Search and Rescue Task Force, about 70 percent of "winter deaths" related to ice and snow occur in automobile accidents directly attributable to weather conditions.

Another 25 percent occur to people caught out in storms. This includes hikers, hunters, people who have abandoned their cars, and anyone else with or without good reasons to be out in the storm. Of those who die as a direct result of exposure to the cold, half are over 50 years old, and 70 percent are male.

There are numerous kinds of lean-tos you can make if you need shelter from the snow. They can be constructed using branches, boughs, and even lined with trash bags. Remember, all you're trying to do is stay sheltered and dry for a day or two, so beauty and durability are not important.

If you are going to be caught out in a storm, the overwhelming chance is that it will be when you're out in your car. So, what can you do? What can you carry in your car to improve your chances of survival? It would be wise to take the advice of Jackie Clay and have a survival kit in your car. (See article in Issue #55, which is in *A Backwoods Home Anthology, The Tenth Year.*) But, in addition, in the trunk of my car I always have a military surplus entrenching tool (folding shovel). If you can find one made for the German Army, they're better built and more versatile than the American-made versions. The ones made for the commercial market are usually flimsy.

I also carry a spare set of clothes: Footwear, socks, flannel shirt, and a couple of quilted flannel shirts. One of the things I keep telling women, particularly women with office jobs, is to carry a pair of walking shoes in their trunks.

I also carry a few butane lighters and some of the treated fire-starting blocks. I even carry a few full-sized heavy-duty trash bags. They make impromptu but effective rain panchos.

It's all cheap stuff, and it takes very little space. I wouldn't drive around without a spare tire, so I don't drive around without stuff that could save my life when I'm in the North Country during winter.

Another item I carry is a pair of military-style ground mats. They're great to lay on for prone-position shooting, but they'll also insulate you from the cold ground or even snow if you have to sleep outdoors.

Blizzards today will be met with a whole new set

of tools. With today's cell phones, loved ones are less likely to be "missing" for weeks at a time, as they were in the aftermath of the Great White Hurricane. With today's weather technology, including satellite photos and up-to-the-minute reporting, more will be known about impending storms. Still, there will be a surprising number of individuals who will venture out into the storms anyway, and not unsurprisingly many will become victims.

What to do if you're caught out in a blizzard

If you're caught in a storm, find shelter. If you have to, build a lean-to. Trash bags make excellent coverings for a lean-to.

Keep dry. Cold water can suck all of the life-giving heat right out of you. Cover every exposed part of your body. In particular, keep your head covered. (As much as 20 percent of your body's heat is lost through the top of your head.)

Unless you've built one before, don't expect to build a snow cave to save yourself. For one thing, they're not easy to build. For another, you're likely to get wetter from sweating and from melting snow trying to build it. Cold and wet are a deadly combination in a blizzard.

If you can, build a fire. A fire not only provides heat, it draws attention. Rocks around a fire will absorb and reradiate heat. A wall, even a makeshift wall (another use for a trash bag), will reflect heat. But if you're near trees, beware of snow in overhanging branches. Snow suddenly falling from overhanging branches can suffocate a hard-built fire.

Unless you absolutely have to, do not abandon your car. Rescuers will find it easier to find a car than they will a hiker stumbling around in the backcountry. However, be careful. Cars do not retain heat well, though they will keep you dry. It's a good reason to keep blankets in your trunk. But also keep in mind that cars can get buried in snow drifts.

If you run your engine for heat, make sure the exhaust doesn't get covered because, instead of dying of exposure, you may kill yourself with carbon monoxide poisoning.

Finally, if you get thirsty, **don't eat ice or snow**. The amount of energy required to melt ice or snow is greater than you think. If you're cold now, the ice or snow you ingest will lower your body temperature even further with possible fatal consequences.

A story that sticks with me is one I read years ago. A couple in the Northwest, taking advantage of some early spring weather, went with their newborn into the mountains. A freak storm came up, stranding them. Though they were lightly dressed, they were afraid they wouldn't be found, so they abandoned their car and began walking. The mother was nursing. She felt compelled to eat snow so as to produce enough milk to feed her baby. The father didn't.

But as a result of ingesting the snow, coupled with the fact that they weren't wearing warm clothes, the mother's body temperature fell dangerously. When rescuers finally reached them, the woman was dead, her husband and baby were still alive. The tragedy is that the baby, though uncomfortably hungry, could have weathered the hunger just fine until help arrived, and all three could have survived.

Again, if thirst becomes overwhelming, and the only source of water is ice or snow, don't eat it. Find a way to melt it first, and don't use your body's heat to do so. Use a fire, use the sun, or even the heater in your car.

In fact, if you can find a heat source to melt it, get it as warm as possible. Drinking the water warm is an even better way to ingest it when you're cold.

Last, avoid alcohol. Alcoholic drinks are diuretics. They will not quench your thirst, and they can contribute to a reduction in your body's temperature.

If you live in the North Country, blizzards are a fact of life. Learn to live with them. And learn to survive them. Δ

Modify your oven to bake great bread

By Emily Buehler

Making bread at home is a long process—kneading the dough, waiting while it rises, shaping it into a loaf, and then waiting while it rises again. But in the end, the golden, crusty, voluminous loaf of bread is worth all the trouble. Too often, however, after all that time, the results are disappointing—the loaf doesn't rise well or the crust is dull and pale. The oven can be a key contributor to these unsatisfactory results.

How can the home baker achieve great bread without a professional bread oven? Understanding how dough acts in the oven and what bakery ovens have that home ovens lack leads to simple modifications the home baker can make to improve his or her oven greatly.

Dough rises, or expands, because of gas produced in the dough by fermentation reactions. This expansion occurs throughout the bread-making process, with a final burst of expansion occurring in the oven. What causes this final expansion? The heat of the oven speeds up the dough's chemical reactions, increasing gas production. In addition, carbon dioxide molecules dissolved in the dough turn into gas molecules at higher temperatures, and gas bubbles in the dough expand when heated. These effects of the heat all increase the size of the dough as it bakes into bread. This final expansion occurs in the first 10 minutes the dough is in the oven. To maximize these effects, it is important to have a hot oven the moment the dough enters.

A good bread oven does not lose heat when the door is opened. Traditional deck ovens consist of giant slabs of concrete heated up to the oven temperature. These slabs, once heated, are able to radiate enough heat to maintain the oven's temperature even when the door is opened. Other ovens have thick brick walls to maintain the heat or are designed to reheat very quickly.

Unfortunately, home ovens lose most of their heat when the door is opened. Once the cold dough enters, the oven must regain the lost heat. By the time this happens, it is too late. The yeast cells are dying, gas-producing reactions are slowing down, and the crust is forming on the loaf, preventing expansion.

How can a home oven be kept hot, even when the door must be opened? One simple trick is to preheat the oven too high. For example, a basic loaf made with flour, water, yeast, and salt bakes at a temperature of 450° F. Preheat the oven to 500°. Put the dough in as quickly as possible, shut the door, and turn the temperature down to 450°. The oven temperature will have dropped, but it will be closer to 450° than it would have been without the extra preheating.

Another solution is to bake bread on a pizza stone. The stone must be preheated with the oven. Introducing a cold stone with the dough would exacerbate the problem of lost oven heat. When the dough is placed on the stone and the oven door is shut, the stone radiates heat, reheating the small oven and providing heat to the dough. Extra stones in the oven can increase this effect. Some bakers place a second pizza stone on the rack over the baking rack so that heat radiates down from above the dough. If you plan to line your whole oven with stones, make sure to leave space at the sides so that heat can circulate.

Cheaper alternatives exist as well: Flat stones from a lumber or garden store can be used in place of a pizza stone. In addition, any stone or brick can be used to help hold heat in the oven, whether or not the dough sits on it. Just preheat the oven long enough to ensure that the stones are fully heated.

A second benefit of professional bakery ovens is their ability to steam dough once it enters the oven. The steam condenses on the relatively cool dough, forming a layer of water. This water slows crust formation, allowing the dough to expand for a longer period of time. Sugars in the dough dissolve into the water layer, increasing their concentration at the surface and eventually contributing to the browning of the loaf. More steam generally results in a thicker, browner, shinier crust.

The obvious, but not very effective, method of producing steam in a home oven is to use a spray bottle, spraying water in the open oven door. This small amount of water does little. Instead, the spray can be applied directly to the dough just before it enters the oven. It may be more effective to use a brush or hands—just wet them and wipe them over the entire surface of the dough, producing a good coating of water.

Some home bakers have devised effective ways to steam the oven instead of the loaf. An oven-safe cup of water in the oven 15 minutes before the dough enters will produce a steamy oven. Much of this steam may be lost when the oven door is open, but the water will continue to steam the oven after the door closes. Remove any remaining water after the dough has been baking for 15 minutes so that the oven will dry out and the crust will form.

A more dramatic oven-steaming method is to preheat a cast iron pan with the oven, on a rack below the baking rack. After the dough enters the oven, carefully pour a cup of water onto the hot pan and quickly close the oven door. The water will evaporate rapidly into a cloud of steam.

Proper use of heat and steam can do wonders when baking a loaf of bread. With a few simple tricks, your oven will be baking like a bakery oven in no time. Δ

Build a poured slab foundation for your new home

By David Lee

In the last issue of *Backwoods Home Magazine* I showed you some ways to prepare a building lot for a home. This time I will tell you about my favorite type of foundation, the poured slab. But, this is not just a simple slab, such as the floor of a garage. There are clever things you can do to make that big block of concrete an integral part of the home that will be built on it, while saving labor and materials.

Before exploring the benefits of the slab, let's consider the reasons it may be a better choice for your new home than a below-grade concrete basement-type foundation.

One factor is the cost. A basement is an extensive and expensive construction job. There is a big hole to dig with potential problems caused by what might be found down there. Blasting ledge or dealing with a high water table can raise costs to a very high level. After the basement is built comes the expense of putting the site back together around it. Lots of money involved here.

The time involved in putting in a full basement is an inconvenience to say the least. Organizing the various contractors, material deliveries, and utility hookups while accommodating weather delays is hectic. Keeping an organized time schedule is at its most difficult during the basement-building stage of home construction.

Maintenance of a concrete basement over the life of a home is a significant concern. Dampness is a common problem. Various gases collect down there—like radon, methane, or natural gas—that can be dangerous, sometimes lethal. Cracking of basement walls from outside earth pressure, frost, and plant roots occurs over time. And, of course, flooding and earthquakes cause damage in some areas. These are all potential repair situations you would not have with a slab foundation.

Very often a basement evolves into an expensive, problematic storage space. For the materials and labor spent on a basement, you could build an above-ground storage building, a garage, or more house.

The stone wall is built with mortar from bedrock to about 6" above the highest point of ledge and is level to within about an inch. The enclosed area is filled with course rocky gravel delivered through a hole left in the wall that will be completed later.

Preparing for the slab

Building a slab foundation involves two major stages. First is the preparation of the form, which takes as many days as you need, working serenely and carefully with lots of planning and measuring. Second is the pour, a one-day period of high-intensity work and worry that will become one of those days in your life you never forget, but in a good way.

Let's start the preparation. Assuming your lot has been developed to the point where we left off in issue #101, the site of your house has had the vegetation scraped off and some gravel has been spread. You also have a water line, septic pipe, and electric wire leads exposed within the footprint of the house.

Now is the time to examine the soil under your site. I've worked with four general classes of substrata while building. Clay, sand, and fairly solid sedimentary soils are quite stable and don't swell or get too mushy with changes in water content or temperature. A simple elevated gravel bed about a foot thick overcomes what faults or shortcomings these soils do have.

Forest or heavy vegetation with lots of roots into deep soil requires a backhoe to dig below grade a foot or two or three to cut away the tangled stuff and replace it with rocky (around here called "boney") gravel. The regular (¾ to 1½" sized gravel) bed is built up over that.

With soil that is wet or swampy part of the time or all year round, you need a dry "island" for your slab, so a boney gravel bed with some regular gravel on top must be built up. The elevation of the gravel bed depends on the depth of standing water you expect to encounter during the life of the home. If you have a site like this, maybe you should consider setting a boat there to live on instead.

The fourth class of substrata is ledge above and/or below grade. Some of the very best home sites I have worked with were on ledge. There is nothing like rock for a solid foundation. I build a mortared stone wall from the bedrock up to a height that puts the top of the slab 12" or more above any flood danger, and the wall becomes the base for the forms of my foundation. The area and volume inside the stone wall perimeter is filled with boney, then regular, gravel. See the pictures.

The stone wall has been built up from bedrock. The area inside the walls has been filled with gravel and leveled off. Permanent form boards are being mortared precisely into position and made level. Note pin in center of large circle as a reference point for all measurements.

Photographs included with this article are from several 12-sided homes that I have built, so you may have to use a little imagination to understand the same procedures with a rectangular house.

The permanent form boards have been mortared into place and leveled to within about ¼". The under-slab inclusions are being buried in the gravel fill. Note trees left near foundation for shade.

The contractor who digs the dirt and does the hauling will spread and level the gravel bed. The ones I have hired do a pretty amazing job of getting the pad level. Be sure you have stakes with ribbons marking the dimensions of your house plus about two feet of gravel beyond those dimensions for sloping the bed to the surrounding ground.

I know there are numerous variations in home sites, but the built-up gravel bed or stone wall (perhaps a concrete block wall) with gravel fill will, with the least effort, get you to the point where the slab will be safe. The idea is to rest the slab on a leveled bed of gravel, maybe crushed rock if you like. The gravel bed acts as a gasket that protects the slab from fluctuations in the earth, provides water drainage, moderates temperature extremes, and does other things we will get to shortly.

Let's review. You dealt with the subsoil by scraping and graveling or with

A vapor barrier covers the whole foundation and is held down by scrap roofing pieces. Six-inch mesh reinforcing screen is in place with ½" reinforcing rods inserted into holes drilled in the form boards. Look closely to see the boxed openings in the foreground and upper left of the picture.

a stone or block wall (sometimes called a frost wall) filled with gravel and you were careful not to damage the water line, septic pipe, or any other items to be connected to the house later. Now you have a fairly level gravel pad built up 12" or more above grade that is able to prevent rainwater from getting deep enough to overflow your soon-to-be-poured slab.

Setting up the forms

Now it is time to set up the forms on the gravel bed. A concrete slab about 6" thick is just right for most buildings, so that is what I will describe here.

The big day. The mason orders the concrete and brings helpers, extra chutes, and expertise. Note plumbing pipes and boxed-out holes for utilities.

Contractors who build slabs nail up 2x6 boards around the perimeter, squared, leveled, and held in position with wood or metal stakes. They pour the concrete, strip away the boards the next day, and they are done.

We are going to get a little more involved than that. The form boards will become permanent parts of the foundation. I use the straightest 2x8 or 2x10 pressure-treated dimensional lumber I can buy for my forms. These forms are going to enclose and insulate the slab while assuring levelness and much more.

Set the form boards in position and assemble them with screws. Definitely use screws for this work. Driving nails vibrates the whole structure so much it makes accurate positioning nearly impossible. Back up butt joints in the forms with treated lumber attached to the inner side of the forms, and be generous with the overlaps. Two thicknesses of form lumber insulate the slab twice as well as one and make it stiffer.

Use a shovel, a rake, a level, tape measure, whatever, and whoever else you need to "settle" the whole form down into the gravel bed until 6" of it is left showing above grade. Get it level everywhere. I recommend using a water level for this job. (Google it if you need to learn how to build one.) At the same time, bring the form into square by measuring across the corners. Be really sure the sides are exactly the right lengths. Sight along the tops of your form boards and straighten any bulges in the sides, too. Expect to spend a couple of days on this part and be very fussy about getting everything perfect; perfect meaning within ¼" level and ½" square. You will be a happy builder later by taking the time and making the effort now.

If your version uses a stone or block wall to enclose the gravel bed, set the form—in this case, 2x6 pressure treated lumber—on top of the stonework. Use small batches of premixed mortar to stabilize the form in as many places as needed, while getting it level and square. See the pictures.

You may need to drive stakes around the outside of the perimeter to hold the form boards firmly in place. You can temporarily attach the stakes to the form boards with screws. The screws will also help the form stay level. Be sure nothing rises above the top of the form. Screed boards and other things will be sliding along the form later, and you don't want to impede them.

Use your rake and shovel to pack gravel up against the outside of the form and level out the gravel inside the form to about 6" below the top.

Let's check. The form is assembled with pressure-treated lumber, 2x8 or 2x10 for gravel beds, 2x6 for stone wall versions. The form is perfectly level and square and held firmly in place by stakes, packed gravel, and blobs of mortar where needed, and the interior space is raked level to a depth of about 6". Just to be sure, check again to make certain it is level and square.

Here are more form details. Notice boxed-out openings covered by 6-mil plastic to keep them clean. PVC drains to be buried under the slab pass through screen mesh, reinforcing bars, and vapor barrier. Note the shaped-in-place footing in the lower right-hand corner compensating for an elevation difference. Also note temporary bracing holding form board in position. When the pour is done, this makes a strong one piece foundation. The form boards are permanent.

Installing insulation and the vapor barrier

At this point you have an option to consider. If you live in a cold climate, you can insulate the slab by laying down foam panel insulation. It comes in several thicknesses, but 1" is most practical and economical. The insulation factor is important, but even more significant is the "thermal break" provided between the cold ground and your warm slab. Be sure to increase the depth from form top to gravel bed by the thickness of the insulation you use.

A product called Tekfoil (find it at www.farmtek.com) also works well for this purpose. It is thin enough to not need the extra form depth.

Next comes a very important part of this project. A six-mil vapor barrier is laid over the whole area and brought up the sides of the form. Staple it in place on the inner sides of the form, and use scraps of rolled roofing or old asphalt shingles to keep it from billowing up in the wind and to give some protection from foot traffic. The roofing scraps can be left in place and concrete poured over them later. Keep the vapor barrier as free of holes as possible. The vapor barrier will keep the slab dry and avoid mildew and other osmotic water infiltration problems later, especially important if you plan to paint, tile, or carpet the slab. A dry slab also insulates better than a damp slab.

Reinforcing the slab

Now it is time to turn the common slab into Super Slab. We do that by using two kinds of reinforcing materials. The first are steel reinforcing bars, often called rebar. I recommend ½" diameter rebar in 20' lengths because they are big enough to do the job but light enough and flexible enough to be manipulated by normal people.

I start by placing pieces of rebar parallel to and about 6" in from the form boards all the way around the form, bending them carefully around corners. Then I add a second set of rebar about 12" in from the form boards all the way around the form, overlapping the ends. They will be tied together later. Next, I make a rebar grid by placing pieces every 3 feet and adding another set of rebar pieces 90 degrees to the first set.

The closely set rebar reinforces the more vulnerable edges and corners of the slab, and the 3' grid work gives strength to the center. If there is to be some extra weight on the slab, a fireplace for instance, extra rebar should be laid under that area.

Next comes a little job that will make your slab even stronger. Wherever the end of a piece of rebar meets the form, drill a ⅝" diameter hole through the form about 3" down from the top. Push the rebar into the hole but not so far that it sticks out the other side. This holds the rebar in position laterally and keeps it cen-

The "screed" board, pivoting around the center pin and sliding over the form boards, establishes a level concrete surface. Lots of big strong helpers make the job easier.

tered in the middle of the thickness of the slab during the pour. Doing this also helps hold the form against the concrete when it has cured. Cutting rebar is not easy. When a piece is too long, I bend it rather than cut it. Extra steel here and there in the slab is fine.

The second reinforcing material to add is 6" mesh screen sold especially for this purpose. It comes in rolls 5' wide that cover 750 square feet. Buy enough to cover the full slab area and some extra. Overlapping of the layers is a good thing. Getting this stuff unrolled, bent into reasonably flat pieces, and cutting it is hard work. Besides being difficult to handle it is usually rusty, and if it's not rusty it'll probably be oily. Wear gloves, use a good set of heavy-duty two-handed wire cutters, and be careful.

Lay the mesh in the form and tie it to the rebar with wire ties in many, many places until the whole mess is thoroughly knitted together. Pieces of brick or stone 2 to 3" thick placed under the rebar at the cross-joints will get the rebar up off the bottom of the form and keep it centered in the concrete as it cures. This process will not come out as tidy as I make it sound, but do your best. Just be sure when you site across the form boards nothing is sticking up above them.

Special features

This next part of the project really makes the slab a superior piece of construction. We are going to include a number of features you won't find and wouldn't expect in a common slab foundation. A number of items can be embedded in or buried under the slab to save labor and materials later. Let's consider some of them.

When I build a slab, I bury as many electric wires as I can under the slab in the gravel bed. I enclose these wires inside PVC pipe to prevent damage and keep them dry. Each wire starts in a boxed-out opening nearest the appliance or circuit it will serve, passes under the slab, and comes up through the slab inside a central boxed opening. This central opening is also where the main power wires enter the house. See *Backwoods Home Magazine*, issue #101, page 8, for more about underground power lines. The wall above this central opening will be the location of the main electric service panel.

Here is an example. Routing the wires for your electric range down through the slab beneath the range, through the gravel bed inside PVC pipe, and back up through the slab just below the electric service panel is good planning for several reasons. This is the most direct path the wire could take. The usual route would be through drilled holes in wall studs all the way around the house, leaving wires vulnerable to punctures from nails, screws, or tools. And don't even think about removing that wire if it malfunctions. Lots of work and materials are saved, and you get a safer house, by burying the wires beneath the slab.

Direct routing under the slab is especially convenient for big stiff wires that service water heaters, stoves, and pumps, and it works just as well for other circuits. Run the wires through PVC pipe of a size that allows the wires to slide easily, ¾" for #12 wires, and 1" for #10 or #8 wire. Connect the pipes with unions, glued just like you would if you were doing plumbing, but here it will keep water out instead of in. Route your pipe from a drilled hole in the lower part of a boxed-out opening under where the appliance will go, straight to a drilled hole in the lower part of the boxed-out central opening that will be below the main electric service panel. (More about boxed-out openings in a little while.) This will allow you to change wires by securing a new wire to the end of the old one and pulling the old wire out at the same time you pull the new one through if it ever becomes necessary to change it at a later date. You should not use any elbows in the PVC pipe because they constrict the movement of the wires. The flexibility of the PVC pipe makes elbows unnecessary anyway.

Several wires can be passed through one PVC pipe if it is big enough and they are all going to the same location. Just be sure to use unions and glue so water can't infiltrate the pipe.

I am sure you have already figured out other things to bury under the slab. The fuel line from your oil tank to the furnace is one. Be sure it is in PVC pipe or something similar because the oil company insists on that.

I have buried the cold air return ducts for the hot air furnace system under the slabs of my homes. It is the very best, most efficient location for them and the easiest place to build them in. I use 4" flexible plastic drainpipe (see pictures). I start six or eight tubes from a central plenum chamber (another boxed opening) next to, or under, the furnace and route the tubes to floor grills mounted on boxed openings around the perimeter of the slab. Pulling air from these perimeter locations of the house to the intake of the furnace makes the warm air distribution through the house more thorough. It is another way to save on labor and materials later when the furnace ductwork is installed.

The first runs of 1½" PVC for your central vacuum system could be under the slab. The shortest, most direct routing of pipes for a vacuum system is best. You can use elbows in these pipes—air bends easier than wire.

Let's not forget plumbing. Drainpipes for sinks can be carefully planned and buried under the slab. Be sure to slant the pipes down at a proper angle toward the septic tank. If you are a real precision planning genius, you can install the flanges and drain pipes for toilets and the drain and trap for a shower. It is complicated but possible.

Supply plumbing can be routed below ground to save time and pipe. However, freezing is a factor you need to consider as you run the water supply pipes under the slab. Pipes a couple of feet or more inside the perimeter of the slab should not freeze unless you are up near the arctic. You can judge whether or not to do this and the need for foam wrap, heaters, and all that, in your area but one very good idea is to make a drain point in your water supply system that lets all the water be drained from all your pipes at one location. Many people leave their homes empty for weeks or months at a time, especially in winter, and having the ability to thoroughly and conveniently drain the water is a real bonus. You can design

One of the best reasons to hire a professional mason for a day is this gadget. It brings up the "fat" in the concrete and leaves a super smooth, finish-floor quality to the concrete.

This tool is called a "float." With skill and patience, it can impart a very smooth finish on a concrete surface. Tilting it slightly up and down while sliding it back and forth on the concrete surface is a Zenlike experience.

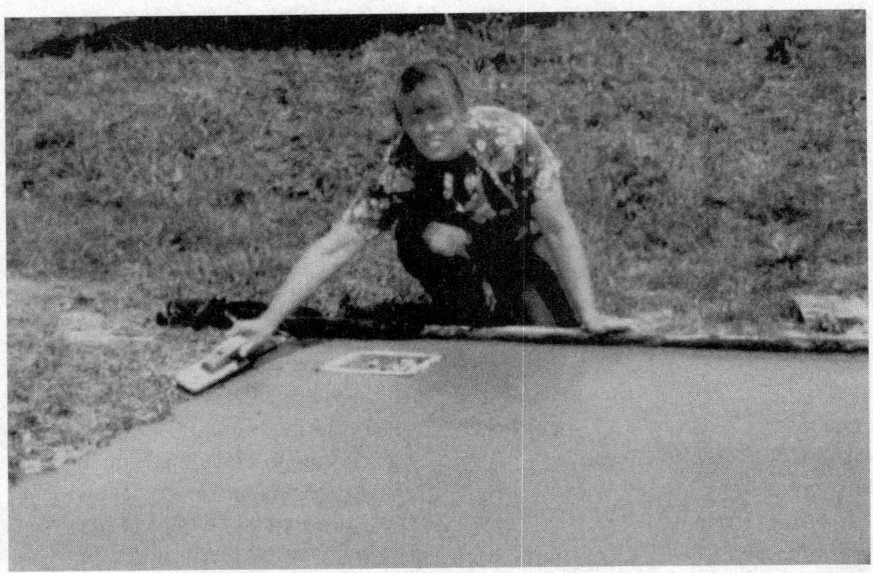

Here, an attractive mason's assistant is using a magnesium hand trowel to smooth the concrete around a boxed-out hole, making sure it is level and the wood is kept clean.

and incorporate this into your plumbing plan and bury it all under the slab.

Remember back when I said the preparation of the form would take many days? I wasn't kidding. But there is more, and it is all worth the trouble.

If you are planning on having a fireplace, woodstove, or wood furnace, you can build a passageway to bring outside air under the slab directly to the air inlet of your wood heater. One piece of 6" or two pieces of 4" drainpipe supplies all the air you need. Screen the outside end to thwart animals and bugs and have a way to close it at the indoor end when it is not in use.

Do you have some precious items you want to keep hidden and safe? Consider making a below-ground hiding place. Burying a container, preferably of heavy plastic, positioning its top (with a cover) flush with the top of the slab in a location of your choice on the floor plan is easily done during preparation. Containers set into the ground below the slab will take on ground temperature and are good cool storage places for certain foods, too.

So far all these items are to be buried in the gravel bed after the form is set and leveled but before the insulation, vapor barrier, reinforcing rod, and screen are installed. Now is the time to build the boxed-out openings that will give you access to the ends of these various supply lines.

Boxed-out openings are made with the same pressure-treated lumber as the forms, and their tops must be level with the top of the forms so the screed board and power trowel will slide over them during the pour. These boxes will vary in size according to what function they are to accommodate. Most of them will be attached to the inner side of the form boards that will hold them in position. Others will be out in the form and must be held in place by stakes or other means to keep them level with the finished top of the slab.

The walls of the house will rest on top of the permanent form and extend onto the slab a few inches. Take this into account when installing the boxed-out openings. As an example, the opening for the kitchen range wire needs to be about 6" wide and extend in from the form board about 10" to clear the wall plate and allow for working room inside the hole. See the pictures for more examples.

When you have built all the boxed-out openings, roll and tuck the wires inside the openings, stuff rags around them to keep them clean, and staple tough plastic over the top of the box to keep out concrete during the pour. Some openings will have pipes or wires protruding up above the form

Foundation and floor are all done, and the stones for the fireplace are displayed for the next stage of construction.

that cannot be tucked below the form top, such as where the water lines and power wires come up through boxed openings in the slab. You will just have to work around them on Pour Day. Poor you. But try to keep these protrusions to a minimum.

There is one more convenience you can build into the form. Maybe your floor plan calls for an interior wall to set on the concrete slab. You could use builder's glue and masonry nails to attach it, but I have been disappointed with these methods in the past. What I do is embed a pressure-treated 2x4, wide side up, in the concrete exactly under the location of the wall. It is held in place with stakes, screws, or whatever gets it level with the top of the form and holds it steady while the concrete is poured. A wall plate screwed to this base is very secure.

If you are planning to install a wood floor on top of the slab, say in the kitchen area, you could embed a grid of 2x4 pieces there to accept the flooring nails. These 2x4 pieces will have concrete around and under them and provide a very solid surface to attach the flooring that can be reused later when it is time to pull up the old floor and install a new one.

Let's catch up. The form is screwed together, settled, leveled, squared, and secured with stakes and mortar on the gravel bed or stone wall. You dug, shoveled, and raked, and packed all the wires, pipes, ducts, plumbing, and hidey holes into the gravel. Next came the boxed-out openings and connections involved, along with provisions for keeping them clean and free of concrete, and not much sticks up above the height of the form boards to interfere with leveling the concrete. Then you added the insulation, vapor barrier, rebar, and screen, which has all been stapled, staked, and screwed in nice and solid so the concrete and the people helping pour it will not dislodge anything.

Now comes a little job that will thoroughly bond all these things together forever. Take a few hundred 3" long dry wall screws and screw them about 1" into the inner walls of the forms, boxed out structures, and the sides of those 2x4 pieces to be embedded in the concrete. When the concrete cures around the screws, it will bond all the wood parts tight to the concrete.

There. Check one more time to be sure the form is level and square, fix any little flaws, and your preparation of Super Slab form is done.

Setting up for the pour

About now, or maybe a little before now, is time to make the acquaintance of your local mason contractor and have him or her come and see your job. You are going to need this person's crew, tools, and expertise to plop the concrete into your form, make it level, and smooth it up to floor quality. All that will be accomplished in one day that starts very early.

Let the mason calculate the amount of concrete you need and have him order it for you. "Civilians" ordering concrete are put further down the list than contractors and may only be able to get late morning or afternoon deliveries. Having the concrete delivered early in the morning gives you the whole day to work it, and that's just what you want. The mason's relationship with suppliers gives you a better chance for an early delivery.

Concrete mix is available in a number of variations. The usual is a 5½-bag, or "sidewalk," mix. That means 5½ bags of cement per yard (27 cubic feet) of concrete, and it is fine for most applications. More cement per yard is available, and there are additives such as fiberglass strands and other surprising things. You can have a nice philosophical discussion with the mason about the merits of each and decide whether you want to spend more money for these extras.

Be clear that you want the concrete polished with a power trowel. It gives a nice smooth level finish.

As walls are stood up, they are attached to the permanent form boards around the perimeter of the foundation, accurately aligned, and firmly connected to the foundation. Building time and labor are saved and the wall is automatically leveled at the same time.

Professionals have these machines and know how to operate them without injuring too many bystanders. Hand troweling the floor surface looks great if done by an old pro, but all the ones I knew are retired or dead.

If your form is long and you have a distance of more than 20' between the concrete truck and destination for the "mud," your pour will require an extra "chute" or two more than the ones that come with the concrete truck. The mason will most likely notice this, but ask anyway. The alternative is muscling it back in there with wheelbarrows, which is worse than chain gang work and may damage the delicate handiwork you did during preparation. The mason can bring more chutes if needed.

Discuss a screed board with the mason. He may have one, or he may have secret ways unknown to normal people for not needing it, but you can offer to nail together some dimensional lumber to make one. These things are very long and hard to transport on vehicles, so he may welcome your offer and you can build one you know is straight. I have a 4" by 4" square by 36' long very smooth, rigid, and straight aluminum thing that used to support an ESSO sign. All the masons around here covet this tool and ask to borrow it sometimes. It conveniently breaks down into three pieces. I may leave it to one of them in my will.

You will appreciate the crew the mason brings with him. Having several burley helpers who know less than the mason, but more than you, about concrete pouring is comforting during the tense hard work of getting tens of thousands of pounds of fast hardening concrete in place and looking pretty. You get to hear the latest masonry jokes, too.

The day of the pour

Here are some tips to make the best and most of this important day, the Day of The Pour. Have plenty of water on hand for cleaning concrete off tools, boots, and clothes. If you do not have running water on site, bring plenty of water in buckets. Clean any concrete off whatever collects it as soon as possible, especially skin, because it can give you a chemical burn.

Bring plenty of drinking water for the day for everyone. Snacks rather than a big meal will keep you active and ward off fatigue. You should be there all day fussing over details, like smoothing over chipmunk footprints and such, until the surface is setup enough to stay smooth. Use some of the "fuss time" to scratch your names and date into the slab for posterity.

Wear calf-high or taller rubber boots for wading in the mud, but bring regular work shoes to wear after the mud is in place. Wear good work gloves and a hat. Bring your own garden rake and hoe to keep the site cleared of debris. Bring a trowel or your wife's biggest spatula for detail smoothing around the edges of the form and boxed-out openings.

This is important: Have a place along the path the concrete trucks use where they can wash out the last remnants of concrete. It will leave a little pile of sand and rock with a bit of cement you can use as fill somewhere later.

I've saved the best tip for last. When the concrete trucks come they always bring extra concrete. Have a place for them to dump that extra. You may or may not be paying for it, and if you don't use it, the truck takes it back to the plant and pours it into forms for Jersey barriers and boat moorings.

A method I use is to lay a big sheet of 6-mil plastic on a flat area of the lawn or driveway where the truck has convenient access. Then have them dump the concrete onto it. Rake it out to a thickness of 2 to 3". Use a hoe to divide the slab into manageable sizes in whatever shapes you like. After it has cured, you have a big outdoor mosaic floor you can move, in pieces, to where you want it when landscaping later.

I also make concrete "pancakes" or patio stones by taking big shovelsful of wet concrete, "plopping" them onto a plastic covered surface, and shaping them into circular, square, or sculpted pieces. If your plastic sheet is on top of a textured surface, such as grass or pebbles, they will create a very interesting texture. You can also embed things in your patio stones while they are curing. You can even use colored chalk sprinkled on and smeared into the top surface of your stones. Masonry supply stores have colored chalks in convenient amounts for this purpose.

I have had as little as ½ yard to as much as 3 full yards of extra concrete on jobs I've managed. The work of shaping the extra mud into useful forms gives me something to do after the mason is gone and I am puttering around smoothing out details on the slab.

After a good night of well-deserved sleep, go back and enjoy your accomplishments. Besides all the goodies embedded in or under the slab, you now have the first floor of your home. After a minimum of six weeks' cure time, you can put your first coat of paint on it to seal the surface.

I recommend leaving the boxed openings covered until you need to get into them. After you have made the connections, fill the opening with builders foam where appropriate. This will complete the insulation and vapor barrier qualities of the slab.

And, there you have it. A slab foundation can be much more sophisticated than you might have thought. It is hard work, and there is a lot to consider, but many of the details described here are also useful when constructing buildings smaller than a house.

Good luck with your lot and foundation plans. Δ

Ask Jackie

If you have a question about rural living, send it in to Jackie Clay and she'll try to answer it. Address your letter to Ask Jackie, PO Box 712, Gold Beach, OR 97444. Questions will only be answered in this column. — Editor

What grows in clay soil?

I live in SW Wisconsin and we have 3 acres of land that we would like to plant to some sort of income producing vegetables. Our land is clay soil. What vegetables would you suggest?

Shelly Schweiger
Viola, Wisconsin

If I had your land, here's what I would do. Plant one acre of it to a good green manure crop, high in organic matter. Buckwheat or rye would be good, for instance. When it is quite high, cut it and till it under. Repeat as often as you can in that one season. This will vastly improve that land in one summer. In the fall, try to work in at least a few inches of rotted manure.

We farmed in northern Minnesota for years on heavy clay soil, growing 3 acres of market garden. The first years were a little tough. Root crops are about out until your soil is in better shape. If you can, alternate your growing for 3 years, working in green manure into an acre you can leave fallow each year.

The first year on our farm I had to plow the garden to "dig" carrots; a fork wouldn't penetrate the dry clay soil. The last year there, you could stick your arm up to the elbow in black, loose soil. It was all that organic material worked in by the ton: Green manure, leaves, rotted compost and straw.

Crops that did the best on our not-so-improved soil at first were sweet corn, tomatoes, cucumbers, and salad greens of fancy varieties. The sweet corn and tomatoes are not too labor intensive, but the cucumbers and salad greens are. All of these crops are in high demand and bring good prices if you do your footwork and keep them in good shape from planting to market.

Avoid such crops as strawberries, peas, or bramble berries; they are just too labor intensive unless you have a great setup and lots of help.

There is a great market for fresh produce, especially organic produce, sold by the grower either at roadside stands or Farmers' Markets.

— Jackie

Cherry tomatoes and pigweed

The place we picked for our garden has done well, except I learned from the previous owners that one of them dumped tons of cow manure in the garden spot. This has done two things: The good thing is the tomatoes love it. What do I do with all the cherry tomatoes? I have hundreds. I canned some, we eat a lot, I've given them away, they just keep coming. What else can I do with them? Second thing: That cow manure? It's also loved by pigweed. I couldn't keep up with it and it took over my garden. How can I get rid of it? Thanks for all your help and answers; I see your homestead is coming along nicely and David is so grown up!

Marty Young
Huntington, Massachusetts

There's lots you can do with those tons of cherry tomatoes, Marty. If you can buy a Victorio Food Strainer for about $56 or can borrow one, you can simply pour them into the hopper and turn the crank. Tomato puree will come out the chute and the skins and

Jackie Clay

seeds will be forced out the end of the screen. It's that easy. No peeling, no coring. I really love mine. You can also spend more and get the stainless steel version (mine has a plastic hopper and chute; it's also very sturdy and more than 15 years old with lots of use).

You can then make tomato sauce, spaghetti sauce, catsup, chili, etc.

Or you can simply core them and cut them in half, lay them on a tray of your food dehydrator, and dry them. They're awfully good for a snack or on a pizza. They dehydrate easily and quickly. You want them to be tough and leathery-dry; brittle is not necessary. But you want NO moisture in them. If you store them in a glass jar and you see any condensation forming on the glass in the first days, dry them some more or they will mold. No dehydrator? You can also line your cookie sheet with parchment paper or even a brown paper bag trimmed to fit and lay your tomato halves on that in your oven at the very lowest setting; if that's too high, leave the door open a crack. You want about 140 degrees or so; you don't want to cook the tomatoes. Turn them over once, and that's that. I use only the pilot in my gas oven with the door closed or else the warming ovens and oven of my wood range with the door open and the oven damper open so it doesn't heat.

Okay, on to the pigweed. The ranch we bought in New Mexico had the same problem. Only they didn't haul cow manure to the garden. I chose the cow yard for my garden. I did that for the only good black dirt on the place. Crops did very well, and the pigweed grew so rank the first year that we actually cleared overgrown rows with a chainsaw!

The answer is keep at it and don't let them go to seed! Chainsaw them down if you must, but don't let them go to seed or you will just have more pigweed next year. In the spring, pull every small pigweed plant you can't till or hoe. Right after watering or a rain is perfect; they pull very well then. Did you know that you can eat pigweed? In New Mexico, my spinach didn't amount to much, so I picked those little, tender seedlings and snapped the tender leaves off those a little larger. Then I canned them; we couldn't tell the pigweed from spinach very much. We actually liked the pigweed better. It was sweeter and had more flavor.

Now you can't gorge yourself on pigweed because it does have a tendency to accumulate nitrates in heavily fertilized areas and some Western areas. But, it would require eating a lot of pigweed to have any trouble. Spinach also does this and we certainly aren't leery of eating spinach. Including it with a meal once in a while is a good thing. It's high in Vitamin A and C and also contains considerable iron and calcium.

Once you look on pigweed as a food, it seems like your battle is half won. It will take you several years to completely win the pigweed war, but you certainly can do it. Mulching once your rows are clean will also help. Wait until your plants are several inches high, then mulch with eight inches of clean straw, leaves, or other organic material. Any pigweed seedlings that do squeeze through the mulch will be very easy to pull out.

— Jackie

Fuzzy/fizzy tomatoes

I just peeled and cooked six tomatoes from my garden with onion and garlic with the intention of making a fresh sauce. When I tasted the broth for salt, I discovered that it was fuzzy/fizzy like something was spoiled. But everything is fresh!

It's not boiling away either. What would cause that? Is it safe to eat?

Jeanne Johnson
Keene, New Hampshire

No, Jeanne, your sauce is not spoiled. This is a perfectly normal reaction when tomato sauce is about halfway cooked down. The "water" is at the bottom of the pot while the fluffy bubbly sauce is floating on the top. Even when I cook down my big roaster pans full of tomato puree in the oven overnight this happens. But when I stir it, it once again looks more normal. I find this happens more with tomatoes that are almost ripe, but not dead ripe. It's really not a problem and when you continue to cook down the sauce, it will look more like tomato sauce instead of a strawberry soda. ***— Jackie***

Hopi Grey Squash, thick peppers, root cellaring

This year I finally located some Hopi Grey Squash seed and planted about eight hills. Seven of them came up and looked good until about the end of June, early July when the leaves on six of the vines started turning yellowish. The vines began turning brownish and were dying. Some research suggested that this might be due to squash vine borers. I've never successfully grown winter squash in the garden, so maybe that's the problem. How do I deal with squash vine borers? Some of the vines had started producing squash, but they're not mature. Can I still use them?

I thought I might still have success with the remaining healthy vine. But the unusually dry conditions attracted the deer to our garden (which is located about 20 feet from the house), and they ate my last Hopi Grey Squash vine! I'd heard that deer didn't like squash. Any suggestions for a better outcome next year?

For both sweet and chile peppers, is there a way to encourage nice thick-walled, meaty peppers? Even with varieties such as California Wonder pepper, the walls of the peppers aren't all that thick. There's nothing better than fresh-roasted chile peppers on a nice fall day, but the thinwalled ones are a real challenge to peel.

I recently have been reading a book on root cellaring and it seems like an easy way to preserve a lot of crops. While canning is great, it is a fair amount of work and mess, and it would seem that root cellaring would be a lot easier. With your huge gardens, have you ever tried it?

How did you move your homestead from Montana to Minnesota cost effectively? So much equipment and tools are required, and animals, too, that it almost seems like a fleet of big trucks would be required.

Thanks for the great column.

Diane Unger
Middletown, Virginia

Whew! Let me breathe and think. Yep, deer DO like squash vines, squash, and then melons, tomatoes, cukes and beans, not to mention corn and carrots, potatoes and flowers. Don't believe people who tell you, "Oh, rabbits don't like onions" either.

You just may be right with the squash borers, although you usually will see part of the vine suddenly wilt and start to die. Then, on examination of the vine, you can see a small hole with dark sawdust coming from it just where the vine is starting to wilt. If you carefully cut into the hollow vine with a pocket knife, you can see the grub and flip him out and squash him. Then, if you will bury about a foot of the vine where the hole was, the vine will sometimes revive and send out roots, going on to produce.

If you are having such a time with squash on your place, why don't you try raised beds? Use either two tires stacked on top of each other, filled with good soil, or wooden raised beds. Then, as the vine gets larger, cover it with a piece of floating row cover. This will help keep mama squash bug from laying her eggs on the squash vine.

Yes, you can use immature winter squash as you would summer squash. Don't try to store them because they will rot.

Fence your garden. As you'll see in my *Starting over, Part 12* this issue, I fought the deer battle and won. You can, too.

To get nice thick walls on your peppers, first choose varieties that have thicker walls to start with. Make sure that the description in the seed catalog says "thick walls," for some just don't have them to start with. Then when you plant your peppers, sprinkle a handful of bone meal around the plant and use a mild organic fertilizer, such as a kelp/fish emulsion, when the little peppers are growing. Then water the plants well when there isn't any rain. Water makes juicy peppers.

Root cellaring is great. I finally have a cellar built in my basement, but it isn't a silver bullet. I still can a lot of my food, for I've carried out buckets of soft and rotten produce, come spring, too. Once it's in a jar, it won't spoil. So when I root cellar food, I keep right on canning and drying it, right through the winter. That way, we have the best of both worlds. There's nice fresh potatoes, apples, squash, onions, carrots, etc. But, I slowly can what we won't use instead of carrying it all shriveled and rotten out to the pigs and chickens, come spring.

We felt that our move to Minnesota from Montana was cost effective as we planned very carefully. As land was so much more costly out there, and we had a nice home that we sold, we could afford to rent a U-Haul truck and flatbed trailer. We packed all our household, tools, and equipment on those. My late husband drove that rig, while I followed with our '85 Chevy pickup with our dogs in the camper and our horses, goats, sheep, one chicken, and a duck in the stock trailer. Water buckets, hoses, and hay were tied on the sides and over the fenders of the trailer. (We did look a little like the Beverly Hillbillies!)

I had already made a trip out alone with our Suburban towing our camping trailer, earlier in the year, and left it here. It wasn't a cheap move, but we felt it was more than worth it. We got a great 80-acre piece of raw Minnesota woods with water on it, and now there's the house, and the homestead is definitely looking up. Would I do it again? U betcha!

— Jackie

Differing jam recipes

My husband and I have recently begun canning for ourselves, and we are really loving it. We are noticing that instructions are different for jams; everywhere we look when it comes to how much sugar to add and what temperature it's ready to be canned at. For example, the Ball canning book is different than the instructions in the Ball pectin. Can you explain this? Also I have begun baking our own bread. My first attempt was with banana bread. My question is about flour. We're trying to eat healthier and heartier. I do not like white all-purpose flour, so we've switched to whole wheat. Our first attempt with it made the bread overflow the pans. Are measurements different when using whole wheat instead of white?

Jaime Hogsett
Franksville, Wisconsin

There is no one recipe for even one kind of jam. Or anything else you may want to cook. There are dozens and dozens of different ones, all of which work fine. Any time I make a food, I choose a recipe (usually one that has worked well for me before, but I do experiment) and follow it.

Some jam recipes use juice for part of the pectin needed to jell the jam. Others use only the pectin in the fruit. Still others use powdered or liquid pectin. Some, you only add sugar and boil and boil to get the jam to jell. Don't let it worry you; they'll all work fine. If you have limited fruit for your jam, you might use a powdered pectin product because you get more end product with your recipe. If you have lots of sugar and time, as well as plenty of fruit, you can choose a recipe without powdered pectin to save money. Again, there is no "right" recipe. Good canning!

— Jackie

Raw cow's milk

I have been thinking about purchasing a cow for milk but would like to know if it is safe to drink milk right from the cow or should it be processed somehow?

Julie Guenter
Ingleside, Texas

If drinking raw milk would harm me, I'd be dead. I've consumed raw cow and goat milk for more than 40 years and much prefer it to "processed" store milk. Yes, you can pasteurize it, but that kills some of the beneficial enzymes in it.

Make sure your cow is well cared for and has been tested for brucellosis and T.B.

I feel that there are certainly a lot more things to worry about in our daily diets today, with all the chemicals, herbicides, fertilizers, insecticides, preservatives, genetically engineered foods, etc., than drinking raw, fresh milk from a healthy, well cared for family cow. ***— Jackie***

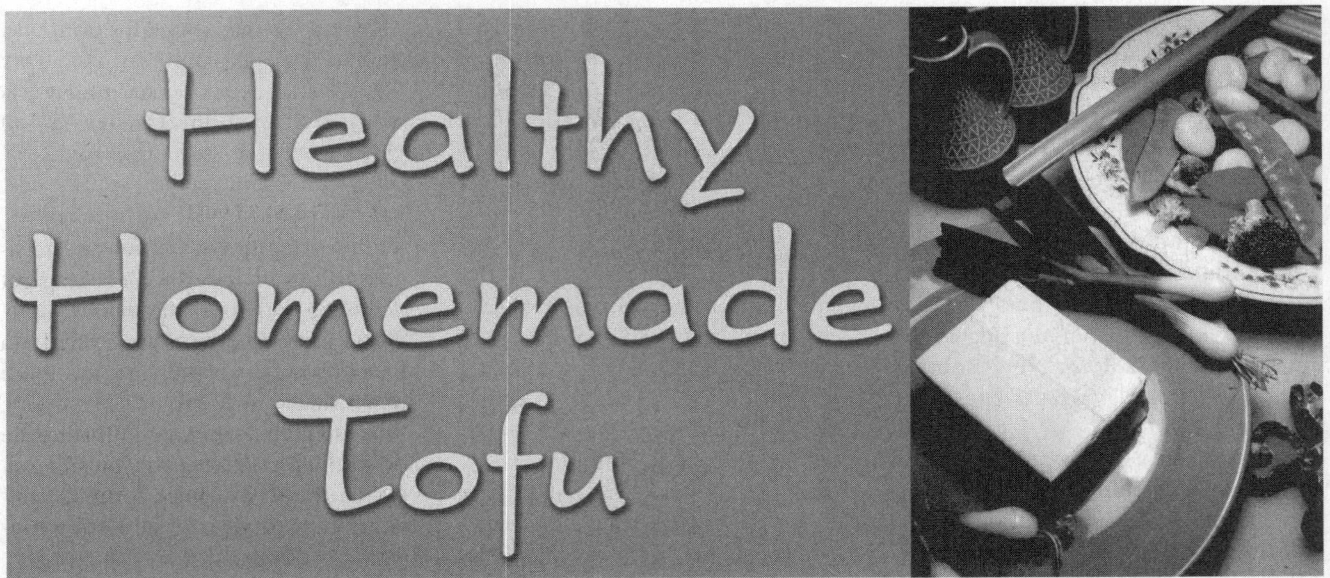

By Linda Gabris

Years ago when I first started making my own tofu, it was done out of necessity. Living in rural countryside miles from the nearest store, making tofu was the only way I had of keeping a ready supply on my icebox shelf.

In spite of the fact that today I live within easy walking distance of several well-stocked supermarkets that carry a delightful array of various types of tofu, quite often I still get the urge to make a batch of my own. Making tofu is a fun pastime that's super easy and economical to boot.

Like baking bread, there's something almost spiritual about creating this wonderful healthy food to share with loved ones. But what I appreciate most about having a supply of tofu on hand is that it is the most versatile item on the refrigerator shelf. Tofu is a great base for everything from soups and salads to main courses and desserts.

So get ready to make tofu—the miracle food item known by health gurus around the world as the protein source of the future.

Following is a cherished recipe that is known as the Japanese Farmhouse method and is easy to follow and virtually foolproof.

From start to finish, the tofu will be ready in about an hour. The recipe makes approximately 40 ounces.

Before starting, assemble needed utensils. Most are common kitchen tools that you more than likely will have on hand, and what you don't have, you can purchase cheaply at yard sales or any store that sells kitchen wares. Or, you can buy a tofu-making kit that will contain all needed materials.

Utensil list:

- 8 quart or bigger cooking pot with a lid
- a tea kettle kept whistling
- a "pressing pot" or deep basin, about 8 quarts
- large colander that will sit on its own in the mouth of the pressing pot
- about an 18" square of cheese-cloth
- "forming container". I made mine out of a bread loaf pan by drilling eight 3/8" diameter holes in the bottom, eight same holes in each side, and four on each end. After holes are drilled, file them smooth and wash well to remove drill dust.
- electric blender, food or grain mill
- long-handled wooden spoon
- spatula
- potato masher
- measuring cup
- fine mesh strainer
- dipper or ladle

Ingredients:

You will need 1½ cups of soybeans. I buy organically grown soy beans for the best of good health as some countries still use pesticides and herbicides in their growing fields.

Wash beans, cover with 6 cups of water, and soak overnight. The beans will swell almost double in size overnight, producing the highest amount of soymilk possible. Drain before using.

A word about coagulants

There are several basic tofu coagulants that a home tofu maker can use. Some tofu connoisseurs vouch that the best flavor comes from nigari (bittern).

Natural nigari, which is most often used in traditional Japanese recipes, is available at health food stores or shops that specialize in tofu-making supplies. It is noted for producing slightly sweet tofu.

Ingredients needed for making homemade tofu

Refined nigari (magnesium chloride or calcium chloride) can be purchased where tofu-making supplies are sold, at a pharmacy, or ordered from a supply house. Recipe calls for 2 teaspoons of nigari.

In the olden days, many home tofu makers such as myself made our own liquid nigari by bundling up a handful of moist natural sea salt in a sack and hanging it over a bowl for collecting the drip; 2 teaspoons full is enough for a batch of tofu.

Common Epsom salts or calcium sulfate (refined form of Epsom salts) was the earliest coagulant used by Chinese tofu makers. It can still be used today and yields higher bulk and softer tofu than other products. If using Epsom salts, you will need 2 teaspoons full.

Old World coagulants like lemon juice, lime juice, and apple cider vinegar can also be used, producing a more granular, tart tofu. You will need 4 tablespoons of freshly squeezed juice or 3 tablespoons high-quality apple cider vinegar.

The best way to decide which you prefer is to experiment until you find the one that suits your tastes to a T.

Getting started

Fill tea kettle with water and measure 8 cups of water into cooking pot and bring both to a rolling boil.

Line colander with moistened tea towel and set over pressing pot. Place in the sink.

Moisten cheesecloth and line inside of forming container. If you plan on saving the whey, place forming container over a bowl for collecting run-off.

Put half the soybeans into blender along with 2 cups hot water. Use 1 cup of tap water and 1 cup of boiling water from tea kettle to reach about 175° F temperature, which is ideal.

Cover and puree at high speed for 2 minutes or until smooth.

Add to the boiling water in the cooking pot. Turn off heat and cover pan.

Puree other half of beans and add to the cooking pot.

Rinse blender out with ¼ cup hot water and add to the pot.

Stir bean mixture for 3 minutes in cooking pot over turned-off heat.

Pour contents into colander. Using spatula, clean out the cooking pot.

Force liquid through strainer by twisting cloth and pressing with a potato masher. Try to extract as much of the soymilk as you can.

Untwist cloth and stir solids, which are known as the okara. Pour 2 cups of boiling water over the okara to rinse off remaining milk. Press through.

Pour soymilk into cleaned-out cooking pot, reserving okara for other uses. (See following.)

Bring soymilk to boil, stirring constantly. Reduce heat and simmer 8 minutes.

Homemade tofu

Tofu stir fry

Remove soymilk from stove. Measure coagulant into 1 cup of water and stir until blended.

Vigorously swirl soymilk with wooden spoon while slowly blending in 1/3 of the coagulant. Let swirling stop.

Repeat. Cover and let stand 3 minutes for curds to form.

Slowly stir in last of the coagulant, working it through the upper layer of curdling soymilk.

Cover pot and let stand 3 minutes or twice as long if using Epsom salts.

Uncover, stir surface layer again for a few seconds, pushing spatula around sides of pot to loosen milk from curds. By this time curds will be forming on top of the whey.

Place pot alongside forming container. Using a fine mesh sieve, press into curds and let the whey collect into the sieve. In this manner, ladle all of the whey out of the pot and empty over cheesecloth into the forming container.

When all of the whey has been lifted away and strained into the forming container, gently ladle the curds into the forming container, one layer at a time.

Draw up cheesecloth over curds and cover pan with heavy weight, like a foil-wrapped brick or other heavy object that will fit nicely over the pan. I use an old cast iron sad iron, which fits perfectly into my pan. Let set 20 minutes.

Fill sink with cold water. Remove weight and submerge tofu-filled container into the water.

Slip tofu from pan and gently, working under water, unwrap and cut in half.

Leave tofu in water for 5 minutes or until firm.

Using a plate, slip under the cakes and lift out.

For fresh use within a day or two, cover with plastic wrap and refrigerate until ready to use. If keeping longer than a few days, store tofu immersed in water in fridge, changing water daily, and it will keep up to a week.

Don't fret if your first couple batches of homemade tofu do not turn out perfect. In the case of tofu, practice really does make perfect. You can still eat the tofu even if the cakes are a little lopsided, flat, or not as plump as you wished them to be.

Some common problems for failed or not perfect tofu are listed below.

• soybeans were too old, thus were poor yielding

• beans were not ground fine enough

• the pressing sack was too tightly woven

• coagulant was not added properly. You really must add 1/3 at a time—stirring in a swirling fashion—and wait as indicated in the directions for best results. Too much coagulant added too quickly can cause crumbly texture.

Now that you've got a delightful batch of homemade tofu to work with, below are a couple tasty recipes to show it off in the finest of fashion.

What to do with the protein-rich okara

In Japan, where there are many tofu shops producing an enormous amount of okara daily—much more than needed for human consumption—excess okara is used as animal feed. You can mix okara into pet food for a boost of extra nutrition. Or feed it to your livestock. Chickens enjoy it, as do pigs and other domestic animals.

Okara can be roasted to remove excess moisture, then added to breads, muffins, cookies, or other dishes as a nutritional boost.

I like to roast mine in a heavy cast iron frying pan, but any heavy-bottomed skillet will do. Put okara in pan over medium heat and stir until it is light and dry. Or spread on baking sheets in 350° F oven and heat for 10 minutes or until moisture is gone.

Okara supper patties:

1½ cups okara
1 cup cooked mashed black beans
½ cup whole wheat flour
1 minced onion
½ cup minced red or green sweet pepper
½ cup finely grated carrot
2 cloves minced garlic
2 Tbsp. soy sauce
seasoned salt and pepper to taste
vegetable oil for frying

Tofu soup

Combine all ingredients, mix well, and shape into patties.

Roll in flour and put in fridge to set for about 1 hour.

Heat oil to 350° F in large skillet. Fry patties until crisp and golden.

Makes 6 patties.

Okara granola:

2 cups okara
6 Tbsp. liquid honey
3 Tbsp. oil
1 Tbsp. vanilla
pinch ground cinnamon and nutmeg
extras: currants, raisins, nuts, seeds, dried fruit, shredded dried coconut or other favorite bites that you like in your granola

Heat oven to 375° F. Combine first five ingredients and spread on baking sheets. Toast, stirring constantly, for about an hour or until golden. Remove from oven and cool. Mix in any extras you wish. Store in airtight container. Serve in traditional manner as a breakfast food or put a handful in a plastic baggie and give to the kids to carry as a pocket treat, which is much healthier than a candy bar to snack on.

Tofu appetizer or luncheon dish:

Here is one of the quickest and easiest ways to enjoy fresh homemade or store-bought tofu.

Allow 4 ounces of well-chilled tofu per serving for appetizer, 6 to 8 ounces per serving for lunch special. Cut tofu into 1" cubes. Place on attractive serving platter, sprinkle with soy sauce, and surround with little dishes of dunks like finely chopped green onion, toasted or black sesame seeds, grated green pepper, bonito flakes, slivered gingerroot, or anything else that tickles your fancy. Dip cubes into dunks and enjoy.

Versatile tofu soup:

6 cups water
¼ cup soy sauce
2 Tbsp. sesame oil
drop of hot pepper oil, if desired
5 dried shiitake mushrooms, broken into tiny pieces
seasoned salt and black pepper to taste
vegetables of choice: carrots, celery, broccoli, water chestnuts, snow peas, red, green or yellow peppers, cabbage or bok choy, onions, etc.
1 cup cubed tofu

Put first 6 ingredients into soup pot and bring to a boil. Taste and adjust seasoning.

Add vegetables and simmer until tender.

Add tofu and heat 3 minutes.

Serve garnished with finely chopped green onion.

Tofu morning scramble:

Here is a delightful recipe that takes the place of eggs in the morning. This is especially nice for those who can't eat eggs or those who simply like a refreshing change of pace.

1 finely chopped onion
½ finely chopped red sweet pepper
1 clove minced garlic
olive oil
1 cup crumbled tofu
pinch each of turmeric, cumin, and black pepper
1 Tbsp. soy sauce

Heat oil in skillet and sauté vegetables until soft. Add tofu and remaining ingredients, and cook until liquid has evaporated. Garnish with finely chopped chives or green onions. Serve in the fashion of scrambled eggs with or on toast. Serves 2.

Easy tofu stir-fry:

Heat 2 tablespoons sesame oil in wok or skillet. Add 4 cups of your pick of vegetables: sliced celery, carrots, onion rings, cauliflower or broccoli broken into flowers, snow peas, peppers, mushrooms, Chinese radish, cabbage or bok choy. Stir fry until vegetables are just tender, about 3 minutes. Add 1 cup cubed tofu, 2 tablespoons soy sauce, and 1 tablespoon chili oil, and stir fry gently for 2 minutes. Garnish with sesame seeds and finely chopped green onion. Serves 2, but recipe can be doubled.

Variation: Add 1 cup of thinly sliced chicken or beef strips and stir fry about 4 minutes or until almost tender. Δ

Water development for the homestead

Ponds, cisterns & tanks

By Roy Martin

In most areas, wells or springs are able to provide water sources for the homestead, but there are places where groundwater is either not available or where it is desirable to accumulate it in storage structures. For the purposes of this article, ponds will refer to water storage structures that are created with dams or that are relatively large holes excavated in the soil to hold water. Cisterns are buried tanks or covered in-ground structures for water storage, and tanks are above-ground or partially in-ground water storage structures.

Ponds

Farm ponds are water-holding structures that may receive their water from one or more sources. The pond is able to store water for future use, but it is usually not suitable for supplying potable water because it may contain numerous bacteria or other organisms that are harmful to humans. Pond water is normally used for livestock water, small-scale irrigation (such as for vegetable gardens or a few fruit trees), raising fish or domestic waterfowl, wildlife, and fire protection. Most farm ponds collect runoff water from surrounding lands, so they may have fecal contamination from livestock manure. Runoff may carry the manure and its organisms into the pond, or livestock may defecate directly in the water while they are drinking.

Pond construction:

Most ponds consist of a small dirt dam constructed in a water channel to intercept and store water from rain and snow that falls upslope from the dam. This means that the pond depends upon water from precipitation, and there must be enough water flowing over the surface of the land to collect behind the dam. You need to make a preliminary dam site selection in a drainage that is in the area where water is needed. Ideally, the natural features of the area will allow placement of the dam in a narrow area in the drainage to minimize the amount of dirt to be moved, plus the drainage will open up behind the dam site to maximize the water storage area of the pond.

The area behind the dam, or the watershed, needs to be evaluated to see if there will be enough water flowing into the dam to fill it in a year with average precipitation. If possible, look at ponds of similar surface area and depth in your area that have water in them. Use topographical maps (these may be purchased at most sporting goods stores). If you can't easily find maps in your area, talk to your Natural Resources Conservation Service (NRCS) conservationist or county Extension Service agent to find out where you can purchase them. These officers can also give you information on the amount of runoff you can expect on your land considering the annual precipitation, the size of the watershed, and the amount of water that soaks into the soil or evaporates. Check the state regulations pertaining to pond construction and use. Some state water regulations require permits for pond construction and use.

Roy and granddaughter, Annie Acosta, pump water from the cistern.

Calculate the amount of water available to fill a pond by multiplying the area of the watershed determined by outlining the watershed on a topographical map, and determining the number of acres. Multiply by the amount of annual precipitation in feet and fractions of feet, minus the losses to the soil, vegetation, and evaporation. Again, the NRCS conservationist or Extension agent may be very helpful. This will provide the number of acre feet of water that is available for storage in the pond. One acre-foot is equivalent to one acre being covered by water one foot deep. There are 43,560 square feet per acre and approximately 7 gallons per square foot, so that is a lot of water. If you have time before construction of the dam, it would be wise to observe the runoff in that drainage where you plan to place the dam. During intense rainstorms or at the time of rapid snowmelt, see how much water would be flowing into the dam. This will provide you with a sense about how water will flow into and fill your planned pond. If no water flows down the drainage, even during a hard rain, it may not be feasible to have a pond on that site. On the other hand, if a heavy rain produces flood conditions in the drainage, there may be too much water for your small pond to safely contain.

After it appears that your proposed site will have enough water, check the soil to determine whether or not it is suitable for dam building. If all the soil at the site is very sandy, it will not make a good dam. Soil for dam construction should have enough clay content to allow it to compact well so it will hold water. Usually the soil in the bottom of the pond should be excavated for use in the dam construction, as that will enlarge the basin for water storage.

The size of the dam itself will be determined by the amount of water needed and the amount of time and money that can be dedicated to the dam building project. Two major considerations must be considered in determining how much dirt will be moved: The size of the dam itself; and the size for a spillway. Any dam that collects runoff must have a suitable spillway to take away excess water when the dam fills. This spillway must be low enough below the top of the dam to avoid overtopping and must be located so the water is carried away from the dam structure to avoid erosion of the dam. The spillway should be as wide and flat as possible to minimize erosion risk and should be able to handle the highest estimated flow of water in the drainage. It should be constructed at one end of the dam, away from the fill of the dam itself, in undisturbed soil. If practical, line the spillway with stone to help prevent erosion.

The spillway is in the foreground and is several feet lower than the top of the dam, allowing excess water to flow out of the pond without causing the dam to erode.

Construction of the dam will require the movement of large amounts of dirt. Although same large earthen dams have been constructed by hand or with animal power in the past, the use of machinery is so much more efficient that it is unlikely that anyone in this day would decide not to use it in such a venture. The choice then comes down to contracting with someone who has the equipment or purchasing your own equipment. It may be that you will need earthmoving machinery for other work on your land, and it will pay to investigate purchasing older equipment that still works well if it is used gently. It is not uncommon to see older Caterpillars or other dozers for sale for a few thousand dollars. Just be sure to have someone knowledgeable about heavy equipment help you in selecting a machine that will serve your needs. Another option is the use of farm machinery with blade or bucket, but a much smaller pond will probably result from the use of this less suitable equipment.

Begin the construction after the site has been selected, the size of the dam has been decided, and the exact location of the dam and spillway selected. The first step is clearing the vegetation and topsoil from the area to be covered by the fill dirt that will form the dam. This will help prevent the formation of channels that may allow water to undercut the dam. It is necessary to form a bond between the dirt being moved in to form the dam and the soil that is in place under the dam to make sure there is nothing that will prevent the formation of that bond. It is best to construct a key-way by excavating a channel two to four feet deep in the soil that will be directly under the top of the dam. The key-way will be filled as the dam is built to further ensure the bonding of fill material and the original soil.

I like to place a pipe with a valve on it through the base of the dam to allow use of the water below the dam itself. This allows for more sanitary livestock water than watering directly from the pond or for minor irrigation systems for watering gardens or fruit trees. With proper treatment, the water from ponds can be made safe for household use, but this should be way down on the list of possible sources for potable water. The pipe going through the dam should have corrugations in it or some baffles on it to prevent possible flow of water along the outside of the pipe. I have installed pipe to make a siphon over the top of a dam, but it is a lot easier to put the pipe through the dam during construction. The pipe should be in place as soon as the key-way is filled so that all of the water above

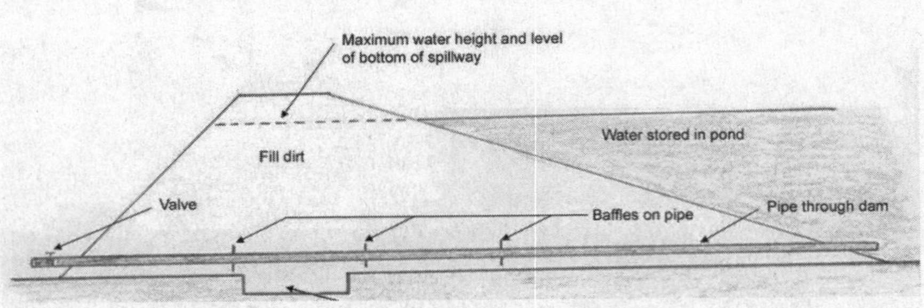

Cross section of a dam constructed for a pond. The pipe allows tapping the water for livestock or small irrigation system.

the original level of the drainage channel will be available for use.

Construction of the dam should be done when there is little danger of runoff so the dam will not wash away during construction. A lot of work can go down the drain in just a few minutes if a flash flood hits during construction and the water washes over the top of the partially constructed dam instead of through the spillway that is designed for overflow. Of course, unseasonably heavy rains can happen, and there is no way to plan for that. If you are building the pond in an area that may have rainfall during any season, install a culvert pipe through the base of the dam with a headgate on it so it can be closed off after construction is finished. This culvert should be large enough to handle normal runoff during the season in which the dam is constructed. That way, runoff coming at any time can flow through the culvert, and construction that is already done will not be adversely affected. It will also come in handy to drain the pond to clean it out if that becomes necessary in the future. If a culvert has to be used, that will add considerably to the cost of the pond unless you can find some older, used culvert. Sometimes the county road department will replace culverts when they are widening a road or making other changes, and the old culverts may be sold at greatly reduced prices or may even be available free. Check with your county road superintendent to see if any are available.

Begin actual construction of the dam itself by pushing dirt with the dozer to form a pile of dirt all along the area where the dam will be built. Take as much of the dirt as is possible from the area where the pond will be. The more dirt taken from the pond basin, the more water can be stored there. You may also use the dirt removed from spillway construction for fill material. Avoid areas of sand and gravel since these will not compact well in the dam. Continue pushing dirt until a dam is formed that is at least four or five feet higher than the bottom of the spillway. Some settling of the fill in the dam will take place over time. The dam should have a three-to-one slope on the upstream side to ensure that the water will not exert too much pressure, causing the dam to fail. That means that for each foot of drop from the top of the dam to the bottom of the fill, there should be three horizontal feet of fill. I like to make the top of the dam at least 10 feet wide. The slope of the downstream side of the dam is not as critical as the upstream, or water side. A one-to-one slope on the downstream side is adequate. Finally, make sure the surface of the dam on all sides is relatively smooth and compacted.

The top, both upstream and downstream sides, and the spillway should be planted to a grass that is well adapted to your area. Grass seed may be broadcast by hand or with a small, hand-cranked seeder. Then, drag a section of harrow, tree limbs, or something else that will put the seed into the soil surface over it, so the

Pond constructed in bottomland that intercepted the aquifer so water flows in from underground

seed will be covered. Even running the crawler tractor over it will help as the tracks will push much of the seed into the soil, allowing a large percentage of germination. I have also planted grass seed by driving an ATV with knobby tires all over the area. The grass cover will help prevent erosion of the soil that has been disturbed. Never plant trees or shrubs on a dam as the deeper roots may eventually die and decay, leaving channels that the water can follow, putting the dam in danger of failure.

Ponds may also be constructed in bottomlands or anyplace there is a shallow water table by simply digging out a pit that goes into the water. In these cases, the water fills the pond by flowing under the surface of the soil and into the hole. There will be water in this type of pond as long as the water level in the shallow aquifer stays above the bottom of the pond. Or, when it floods, water may cover the area where the pond has been excavated and it could be filled with sediment.

Spring-fed ponds may also be constructed, catching the flow from a spring in a small dam or an excavation. I especially like these ponds for raising fish. In Oregon, I had a very small spring-fed pond that was probably not more than 20x50' and I very successfully raised trout in it. Of course, they had to be fed in such a small pond, but it was enjoyable to feed them every day, and they provided a lot of recreation and food. Some of them grew to well over five pounds.

Protecting the watershed:

The quality of the water in the pond and the useful life of the pond are dependent upon the condition of the land that comprises the watershed. If water flows from cultivated land that is easily eroded, the water flowing into the pond will carry soil and fertilizer into it, creating dirty water that will silt-in the pond and that will grow abundant algae and bacteria. On the other hand, if the watershed is well-managed pasture or woodland, the water will be clear and free of pollutants. Cropland that has grassed waterways and that is farmed in such a manner that there is very little erosion can also yield runoff that contains a minimum of pollutants.

Old dozers like this 1951 D7 are often available at a reasonable price and are suitable for pond construction and other dirt moving on the homestead.

In areas where sediment in the water is a fact of life, such as many desert areas, it may be wise to dig small basins in the drainage channel upstream from the dam you have constructed for your pond. These can be small, scooped-out areas that will slow the water before if flows into your pond. Slow-flowing water will not carry much sediment, so it will be deposited in the silt trap basins, preventing it from going into the pond. The sediment can then be scooped out with the dozer or a tractor bucket, and it will be ready for the next runoff event.

Where livestock graze in the area of the pond, in addition to using proper grazing practices, it is wise to fence off the pond area itself. Livestock watering should not be done in the pond because they tend to pollute their own water source. Use the pipe placed through the pond to fill a watering trough located somewhere below the pond. A strategically placed pond can be used to deliver water through a gravity pipeline to more than one water trough. Plastic pipe can go to several pastures and water levels in the troughs regulated by simple float valves.

Pond and dam maintenance:

Properly constructed and managed, a farm pond will provide water indefinitely for homestead needs. Prevention is the best management technique, so management of the land around the pond, the watershed area that feeds water into it, is the best way to ensure water quality. Grazing the land should be under strict management so a good vegetation cover is maintained. Checking the dam and spillway regularly for small eroded areas or rodent burrowing is important. Those areas should be repaired and burrowing animals controlled. The fence around the pond needs to be kept in good repair to prevent livestock from direct access to the pond water.

Some ponds may be infested with waterweeds and algae. There are chemical treatments to control these water pests, but fish may also control them. Grass carp and other species eat the vegetation in the pond and keep it open. Check with your local Extension agent to find out which fish are suitable for your pond and to determine the best way to control weeds and algae.

Cisterns

Cisterns are covered structures used to store water in the ground. They often collect water from the roofs of homes and other buildings. Many older rural homes had cisterns, either because there was not an aquifer within reasonable depth for a well or because the well water was highly mineralized. I have known women who would cook dry beans only with cistern water because beans cooked in the hard well water seemed to just get harder. The collected rainwater had no minerals, and the beans would cook up quickly in it.

In a few areas, well water is not an option, and cisterns are a way to collect water for household use. In those areas, water must be hauled from town and piped into the cistern when there is not sufficient rain to fill it.

The Persians constructed very sophisticated cisterns, filling them with runoff or with water from irrigation canals. Many of the older towns have cisterns constructed into the complex that makes up the bazaar, or old business area. Some have huge domed roofs constructed of masonry with no reinforcement. Others are small buried tanks that collect runoff water, and the roofs over them protect the water from evaporation.

I saw an old water system in an irrigated desert community in Utah that took water from the irrigation ditch to fill the cistern. The irrigation water from the river was muddy so they had an open-topped, shallow tank that held the water and allowed it to settle out some of the mud. It then went through a homemade sand filter to clean it further and then into the cistern where it was pumped out as needed for home use.

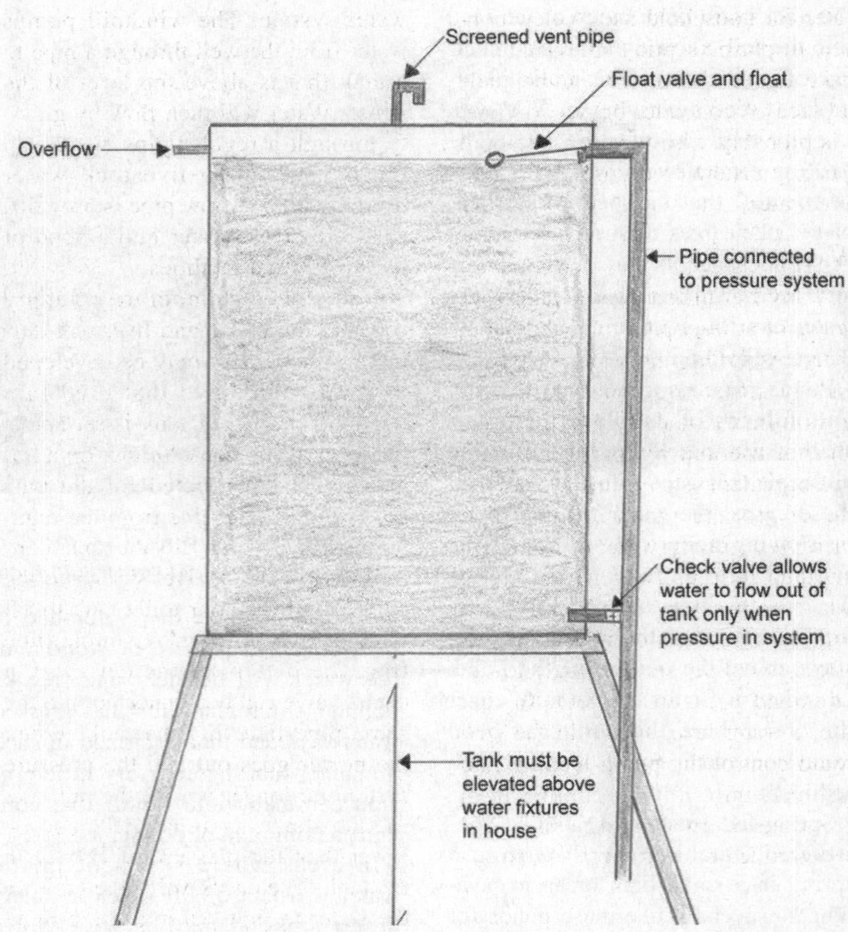

An elevated tank can be used with a pump and pressure system to provide an emergency water supply when electrical power is interrupted.

For practical purposes, cisterns for the homestead are useful for using water collected from roof gutters to provide either regular water for the house or emergency water when the power to the well pump is off. A small pitcher pump will provide ready access to the water. In some areas, especially near cities, rainwater and dust washed off of the roof may contain pollutants you don't want to drink. If this may be a problem, have the water from your cistern tested. You may also have a diversion from the pipe feeding to the cistern. When a light rain falls and during the first few minutes of a hard downpour, the diversion is left running onto the ground surface and then it can be manually changed during hard rains to fill the cistern with water that is less likely to contain pollutants.

I used a 400-gallon plastic tank for my cistern. I dug a hole deep enough so its top would be about a foot below the ground surface. I then filled it with water to keep it from caving in and backfilled around it. All of the drain spouts from the gutters of the house were put into buried PVC pipes that take the water to the cistern. I built an overflow into the tank so excess water will flow away from it. A platform was constructed over the top of the tank and an inexpensive pitcher pump installed to remove water for household use. A new concrete or plastic septic tank would also make a good cistern or it can be made in place of concrete, brick, or stone. It is probably wise to seal a site-built masonry cistern to ensure that it will hold water.

Water tanks

By my definition, water tanks are above, or at least partly aboveground, structures for storing water. They are usually situated so that the water flows from the tank by gravity to the point of use and are part of another type of water system. I mentioned the use of storage tanks as part of a spring-fed gravity water system in a previous article. They may also be part of a well system. Low-yield wells may pump into either a tank or cistern to collect enough water to run a demand pressure system. In that case, a water-level switch in the well would control the pump feeding into the tank and another pump would take water from the tank and would be controlled by a pressure switch.

A tank like this was buried to use as a cistern.

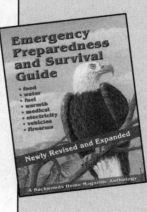

Water tanks were often used in conjunction with a well and windmill water system. The windmill pumps water from the well through a pipe to a tank that is above the level of the house. Water will then flow by gravity through a regular pipe system to the house and to livestock water troughs. An overflow pipe is provided to divert excess water into a pond or livestock water facilities.

A system to temporarily supply water to the house and livestock during power outages may be developed in a way similar to that used in a windmill system. A tank is set above the level of the house (either on a hill or a tower constructed for the purpose) and a water line from the regular pressure system fills the tank, controlled by a float valve, similar to the one that allows your toilet tank to fill without overflowing. A simple pipe from the bottom of the tank with a check valve can be connected into the same pipe that fills the tank. When the power goes out and the pressure system no longer works, the pressure in the water system will become lower than the pressure of gravity in the tank. The check valve then allows the water to flow out into the system. Another check valve between the pressure switch and the well keeps the tank water from emptying into the well. The water pressure in the house will be much lower with the tank than with the regular pressure system, but it will provide emergency water. It will be a limited supply, however, so anytime the house is dependent upon the tank, strict water conservation measures should be employed. It will be a temptation to think of everything as normal with this system, but the water supply will be limited to the volume of the emergency water tank.

In areas that have cold weather, tanks will have to be protected from freezing. Some old farm water towers had siding on them, all the way to the ground. Combined with insulation, this would keep the frost out of the pipes going to the tank. In extreme cold, a stove would heat the room at the base of the tower, and the heat would keep the entire system from freezing. When the tank is sitting on the ground surface, taking the pipe into the center of the bottom of the tank will prevent freezing in most climates.

The use of water storage structures such as ponds, cisterns, and tanks can provide additional supplies of water to the homestead. With wise planning and construction, they will become important aids in providing an easier and more independent lifestyle. Δ

The last word

Who's supposed to protect *our* rights?

Who is supposed to protect our rights? The President? The Congress? The courts? The police? Before you answer, let me remind you of something: Our rights are supposed to protect us *from* the President, the Congress, the courts, and the police.

Now, most people think it's the job of the Supreme Court to protect our rights. But you know something? There's no provision in the *Constitution* for the courts to adjudicate our rights. I know the Supreme Court makes rulings on them all the time. It has for the last 200-plus years. But the idea that the Court, a branch of the federal government whose members are appointed by the President and confirmed by the Senate, is allowed to decide which rights we are allowed to exercise is a *tradition*, not a part of the original *Constitution*. It's not even a constitutional amendment.

Where did the idea of the Supreme Court making these decisions for us come from? Actually, it came from the early days of the Republic when, in 1803, with the decision *Marbury vs. Madison,* the concept of judicial review was established. Judicial review wasn't a big hit at first, but it grew until, today, the overwhelming majority of Americans believe that the courts are *supposed* to be the adjudicators of our *God-given* or *natural* rights.

The good news is that the Court used to (usually) rule *for* the individual and against the government when questions of individual rights were brought before it. The bad news is that since the early part of the 20th century, and especially since the explosive growth of Big Government that started during the Great Depression, the courts have reversed that trend and typically now rule *against* the individual and for Government.

So, if not the courts, who's *supposed* to decide what our rights are? *We are.* And the reason we are in danger of losing our rights like this is because We the People don't stand up to the very people our rights are supposed to protect us from.

Okay, you may stand up, and certainly I do, but the fact is, a handful of people here and a handful there cannot protect the rights of a nation of 300 million people if the overwhelming majority of them don't care. The obvious question now is: Can the citizens actually make a difference? Can they get control of and protect their rights? Of course they can—if they care.

Let's do a thought experiment. It'll be an easy one. Let's say the Congress writes into law that the United States will, from this moment on, officially be Moslem (I could have said Buddhist, Baptist, Jewish, or whatever, but I think you see where this is going) and the practice of any other religion is to be prohibited. How many people do you think would go around saying, "Well, it's official. Congress has made it a law, and the courts have rules, that I can't be Catholic (Mormon, Methodist, etc.). Guess I'll no longer worship as I please."

Compliance, of course, would be nearly zero. No matter what the courts did, no matter who the police arrested, there would be no compliance with the law. In fact, it may go beyond noncompliance. There could even be open revolt.

On the other hand, say just Unitarianism was outlawed. Well, there may be protests, there'd even be court arguments by the ACLU, but most people would go on about their business because, well, let's be honest, most of us aren't Unitarians, so we wouldn't care.

And this is how we are losing our rights to free speech, a free press, our rights to bear arms, and even our rights to worship as we wish. They've taken them away a little at a time. Free speech? It's not removed all at once. In politics it's now restricted to "free speech zones." Congress passes a law making it illegal to criticize incumbents by name for their performance for 60 days before an election (the McCain-Feingold law, which, in effect, says you can't place ads to tell people who's screwing up in office in the 60 days before an election when it would most matter because that's when people are most apt to be paying attention). Did you stand up and yell, "No!" They passed this despite the fact that the Constitution plainly states:

Congress shall make no law respecting an establishment of religion, or prohibiting the free exercise thereof; or abridging the freedom of speech, or of the press; or the right of the people peaceably to assemble, and to petition the Government for a redress of grievances.

Where were you when *your* representatives and senators passed the PATRIOT Act, taking away even more of your rights? Where were you when *your* President signed it into law? What about when the RICO Act, which denies we have any property rights, was passed in 1970? Were you yelling and screaming when Congress, the President, and the courts were denying you have a right to your house, your car, and even your cash? Where were you when the DEA, the FDA, and the courts said you have no right to determine what you put into your body. Get it? You don't own that—your body—anymore either. You did, but not now. Where are you every time *your* Supreme Court says it's okay if yet another right is abrogated? I would imagine you didn't care when they did any of these things because you didn't think any of them affected you. I would guess you probably didn't even know what was being taken away.

Okay, some of us screamed, some of us protested, but a handful of us alone can't save the rights of 300 million.

Once again, who's supposed to protect our rights if it's not the job of the very people those rights are supposed to protect us from? That's right, we are.

And, if in a year, five years, ten years...the voting booth, the letter writing, and resistance don't work, remember what Thomas Jefferson said: "The tree of liberty must be refreshed from time to time with the blood of patriots and tyrants."

— John Silveira